Readings in American Folklore

Readings in American Folklore

Edited by

Jan Harold Brunvand
UNIVERSITY OF UTAH

W · W · NORTON & COMPANY
New York · London

W. W. Norton & Company, Inc., 500 Fifth Avenue, New York, NY 10110
W. W. Norton & Company Ltd, 10 Coptic Street, London WC1A 1PU

Library of Congress Cataloging in Publication
Data
Main entry under title:
Readings in American folklore.
    1. Folk-lore—United States—Addresses, essays,
lectures.   2. United States—Social life and cus-
toms—Addresses, essays, lectures.   I. Brunvand,
Jan Harold.
GR105.R4   1979   390'.0973   79-11189
ISBN 0-393-95029-8

7 8 9 0

ROGER D. ABRAHAMS, "Folklore in Culture: Notes Toward an Analytic Method," *Texas Studies in Literature and Language* 5 (Spring, 1963). Copyright © 1963 University of Texas Press. Reprinted by permission of the author and publisher.

JOHN Q. ANDERSON, " 'Miller Boy,' One of the First and Last of the Play-Party Games," *North Carolina Folklore Journal* 21 (1973).

LOUIE W. ATTEBERY, "The Fiddle Tune: An American Artifact," *Northwest Folklore* 2, no. 2 (1967). Reprinted by permission.

RONALD L. BAKER, " 'Hogs Are Playing with Sticks—Bound to Be Bad Weather': Folk Belief or Proverb," *Midwest Journal of Language and Folklore* 1 (1975). Reprinted by permission of the author and the publisher.

MAC E. BARRICK, "The Migratory Anecdote and the Folk Concept of Fame," *Mid-South Folklore* 4 (1976). Copyright © 1976 *Mid-South Folklore*. Reprinted by permission.

L. MICHAEL BELL, "Cokelore," *Western Folklore* 35 (1976). Reprinted by permission of the California Folklore Society.

DAN BEN-AMOS, "Toward a Definition of Folklore in Context," *Journal of American Folklore* 84 (1971): 3–15. Reproduced by permission of the American Folklore Society and the author.

CHARLES BOND, "Unpublished Folklore in the Brown Collection," *North Carolina Folklore* 20 (1972).

JAN HAROLD BRUNVAND, " 'The Lane County Bachelor': Folksong or Not?" *Heritage of Kansas: A Journal of the Great Plains* 10, no. 1 (1977). Reprinted by permission.

———, "New Directions for the Study of American Folklore," *Folklore* 82 (1971). Reprinted by permission of The Folklore Society.

TRISTRAM P. COFFIN, " 'Mary Hamilton' and the Anglo-American Ballad as an Art Form," *Journal of American Folklore* 70 (1957): 208–214. Reproduced by permission of the American Folklore Society and the author.

KAY COTHRAN, "Talking Trash in the Okefenokee Swamp Rim, Georgia," *Journal of American Folklore* 87 (1974): 340–356. Reproduced by permission of the American Folklore Society and the author.

———, "Participation in Tradition," *Keystone Folklore* 18 (1973). Reprinted by permission of The Pennsylvania Folklore Society.

IDA M. CROMWELL, "Songs I Sang on an Iowa Farm," *Western Folklore* 17 (1958). Reprinted by permission of the California Folklore Society.

LINDA DÉGH, "Symbiosis of Joke and Legend: A Case of Conversational Folklore" from *Folklore Today: A Festschrift for Richard M. Dorson*, edited by L. Dégh, H. Glassie, F. J. Oinas (Bloomington: Indiana University, 1976). Reprinted by permission of the author and the Folklore Institute.

ROLAND B. DIXON, "Some Coyote Stories from the Maidu Indians of California," *Journal of American Folklore* 13 (1900): 267–270.

RICHARD M. DORSON, "Folklore at a Milwaukee Wedding," *Hoosier Folklore* 6 (1947): 1–13. Reprinted by permission of the author and the publisher.

———, "Heart Disease and Folklore," Folklore Preprint Series (Bloomington, Indiana), vol. 1, no. 10 (April, 1974), pp. 1–14. Reprinted by permission of the author and the publisher.

ALAN DUNDES, "On Game Morphology: A Study of the Structure of Non-Verbal Folklore," *New York Folklore Quarterly* 20 (1964). Reprinted by permission of the New York Folklore Society.

———, "Metafolklore and Oral Literary Criticism," *The Monist* 50, no. 4 (1966). Reprinted by permission of the author and the publisher.

SYLVIA ANN GRIDER, "Con Safos: Mexican-Americans, Names, and Graffiti," *Journal of American Folklore* 88 (1975): 132–142. Reprinted by permission of the American Folklore Society and the author.

BESS LOMAX HAWES, "Folksongs and Functions: Some Thoughts on the American Lullaby," *Journal of American Folklore* 87 (1974): 66–71. Reprinted by permission of the American Folklore Society and the author.

WILLIAM HUGH JANSEN, "The Surpriser Surprised: A Modern Legend," *Folklore Forum* 6 (1973). Reprinted by permission of the author and the publisher.

AILI K. JOHNSON, "Lore of the Finnish-American Sauna," *Midwest Folklore* 1 (1961): 33–39. Reprinted courtesy of the publisher and the author.

WARREN KLIEWER, "Collecting Folklore Among Mennonites," *Mennonite Life* 14 (1961). Reprinted through the courtesy of *Mennonite Life*.

SHIRLEY MARCHALONIS, "Three Medieval Tales and Their Modern American Analogues," *Journal of the Folklore Institute* 13 (1976): 173–184. Reprinted by permission of the author and the publisher.

HOWARD WIGHT MARSHALL, "Mr. Westfall's Baskets: Traditional Craftsmanship in Northcentral Missouri," *Mid-South Folklore* 2 (1974). Reproduced courtesy of the publisher.

ALBERT J. PETERSEN, "The German-Russian House in Kansas: A Study in Persistence of Form," *Pioneer America* 8, no. 1 (January, 1976). Reprinted by permission of *Pioneer America*.

PATRICIA K. RICKELS, "Some Accounts of Witch Riding," *Louisiana Folklore Miscellany* 2, no. 1 (August, 1961). Reprinted by permission of the Louisiana Folklore Society.

JOHN A. RICKFORD AND ANGELA E. RICKFORD, "Cut-Eye and Suck-Teeth: African Words and Gestures in a New World Guise," *Journal of American Folklore* 89 (1976): 294–309. Reprinted by permission of the American Folklore Society and the authors.

ARCHER TAYLOR, "Method in the History and Interpretation of a Proverb," *Proverbium*, no. 10 (1968). Reprinted through the courtesy of The Finnish Literature Society.

JUDY TREJO, "Coyote Tales: A Paiute Commentary," *Journal of American Folklore* 87 (1974): 66–71. Reprinted by permission of the American Folklore Society and the author.

ROGER WELSCH, "The Cornstalk Fiddle," *Journal of American Folklore* 77 (1964): 262–263. Reprinted by permission of the American Folklore Society and the author.

———, " 'Sorry Chuck'—Pioneer Foodways," *Nebraska History* 53 (1972): 99–113. Reprinted by permission of the author and the publisher.

WILLIAM A. WILSON, "Folklore and History: Fact Amid the Legend," *Utah Historical Quarterly* 41 (1973): 40–58. Reprinted by permission of the Utah State Historical Society.

ROSEMARY ZUMWALT, "Plain and Fancy: A Content Analysis of Children's Jokes Dealing with Adult Sexuality," *Western Folklore* 35 (1976). Reprinted by permission of the California Folklore Society.

Contents

Section 3
Analysis and Interpretation of American Folklore

Section 4
Some Theoretical Perspectives in American Folklore

Preface

Many teachers and students using *The Study of American Folklore* in introductory courses have asked for more examples of American folk materials and additional samples of scholarly analysis. These supplementary materials, it was pointed out, could provide classes with subjects for discussion and models for term projects. Book-length studies and folklore journals may serve such purposes, but regular class use puts a considerable strain on the university library and the student's textbook budget; besides, the desired volumes are not always available, and books and journals always include materials unsuited for teaching along with those that are usable. What is needed is a single volume of well selected examples and studies arranged for the use of beginning students of American folkore and furnished with notes and commentaries directed specifically to their interests.

The present volume is designed to meet these requests by bringing together a number of exemplary but relatively brief collections and studies of American folklore, drawn primarily from the scholarly folklore journals. These articles were chosen to illustrate a variety of approaches and folklore genres; they are rich in actual examples of folk materials and are above all well written and thought-provoking. Many are definitive studies cited in the bibliographic notes of *The Study of American Folklore*; others appeared in journals only recently. While the collection is intended primarily to supplement my established textbook, it also stands on its own as another introduction to American folklore study using examples of scholarship rather than definitions, descriptions, and summaries of major writings.

Journal articles were chosen rather than chapters from books so that studies could be presented in full, exactly as they were originally published. This method has the added advantage of presenting examples of writings from the smaller and specialized journals not available in many university libraries. An effort has been made to limit the number of selections from the large and better known periodicals in order to dip into a variety of lesser known but often equally scholarly and readable ones. By the same token, selections were not included if they had appeared relatively recently in other books of reprints, and only a few folklorists are represented more than once. Thus, for most students and many teachers some of the materials gathered here will be fresh and perhaps otherwise unavailable on their campuses.

The articles are arranged in four sections: collectanea, context, analysis, and theory. Introductions to the sections and to each selection relate the articles to the section themes and to each other. Not all folklore genres are represented, but typical examples are given of oral, customary, and material folk traditions from a wide scope of American folklore and folklife topics. For several major genres (e.g. proverbs, folktales, folksongs) there are representative selections in each of the first three sections to illustrate increasingly more analytical approaches to common topics. Each section includes selections on minority ethnic, immigrant, racial, and regional group traditions, although (as in *The Study of American Folklore*) the majority of material deals with Anglo-American folk cultures.

The somewhat different systems of documentation used by the various journals have not been changed, and only obvious typographical errors have been corrected. In a few instances (mentioned in the notes) new information or updated references supplied by the original authors have been added. The editor has also added a few explanatory footnotes; these are clearly distinguished from the original footnotes by square brackets.

The classroom uses of this anthology, of course, should not be limited to the specific themes suggested for each section. Students might, for example, try to supply the typical context for collected materials presented in Section 1, to interpret the material in Sections 1 or 2, or to collect more examples for study along the lines suggested by the interpretations in Section 3. All of the earlier sections contain materials which might be approached by the theories discussed in Section 4, and all of the authors represented have published other excellent studies which might be consulted.

A frankly pedagogical volume of selections like this one, of course, cannot claim to represent fully the folk traditions of this or any other nation. The regions and folk groups of the United States are simply too large and diverse to admit of packing them between the covers of one book. Thus, while a variety of places and peoples is represented by these selections, the coverage of many kinds of lore or of folk groups is sketchy in comparison to the rich materials gathered in more specialized books, articles, and archives. These gaps are as apparent to the compiler as they will be to his readers, but it is hoped that this reader will be useful for what it does include and will be regarded as another reliable guide-post to American folklore studies. The headnotes to these selections, along with the bibliographic notes to chapters in *The Study of American Folklore*, suggest ways of getting further into this fascinating field. In this reader you simply meet some notable American folklorists on their own turf—the scholarly folklore journals.

Readings in American Folklore

Collections of American Folk Materials

The nine selections in this first section are primarily collections, either oral texts or descriptions of customary and material folk traditions, annotated with references to further examples found in other publications. The collectors or editors describe how the material was assembled and which written and printed sources were consulted. Whenever possible, standard bibliographic and classificatory references are cited, although some important works for individual genres may not have been published at the time that these original articles appeared. The mode of presentation of the material ranges from a mere classified listing of items or a "finding list" (in which only selected items are quoted) to a full narrative presentation in which the collected material is introduced into a general discussion of the form. Although a few of these articles do include contextual or interpretive matter, in general they emphasize the material itself, and as such they furnish good examples of annotated collections which students themselves might want to prepare.

A wide range of American folk material is represented here, even in this very limited space: folktales and legends, folksongs and ballads, several short oral genres, beliefs and customs, and one example of a folk craft. (The order of selections is roughly the same as the order in which genres are given in The Study of American Folklore.) One article contains a small sample of folk music, and two employ drawings in the documentation of a folk tradition. Much of the material is Anglo-American, but American Indian folklore, black tradition, and some ethnic and immigrant lore are also represented. Besides the material collected directly from oral tradition, one article contains lore written out by informants, and one batch of material was collected by a recent folklore class. One essay gives advice on collecting folklore with examples included. The historical periods of these examples range from original Native American culture to pioneer lore and later settlements, finally up to the present—from Coyote stories to "cokelore." There is some regional lore and a sample of semi-religious folklore. Seven different journals are quoted with dates from 1900 to 1976.

It is impossible to claim that nine articles do justice to the whole spectrum of American folklore, and so this section must be regarded as representative. It is also true that some of the finest American folklore collections are in book form rather than journals, and much material lies unpublished in archives. The ideal of collecting the full surrounding context for each performance of folk material can barely be approached in most journal articles; that is the aim of most of the studies in Section 2. Despite these shortcomings of the item-oriented approach, however, it is valuable to have the texts themselves reliably quoted or described, and authoritatively annotated, as a basis for further study and analysis. All of these selections are worthy examples of that modest but important goal.

UNPUBLISHED FOLKLORE IN THE BROWN COLLECTION

Charles Bond

North Carolina Folklore is an enormous and varied collection that was compiled by Professor Frank C. Brown of Duke University, then edited and annotated for publication between 1952 and 1964, after his death, by a group of folklore specialists. The resulting seven-volume work is indeed a monument of American folklore materials; however, as this study by a Duke University folklore student reveals, Brown's complete collection was not published. The items of only one traditional genre were included in full as they were collected, and two genres of collectanea (folk sermons and place-name origin stories) were entirely unrepresented in the printed volumes. In fact, it appears that full publication of the remaining material would constitute a substantial eighth volume for the series. Such complete publication of the Brown collection seems unlikely now; consequently, the major value of Bond's article is to call attention to his "Tabulation" of these items and to provide some examples of unpublished materials so that other folklorists may be inspired to consult them for their studies. Collection and classification of folklore facilitate eventual analysis of it, and the reader is given a small cross-section of typical folklore of one state to compare with traditions of his own region. (The beginning folklore student, of course, should familiarize himself with The Frank C. Brown Collection of North Carolina Folklore in its entirety.)

It is revealing of trends in folkloristics to see which folklore types were slighted or ignored. Proverbs—fixed-phrase sayings with a long scholarly tradition—were published, but more general and less structured "items related to folk speech" were not. "Folk Sermons" have only recently come into their own as a subject for research, and doubtless Brown's unpublished texts will eventually be consulted by such specialists as Bruce A. Rosenberg, whose book The Art of the American Folk Preacher appeared in 1970 (New York: Oxford University Press). Most of the unpublished songs and ballads are of the "miscellaneous" type frequently overlooked by past folklorists but increasingly investigated nowadays. (If the collection had been edited in the 1970s, probably most, if not all, of the songs would have been included.) Fortunately, Brown had the foresight to collect these songs along with the more highly regarded types (ballads, spirituals, work songs, etc.), thus leaving us a valuable record of the song repertories of his informants. Some black American folklore collected by Brown was also apparently suppressed in the published material and is sampled by Bond.

The examples of unpublished folklore which Bond includes may be compared to others in print in order to see the variations from North Carolina forms. For instance, the same pictorial folktale collected by Brown in 1922 and Bond in 1971 was described by Maud G. Early in the Journal of American Folklore, Vol. 10 (1897) but without the alternating actions of characters named "Jack and Tom." (Possibly these names derive from the "Jack Tales" [Americanized Märchen, fairy tales] that are told in North Carolina.) Another pictorial tale involving a different drawing (of a big bird) appears in the children's classic by Laura Ingalls Wilder, On the Banks of Plum Creek (1937), and a variant of this one called "The Mystery Pet" appears in Jan Harold Brunvand's A Guide for Collectors of Folklore in Utah (Salt Lake City: University of Utah Press, 1971).

It is a mystery why some of these materials (including the legend Bond calls "the gem of the collection") were left unpublished by the editors. Certainly "The Brown Mountain Lights" is a well told and interesting supernatural legend text with just a hint of the narrator's context in the collector's note. Perhaps a greater mystery is why Brown himself never published any of the riches he had assembled. For some speculations on this matter see Alan Dundes' provocative essay "On the Psychology of Collecting Folklore" in the Tennessee Folklore Society Bulletin, Vol. 28 (1962), in which Frank C. Brown is cited as a prime example of a folklore collector who declines to published his findings—not, apparently, an uncommon phenomenon.

THE FRANK C. BROWN COLLECTION of North Carolina Folklore is the largest, most homogeneous collection of its kind in the United States, with more than 38,000 items, ninety-five percent of them collected in North Carolina. The collection was assembled during the first half of this century primarily by Dr. Brown, for many years Secretary-Treasurer of the North Carolina Folklore Society, as well as member and Chairman of the Duke University Department of English.[1] Upon his death in 1943, Dr. Newman I. White, his colleague at Duke, assumed the great task of preparing the collection for print. Dr. White's initial organizational efforts and the subsequent editorial assistance of many other specialized scholars eventually led to the publication of the seven-volume Frank C. Brown Collection of North Carolina Folklore, issued by the Duke University Press (1952–1964).

1. Dr. White presents a thorough history of the Collection and its collector in his "General Introduction to *The Frank C. Brown Collection of North Carolina Folklore* (henceforth referred to as *Brown*), I, 12–28.

Since publication, the volumes of the *Brown Collection* have served as an important source of reference for students of folklore. The scope of genres in the *Collection* and its great number of entries within those genres—in short, the collection's size—make it valuable. Dr. Brown's approach to folklore was to "collect everything of *possible* value,"[2] so, *in toto*, the Brown Collection transcends the collections of "curious survivals" common to the era and approaches in many respects a raw ethnography, full of the details of the cultural anthropology of North Carolina. Dr. White best summarized the nature and importance of the Frank C. Brown Collection:

> As to how the collection was assembled, the answer is in every way I know—sound recordings, noting down from dictation, extensive materials in manuscript at first and second hand from students, large manuscript collections from other collectors, clippings from news-papers, traditional family documents, etc., etc., . . . So large a col-lection amassed so persistently over nearly a third of a century almost entirely from one limited, homogeneous region, may properly be ex-pected to yield a full and sound picture of the whole folk background of that region—and so also of similar ones. . . .[3]

It is now nearly three decades since Dr. Brown died, and nearly two decades since the first three volumes of the *Brown Collection* were published. A new generation of folklorists is rising with new interests and emphases. With our perspective changed not only by these new approaches, but by the passage of time itself, a re-examination of the entire Brown Collection seemed in order.

But what kind of re-examination? In April of 1970, I undertook an initial investigation and discovered that the entire collection was in temporary storage, and that the only indexes available were the orig-inal incomplete catalogues prepared for the editors in 1945. With ample space in Duke's new Perkins Library, the collection was soon moved to its present location in the Manuscript Department. Turning to Professor Paull Baum's "Foreword" to the published Collection, I found the following passage:

> It should be stated clearly that though much is given, much re-mains, and that the editors have omitted a great deal. In fact, a

---

2. *Brown*, I, 20.

3. Newman I. White, "The Frank C. Brown Collection of Folklore: Its Organ-ization, Classification, and Publication," p. 4. This paper was delivered before the General Literature Group of the Modern Language Association, New York, De-cember 28, 1944, and a manuscript of the text is among "The Editors' Papers" in the collection. Those "Editors' Papers," by the way, document the great labors of scholarship that went into the preparation of the seven volumes. It was indeed a twenty-year odyssey for the collection, from Dr. Brown's attic to press. In reading the "Editors' Papers," one gains a great appreciation of the efforts of Dr. White and all the other scholars invoived.

tabulation of their rejections was once planned, but has been suppressed, for the complete Collection with multiple indexes is now
accessible in the Duke University Library.[4]

Realizing that the catalogue of the collection had to be made complete,
and aware at the same time that all unpublished items should be
reviewed, I adopted Dr. Baum's abandoned plan for a tabulation as a
means of achieving both of those goals. It took some twenty weeks of
work to complete my inclusive Tabulation of Unpublished Items in the
Brown Collection (over 300 typewritten pages and 2,000 file cards of
verbatim texts), as well as more than thirty hours of Dr. Brown's later,
higher quality field recordings. My Tabulation was geared primarily for
general use in the Manuscript Department.

Only one assistant editor, I discovered, had published all of the
contributions for his genre: Professor Archer Taylor included every
riddle in the collection.[5] On the other extreme, the tabulation for some
genres yielded hundreds of unpublished items. For example, an item-by-
item check of the 6,000 proverbs in the collection uncovered more
than 900 that were not printed; likewise, more than 1,000 other items
related to folk speech were omitted. Surprisingly, there were two completely "untouched" genres: Folk "Sermons" (24 items, mostly
humorous), and The Origin of Place Names (currently being edited by
Mr. Edward S. Haynes of Duke University). In other areas, there were
58 unpublished games, 129 unpublished rhymes, 80 unpublished customs, and 49 unpublished tales and legends. Dr. Wayland Hand, of the
University of California at Los Angeles, informs me that he is reviewing the Collection's unpublished beliefs for possible publication, and
will ultimately return these to the Duke Library. That leaves only the
songs and ballads, and it is hoped that in the near future I can place
into print Dr. Hudson's and Dr. Belden's complete, collated checklist
of the 447 unpublished songs and ballads. Suffice it to say that most of
these songs are vintage Tin Pan Alley—sentimental, homiletic, and the
like.

In closing, let me again invite folklorists to peruse the Tabulation,
listen to the tapes, and survey the entire Frank C. Brown Collection in
the Duke Library. In so doing, they will discover, as I have, that the
rhymes and games, the gruesomely worded superstitions, the sentimental songs of home and mother, can indeed help us paint more
clearly and honestly the portrait of North Carolina's past.

4. *Brown*, I, xi.

5. This author is responsible for supplements to the first three volumes. All
music in the collection was apparently printed in Volumes IV and V, although a
number of tune variants heard on Brown's sound recordings were not transcribed.

I have appended examples of the rich unpublished materials in the Collection.

Game. The Tale of the Wild Cat

Originally contributed to the Frank C. Brown Collection by the Misses Jean and Hallie Holeman of West Durham, circa 1922. In 1971, I collected the same drawing game from a Duke student who lives near Kinston. She had learned it from her grandmother, also a native of Eastern North Carolina.

Tom said he believed he would build him a house, and this is how he did it.

Jack said he believed he would build him one just like it.

Tom said he would put a chimney on his house.

Jack said he would put a chimney on his.

Tom said he would put a window in his house.

Jack said he would put one in his house.

Tom said he would put some walks in his yard.

Jack said he would put some in his yard.

Some distance from the house was a spring.

Tom said he would run down to the spring to get a bucket of water.

When there, he thought he would run up the hill a short distance to look about a little.

He came back, picked up his bucket and started on his way home.

He went a short distance and fell down. Up he got, but in a short time, he fell down again. He got up, went on quite a distance and fell down again. He got up and in a little while fell again. When he got up this time, he reached home safely.

GAME. MISS LUCY, OR TWISTIFICATION

In his introduction to the Games, Professor Paul G. Brewster expresses his regret that more black children's material was not collected (*Brown* I, p. 33). Ironically, the Tabulation revealed that more black children's games were excluded than were published. "Miss Lucy, or Twistification" is one of several from the Maude Minnish Sutton collection of children's lore. The music for this and six other Sutton games appears in the *Collection*, V, 545–551.

"Miss Lucy" is a song that is used to play a sort of dance game called Twistification. We picked it up from a group of Negro children playing ring games one summer evening. The game was intricate, and we judged that a good deal was improvised.

> I went down to see Miss Lucy
> Oh I'd never been there before
> Last time I saw Miss Lucy
> She was rollin' on the floor.
>
> Roll on the floor
> Roll on the floor
> Roll on the floor
> Till life's roll is o'er.
>
> As I was a-goin' down the road
> I met a rabbit and I met a toad
> And ever time that toad would sing
> The rabbit cut the pigeon wing.
>
> Roll on the floor, etc.

This dance was more of a romp than a game played by formula. One little black urchin would turn handsprings through the ring at the "Roll on the floor" line. Another would Cut the Pigeon Wing[6] at intervals. They varied the above song with:

> Sugar in my coffee
> The rabbit hipped
> The rabbit hopped
> The rabbit bit off
> The turnip top.
>
> A little more sugar in my coffee, O.
> I do love sugar in my coffee, O.
>
> I do love liquor
> And I will take a dram
> I'd ruther be a nigger
> Than a pore white man.
>
> A little more sugar in my coffee, O.
> I do love sugar in my coffee, O.

An old mammy sitting near by where the games were being played told us that "the Chillum were juest a rabbit dancin'."

RHYME. I KNOW ENO

Miss Eleanor Simpson of East Durham contributed this ingenious tongue-twisting wit-mixer in 1923. Today I would certainly be remiss if I did not dedicate it to Dr. Holger O. Nygard, Duke's well-known ballad scholar, whose laudable efforts have done much toward preserving the natural beauty of the Eno River.

> I know Eno, you know too.
> In fact we all three know.
> We know Eno, he knows you.
> You know, I know Eno.

RHYME. TROT A HORSE

The following two variants of this bouncing rhyme present contrasting viewpoints, showing, I believe, that so many of our problems may have their roots in simple things.

---

6. [Jump and click the heels together.]

A. From Mrs. Nilla Lancaster of Wayne Co.

> Trot a horse, trot a horse, my little man,
> Better mind out you don't fall down.

B. From Valeria Johnson Howard of Roseboro, Sampson Co.

> Trot a little horse and go to town
> Take a load of buckshot to shoot a nigger down.

BELIEFS AND CUSTOMS

You must pinch a baby's nose for nine mornings after birth to make the nose pretty. Sometimes a clothes pin is used. Rub a baby's head while it is little to make it a nice shape. (Paul Green, Chapel Hill, from Eastern N. C., 1926–'28)

Painters (Panthers) can smell childbirth blood for miles (Anon.)

A cat should not be permitted in a room with a corpse. (Louise Lucas of White Oak, Bladen Co.)

Put a saucer of salt on a corpse to keep it from swelling. (Anon.)

Hair Color Restorative: sage tea. (Kate S. Russell of Roxboro, Person Co.)

Homemade Coffee: roasted bran and molasses (John F. Doering of N.Y.), or parched wheat (Kathleen Mock of Davidson Co.).

Horse Fiddle: Instrument used in belling a newly married couple, composed of a large box made of thick boards with one end left open. A well-rosined plank is used like the bow of a violin, and two men push it back and forth over the open sides of the box. Two sides of the box take the place of the strings of the violin, and the whole box acts as a sounding board. (From a longer description of wedding customs by Fred Ketcham.)

PROVERBS AND SAWS

HAND: Keep your hand upon the throttle and your eye upon the rail. (Paul Green, Chapel Hill; originally from hymn "Life's Mountain Railway to Heaven.")

JOY: Joy go with you and peace behind you, / But never quite catch up with you. (Gertrude Allen Vaught of Alexander Co.) Joy go with you, you'll leave peace behind you. (Anon.)

NINETY-NINE: Ninety-nine pounds is an old hag's weight. (Anon.)

SAID: Least said, soonest mended. Little said is soon mended. Least said the better. (All Anon.)

SCRATCH: He scratched his cakes and poured syrup down his back. (Paul Green)

SUN: The sun should never set on anger. (Paul Green)

WOOD: Don't put no 'pendance in dead wood. (Paul Green)

LEGEND. WHAT CAUSED THE BROWN MOUNTAIN LIGHTS

Narrated by Mrs. Ira Vance of Pineola, c. 1941, as told by Granny Clark.

(The following unpublished legend is, in my opinion, the gem of the collection. In this murder mystery with its supernatural resolution, the action centers on North Carolina's most famous phenomenon, the Brown Mountain Lights.[7] As if these elements were not titillating enough for the folklorist, the story is told in the first person, *and,* according to a note by Brown, within earshot of the villain's sister.

(Such a curiosity-rousing narrative naturally brought out the detective in me: What is fact, and what is fancy in this tale? Who are the characters, and where are the landmarks? So I wrote Mrs. Vance, the narrator, and learned sadly that ill health has rendered her unable to recall any of the facts. At the same time, editor Stith Thompson cannot recall why the tale was not published. Obviously, though, Professor White had expected the inclusion of some Brown Mountain material, as evinced by his authoritative notes on the Lights, *Brown* I, 628–630.

(So I present the mystery of "What Caused the Brown Mountain Lights," and, trusting that time has not completely concealed the answers, I call on my fellow sleuths and folklorists to investigate and report until all of the facts are known and the case is closed.—C.B.)

Well, I'll tell you now what caused the Brown Mountain Lights. There's lots of folks thinks they are caused by minerals—different kinds of minerals or something like that, but I know that it wasn't caused by that. I know why it is caused, because there wasn't any lights there before this tragedy happened.

Now Jim was a mean and cruel man and he had the most lovely little wife you ever saw. She was just as good and *clever* as she could be. Her name was Belinda, and Belinda was expecting to have a baby and Jim was just as mean to her as he could be, and he was kind of sparking another old woman that was around there in the country. Her name was Susie. He was crazy about her, and so one day Belinda was not feeling so good, and folks missed her out of the community, and

7. [Small balls of red or orange light that have appeared at irregular intervals since about 1913 moving about on Brown Mountain.]

some folks went over to her house one day and asked Jim where
Belinda was, and he says, "Oh, Linda, she just put on her old bonnet
and left the other day and she hasn't come back yet."

Folks got to looking around and found blood on the door steps and
blood on the gate and down the road where there was wagon tracks.
And so folks got to hunting for Belinda, and, way about ten or twelve
miles away from where they lived, they found Belinda's bonnet. And
immediately after they found the bonnet, they got to searching all
through the woods for Belinda, and all of a sudden fire got out and
swept the whole country out. And so of course if there was any more
clues as to Belinda's whereabouts, it was destroyed when the fire passed
through; and immediately after that the Brown Mountain Lights came.

And so I watched and I watched the Brown Mountain Lights and I
decided there was something quare about it, and I was going to find
out what it was. So one night I kept seeing the lights go up and come
down and go out, and there would be two or three lights that would
come up and go down, up and down and out, and up and down, so I
decided I would get the position of those lights located on Brown
Mountain and in the daytime I would go and search it out and see
what caused it.

So I went over there with a couple of my friends and we came to the
face of a big cliff, and I climbed around and got on top of the cliff and
looked down at the bottom, and I saw a pile of stones laying down
there at the foot of that cliff. And I says, says I to myself, "The Lord
didn't put them stones there. That's been put there by the hand of
man."

I climbed down off the cliff and went down there and unpiled those
stones and what do you suppose I found? I found the skull of a grown
person and the skull of a baby. You know folks say the skulls of
murdered people never decay, and I have heard all my life that if you
ever took the skull of a murdered person and got it over the head of
the person who murdered the one who was murdered, and asked them
about it they couldn't tell a lie; they would have to tell the truth.

So we picked up those skulls and took them back to Jim's house and
put them in the loft and we kept watching and watching until one day
we found him sitting right under those skulls and I just popped right
up and asked, "Did you kill Belinda?" And he raised up and turned
just as white as a sheet and trembled, and the sweat just poured off him
and he didn't say a word.

It passed off that he was just about as mean to Susie as he was to
Belinda, and Susie was afraid to say anything, afraid he would beat her
and maybe kill her. So it passed off till his health began to fail and he
got sick, and oh he had the awfulest time in the world. He was all the

time a-screaming and hollering and had a stick in his hand beating it in the air and saying, "Oh Belinda, get away, get away, get away, take that crying baby away!" And he just screamed and screamed and did that way for weeks and weeks.

The folks at that time let their cattle all run in the range, and they had their calves penned up so the cows would come so they could get the milk, and hogs and everything run out in the woods then; and the evening that Jim was about to die he was worse than usual. He had been screaming all day and fighting Belinda away from him all day long, and it looked like he was completely exhausted. He had gotten to where he couldn't raise his voice and he had just about passed fighting with his stick, and all of a sudden all the chickens began to cackle and the roosters began to crow, and the ducks began to quack, and the geese began to holler, pigs began to squeal, cows began to bawl, and horses began to neigh, and the gate flew open and we looked out and saw a black cart backed right up to the door. It started pulling out and when he started to leave the door, there was a big black ball laying in the black cart, and Jim was dead.

(Note by Brown: After Mrs. Vance finished dictating, she said: "I should have been more careful about relating this story because Granny—Jim's sister—may still be out in the kitchen." The daughter went to look and reported that Granny was still there.)

SOME COYOTE STORIES
FROM THE MAIDU INDIANS
OF CALIFORNIA

Roland B. Dixon

For about thirty years following the founding of the American Folklore Society in 1888 the pages of the Journal of American Folklore were largely given over to the publication of texts in order to fulfill one of the society's main purposes of preserving "fast-vanishing relics" from extinction. A high percentage of these texts were American Indian narratives, and the ones in JAF, combined with hundreds of other Indian tales published in anthropological journals, in government reports, and in monographs and books, constitute what folklorist Stith Thompson has referred to as "by far the most extensive body of tales representative of any primitive people."[1]

The following four stories from Roland Dixon's fieldwork in northern California are of the type widely known in American Indian tradition as "trickster tales." The trickster hero is mentioned in an essay by Roger D. Abrahams, "Some Varieties of Heroes in America," as one who "expends much of his energy in antisocial or anti-authoritarian activity." He is, Abrahams suggests, "an approved steam-valve for the group . . . allowed to perform in this basically childish way so that the group may vicariously live his adventures without actually acting in his impulses."[2] Coyote in these four Maidu stories acts the typical role that in other Native American groups was played by Raven, another animal, or a man. He is capricious and violent, a liar and robber, incestuous and bigamous, and he brings harm and destruction to himself as well as to others. But at the same time he feeds some hungry birds, gives haughty creatures their comeuppance, and even experiences a god-like resurrection after injury and death. We can well understand Thompson's opinion (Tales, p. xviii) that for the non-Indian reader "perhaps the most incongruous feature of the trickster tales is the frequent identification of the buffoon with the culture hero." Yet, despite all the apparently alien aspects of his character, occasionally one of Coyote's adventures seems quite familiar; for example, the story of "Coyote and the Fleas" is an obvious variant of the well known "Pandora's Box" theme (Motif

---

1. The work from which this quotation comes contains a good selection of typical Indian tale texts: see Tales of the North American Indians, selected and annotated by Stith Thompson (1929; Bloomington, Indiana: Midland Books paperback edition, 1966).

2. Journal of the Folklore Institute, Vol. 3 (1966), p. 342.

C321.),[3] while his role as a "marplot" corresponds to the actions of Loki in Norse myths.

Lacking context and background information, these translated texts —isolated in print from the traditional oral culture—pose many puzzles. Is Coyote to be pictured as an animal, a human being, or some kind of amorphous combination of the two? He interacts mostly with other animals, it is true, but they all seem to live in camps and huts, use fire and tobacco, cook their food, carry Indian weapons, and take part in gambling, funerals, and other human activities. In the third of these stories Coyote's shape is clearly animal-like with hide and tail, but in the fourth he is said to be married to an "old woman."

The essay by Judy Trejo in Section 2, "Coyote Tales: A Paiute Commentary," fills in some of the performance and cultural context for the telling of such tales in Indian families. (Among other things, she indicates that sometimes Indian children too were confused about the possible human or animal shape of the trickster.) We also observe here that just as Dixon's four texts all end with a formula sentence ("People can call me Coyote."), the narrations began, as European fairy tales do, with another formula. Further, Trejo's texts from Idaho, Oregon, and Nevada include several variations on themes found in Dixon's California versions, and she provides personal interpretations of the Paiute tales. Non-Indian readers might study only the texts in these two collections first and then attempt to list possible meanings they seem to embody before reading Judy Trejo's account of the "lessons" which Indian children sensed in them. For further analysis of the trickster hero see Paul Radin's The Trickster: A Study in American Indian Mythology (New York: Philosophical Library, 1956).

(THE Coyote stories here given were collected as part of the work of the C. P. Huntington Expedition during the summer of 1899, among the "Koyoma" or Maidu of the higher Sierra in the vicinity of Genessee and Taylorsville, Plumas County, Cal. The Maidu, both of the Sierra and of the Sacramento Valley, have a large number of such stories in addition to others of a more serious nature, in which the Coyote acts as a marplot to the plans of Kodoyanpe, the Creator.)

THE COYOTE AND THE GRIZZLY BEARS

LONG AGO THE COYOTE and the Grizzly Bears had a falling out. There were two Bears who had a couple of small birds, called Pitsititi.

---

3. See Stith Thompson, *The Motif-Index of Folk Literature*, 6 vols. (Copenhagen: Rosenkilde and Bagger, 1955–1958), the standard classification of narrative units or "motifs" in folktales.

Whenever the Bears went down to the valley to get berries, they left these two birds at home. Once, while the Bears were away, the Coyote came to the Bears' camp, and asked the two little birds whether the Bears gave them enough to eat. Said the little birds, "No, they do not; we are always hungry." The Coyote then asked whether there was any food in the camp, and the birds told him that there was, the Bears keeping a large supply on hand. Said the Coyote, "If you will show me the food, I will get up a fine dinner, and then we can all eat." The little birds agreed, and the Coyote prepared the food, and all had a great feast. When they were all through, the Coyote took up a small stick from the ground, thrust it into his nose to draw blood, and then with the blood marked a red stripe on the heads of the birds, and said, "When the Bears come back and ask you two who did this, say, 'The Coyote did it.'" Then the Coyote went off down the hill into the valley where the Bears were picking berries, and shouted from the side-hill, "Get out of there! That ground belongs to my grandmother." Then he went back up the hill to his own camp.

The two Bears came home, and when they saw the birds, asked them who had been there and painted their heads with red. The two little birds answered that it was the Coyote. The Bears were very angry. They wanted to have their revenge, so they set out for the Coyote's camp. Before they reached it, however, the Coyote had made all his preparations to receive them. He let the fire go out, cluttered up the camp with filth, then lay down beside the fireplace, and blew the ashes up into the air, so that they settled on him as he lay there, and made it appear as if he had not been out of the camp for a long time. He meant to deny everything that the two little birds had said, and claim to have been sick for a long while.

The Bears on their part had made plans also. Said one, "I will go in after him, while you stay by the smoke-hole outside, and catch him if he tries to escape by that way." They both carried sharp-pointed digging-sticks. The first Bear went into the hut, and asked him what the trouble was, and the Coyote replied, "Oh, I'm sick." To this the Bear said, "I don't believe you. You have been down at my camp, and made trouble there." "No, I haven't," said the Coyote, "I've been sick up here for a long time." "But the birds said that you had been down at the camp, and had marked their heads with red, and eaten up all the food," replied the Bear. The Coyote, however, stoutly denied that he had been to the Bears' camp, and repeated the statement that he had been lying sick in his hut for a long time. "I've been here sick," he said, "and have heard the children playing round outside, but no one has come in to see how I was." At this moment the Bear made a thrust at the Coyote with the sharp stick. The Coyote dodged, crying, as he did so, "Whee." The Bear struck again, but this time the Coyote jumped up through the smoke-hole, and escaped. The other Bear, who was stationed at the smoke-hole, struck at the Coyote as he passed, but missed him.

As soon as he was clear of the hut, the Coyote ran to a big log, where he had hidden his bow and arrows. The Bears followed as fast as they could, crying, "Hurry up, there, hurry up! We'll catch him, and make a quiver out of his skin." The Coyote jumped over the log to where his bow was, and got it and his arrows all ready. He waited for the Bears to jump up on the log. The one that had been at the smoke-hole reached the log first, jumped up on it, and was shot by the Coyote at once. The other Bear came next, and was likewise shot by the Coyote. When he had killed both the Bears, he came out from behind the log, and said, "All people can call me Coyote."

COYOTE AND THE FLEAS

The Coyote was walking along a road one day, and came to where a Mole was working. He stood and watched the Mole for a while, then stuck his foot down in front of the Mole, and kicked him out of the ground, saying "Hello, Cousin." The Mole had a little sack that he was carrying, and the Coyote, thinking that it contained tobacco, said, "Here, give me a smoke." The Mole replied, "No, I have no tobacco." The Coyote answered, "Why, yes, you have; you have some in that little sack." The Mole repeated that he had no tobacco, that there was none in the sack. "Let me look in the sack," said the Coyote. "No, you can't look at it," said the Mole. "Well, then, if you won't let me, I will take it away from you," and the Coyote grabbed the sack, and took it away. He opened it, and found that it was full of fleas. They jumped all over him, and began to bite him. The Coyote cried out, "Take it back, Cousin, take it back," but the Mole had run to his hole, and disappeared. The Coyote was left to howl alone. After a while he looked around, and said, "People can call me Coyote."

COYOTE AND THE GRAY FOX

The Coyote was going up over a hill into a valley that lay on the far side, when he saw a Gray Fox coming down the valley along the foothills. The Fox kept crying out, as he thought that the Coyote would not come into the valley while he was there. The Coyote said to himself, "What can he be crying out so loudly for?" In order to see what was the trouble, the Coyote trotted down the hill towards the Fox, and coming within a hundred yards of the Fox, said, "I'll bet that is my cousin." He caught up with the Fox, and asked what had been the cause of his crying and hallooing so loudly. The Fox answered that he had been gambling, and had lost his hide, which the winner had taken to make a quiver of. (This was a lie, but the Fox knew that the Coyote always believed everything he was told.) The Coyote said, "How do you fellows take your skin off in that way?" "I cannot tell you how it is done," said the Fox, "but I could show you if I only had some one to work on." "Does it hurt much?" asked the Coyote. "Oh, no, not generally; if it does, however, you have to keep perfectly still," replied the Fox. "Well, if it does not hurt much, you had better try it on me; I want to see how it feels." Now this was just what the Fox wanted, so he said, "All right, lie down here, and I'll see if I can do it for you." Pretty soon the Fox had all the Coyote's hide stripped off, except the tip of his nose; when he got this far, he just broke the end of the nose off, thus killing the Coyote. Then the Fox laughed and shook the skin, saying, "I'll make me a Coyote-quiver for my arrows out of this," and went off, leaving the Coyote lying there. By and by the Buzzard came along, and picked out the Coyote's eyes. While he was eating them, the Coyote came to life, jumped up, and cried, "Who is that that is digging my eyes out?" But his eyes were both gone, and he could not see anything. He crawled about in despair, but soon came to a pine-tree where he found a lot of gum. He took two pieces of this, stuck them in his eye-sockets, and made a pair of eyes of them. When he had done this, he found that he had lost his tail. So he picked up a bit of a branch that was lying on the ground near by, and stuck it on for a tail. As he went off, he said, "People can call me Coyote."

How the Coyote Married His Daughter

One of the Coyote's daughters was a very beautiful girl. The Coyote was very fond of her, and was always scheming as to how he might succeed in marrying her. One day a plan occurred to him. He made believe that he was sick, and lay there, groaning. He told his family that he was going to die, and instructed them to prepare a scaffold three or four feet high of boughs, etc., to burn his body on. The Coyote's wife and daughters prepared everything according to directions, and gathered a great quantity of sage-brush to put under the scaffold when the time came to burn the body. The Coyote told them that when they had once started the fire, they were to go away at once, and not look back. Soon after telling them this, the Coyote made believe he was dead. His family carried out his orders, and having lit the fire under his body, went away, crying. As soon as they were gone, the Coyote jumped down from the scaffold, and went off. Two or three days after he came back, and meeting his daughter, made love to her. After a while he married her. A week or two after they were married, the old woman who had been the Coyote's wife before suspected that there was something wrong. She suspected that the man who had married her daughter was really her own husband whom they had thought dead. One day, when the Coyote had gone out hunting, the old woman said to her daughter, "I think that you have married your father." The old woman knew that the Coyote had a scar on the back of his head, which was due to an old wound. So she told her daughter to try to get her husband to let her hunt for lice on his head, when she would have an opportunity to see if he had a scar. After several days the young girl succeeded in getting her husband to let her hunt for lice on his head, and in a minute she found the scar. She said, "Now I have found you out; you are my father." The Coyote jumped up and laughed till his sides ached, then he said, "People can call me Coyote."

COLLECTING FOLKLORE
AMONG MENNONITES

Warren Kliewer

In the framework of a brief collector's guide for amateur folklorists (which also constitutes a good review essay for beginning students) Warren Kliewer introduces a number of sayings and rhymes current among Mennonites in midwestern America. (Mennonites are members of a Protestant denomination founded in the sixteenth century in Switzerland; they spread throughout central and eastern Europe, and in the early eighteenth century began to emigrate to North America). Operating with a traditional definition of folklore, Kliewer has specialized in oral lore, particularly proverbial speech, which he found so common in people's daily usage (unlike songs and other forms) that he often collected examples simply by listening in on conversations. He concludes the discussion with sixteen new examples to add to the 117 he had previously published (see footnote 3), giving both the native dialect and a free English translation in order to capture both text and texture (style).

Besides providing a sampling of folk sayings among this conservative immigrant, religious, and regional group, the article allows a comparison between folklore items that are simply listed versus those placed in a cultural context. It is difficult to understand just what the saying "Handling is teaching" might mean without a description of its occurrence in use; the same would be true of "There is no kettle which can't be fitted with a cover" had Kliewer not explained that it applies to bachelors searching for mates. (He does not comment on the possible sexual symbolism of cover atop kettle which may underlie the domestic source of the literal image.) But even the suggested context fails to clarify the proverb "Bitter in the mouth is healthy for the heart." How is this an answer to a reproachful husband, as Kliewer describes it? Is this proverb ever applied to the taste of medicine instead?

That the Low German Mennonite tradition of proverbs is a rather esoteric one with mostly insiders' references and meanings is also shown by the relatively few correspondences to popular English sayings. We might relate the comparison "money like manure" to the expression "filthy rich," and Kliewer's example number 126 seems roughly analogous to the saying "sour grapes" which alludes to Aesop's fable, but few other Mennonite proverbs come even this close to the English tradition. (Number 125 may have something of the force of the traditional English comment on writers of graffiti, "Fools' names and fools' faces are often seen in public places," however.) Expressions such as "All in a row like Klassen's cows" are totally opaque to someone not part of the culture where it is current, although Kliewer's citation of a variant form shows that it is still living folklore among different speakers within that culture.

A review of the large published literature of Pennsylvania German folklore would turn up many more parallels˙ for these proverbs and others much like them. A similar collecting project among other immigrant groups could result in an equally rich assortment of folk sayings.

Kliewer has corrected and amplified his article especially for this reader.

———————

When I first began collecting Mennonite Low German[1] folklore several years ago, I entertained the hope that my efforts would not only preserve some valuable traditional material but also stimulate others to make their own collections. I hoped that others would search their own memories, their own locales in an attempt to compile more examples of the lore passed on from previous generations, for collecting folklore becomes most effective when it is carried on by many people living in many different places. While the professional student of folklore is able to do much toward the preservation of traditional material, he never is able to understand· local traditions quite as well as the person who has lived in the locality for many years. In other words, the amateur who collects folklore as a hobby can perform a valuable service while enjoying himself. An amateur collecting folklore among Mennonites is likely to preserve, in a way that no one else could, traditional lore of great value both to scholars and to future generations of Mennonites. It is for this reason I should like to suggest some of the problems which one is likely to encounter while collecting folklore in a Mennonite community, and to suggest some of the ways in which these problems can be solved.

What Is Folklore?

The first problem which one will encounter when beginning to collect folklore—perhaps the most fundamental problem—is the ques-

1. The Mennonite Low German dialect (*Mennonitische Plaut Dietsch*), also known as the Swiss-Volhynian dialect, originated in northwest Germany and was carried by the Mennonites to the area of Volhynia in the Ukraine in the seventeenth century, and from there to North America in the 1870s. It was not a written language until this century, when a written alphabet for the unique sounds was devised by several Canadian writers.

tion of what one is looking for. Exactly what is folklore? What is it that distinguishes it from all the other things which people talk about and write about? I shall not attempt a complete definition of the subject, but I can suggest a few qualities which inhere in the term and a few qualities which are not relevant to the interests of the folklore collector.

For one thing, the question of whether or not a statement made in folk tradition is true is usually of slight importance. Proverbs, for example, sometimes make statements which are true, while folktales or songs are usually not true or even based on fact. But proverbs are not for this reason more interesting or valuable in collecting folklore. Even if they were, one could frequently find a situation in which a proverb would not apply or even find another proverb to contradict the first. This can be illustrated with a few proverbs which I collected some time ago in Mountain Lake, Minnesota. There was one proverb which was sometimes used as a kind of rough consolation for bachelors unable to find mates or for their feminine counterparts: "Doa es tjeen Groape woa nijh 'n Datjsel to pausst." (There is no kettle which can't be fitted with a cover.) Yet we all know that there were some who didn't find a *Datjsel* and who must have thought that the proverb conveyed more irony than consolation. Nor is it hard to find proverbs which contradict each other. A thrifty husband who wanted to reproach a wasteful wife could fall back on a well-known proverb: "Waut dee Maun met dem Ladawoage nenbringe kaun, daut kaun dee Fru met dem Schaldoak erut droage." (What the husband can bring in with the wagon, the wife can carry out with her apron.) But if the woman was as resourceful as she was wasteful, she could answer with another proverb:

> Betta em Mund
> Es dem Hoate jesund.
> (Bitter in the mouth
> Is healthy for the heart.)

The truth or untruth, then, of a statement or rime is not the test by which we judge whether it is folklore.

Nor can we judge folklore by its emotional qualities. Perhaps there are a few emotions not to be found in folklore, but it nevertheless conveys a wide variety of moods and attitudes: happiness, sadness, optimism, morbidity, anger, tolerance. One can readily find the feeling of resignation in a folk proverb like the following: "Wann daut 'Wann' nich wea, wea maunchelei aundasch." (If it were not for "if" then many things would be different.) One can find proverbs expressing a feeling of well-being, as in this one: "Jemietlichkeit es et haulwe

Leewe." (Complacency is half of life.) Anyone who is familiar with folklore is aware that much material is ribald, vulgar, or even obscene. In this case perhaps a rather more polite example would suffice: "He haft Jelt aus Mest." (He has money like manure.) Ridicule is a common attitude of the folklore which one can find among Mennonites: "Harschoft en Schwien woare hinje jefäat." (Upper class people and pigs are hauled in the rear.) Some folk sayings express hostility—sometimes bluntly and some ironically—as in the following two examples. "Hee weet nich veel; dee es bloss hinja dem Owe opjewosse." (He doesn't know much; he grew up behind the oven.) "Wo daut Oas es, doa saumle sich de Odlasch." (Where there is carrion, there the eagles gather.) Very often, especially in the rimes which are recited for children, one finds folklore of nonsense, which seems to be simply for the love of nonsense. This next example is a rime recited by an adult who counts off the poetic lines on a child's fingers.

> Tjleena Finja
> Goldrinja
> Langhauls
> Buttaletja
> Lustjetjnetja.
>
> (Little finger
> Gold-ringer
> Long-neck
> Butter-licker
> Louse-cracker.)

Thus, in collecting folklore we cannot expect to find emotions of only one kind. It is more likely that we will find a wide range of feeling.

"Mennonite" Folklore?

Finally, I would suggest that in collecting folklore among Mennonites we are unlikely to find anything that is in any obvious way unique to Mennonites. To be sure, we might find some unique qualities, some unique turns of phrases, but these qualities will be subtle and quite hard to find. The broad outlines of Mennonite folklore will be like American folklore in a few respects and in even more ways like the wide-spread folklore of German-speaking cultures. I can illustrate this with a story which I have collected from as far north as Mountain Lake, Minnesota, and as far south as Fairview, Oklahoma. It's a well known story. A man, you will remember, was emigrating from Russia to the United States. When he landed in New York, he was obviously impressed, and he said, "Na, wann New York so groot es, wo groot mott Hillsboro senne." (If New York is so big, how big must Hillsboro be.) It so happens that this same story is told in Lindsborg and Salina about an imigrant from Sweden who said the same thing, substituting Lindsborg for Hillsboro. In other words, Mennonites share this story with other American immigrant groups.

Likewise, it is not hard to find portions of folklore which are shared by other German-speaking groups. For example, I have been able to collect a fragment of a song which begins: Ringel, ringel, Rosenkraunz." This was collected in Mountain Lake, Minnesota, and although the rime is incomplete, the fragment suggests that a game similar to the English game, "Ring around the Rosy," once existed in that community. A similar rime has been given to me by William Gering who grew up among the Swiss-Volhynian Mennonites near Freeman, South Dakota.

> Ring around de Rosa,
> De Buben haben Hosa,
> De Mäden haben Reck;
> Dann fallen alle in der Treck.

> (Ring around the rosy,
> The boys have pants,
> The girls have dresses;
> Then all fall into the dirt.)

It seems likely that the game did not travel from one American Mennonite community to another but that both versions developed from a common German origin.

Thus, we cannot say that folklore is necessarily true or untrue; we cannot limit folklore to serious emotions or to ridiculousness or to wit, for it includes all of these; and we do not begin collecting folklore with the intention of finding some unique cultural characteristics. We can, however, define folklore to include all these elements of a culture or a society which have been passed, frequently with changes, from an older generation to a younger or from one place to another by means of an unwritten tradition. This unwritten tradition may include customs, such as the manners of courtship and marriage, or it may include what is known as material culture, for example the local custom of planting hedgerows as fences, or it may include folklore of language: songs, proverbs, stories, riddles, and games. Though history may be valuable in itself and though it may in the course of time turn into folklore, history as such is not folklore. For the folk tradition conveys not only the content of an idea but also the form. The folk tradition will not only convey the substance of what happened in a story but will also dictate the form in which the story is to be told.

COLLECTING FOLKLORE

With this definition in mind, I should like to suggest a few things to observe when collecting folklore. The first of these is an attitude. I would suggest that it is absolutely necessary for the collector of folklore to believe in the value of the traditional material which he is collecting. Everything is valuable to the folklorist. Nothing is worthless, even though it may seem trivial in itself. Again and again I have had informants tell me that they knew a rime or a proverb, and then they would add, "But you really wouldn't be interested in it. It's awfully foolish." Little did they know how excited I was likely to become. I remember one informant who told me he knew a song that was much too silly to repeat. After I tried to assure him that I really would be interested, he finally consented, and he recited a little High German[2] rime that was the most exciting discovery I had made in a whole month. For during that month I had been trying unsuccessfully to find evidence of real folk songs among Mennonites. And though my informant had forgotten the tune, he had given me the first evidence that folk songs had been popular. The rime goes as follows:

> Meine Mutter hat gesagt,
> "Heirat keine Bauersmagd,
> Heirat eine aus der Stadt,
> Die die Tasch' voll Geld hat."

> (My mother said,
> "Don't marry a farmer's daughter;
> Marry one from town
> Who has her purse full of money.)

As you can see, my informant was right: the song is a little bit silly. Yet in the context of the thing which I was searching for, the discovery of this rime was extremely significant.

This feeling that every bit of folklore is valuable leads directly to the second rule which one should follow in collecting folklore. If the folklore collector values his material, then he is likely to record everything with accuracy. Perhaps a general accuracy could be taken for granted, but in collecting folklore it sometimes becomes necessary to be accurate in recording even the slightest variation in sound. Part of the interest in studying folklore is in the study of the slight changes which take place in its passing from generation to generation or from place to place. One proverb which I collected in Minnesota illustrates how a slight change in sound can make a great difference in meaning. The variant of the proverb which I collected reads:

2. [The standard German dialect, native to southern and central Germany.]

Aule en 'ne Reaj
Aus Klosses Tjeaj.

(All in a row
Like Klassens' cows.)

When I first heard this form, I was surprised and I asked to have it
repeated. But the proverb was again stated in the same form. The
reason for my surprise was that the proverb has another common
form which reads: "Aule eene Reaj," etc. The change from one form
of the proverb to another is small and is not hard to explain; yet this
small change in sound alters the meaning significantly. The difference
between the two is the difference between saying "All in a row" and
"All one row."

ACCURACY IS NECESSARY

Accuracy in collecting folklore extends to more than just the recording of sounds; it includes a recording of the time and the place
when the folklore was collected. It is important to know whether a
particular folk song was sung in 1960 or 1930 or 1900. It is important
to know that a particular proverb was collected not only in Mountain
Lake, Minnesota, but also in Buhler, Kansas, for the folklorist can use
both kinds of facts to determine the age of the traditional material as
well as its stability and resistance to change. Most of the proverbs
which I have found in Minnesota seem to have a wide distribution.
They are found in other Mennonite communities of Russian and
German background and some can be traced to the communities in
Germany where the Mennonites came from. Thus, we can conjecture
about the age of a proverb which I have found in two versions. The
Low German form states:

Scheen-Smack
Moakt 'n Battelsack.

(Good taste
Makes a beggar's sack.)

The other version of the proverb is Pennsylvania German: "Wohlge-
schmack bringt Bettelsack." It is likely the proverb is so old that it was
acquired by the ancestors of present speakers of Low German and
Pennsylvania German before either of them left Europe.

I should like to suggest a final kind of accuracy which the collector
of folklore would observe, and this is accuracy in noting whether the
material he is collecting comes from a dead tradition or from a living
tradition. That is, the collector will be interested in whether the mate-

rial is part of the everyday lives of the people or only something which they remember having been common in the past. Perhaps the clearest example of a dead tradition is the song. As I suggested above, I had considerable difficulty finding songs with words in Low German. One person after another told me that there were no Low German songs and there never had been. Well, I finally did find a few—four of them, to be specific—but two of them were remembered with great difficulty. After singing the songs, my informant told me, "I haven't thought about that song for thirty years." In at least one place, therefore, the Low German song is a part of a dead tradition.

But Low German proverbs are far from dead, and in fact are so very much alive that I was able to hear them in conversation after conversation. Since proverbs seem to be embedded in the language almost as much as the vocabulary itself, they seem to survive as well. And since a proverb usually comments on a basic, ever-recurring human situation, it is likely to be revived as often as the situation comes up. As a result I found that I was sometimes able to collect proverbs simply by standing on a street corner on a Saturday evening and listening to people talking. One time, I remember, when I was talking to a man whom I had not seen for several years, he said to me, "Jung, du best so utjestrajt aus 'n Rejenworm." (You're as stretched out as an earthworm.) Now this was a living folk tradition. The proverb came to mind naturally and without a bit of strain on his memory.

Perhaps still another illustration of the life of the Low German proverb tradition is that although I published a collection of proverbs from Mountain Lake, Minnesota, about a year ago, I continue to find more and more new proverbs. I should like to conclude with a brief appendix of these new proverbs. These proverbs have all been collected since 1959 and thus are all current. It is likely that they might also be found in other communities.

I. COMPLETE SENTENCES[3]

118. Fe dem Doot es tjeen Krut jewosse. (No weeds have grown up for death.)

119. Hee tjemmt fe aule Drockichtjeit nich aun 'e Oabeit. (In spite [or because] of his busyness he never gets around to working.)

120. Haunteere
     Deit leere.
     (Handling is teaching.)

3. The organization of these proverbs resumes the sequence of my previous collection of Low German proverbs in *Mennonite Life*, XV (April, 1960), 77–80.

121. Hee es met Joacobs Heene opjefloage. (He has flown up with Jacob's chickens. The proverb is an answer to the question, "Where is he?")

122. Fe daut Jewesene jeft dee Jud nuscht. (For that which was the Jew will pay nothing.)

123. Dee Kleagste jeft aum easchte no. (The cleverest one gives in first.)

124. Dee Krankheit tjemmt jefloage;
Dee Jesundheit tjemmt jekrope.
(Sickness comes flying;
Health comes creeping.)

125. Dee Kuckuck schrijt sien eajne Nome. (The cuckoo screams its own name.)

126. Wann dee Mus saut es, es et Koorn betta. (When the mouse is full, then the kernel is bitter.)

127. Wäa den Schode haft dauf fe den Spot aul nich sorje.
(He who has misfortune need not worry about ridicule.)

II. Proverbs with Verbs

128. Met dee eagne Schaund to Bad gone. (To go to bed with one's own shame.)

III. Proverbial Comparisons

129. Daut eena hoat enn schwoat woat. (So that one becomes hard and black.)

130. Daut eenem daut Heere en Seene vejeit. (So that one's hearing and sight are deranged.)

131. Daut eenem de Verstaunt stell steit. (So that one's understanding stands still.)

IV. Interjections

132. Jistresche Dach. (Yesterday's day. This proverb is spoken in answer to "What are you looking for?")

133. Rund om en dom. (Round about and stupid.)

SONGS I SANG ON AN IOWA FARM

Ida M. Cromwell. Collected by Eleanor T. Rogers
Edited with notes by Tristram P. Coffin and
Samuel P. Bayard

This article preserves traditional oral lore that has been classified and annotated according to scholarly standards. Songs from Midwestern rural tradition at the turn of the century were recollected by an Iowa farm woman, then analyzed by specialists in ballads (Coffin) and in American folk music (Bayard). As the folklorists suggest, publication of the totality of an informant's repertory has been uncommon in American folklore studies, but it must be pointed out that ideal comprehensiveness has not been achieved here either. Only a portion of Ida Cromwell's songs are given in full, and we are not told exactly where in Iowa they were sung, how they were collected—whether sung or recited, recorded or written—and in what order the informant presented her songs, all of which are important details for the study of a total repertory in its traditional context. The value of the article, then, lies (like most essays in this section) mainly in the range of items represented, not in any specific conclusions about function or meaning. A "finding list" approach, as Coffin and Bayard term it, documents the mere existence of specific pieces of folklore and makes them accessible to other collectors and scholars.

But even the brief informant's introduction gives us some revealing details about the singing tradition from which the songs come. They were "recollected" to mind and discussed in the past tense; thus, it is a memory culture, not living folk tradition. They were sung at social gatherings or while walking to and from such gatherings, and they were learned orally (even if some originated in print), usually from relatives and visitors. The songs were performed by groups without instrumental accompaniment, and they were combined with recitations and other spoken pieces in stage programs. Such details as these, doubtless very commonplace to Mrs. Cromwell and her fellow Iowans sixty years earlier, are valuable windows into the past for the later study of rural American singing tradition. Similar details about current traditional singing at children's camps, in families, in occupational groups, and the like would be equally interesting to future scholars and should be preserved by present folklore collectors.

The subjects of the orally-disseminated songs of this period (war, tragedy, love, etc.) and their attitudes (piety, puritanism, sentimentality, etc.) are typified in this collection. This impression could be verified and possibly expanded upon with reference to other collections in folklore journals (such as Louise Pound's "Traditional Ballads in Nebraska," *Journal of American Folklore*, vol. 26 [1913]) or in any of the larger folksong collections, such as those used to annotate this article.

Sometimes the songs are reworked British importations, but facts from recent events appear too, such as the assassination of President Garfield by Charles Guiteau in 1881 or the sinking of the battleship Maine in Havana, Cuba, in 1898. The stereotyped image of the black man conveyed in "Kitty Wells" is typical of songs of this period, some of which still circulate orally today. Possibly the singing of "The Lord's Prayer" and other religious texts may still be practiced in some regions, perhaps in church camps for young people. All of these types and topics would be good subjects for interviews with elderly informants whose memories might be jogged by simply using this finding list as a questionnaire. The person doing such research may conclude that Coffin and Bayard were premature in fearing the "final submersion" of the oral song tradition by popular culture.

Mrs. Cromwell's Introduction

THE SONGS I HAVE RECOLLECTED were used in all the entertainments the young people had in central Iowa over sixty years ago. We had a "Literary Society" and there was always singing in groups and duets by girls. We used to walk to church services held in the schoolhouse. We sang on the way, going and coming. Schoolteachers trained their pupils, so we had what were known as "Exhibitions." The programs were dialogues, recitations, and songs; but—as we had to walk several miles—we sang on the way. On Sunday afternoons we would gather, first at one home and then another, and sing. We had no musical instruments to accompany us, but we just sang anyway.

I never saw the songs in print. We learned them from different sources. If some person visited us—a friend or relative from Wisconsin or Illinois—they brought new songs which they sang and we copied them.

—I.M.C.

Editor's Introduction

THE MODERN COLLECTOR seldom prints everything that his informant sings to him. Usually, in the interests of scholarship, he winnows as he edits, separating the traditional songs that have oral histories from the commercial songs that are close to print. Perhaps this widespread practice has led many of us to underestimate the influence and popularity of nineteenth-century urban pieces among twentieth-century informants.

Ida Cromwell's recollections of the songs she once learned at social gatherings and in family groups gives without doubt an accurate cross section of what was sung in a typical Iowa farming community two or three generations ago. As such, this manuscript is an important document for sociologists, local historians, and folklorists. True, most of the songs have limited oral traditions. Some have no oral currency at all. But the collection illustrates a phenomenon that has been common in America during the past century: the flooding and final submersion of a genuine oral tradition by popular sheet music and minstrel pieces. And it illustrates as well the rather brief life that this commercial music had under conditions not unlike those enjoyed for centuries by the older folk products. Indirectly, the manuscript reveals much about the demise of the Child ballad,[1] the changes that have come into folk singing styles, and even the popularity of hillbilly and tin pan alley matter with the "folk" of today. Here, then, is the material that reflects in folklore what the spread of printing and the rise of mass education reflect in our literary history.

Mrs. Cromwell's songs have been divided into five groups: I, Songs with Extensive Oral Traditions; II, War Songs; III, Humorous Songs; IV, Parlor Songs and Songs of Sentiment; and V, "The Lord's Prayer." The pieces of Group I, all ballads, are published in full with words and music, as are "The Dying Nun," "Kitty Wells," and "Christine Le Roy" in Group IV. Ballads and songs in all other categories, except "Tough Not! Taste Not!," "Alone," and "Forsaken" in Group IV, are presented on a finding-list basis only, with titles, first stanzas, and bibliographical references given.

Group I consists of material that is widely established among the folk singers of America. Though it may at one time have had the sentimental and melodramatic trappings of the other songs in this collection, it has nevertheless been with the folk long enough to get or to begin to get those highly prized qualities of compactness and objectivity. Group II is matter from the wars of the nineteenth century, and stands in relation to those conflicts as "Don't Sit under the Apple Tree" and "There'll be Bluebirds over the White Cliffs of Dover" do in

---

1. [Variants of the old British ballads assembled in Francis James Child's five-volume *The English and Scottish Popular Ballads* (1882–1898) are now always referred to in scholarship by their "Child numbers" and titles. The editors' comment here suggests that Child ballads have been replaced in tradition by newer ballads and songs. Tristram P. Coffin's study of Child 173, "Mary Hamilton," is in Section 3.]

relation to World War II. Group III involves humor of the sort characteristic in the music halls of a century and more ago. Out of this background rose better-known folk songs, such as the comic "Springfield Mountain" and "Ole Bangum." Group IV, by far the largest group, is representative of material that has fed oral tradition to a degree (for example, "Kitty Wells," "The Dying Nun," and "Christine Le Roy" are well known to collectors); but this material has not been in oral circulation for many generations and it has gained almost nothing from oral tradition but anonymity. However, the line between a song like "Kitty Wells" and a song like "Young Charlotte" is fine indeed. Group V is, of course, merely a musical paraphrase of the most famous of all prayers.

A bibliography is given on page 51. Bibliographical references are designed to start the scholar on the road to building up a list of versions and variants from other collections. No effort has been made to make these citations complete, although in each case an effort was made to cite collections which contained further references. In a few cases, no parallel texts were located. However an exhaustive search through nineteenth-century sentimental tradition would undoubtedly turn up sources for this unidentified material.

T.P.C.

S.P.B.

GROUP I: SONGS WITH EXTENSIVE ORAL TRADITIONS

The Butcher Boy (Laws P-24)

Laws, *ABBB*, 260, and Belden, 201 f., print extensive notes to this popular story of thwarted love and tragedy. Stout, 37, records it from Iowa. The tune, probably some form of the traditional British setting, is difficult to identify as it appears below.

In Jersey City[2] where I did dwell,
Lived a butcher boy I loved so well.
He courted me, stole my heart away.
And now with me he will not stay.

2. [This New Jersey place name reveals the American origin of "The Butcher Boy." The ballad also gained wide popularity in Britain, where some versions begin "In London town where I did dwell."]

There is an inn in that same town,
Where my lover goes and sits him down.
He takes strange girls upon his knee,
And he tells to them what he once told me.

'Tis a grief to me, and I'll tell you why,
Because she has more gold than I.
But her gold will melt and her silver fly,
And in time of need, she'll be poor as I.

I went upstairs to make my bed,
And nothing to my mother said.
My mother she came up to me,
Saying, "What's the matter, my daughter dear?"

Then my father he came home,
Saying "Where is my daughter gone?"
He went upstairs, and the door he broke,
He found her hanging by a rope.

He took his knife and cut her down,
And on her breast these lines he found:
"O what a silly girl am I,
To hang myself for a butcher boy.

"Go dig my grave both wide and deep,
Place a mark stone at my head and feet.
And on my breast place a turtle dove,
To show the world I died of love."

The Dying Cowboy's Lament (Laws B-1)

The only unusual thing about this Anglo-American song is the name of the bar, Tim Sharrow's. See Laws, NAB, 131, and Belden, 396, for discussion and further bibliography. Pound, 26, and Stout, 103, list the song from Nebraska and Iowa. The tune is the common American folk-form of "My Lodging is on the Cold Ground" ("Fair Harvard" and "Believe Me If All These Endearing Young Charms"). It is more frequently found attached to "Mary and Willie," a returning lover ballad.

As I rode down to Tim Shar-row's bar - room,
Tim Shar-row's bar-room one morn-ing in May; It's whom should I spy, but a
hand - some young cow-boy, All wrapped in white lin - en, though fit for the grave.

As I rode down to Tim Sharrow's barroom,
Tim Sharrow's barroom one morning in May;
It's whom should I spy, but a handsome young cowboy,
All wrapped in white linen, though fit for the grave.

"I see by your outfit that you are a cowboy,"
These words he did say as I slowly passed by;
"Come sit down beside me and hear my sad story,
I am shot through the breast and they say I must die.

"Then beat the drum slowly,
And play the fife lowly,
And play the death march as they carry me along;
Take me to the valley and plant the sod o'er me,
For I'm a young cowboy, and I know I've done wrong.

" 'Twas once in my saddle I used to go dashing,
'Twas once in my saddle I used to be gay;
I first took to drinking, and then to card playing,
Got shot through the breast, so I'm dying today.

"Go break the news gently to my gray-haired mother,
And tell the news softly to my sister so dear;
But not a word of my wrongs do you mention,
As they gather around you this sad story to hear.

"But there is one more dear than a sister,
What will she say when she hears I am gone?
Perhaps a more worthy young fellow her love will win,
His affection may win, for I know I've done wrong.

"Go get me a drink of pure cold water,"
The poor fellow said,
But e'er I returned his soul had departed—
And gone to his Maker,
The poor cowboy was dead.

Young Charlotte (Laws G-17)

This is a standard version of the widely collected "Young Charlotte" ("Fair Charlotte") ballad. See Laws, NAB, 214–215, and Belden, 313, for a discussion and bibliography for this song, which is in most extensive American collections. Pound, 19, and Stout, 51, list it from Nebraska and Iowa, respectively. The tune used here is reduced to the repetition of a final phrase, so that positive identification is all but impossible.

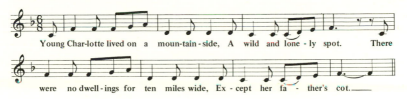

Young Charlotte lived on a mountainside,
A wild and lonely spot.
There were no dwellings for ten miles wide,
Except her father's cot.

> And yet on many a winter night,
> Young swains were gathered there;
> For her father kept a social board,[3]
> And she was very fair.

One New Year's Eve as the sun went down,
Far looked her wistful eye,
Through the frosty windowpane,
As the merry sleighs dashed by.

> At the village fifteen miles away,
> Was to be a ball that night,
> And thought the air was piercing cold,
> Her heart was warm and light.

"O daughter dear," her mother said,
"This blanket round you fold,
For 'tis a dreadful night abroad,
You will catch your death from cold."

> "O nay, O nay," young Charlotte cried,
> And she laughed like a gypsy queen,
> "To ride in blankets muffled up,
> I never would be seen.

"My silken cloak is quite enough,
You know it's lined throughout,
And there is my silken scarf
To twine my head and neck about."

3. [Was a generous host.]

Her bonnet and her gloves were on,
She jumped into the sleigh,
And swift they sped down the mountainside,
And over the hills away.

"Such a dreadful night I never saw,
    My reins I scarce can hold."
    Charlotte smiled and then replied
"I am exceeding cold."

He cracked his whip, he urged his steeds,
Much faster than before,
And thus five other dreary miles,
In silence were passed o'er.

Spoke Charles, "How fast the freezing ice
Is gathered on my brow."
Charlotte smiled and then replied,
"It's growing warmer now."

Onward still the horses sped,
Nor check their speed one mite,
And then at last the village lamps,
And the ballroom came in sight.

He called her once, he called her twice,
She answered not a word,
He asked her for her hand again,
But still she never stirred.

He took her hand in his, 'twas cold,
And hard as any stone;
He threw the mantle from her face,
And the cold stars on it shone.

Then quickly to the lighted hall,
Her lifeless form he bore;
Young Charlotte's eyes were closed for aye,
Her voice was heard no more.

Corilla (Laws F-1)

See Laws, NAB, 184, and Belden, 324, for a start on the bibliography of this not unusual text of "The Jealous Lover" ("Florella")
ballad. It is known in Nebraska and Iowa. See Pound, 17, and Stout,
50. The tune is apparently a form of the same fragment that is used
for "Young Charlotte," above.

Down in a valley lonely, where none but willows grow,
There lies our own Corilla in a dark and silent grave;
She dies not brokenhearted, nor of long illness fell,
But in one moment parted from the home she loved so well.

One night when the moon shone brightly around her cottage door,
Then to her cottage window her treacherous lover came;
He said, "Come love, let's wander down through the meadows gay,
Where, undisturbed, we'll ponder upon our wedding day."

Down in a valley lonely, where none but violets bloom,
For none but you, Corilla, we would have hither strayed;
"Down in the woods I have you; you cannot from me fly,
No mortal hand can save you—Corilla, you must die."

Down on her knees before him, she pleaded for her life,
But into her snow-white bosom, he plunged a deadly knife;
"O Edward, I'll forgive you," was her last and dying breath,
Soon her heart ceased beating, and her eyes were closed in death.

On the Banks of Opeedee (Laws F-5)

See Pound's "On the Banks of the Old Pedee" from Wyoming in her
American Songs and Ballads (New York, 1922). Old Pedee songs are
of course versions of the widespread "On the Banks of the Ohio."
Laws, NAB, 187–188, and Randolph, II, 137, give discussion and
bibliography. The tune is a worn-down version of the melody normally
used for this song.

One night I went to see my love,
And we walked a little way.
As we walked, we talked about
When should be our wedding day.

"Only say that you'll be mine,
And our like shall happy be,"
As we strolled along the banks,
Of the beautiful Opeedee.

"No," said she, "that cannot be."
"Then," said he, "your life I'll take."
"Take my life, you take in vain
What you ne'er can give again."

He seized her by her long black hair,
As she fell upon the ground;
And drew her to the river's bank,
There to see his darling drown.

Charles Guitto (Laws E-11)

This common song is given here in fragmentary form. Laws, NAB, 176, and Belden, 412, give extensive references, as do most American collections. Pound, 20, lists it from Nebraska; Stout, 110, from Iowa. The tune is a common one, often found with "The Lake of Pontchartrain," and can be compared with the tune to "Betrayed" below and to "Polly Wolly Doodle." Professor Bayard heard a ballad in Ukrainian sung to it in Williamsport, Pennsylvania, during the 1930's. The singer had learned the music and text in his native village in eastern Poland many years before.

My name is Charles Guitto,
My name I'll never deny,
I leave my aged parents,
In sorrow for to die.

And little did they think I,
While in my youth did bloom,
Would be taken to the scaffold,
To meet my fatal doom.

The judge he read my sentence,
The clerk he wrote it down,
And on the thirtieth of July,
I'll meet my fatal doom.

And there upon a scaffold,
Upon a scaffold high,
For the murder of James A. Garfield,
I know that I must die.

GROUP II: WAR SONGS

The Last Charge (Laws A-17)

This song is printed in Belden, 383–387, in much the same form that it appears here. Both Belden and Laws, NAB, 127, give bibliography and notes. Pound, 39, found it in Nebraska. The tune, like the one for "Young Charlotte," is hard to identify as it has been worn down to the repetition of a phrase.

'Twas just before the last fierce charge,
Two soldiers drew their reins;
With touch of hand and parting word,
They ne'er might meet again.

(first stanza only)

A Pardon that Came too Late

This song, probably written by Paul Dresser, is listed by Pound, 39, from Nebraska and can also be found in Randolph, IV, 171. The tune is not distinctive enough to identify and resembles many common strains.

A fair-haired boy in a prison cell
At sunrise was to die;
In his lonely cell he sat alone,
From his heart there came a sigh.
Deserted from the ranks they said,
The reason none could say,
They only knew the orders were,
That he should die next day.

(first stanza only)

My Sweetheart Went Down with the Maine

See Randolph, IV, 139, for another text of this song collected from oral tradition. The tune, like the one to "A Pardon that Came too Late," is not distinctive enough to be identified.

> Out on the high seas he sailed,
> Under the red, white and blue;
> Faithful to country and home,
> Faithful to captain and crew.

(first stanza only)

Group III: Humorous Songs

No Sir!

This song is given, with bibliography, in Randolph, III, 1–4. See also Pound, 43, who lists it from Nebraska. It is a stage song, apparently inspired by "Oh No John." The tune is not a folk melody, nor is it associated with traditional forms used with the older English folk song.

> My father was a Spanish merchant,
> And, before he went to sea,
> He told me to be sure and answer,
> "No!" to all you said to me.

(first stanza only)

Miss Fogarty's Christmas Cake

(Tune: same as "Theater Fire" below.)

A more complete, but quite similar, text of this song is given by Morris, 439. Randolph, III, 245, also prints a version entitled "The Biscuits Mis' Flanagan Made."

> I sat by my window one evening,
> And the letter a man brought to me
> Was a little gilt-edged invitation
> Saying, "Gilhooley come over to tea."

(first stanza only)

Over the Garden Wall

This song was a music hall hit of the 'nineties. Randolph, IV, 392, includes a chorus from oral tradition and a brief discussion. Pound, 58, lists it from Nebraska. The tune has been adapted from the familiar Germany melody, "Ich bin der Doktor Eisenbart."

> My love stood under the walnut tree,
> Over the garden wall,
> Many a time I've kissed her there,
> Over the garden wall.

(first stanza only)

GROUP IV: PARLOR SONGS AND SONGS OF SENTIMENT

TEMPERANCE

Touch Not! Taste Not!

(Tune: "Maryland, My Maryland")

Ray Browne of the University of Maryland says a song strikingly similar to this one appears in *The Prohibition Methodist*, 68, attributed there to Rev. John O. Foster, A.M. In such forms the song is three stanzas, with a "Touch not, taste not, handle not" chorus.

> Strong drink is raging. God hath said,
>> Touch not! taste not! handle not!
> And thousands it hath captive led,
>> Touch not! taste not! handle not!
> It robs thy pocket of its cash,
>> Touch not! etc.
> And all thy hopes of pleasures dash,
>> Touch not! etc.
> 'Twill scourge thee with a cruel lash,
>> Touch not! etc.

Alone

This text is a standard stanza from the temperance song "Don't Go Out Tonight, My Darling," which is printed in Brown, III, 51, and Randolph, II, 434. The tune is a fragment of a melody that equally resembles "What a Friend We Have in Jesus" and "Way Down Upon the Swanee River." However, the reader should consult the notes to "Kitty Wells," below, as the tune may well relate to this melody also.

> Don't go out tonight, my darling,
> Do not leave me here alone.
> Stay at home tonight, my darling,
> For I'm lonely when you're gone.
>
> Oh, My God, he's gone and left me,
> With a curse upon his lips.
> Who can tell how much I suffer,
> From the cursed cup he sips.

DEATH

The Dying Nun

Belden, 218, gives a text of this song without discussion. Pound, 21, lists it from Nebraska. The tune is a common air, normally associated with this piece and probably originally a hymn melody.

Let the air blow in upon me, let me see the midnight sky,
Stand back sisters from around me. O it is so hard to die,
Lift my pillow up dear Martha; Sister Martha you are kind.
Come and stand alone beside me, ere I leave you all behind.

Take my hand so cold and frozen; once it was so small and white,
And the ring that falls down from it, clasp my finger round so tight.
Little ring they thought so worthless, that they let me keep it there,
Only a plain golden circlet, and a lock of Douglas' hair.

Read his letters to me, Sister, then place them close to my heart,
But the little ring he gave me, never from my finger part.
Douglas, Douglas, I am coming. Yes, and soon I will be there,
Oh, I hear the angels calling; Death will bring you back your Claire.

I was thinking of some music that I heard long, long ago.
Oh, how sweet the nuns are singing in the chapel, soft and low.
Oh, my father and my mother, will you not forgive the past?
When a stranger comes and tells you, that your stray lamb died at last?

Sister Martha, Sister Martha, you are kinder than the rest,
Take my hand and hold it gently, while I lean upon your breast.
Sister Martha, Sister Martha, has the moon gone down so soon?
Oh, this cell is cold as winter, though I know it is but June.

And of all who used to love me, who will love me when I'm dead?
Only you, O Sister Martha, keep the last watch by my bed.
Sisters on your white beds lying, sleeping in the pale moonlight,
Through your dreams come no message. Clara dies alone tonight.

The Blind Girl

See Belden, 276, for a similar text and bibliography. Stout, 79,
found the song in Iowa. The tune is not distinctive enough to be
positively identified.

They say tonight, dear Father,
That you'll wed another bride;
That you will clasp her in your arms,
Where my dear Mother died.

(first stanza only)

Put My Little Shoes Away
(Tune: same as "The Dying Nun")
See Randolph, IV, 178, for similar texts and a few references.

Mother, come and bathe my forehead,
I am growing very weak;
Let one drop of cold water,
Fall upon my burning cheek

(first stanza only)

Theater Fire

The tune of this song is similar to that used for "Young Charlotte" above. The text could not be identified by the editors. It may refer to a local tragedy.

The doors were open at seven,
The curtain rolled up at eight;
Those who got seats they were happy,
But angry was those who were late.

(first stanza only)

TRAGIC LOVE AND BETRAYAL

Kitty Wells

Cox, 395, and Brewster, 357, give adequate references and notes to this popular broadside and songster ballad. Pound, 65, and Stout, 81, list it from Nebraska and Iowa. The tune used here is not the one the song is normally sung to. This tune is related to "Massa's in the Cold, Cold Ground" and to the melodies used with "Alone" and "Christine Le Roy" in this collection.

You ask what makes this dark-ey weep,— Why he, like oth-ers is not gay, What
makes the tears flow down his cheek,— From ear-ly morn till close of day?
My sto-ry, dark-ies, you shall hear,— As in my mem'ry plea-sure dwells, 'Twill

Ida M. Cromwell

cause you all to drop a tear,____ On the grave of my dear Kit-ty Wells. The

Chorus

birds were sing-ing in the morn - ing, The myr-tle and the i - vy were in bloom, The

sun the tree-tops was a - dorn - ing, That was when we laid her in the tomb.

You ask what makes this darkey weep,
Why he, like others is not gay,
What makes the tears flow down his cheek,
From early morn till close of day?
My story, darkies, you shall hear,
As in my mem'ry pleasure dwells,
'Twill cause you all to drop a tear,
On the grave of my dear Kitty Wells.

> The birds were singing in the morning,
> The myrtle and the ivy were in bloom,
> The sun the treetops was adorning,
> That was when we laid her in the tomb.

I shall never forget the day,
When together we roamed the dells;
I remember well I kissed her cheek,
And named the day I'd marry Kitty Wells.
But Death came to my cabin door,
And took from me my joy and bride.
When I found she was no more,
I laid my banjo down and cried.

The Springtime has no charm for me,
Though the flowers are blooming in the dells;
I cannot see the lovely form,
The form of my sweet Kitty Wells.
I often wish that I was dead,
And laid beside her in the tomb;
For the sorrow that bows down my head,
Is like the deepest midnight gloom.

Betrayed

The tune is a mazurka and song of German origin. See Jackson, 329, and his note to No. 24. The text was not identified.

We met in a crowd,
I thought he would shun me,
He came. I dared not look,
For his eyes were upon me.

(first stanza only)

Forsaken

The tune is a version of the "Lord Randal" tune, in a set showing the common Anglo-Irish feature of the second or B strain's ending on the fourth of the scale. Otherwise, it is not too far removed from the "Polar Bear"—"Sweet Betsy from Pike" sets. The text was not identified.

Forsaken, forsaken, forsaken am I,
Like a stone in deep water,
My cherished hopes lie;
I go to the churchyard,
My eyes fill with tears,
For there my love sleepeth,
I'm forsaken indeed.

Christine Le Roy

Randolph, IV, 314, and Pound, 38, list this ballad which is encountered from time to time by American collectors. The tune seems to be similar to the settings for "Alone" and "Kitty Wells" in this collection.

No, Brother, I'll never be better,—— It is useless in telling me so; This aching heart only is waiting For a resting place under the snow.

No. Brother, I'll never be better,
It is useless in telling me so;
This aching heart only is waiting,
For a resting place under the snow.

I have only been dreaming, dear Brother,
How happy our home was with joy;
Till a serpent crept into our Eden,
In the fair face of Christine Le Roy.

She came with the face of an angel,
To greet me a lifetime of joy;
But my heart shrank with fear of that demon,
In the fair face of Christine Le Roy.

    The jewels gleamed bright in her tresses,
    And over her snowy white brow;
    And sparkled like dew in the sunlight,
    On her fingers as white as the snow.

When she placed her soft hand in my husband's
I knew he thought me but a toy;
By the side of that radiant beauty,
The beautiful Christine Le Roy.

    But one year passed away and my Harry
    Grew colder and colder each day;
    Then I knew that the wiles of that demon,
    Had so carelessly led him astray.

Till at last one bright evening I found them,
It seemed my heart's life to destroy;
Hand in hand with her head on his shoulder,
Sat Harry and Christine Le Roy

    So brother be kind to your darling,
    My heart was grown sickened and faint;
    When I think of the wiles of that demon,
    In the beautiful face of a saint.

When I sleep 'neath the snowdrifts of winter,
Where no heartache nor pain can destroy;
You may tell them they've murdered. O Harry,
God forgive you and Christine Le Roy.

Two Loves

The editors were not able to identify this sentimental song, nor is the tune distinctive enough to place.

    The woman he worshipped only smiled,
    When he told her his passionate love;
    But the other somewhere
    Kissed her treasure most rare—
    A book he had touched with his glove.

                (first stanza only)

Widow in a Cottage by the Sea
(Tune: same as "The Dying Nun")
Randolph, IV, 160, gives similar texts and a brief bibliography.

Just one year ago today, love,
I became your happy bride,
Changed a mansion for a cottage,
To dwell by the ocean's side;
Then you told me how you loved me,
And how happy we would be,
But tonight I am a widow,
In a cottage by the sea.

(first stanza only)

The Gypsy's Warning

This song and the reply have been widely found in the United States. Brewster, 273, and Cox, 439, give adequate discussion and texts of both songs. Pound, 43, lists "The Gypsy's Warning" from Nebraska; Stout gives both the warning and answer from Iowa. The tune is one commonly used with the songs.

Do not trust him, gentle lady,
Though his voice be low and sweet,
Heed him not who kneels before thee,
Softly pleading at thy feet.
Now thy life is in its morning.
Cloud not this, thy happy lot,
Listen to the gypsy's warning,
Gentle lady, trust him not.

(first stanza only)

Answer to Gypsy's Warning

Lady, heed thee not her warning.
Trust me, thou shalt find me true,
Constant as the light of morning
I will ever be to you.
Lady, I would not deceive you,
Fill thy guileless heart with love,
Trust me, Lady, and believe me,
Sorrow thou shalt never know.

(first stanza only)

Blame Yourself If You're Sold

Neither the text nor the tune of this song was satisfactorily identified. The tune is not distinctive enough to place.

This world of ours is a very queer place, and people all find it so,
For you never can tell what the day may bring forth,
And the future no man can know.

The many mistakes of a comical kind committed by young and old,
Is the fault of him who gets in a scrape,
So blame yourself if you're sold.

(first stanza only)

NOSTALGIA

White Wings

See Randolph, IV, 295, for a similar text and brief discussion. The
tune is not distinctive enough for positive identification.

> White wings they never grow weary,
> They carry me cheerily over the sea.
> Night comes and I long for my deary;
> I'll spread out my white wings,
> And sail home to thee.

(first stanza only)

When We Parted

The editors were unable to identify either the text or the tune of this
song. The tune is not distinctive enough to place.

> We parted in silence, we parted at night,
> On the banks of that lonely river
> Where the fragrant limes their boughs unite,
> We met, and we parted forever.

(first stanza only)

The Bells

There are many "bells" songs in nineteenth-century sentimental tradition, but the editors did not locate a parallel to this one. The tune,
however, is a fragment of the hymn "O Happy Day that Fixed My
Choice on Thee, My Saviour and My God."

> Those evening bells,
> Those evening bells,
> How many a tale
> Their music tells.

(first stanza only)

COURTING

Sparking Sunday Night

Spaeth, 95, prints a complete version of this song. Randolph, III, 92
and 228, gives two songs of the same title from oral tradition in
Missouri. Both of these texts show similarities to Mrs. Cromwell's

lyric, but they are not similar enough to warrant calling them variants. See Randolph also for references to other nineteenth-century songs on the same theme. The tune is not distinctive enough to identify.

> Sitting in a corner on a Sunday Eve,
> With a tapered finger resting on your sleeve,
> Twilight . . . are casting and on her face they light,
> Bless me it is pleasant, sparking Sunday night.

(first stanza only)

Over the Bannister

The editors did not identify this text. However, the tune is another setting of the one used for "Charles Guitto," above.

> Over the bannister leans a face,
> Tenderly sweet and beguiling,
> Gazing into the one below,
> Over the bannister smiling.

(first stanza only)

GROUP V: "THE LORD'S PRAYER"

(Tune: "Home, Sweet Home")

The practice of singing "The Lord's Prayer" to familiar tunes was not unusual in the nineteenth century.

> Our Father in Heaven, we hallow Thy Name,
> May Thy Kingdom so holy
>   On earth be the same.
> Give us daily our portion of bread,
> It is from Thy bounty that all must be fed.
> Forgive our transgressions and teach us to know
> The humble compasison
>   That pardons each foe.
> Keep us from temptation, from weakness and sin,
> And Thine be the glory, forever. Amen.

BIBLIOGRAPHY OF BOOKS CITED IN THE NOTES

BELDEN, H. M. *Ballads and Songs Collected by the Missouri Folk-Lore Society* (The University of Missouri Studies, XV, No. 1, Columbia, Mo., 1940).

BREWSTER, PAUL G. *Ballads and Songs of Indiana* (Indiana University Publications, Folklore Series No. 1, Bloomington, Indiana, 1940).

WHITE, NEWMAN I. (General Editor). *The Frank C. Brown Collection of North Carolina Folklore*, Vols. II, III (Durham, 1952).

Cox, J. Harrington. *Folk Songs of the South* (Cambridge, Mass., 1925).

Jackson, George P. *White and Negro Spirituals* (New York, 1943).

Laws, G. Malcolm, Jr. *American Balladry from British Broadsides* [ABBB] (American Folklore Society, Bibliographical Series, VIII, Philadelphia, 1950).

Laws, G. Malcolm, Jr. *Native American Balladry* [NAB] (American Folklore Society, Bibliographical Series, I, Philadelphia, 1950).

Morris, Alton C. *Folk Songs of Florida* (Gainesville, Fla., 1950).

Pound, Louise. *Folk-Song of Nebraska and the Central West, A Syllabus* (Nebraska Academy of Science Publications, IX, No. 3, Lincoln, 1915).

Randolph, Vance. *Ozark Folksongs*, Vols. II, III, IV (Columbia, Mo., 1948–1950).

Spaeth, Sigmund. *Weep Some More, My Lady* (New York, 1927).

Stout, Earl J. *Folklore from Iowa* (Memoirs of the American Folklore Society, XXIX, New York, 1936).

SOME ACCOUNTS OF
WITCH RIDING

Patricia K. Rickels

Frequently the teacher of folklore courses has the experience of discovering through the efforts of his or her students the continued vitality of a form of folk tradition thought to be long forgotten. In this instance the instructor was not even teaching a specific class in folklore, and the studets' own self-awareness about their supernatural experiences must have matched their professor's fascination with the stories that were written down. Actually, these accounts are not so much "texts" of folk legends (although they are the stuff of legendry) as they are first-hand descriptions of personal experiences interpreted by the individuals according to their family, religious, and general cultural backgrounds. The closest folkloric category for them would be Swedish folklorist Carl W. von Sydow's term "memorate," and an important analysis of this kind of proto-legend formation is Lauri Honko's "Memorates and the Study of Folk Beliefs," Journal of the Folklore Institute, vol. 1 (1964). (Related references are listed in The Study of American Folklore, p. 122.)

Patricia Rickels' analysis of the data on cauchemar (nightmare) she collected from her black students takes this study much beyond merely collecting instances of a folk belief. Her approach is comparative, historical, contextual, and in a speculative way psychological. Her findings have implications for studying American history, religion, literature, and, of course, the interrelations of various American folk-group traditions. Her concluding distinction between the attitudes of older and younger generations of black French-Catholic people regarding cauchemar should be tested against later collections of Afro-American folklore from all regions of the country and, whenever possible, by further fieldwork.

It should be pointed out that these informants' written language is not the same as their unselfconscious oral tradition would be, although both student writers display some indications that spoken idioms influence their writing. Still, handwritten texts are suitable for research when the point of the study is information and self-commentary about a tradition and not the nuances of oral performance style.

AT THE TIME OF THE NEW ENGLAND witch trials, no charge was more common than that the accused had "ridden people," that is, leaped upon them as they slept and "grievously oppressed them."[1] The word nightmare, commonly used today to mean merely a bad dream, is also defined by *The American College Dictionary* as a "monster or evil spirit formerly supposed to oppress persons during sleep." Here the word *formerly* implies that witch-riding is extinct in America. The fact that it survives in American Negro folk tradition is recognized by Richard Dorson when he speaks of "the luminous ghosts who alarm colored folk at dusk dark, and the shape shifting witches who straddle them in bed."[2] That it survived among Louisiana Negroes a generation ago is attested by two brief mentions of witch riding in *Gumbo Ya Ya*.[3] The accounts presented here will demonstrate that the belief is still both widespread and deeply entrenched among Negroes in the French-Catholic culture area of southwestern Louisiana.

At the suggestion of Wayland Hand, president of the American Folklore Society, I began in 1958 to collect folklore from my students at the University of Southwestern Louisiana. Such a project is bound to be full of surprises; my first was discovering a student who had been ridden by a witch.

A serious-minded Negro in his mid twenties, a native of Abbeville, a Catholic, he speaks both French and English. His full account is given below, just as he wrote it, because he represents a paradox perhaps not found in America since the seventeenth century. Like Cotton Mather,[4] he is intelligent, literate, sophisticated about most things, but full of a simple faith in the "wonders of the invisible world," wonders which he describes in direct, concrete, and often colloquial language, though employing generally a finished prose style.

Prologue

Few people are willing to admit that superstition has some truth in it. Those who believe in such far fetched ideas are regarded as ignorant. Whether I am called ignorant or not, I do believe to a greater degree than most people. I have good reason to believe in witches, however, as you will discover when you read this story. The story is true, believe it or not, as you may.

The Ride of the Witch

My grandfather was regarded as the best storyteller in our community. Almost every night the boys and girls in our neighborhood

1. *Narratives of the Witchcraft Cases, 1648–1706*, ed. George Lincoln Burr (Charles Scribner's Sons, New York, 1914), pp. 225–227 and *passim*.

2. Richard Dorson, *American Folklore* (University of Chicago Press, Chicago, 1959), p. 185.

3. Lyle Saxon and others, *Gumbo Ya Ya* (Houghton Mifflin Company, Boston, 1945), pp. 258, 545.

4. [New England Puritan clergyman and author, 1663–1728.]

would assemble in the parlor of our home to listen to the old man.

One evening, while grandfather was in the midst of about ten small children and getting ready to begin his session of storytelling, I tip-toed into the room inconspicuously, for I did not want to interrupt his guests. In the meantime, he had begun to tell the tale of the witch. He described her as being tall and bony. She had a mouth almost bare of teeth with the exception of one long tooth in the center of the upper part of her bridge; a long nose with several pimples scattered around and near the tip; long, gray, stringy hair which resembled the threads of a soiled mop; fingernails about an inch long, and a complexion as white as a sheet. She was attired in a dingy black dress and wore a pointed black hat.

Grandfather went on to say that her evil duty, among others, was to sneak into the homes of bad boys and girls and haunt them while they slept. This occurred usually after midnight when she was certain that everyone was asleep.

This is how she went about her task of haunting; first, after entering a home, she would go from room to room in search of a victim to ride, but the only way she could ride the victim was to find him sleeping on his stomach; second, if the conditions were contrary to her expectations, she would then use force to roll the sleeping person over. The moment the witch rolled him over, she would pounce on his back and ride the daylights out of him. This was surely an experience he would never forget.

The only way to get her off your back was to pray, said grandfather. The witch was afraid of prayers. If one had the power to make the sign of the cross or utter a prayer, she would immediately leave the house. The prayers, however, had to be heard by the witch or otherwise they were of no use. She fought with all her might to prevent the mere thought of someone saying a prayer.

After grandfather had finished telling spine-tingling tales, the children were too afraid to go to their homes. It was dark, and they were afraid that the witch would attack them if they dared to venture alone in the night. He told them that if they would run fast and make a lot of noise the witch would not attack them; so finally they decided to leave. You should have seen them run. We could hear their noise blocks away.

I retired to my room and prepared for bed, but after putting out the light, I could imagine that I was seeing all sorts of eerie things around my room. Then I saw something weird coming toward me, crouching and lifting its arms high above its head. It was the witch! She made a wild leap for me, clutching desperately for my head; made a loud screeching noise which sounded like the noise of a bird of prey, preparing to attack its victim. I screamed! I immediately pulled the blankets over my head in a vain attempt to blot out the vision of that horrible creature. But she kept diving in on me, again and again. She tried with all her strength to roll me over, but she could not manage to do it. The bed was wet with the sweat from my body as I lay there helpless and pleading.

Several hours later, when everything had quieted down, the witch led me to believe that she had gone. I was too scared to believe that she had really left the room, and too tired to uncover my head. So, I remained motionless under the blankets until I could find strength to move the tired muscles in my body.

My weariness led me into a deep slumber, and somehow, during a bad dream I happened to roll over on my stomach and she hopped me just as fast as ever. Realizing that in my position I could not defend myself, I resorted to making outcries for help, but no one heard me, because no matter how wide I opened my mouth to yell, no sounds would come out of me. If you could but imagine how horrible a situation such as that could be, you would pray that this would never happen to you.

Two nights of those vicious attacks by the witch and I was almost a nervous wreck. In the meantime, however, I had told my mother about all the things that had happened to me. My mother was despondent and she did not know what to do. I begged for her help, but did not know what possible assistance she could give me, except perhaps, to keep a constant watch over me during the nights that followed.

On the third night the witch jumped me again, but that time I gave her a run for her money. I fought her like a savage with all the strength I could muster, but I could not shake her off of my back. She pinned my arms to my sides and used them as reins to subdue all the fight within me. I made a vain attempt to pray out loud, but that only provoked her to a greater degree of contempt for me. She became more violent than ever, and rode me completely out of my bed onto the floor; then steering me toward the stairs, she proceeded to guide me to the very top. There was an opened window, screenless, just above the landing. Her intention was to ride me completely out of the house through that window. Death loomed over me like a dark cloud, waiting cautiously to engulf me. I did not want to die and I pleaded with her to set me free. But she was determined to take me with her. Her mind was made up and there was nothing I could do or say to change it.

Meanwhile, my mother had pulled a bed check on me. When she could not find me in bed she began a mad search through the house for me. By the time she found me I was almost ready to jump out of the window. Upon seeing this, mother became almost hysterical; screaming at the top of her voice she came running to aid me, and reached me in the nick of time, for a minute more and I would have been a goner.

As I stood there staring blankly into space, Mother held my hands and cried pitiously, for the witch had almost cost me my life.

Now I am a grown man and I am still plagued by the witch. However, through experiences I have learned to cope with her. That is, I don't sleep on my stomach any more. And if I have occasions to roll over during a bad dream, and she should hop on me, well, the story is different now. I have found the strength to make the sign of the cross and utter a vociferous prayer.

I asked this man why the witch chose him to ride. His answer was, "The only reason I know is that I was sleeping on my stomach." I asked him whether he had ever told the priest about the witch. "No," he replied, "I never thought about mentioning it to my confessor."

This turned out not to be an isolated case. When my American literature class next read Cotton Mather's account of Bridget Bishop, I asked whether the stories of her riding people reminded them of anything they knew. Everyone looked blank except the one Negro in the class—a French major, an ex-seminarian, and an excellent student. He said, "Why, it sounds like *cauchemar*." He went on to explain that he knew people who believed in a spirit that rode sleeping persons and agreed to make inquiries about it in his home town, St. Martinville, Louisiana. The following is his English version of a story told to him in French by an eighty-six year old Negress, a native of St. Martinville.

"My husband had been living a bad life. A bad woman called Big Marie had hoodooed him[5] in his coffee. He stopped going to church and would come home after twelve almost every night. I knew that he was coming from Big Marie's house, so I would make him sleep alone in another room.

"One night I heard him straining and coughing and trying to call for help. I lit the lamp and ran to his room. He was trying to push someone away from him.

"I knew that Cauchemar must have had him. So I turned him on his side. Soon as I turned him on his side, Cauchemar left him. So he tried to show me that Cauchemar was leaving out of the door, but only he could see him, I could not. I told him to say his prayers and go back to sleep, but he was too scared to sleep. He sprinkled holy water all around his bed and spent the whole night with the lamp lit.

"What do you think would have happened if you had not waked your husband?" I asked. "Cauchemar would have choked him to death," she replied. Upon being asked if she knew of anyone whom Cauchemar had choked to death, she said that many people who are thought to have died in their sleep of natural causes were in reality strangled by Cauchemar.

"Do you know of anyone else who was caught by Cauchemar?" I

5. [Brought bad luck on him by magic means, in this instance by adding a potion to his coffee.]

asked. "That used to happen to a lot of people a long time ago," she replied. "But people have screen doors today. And, you see, Cauchemar has to count every little hole in the screen before he can enter the house. If he makes a mistake he has to start all over again. That's why he doesn't bother people any more."

"Did he ever bother you?" I questioned. "Oh, yes," she said. "But as soon as I feel him getting on me from my feet, I just turn on my side and he leaves me alone."

"Why doesn't he bother you on your side?"

"I don't know, but he can only catch you when you are lying on your back. If you are fast enough you can roll on your side before he gets a good grip on you and he will have to go."

"But what does he do? How does it feel when he is at you? Does he touch your whole body?" She paused in amazement at my apparent ignorance.

"Oh, yes, he touches you all over—even your head. In whatever position he finds you, he will try to hold you. If he gets a good grip, no matter how hard you try you cannot move. You may try to scream, but no sound comes out. Sometimes when he would catch my brother, my brother would strain so much that his neck would be stiff the next day. That's why it's so good to have someone sleeping with you, so he can wake you up."

We might note here in passing that just about everybody in this family was witch-ridden at one time or another.

Still another student in another class had something to report. This one, an eighteen year old Catholic Negro girl from Carencro, Louisiana, says she understands French but cannot speak it. She wrote the following account in a remedial English course.

One night a friend of mines came to my house to sleep with me. During the middle of the night it seemed as though I had awaken and heard a voice through the window, which was up, asking a question in a soft voice 'Which one it is?' I tried to call my mother but the words couldn't come out. All I could have done was stay in one place and trimble. A few minutes after I heard the voice again asking the same question. After I really woke up I started thinking that it must have been a *Quesma*[6] because I was sleeping on my back and when I heard the voice I couldn't get up or call anybody. That happened about three summers ago.

My white students do not seem to know this tradition, though they are ready enough to report their beliefs in other supernatural phenomena. One Youngsville, Louisiana, girl does remember her grandfather's speaking of *cauchemar* as "a spirit that colored people believe in."

6. [Witch.]

And among Negroes around Lafayette, the belief persists everywhere. I asked two older colored persons and both of them were full of information. The first is a woman of about fifty who has lived all her life in Breaux Bridge, Louisiana, speaks English and French with equal ease, and can read and write fairly well. She works as a servant, her husband as a carpenter's helper, and between them they maintain a high standard of living, sending all their children through high school and some on to college. She is not sure whether *cauchemar* is anything more than a bad dream but is inclined to believe, because she has had other experiences with the spirit world. For instance, her mother, when she had been dead for twenty-two years, once got into bed with her and her husband. They could not see her but could touch her and hear her voice. "*Cauchemar*," she says, "is the spirit of an unbaptized person that chokes you in the night. It comes to scare Catholics who need to go to Communion. It happens when you are lying on your back." "If it happened to you, would you tell the priest," I asked. "Oh, no," she replied. "Those priests don't like hoodoo! They're always talking against it. They say if you fool with hoodoo, you're fooling with the devil. Just last week the priest said, when he preached the Gospel, 'All you peoples that got a dime in your leg[7]— that's hoodoo!' All the people laughed, because plenty of them *got* a dime in their leg right then! No, ma'am, I wouldn't tell that priest anything—just go on to Communion." (Notice here the curiously confused theology: a spirit sent, presumably by God, for the edification and reformation of the victim, is at the same time interpreted as a manifestation of voodooism, forbidden by the Church.) I read her the account of one of Bridget Bishop's victims, written down in Salem, in 1693, and she approved it as "Just right." When I told her that some of my students believed an attack by the *cauchemar* did not mean you had done anything wrong, she took this as just one more example of the younger generation's flippancy which will bring about their ruin.

I also discussed *cauchemar* with an "old style" Negress, an elderly woman who lives with her tenant farmer husband in the country near Milton, Louisiana, has no new-fangled ideas, and has never been to school. She speaks English well but calls herself a Creole. She boasts that she "can't even understand Cajun" but talks "better Creole than Mayor Morrison on T.V." She has had experience with *cauchemar* and knows many others who have also. It is the spirit of an unbaptized person who jumps on Catholics who have been remiss about their prayers. The spirit takes the form of an old grey haired woman. It is visible only to the victim, whom it attacks when he is in bed but

---

7. A hole is punched in a dime and it is tied around the leg to ward off illness.

"Cauchemar stops everything." At last one can outwrestle the thing, manage to say a prayer, and hope to avoid further encounters by being faithful in his prayers from then on. I asked her whether a person's leading an immoral life would bring the attack of the spirit. She had never heard of that. I asked if she had ever told the priest about her experience with *cauchemar* and she said, no. I asked whether *cauchemar* was the same as a witch. "Well," she said, rather dubiously, "some peoples calls it a 'wench'." The word was obviously not familiar to her.

Richard Dorson has remarked that some Negro tales of witch riding "strongly echo the Salem witchcraft records of seventeenth-century New England."[8] A number of such resemblances might be cited in the accounts I have collected. The basic similarity is obvious: one of the faithful is attacked in his sleep by a mysterious being who chokes off his breath until repelled by the force of prayer or until a second person takes hold of the victim. And many of the details are strikingly reminiscent of Salem: the appearance as an ugly old woman, the entry through a window, the stopping of the power of speech of the victim, the invisibility of the witch to all but the victim. But the differences from Salem accounts are about as striking. Most important, in New England, the witch was an identifiable person in the community, in league with the powers of evil. From this fact arose the whole quality of the witchcraft cases in Salem. They were matters of public interest, ecclesiastically and legally. There was a criminal to be brought to justice under the edict "Thou shalt not suffer a witch to live." The accounts I have presented clearly show *cauchemar* to be unconnected with persons known to the victim. It may be a good, rebuking spirit, or a bad, malicious spirit. But it is a spirit, not a person in league with the devil. Thus there is no legal problem. The experience is a private one, so private that even one's priest is not ordinarily told of it, much less an officer of the law. There are other notable differences from the Salem pattern. The emphasis placed by all my informants on the importance of the position of the sleeper has no parallel that I have been able to discover. And this is the one condition insisted upon in all five accounts. Whatever else brings a witch to ride you, you must be lying in a certain position or the spirit will be unsuccessful. There is no mention of shape-shifting or of animal familiars in any of the accounts. The Catholic sacramentals—the sign of the cross, the holy water—are certainly not echoes of Cotton Mather's Salem. One of the most interesting contrasts between Salem and Southwest Louisiana witches is their color. The witches who plagued white New Englanders

8. p. 185.

were often black. The devil was dark-skinned, and so were those who dealt with him.[9] Conversely, the witch who rides Louisiana Negroes is white. The sociological implications here may be illustrated by the remark of a New Orleans Negress quoted in *Gumbo Ya Ya*: "I seen plenty of witches, too. Them things ride you at night. . . . I think lots of white peoples is witches. Others is just plain bitches."[10] Finally, we might note the enormous difference in emotional attitude between the witch ridden of 17th century Massachusetts and 20th century Louisiana. Hysteria was the order of the day there and then. Yet only a few persons were bewitched in New England, whereas many in Louisiana seem to be troubled by *cauchemar* at one time or another. And we cannot quite accept the view expressed by Christina Hole that "to-day what was once a universal creed has, for most people, sunk to a shamefaced and only half-acknowledged superstition, shorn of its worst terrors, and never again . . . to influence our lives in any serious manner."[11] My informants were not shamefaced, and two of them believe that *cauchemar* can kill his victim.

Whatever its likenesses to and differences from the classic New England pattern, the witch-riding tradition in Louisiana must, like every folk tradition, serve some need in order to survive. Kittredge remarks that all the theology of witchcraft has the same origin: the need to explain bad things that actually happen to people.[12] *Cauchemar* functions in just this way. It provides an acceptable explanation for otherwise mysterious phenomena: bad dreams, sleep-walking, waking up with a stiff neck, or even death in sleep. Witch-riding is adequate as an explanation of all these things. But the motivation of the witch is sketchy in most of these cases. Logically a witch should have a reason for riding a victim. The primary reason in Salem was personal revenge or spite, but the absence here of any attempt to identify the witch with a known person rules out that motive. There was an elaborate mythology connected with witchcraft in Western Europe, and to a lesser degree in England and New England. Both the doctrine of the *incubus* or *succubus* and that of the Witches' Sabbath were apparently related to witch riding. The *incubus*, a male spirit, and the *succubus*, a female spirit, descended on sleeping persons for the purpose of having sexual intercourse with them. There is no direct survival of this belief in local witch riding tales; however, a remnant of

9. *Narratives of the Witchcraft Cases*, pp. 261, 298, 312, 326, 344, 355, *etc.*

10. p. 298.

11. Christina Hole, *Witchcraft in England* (Charles Scribner's Sons, New York, 1947), p. 19.

12. George Lyman Kittredge, *Witchcraft in Old and New England* (Russell & Russell, New York, 1956), pp. 4–6.

the *incubus-succubus* tradition may perhaps be preserved in the insistence on the importance of the position in which the victim lies. Since a man is attacked when lying on his stomach, a woman when lying on her back, this could be a relic of the tradition underlying the etymology of *incubus* (one who lies on) and *succubus* (one who lies under).

A clearer connection may perhaps be made with the Witches' Sabbath. There seems to be a survival in the first account given here of the tradition that witches sometimes use their victims for transportation to the Witches' Sabbath, often, but not always, turning them into horses by means of a magic bridle. The victim recalls: "She pinned my arms to my sides and used them as reins to subdue all the fight within me. . . . She became more violent than ever, and rode me completely out of my bed onto the floor; then steering me toward the stairs, she proceeded to guide me to the very top. . . . Her intention was to ride me completely out of the house through that window." He was afraid for his life, because he assumed he would fall and be killed. Here we have the idea of being ridden like a horse without the logical accompanying idea of a destination which the witch needs a mount to reach. Negro witch riding stories from other parts of the South often have this element more clearly defined, even when the Witches' Sabbath is not the specific destination. Mark Twain has Jim in *Huckleberry Finn* tell how "the witches bewitched him and put him in a trance, and rode him all over the State, and then set him under the trees again, and hung his hat on a limb to show who done it. And next time Jim told it he said they rode him down to New Orleans; and, after that, every time he told it he spread it more and more, till by and by he said they rode him all over the world, and tired him most to death, and his back was all over saddle-boils. Jim was monstrous proud about it, and he got so he wouldn't hardly notice the other niggers."[13] There is a Virginia Negro ballad about a victim being ridden by witches to a fox hunt.[14] My informant has apparently kept the terminology of mount and rider but not the idea of purpose in the ride beyond mere malice on the witch's part. He has never heard of the Witches' Sabbath as such.

The source of our local witch-riding tradition is a complex problem. Dorson insists on a European rather than an African origin on the basis of Christian elements. If we accept this premise, it is still difficult to fix a European source.[15] Spain, England, and France all brought witchcraft with them to the New World. That the belief lingered long

13. Chapter 2.

14. R. Meikleham, "A Negro Ballad," *Journal of American Folklore*, VI (1893), 300.

15. p. 185.

in Spanish America is shown by the burning of two witches in Mexico as late as 1874.[16] The Catholicism of southwestern Louisiana seems to argue against penetration of the New England Puritan witchcraft beliefs. It seems most likely that the French brought witch-riding to Louisiana as they did that other, and perhaps related, survival from the middle ages, the *loup-garous*, the werewolf of the bayous. And African origin of some aspects of the local tradition cannot be entirely dismissed. The Negroes concerned clearly connect *cauchemar* with voodoo, and their instinct in this may not be altogether wrong, for the African tradition of the *loa* has much in common with *cauchemar*. The *loa* is a spirit which possesses a human being, though usually with his consent and when he is awake. The similar use of equestrian images to express the relation between possessed and spirit is especially striking. The *loa* is said to take a person as a "mount" and to "ride" him.[17] Puckett, in his *Folk Beliefs of the Southern Negro* notes that "the beliefs relating to burial, ghosts, and witches show certain broad similarities both in Europe and Africa."[18] He believes that Afro-American beliefs result from contact between these two cultures.

The reason why Negroes and not whites preserve the belief may be simple cultural lag, perhaps reinforced by voodooism. Puckett found in his investigation that southern Negroes were "in part, at least, custodians of former belief of the whites."[19] Especially among illiterate Negroes in rural areas he discovered many fragments of earlier European thought. The witch-riding tradition, though still a very lively one in our Negro-French-Catholic cultural community, is losing its moral force. The older generation believes *cauchemar* has a real significance: to punish or warn against wrong doing. The younger generation believes the experience is just something that happens without any real reason or meaning. Probably the next step will be for witches to stop riding altogether.

16. Henry Charles Lea, *Materials Toward a History of Witchcraft*, ed. Arthur C. Howland (T. Yoseloff, New York, 1939), III, 1528.

17. Alfred Metraux, *Voodoo in Haiti*, trans. Hugo Charteris (Oxford University Press, New York, 1959), pp. 120–122. Also, in this connection Newbell Niles Puckett notes that in New Orleans and parts of Mississippi a "voodoo doctor" is sometimes spoken of as a "horse." *Folk Beliefs of the Southern Negro* (University of North Carolina Press, Chapel Hill, 1926), p. 159.

18. p. 165.

19. p. 2.

THE SURPRISER SURPRISED:
A MODERN LEGEND

William Hugh Jansen

The following essay adopts an unusual and very effective mode of presenting folk narrative collectanea in which all of the actual texts are given in full, classified according to subtypes, and furnished with a running commentary on their possible functions and meanings. The order in which the subtypes and variants are presented is based on the collector's theories about the history and development of the basic story. While many of the variants are not highly distinctive in themselves, the weight of accumulated evidence is impressive, and Jansen's apt discussion of the constants and variables in the tradition makes a convincing case for his conclusions. This essay is a fine example of how much may be learned about a particular tradition simply by collecting patiently over a period of time, studying the details of each item closely, and drawing inferences from their variations.

There is a somewhat wider range of "nude surprise party" narratives than Jansen includes here; other variations on the theme are alluded to in The Study of American Folklore, pp. 111–12 (related references, p. 122). For example, the one about a housewife caught doing her laundry in the nude by a gas-meter reader also involves what Jansen calls the Freudian symbolism of a descent down stairs before the shocking conclusion.

Probably some folklorists would disagree that the B version, "the Flatulent form" of the tale, is indeed a close relative of the nudity legends. (They could argue, at least, that the logical order of texts might be A, C, B.) Since Jansen has only four versions of B to report, and one of them is literary, he expresses his own doubts on the matter. This is an excellent question for youthful folklore students, presumably part of the group which circulates such legends, to test with their own fieldwork and analysis. Just as Jansen collected some of his texts after reading earlier versions he had found to folklore classes, it is probable that members of later folklore classes reading his essay will be able to remember the versions they have heard. With this wider readership and response to Jansen's study, it seems likely that the analysis of the "surpriser surprised" legends is not yet completed.

ABSTRACT—WHAT FOLLOWS IS A MODERN LEGEND, presented in twenty-eight variants with diverse comment upon some of those variants. This legend has a demonstrable life span of forty-five years and is possibly much older. The variants here presented were heard in an area that spreads from Utah to Wales and from Texas to Massachusetts. The non-appearance of states and countries indicates only, I would guess, a lack of collecting or publication of modern legends in those areas. The twenty-eight variants seem to justify the inference that this legend has split into three versions or sub-types, one of which may imply the absorption into our legend of another more recent legend.

I first encountered this narrative in 1935, I think in December. A Junior Master in a prep school, I was lounging with several students in the suite of our House Master, David Thomas. Ghost stories and eerie personal experiences were being repeated. After a desultory pause, Dave volunteered to tell a true story (they are always true stories, of course). This is the story as I heard Dave perform it then and several other times during the next eighteen months. *Perform* is particularly apt for David Thomas, for his narration was very precise, marked by almost literary sentences, profuse gestures, facial animation, and darting glances at various auditors—and, seemingly, great personal conviction. Although he talked dramatically, his narrative speed was considerably slower, more measured, than his normal conversation rate.

A-1

(Collected in Massachusetts, but evidently recently from New Jersey. Collected in December, 1935.)

This happened about a year ago. The girl's family lives in the town where my brother teaches, in North Jersey. She commuted, lived at home, helped out her family. They didn't have much, ever since the Crash. My brother says, "A nice girl, real quiet, shy."

She'd been engaged forever to this fellow who worked in the same office with her. Poor kids, they couldn't afford to get married. He lived in the City and helped his folks. But being in love, being in the same office, all that, they saw a lot of each other. They celebrated everything together: Christmas, New Year's, Labor Day, the 4th of July, his birthday, her birthday, even their anniversary—you know, anniversary for their engagement. And this had been going on for some time, maybe three-four years.

About a year ago in the spring, her birthday was coming up and it was going to be on a Saturday, and her boy friend, he wanted to do something big for her. Maybe on her birthday she would stay in

the City and they could go to a matinee and then have dinner and
dance in Chinatown and he'd ride out to Jersey with her afterwards
on the milk train. The late trains are sort of fun on Saturday nights.

But she was practical—good, common-sense kind of girl, and she
said no, they couldn't afford it. But she had an idea. She thought
the boss would give her Saturday morning off and she'd stay home
and shop and cook him the best meal he ever had and he could
come out on the early afternoon train and they'd have most of the
day to themselves, just the two of them. Well, he protested. He
wanted to do something—it was her birthday, wasn't it? But the
next day he gave in and they went ahead with her plan.

And on her birthday he came out from the City and went to her
house and brought her chocolates and flowers. And they sat around
and talked and had a good time with her parents until just before
dinner time, to his surprise, her parents got up and left for the evening so he and the girl could be together. And they had just a real
nice dinner, lace tablecloth, candles and everything—and she had
cooked a real meal. Finally about half past seven she says, "I've
got a present for you. It's upstairs. I'll go and get it and bring it
down to you in the living room."

And he says, "Well, gee, you didn't have to do that. This meal's
enough. Besides it's your birthday." Says, "I'll tell you what, let
me help you with the dishes, first."

She argues a little bit, but when he says, "Just like we're married,"
she gives in and they do the dishes.

By this time it's way after 8 o'clock and she says, "Can I give you
your present now?"

"Oh, sure," he said and went around turning off the lights.

She went to her room and took off all her clothes. I don't think
she was desperate or anything like that—it was just she was so
much in love and he was so patient. Anyway, here she came, without a stitch on, down the stairs in the dark and into the middle of
the living room. And she said, sort of embarrassed, I suppose, "You
can turn the lights on now, Henry."

And he did, and there was everybody from their office, jumping
up and screaming, "Surprise! Surprise!" Henry had brought them
there to give her a surprise birthday party.

Well, she fainted dead away. And when she came to, she couldn't
recognize anybody. Still can't. She's in the State Asylum. They say
she's hopeless.

Isn't that something? Isn't it awful? Can you just imagine?

As I was to realize over the years, this is an excellent representative
of what I deem the main form of the legend, though probably not the

oldest form. O. Henry-like irony[1] and all, this variant has about all the features that appear in one or another of the other forms of what I shall call sub-type A. The narrator's attitude implies a horror at the misfiring of good intentions, a sympathy with the couple's plight caused by the long delay of their marriage (forget not that 1935 was still within the Great Depression), a tacit approval (or understanding at least) of the physical aspects of sex (how mealy-mouthed can a scholar be?), and a kind of testimony to the bad luck inherent in what Thompson's *Motif-Index* (Chapter U) dubs "The Nature of Life." The occasion upon which the event occurs is an anniversary, as it is in every one of the fifteen variants of A; in fact, it is the girl's birthday, as it is in seven of the fifteen. The aftermath of the event here is tragic, as it is in nine of the fifteen; it is insanity specifically, as in six of those nine.

In sub-type A there are several persistent details. Unexpected, embarrassing exposure of one or more people in the nude is, of course, a crux in all but one variant of A and can hardly be called a mere detail. But in this, as in seven other variants, the exposure is preceded by a descent down a staircase into the dark—a symbol which could certainly warm the heart of a Freudian or, for that matter, of a fundamentalist. Also in this variant the instigator of the unfortunately abortive sexual action is the female, as it is in three other accounts and as the male erroneously thinks it is in yet three more variants.

A-2

(Collected in Kentucky from a woman who had heard it from her husband in 1959 in Illinois at a story-telling session. Another participant in the same 1959 session insisted the event had taken place in St. Louis and "even named the institution in which the girl had been confined." The man the informant's husband had heard it from "had sworn that it had actually happened in Decatur and that the girl had been committed to an institution in Jacksonville, Illinois." The informant reported that her brothers in East Chicago, Indiana, also knew the tale.)

A young couple had been engaged for a short time and were soon to be married. They were spending the evening together in her home, alone. For some reason they were both naked. While in this condition, they decided to go down into the basement to look over their wedding gifts. He was carrying her down the steps when sud-

---

1. [Pen name of William Sydney Porter, American author of short stories who was famous for his ironic surprise endings.]

denly the lights went on and a bunch of people yelled, "Surprise!" The girl had a nervous breakdown and was committed to an institution.

In this passive, summary, fragmentary variant, the important thing, perhaps, is what has not been summarized, but kept in full detail: the fact they were to be married; the boy, naked, carrying the girl, naked, down the stairs into the dark basement; and the tragic insanity. This is the first time that we encounter the carrying motif, which occurs in many variants, and the first time both boy and girl are naked. In such a passive form of the story it is hard to derive the narrator's attitude, but perhaps the mention of the wedding gifts would imply the presence of sympathy for the couple and again a sense that theirs was tough luck.

A-3

(Collected in Kentucky from a girl who had heard it in 1959 and believed it had happened in Somerset. The same informant had also heard it about the same couple in Somerset but with the occasion being a bridal shower.)

There was a young couple of well-to-do families who were engaged to be married. On the girl's birthday, the two of them went out, but returned home rather early. Upon returning to the girl's home it was discovered that the parents were away. The two of them decided to do something "different" and removed all their clothing. Soon thereafter, the telephone rang. When she answered it, the girl was asked by her mother to please go to the basement and turn off the automatic washer, which she had forgotten. When the conversation ended, one of the couple decided it would be fun if the boy carried the girl downstairs piggyback. This they proceeded to do, and when they reached the bottom of the stairs, the lights came on and a large group of friends and relatives yelled, "Surprise!" The girl, I was told, had a nervous breakdown and was institutionalized. The boy has neither been seen nor heard of since.

This variant differs little from the preceding ones, except that it introduces piggyback transportation, a detail that stuck in several narrators' minds. Also, it very carefully establishes the fact that neither member of the couple instigated the sexual play. It is probably intended that this innocence should be remembered so that it will increase the shock when the hearer learns that both young people suffered tragedy as a result of the well-intentioned Surprise. (Usually,

if a tragic end is specified in the narrative it is for the girl alone.)
A most passive and pallid form is:

A-4

(Collected in Kentucky from a girl who heard it in 1961 in North Platte, Nebraska.)

A young couple, recently married, were living with the parents of one of them. The mother was leaving for downtown and asked them if they would go down to the basement at a prescribed time and take the laundry out of the dryer. This they did, but in a state of nakedness, and when they reached the basement, the lights were turned on and a group of their friends were on hand for a party in honor of their marriage.

Although the story retains the outlines, it has lost most of its motivation and all of its point. It still keeps the Freudian symbolism, but is almost an example of how not to tell a tale.

The next, although also passive and too compact, retains most of the points from some of the better-told variants.

A-5

(Collected in Kentucky, heard in 1961 at a party, no particular locale mentioned.)

A girl and a boy are going together. The girl's family are away for the weekend. She invites her boy friend over. In the course of the evening's lovemaking they decide to go upstairs to bed. After a time they hear noises. They both get up and in the nude go downstairs to investigate. Suddenly all the lights are turned on. The girl's friends have come to give her a surprise birthday party. This shattering experience is the end of this romance.

Certainly, here the suggestion is that the girl is the instigator and there is implicit in the last sentence, perhaps, a bit of moral censure. Interestingly, it might be pointed out that this variant was collected by a girl from a girl who had heard it from a girl.

A-6

(Collected in Kentucky in 1970; heard in Louisville)

A girl was invited to spend the night with her best friend, whose family was on vacation. On arriving at her friend's house, the invited girl was met with a note from her friend saying that she had gone to Cincinnati with an old boy friend who had shown up unexpectedly. The note said that she would be home about three or four A.M. and she still wanted the girl to stay.

The invited girl did not want to stay in the house by herself; so she called her boy friend and asked him to come over. One thing led to another and soon they were both stripped down to the nude. All at once a key turned in the lock and the girl's friend burst in, accompanied by about ten of their mutual friends, yelling, "Surprise!" They had arranged a surprise birthday party for the girl, whose birthday was in a few days.

The boy left town soon after and the girl is said to have had a mental collapse.

Although the symbolism has disappeared and the story has lost some organization, it does insist upon the girl's loneliness, it does stress that she is the instigator of the sexual play (both of these are important details in the C version of our story), and it thrashes around to make the point that the event marked an anniversary, or nearly so. In the last sentence, the announcement of a double tragedy may also imply at least a leaning toward the that's-tough-but-that's-the-way-life-is philosophy. And need I point out that such a philosophy is a prerequisite to the Evil Eye syndrome?[2]

The next variant has a strange origin. It was left on a reel of tape in gratitude by a young man who had borrowed the tape recorder. The owner of the tape recorder transcribed the story as a gift to me and accompanied it with a note that the teller "swears to the truth of the story; he knows the couple." The style, of course, smacks more of English Composition 101 than of oral-aural narration. Yet the variant is remarkably complete and it does introduce a fortuitous religious element that is one of the persistent details of both Version A and Version C.

A-7

(Recorded in 1970 in Kentucky.)

It seems that not long ago a young couple were engaged to be married. At the time when the following events occurred the two were to be married in less than two months.

Sherry was a very shy, unassuming girl. She had led a fairly sheltered life until she met Ricky. Sherry's father was a deacon in one of the churches in town and she was also an only child.

---

2. [One may sometimes transmit bad fortune to another by a look or stare called the evil eye, even without intending any harm or knowing that harm is being done.]

Ricky, on the other hand, was a boy of pretty wide experience. He was as loud as Sherry was quiet and had been quite a hell-raiser until he met Sherry and asked her to marry him.

It seems that Sherry and Ricky were at her home one afternoon several weeks before the wedding. They were sitting in the parlor conversing pleasantly with Sherry's parents when her parents decided to go visit the preacher at the parsonage.

"Now, Sherry," her mother said, "we'll be back in about three hours. I've just put some clothes into the washing machine and they'll be finished in thirty minutes. Would you go downstairs and put the load into the dryer?"

Sherry agreed. Her parents then left to visit the preacher. The couple, with some time on their hands, proceeded to engage in a little premarital sex. After twenty-five minutes or so of love-making, Sherry remembered the wet clothes. Ricky, however, was somewhat reluctant to run downstairs and put the clothes into the dryer. He tried unsuccessfully to talk Sherry out of going downstairs. Sherry began to put her clothes back on, but Ricky, with unfailing logic, suggested that they both go downstairs as they were. Getting dressed, he pointed out, and then getting undressed again upstairs was really a waste of time. Sherry hesitated but then agreed. Ricky began to tease her and the two broke into uncontrollable laughter. In the spirit of the moment Sherry rode downstairs on Ricky's shoulders. Giggling and carrying on, the two reached the foot of the stairs and Ricky flicked on the lights in the dark basement. There, before the couple, were Sherry's two aunts, uncles, several cousins, the preacher, the members of the church choir, and several other family friends. It seems that Sherry's parents had planned to surprise the engaged couple with a shower.

Both parties gasped and Sherry screamed. Ricky quickly turned the lights off again, dumped Sherry from his shoulders and the two ran back upstairs and slammed the stair door behind them. Downstairs the parents somehow managed to dismiss the shocked shower party. Upstairs and clothed, Ricky was trying to calm the hysterical Sherry. Her parents came upstairs and the girl's father told Ricky it was time that he left. Exit Ricky. Soon afterward Sherry suffered a nervous breakdown and the engagement was broken.

The characterization of the young couple is unusually full, but it coincides with what is implicit in some other variants. There seems to be a conscious flouting of religion (her father was a deacon, her parents were visiting the preacher, the preacher was present at the denouement)—and perhaps just a suggestion that the tragedy would not have been so great were the religious condemnation of sex and nudity less severe. The symbolism of the piggyback ride down the stairs into the dark, with both partners nude, is enhanced by the fact that it is the young man himself who turns on the light! In this connection, note that the young man, rather than the young woman, is the instigator of the sexual play in this variant.

A-8

(Recorded in 1967 in Kentucky from a girl who had heard it in North Carolina.)

Gosh, one time there was a couple that had just gotten into their new house. They immediately went upstairs, took off their clothes and went to bed. Unfortunately the phone rang downstairs—so— nude, and still clinging to each other, they both went downstairs in the dark to answer the phone. When they reached the bottom of the stairs all the lights flicked on and a group of friends and neighbors yelled, "Surprise!"

This passive, harmless form contains little of interest except the rather startling preservation within its innocuousness of the Freudian naked journey down into the dark.

The next four variants have almost enough in common and are almost sufficiently different from A-1 through A-8 to warrant setting them up as a separate version. In each, the occasion is *his* birthday; in each, he thinks erroneously that she is the instigator and thus willingly deluded, *he* becomes the instigator; in each, sexual appetite seems to be implicitly decried rather than sympathized with; and, in each, the narrative has become more nearly a joke than a legend. Note the opening of:

A-9

(Collected in Kentucky from a young lady who had heard it in 1962.)

I heard this story as a joke. In this version, the setting was an office, the two main characters being a female secretary and a new male accountant.

The secretary was a single, very attractive young woman and the man promptly asked her out. She refused him many times and he became more and more determined to win her favor and take her out.

Finally, after many weeks of consistent efforts, the secretary approached the man and invited him to her apartment for dinner. All through the meal she hinted at a surprise for him. Instantly drawing his own conclusions, the man became very excited.

After dinner she excused herself and stated that she was going to prepare for the surprise. Completely mistaking her true meaning for one of a sexual nature, the man removes all his clothes and when she asks him if he is ready, he immediately answers yes and she flings the door open, revealing the entire office staff, gathered to celebrate his birthday.

A-9 suggests a moral judgment and a practical judgment. The young man was blinded by his sexual passion. We laugh at him because he is naked, rather than cringing at his misfortune as we did in A-1. We laugh at him, too, because he made a mistake, and all prior evidence should have helped him to avoid the mistake.

A-10

(One of the two conventionally published variants of this legend, A-10 appeared in J. M. Elgard, ed., *More over Sexteen* [New York: Grayson Publishing Company, 1953], p. 50.)

The boss of a medium-sized office hired a steno who was out of this world. She had looks, personality and clothes. After looking at her for a few weeks, the boss, a married man, decided that he was going to take her out some night. He approached her and asked if she would like to celebrate his birthday with him at some secluded night spot. She said she would have to think about it.

The next day she consented to go, but offered they go to her apartment. To himself, as any other normal man would have commented, "Better than I planned."

The night of his birthday they went to her apartment and had cocktails, appetizers, dinner, and some drinks. After a short time she said: "I'm going to my bedroom, honey, and you can come in in five minutes." After five minutes were up the boss disrobed. He knocked on the bedroom door. The voice from behind the door in a sweet tone said, "Come in." A twist of the doorknob and the door swung open—only to find the rest of the office force singing, "HAPPY BIRTHDAY TO YOU!"

Unlike A-9, this strangely elliptical variant insists upon the married state of the man and thus, I think, we are meant to understand that he has added adultery to his sinfulness. Therefore, the moral judgment is harsher—and the laughter is louder. Incidentally, I owe Alan Dundes thanks for sending me the copy of A-10.

A-11

(Coming from what Dundes calls the "Paperwork Empire," A-11 was in 1969 circulated, printed on one side of a sort of 8 × 11 broadside, in the University of Kentucky's Medical Center. A copy was presented to me by one of my students in 1971.)

Two men sat at the Club and one said, "Say, how is that gorgeous secretary of yours?"

"Oh, I had to fire her."

"Fire her? How come?"

"Well, it all started a week ago last Thursday, on my 49th birthday. I was never so depressed."

"What has that got to do with it?"

"Well, I came down for breakfast and my wife never mentioned my birthday. A few minutes later, the kids came down and I was sure they would wish me a Happy Birthady, but not one word. As I say, I was most depressed but when I arrived at the office, my secretray greeted me with 'Happy Birthday' and I was glad someone remembered. At noon time she suggested that it was a beautiful day and that she would like to take me to lunch to a nice intimate place in the country. Well, it was nice and we enjoyed our lunch and a couple of martinis. On the way back, she said it was much too nice a day to return to the office and suggested that I go to her apartment where she would give me another martini. That also appealed to me and after a drink and a cigarette, she asked to be excused while she went into the bedroom to change into something more comfortable. A few minutes later, the bedroom door opened and out came my secretary, my wife and two kids, with a birthday cake, singing, 'Happy Birthday' and there I sat with nothing on but my socks."

More complicated than A-9 or A-10, A-11 still suggests a moral judgment. The man is clearly the aggressor; he is laughed at not only because he is discovered in an embarrassing situation and nude, but also because he underestimated his wife's memory, overestimated his secretary's pliability, and overestimated his own sexual appeal. He is a high-class schnook or a noodle. And, of course, there is a kind of punishment: the gorgeous secretary undeservedly loses her job; and the boss can no longer enjoy the scenery in his office.

A-12 is one of my real prizes. Gerald Thomas, member of the Romance Languages Department of the Memorial University of Newfoundland, heard of my interest in the Surpriser Surprised and most kindly sent me his variant of the story.

A-12

(Most probably heard in school from 1957–59 in South Wales, otherwise heard at University College of Wales in 1959–63. Written down in 1970 in Newfoundland.)

Well, there was this businessman, see, and in his office he had a very pretty secretary. One day, it was his birthday, and his wife forgot to wish him "Happy Birthday." All day long he was in his office growing more and more upset at his wife's forgetfulness. By the time evening was approaching, he was quite angry. His secretary had noticed his ill-temper and, being a good secretary, had done everything possible to calm him. Finally he confided in her. "My wife has forgotten my birthday. It's the first time ever!"

"Oh, that's really too bad," says the secretary. "I'll tell you what, why don't you come round to my apartment after work and have a quiet drink before you go home?"

Well, the boss was suddenly struck by the idea that it might be a good thing. He really was angry with his wife. So after work, they went back to her apartment. She poured out drinks for them both and they chatted about this and that. The boss was growing more and more appreciative of his secretary's good looks and pleasant company. Another drink and he was looking at her with more than mere appreciation. So you can imagine his feelings when, with a coy smile, she lowered her eyes and said, "I'm going into the bedroom to get into—er—something comfortable."

He couldn't get over his good fortune. His beautiful secretary was making him a birthday present of herself! Without wasting any time he stripped off his clothes and stood in eager anticipation before her bedroom door. His excitement rose to fever pitch when a langorous voice murmured, "You can come in now, darling."

With one jump he opens the door and rushes in, stark naked. His wife, children, secretary and all his staff are standing there with a big sign saying: "Happy Birthday to You."

Worth recording here is some of Professor Thomas' comment on this variant. "The joke obviously made a considerable impression on me since I have kept it in my own repertoire ever since. I think it must be the absurdity of the final situation, coupled with the relief that it was not me in that situation which I found so amusing . . . probably . . . addressed to a mixed audience. . . . if I told the joke as a student to male friends, I would probably have included some more scabrous detail about the man's physical state before going into the bedroom.

"I . . . don't tell the joke for the same reasons now as I used to. As a schoolboy, the emphasis was more blatantly on the sexual encounter, whereas now it probably lies on the incongruity of the final act."

But the real prize was given to me by Mrs. Berniece T. Hiser, "itinerant Appalachian," as she bills herself.

A-13

(Collected by and written down by Mrs. Hiser on her first teaching job in August, 1927, in Perry County, Kentucky. The [original] footnote is also Mrs. Hiser's, as is the phonetic spelling.)

Well, sir, I allus knowed that Sile is a hot old piece of stuff. I could a treaded[3] her these last ten years any time I chose, but I didn't choose. Not but what old Sile is good-looking, and so fat rain water wouldn't run offen her back, but she is too old for me. And, besides, I woultn't cuckoll[4] old Sibo, for me and him was raised together like two in a bed.

Other fellers weren't so particular though. They was one of these here fellers at works on the road gang a buildin' the highway up Troublesome from Jackson and fur parts to Hazard seed old Sile and fell fur her the wust way, but he couln't or hatn't made it to first base with here. But one night old Sibo went, as he said, to take the night with his kin in the Betty Fork of Troublesome in Knott County. Hearing of this, this ferrin feller rid up and lit at Sile's door.

Fell out hit was Sile's birthday and she felt like giving herself a treat, although she kep him on tenters, wouldn't tell him for God shore. But she did send the young uns off to their Granny Combs's, and bid the ferrin feller sit in the front room before the fire while she cooked their supper in the other room.

She put on taters to fry and heared the feller a-singing' "Dig a hole in the meader." This put old Sile in the mind of things so she set the taters on the back of the stove so they woultn't burn, and took off all of her clothes, and went into the big house where he sot in front of the fire, and her naket as a bird's eye.

Now, old Sibo had heared of these here quare women on Troublesome a-givin' surprise birthday parties, so he'd got one up for his womarn, asked in all her neighbors and her Pap and Mom and other relates; and just as Sile come into the front room naket from the kitchen house and the ferriner leaped to his feet and run to meet her, Sibo and the company come in the front door a-hollerin', "Surprise! Surprise!"

That's why old Sibo is divorcin' Sile. And that's the God's truth; and a man can't blame him, neither.

3. [Had sexual intercourse with.]

4. "Cuckoll" is a verb in the Kentucky Mountains, past tense "cuckolled," even though a smart alec ferriner says "cuckold" is never used in East Kentucky. In my fifty-five years there, I never heard "cuckold" used as a noun.

I think this is a marvelous form of Version A. It is so fabliau-like[5] that one expects to find it indexed at least in Thompson's *Motif-Index* and in Baughman's great work *The Type and Motif Index of the Folktales of England and North America*, but I fail to find it in either work. Although there is clearly explicit disapproval of adultery, a somewhat ambivalent attitude towards sex as fun, and an indubitable identification of Sile as the instigator, Sibo comes' through as a fairly pallid character, and one cannot avoid the impression that, if it hadn't been for those newfangled ideas about surprise parties, Sile wouldn't have had the opportunity to cuckold her husband, and just everybody would have been happier all-around. In other words, Sibo brought it on himself by being unnecessarily pretentious.

A-13 has all the characteristics of the A version: the narrator's attitude, however perfunctory, shows disapproval of adultery and of Sile's willingness and suggests at least a sympathy for Sibo. The occasion is Sile's birthday. The aftermath is tragic (divorce was shameful in the mountains in the '20's).

Although mountain houseplans don't allow the Freudian symbol of the descent of the staircase into the dark, the narrative almost spells out a Freudian symbolism for "Dig a hole in the meader," and perhaps something could be made of the preparation of a meal on the stove being interrupted by disrobing. The preacher is not present at the exposure scene, but the presence of "Pap and Mom" would be almost as shocking.

There are two more or less aberrant forms of the A Version.

A-14

(Collected in Texas in 1961.)

A woman in Austin had been complaining of late to her husband that she had not been getting enough attention. On her birthday the husband came home early to make up for his inattentiveness, undressed, and began wandering from room to room of their well-built, rambling, ranch-style house. He opened the door to the living room to find his wife and her bridge club playing cards. The shock of the experience caused him to have a nervous breakdown from which he never recovered. He is said to be in the Austin State Hospital for the Insane in the psychopathic ward, his hair white, an old man.

This peculiar, emphasis-less story may imply a bit of fault to both the wife for her sexual appetite and to the husband for his desire to

---

5. [Comic and usually ribald medieval tales, such as Chaucer's "Miller's Tale."]

prove his manhood, but I rather think it approves of sex and disapproves of bridge clubs that cause disaster. Certainly, there is sympathy for the male and his insanity is understood to be a tragic aftermath. The Freudian symbolism has changed to seeking from room to room and opening closed doors. Again, the occasion is a birthday. And here the man is directly the instigator of the sexual action, although indirectly the woman with her complaining may be considered the instigator.

Further from the norm is:

A-15

(Collected in 1970 in Kentucky.)

> There was this Baptist couple who were real important people in the church. It was the woman's birthday and her husband had planned a surprise birthday party for her. While she was upstairs taking her shower that night, the minister and the rest of the church people were led in by the husband and hidden behind chairs in the living room. His wife, upon finishing her shower, walked down the stairs and stood naked at the bottom and hollered, "Come and get it while it's clean!"

Brief as this joke is, there can be no doubt of its belonging to Version A. Peculiarly anti-clerical, this variant has the couple as important in the church, has the minister present along with the "rest of the church people," and may be implying that the church is responsible for the shame or horror in the situation described. Again, there is the Freudian staircase, the birthday as the occasion, and the woman as instigator. Interestingly, it would be possible to build a case for close basic similarities between this A-15 and the fabliau form A-13.

The B version, the Flatulent form, exists for me in only a few variants. The essential difference between A and B is that in the latter the cause of embarrassment (the surprise for the surprisers) is the breaking of wind rather than an appearance in the buff. Other differences will be pointed out in the discussion of the several variants.

It is tempting to suggest bowdlerization as a cause for the difference, but it is of course conceivable that a separate tale about surprises existed and picked up some elements from our legend. It is conceivable but I doubt it.

B-1

(Written down from memory in March, 1972, in Kentucky by a girl student who had heard it about six months earlier.)

One night a girl had a special blind date with a guy that she really wanted to impress. He was really nice looking and had a real friendly nature. He and the girl sat in her living room with her parents for a while and having a real enjoyable time before they were to go out on their date. After a half hour or so, he stood up and made moves to leave, shook the father's hand and helped the girl with her coat. As they went down the girl's front porch steps—now in the dark— he told her that he really liked her family and that he thought she looked real pretty. The girl got a little embarrassed, partly because she was glad that he'd said that and partly because she felt a little gas building up. He walked her to his stationwagon, opened the door on the passenger side for her to get in, closed it and walked around the back to his side. The girl, noticing his position outside the car, promptly relieved herself and gave him a big smile a few seconds later when he opened the door. He got in, fooled to get the key in and started it, adjust the rear view mirror, and turned to the girl, saying that he was sorry, but he'd forgotten to introduce her to the couples in the backseat.

Although the "couples in the backseat" are hardly surprisers, they are certainly surprised. I am told that in some variants the occupants of the backseat are the boy's parents to whom he is intending to introduce his girl friend. The courtship theme might be considered a parallel to the engagement or recent wedding theme in so many of the A and C variants. Although the horror of the anxious girl is not mentioned, it is certainly implied and thus might be held to be a tragic aftermath. Of course there is no anniversary theme and the scene has been shifted from the inside of a house to the inside of a car—perhaps a sign of modernization.

The next variant was supplied by a colleague who had heard me read an A variant.

B-2

(Written down March, 1972, in Kentucky from the memory of having heard a ten-year-old boy tell it in Detroit, Michigan, in about 1935 "as a true story.")

There was a man who was extremely fond of baked beans. He ate them at every opportunity, but he had one great difficulty: whenever he ate baked beans, he had great problems with gas. The older he became, the greater the amount of gas.

He finally realized that he would have to give up his favorite food if he wanted to keep his friends. And so he went for several years without eating beans. Eventually, he married a young and beautiful girl. She was very fond of baked beans, too, and when she offered to fix some for dinner, he asked her not to. He told her his problem and although she didn't appear to believe him, she agreed not to fix the beans.

They had been married only a few months when his birthday arrived. As he left the house that morning, his wife told him to be sure to get home from the office early as she was planning a special treat for him.

That day at lunch, baked beans were on the menu, and he almost weakened, but remembering his old problem, he did not. That evening, he arrived home promptly and started for the kitchen to see what his wife was preparing. She shooed him out before he could see and told him to stay in the dining room.

After a while, she came in carrying a large, covered casserole. She placed it on the table and with a warning to him not to peek, she returned to the kitchen. His curiosity became too great to bear, and he opened the casserole. Beans! Beautiful, baked beans! He couldn't stand it another minute. Looking around to be sure that his wife could not see him, he picked up a spoon and helped himself to a large mouthful of beans. They were delicious! But all of a sudden, the old feeling of gas came back upon him. Somehow, he had to expel the gas without letting his wife realize that he had been sampling. Looking around, he saw the window—and he opened it, turned his back to the outdoors, and relieved himself of the gas. He closed the window and walked back into the center of the room, looking very innocent.

But the beans were too tempting. Again he sampled the beans, and again he had to go to the window. And a third time, the same. Just as he was wondering whether to try the beans again, his wife came into the dining room. She lit the candles on the table. As he prepared to seat her at the table, he heard a loud, "Surprise!" behind him. He turned around to see his parents, closest friends, and minister issue forth from behind the draperies in the dining room. He fainted.

The Pandora's box motif ("don't peek") is unique to this variant of the legend. Otherwise, it shares with the other B variants the motif of unsuccessful concealed embarrassment (the flatulence). And it shares with the overall legend mentions of the wedding and of the office and, much more significant, the themes of the good intentions of the bride-planner of the surprise, of the occasion being a birthday, of the surprisers' being surprised, of the minister's presence, and of the young man's fainting in embarrassment.

The next variant was also inspired by my reading. I read A-1 in a folklore class and one of the students wrote down her memory of a story told by her husband. Very interestingly, she was embarrassed to tell me the tale and admitted she thought it "dirtier" than A-1.

B-3

(Written down in Kentucky in 1971 from the memory of an earlier narration in Kentucky.)

> There's the story of the birthday man who suffers gastric distress following a big meal of beans.
> Told to sit alone in a darkened room awaiting a birthday surprise, he takes the opportunity to give vent to a long series of raucous explosions. Then, of course, the light is switched on suddenly, and twenty people begin to sing, "Happy Birthday."

The last B variant is a literary recording of the legend, which was pointed out to me by a colleague.

B-4

(From Carson McCullers, *The Heart Is a Lonely Hunter*, Bantam Books, 1970. The novel was originally published in 1940 by Houghton-Mifflin Company.) (Biff Brannon has been reviewing his life and remembers his twenty-ninth birthday when his sister-in-law Lucile had invited him to drop by her apartment.)

> He expected from this some small remembrance—a plate of cherry tarts or a good shirt. She met him at the door and blindfolded his eyes before he entered. Then she said she would be back in a second. In the silent room he listened to her footsteps and when she had reached the kitchen he broke wind. He stood in the room . . . blindfolded and pooted. Then all at once he knew with horror he was not alone. . . . At that minute Lucile came back and undid his eyes. . . . the room was full of people. . . . He wanted to crawl up the wall. . . .

Again there are the birthday, the well-intentioned surprise party that misfires, and the unsuccessful concealment of embarrassment. There is also a kind of sorry aftermath: when he discovers he can't crawl up the wall, the embarrassed Biff drinks a quart of whisky. Even the word *apartment* brings an echo from various other variants. It is interesting to conjecture whether there is any influence between B-4 and B-3. Beans, which of course are peculiar to the B variants, are not mentioned in B-4 and neither is the singing, or shouting, of "Happy Birthday," but the image of the unhappy victim is strikingly similar in the two variants.

Version C tells a story very like that generally implied in Version A: a young couple (always a couple, rather than one of the two) is unintentionally (usually) exposed naked at the beginning of a surprise party and frequently there is a sad aftermath. The Surprisers in the C-variants are less conspicuous than those in the A-variants, but nevertheless they are surprised. The focus is more on the victims in the C-variants and a part, at least, of their activity is invariably baby-sitting. The time span of the C-variants is exactly ten years—one-quarter that of the A- and B-variants—and it is perhaps because of this that more homogeneity exists among the C-variants than among the others. Possibly, of course, the C-version was once an independent story and has received influence from the older (?) tale that is the A-version. But it is my conviction that C is merely a timely modernization of A. If it is not, the number of persistent details common to both versions is phenomenal.

Regard:

C-1

(Heard in 1961 in Kentucky and recorded a year later.)

A young couple, whose wedding was in the near future, were asked to sit with the boy's brother's children one evening. They agreed to keep the children. After bathing and feeding their charges, the couple put them to bed. After watching television for awhile, the boy and girl began petting. They decided to make the most of their opportunity. The both undressed and got into bed, not expecting the parents until much later. Before very long, the telephone rang. The boy got out of bed and answered it. It was his brother, telling him to check the furnace in the basement. The brother had forgotten to add enough coal.

The boy and girl decided to go downstairs together. They got a flashlight and started toward the door. Neither had bothered to dress because they were alone in the house. They opened the basement door and started down the steps. They were giggling with excitement and half-embarrassment. When they reached the bottom of the steps, the basement lights flashed on and there was a shout—"Congratulations!" The families of the couple had thrown a surprise shower!

The girl, completely horrified, fainted and the boy dashed up the steps.

If there was any more ending to the tale I don't remember it. Also, I'm hazy about the reason the brother asked them to go to the basement. I think it was to check the furnace.

The narrator's feeling that there should be more to the ending may reflect a forgotten tragic detail. Otherwise, the variant is typical: sympathy for the couple, implicit disdain for a society that makes sex shameful, the Freudian descent into the dark (again emphasized by descriptive detail—giggling, excitement, embarrassment), and a suggestion that good intentions have gone astray.

The next variant, fragmentary (I think), puts a very heavy emphasis upon sympathy for the couple and an implicit justification for their incontinence. Note again that the background is one of baby-sitting.

C-2

(Collected in Kentucky in 1970.)

Once there was a couple in our town who had been going with each other for a few years, but they had decided they weren't going to get married until the guy had finished college. Well, it so happened that this one weekend when he was home to surprise her, that she had promised a neighbor she would baby-sit for them while they went to a movie. Being the nice guy that he was, he told her that he would sit with her while the neighbors were out. As the evening went by, the children were sent to bed, and the couple sat on the couch making up for all the time he had been gone. Well, it got to the point that they decided—why wait?—they were going to be married in a few weeks anyway. Well, just as they had undressed, in pops the neighbors with a whole gang of people with a big surprise party they had planned for the couple-to-be.

This is a peculiarly unbalanced variant. It is as though the introduction were given in full and the rest of the tale had collapsed. The only detail that points to narrative skill is the anticipation of *surprise* in the boy's reason for coming home from college. Certainly, the Freudian symbolism and the denouement have disappeared completely.

More complete, even though it shows signs of haste, is:

C-3

(Heard in 1962 in Kentucky.)

A couple that had been going together for quite a while were baby-sitting one night. While sitting on the couch, the situation became quite involved and one thing led to another. Suddenly the telephone rang. It was the father of the children with whom they were baby-sitting. He asked the couple to go down to the basement and turn the furnace up. The boy picked up his girl friend and carried her downstairs in his arms. Both were naked. As they reached the bottom of the stairs the light was switched on and their friends yelled, "Surprise!" It was the girl's birthday.

This is told as actually having happened. The girl is supposedly in a mental institution as a result of the shock and humiliation.

This story is so skeletal that it is hard to determine the narrator's attitude. Perhaps the first sentence suggests a sympathy for the couple that is reiterated in the last sentence—a pattern that Axel Olrik[6] would have hailed. The Freudian symbolism is, however, quite complete.

Differing only in insignificant detail from C-3 is:

C-4

(Collected in 1961 in Kentucky.)

An engaged couple were baby-sitting. It was only a few weeks before they were to be married; so they decided "What the hell, why wait? Just two weeks." They both undressed. A little while later the phone rang. It was their friend for whom they were baby-sitting. She said she had left her washer on in the basement, and would they go down and turn it off? Since they just had to go to the basement they decided that wasn't any point in getting dressed, so they went down together. Just as they were feeling their way down the stairs, the lights went on and the people yelled "Surprise!"
As a result the girl went crazy and left town.

The peculiar double disposal of the female victim may spring from a faulty memory of "The girl went crazy and the boy left town."

C-5 is particularly graphic in the passage which incorporates the Freudian symbolism that seems to have stuck so firmly in so many informants' memories.

C-5

(Collected in 1961 in Kentucky.)

A young girl, who was engaged to be married, was asked to baby-sit with her young cousin. She agreed to do so, and invited her fiancé to sit with her. During the course of the evening they became passionately inclined, took off their clothes, and frolicked about the house. While giggling and pushing one another around, the boy heaved the girl on his back in piggyback style and bounced her through the rooms. Going past the door to the basement, they heard a sound, and the boy teasingly said he was going to take her

6. [Danish folklorist whose concept of "epic laws" to explain how folktales become increasingly stylized in retellings was an early attempt (1908) to deal with oral narrative structure.]

down in the basement with the spooks. He gropingly took her down the stairs in the dark. When they reached the bottom, a light came on and the girl's parents, the minister, and many prominent people of the community jumped out from their hiding places and yelled, "Surprise!" They had arranged a surprise bridal shower for the couple. The boy dropped the girl from his back, ran up the stairs, grabbed his clothes, and fled from the city. It was later learned that he had joined the Navy, and never again contacted the girl. The girl lost her mind, and was committed to an asylum.

Here once more we have the strange recurring detail of the ministerial presence, that somehow makes the horror the greater, and that can only imply a latent anticlericalism and a latent sympathy for those who yield to the temptations of premarital sex. Indeed, I suppose the anticlericalism entails condemnation of those forces which made me use *temptation* instead of *attraction* or *summons* in the preceding sentence!

Very similar to C-5 except that it does not dwell upon the tragic results of the double-surprise is:

C-6

(Collected in 1970 in Kentucky.)

This story was told to me by my roommate last summer (1970). He heard it from a person he had known when he lived in the dorm during the previous spring semester here at UK [the University of Kentucky]. The incident happened to some friends of this person in Northern Kentucky, where he was from. It is supposedly true.

The couple was engaged to be married. They were at the home of her parents. The parents were going out somewhere that evening and the young lady was supposed to baby-sit for her young brother, who was already asleep. She was also instructed by her mother to take the laundry down to the basement and put it in the washer.

After the parents had left, the young couple began to entertain themselves, engaging in the age-old custom of petting. After a while and a moderate amount of coaxing and persuading the young man convinced his wife-to-be that since they would soon be married and no one would know the difference anyway, there would be nothing wrong with making love.

They went upstairs to her bedroom, took off their clothes, and got in bed. At this point she remembered the laundry her mother had told her to put in the washer. She insisted that she had to do it because her mother would want to know why it wasn't done if she failed to do it.

The young man helped her carry the laundry basket down the stairs. Both were still unclothed. As they approached the bottom of the basement stairs the lights went on and they heard someone yell "Surprise!"

Their pastor, their mother and father, and their church youth group were giving the couple a surprise engagement party.

Again, the Freudian symbol is present, though made little of; but because of its position both close to the end of the story and yet first in a series, the ministerial presence is given extraordinary, if unknowing, significance and again must indicate anticlericalism.

The next aberrant variant had strange and ambivalent attitudes that may spring from two facts: 1. it was collected from a non-Mormon Utah native; 2. the informant, at the age of retirement, struggles valiantly to empathize with the young "in" generation.

C-7

(Collected in 1970 in Kentucky.)

In a small town in Utah, the story goes, the daughter of a Mormon minister volunteered to baby-sit her younger sisters while her parents attended a church celebration.

Although members of this faith are very strict about misusing their bodies, this teenage girl did not seem to maintain the beliefs which were taught to her by her parents.

After her parents left their home, the girl decide to indulge in a few of the habits which her parents disapproved of strongly. She smoked numerous cigarettes, drank several beers and invited her boy friend over to entertain her while her parents were gone.

The girl became quite drunk and forgot all about her baby-sitting chores, but she did remember her boy friend. Around 10:30 P.M., she decided to go to bed, accompanied by her boy friend.

Her parents came home about 11 P.M. and found their daughter in bed with her boy friend. Although the couple had done nothing morally wrong, the family became extremely humiliated and consequently, left town within twenty-four hours.

This rather startling variant does, I think, belong to Version C: the baby-sitting, the unconcealed anticlericalism, and the sympathy for the revolt against the Establishment, all bespeak relationship to the C Version of the Surpriser Surprised. I suppose the shame and the disappearance of the family are deteriorated remains of what usually appears as a tragic ending for the girl and the boy.

The seven preceding variants of C all, I assert, belong to young audiences: baby-sitting, sympathy with passion, anti-Establishment implications, anticlericalism, bitterness with postponement of living an adult life, tacit approval of premarital sex, complaint about bad luck in the way of life—all are part of the existence of youth.

The last two variants belong to a very different audience, an audience that employs baby-sitters, that is suspicious of youth, that has no sympathy with excuses for premarital sex, that hesitates to trust its babies to the care of "irresponsible" youth.

C-8

(Collected in Kentucky in 1970 from an informant who had learned it while with the U.S. Army overseas.)

> Once upon a time, I knew of a baby-sitter who got caught red-handed. This young chick was a baby-sitter in order to earn a little money so she could go to school. She worked weeknights and every weekend. One Saturday night she was baby-sitting and thought that it would be a good idea to invite her boy friend over to spend the evening with her. She gave him a buzz on the telephone and asked him to come over.
>
> The young lover wasn't very long in getting there. She told him to make himself at home. He went straight to the icebox. He got himself a small snack and returned to watch some television. Well, he and the chick were watching the television and one thing led to another. They decided to make love because they were going to be married next week and besides, this wasn't something new to them. They took each other's clothes off and started to get with it when the telephone rang. It was the woman who was having the young girl to baby-sit for her. She said that she had left the heater off in the basement and was afraid that her pipes would freeze up. So the young chick said that she would go downstairs and turn it on. The young man said that he would go with her to keep her warm. So off they went. When they got to the top of the basement stairs, they turned on the light. Surprise! There was the preacher, the doctor, her parents, his parents, and a bunch of friends. They had all come to give the young couple a surprise bridal shower because they were so nice. The young chick went insane and the young lover left town and was never heard of again.

C-8 gives a unique twist to some of the persistent details common to the variants of the Surpriser Surprised. Although the couple is long engaged, the narrator's attitude sours as he remarks sardonically on their sexual experience and upon their being "so nice." The Freudian symbol is twisted into the bad dream in which the nude couple are framed in the light at the *top* of the stairway looking down at a sea of shocked faces. The ministerial presence merely reinforces the righteous moral disapproval explicit in the idiom "caught red-handed." And the tragic ending, seemingly anticlimactic, may be just retribution rather than tragedy.

C-9 is kin to C-8 in its rectitude, but has lost the element of the double surprise. In C-9 the surprise is a trap and the surprisers have their suspicions fulfilled. Again, it is obviously a story for the older generation and like C-8 it leaves a bad taste in the mouth.

C-9

(Collected in 1961 in Kentucky.)

One night a girl was baby-sitting, and she called her boy friend to come over. When he arrived, they went to the bedroom upstairs and undressed. Suddenly, the girl remembered that the woman had told her to put the clothes out of the washing machine and into the dryer. So, she told her boy friend that she would have to go to the basement and take care of the clothes. He insisted on going with her because it was dark. So she told him he could. As they started down the basement steps, he picked her up and carried her because the step at the bottom was loose and the girl might fall. When they reached the bottom step, she reached up and turned on the light and suddenly they heard, "Surprise!" They looked around, and there were all the friends of the people who lived in that house. They had planned this to see if their suspicions of the babysitter were true.

This was supposed to have actually happened in Mayfield, Kentucky.

We can hope that this malicious little narrative is a badly decayed form of the Surpriser Surprised. It could, of course, be an early version of an independent story that got sucked into the pattern of the longer-established, more common tale that I have designated Version A. But the dalliant baby-sitter, the naked descent of the couple to the basement (this time down two flights of stairs), the shout of "Surprise," all belong to the Surpriser Surprised, and without these details there wouldn't be much to C-9; therefore, I choose to think of C-9 as a distant form of the same tale that gives us variants C-1 through C-8.

In summary, we have twenty-eight variants (six of them quite noticeably divergent) that divide into three versions: A, with fifteen variants; B, with four variants; and C, with nine. Statistically, the twenty-eight texts have the following features as narratives:

In most of them, more than one *attitude* is implied on the part of the narrator. Perhaps surprisingly, thirteen of the texts imply an approval of sex as fun; ten texts suggest a sympathy for the flagrant couple because their marriage has been postponed. Ten narratives express dismay at the unhappy outcome of the good intentions with which the surprise party had been planned. Five variants imply or express discontent with puritanical standards that hold nakedness or sex as lewdness. However, six express condemnation of the unbridled passion of one or both members of the exposed couple. Five imply that the defeat of good intentions is one of the "ways of the world"— *c'est la vie*. Three give warnings about the irresponsibilities of baby-sitters. One expresses sympathy with the point of view that loneliness is ample justification for an invitation to illicit sex, and another one sympathizes with the awkward shyness of a newly-wed couple vis-à-vis each other.

The *occasion* for the party essential to the tale is in fifteen instances a birthday (eight times the girl's; seven times the man's); in nine accounts (in one of them it is also the girl's birthday) it is a pre-wedding "shower"; in two instances it is a housewarming; in one, a trap for feckless baby-sitters; in one, a blind date; and in one it is not specified.

The *aftermath* when specified—in eleven texts, it is not specified—is tragic in varying degrees. In seven instances, the girl goes insane; in one, she faints; in one, her family disappears; in one, her engagement is broken; in another, she loses her husband via divorce; in one, she loses her job. In four instances, the male disappears, joins the navy, runs away; in one, he becomes insane; in another, he becomes drunk; and, in another, he faints.

Frequently, the narrative is quite explicit about the *instigator* of the sexual play which leads to the embarrassing exposure of the naked person or the naked couple. Although in nine instances the narrative is not explicit on this point, in eight instances the girl is clearly the aggressor, and in seven the instigator is the male. In the B version, of course, this determination does not apply.

And, finally, there were the *persistent minor details*. The intriguing descent of a staircase down into darkness occurs in fifteen of the variants, and in five there is the motif in which the naked lover carries or "piggy-backs" his naked sweetheart to the unexpected exposure. And in seven of the variants, a preacher is specified as one of those present. In all but two of these instances, the ministerial presence is a kind of key to an anticlericalism in the variant.

The Surpriser Surprised has been checked against the Thompson *Motif-Index of Folk-Literature*, the Baughman *Type and Motif-Index of the Folktales of England and North America*, the Christiansen

Migratory Legends, and the Dorson *Folk Legends of Japan.*[7] To the best of my knowledge it does not appear in any of these.

I should like, in closing, to propose as possible motifs for the A and C versions of the Surpriser Surprised:

F 1041.8.15*	Madness from exposure while naked.
N 384.0.1.4*	Madness from embarrassment.
Q 241.5*	Adultery (or premarital sexual intercourse) revealed accidentally during good-intentioned surprise.
Q 495.4* or Q 589.6*	Naked appearance before friends as punishment for dalliance.
U 190.*	The frustration of good intentions.
Z560*	Good intentions have evil results.

Last, and most important of all, let me thank most profusely those who supplied the basic materials upon which this meditation has been based: my colleagues past, David Thomas, and present, Mrs. Kathleen A. Smith and Herbert Billiland; my folklorist peers Mrs. Berniece T. Hiser, Alan Dundes, and Gerald Thomas; and my informants and former students of the last ten years whose names are arranged in alphabetical order: Helen Graham Baughman, Carol Beesley, Billie K. Broaddus, Dora June Burgess, Robert B. Eidson, Nancy Gilpin, Don Graham, Susanna Hall, Mary Ann Harris, Ovida R. Head, Linda Hoffman, Sue Illman, Ann Kennedy, Jeannie Leedom, Dorothy Mason, Mary Ann Moody, Corley Revell, Carmen Rodriguez, Thomas N. Sanders, Susan Vessels, Sharon Walter, and Betty Jo Webb. Without them, there could have been no paper.

7. [Stith Thompson, *Motif-Index of Folk Literature,* 6 vols. (Copenhagen: Rosenkilde and Bagger, 1955–1958); Ernest W. Baughman, *Type and Motif-Index of the Folktales of England and North America* (Bloomington: Indiana University Folklore Series, no. 20, 1966); Reidar Th. Christiansen, *The Migratory Legends* (Helsinki: *Folklore Fellows Communications,* no. 175, 1958); Richard M. Dorson, *Folk Legends of Japan* (Rutland, Vermont, and Tokyo: Charles E. Tuttle, 1961). The stars on the motif numbers indicate that these are numbers which Jansen proposes to add to the indexes at appropriate places in the system.]

LORE OF THE
FINNISH-AMERICAN SAUNA

Aili K. Johnson

As a member of the Finnish-American community in Michigan, Aili K. Johnson assisted noted folklorist Richard M. Dorson on his 1946 collecting tour in the Upper Peninsula. (See Dorson's Bloodstoppers and Bearwalkers [1952; Cambridge: Harvard University Press paper back 1972].) As a folklorist in her own right, she published the following essay surveying the history, uses, and folk traditions surrounding the Finnish sauna in the United States. Her discussion should be especially interesting to American readers now that saunas have become widely popular in gymnasiums, health spas, hotels, and private homes that are far removed from any traditional Finnish-American context. The situation is perhaps comparable to such examples as fast-food chains specializing in ethnic foods, hibachi and stir-fry cooking at home by non-Orientals, current clothing fashions inspired by European peasant or gypsy garb, and the general popularity of several forms of foreign martial arts and exercise systems. Such "borrowings," of course, are an old part of American culture, extending to a great many of our institutions ranging from the system of government to holiday customs and children's games.

The sauna seems to have taken a typical course for many such cultural transplants, from a stage of almost ritual practice and meaning to a loss of these significances as the custom becomes mainly recreational and social or is beginning to be accepted by "outsiders." Johnson documents the early appearance of such acceptance in her concluding examples of intergroup sauna lore and Finnish (or "Finglish") dialect stories which give an exoteric view[1] of the Finns' devotion to the sauna.

An important newer study to read in connection with this essay is Yvonne R. Lockwood's "The Sauna: An Expression of Finnish-American Identity," Western Folklore, vol. 36 (1977). Her research was carried out in Michigan's Upper Peninsula thirty years after Dorson and Johnson collected there. The theoretical perspective is enlarged by reference to the scholarly literature about ethnicity, ritual processes, and conceptual aspects of space and time. The data base is improved by close observation of sauna behavior and study of attitudes towards sauna use.

---

1. See William Hugh Jansen's essay "The Esoteric-Exoteric Factor in Folklore," *Fabula*, 2 (1959), 205–11, repr. in Alan Dundes, ed. *The Study of Folklore* (Englewood Cliffs, N.J.: Prentice-Hall, 1965), pp. 43–51. An exoteric view is one from outside the culture.

Of particular interest in Lockwood's study is her description of the enculturating role of sauna usage for Finnish-American children. She interprets the practice in these terms: "To grow up Finn is to partake properly in the weekly sauna. But to be Finn also means to persevere, to stick it out in the heat, not to give up." One wonder if there are not similar "tests" or "lessons" taught by participation in tradition among other ethnic groups: must a Basque child learn to deliver (or at least to tolerate) the ear-splitting Basque yell, or do Mexican-American youngsters test themselves by means of the hotness of chilies they can eat, or should a good Norwegian learn to like lutefisk (codfish preserved in lye)? If these or similar statements about "ordeals" might be valid for other ethnic groups, then we could expect to paraphrase Lockwood's conclusion about Finns in appropriate terms for them: "The affirmation of their identity is communicated in the sauna performance." (The term "performance" in behavioral analytic terms refers to any action that is part of the traditional participation in a particular custom.)

THE *sauna*, THE HOT-AIR BATH of the Finns, was first brought to America in 1638, by Finnish immigrants from Sweden to the region of the Delaware River. The Finnish historian, S. Ilmonen, states in his account of these immigrants[1] that their earliest colonial map shows a place name, *Sauno*, where Philadelphia was to be founded by William Penn forty-three years later.

No trace of these early *saunas* seems to appear in subsequent American history or folklore, for although Robert Beverley, in 1705, in *The History and Present State of Virginia*,[2] indicates a similarity between the sweat house of the American Indian and that of the Finns and Muscovites in Europe, he makes no reference to the *sauna* in America.

It was not until the 1860's that succeeding waves of immigration from Finland again brought to this country the *sauna*, with its ancient heritage of shamanism[3] already modified by the Lutheran church. Further changes were to take place to conform with the folkways and mores of the neighboring "toiskieliset" ("Other-tongued ones"), such as the building of a dressing room adjacent to the *sauna*, the construction of a chimney for the hearth, to conform with safety regulations and insurance company requisites.

The *sauna* still exists, however, as a folk cultural institution wherever Finnish Americans live, retaining its most important traditions

1. *Delawaren Suomalaiset*, S. Ilmonen. Karisto, O Y, n.d. Pp. 104–105.
2. *History and Present State of Virginia*, 1705, Robert Beverley. Pp. 218–219.
3. [Magic performed by a shaman, a priest who acts as a medium between this world and the world of good and evil spirits.]

and tabus in rural areas. The commercial steam bath of the cities, sometimes accepted as a substitute for the hot-hair bath, is not regarded as a "truly Finnish" *sauna* by even the younger Finns.

To understand the uses of the *sauna*, a brief description is necessary. The immigrant farmer frequently builds his *sauna* of cedar or pine logs before he builds his house. The bathchamber is usually square with a square fieldstone hearth in one corner and a three-tiered wooden platform extending from wall to wall at one end of the chamber. These, and the bathwhisks[4] of leafy boughs, are the requisites of all Finnish baths, ancient or modern.

The earlier type of *sauna*, the *savu-sauna*, or smoke-*sauna*, is still found in some rural areas and is generally preferred by the older Finns. It differs from the modern farm *sauna* in that it has no chimney. The fireplace, about four feet square, is built of field stone without the use of bricks or mortar, and the fragrant smoke from the wood fire encircles the log walls, the triple-tiered platform, the beams of the low ceiling, and escapes from a small vent near the ceiling.

Grandfathers will tell you that only this ancient type, the smoke-*sauna*, is a Finnish *sauna*. It is built without a chimney because smoke is pure and cleansing; its fragrance is healing. No bricks or mortar can be used, because these give off unwholesome steam which prevents the *sauna* from becoming hot enough[5] to dry the perspiration of the bather as it forms. A steam bath is weakening, but a hot air bath, with a rinse in pure water, gives one strength. There must be no iron in the fireplace, or on the wooden tubs for water, or elsewhere in the *sauna*, for iron rusts, and rust is poison.[6] The bathwhisks must be made with care, of cedar,[7] a "living" tree that remains green throughout the winter. John Erkintalo,[8] however, finds that ironwood is a tree of hardness and strength, so he prefers ironwood boughs instead of cedar, or the traditional birch of Finland.

The modern *sauna*, despite the chimney, bricks, mortar, and iron, retains, however, some of the ancient traditions of the smoke-*sauna*. No child is permitted to play in the bath-chamber, no cat or dog allowed to enter. No dead are brought to lie here, for the odor of death, "Kalman haiju," is an evil odor. No menial, defiling tasks are permitted in the *sauna*, such as the smoking of meats, boiling of wash water, or cooking of foods lest they spoil the *sauna* with their alien

---

4. [Small whip-like bundles of branches and leaves used to beat the body to heat and cleanse it during the *sauna*.]

5. 170 to 230 degrees Fahrenheit.

6. Informant: Henry Hankila, Mass, Michigan.

7. The traditional birch boughs are sometimes used; the cedar is more common.

8. Immigrant, Forest Lake, Michigan.

smells. Many Finns never enter the bath-chamber wearing shoes, even to build the fire, but keep a pair of house slippers for this purpose in the adjacent dressing room.

One old country use of the *sauna* seems profane to the American Finn: that of the top bathing platform for the heating of barley into malt. This board was called the *mallas-lauta,* the malt-board. My father explained to me that the older folks considered the making of ale no sacrilegious task, for the ripening grains had the "element of life." This traditional use of the *sauna* was ridiculed by the Temperance Society American Finn of the early twentieth century in the jeering name given to the dance halls adjoining the old-fashioned saloons. They were called *mallas-saunat,* malt-*saunas,* and the term expressed disapproval of ale-making as well as the beerhall of America.

The old smoke-*sauna* had three important uses: it was the sanctuary devoted to ritual cleansing, healing, and birth. The modern *sauna* is used for cleansing and healing; its dressing room may sometimes be used as a craft shop for "clean" tasks, like the weaving of rugs, the making of birch bark shoes, or woodcarving.

The Sabbath of the older Finns begins on Saturday, at sundown, with the ritual cleansing. Even a third generation American Finn will say, after his bath, "I feel clean inside and out; all the week's evil is washed out of my system," or, "Now I am clean enough to go to God's house."[9] Another clue to the importance of cleansing in its relation to religion lies in the tabu against swearing or becoming angry in the *sauna.*

Many of the social aspects of the *sauna* have been retained. It is still the custom to invite guests to bathe in your *sauna* on Saturday night. They bring with them their own towels and often a cake or coffee bread for the after-*sauna* coffee party.

Men and boys[10] go to the *sauna* first, while it is at its hottest. The young men vie with one another to see who can lie on the top platform the longest, who can roll in the snow the greatest number of times, or who can reach the lake or creek first for a cooling rinse. He who succeeds is, of course, the "strongest."

Women and children bathe next. The children are given instruction in the ritual of cleansing, encouraged to stay in the bath a long time, and to sit on the top platform where the heat is greatest, in order that

---

9. Many rural Finnish communities hold dances on Sunday night, for the Sabbath has ended at sundown on Sunday. It is considered wicked to dance on Saturday night, even in non-religious groups. The Lutheran Church frowns upon dancing at any time.

10. American Finns never follow the ancient custom of having a woman attendant in the bath, nor that of having both sexes of different families bathe together (except with young children).

they may become strong and hardy. Sometimes a nonsense rhyme is chanted as a mother pours rinsing water on her child's back. "Resputa, resputa, resputa, respun, respun, respun," she sings.

Occasionally a crying child is admonished with an old nursery song:[11]

Piis, piis, pikkusta lasta,	Hush, hush, little child,
Mikä sille lapselle tuli?	What has come upon him?
Vai liekkö tuon pappa säikkytänyt	Has his papa frightened him
Saunan savisella tiellä?	On the clay path to the sauna?

The young women among the guests and family are the last to bathe.

When guests are not present, the family of mother, father, and young children bathe together. As a result of this custom of cleansing, the Finnish child grows to adulthood with no feeling of shame or curiosity about the human body. Sex is never synonymous with nakedness in his mind.[12]

The *sauna* is still used in healing by the immigrant healer. Rarely does he use magic properties, such as graveyard mold, sweat from a stone, or excrement. He may chant a charm or two, but massage alone is usually considered sufficient, since he is believed to have a "divine gift." A Finnish proverb states that illness is brought by God. "Ei tauti tartu eikä rutto rupea ilman tahotta Jumalan." ("No illness clings, no plague begins, without the will of God.") Likewise, God is the great healer. Old Eli, an Upper Peninsula masseur answers, when asked if he "says a prayer or two" (i.e. chants a charm), "My prayers are my own; God is the healer. I am only the go-between."

The *sauna* is now not completely necessary for healing, for Herman Maki,[13] in speaking of the seer and prophet, John Bjorklund, tells the following anecdote:

"John Bjorklund had just come in from the *sauna* to the lumber kitchen when he saw Jack Kivisto groaning with a toothache. He laughed and said, 'Are there still foolish Finns who suffer toothache? I am weak from the steam[14] of the *sauna*, but I shall try to cure you!' He stood behind Kivisto, took the man's chin in his hands and massaged it. 'Now bite your teeth together,' Bjorklund said at last, and at once Jack's toothache was gone.

"Many years later, Jack would tell the men down in the mines when

---

11. Sung to traditional Finnish tune *Velin Surmaaja* (version: Child ballad No. 13).

12. Lauri Lahti, Flint, Michigan. Aged 38, second generation.

13. Immigrant story teller, Palmer, Michigan. Told to R. M. Dorson.

14. The implication of the remark is that this was a modern *sauna*.

they complained of toothache, 'Why don't you get your toothache cured forever, as I did mine?' "

The masseur is still a recognized healer, regarded with respect by old and young alike. Not so with the cupper, the bleeder, for innumerable anecdotes are told by younger Finns about anemia and death resulting from this practice. Older folks, under seventy-five years of age, however, are often convinced that they should be bled twice a year, spring and fall, to relieve them of "bad blood" causing rheumatism or high blood pressure.

The cupper, like the masseur, officiates in a warm *sauna*. His (or her) tools are simple: cows' horns, well scraped and cleaned, and a sharp instrument to prick the skin. The modern cupper uses horns of glass, designed to simulate animal horns, and an instrument which makes innumerable tiny punctures in the skin at one swift stroke. The charge to the patient is usually five cents a horn, and as many as forty horns are required for an acute illness. Formerly blood-stopping charms and healing charms were known by the cupper.

The third important use of the *sauna* has almost disappeared in America, along with the midwife whose function it was to heat the *sauna*, to prepare the waters, and, long ago, to say a charm to bring an easy birth, or to stop the blood from flowing. Old grandmothers tell many anecdotes of birth in the *sauna*, of the strength of the mother, her joy at carrying the baby back to the *tupa* in her arms, her readiness to assume her household tasks within a few hours after birth.

The frequent and casual mention of the *sauna* in traditional folktale and folksong reflects these principal uses of the *sauna*, as a place for cleansing, healing, and birth.

The following tale of Herman Maki, of Palmer, Michigan, expresses the faith of the Finn in his *sauna*.

THE SAUNA[15]

They say that the *sauna* was at one time a holy place, where one had to be careful how one spoke. Even in my time men do not swear in the *sauna*.

There is a good story about the powers of the *sauna*. It shows that even the Russians knew about the Finnish *sauna*.

Three Russian peddlers were crossing a lake on the ice. They carried heavy knapsacks, filled with woollen shawls, and other such things. They came to the other shore, where there was a large opening in the ice, from which water was carried for cattle by horses and sleighs.

15. Told to R. M. Dorson and A. K. Johnson, September 4, 1946.

As nightfall was approaching, the men did not see the hole in the ice, and the man in the middle fell in, knapsack and all. The others paid no heed, but went on to the nearest house by the lake, and asked for a lodging for the night. As Russian peddlers are known to pay well, they were allowed to stay.

They arose the next morning and asked, "Will the good wife heat the sauna? Make it hotter than usual."

The housewife, knowing they would pay well, heated the *sauna* as hot as she could.

Then the Russians took woollen blankets, and a couple of log-grappling hooks from their knapsacks, and went out to the lake where they fished out their comrade who had drowned the night before. They wrapped him in blankets, and carried him to the *sauna*. They remained in the *sauna* for four hours. Three men walked out and continued on their journey.

There is a Finnish proverb, "Jos ei terva, suola, ja sauna, paranna, kuolema ottaa." "If tar, salt,[16] and the *sauna* cannot cure you, death will take you." It is quite true, you know.

The following anecdote is the only off-color joke the writer has encountered, pertaining to sex and *sauna*: The trenki (hired man), the old master, and the young wife were bathing in the *sauna*. The young wife suddenly cried out, "More soap for the old man's eyes."

At one time the Cornish neighbors of Finns regarded the *sauna* with horror as a dangerous, heathen custom. Old Finnish miners still tell stories about the sheriff in Bessemer who "hung around the Finnish boarding house on Saturday night, ready to arrest a man if he stepped out of the house in his bare feet."

The attitude of the "Kosen-jäkki"[17] has changed, for he will now tell you, with genial humor, that he has a fine *sauna* at his camp. "And why not?" he asks. "Didn't the Finns steal our pasties and call them Finnish pasties? Why can't a good U.P. Cousin Jack have a genuine Cousin Jack *sauna*?"

The following anecdote, current in the Upper Peninsula, became popular in the army during World War II. In the earlier versions, collected in the Upper Peninsula before the war, the leading characters were Finnish and English missionaries in the south sea islands. The army version makes them three American soldiers from the Upper Peninsula, in the South Pacific area. The boys, one of whom is called

16. Maki uses the Americanized "temperance" version of the old proverb substituting "salt" for the word "spirits." Salt is also considered a strengthening substance, used internally and externally.

17. "Cousin Jack," one of English background.

Urho, are captured by natives, hostile cannibals. They are placed in a huge cauldron to boil, covered with a heavy lid. After four hours of cooking, Urho, the Finnish boy, knocks on the lid. The surprised native chief removes the cover from the cauldron, and out pops Urho's red face. He waves his arm and shouts, "W'at blace da dowel? Dis iss da pest *sauna* I haf had since I leave da Is'peming."[18] This anecdote is one of the many popular Finnish dialect stories of the Upper Peninsula, first told by the "outsider," now enjoyed by the Finnish American himself.

To the Finn, however, there is really very little humor in his concepts of the *sauna*. The structure of the old *sauna* has changed, superstitions are forgotten, magic charms have almost died out, but the ancient belief still lives in the heart of every Finnish American; his *sauna* is the antithesis of all evil, death and decay; it is a symbol of life, strength, healing, and goodness. "The *sauna* brings you a little nearer to God."[19]

18. There were five versions; two were pre-war, the earliest told by a Swede, the other by a Finn. Of the three post-war versions, one came from a second-generation Cornish American, and two from Finnish Americans, second generation.

19. The same thought has been expressed to me by many older people, some a little apologetically through fear that they might be thought superstitious.

COKELORE[1]

L. Michael Bell

This mini-survey in modern folklore demonstrates that oral traditions may be associated with products of mass production and that one need not go beyond one's daily routine to collect folklore. Like Patricia Rickels' essay above, this one contains folklore collected in college classes; like William Jansen's study, it deals mostly with the folklore of urban adolescents. Considering only the corrosive properties that Coca-Cola is credited with in oral tradition, it seems surprising that the drink continues to be so popular. Either people do not really believe the folklore, or they have a deep-seated wish to live dangerously!

Bell's brief discussion suggests two directions for further research: first, wider collecting and analysis of "cokelore" itself, and second, the possibility, as he puts it, of "a self-economizing selective principle of traditional lore." This latter point might be studied by collecting the folklore of other manufactured products, such as Kleenex, Saran Wrap, Kentucky Fried Chicken, various beers and liquors, and certain automobiles or other machinery. An interesting related study of urban lore is Frank M. Paulsen's "A Hair of the Dog and Some Other Hangover Cures from Popular Tradition," Journal of American Folklore, Vol. 74 (1961). Of the hundreds of hangover cures given here, only one mentions Coca-Cola, and it is a common example in Bell's collection as well: "Take three aspirin with a coke." Two studies of sexual folklore involving manufactured products appeared in one recent volume of Western Folklore (Vol. 32, 1973): Eleanor Long, "Aphrodisiacs, Charms, and Philtres," and George W. Rich and David F. Jacobs, "Saltpeter: a Folkloric Adjustment to Acculturation Stress."

MOST OF US KNOW AT LEAST ONE ANECDOTE—often told by a dentist—about the corrosive or otherwise pernicious properties of Coca-Cola.

1. L. Michael Bell (instructor) made the assignment and wrote the article. Material was collected by Roland Aden, Margot Barnett, Jeffrey Bartlett, Barbara Hanson Baumgartel, Linda Beckley, Elaine Boutilier, Samuel Broyles, Phyliss Burgreen, Laurel Clark, Florence Cooley, John Dakin, Margaret Diederich, Timothy Ford, Gerald Franchère, Barbara Galicia, Paula Graves, James Green, Mary Hahn, Douglas Harrington, Laurie Helma, James Herrington, Sally Horner, Leslie Jones, Debbie Kelso, Paula Kermiet, Barbara Kushner, Phillis Leftin, Cathie Light, Anne McGovern, Douglas Meyer, Mark Nagel, Nadine Nakazono, Sally Nogg, Cathy Orr, Russell Page, Vivian Pearlman, Kay Pennington, Cynthia Powers, Philip Price, Salley Rhea, Andrea Richtel, Sanford Rothman, Robert Rotz, Eileen See, Joan Shahinian, Darlene Shigemoto, Tracy Siler, Ronda Smith, Daniel Snepenger, Nancy Spier, Ellen Stewart, Mary Anne Thomas, Susan Tobias, Larraine Vollmert, Engberdine Voûte, Kelley Waite, Lee Walker, Joni Weiner, and Diana Wilcox.

Around twenty years ago in Pennsylvania, my dentist told me how an extracted tooth, dropped in a bottle of Coca-Cola, dissolved in three days; he told my younger sister of a couple he knew who had driven through a road construction site and had their windshield spattered with a tar so persistent that nothing but "Coke" could clean it off.

This sort of lore, with its frequently anecdotal structure, occupies a category which is intuitively well-defined but has only recently been treated and sub-categorized by folklorists.[2] The lore of Coca-Cola, in particular, would seem to fit into at least two categories: 1) folk beliefs regarding food and drink; 2) a category in which "a well-known business concern (such as Pepsi-Cola) may become associated with a particular legend."[3] In order to find out how pervasive and varied this lore might be in modern oral tradition, the one hundred students in English 322 (Introduction to Folklore) at the University of Colorado were asked to report any such anecdotes they knew personally or could collect from any three additional informants on campus.

Sixty students completed the assignment. Some had canvassed more than three informants (to a high of nine), some fewer, and some phrased their reports ambiguously on this point. Allowing for this fact, and for potential overlap, the population from which the following sample is drawn can be estimated at between 240 and 260 persons, and the age range for the bulk of informants, can be fairly certainly established between 18 and 25 years of age. Collectors were not asked to specify age, sex, or other characteristics of their informants, although some did. Nonetheless, a population as uniform as that at most state universities can be assumed. The class (exactly one hundred students) can probably be taken as a representative cross-section of the student body as a whole, since it included a fairly even distribution of majors in twenty-seven different disciplines. Fifty-one students were female and forty-nine male. Approximately half the students were Coloradoans, but at least 22 other states were well-represented (with the exception of under-representation in the Deep South and Pacific Northwest). The class contained a considerable ethnic mixture.

In the oral tradition of the modern college campus, Coca-Cola would appear to be a nearly universal solvent. A quick survey of its corrosive properties, as attested by our informants, will serve as an illustrative prelude. Coke will dissolve teeth, dentures, and fillings; the lining of the stomach of humans, cadavers, and rats; nails, bolts,

2. See Duncan Emrich, *Folklore on the American Land* (Boston, 1972), 330, on the "urban belief tale"; Jan H. Brunvand, *The Study of American Folklore* (New York, 1968), 90–92 [2nd edn., pp. 110–112], on the same; J. Barre Toelken, "The Folklore of Academe," in Brunvand, 317–337 [372–390].

3. Brunvand, p. 91 [2nd edn., p. 111].

pennies, nickles, spoons, and the linings of aluminum containers; meat, especially hamburgers, hot dogs, steak, and bacon; mice, bats, flies, and chicken bones; car paint, enamel, fingernail polish, and the fingernail itself; its own paper cup, straw, and bottle; gum, marbles, barnacles, and upholstery; a block of wood; and battery casings. It will remove rust from nails, car engines, tire rims, exhaust pipes, chrome, and water pipes; corrosion from battery cables and terminals; grease from dirty parts and stove grills, shellac from carburetors, bugs from radiators, and tarnish from pennies; and it will clean windshields and drains.

Four students reported finding that Coke will "renew (or "start") batteries if poured over the battery," probably a loosely-understood variant of another informant's claim that it will substitute for battery acid. Others reported that it will substitute for starter fluid and liquid wrench—a folk-generic (actually a copyrighted brand name) for a penetrating solvent which dissolves rust. The belief that it will substitute for starter fluid shows an apparent confusion between the properties of acidity and volatility.

Some of the other properties claimed for Coca-Cola, though rarely reported, are so specific and vivid that they deserve inclusion here. The following were reported by one student each. Coke will tenderize steak; "cook" hamburger and bacon; "hardboil (rubberize) an egg (takes a week)"; throat becomes . . . so transparent from drinking the coke[4] that one can see the bubbles of the coke as they go down"; "A girl supposedly drank a case of coke a day and developed a fissure down the center of her tongue, splitting it in two."

Before dealing with further details and variants of such properties, three fairly frequent responses should be mentioned which do not necessarily reflect acidity or corrosiveness. The first is the long-standing belief (going back at least to the instructor's high school days in the 1950s) that Coke with aspirin will make you drunk. The second is the more recent belief (gaining popularity in the 1960s) that Coke makes an excellent contraceptive douche. Seven informants knew of the first property and four of the second, not including one intriguing blend: "Coke & aspirin as a contraceptive" (administration not specified). This was one of several diverse hybrids, such as, "When aspirin [is] put in coke it forms acid," "Washing down aspirin with Coke would upset your stomach." A third, slightly less frequent response in this category was that Coke is addictive, containing some form of "dope" (not specified) which "can get you hooked" and give you

---

4. Variant capitalization of "Coke" in this article will reflect student practice, since the variation may have some significance (see note 8 below). In other respects, spelling vagaries have been corrected.

withdrawal symptoms or the "coke fit" (similar to a nicotine fit in smokers).

One of the areas of widest variation within a given category was the time required for Coca-Cola's solvent action. Not all responses included a time element, but the high proportion of those which did include one indicate clearly that this element is an essential sub-motif of the lore. For instance, the time it takes the drink to dissolve the (lining of a) live human stomach varied from two days to one year— the year spent drinking Coke at the rate of a bottle a day. (A cadaver's stomach will dissolve overnight, according to the physician father-in-law of one student.)[5] The time required to dissolve a tooth immersed in Coke varied from eight hours to three days, with "overnight" being the most common response. (One informant, however, spontaneously transferred this property from Coca-Cola to stannous fluoride, the key ingredient of fluoridate toothpaste.) The time required to dissolve meat extended from overnight to one week. Perhaps the most dramatic acidity exhibited by Coke appeared in the belief of one informant that Coke would dissolve a nail in half-an-hour, or a spoon in two days.

Typical of the "urban belief tale" or "migratory legend," few of the reported beliefs were traced to personal experience, but some declared the source of the primary experience to be a close acquaintance.[6] "My older cousin never heard the story of the tooth and coke, but has used coke *himself* to loosen a nut and bolt, and it did work." "The . . . person said he had done such an experiment in junior high school, and though the tooth did not disappear, the decay was frightful enough to

5. The full citation is given here verbatim, since it contains an ancillary detail of considerable interest:

> Story version came fr. my father-in-law who is a doctor in Paducah, Kentucky: Medical student had stolen a cadaver's stomach & placed it in a tub of coke overnight—the stomach was dissolved the next morning.

The stealing of the cadaver's stomach puts this anecdote squarely in the area of Motif N 384.0.1.1, "The cadaver arm." However, this and other evidence suggests that the prank of stealing a cadaver (or part of one) ought to be identified as a separate motif, not necessarily to be included under "Unlucky Accidents" in Stith Thompson's section N, "Chance and Fate" (*Motif-Index of Folk Literature*, Vol. 5, Bloomington, 1957). It is apparently the death from fright of the victim of the prank which causes this motif to be lumped under "Unlucky Accidents." Toelken, p. 327 [381], cites a traditional prank involving the theft of a cadaver with no consequences (or intent) more horrible than probable disgust on the part of beholders. The instructor, and others of his acquaintance, know similar variants, in which the purpose of the theft is to give a shock to some such unsuspecting functionary as a collector in a highway toll booth.

6. "The touchstone to them [urban belief tales] is that they are either actually believed by the teller or reported by him as being the true experience of someone else" (Emrich, 330). "As with most Urban Tales . . . there is an attempt to authenticate the incident by making reference to the source of the story, usually a trusted friend who knows one of the people to whom it happened" (Toelken, 323 [377]).

make him swear off soft drinks in favor of dental floss." "[Coke] dissolves . . . hot dogs (1 week—from an experiment in junior high)."

Some of the reported beliefs overlapped with another type of urban belief tale, the horror story associated with commercially packaged food: repulsive remains found in a factory-sealed can or bottle. The most elaborate of these goes as follows:

> In the plant a man discovered a mouse in one of the bottles of coke on the assembly line. Machines were stopped but the mouse could not be found in any of the bottles.

The mouse's fate might be spelled out by another version:

> Coca-Cola bottling companies were discovered to have unsanitary conditions resulting in having flies bottled in coke. People do not have to worry since they will be completely dissolved by the time you drink it.

That last thought, however, might not comfort the believer of the following slightly confused story:

> When let sit for a few days, different insects can be seen and dirt can be skimmed from the top.

Finally, another of these shows the strongest overlap with the "mouse tail in a Pepsi-Cola bottle" tale-type cited by Brunvand:[7] "Someone received a bottle from a machine containing only the skeletal remains of a bat." This area of urban lore often exhibits what market researchers call "brand name fidelity." Although Coke has poached here on Pepsi's territory, the assembly line, only one student reported any Coke lore specifically attributed to another brand name: "Pepsi will dissolve any fabric if not washed out within an hour or two."

This last fact, however, does not necessarily indicate that Coke completely dominates the market in soft-drink lore; it may also reflect the fact that "Coke" is to some extent a folk-generic for "soft drink." Although the generic quality of this name is not reflected in standard American dialect maps,[8] it is shown in two other manifestations: undergraduate usage and certain Coca-Cola advertisements. Since about 1966, the instructor has casually surveyed all of his "History of the English Language" classes on this particular dialect item, and a

7. Brunvand, p. 91 [111].

8. The standard survey is plotted in Hans Kurath, ed., *Linguistic Atlas of New England*, Vol. II, Map 312 (Providence, R. I., 1941). Other studies have found "Coke" and possibly even "Coca-Cola" as a folk-generic; see Ruth Schell Porter, "A Dialect Study in Dartmouth, Massachusetts," *PADS*, 43 (April 1965), 15. Porter implies (p. 8) that her questionnaire was administered orally, which suggests that her capitalization of the response "Coke" on p. 15 may not accurately reflect the informant's concept of the term.

few students always indicate that they have heard "coke" along with "pop, soda, tonic," etc., as a generic for "soft drink." Further, the Coca-Cola Company frequently advertises in Journalists' trade publications, such as *Editor & Publisher*, the fact that "Coke" is a registered trademark.[9] This is a practice adopted by other proprietors of trademarks which have become folk generics, such as Fiberglas, Scotch tape, and Kleenex. Their advertisements suggest that journalists use a legal generic, and usually supply one: "glass fiber," "cellophane tape," "facial tissue." In other words, part of the reason why there is so much Cokelore and so little Pepsi lore is that "Pepsi" is not a folk-generic.

The rough study conducted at Colorado suggests some directions for further work on this topic. First, much more precise information could be gleaned by identifying informants by age, sex, and home area, and by when and how they received the lore (from dentist, sibling, friend, and so on). Regional variants in this belief-area might be particularly interesting, since quite restricted localizations are often displayed by such teenage and campus lore. (One student in the class, engaged in another project, found some striking geographic restrictedness in the lore of Paul McCartney's death.) Second, traditions of Coca-Cola emphasizing features other than its corrosiveness might be more thoroughly investigated. Such inquiries might be useful in testing the currency of former traditions; for instance, our survey found no direct evidence for the persistence of the once-reputed belief in the cocaine content of Coca-Cola.[10] They might also unearth further legendary properties in addition to its supposed contraceptive, intoxicant, and narcotic action.

Despite the casualness of our method, can any general conclusions be drawn from our study, beyond the fact that Coca-Cola is widely believed to be corrosive to an unhealthy degree? Only one noticeably broader pattern was found in our data: that hardly any of our informants had heard more than one or two items of this lore, although very few—about 23—had heard none at all. If the lore is as widespread as it seems, what accounts for the dearth of variation in any given individual?

9. No less than the United States Supreme Court established the company's proprietary rights to the name "Coke." Some details of the litigation in question are given in H. L. Mencken, *The American Language*, Supplement One (New York, 1945), 346.

10. It is worth mentioning here that dialect fieldworkers in the United States have also found "dope" as a folk-generic for "soft drink," frequently enough to include it in their questionnaires; and that the well-known use of "coke" for "cocaine" has caused the Coca-Cola company some consternation in the past. See Alva L. Davis, Raven I. McDavid, Jr., and Virginia G. McDavid, eds., *A Compilation of the Work Sheets of the Linguistic Atlas of the United States and Canada*, 2nd ed. (Chicago and London, 1969), 48–49; and Mencken.

As one participant observed: When all the variants of 'Cokelore' are assembled, the belief loses, rather than gains, functional impact; it loses plausibility not only from the introduction of relativeness but from the sheer volume and diversity of detail. Somewhere in this observation may be, in embryo, evidence for a self-economizing selective principle of traditional lore—a principle which could help explain the organizational economies of other forms of folklore, such as legends and tales.

COCA-COLA LORE SURVEY, UNIVERSITY OF COLORADO, JANUARY 1975[11]

Corrosive Properties		*Non-corrosive Properties*	
Dissolves teeth	28		
Dissolves meat	12		
Dissolves nails	12		
Cleans rust from metal	12		
Dissolves stomach lining	10	Coke + aspirin = intoxicant	7
Dissolves car paint	9	Contraceptive douche	4
Dissolves pennies	4		

Items reported twice: Cleans windshields; dissolves dentures; "renews batteries"; "starts batteries"; replaces Liquid Wrench; contains "dope" and gives you "Cokefits"; contains more caffeine than coffee.

11. These statistics are offered with the reservations so well enunciated by Toelken, 337, n. 14 [390, n. 18]: Because of the often inescapable lack of rigor in such surveys, "the specific statistics are not consistently reliable except to indicate generally that a particular traditional item is current, or well known in detail, or in disuse."

THE CORNSTALK FIDDLE

Roger L. Welsch

The following note is a concise, straightforward example of how to document a simple artifact of material folk culture. It provides the dimensions, the manufacturing process, the use, and some of the contextual background for the artifact, clarifying these points with a drawing. Anyone should be able to follow the directions and make a cornstalk fiddle himself or herself.

Further background on Great Plains pioneers' uses of corn are given in Welsch's essay " 'Sorry Chuck'—Pioneer Foodways" in Section 2. To his list of uses for corn one might add smoking dried cornsilk (although this may be more a joke than an actual practice) and making autumn decorations from dried corn stalks and ears. We should also remember the continued manufacturing and use of corn-cob pipes (General Douglas MacArthur's trademark) and the ongoing popularity of various breakfast cereals made from corn, plus the apparently eternal association in the United States of popcorn with going to the movies.

Other collections of multiple uses of farm products might be applied to fruits like apples (pies, sauce, cider, vinegar, apple-head dolls, etc.). Other simple toy noisemakers are willow whistles, window rattlers, folded-paper "poppers," and the "dumbull" or "scrauncher," as described by John C. McConnell in the Tennessee Folklore Society Bulletin, Vol. 25 (1959).

THE CORNSTALK FIDDLE:—The Nebraska pioneer folk culture relied to an astonishing degree on the versatility of corn, almost equalling the Asian reliance on bamboo. The cobs were used for pipes, toilet tissue, and accurate heat gauges in cooking ("Seven cobs for an angel food cake"[1]). The grain itself was used popped and unpopped to decorate the soddy,[2] it was fed to the animals, and it was prepared for human fare in an unbelievable variety of ways: popped, roasted on the cob, roasted and used as a coffee substitute, popped and served with milk as a breakfast cereal, ground for corn meal, parched, boiled into hominy or soup, and grated for puddings.[3] Husks were used to stuff mattresses.

1. Mrs. Joyce Henry, North Platte, Nebraska.
2. [A house made of prairie sod stacked like bricks.]
3. *Early Nebraska Cooking*, collected by Workers of the WPA Writers' Program (Lincoln, Nebraska, 1940), Nebraska Folklore Pamphlets, number 28, *passim*.

Children made a variety of toys from the plant: darts from the cobs, spears from the stalks, dolls from the husks, and—perhaps the most amazing of all the products of the corn plant—the cornstalk fiddle.

The two fiddles that I have measure 23 and 21½ inches long; both bows measure 14½ inches. Each fiddle uses three sections of the stalk, each bow two. The fiddles have two strings and the bow has one; the strings are made by slitting the section between two joints so that thin slivers, with the ends still attached to the stalk, can be raised from the stalk by means of two bridges (see illustration).

When the strings are wetted and the bow drawn firmly across the strings, a soft, scraping tone is produced. Differences in the tension, width, and length of the strings enable the instrument to produce two distinct tones. My informant, Mr. Heye Rademacher of Auburn, Nebraska, said, however, that they were used only as toys and there was no attempt made to play tunes on them.

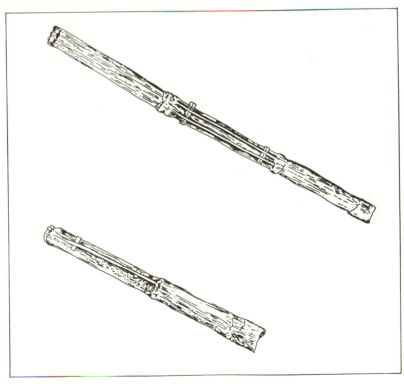

Illustrations by Walter R. Jaeckle, University of Nebraska

Folklore in Context

Although the articles in this section also contain examples of collected folklore, the emphasis is on the social and cultural contexts in which American folk traditions thrive. With one exception, these articles were published in the 1970s, as it has been only recently that American folklorists have adopted a more present-oriented contextual approach. (The first article is the exception, and it is included to show the change in one folklorist's approach over two decades.) All of these studies to some degree meet the standard called for by Alan Dundes in his 1966 essay on "metafolklore" (see Section 4) for "fewer texts and more contexts."

In general the selections are arranged to illustrate increasingly detailed and sophisticated analyses of setting, audience response, and performance style. The first articles simply describe the situations in which folklore is transmitted; later selections analyze regional and family settings more closely, and the concluding essays discuss some of the ways context influences genre classifications, functions, and other social interaction patterns. Accordingly, in some of these studies the folklorist is an outside "collector," but in others he or she becomes a participant-observer. (It is interesting to note how frequently the folklorist seems to be thrust into this role accidentally rather than cultivating it deliberately.) Like the articles in Section 1, a range of folklore types, folk groups, times, and regions of the country is covered. Several of these articles complement the text collections of Section 1 by furnishing more information on performance and setting; this is especially true for the articles on Coyote tales, proverbs, folksongs, and modern legends.

The study of context is still in an infant stage in the United States, but several points of interpretation about the effect of environment on folklore transmission and style can be made. First, as several of these selections illustrate, the American family has been a strong conserving and shaping force on our folk traditions. Also, not only do groups, whether ethnic, immigrant, or regional, preserve distinctive folk traditions, but individuals too may perpetuate a tradition, such as the basketmaker studied by Howard Wight Marshall. And a most important principle that emerges in several studies is that not simply the folk performers and audiences but the folklorist as well has an identifiable influence on what is performed and in what manner. The best analyses of this process are in the essays by Kay L. Cothran and Linda Dégh.

FOLKLORE AT A
MILWAUKEE WEDDING

Richard M. Dorson

In the early summer of 1946, Richard M. Dorson, then a relatively in-experienced folklorist, found himself in two quite different settings—one rural and one urban—both of which turned out to be rich in folk traditions. With a resourcefulness typical of his prolific career in American folklore, Dorson converted the distraction from his fieldwork project into another opportunity for collecting. The major result of his planned fieldwork in the Upper Peninsula of Michigan was the book Bloodstop-pers and Bearwalkers (Harvard University Press, 1952); the result of the weekend digression to Milwaukee was this modest article in a regional folklore journal.

Although Dorson's chief concern at the time seems to have been the "harvest of folklore" he could gather even in a big city, he does a credible job of sketching out the immediate context of a wedding party as source and stimulation for folk transmission. Surprisingly, none of the traditions passed on to him dealt directly with weddings—normally a rich subject of folklore—but were prompted by other timely events, notably the recent end of World War II. Probably Dorson's own presence as a folklorist, replete with exotic tales from his ongoing research, had a strong influence on what sort of lore he was told; and even the folklorist here is a source of tradition, telling his own version of a war story. (The technique of eliciting lore by first performing some is often a useful collecting ploy, although it does introduce new elements into the context.)

It would appear that the Milwaukee wedding was not quite as remote from the Peninsular culture as Dorson suggests. Not only are several of the folklore items paralleled in the Michigan collection (see footnotes 8, 9, and 14 plus some in-text references), but also one main informant, Mrs. Ladwig, had been brought up in a Michigan lumbering center. The German lore is somewhat similar to ethnic-group traditions Dorson was getting in his fieldwork. Still, as he points out, the environment here is much more middle class, urban, educated and sophisticated than was true in the Upper Peninsula, and the folklore reflects this.

In general, it is fair to say that the wedding party was not a true "folk group" in the sense of an established combination of people shar-ing traditional ways and knowledge. Instead it was an ad hoc group of people loosely related by marriage and acquaintance having enough in common culturally to communicate similar traditions when the leisure

time to do so was made available. Other such situations that collectors
might exploit are social gatherings for holiday celebrations, family re-
unions, or parties.

Dorson's annotations are minimal, designed to validate the tradi-
tionality of a few items rather than to provide exhaustive citations.
Virtually all of his material, however, could be annotated in detail from
standard reference works (some of which were not published in 1946).
In the last essay in Section 2, for example, Linda Dégh identifies a
Hungarian-American variant of the first story Dorson gives as being
Tale Type 1676B (see her footnote 10). A category "not yet recognized
by folklorists" which Dorson identifies as "the personal amorous misadventure" has since come more to the forefront in recent articles (including some by Dorson himself) concerning the personal experience
story as folk narrative.

In recent field projects, Richard M. Dorson has entered the most
congested city centers themselves as places to collect and do research.
He introduces a group of studies in such urban folklore done by his
students at Indiana University in an essay titled "Hunting Folklore in
the Armpit of America," Indiana Folklore, Vol. 10 (1977).

WHEN AND WHERE FOLKLORE is to be found remain puzzles to con-
found those who collect popular story, saying, and song. Especially in
the United States these questions provoke controversy, since the clear
lines of Old World social division that demarcate an illiterate peas-
antry rich in lore are blurred by an enveloping middle class culture.
Still there are those who seek this nation's folklore in hill country
pockets or concentrate on the Negro and the Indian and the unas-
similated immigrant, as the lowest culture levels available. Without
ever accepting their premises, I still followed somewhat this thinking in
selecting the remote and self-contained Upper Peninsula of Michigan
for intensive field collecting in the spring and summer months of
1946. In the midst of this project I had occasion to visit Milwaukee,
due south of me, the week end of June 1, to act as usher at the
wedding of an old college friend. I packed away my notebooks, and
drove away from the country of Chippewas, shackers, lumberjacks,
miners and Finns, which has no town over 16,000 in population, to
the metropolis of over half a million.

But oddly the wedding week end was to yield me a good harvest of
folklore and some new insights into its processes, and I soon had my
notebooks out again. The experience afforded two useful lessons. A
group with urban backgrounds, a high level of education, and an

adequate economic situation is not bereft of tradition—quite the contrary. And a wedding offers a good opportunity to pick up folklore; since the group is festive and in a storytelling mood, it has leisure for talk. It includes long-separated friends who reminisce, and it brings together strangers with varied knowledge who are fused together briefly in a congenial intimacy. The material presented below was evoked, quite unexpectedly, from such a wedding group during a space of three days. Generally collectors extract tradition over a lengthy stretch of time; but what exists in the memories of a casual group at a specific point in time and place may inform us more of the vitality of folklore.

All the members of this wedding party, without exception, contributed some item of folklore—bride and groom, ushers, sisters of the principals, the bride's mother and brother-in-law, the latter's mother, with whom the groom and I stayed one night, as well as friends and acquaintances. In this circle were persons knowing war stories, German folktales, Pennsylvania superstitions, Michigan tragic ballads, and urban nonsense tales. When I began recounting some of the more fantastic narratives I had heard in the Upper Peninsula, they started to recall items from their own folk-knowledge; and in the course of the week end this tendency gathered momentum, as more people entered the circle. However there were other times when storytelling developed quite spontaneously, in the hotel bedroom or at a home, with one story suggesting another and all the audience eagerly listening, in the manner of any cracker-barrel crowd. That such tales dealt with unusual autombile mishaps—such as stealing a tire that has parted from its vehicle while it is still rolling—or startling amatory adventures—such as dating a snake-charmer, and her snake—rather than more time-honored themes, does not invalidate their folklore quality.

On the first evening I spent in Milwaukee, the bride and groom and their contemporaries began reciting superstitions, and stimulated each other to recollect a number.

SUPERSTITIONS

Verne has a bunch of grapes on his arm; you can even see the stem. His mother must have wanted grapes when she was carrying him.

If you drop a knife when eating it means a man is coming. If you drop a fork it means a woman. A spoon means children.

If the hem of your skirt is turned up it means you are going to be kissed.

White thread on your suit means a blonde is thinking of you.

If you see a nun, spit three times for good luck. I saw a whole procession pass once and it nearly wore me out but I thought I better do it for every one anyway.

Count 100 white horses or 100 straw hats and then make a wish.

Deaths come in threes.

For a black cat crossing your path make a circle with your toe in the first dirt you find; put a cross in the circle, then spit on the center of the cross.

If you put your dress on inside out, leave it on that way.

If you step on an ant, it will rain.

Bad luck: hat on a bed, shoes on the table, opening an umbrella in the house.

Actors say that whistling in the dressing-room is the worst thing anyone can do.

I know people who insist on going out the same door they came in. If they come in by the front they won't go out by the rear.

If you lose something, spit on the palm of your hand, tap your palm with the forefinger and middle finger of your right hand and say, "Spit spat spo, where did the ring go?" Then follow the direction of the spit. We used to do that for books and tops we lost.

Flick your butter onto the plate. If it lands sideways that means you are going to get a letter. We used to do that all the way through boarding school; if it landed on edge we'd immediately run out for the mail.

> Find a pin and pick it up,
> The rest of the day you'll have good luck.
> Find a pin and let it lie,
> In great want you're sure to die.

My aunt Blanche, who used to live near Edinboro, Pennsylvania, told me that if you rub a wart with one-half of a navy bean, then take both halves and tie them together with a piece of silk thread and bury the whole in the earth, it will disappear by the time the full moon comes around again. She said hers *did*, too.

(Although these superstitions were considered comical by their carriers, they were nevertheless followed in practice, as for example the spitting on seeing the nuns. The gods of luck still require their propitiation; surely there *is* such a thing as luck, and why take a chance? A lawyer told me, later in the week end, with great seriousness, "I never dress without first putting on my right stocking, then my left, then my right shoe, then my left. I wouldn't think of doing it any other way." "Why not?" "Do you think I want the roof to fall in on me?" he said, and glared at me belligerently.

To convince the skeptics, narrators would give case evidence of occult phenomena.)

A bird flying against the pane is a messenger of death. My mother-in-law told me how her little girl Marion was playing on the floor when that happened, and she died a week later of the measles. She would say, "Minnie, look out when a bird flies against the window."

When I was in St. Louis there was a Negro who used to find water with a willow rod. I've seen him do it. He'd go down to the bank and cut a branch from a growth of fresh willow—it had to be willow and it had to be fresh growth. Then he would hold the branch by the forks and walk along till he came to water; it would point down, and when he passed the spot it could point up again. He dug a well for us.

GERMAN LORE

(One close relative of the family was known for her stock of Old Country sayings and beliefs, and contributed these Milwaukee German items.)

Dreams

I'm not superstitious, but I can dream of things that are going to happen. Old things, like old furniture, mean good luck. I dreamed once of old lace that crumbled in my hands when I picked it up. A week later I sold my house that had been up for sale a long time.

Clear water is good, muddy water is bad. Dogs and horses are good. A wedding or teeth means death—oh, I don't like to dream of teeth. Blood is bad; my daughter Grace dreamed of blood on a chest, and she got divorced right after.

I dreamed of two birds in a cage once. They wanted to get out, and I tried to make them stay, but one got away. My daughters Lil and Grace were 22 and 16 then; Grace was very sick with appendicitis and pneumonia and Lil wanted to get married. I asked her not to, until Grace got better, but she did anyway. So I lost one of my birds.

Sayings

Spiel im feuer, piss im bett.

Bier auf wein, lasst das sein,
Wein auf bier, das iss fein.[1]

1. ["Play with fire, piss in the bed."

"Beer after wine, leave it alone,
Wine after beer, that's just fine."]

Folktale

My mother told me this, in Hanover, as an actual happening that had been told for generations. Two soldiers made a bet that one couldn't stay all night at the graveyard. The other was to come in the morning and pay him the bet if he were still there. That was in the days when the soldiers wore long capes. The one went to the grave-yard and sat down on a grave. To pass away the time he drew out his knife and started whittling on a stick. At last growing tired, he lay down to sleep and struck the knife in the ground. But in the darkness he put his knife through his cape. In the morning when the other soldier went to the graveyard he found the man dead.

He thought the one underneath was pulling him down, you see.[2]

War Tales

Parachute-Tester

(Several of the younger men and one of the young women had seen service and brought back humorous army, navy and air corps anec-dotes. Bill Gresham told me at lunch some jokes played on new trainees coming into boot camp.)

When I was working in the Classification Division at the Great Lakes boot camp, we used to have some funny experiences with fel-lows who were hard to give ratings[3] to. Whenever a smart aleck came in, we would give him this particular one. I did it myself with one trainee who had a good education and was disappointed because he didn't get a commission, so he turned up his nose at all the ratings I mentioned to him. Finally I called over to one of the other classifiers and said, "Dick, have we got anything for this man; he doesn't like any of the ratings we've got here." Dick called back, "Why yes, there's a new one that just opened up that requires special ability." Of course the fellow pricked up his ears. "It's Tester of Rejected Parachutes. You know nylon is scarce, and we want to be sure that we're not throwing away good chutes. The plane lets you go from 10,000 feet, so there's plenty of time for them to open. Of course when you land

---

2. I heard the tale in the Upper Peninsula, localized in Canada and in England, and also told as a modern story in two versions. One is set in Wisconsin, and has as the condition of the bet that the watcher must plant a stake over the grave; crawling up to the spot at night he drives it through his coat. The other is told on American soldiers in World War II at a French cemetery; the watcher plants his bayonet through his raincoat.—R. M. D. See *HFB* 1:59 August, 1942.—The Editor.

[Explanation of tale: Having stuck his knife through his cape and into the ground, the soldier has pinned himself down but thinks he is being held fast by a corpse from below. Another version of the "Graveyard Wager" story appears below in the article by Linda Dégh.]

3. [Military job classifications.]

you have to fill out sixteen different forms giving all the details of the jump. However, if the chute doesn't open you don't have to fill out the forms."

Silly Question—Silly Answer

One time a young boy of seventeen was in my line, looking very upset and very much from the country. He didn't seem to know how he should be classified, and I went through the whole dictionary of rates, trying to find out just where his experience fitted him. But nothing seemed to be right, so I asked him what they had called him at the company where he worked before he enlisted, thinking that might help. He answered in a weak voice, "They just called me Clarence."

Leg-Pulling

Another time a trainee came into the station who seemed to be from the Kentucky or Tennessee hills. He started looking at the card very interestedly before I finished filling it out, and asked what the initials "ARM" at the bottom stood for. I told him, "Aviation Radio Mechanic," and he then asked, "Does that have anything to do with airplanes?" I said, "Yes, but that is a very difficult rating to qualify for. I think I know just the one for you though." And I called across the way to this friend of mine, "Dick, do we have any openings in aerial submarines?" He called back, "No, but there are some in underwater aircraft." The boy looked startled and asked me if there really were submarines that could fly.

Fool's Errand

That reminds me of a trick that was pulled on me the summer I was working on a freighter. We were anchored to buoys in the water off the Hawaiian Islands. When a ship is tied up at the dock, they put "ratguards," which are shaped like inverted funnels, over the ropes to prevent the rats from running on them onto the ship. So this time they sent me to the first mate to get "fishguards," so that the fish wouldn't swim up the ropes onto the boat. The first mate told me he thought the second mate had them, and the second mate sent me to the bos'n and so on.

Classification Mixup

(One of the ushers had heard this navy folktale.)

There were some funny classification mixups during the war. A math professor by the name of W. E. Smith was commissioned at Ft. Schuyler and then sent to Washington to get his orders. He expected to teach math in one of the naval programs, as there was then a serious shortage of instructors. However, his orders instructed him to proceed to Boston and board a destroyer, where he would find further orders. This considerably surprised him, but his friends insisted that Washington knew what it was doing and that the matter would duly be explained. He went to Boston, boarded the destroyer, and opened his second orders, which read that he was to command the ship in convoy duty to England. Smith called the junior officers together, explained to them his situation, and told them to tell him what to do. He stayed in his cabin all the trip to England. On subsequent trips he learned his way around, took actual command, and shot down several subs.

Some time later Smith received another call to Washington. As he was waiting outside the designated office, he saw another lieutenant pacing up and down and muttering angrily to himself: "How can they do that to me, me a graduate of Annapolis and they send me to teach mathematics at college. And I haven't had any math since my freshman year!" Smith, interested on hearing this, asked the man his name, and learned that it too was W. E. Smith.[4]

(Mary Alice Gresham had flown as a civilian ferry pilot assisting the Army, and as my dinner partner one evening related some flying lore.)

At Clovis, New Mexico, the flyers had a superstition that a painted B-25 was unlucky. Some planes were painted an olive drab color, and it seemed that they were always fouling power lines, or coming in with one engine missing, or cracking up.

They used to send new trainees to get ceiling jacks to raise the ceiling, or to get buckets of propwash.

Landing with One Engine

One story that was told many times was of the instructor at a training field who was taking a personal visit in his little, one-engine training plane during a few days' leave. Toward dark he was running out of gas and was still far from his destination, with the only landing field near a big B-25 base, on which outsiders were strictly forbidden to land. He signalled the landing tower, "Coming in on one engine, coming in on one engine." Immediately the tower ordered the field cleared of all planes and personnel, and sent back landing instructions. The little training job slid down onto the field, and the tower called out, "Clear the field, clear the field, distressed plane coming in on one engine." "That's me," said the instructor.

---

4. This is a story I have heard both before and since, from William F. Sullivan in Boston, and from Alfred R. Jones in East Lansing. It is told as true.

(An ex-army captain remembered these gags.)

During the time when the army was rushing men through OCS[5] as fast as possible because of the shortage of officers, all the bars around the training camp used to carry a sign, "No Lieutenant-Colonels allowed in this bar without their parents' consent."

Stories ran all the way from Long Island to Maine that a German submarine had been captured and a loaf of Bond bread, or movie stubs, found inside her.

Live Ammunition Story

(Although supposedly informed on folklore matters, I had been duped by an army folktale which for several years I implicitly believed, and this I contributed to the War stories.)

When I was teaching in the Army Specialized Training Program, one of my students told me in class one day a tragic thing that had happened at his training camp in Texas. He said that the soldiers were getting experience with live ammunition, which was shot over their heads from machine guns as they crawled on their bellies. As one was crawling along he saw a rattlesnake directly in front of him, and rather than be bitten by it he stood up and was shot dead. The soldier-student told the story with considerable drama, and it always stuck in my mind. Then, this spring when I was traveling in Upper Michigan, three years later, I met a newly discharged veteran who in the course of conversation happened to say, "Did you ever hear that story of the fellow and the rattlesnake, which they fasten on to every training camp in the country?"

CITY STORIES

While every person in the groups, male and female, older and younger, had some tale or tradition to tell, one soon emerged as a standout. Here was the natural-born storyteller, with the talent for comic delivery that soon dominated the circle. Old friends had heard certain stories, and urged him to repeat them; one of some length I heard twice in two days. The use of gesture, tone, pause and idiom cannot be caught in cold print; one must simply record that here was the master narrator as skillful as any corner store or lumber camp bard. The choicest stories also cannot be set down, because they belong to a genre not yet recognized by folklorists, that of the personal amorous misadventure. I noticed that these not only seemed very suspiciously inflated, although told in the first person, but that they ended with patterned punch lines: "And that's the last time I ever

5. [Officers Candidate School.]

went to Baltimore"; "And the major said, 'That's what I call sending a boy to do a man's job.' "

Besides the rather lengthy personal experience story, other types of urban tales were told, such as "Shaggy Dogs" and "Clever Animals." The Shaggy Dog story builds up with a wealth of detail and episode to anticlimax and frustration of the listener. Apparently the first story of this genre dealt with the long protracted search for a shaggy dog.[6] Comical tales about speaking or remarkably intelligent horses and dogs at present enjoy a considerable vogue among businessmen and urban social groups. Other city jokelore included the hillbilly story, the little moron story, and railroad stories. A few of those told follow:

Mysterious Note in French

An American in a French restaurant is handed a note in French by a strange well-dressed woman, who immediately leaves. He asks the waiter to translate it for him. The waiter looks at him, and in horror asks him to leave the restaurant. This experience is repeated several times. Finally in desperation the American takes passage back to the States. On board ship he finds an old college friend who promises to translate the note no matter what it says. He hands it to his friend, but a wind blows it overboard into the sea.[7]

Wrong Man Thrown Off

A man getting on a train at Grand Central Station tells the conductor, "Throw me off the Pullman car when we get to Princeton Junction. I'll be dead drunk, so wake me up; I'll resist so be sure to throw me off no matter how much of a fight I put up." But when the man wakes up the train is in Philadelphia. He asks the conductor why he wasn't put off. "Oh," said the conductor, "no wonder that other fellow put up such a struggle."[8]

6. For collections of Shaggy Dog stories, in which familiar and traditional plots as well as novel nonsense crop up, see three articles in *Esquire* by J. C. Furnas (the last in collaboration with Laurence McKinney), "Don't Laugh Now," May, 1937, 56, 236–237; "Patron Saint of Shaggy Dogs," March, 1942, 30–31; "Dogs Are Getting Shaggier," September, 1942, 46–47. See also Bennett, Cerf, *Try and Stop Me: A Collection of Anecdotes and Stories Mostly Humorous* (New York, 1944), 323–332, "Fireside Book of Shaggy Dog Stories."

7. This story represents an oral-literary-oral descent. The teller later traced down and sent me the printed source she had read—which differed considerably in its ending; the American simply loses the paper without knowing how. Albert Payson Terhune, in his prefatory note, says: "More than 30 years ago a college classmate told me he had heard this strange story from an aged Canadian priest who said it was a folk-yarn long before it was imprisoned in print."

8. I have heard a parallel to this in the Upper Peninsula story of a man who had trained a cub bear to harness; one time when it was full grown he had a terrific tussle before he could harness the bear to his wagon; returning home he found his tame bear asleep on the porch.

Narrow Escape

Two factory workers saw their boss leave the plant at three o'clock in the afternoon and decided to sneak off work. One went home and saw the boss inside with his wife. The next afternoon the boss again left early, and the other worker suggested they duck out again. "I should say not," answered the first, "the boss nearly caught me yesterday."[9]

Checker-Playing Dog

A man and a dog are playing a game of checkers. A friend sees them and expresses surprise at the dog's cleverness. "Oh, he's not so smart," said the man. "I just double jumped him."

MICHIGAN BALLADS

(Quite unexpectedly the bride's mother sang to me two verses of a courting song her mother had used to sing to her, about 1902, in the lumber woods.)

> Madam I have gold and silver;
> Madam I have house and land;
> Madam I have ships on the ocean;
> All shall be at your command.

Ready um a doo—doo dum—doo dum
Ready um a doo—doo dum day.

> I'll not have your gold and silver;
> I'll not have your house and land;
> I'll not have your ships on the ocean;
> I want and I will have a better-looking man.

Ready um a doo—doo dum—doo dum
Ready um a doo—doo dum day.

> Madam you're a saucy maiden . . .[10]

(Later Mrs. Ladwig wrote me in rich detail about the setting in which she heard her mother's songs.) "All of the songs she sang were learned in her girlhood as her married life held no gaiety. She said that her father had been fun-loving and fond of singing. They had lived in Otsego County, Michigan, in the towns of Waters and Otsego Lake which were then thriving lumber centers. Her songs may have been

9. This is told in the Upper Peninsula as a Cousin Jack mining story.
10. Cf. "The Spanish Maiden," in E. E. Gardner and G. J. Chickering, *Ballads and Songs of Southern Michigan* (Ann Arbor, 1939), 418–419, stanzas, 3–5.

local or her father may have brought them from the East. His name was George Van Slyke, of Pennsylvania Dutch origin,[11] I believe. My mother had a marvelous memory. . . . My early childhood was spent in Crawford County, Michigan, where my father had a lumber camp in winter and farmed in summer. My father was stern and there was not much fun at our camp. The men lived in a bunk house a short distance away—we children were not permitted to have anything to do with them. They came into our long lean-to kitchen for their meals but no talking was allowed at table. Sometimes there was a man cook but oftener it was my mother's job. . . . The fare was plentiful but simple—side pork, fried very crisp, boiled potatoes, sauerkraut, turnips and other root vegetables, prunes, canned raspberries and blackberries which grew abundantly in the surrounding woods, a breakfast food named 'Force,' and always loads of wonderful, thin, golden pancakes baked on a huge black griddle. When company came, my mother would change her 'wrapper' for a shirtwaist and dark skirt with a clean white apron. Those *were* occasions."

(Mrs. Ladwig remembers the plots and occasional lines of several songs from her mother's repertory.) "The church was brightly lighted and all was warm within." A mother with her baby was struggling through the snow. She stepped into the church for a moment's shelter. A wedding was in progress. The bride and bridegroom were at the altar. The minister asked if anyone knew of any reason "why these two should not wed." The mother stepped forward: "The bridegroom is my husband, sir, and this our little child. 'What proof have you?' the preacher sternly cried." "The mother lifted up her babe—the little one had died." The last lines tell of the bride's father taking the mother by the arm. "We'll care for you through life," he said, "You've saved our girl from harm."[12]

("Fair Charlotte" was also evidently known to the folksinger.)

Another told of a girl who froze to death on her way to a gay party. Her escort realized that she was freezing when she said that she was "growing warmer" and it tells of his efforts and how they finally reach the party and carry her in but too late.

I remember of one about a tragedy at Top n' Bee (Michigan): "He took her by her lily white hand" and flung her in the dark water to drown.

There was one that mother sang a lot to us children. These are some of the verses.

---

11. [Correctly "Pennsylvania German" (*Deutsch*), but sometimes mistakenly thought of as Dutch.]

12. This is "The Fatal Wedding," by Gussie L. Davis. See Sigmund Spaeth, *Read 'Em and Weep* (New York, 1927) 172–174.

My kitten has gone from her pillow,
My kitten is not in her tree.
Oh who will find my kitten
And bring her back to me.

The dog that lives down by the river
Came out with his naughty old bark,
He frightened my kitty just dreadful,
Just hear her cry—just hark—Meow!

They say that when people get frightened
Their hair will turn perfectly white,
If that is the case with my kitten
She won't have a black hair by night.

Fetching a Canthook

(In her informative letter Mrs. Ladwig added as well a yarn told her by an old time lumberjack from northern Wisconsin.) A Swede entered the logging camp and asked for a job. He knew nothing about the work but had come a long way afoot, was penniless and very hungry. The foreman looked him over and said "You'll do—go up to the shed and get a canthook. The poor Swede started for the shed, desperately wondering what a canthook looked like. He caught sight of a "muley" cow[13] and suddenly brightened. Breaking a branch from a tree, he drove her down to the astonished foreman, announcing triumphantly, "Here she ban—she no can hook."[14]

Note: I should like to express my particular thanks for their contributions to this article to Mr. and Mrs. William B. Gresham, Jr., Mrs. August E. Ladwig, Mr. and Mrs. William Metzler, Mrs. Louis Metzler, Miss Alice B. Gresham, Mr. and Mrs. John J. Guba, Miss Jean McLallen, and Mr. Eli Garfield Gifford.

13. [Hornless.]

14. This lumberjack folktale I have heard several times from old woodsmen in the Upper Peninsula, but not as a Swede story.

HEART DISEASE AND
FOLKLORE

Richard M. Dorson

Ever the Compleat Scholar and full-time folklorist, Richard M. Dorson
even turned his dangerous bout with arteriosclerosis and open-heart
surgery into a successful research project. Just twenty years after the
publication of Bloodstoppers and Bearwalkers, with dozens of other
respected folklore studies to his credit, he found himself at the 1972
annual meeting of the American Folklore Society just before a heart
attack and a new and frightening (but enlightening) adventure with
folklore. One year later at the next annual meeting of AFS he had not
only recovered his health but had produced this sprightly and informative paper describing his experiences and discussing the relationships of
different lifestyles to stress-induced heart ailments. He developed the
theory, perhaps partly in jest, that "folklore lived . . . is the surest preventive of heart disease."

It seems odd that American folklorists who study folk medicine
have paid much attention to fairly trivial ills—hiccups, warts, hang-
overs, etc.—and practically none to the real killers and cripplers, some
of which (especially venereal diseases and cancer) are steeped in folk
attitudes, fallacies, and supposed cures or preventives. Perhaps it takes
a firsthand experience with such diseases, plus a folklorist's special
viewpoint on behavior, to see the possibilities of these subjects. Dorson mentions the "wondrous tales of surgical miracles" he heard from
other patients of the Cleveland Clinic, but what folklorist would have
gone to such a setting just to collect tales, and who but a folklorist
finding himself a patient would think to collect and analyze other
patients' traditions? Even the folklore of the regular habitués of hospitals—the folk group of doctors and nurses—has barely begun to be
sampled. (See Victoria George and Alan Dundes, "The Gomer: A
Figure of American Hospital Folk Speech," Journal of American Folklore, Vol. 91 [1978].)

In the context of being seriously ill and surrounded by invalids and
hospital staff, one might be more receptive than usual to the idea
quoted by Dorson that "disease is tied to the way of life." That is to
say, purely physiological causes cannot account for all incidents of heart
disease, but the kind of society an individual lives in partially determines his chances of suffering from it. Apparently, as some doctors had
suspected and two Indiana-trained folklorists supported with their
studies in Egypt and among Italian-Americans, traditional lifestyles

offer mechanisms that reduce stress and enhance one's chances of avoiding angina pectoris and related complications. *(Carla Bianco's book The Two Rosetos, written as an Indiana University dissertation, was published by IU Press in 1974.) One wonders if the folk themselves may have legends, anecdotes, and beliefs attesting to the life-preserving value of their own "folkloric behavior."*

PART I: THE CORONARIES CLOG: A MEMORAT WITH A MORAL

On Saturday morning, the 18th of November 1972, I was hastening from breakfast to the Joe C. Thompson conference building at the University of Texas, Austin, to catch the opening session of that day's American Folklore Society program. As I mounted the steps a strange and novel sensation overcame me, best described in a phrase I later encountered, as of an elephant stepping on one's stomach. Weakly I turned to retrace my steps to my motel room, but as the crowd was coming toward me, various persons paused to chat and Frances Gillmor accompanied me back discussing a matter of mutual interest, unaware of my distress. Once in the room I collapsed on the bed and slept for four hours. When I awoke the pain was gone.

Since I had stayed up until three a.m. the night before talking with folklore graduate students at the Goldstein-Wilgus open house suite, and then had arisen at seven a.m., I dismissed the matter as a case of extreme fatigue. But the following morning, as I took my place on the panel chaired by Frank de Caro, on "The History of Folkloristics," a twinge returned, and led me to press my hand against my chest and wonder if I could deliver my piece. Carmen Roy, sitting in the front row, noticed my situation and made a gesture of concern. This time the pain passed after a few moments and I was able to say my say. On reflection I considered the sensations as perhaps a natural reaction to a session on structuralism I had unwittingly wandered into, or maybe an internal disorder connected with my idiosyncratic esophagus.

The strange pain recurred on December 6, at the end of a drive to Indianapolis for a board of directors' meeting of a new publishing company, and I nursed it through the meeting with a cup of hot water. Then, during the Christmas break, a fourth and fifth repetition occurred while I was walking casually with Gloria near our home. On December 26th a long and painful seizure made me consider going to the hospital, but the pain finally eased after I stood for some time under a hot shower. My family doctor had left on vacation, and his nurse cautioned me that chest pains were nothing to fool around with.

Two days later came the seventh, now familiar attack, so prolonged and intense that this time Gloria drove me down to the emergency ward of the Bloomington hospital, where I was given an electrocardiogram. The physician on duty diagnosed angina and admitted me for observation for a few days. But my stay in hospitals was to extend through February third of 1973.

Now a chest specialist, Dr. Glen Ley, looked me over. He assured me that blood thinners and anti-coagulants would alleviate the angina, and that I could return home in a few days and continue my preparations for our move to Amherst, where I was to teach at the University of Massachusetts in the spring semester. Personally I did not feel too worried, for although I had over the past year registered some high blood pressure, which led my family doctor to warn me against playing competitive tennis and squash, and some blood sugar, I believed myself in good physical shape. But on the fifth morning, when I was scheduled to go home, the chest pain came again, and for the first time I was given a pain-killing shot. Next morning it recurred once more, the ninth seizure, and now the nurse had me place a tiny nitroglycerin tablet under my tongue, which in five seconds miraculously chased away the angina.

At this point Dr. Ley's mood changed. Pain at rest, he informed me, was serious. He counseled my going to the Cleveland Clinic Hospital for possible open-heart surgery, in which veins from the legs are transferred to the chest to bypass the clogged portions of the coronaries. His diagnosis was "acute coronary insufficiency," the preliminary to a heart attack. As yet the heart showed stress but no damage. Dr. Ley made arrangements for Gloria and me to fly to Cleveland in what was charitably called an air ambulance. The middle-aged insurance man flying it, an ex-marine pilot now bald and paunchy, slipped on the icy ground pulling his toy plane out of the hangar and lay on his back bracing his leg against the nose so the craft would not flatten him, as Gloria, the children and I watched in astonishment. Airborne, we encountered a swirling snowstorm and bundled up—I had been especially warned against cold weather—when the plane's heater went dead. "That always happens when it gets cold," our pilot commented cheerfully. The storm caused him to detour and land us at a different airfield. My heart could not be in such bad shape, I mused, if it withstood that trip.

So on January fifth I entered the famed Cleveland Clinic, located in the squalid and crime-ridden inner city. The events of my first week there are encapsulated in the following letter of January 13 which I circulated to the Folklore faculty and students, university administrators and colleagues, and various friends.

To: Faculty and Students of the Folklore Institute,
         Indiana University
From: Richard M. Dorson
Place: Cleveland Clinic Hospital
Date: January 13, 1973

Dear Everybody:

Thanks for all your good wishes. This Cleveland Clinic is a fantastic place. They have superspecialists in 37 diseases who check you from stem to stern. After examining nine tubes of my blood, a team of cardiologists (all of the doctors move in teams, the top boy and his retinue) marched into my room to give me the once over. Unflinchingly I faced them. "Professor," began the leader (a world-renowned diagnostician), "have you ever had syphilis? Your serology test is positive."

For this I was not prepared. Redfaced I paraded my virtues: no smoking, drinking, coffee, tea, and certainly *never* any hanky panky. My blood pressure rose so much they warned me it might affect my cardiac catheterization the following day. They promised to recheck that particular test. Meanwhile my beloved Gloria, loyal and true, stood by my side breathing words of reassurance while hastily tying on a mouth mask.

The next day I was led down to the catheterization room, strapped to the turntable underneath the cardioscope, and asked to extend my right arm, into which the doctor injected the blue dye that circulates through the arteries. They had me twist while they photographed the passage of the dye. On the basis of the films the cardiologist makes his recommendation: send home on medication, surgery at a future date, immediate surgery, or shipment to the morgue. This is the origin of the saying, "The dye is cast."[1]

At one point in my twistings I found my head right alongside the doctor's ear. As it is very difficult to get the attention of these famous physicians, I took the opportunity to whisper in his ear, "Doctor, do you really believe a clean-cut, all-American type like me, a model and inspiration to our students at the Folklore Institute, could have V.D.?"

He gave me his answer the next day, when Gloria and I sat in his office outside the catheterizing room. "The report was a false positive," he said unemotionally. "You do not have V.D." Then he spread a series of charts across his desk top. "However," he went on (Dr. Razavi is a handsome, glittering-eyed Mediterranean), "you do have some problems. You have arteriosclerosis (hardening of the

---

1. [Dorson is making punning reference to the traditional proverb "The die (singular of "dice") is cast" meaning that an action has been set in motion which cannot be stopped.]

arteries) in all three coronary arteries, diabetes in a moderate stage, excessive cholesterol, high uric acid, high blood sugar," and he mentioned a couple of other highs that Gloria and I could not recognize. "My recommendation is a double bypass transplanting a vein from each of your legs into your chest. Of course your enlarged esophagus will present some difficulty in this kind of open-heart surgery."

I digested all this for a few moments. My eyes met Gloria's, then returned to the doctor. "Look doctor," I said, "I'll make a deal with you. I'll swap all this stuff you've given me for the V.D."

Alas, they do not operate—and I use the word advisedly—that way at the Cleveland Clinic. The only concession Dr. Razavi would make was to suggest that while the surgeons were inserting the new heart veins they could also perforate the cardia at the base of my esophagus that had given me so much digestive trouble since I was fourteen. "It will only take us an extra ten minutes."

It occurred to me with regret that during my stay in the Bloomington Hospital the gnarled projectile of my second big toenail on my right foot, which titillated a number of nurses who trooped in to view it (I jest not), had been sawed off by Gloria the day before we transferred to the Cleveland Clinic.

Otherwise the surgeon could have cut that off too. It would have only taken an extra five minutes.

This letter has proved to be my most successful nonpublication. Chancellor Byrum Carter read it at the monthly meeting of the board of trustees of Indiana University, following the usual announcements of recently deceased and severely ailing faculty members.

The pre-surgery portion of my hospital stay proved extremely pleasant. It was the first vacation I had taken in years, and I enjoyed every moment, since the angina no longer recurred, and Cleveland Clinic permitted the maximum amount of free movement. If you were ambulatory, they let you wander all over your floor. I saw more of Gloria than I had at any time since our courtship. And I met fascinating people, swathed in bandages on every portion of their anatomy, pushing their intravenous feeding poles in front of them, reciting the most wondrous tales of surgical miracles. The patients' lounge at the end of the hall proved a swapping ground of death-defying memorats. There was the poor chap with a cancerous urethra, whose Long Island doctors had given him up, but the Cleveland Clinic urologist fashioned him a whole new organ out of his own flesh. A garrulous woman whose right hand had been mangled to a pulp by a factory machine carried the splintered remains sewn to her abdomen, where her own tissues were renewing the hand. Every conceivable kind of major damage to the human body was treated at the Cleveland Clinic, which handled nothing less than a hernia. Some of these patients had been callers at the clinic for much of their lives. My roommate, garrulous Bob Richards, thirty-one, had undergone twenty-five major operations since at the age of fifteen he had crashed his motorcycle head on into an automobile and pulverized his kidneys.

Late one Friday evening, when I had settled comfortably into my new routine and half suspected the doctors had forgotten about me, a tall stonyfaced young surgeon materialized at the foot of my bed, by the TV, on which I was watching an old James Stewart–Doris Day thriller, and asked in an Australian accent if I were ready to have heart surgery next Monday. I was, and inquired if they were going to do the esophagus too. "Yes, we are going to try it all in one go," he said pluckily.

All the patients scheduled for open-heart surgery are briefed at four p.m. the day before their operation by a nurse who spares no details. One patient, I was told, decided after the briefing to forego the operation and go back to Texas to await his end at home. Another, who stayed on, described the intensive care unit as a torture chamber. The near and dear are no longer allowed into the ward, since too many of them fainted on seeing the state of their loved ones. Suffice to say that the mortal is reduced as near as possible from the animal to the vegetable level. I awoke with a tube down my throat breathing me, two tubes inserted into my chest giving me blood, another in my right shoulder feeding me intravenously, still another attached to my urethra emptying me, and an extra one in my left abdomen that puzzled the nurses, orderlies, and even some of the passing doctors not on my case, one of whom inquired if it was a drainage or a feeding tube. The latter possibility represented my worst fears, namely that my esophagus had blocked and would have to be bypassed, along with my coronaries. My surgeon, Dr. Laurence K. Groves, later informed me that mine was the first case he had encountered of arteriosclerosis complicated by achalasia (the name for my distended, malfunctioning esophagus).

As it turned out, Dr. Groves had decided not to attempt the cardiomyotomy (perforation of the esophagus) considering it too hazardous on top of the three bypasses. The surgeons did remove, in his phrase, "about twelve pounds of sauerkraut" from the esophagus, and as a memento they inserted the extra tube to drain the stomach fluids. Unlike the other patients in the ward, I was not permitted any oral intake of food or drink until my insides thawed out, and for several days the attendant physician would listen with his stethoscope on my abdomen for what he termed "bowel sounds," and I too cocked an anxious ear. The first bowel movement induced in me a state of euphoria, promptly communicated to all my fellow patients and hospital personnel within reach, and celebrated with a feast of bouillon and jello.

As soon as the heart patient is unplugged and detubed, he begins a regime of deep breathing exercises and enforced coughing that threaten to split him open again. He breathes in oxygen for ten minutes from an oxygenator breathing machine, then tries to cough while a burly attendant swats him on the back and exhorts him to try harder to bring up secretions deep in the lungs. If all goes well, the stitches are removed from the chest and legs within nine days. On the eleventh day I was sent home to convalesce. As of today I feel better than ever and everything works, even the trick esophagus.

The surgery for the coronary bypass operation has been described by Thomas Thompson in *Hearts* as the most meticulous and tedious of operations. Surgeons prepare for it by circumcising gnats. They liken the procedure to sewing twenty stitches on the mouth of a piece of quivering spaghetti while attempting to insert it into a palpitating pear. How successful coronary bypass surgery will prove to be over the long haul cannot yet be predicted, since it was only initiated in 1967. The heart surgeons at the Cleveland Clinic report a mortality rate of 6.2% of 1000 operated patients after one year, compared with 11.9% of severe coronary patients who were not operated upon. After three years the percentages compare at 13.4% to 24.9%, on a smaller sampling. The surgeons conclude that the bypass operation reduced mortality by about one-half.[2] Beyond that, the operation demonstrably has restored surgical patients to health and vigor, in contrast to those not operated upon who remain cardiac cripples. Every year some 700,000 Americans die from coronary arteriosclerosis, about one-fourth prematurely before the age of 65. The coronary bypass operation, called "the most frequently performed radical lifesaving procedure in U.S. hospitals, "saves 60,000 Americans who would otherwise swell the total of annual deaths.[3]

Man has found a cure for coronary heart disease. Can he find a preventive?

PART II: FOLKLORE TO THE RESCUE

What causes heart disease, and specifically arteriosclerosis, the filling up of the coronary arteries with fatty tissue that threatens eventually to block completely the circulation of the blood? During my

2. *Time* 102:8 (20 August 1973), "Letters," p. 4.
3. *Time* 102:5 (30 July 1973), "Medicine," p. 71.

convalescence a teeming literature of speculation on the subject seemed to leap at me: in columns of medical advice in the daily papers; in professional journals in the doctor's office; in a long leader article in the *New York Times Magazine*; in a gripping book by journalist Thomas Thompson, *Hearts*, reporting on the experiments with heart surgery at Houston by Michael DeBakey and Denton Cooley; in a *Time* magazine piece on the success of the coronary bypass operation at the Cleveland Clinic, with pictures of active persons good as new after their repairs. As America's number one killer in the 1960s and 70s, heart disease compels increasing attention, discussion, and anxiety. Anyone can be striken, the young as well as the old, and autopsies of American soldiers killed in Korea revealed that many youths in their twenties already showed signs of hardening of the arteries. A graphic metaphor likens the disease to the clogging of pipes with rust and slag; originally the pipes appear clean, white, and gleaming, but in the course of time they silt up, turn ugly red, and show angry furrows as the mounting refuse slowly chokes the blood flow.

Medical opinion has isolated half a dozen factors contributing to coronary heart disease: heredity, obesity, lack of exercise, smoking, excessive fats and sugar in the diet, indicated by high cholesterol and blood sugar counts, and stress. Some kind of syndrome involving several of these components appears in most coronary cases. In my own case the components were heredity, sugar, and the factor most Americans complain of, stress. Save for stress, these causes can be pretty well pinpointed. Americans have become alerted to the risks of smoking tar- and nicotine-filled cigarettes, and of eating too much saturated fats and added sugar. "We are in danger of becoming a nation of sugar junkies," the papers quoted a vegetarian housewife. "We are a society of nutritional illiterates," declared a food expert. But diet is now a national obsession. By contrast, just what is stress, how does one measure and control it? Some physicians divided American males into two personality types, A and B, the one compulsive, tense, gut-driven, the other equable, easygoing, relaxed. The first type fell victim to arteriosclerosis. An American Medical Association sponsored magazine for the layman, *Today's Health*, presented a case study of a Type A personality who dropped dead of a heart attack while running around the track. He was a successful California businessman, owner of a milk-processing and distributing plant, who had consumed a large late lunch with several cocktails after a heavy morning's work, and then knocked off early in the afternoon to keep in shape by running. Overwork, overeating and drinking, and exercise on top of that invited the coronary. Athletes are no more immune than anyone else, for, if seemingly fit, they share the same stresses as other competitive Americans. Exertion and excitement bring on the heart attack. Thomas Thompson gives an example of an urbane University of Texas dean who was discharged from the Houston hospital after the surgeons had installed a pacemaker in his heart muscle. At the airport he learned that he had just missed his flight, but if he hurried he could make another down the line. The dean grabbed two suitcases and ran to the new flight departure desk. His pacemaker popped out, and instead of returning home he returned to the hospital, for two more operations, both unsuccessful, and death.

The cause of stress, we recognize, is our life style, and the correlation between coronary heart disease and the American rhythm of life today is strikingly made in an article by Eric J. Cassell, clinical professor of public helath at Cornell University Medical College, "Disease as a Way of life."[4] Cassell contends persuasively that the basic social and economic patterns of a society determine the kinds and incidence of diseases in that society, regardless of the medical knowledge and health services available. "Simply stated, disease is tied to the way of life." A pacemaker or a coronary by-pass operation will not solve the problem of heart disease if the patient resumes the life style that caused the thickening of his arteries. Cassell offers as an example the attempt in the 1950s of a health research team of physicians and nurses to bring modern health care and facilities to an impoverished Navajo Indian reservation where extended families lived in windowless one-room log and mud dwellings. At the end of five years, the team had reduced tuberculosis and ear infection among children, but had effected no change in the pattern of disease among these Navajo. Their children continued to die of diarrhea and pneumonia in like numbers as before. Antibiotics could not conquer malnutrition and bad sanitation. At the turn of the present century, American children living in ethnic ghettos in crowded industrial cities were dying of the same diseases as the Navajo. By the 1950s the death rate from such scourges as tuberculosis, typhoid, and the diarrhea-pneumonia complex had dropped sharply, not because of the use of new drugs and vaccines, which were not then generally available, but because of improved living conditions. But as the older diseases receded, new ones—cancer, heart disease, strokes—replaced them as an accompaniment to the affluent society. Recently industrialized nations, like the Soviet Union and Venezuela, are proud of the rise in their death rate due to arteriosclerosis, a sign of their increasing prosperity.

What lifestyle can the individual in the affluent society adopt to

4. *Commentary* 55 (February, 1973): 80–82.

avoid the tension and stress that lead to coronary heart disease? The modern lifestyle offers him prizes and rewards he cannot easily forego: status, titles, honors, riches. A folklorist will naturally contrast the rhythm and tempo of modern life with the very different pace and values of traditional societies. To what extent do hypertension and heart attacks affect the folk?

Very little indeed, so long as they resist Americanization, according to a lengthy article beginning on the first page of the *Washington Post* for Monday, April 16, 1973. A special feature written for the *Post* by Bill Richards and headlined "American Ethic Kills Miracle," the story dealt with the town of Roseto in eastern Pennsylvania, whose population of 1600 Italians had in the early 1960s attracted national attention for their seeming immunity to heart attacks. A research team led by Dr. John G. Bruhn, a medical sociologist at the University of Texas medical school's Galveston branch, descended on Roseto in 1961 and reported the rate of arteriosclerotic heart disease as one-third the national average of 3.59 per 1000 males, and only one-fourth the rate of non-Italian towns in the area. Yet the short, heavy Rosetans ate prodigously of *pasta, prosciutto,* and *scarpetti*—"green peppers fried in lard with bread dipped in a rich, lard-based gravy"—at meals lasting up to six hours. The report of Bruhn's team, published in 1965, stated that not one Rosetan under forty-seven had ever suffered a recorded heart attack, and that the Rosetans seemed to live ten and twenty years longer than other Americans. Gravestones of the older immigrants, who first came from the farming village of Roseto, Valforte, Foggia, in 1882, bore witness to their longevity: Fausto Sabatino 1866–1951; Vincenza Gaggiagarro 1878–1953.

A piece in *Time* magazine on the long-lived Rosetans drew my attention, not because of the immunity to heart disease of these overweight, high cholestorol gourmands—an aspect that did not then interest me—but because there was an immigrant rural community, totally Italian, colonized in America from a parent community in the Old Country. The situation offered inviting possibilities for comparative fieldwork and I made it known to Carla Bianco, come over from Rome to work toward the folklore doctorate at Indiana University and eager for fieldwork among Italian-Americans. Carla embraced the idea, understook intensive field forays into Roseto, Pennsylvania and Roseto, Italy, and completed a splendid dissertation on "The Two Rosetos" which is being published by the Indiana University Press. While her interests lay in comparative ethnography and the acculturation process, we did discuss the absence of heart disease among the Pennsylvania Rosetans, and agreed that a likely explanation lay in the successful transition they had made from the Old World to the New, a transition that enabled them to enjoy the fruits of both worlds. In their new setting these particular immigrating Italins had avoided the traumatic interlude of settling in an urban ethnic ghetto and attempting the painful climb into middle-class suburbia, the usual story, as reported for the New Haven Italians by Phyllis A. Williams in *South Italian Folkways in Europe and America.* In eastern Pennsylvania the first comers found jobs in slate quarries at fifty cents a day, alongside English and Welsh miners similarly attracted to the "slate belt," and there they prospered, bought their own homes, and established their own community, which even today is 95% Italian. "They developed a local reputation for their boisterous and close-knit town life." These fortunate Rosetans preserved the ritual solidarity of their traditional culture while enjoying the economic advantages of middle-class America. They ate prodigiously, and lived long.

But Satan entered paradise in the mid-1960s and corrupted Roseto. The town's heart attack rate soared to three times the national average by 1972, and the medical-social researchers rushed back to ascertain the cause. They spotted it immediately, and labeled it "Americanization."

"We were stunned," commented Dr. Bruhn. "There was a very obvious change underway. The men now belong to country clubs and play golf. Their kids drive fancy cars and go away to college. Everyone is making and spending money as fast as they can. In 1961 I never saw a Roseto family sit down to a meal where everyone wasn't at the table together. Now they run in, grab something to eat, and run out again. They used to confide in each other and share their problems and pleasures. Now they compete to show they are doing better than each other."

Between 1961 and 1971 Rosetan family income rose from $7,000 to $11,000. The Rosetans of 1971 possessed color televisions and big cars, and had erected handsome new brick and stone dwellings on empty lots, or remodeled their old homes. Neat front lawns replaced the gardens and orchards once planted in the back yard. "People are living big here now," Mary Cannavo, 72, owner of a luncheonette informed the researchers. "It used to be one big happy family here before. Now it's 'I'm better than you or you're better than me.' Everybody's showing off."

Work and play habits and the once "easygoing lifestyle" of the Rosetans had notably altered over the decade. Upwardly mobile Rosetans commuted twenty or thirty miles out of town to office and managerial positons. Their children departed Roseto for college and then for careers and marriages in the outside world. In the altered life pattern of daily competition replacing the old communal conviviality

Dr. Bruhn found the explanation for the appearance of heart disease. "In Roseto family and community support is disappearing," he concluded. "Most of the men who have had heart attacks here were living under stress and really had nowhere to turn to relieve that pressure. These people have given up something to get something, and it's killing them."

Some medical researchers took issue with Bruhn's analysis. Dr. Ansel Keyes, professor emeritus of public health at the University of Minnesota, challenged both of Bruhn's reports on the grounds that the second was based on the false statistics of the first, which erred because the local doctor reporting on the original medical records in Roseto disliked the term heart attack and refused to recognize any such cases. But Keyes in turn was countered by Dr. Joseph Farace, Roseto's physician for forty-eight years, who flatly declared that his patients never suffered from heart disease in spite of their outrageous dietary habits. In recent years, however, he had been treating Rosetans in the thirty to forty-year-old age bracket for nervous breakdowns that had never occurred there before. "The people who are having heart attacks are the younger generation who work under pressure and sit around worrying about how much money they make," Dr. Farace asserted.

At this point, if we accept the Roseto experience as evidence of correlation between the modern lifestyle and stress-caused diseases, such as arteriosclerosis, we may ask, is there collateral evidence elsewhere? and how does folk lifestyle—or what Hasan El-Shamy calls "folkloric behavior"—relieve stress?

On the first point, here is a newspaper story from Cairo, Egypt, "The Working Woman Enters the Trap of Heart Ailments."[5] The item reports the rise in arterial malfunctions and blood clots (thrombosis) among Egyptian women during the past ten years, the period in which they abandoned their traditional roles to engage in the same kinds of heavily competitive work as men. Of the 179,403 outpatients treated in the internal and cardiac section of Qasr Al-'Aini Hospital over the past year 102,000 were women, and 48,000 of these had heart ailments. A number of suspected heart disease cases actually proved to be nervous conditions reflecting psychological pressures that produced the same symptoms as *angina pectoris*, but the wives continued to insist they suffered from heart ailments so as to win their husbands' sympathy.

As for the question, how do mechanisms in the traditional lifestyle siphon off anxieties and tensions, El-Shamy has written directly on this

5. *Al-Ahram* 99:31547 (25 April 1973), by Ameera Yousif, translated by Hasan El-Shamy.

point in terms of folk practices in Egypt. He writes, "Traditional cultures provide their members with varied patterns of folkloric behavior, the social style and content of which are conducive to dissipation of guilt, anxiety and other forms of stress."[6] What El-Shamy calls "stress-reducing practices" includes both individual and collective expressive forms, and he enumerates such activities as singing, dancing, storytelling, riddling, using proverbs, vocalizing belief, joking, playing folk games, applying folk medicine, and participating in mock fights, verbal duels, religious chants, and sacrilegious rituals. The oral expressive forms reduce and dissipate stress by permitting fantasy fulfillment in the plots of tales and songs and the themes of riddles. Incestuous impulses, status drives, material wants are gratified in these recitals which the folk enjoy and the urban middle classes denigrate. In the kinetic forms of folkloric behavior, such as communal folk dances performed by the urban lower classes, villagers, and Bedouins,[7] the physical movement and their verbal accompaniments release emotional energies in socially satisfying ways. Here is an example El-Shamy gives from the Nubian culture area[8] of a traditional dance ceremony that maintains "emotional equilibrium" in a folk community:

> On the occasion of celebrating the birthday of the five grand-fathers (*annoutchi*) of the Nubian nation, several *kaff* circles were formed on the celebration ground. Scores of young and old men participated actively in the dance while tens of children watched closely. Some women looked on from the tops of their low built houses. The activities climax into wild but highly coordinated leaps attuned to rhythmic clapping and drum beats. The emotional discharge caused by the vehement kinetic activity and accompanied by a verbal activity serves to exalt self, one's own family and social group.
> "I am the artist!" "I am the generous one." "We are the masters of the area." "My brother is working in Cairo." "We are noble Arabs." All are typical utterances repeated with intense emotional involvement until another person forces himself onto the singing floor by saying, "You are an artist, but I am too . . ." Some of the most common themes in these songs are generosity, courage, social prominence, having noble maternal uncles, noble Arab descent, verbal dexterity.[9]

6. Hasan El-Shamy, "Mental Health in Traditional Culture: A Study of Preventive and Therapeutic Folk Practices in Egypt," *Catalyst* 6 (Fall, 1972): 13.
7. [Nomadic desert Arabs.]
8. [The Nile valley of southern Egypt and northern Sudan.]
9. *Ibid.*, pp. 17–18.

Such folkloric behavior, frowned on by the urban middle classes, provides mortals with ego reassurances and satisfactions while avoiding the fierce stress of competitive individualism in modern life.

The hypothesis is clearly framed: folklore lived, not studied, is the surest preventive of heart disease.

CON SAFOS:
MEXICAN-AMERICANS,
NAMES AND GRAFFITI

Sylvia Ann Grider

In contrast to suggestive or editorial graffiti, most often written by other groups (and usually studied by folklorists and sociologists), the Mexican-American culture produces mainly name- or initial-writings that are invariably safeguarded by the untranslatable inscription con safos. There is a useful bibliography of general works on graffiti cited in the first three footnotes of this essay, even though the special context being described here includes a different genre of wall writings from the usual erotic and humorous variety seen in public places.

Sylvia Ann Grider alludes to other cultures' ways of expressing respect for the power of names, and she raises the interesting question of why Chicanos and other American "street-oriented groups," who place such great importance on personal names, frequently put up their names in public places just where they might most easily be erased or desecrated. For the Mexican-Americans, con safos has the power to protect their written names, although there is still the risk that members of other groups (even those in the same school and community) will not recognize or respect the warning. It is interesting that the Anglo-American children's saying "I'm rubber, you're glue . . ." given as a counterpart to con safos is used only in oral tradition, while con safos is always written. (Do any other American groups have written traditional warnings or protection?)

The fieldwork for this article was done in Texas, but published references show a more general widespread urban Mexican-American tradition of con safos. It is notable that the author went beyond merely recording the mute graffiti themselves to collecting also the comments and beliefs of the members of the group responsible for them. Folklore students in any community with a Chicano section could test for themselves Grider's three-part classification of these graffiti and her description of the oral transmission channels for learning the custom. Variant folk explanations of what con safos means would be especially interesting to collect. Knowledge of the con safos tradition gained from reading this article, plus background information in the other works cited on Mexican-American culture, should enable the non-Chicano collector to establish rapport with possible informants.

Frank J. D'Angelo has published the following rhetorical analyses of recent American graffiti: "Sacred Cows Make Great Hamburgers: the Rhetoric of Graffiti," College Composition and Communication

(May, 1974); "Oscar Mayer Ads Are Pure Baloney: The Graffitist as Critic of Advertising," College Composition and Communication (October, 1975); "Fools' Names and Fools' Faces Are Always Seen in Public Places: A Study of Graffiti," Journal of Popular Culture, Vol. 10 (Summer, 1976); and "Up Against the Wall, Mother! The Rhetoric of Slogans, Catchphrases, and Graffiti," in A Symposium in Rhetoric, ed. William C. Tanner, J. Dean Bishop, and Turner S. Kobler (Denton, Texas: Texas Woman's University Press, 1976).

CONTRARY TO POPULAR OPINION, not all graffiti are "dirty," humorous, or erotic. Although the majority of serious studies have dealt with the psychological and sociological analysis of the category of graffiti which Alan Dundes calls "latrinalia,"[1] and, although the popular press has a long history of feature articles on the topic,[2] little investigation has been undertaken to determine the nature and importance of other types of public-wall writing in the United States.[3] This paper

1. Alan Dundes, "Here I Sit—A Study of American Latrinalia," *Kroeber Anthropological Society Papers*, 34 (1966), 91–105; other studies which have dealt with graffiti from a psychological or sociological standpoint are T. Collins and P. Batzle, "Method of Increasing Graffito Responses," *Perceptual and Motor Skills*, 31 (1970), 733–734; E. Landy and J. Steele, "Graffiti as a Function of Building Utilization," *Perceptual and Motor Skills*, 25 (1967), 711–712; Paul D. McGlynn, "Graffiti and Slogans: Flushing the Id," *Journal of Popular Culture*, 6 (1972), 351–356; L. Rudin and M. Harless, "Graffiti and Building Use: The 1968 Election," *Psychological Reports*, 27 (1970), 517–518; L. Sechrest and L. Flores, "Homosexuality in the United States and the Philippines: The Handwriting on the Wall," *Journal of Social Psychology*, 79 (1969), 3–12; L. Sechrest and K. Olson, "Graffiti in Four Types of Institutions of Higher Education," *The Journal of Sex Research*, 7 (1971), 62–71; and Terrance L. Stocker and others, "Social Analysis of Graffiti," *Journal of American Folklore*, 85 (1972), 356–366.

2. A sample of such articles includes J. Brachman, "Graffiti Fit to Print," *New York Times Magazine*, 116 (February 12, 1967), 97–99; "Handwriting on the Wall," *Time*, 92 (November 15, 1968), 56; H. Lomas and G. Weltman, "Washroom Wit," *Newsweek*, 68 (October 10, 1966), 110; and R. J. Walker, "Kilroy Was Here: A History of Scribbling in Ancient and Modern Times," *Hobbies*, 73 (July 1968), 98 N–98 O. A more complete listing of titles can be found in the *Readers Guide to Periodical Literature* listed under "graffiti"; also, consult the "Folklore in the News" section of *Western Folklore*. Popular books on the topic: Richard Freeman, *Graffiti* (London, 1966), and Robert Reisner, *Graffiti: Two Thousand Years of Wall Writing* (New York, 1971). Other representative titles, most of which are rather superficial: Bill Adler, *Graffiti* (New York, 1967); Al Boliska, *It Is Written: A Collection of Graffiti from the Washrooms, Fences, Alleys, Walls, Billboards and Subways of North America* (Montreal, 1968); Bill Leary, *Graffiti: Those Private Scrawls on Public Walls* (Greenwich, Conn., 1968); Morton Mockridge, *The Scrawl of the Wild* (Cleveland, 1968); Robert Reisner, *Great Wall Writing and Button Graffiti* (New York, 1967); and Alan Robbins, *Guide to College Graffiti* (New York, 1967).

3. The most significant contribution in this area of investigation is Herbert Kohl and James Hinton, "Names, and Graffiti and Culture," in *Rappin' and Stylin' Out*, ed. Thomas Kochman (Urbana, 1972), 109–133.

deals with a distinctive type of such non-scatalogical graffiti, the phrase *con safos*, which is used by Mexican-Americans as a unique expression of Chicano attitudes and values.

Personal names and even nicknames are important to all peoples but in varying degrees. Some American Indians, for example, regard a person's name as a vulnerable extension of the person himself. And of course given names and nicknames represent a special device for individualizing and distinguishing persons within any given group. Mexican nationals and those who have immigrated to the United States are no different in this respect. As any tourist in Mexico can notice, Mexicans are prone to attach a special name to anything of importance to them, animate or inanimate, from children to taxicabs to buses, and they usually inscribe the name thereon.[4] Among Mexican-Americans this penchant for naming is especially given graphic expression through graffiti. Throughout the Chicano district of practically any American town, from San Antonio to Los Angeles, one can spot distinctly Spanish surnames, given names, and nicknames written on walls and sidewalks. Especially on the West Coast, this "wall art," composed primarily of stylized names, has achieved the status of folk art.[5] The problem that such public presentation of names creates for the individual who writes them is the necessity for protecting these inscriptions from defacement and further insult because the graphic depiction of the name is regarded as a tangible extension of the person himself. But, if names are so important and so vulnerable that they require almost ritual and mystic protection, why do the Mexican-Americans write them in public places in the first place?

To be able to write their names wherever they please is very important to street-oriented groups because, as Herbert Kohl and James Hinton observe, "To declare one's name on a wall is to claim that name for oneself; it can also be a public announcement of one's role in a peer group. If there are no 'legal' ways to proclaim these important aspects of our cultural life, we invent extralegal procedures."[6] The apparent answer to this question, then, is that Mexican-Americans have devised a means of protection strong enough to protect the graffiti names wherever they happen to be written.

The means by which the Chicano graffitor protects his own name or that of his sweetheart or barrio[7] from erasure or defacement is by writing the phrase *con safos* in conjunction with the name. *Con safos*, an apparent corruption of the Spanish verb *zafar*, is untranslatable.

4. For examples of this see A. Jiménez, "Letreros en Camiones," in *Picardía Mexicana* (Mexico City, 1961), 9–20.

5. José R. Reyna, "Chicano Graffiti of Los Angeles," paper read at the American Folklore Society meeting in Austin, Texas, November, 1972.

6. 124.

7. [Spanish-speaking neighborhood.]

The verb *zafar* can mean "to loosen," "untie," or "clear." *Zafo*, the adjective, means "intact," or "unhurt." Another related adjective, *safado*, means "impudent" or "shameless."[8] The meaning of the related *con safos* is infinitely more specialized in meaning and the phrase exists primarily in association with names. An indication of the linguistic peculiarity and apparent folk origin of the phrase is obvious as soon as one attempts to look it up in a standard Spanish-English dictionary. *Safos* is simply not listed. One reason for this omission may be that the word exists only in unpublished written form while dictionaries and glossaries are based on the standard spoken or published language. However, specialized studies of Spanish-English argot in the United States, one variation of which is *Pachuco*,[9] do note the use of this idiomatic expression. Two such studies present the word *safo*, spelled without the terminal *s*. Haldeen Braddy gives the simple explanation in the glossary of his article: "*safo*—the same to you."[10]

The problem with this definition is its omission of the preposition *con*, which means "with." The phrase is always expressed as *con safos*; never does *safos* appear alone. It is the *con* which seems to give the phrase its reflexive aspect. Lurline Coltharp has a more complete interpretation:

> *Safo*, n. This is used only in the phrase "con safo" which means "the same to you." In order to forestall criticism, if a person writes his name on a wall, he puts C/S after it. Then if a person criticizes, the initials say, "It names it back to you."[11]

A bi-lingual magazine published in Los Angeles has taken the phrase as its title. A standard feature of this magazine is its glossary of idiomatic Spanish expressions, one entry of which explained the term as follow:

> *Con Safos*, n. *caló*, protective symbolism used by Chicano grafitti [sic] artists appearing usually by a person's name or the name of his *barrio*, meaning the same to you; ditto; likewise.[12]

All informed explanations of the term thus seem to be essentially the same. Further corroboration was given me by an informant who said that by writing *con safos* in conjunction with one's name, the

8. Charles E. Kany, *American Spanish Semantics* (Berkeley, 1960), 178.

9. Special studies of this argot or class jargon are George C. Barker, *Pachuco: An American-Spanish Argot and Its Social Functions in Tucson, Arizona* (Tucson, 1950); Haldeen Braddy, "The Pachucos and Their Argot," *Southern Folklore Quarterly*, 24 (1960), 255–271; and Lurline Coltharp, *The Tongue of the Tirilones: A Linguistic Study of Criminal Argot* (University, Alabama, 1965).

10. 270.

11. 256.

12. *Con Safos*, 7 (1971), 65.

writer means, "I free myself from whatever ugly slur you write against my name." Another informant explained the meaning by analogy, saying that it meant the same as the English jingle, "I'm rubber, you're glue; whatever you say bounces off me and sticks to you." In essence, then, *con safos* is a surrogate for a physical bodyguard which can protect a written name only by being written in connection or direct association with it. Just as the reflection in Perseus' shield killed Medusa, it throws the obscenity or slur back upon the defacer of the graffiti name thus protected because no one who knows the function of the phrase is willing to state publicly that he himself is a *puto* or whatever, which is what it would mean if an enemy wrote this or any other obscenity directed toward a protected name. The wish to keep graffiti safe from harm is not unique to Mexican-Americans, however. Although they lacked any such symbol as *con safos*, ancient Romans too felt that their graffiti ought to be left undisturbed. In Pompeii, for example, where wall artists generally signed their works, the following graffito has been recovered: "Scripsit Aemilius Celer, invidiose qui deles aegrotes," which, roughly translated, means, "Aemilius Celer wrote this, and if you're mean enough to spoil my work, I hope you'll be ill."[13]

Although *con safos* itself is exclusively graffiti and seldom appears alone, the explanation and transmission of its function and meaning is through oral tradition. As soon as the children have been in school long enough to learn to write their names and recognize letters of the alphabet, they ask someone who is older and more knowledgeable what the ubiquitous *con safos* means. In fact, they probably recognize this phrase or its initials long before they learn to read. The usual answer to such a query is something to the effect that, "It means that when you write your name and put *con safos* by it nobody will write dirty words over your name." This was the most common answer I received when I asked Chicano high school students in Dallas what the symbol meant and how they had found out about it.[14] Further investigation revealed that many of the students accepted this explanation fully and never considered the matter any further. They knew how the phrase functioned and so were not really interested in its more esoteric ramifications. Since they were bi-lingual and Spanish

13. Helen H. Tanzer, *The Common People of Pompeii: A Study of the Graffiti* (Baltimore, 1939), 95.

14. From 1967–70 I taught on the practically all-white faculty of N. R. Crozier Technical High School in Dallas, Texas, where the student population was pre-dominantly Mexican-American. Integration problems and the route of a new freeway closed the school in the fall of 1971. This paper is based on data gathered for me by my Chicano students. Throughout this paper I will use the terms Mexican-American and Chicano interchangeably, as did my students, without at-taching any special connotative value to either term.

was their first language, a translation of the phrase into English was unnecessary for them. It took many conversations and some active research on the part of my student informants before they could arrive at an explanation of their term that I, a non-speaker of Spanish and a cultural outsider, could understand. They all agreed that they had found out about its function by asking either family members or older friends. Translation or lexical equivalents were irrelevant. One high school junior remembered being told as a small boy by his mother that anyone who violated its taboo would be turned into a frog, a misconception arising from her etymological confusion of *safos* with *sapo*, the noun meaning "toad" or "frog." Various other oral explanations were "You call yourself that," "Back to you in case of bad words," and "No one can put something else where somebody has put something down." Another explanation, stemming from the fact that *con safos* almost always accompanies pairs of sweethearts' names, is that the *con safos* means that "it is no lie that the boy and girl love each other."

Throughout these investigations, there was never any attempt to conceal the meaning or function of *con safos*. There is absolutely no secrecy or covert mysticism involved. The phrase is regarded very matter of factly and there are no prohibitions on who can use it. In fact, my informants were so willing to discuss *con safos* that they volunteered an explanation of a seemingly related expression which I have never seen written or heard used in any other context, *sin safos*. *Sin*, of course, means "without," and if *con safos* is taken to mean "it counts" then *sin safos* means "it doesn't count" or the exact opposite of *con safos*. Regardless, *sin safos* exists only orally by way of explanation of its contrary and is not used itself as graffiti because it would be completely dysfunctional.

Who uses *con safos*? Younger teenagers, both boys and girls, use this protective symbol more than any other age group. Its use does not necessarily connote delinquent involvement.[15] By the time they are juniors and seniors in high school the young people say that they have outgrown writing their names on walls and desks so they no longer

15. Mexican-American juvenile delinquents are usually called *pachucos* (see Note 9 for further bibliography on the term). Nearly all studies of Mexicans in America attribute the whole stereotype of Mexican-American delinquency to the race riots in Los Angeles during World War II. Examples of such studies include Beatrice Griffith, *American Me* (Boston, 1948); Celia S. Heller, *Mexican American Youth: Forgotten Youth at the Crossroads* (New York, 1966); Carey McWilliams, *North from Mexico* (New York, 1968; original publication 1948); Matt S. Meier and Feliciano Rivera, eds., *Readings in La Raza: The Twentieth Century* (New York, 1974); Stan Steiner, *La Raza: The Mexican-Americans* (New York, 1969); and Ralph H. Turner and Samuel J. Surace, "Zootsuiters and Mexicans: Symbols in Crowd Behavior," *American Journal of Sociology*, 62 (1956), 14–20.

need the protective agency of *con safos*. In fact, many will admit that they no longer "believe" in it. The expression is used most extensively by those who have the closest ties with the Mexican cultural heritage, meaning generally those who speak only Spanish at home and whose parents or grandparents immigrated from Mexico. Many of the more anglicized youth shun the use of *con safos* and even seem embarrassed or ashamed of it and there are those who do not know what it means or how it is used. Those who are from more educated backgrounds are least likely to know and use this folk expression. The phrase may also have taken on a *paso por aquí* or "Kilroy was here" aspect, for it is found in such out of the way places as Bloomington, Indiana, where an anonymous "Los Chicanos C/S cccc" is indelibly etched into a sidewalk by the railroad track on the edge of the campus of Indiana University. Although the sentiment was not evident among the Dallas teenagers upon whom this study is based, *con safos* is reportedly used extensively in the anti-establishment Chicano movement in California. In this case the phrase is apparently spoken and has taken on an "up yours, gringo" meaning of contempt for Anglos.[16]

The efficacy of this graffito depends upon a reciprocal understanding and acceptance of its meaning. Any Mexican-American who writes his name in a public place must take the precaution of protecting it by including the *con safos*. But before that protection can function effectively, the enemy who has the urge to defile or insult that name and thus, by extension, the person that it represents or who wrote it, must know and be willing to accept the consequences of the violation of the taboo. If the defiler of the graffito is ignorant of what the *con safos* means and is therefore not subject to the taboo, he has no compunction about attacking the name in any way he wants to, which might range anywhere from marking through the name to erasing it completely or glossing it with whatever obscenities and insults he deems sufficient to show his contempt for the person named in the graffito inscription. On the other hand, in Dallas one way to precipitate a fight with an opposing gang is to write the barrio name without the *con safos* bodyguard, wait until the other gang defaces the name, and then use that act as an excuse for retaliation.[17] This is a similar

16. "Anglo" is the term which Mexican-Americans frequently use to designate the "whites," or native English speakers of the dominant Caucasian culture.

17. Mexican-American gangs in Dallas date from the establishment of the first Mexican ghetto there, the Little Mexico district near downtown. For the earliest and most complete treatment of this complex, see Ethelyn Clara Davis, "Little Mexico: A Study of Horizontal and Vertical Mobility," M. A. Thesis, Southern Methodist University, 1936, and Haskell A. Miller, "Boys' Gangs in Dallas," M. A. Thesis, Southern Methodist University, 1933. The dominant gangs in Dallas today are *El Barrio*, Ledbetter, and City Park. The names of the gangs reflect the sections of the city in which the members live.

type of dare to that expressed in the phrase "to go around with a chip on your shoulder" or, in earlier days, by throwing down the gauntlet as a provocation for a duel. But if the gang name has been protected by the *con safos,* the opposing gang ususally will not bother it because they respect the power of the C/S.

Thus, as long as both parties involved know and respect the use of *con safos,* personal names and nicknames are safe from harm. In the predominantly Mexican-American high school from which these samples were drawn, *con safos* was used so extensively and effectively that even a few Anglos successfully adopted it. However, when the neighboring black high school was closed and merged with this school as a result of civil rights legislation, the epidemic violation of this protective taboo became one of the factors that precipitated cultural frictions between Chicanos and blacks. The incoming black students had no way of knowing what *con safos* meant, and many of them later admitted that they had not even noticed the phrase or if they did, they assumed that it was a Spanish nickname of some sort. Consequently, they wrote their own graffiti sentiments wherever they pleased, with total disregard for a custom that did not directly affect them. As a result of this constant violation of their tradition by these outsiders, most of the Chicanos reacted by no longer writing their now vulnerable names in public places at all rather than by fighting or defacing the graffiti of the blacks, which tended more toward impersonal obscenities or sexually explicit drawings than toward identifiable personal names.[18] Nevertheless, even under such outside pressure, the general use of *con safos* continued as an active tradition among the Mexican-American youth within their own cultural milieu, such as in the Little Mexico ethnic enclave.[19] There, adolescents continued to announce their presence to one another by writing their names for their own world to see. These graffiti are not intended for the outside world; the youth write their names for people who know and recognize them, not for hostile strangers or to deface public property as a sign of their contempt for society. Kohl and Hinton report the following justification for such public writing from one of their informants: "Once I asked him why he put his name on the walls of buildings in his neighborhood. He replied, 'Because all the kids do,' and when I pressed him, he had no response. Yet as he thought more about it he talked of the joy of knowing that other people see one's name and the

18. Reisner, *Graffiti,* and Sechrest and Olson, "Graffiti in Four Types of Institutions of Higher Education," both list "fuck you" as the most common graffito in their collections, and this was also true at Crozier Tech after the blacks enrolled in the school.

19. Davis, "Little Mexico."

sense of satisfaction he felt in seeing his own name next to those of his friends."[20]

Artistically, Chicano name graffiti used in association with *con safos* are highly stylized. The phrase itself is variously abbreviated and is written in varying styles. My approximately 150 collected examples of this graffito show a wide range of individual styles, some of which are so distinctive that they become something of a personal trademark, similar to a monogram, apparently strengthening the sanctity of the writer's name. As the accompanying examples indicate, the simplest graphic expression of *con safos* is the abbreviation C-S, with the letters separated by a slash or a dash but never followed by periods, the standard academic convention for indicating abbreviation. This C-S is often worked into a design, as shown in the examples (see especially Group I). The whole unabbreviated phrase constitutes the next more complex means of expression (see Group II). The words are nearly always written on either side or above and below the protected name, creating an aesthetically balanced design. The letters are always printed, often in the distinctive Chicano west-coast style,[21] and are never written in script. The most elaborate means of presenting *con safos* involves a combination of words, symbols, and lines which completely box in or enclose the protected name (see Group III). There is a strong indication that such framed names have the greatest degree of protection. In such cases the *con safos* literally defines the boundaries of a sacrosanct area within which the name is written. This provides protection for the written name in much the same manner that sanctuaries such as churches or universities, or the familiar "King's X" of children's games, do for a person seeking refuge and safety.[22] The variety of these stylized graffiti is almost endless, although some simple motifs, such as the small circle with the flanking horizontal lines, are quite popular.

Chicano graffiti as a whole is thus fairly standardized, consisting primarily of combinations of personal, gang, and sweetheart names associated with the actual words or initials of *con safos*. Such graffiti are ubiquitous. Unlike many graffiti forms, the names and *con safos* are not necessarily written in public restrooms used by Mexican-Americans. Books, homework papers, walls, sidewalks, clothes, even Christmas tree ornaments become the vehicles for this urge to present

---

20. 112.

21. Good examples of this distinctive calligraphy can be found in the magazine *Con Safos*.

22. My thanks to Archie Green for pointing out the apparent relationship between "King's X" and *con safos*. See Figure 15 in Group IV of the examples of Crozier Tech graffiti for a graffito combining the features of "King's X" and C/S.

personal names publicly. The one medium in which this graphic symbol does not appear is body tattooing, a practice which is widespread among Chicano gang members throughout the United States in the form of the radiant cross, which is inked or cut into the flap of skin between the thumb and forefinger.[23] It is the name *per se* which must be protected, not the individual himself.

What generalizations or conclusions can thus be drawn from such a survey? In the first place, it is apparent that graffiti vary from culture to culture, not just from building to building, as so many serious studies have tried to prove.[24] Furthermore, the graffiti of Mexican-Americans is not regarded by them as a defacement of public property. It is instead one aspect of a communication code which places extremely high value on personal names. Although such names written with the *con safos* are the most common graffiti of Mexican-Americans, these are by no means their only graffiti.[25] The actual distribution of the use of *con safos* has not been investigated, but one assumes from what evidence is available that it appears throughout the United States wherever there are large Mexican-American communities.[26] The origin of the *con safos* graffito is obscure; the extent of its use in Mexico or the other Spanish-speaking countries of South and Central America is not known at this time. Nevertheless, the use of *con safos*

23. The best treatment of this custom is the novel of Floyd Salas, *Tattoo the Wicked Cross* (New York, 1967). See Figure 16 in Group IV for the examples of Crozier Tech graffiti for a graffito combining the feautres of the radiant cross and C/S. There are some examples illustrated in Griffith, *American Me*, 47.

24. See Note 1 for bibliography. Significant studies of the graffiti of other time periods and other cultures include Edda Bresciani, *Graffiti démotiques du Dodécaschoene* (Cairo, 1969); Henry Field, *Camel Brands and Graffiti from Iraq, Syria, Jordan, Iran and Arabia* (Baltimore, 1952); Violet Pritchard, *English Medieval Graffiti* (Cambridge, 1967); Heikki Solin, *L'Interpretazione delle Inscrizioni Parietali: Note e Discussioni* (Faenza, 1970); Helen H. Tanzer, *The Common People of Pompeii: A Study of the Graffiti* (Baltimore, 1939); Emilio Tiberi, *La Contestazione Murale: Una Ricerca Psico-sociale sul Fenomeno Contestatario Attraverso lo Studio di Graffiti e di Comunicazione de Massa* (Bologna, 1972); Ivan I. Tolstoi, *Grecheski graffiti drevnikh Gorodov Severnogo Prichernomor'ia* (Moscow, 1953); and Veikko Vaananen, *Graffiti del Palatino* (Helsinki, 1966).

25. For examples of Mexican graffiti and latrinalia see A. Jiménez, "Grafitos en los communes," in *Picardía Mexicana*, 118–138 and *Neuva Picardía Mexicana* (Mexico City, 1971).

26. There are distinct Mexican-American communities throughout Texas, the Southwest, and California, as well as in St. Paul, Minnesota (see Norman Goldner, "The Mexicans in the Northern Urban Area," in *Readings in La Raza*, 90–94), Detroit, Michigan (See Norman D. Humphrey, "Detroit Mexicans," in *Readings in La Raza*, 45–50), and Chicago, Illinois and vicinity (see Richard M. Dorson, "Is There a Folk in the City?" in *The Urban Experience and Folk Tradition*, Publications of the American Folklore Society Bibliographic and Special Series 22 [Austin, 1971]; Anita Jones, "Chicago's Mexican Colonies," in *Readings in La Raza*, 51–55; and Julian Samora and Richard A. Lamanna, *Mexican-Americans in a Midwest Metropolis: A Study of East Chicago* [Los Angeles, 1967]).

is a distinctive cultural trait of Mexican-American youth which reveals the importance of their names to them for, as Kohl and Hinton conclude, "Inscribing one's name on a wall involves more than the immediate pleasure of writing where one is not supposed to. It may have to do with the important roles names play in our lives and in a larger sense, in the whole fabric of life in the society of men."[27]

ADDENDUM

After this paper was already in press, the following significant item was brought to my attention. As with the novel mentioned in Note 23, *Tattoo the Wicked Cross*, the following literary description describes the function of *con safos* as effectively as any scholar could do and thus re-emphasizes the interrelationship of folklore and literature. The following passage is from Joseph Wambaugh, *The New Centurions* (New York, 1972 [originally, 1970]), 105.

This was a gang neighborhood, a Mexican gang neighborhood, and Mexican gang members were obsessed with a compulsion to make their mark on the world. Serge stopped for a moment, taking the last puff on his cigarette while Milton got his notebook and flashlight. Serge read the writing on the wall in black and red paint from spray cans which all gang members carried in their cars in case they would spot a windfall like this creamy yellow irresistible blank wall. There was a heart in red, three feet in diameter, which bore the names of "Reuben and Isabel" followed by "mi vida" and there was the huge declaration of an Easystreeter which said, "El Wimpy de los Easystreeters," and another one which said "Reuben de los Easystreeters," but Reuben would not be outdone by Wimpy and the legend below his name said, "de los Easystreeters y del mundo," and Serge smiled wryly as he thought of Reuben who claimed the world as his domain because Serge had yet to meet a gang member who had ever been outside Los Angeles County. There were other names of Junior Easystreeters and Peewee Easystreeters, dozens of them, and declarations of love and ferocity and the claims that this was the land of the Easystreeters. Of course at the bottom of the wall was the inevitable "CON SAFOS," the crucial gang incantation not to be found in any Spanish dictionary, which declared that none of the writing on this wall can ever be altered or despoiled by anything later written by the enemy.

27. 119.

REPRESENTATIVE GRAFFITI FROM DALLAS, TEXAS *

GROUP I: SIMPLE C/S

Figure 1

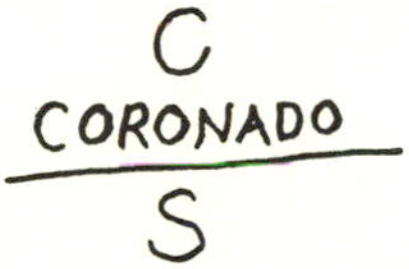

C
CORONADO
S

Figure 2

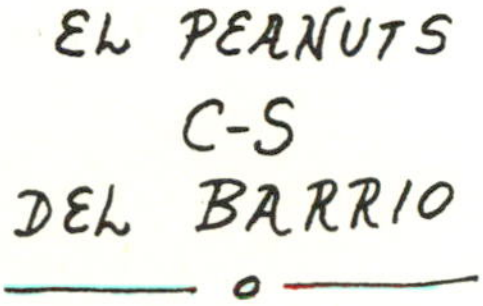

EL PEANUTS
C-S
DEL BARRIO
———— o ————

Figure 3

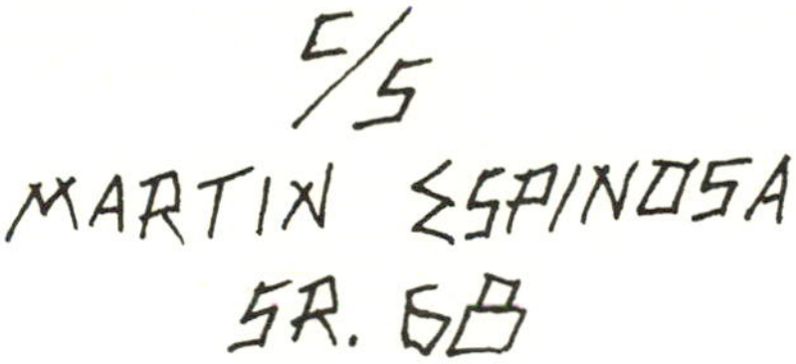

C/S
MARTIN ESPINOSA
SR. 6B

Figure 4

C/S
RAYMOND GALVAN
CON
YOLANDA PINEDA
C/S

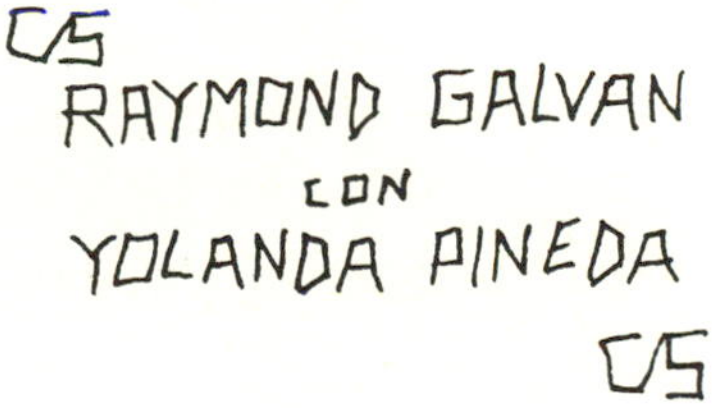

* Sketches are by the author. They are not to scale.

GROUP II: SIMPLE CON SAFOS

Figure 5   *Figure 6*

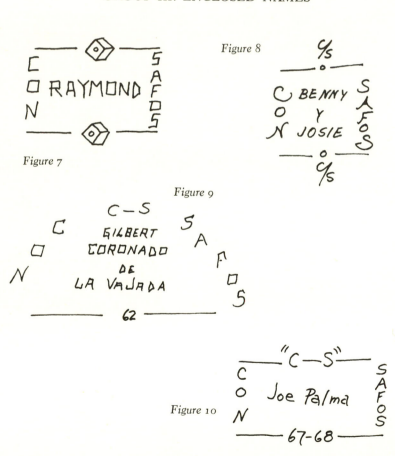

GROUP III: ENCLOSED NAMES

Figure 8

Figure 7

Figure 9

Figure 10

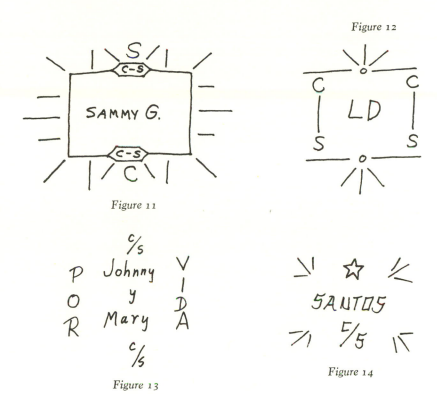

Figure 12

Figure 11

Figure 13

Figure 14

GROUP IV: COMBINED MOTIFS

Figure 15

Figure 16

"SORRY CHUCK"—
PIONEER FOODWAYS

Roger L. Welsch

When a traditional context of the past cannot be observed in person, it may be possible to reconstruct it in part by gathering cultural data from surviving literature or folklore. In this instance, one aspect of the Great Plains pioneer's daily life—foodways—is revealed in songs and tales, sayings, reminiscences, and recipes found in older writings or folklorists' studies. Attitudes toward food and uses of specific foodstuffs tell a great deal about a particular society and its values, as do the oral folklore and customary behavior found in that same culture. While studies of foodways or "ethnocuisine" are relatively new in the United States, interest in the subject is growing, as indicated in Chapter 21 in The Study of American Folklore.

Many of Roger L. Welsch's findings about pioneer food attitudes are probably still part of Midwestern traditions; some usages vary depending upon the origins of settlers, available food supplies, the period of settlement, and other factors. But certainly Welsch's approach to foodways study could be applied to other regions; for example, he first distinguishes general categories of foods recognized by the folk (i.e., immigrant, American, and Indian) and then suggests some analytic categories. The kinds of data collected here include modes of preservation and preparation, staple foods, holiday foods, acceptance of wild foods, kitchen equipment, and folk traditions about foods. A student might begin his own research by trying to describe in a detailed and objective manner his family's traditional foodways insofar as they seem to be distinctive and noncommercial. It would be worth asking too whether somewhat derogatory idiomatic terms for food (such as "chuck" and "grub") are current in folk speech. ("Sorry chuck" means, roughly, "low grade food"; the phrase appears in the Western folksong "The Buffalo Skinners": "He fed us on such sorry chuck, I wished myself 'most dead.")

That many of the quoted food sayings and anecdotes are typical of Great Plains humor or stoicism does not necessarily mean that this folklore is original or unique to that area. Other places too have stories similar to the account of getting "unmoused butter," and other people tell anecdotes about a preacher coming to dinner. One striking example of the recurrence of similar folklore in widely separated places is the description of a menu consisting entirely of corn meal. In Romania, where the corn-mush staple is called mămăligă, one peasant's joking description of his steady diet goes as follows: "Well, there's cold mămăligă, mămăligă and milk, mămăligă and butter, mămăligă and onions, and there are boiled potatoes, fried potatoes, baked potatoes, cold potatoes . . ." (This version is quoted from Julian Hale, Ceauşescu's Romania, A Political Documentary [London, 1971], p. 78.)

Besides Welsch's other publications on Plains folk culture cited in his footnotes, the student should consult his well illustrated essay "Shelters on the Plains" in Natural History, Vol. 86, No. 5 (May, 1977). An excellent example of foodways data extracted from another body of Western American folklore is Charlie Seeman's article "Bacon, Biscuits, and Beans: Food of the Cattle Trails as Found in American Cowboy Songs," Arizona Friends of Folklore Word, Vol. 4, No. 3 (October, 1974).

IF THERE IS ANY ACCURACY to the German proverb "Man ist was man isst" (one is what he eats), knowing more about the Plains pioneer's food would help us understand him. Indeed, a knowledge of the homesteader's menu may be necessary to an understanding of his home life, literature, and folklore. Contemporary songs contain frequent allusions to pioneer foods—rarely complimentary:

> I am looking rather seedy now while holding down my claim,
> And my victuals are not always of the best . . .
>
> Yet I rather like the novelty of living in this way,
> Though my bill of fare is always rather tame."
> —from "Little Old Sod Shanty"

Oh, they churn the butter well
  In Kansas.
They churn the butter well
  In Kansas.
They churn the butter well
And the buttermilk they sell
And they all get lean as hell
  In Kansas.

Oh, potatoes they grow small
  In Kansas.
Potatoes they grow small
  In Kansas.
Oh, potatoes they grow small
And they dig 'em in the fall
And they eat 'em hides and all
  In Kansas.
  —from "In Kansas"

Of course, the entire song and its title, "Starving to Death on My Government Claim," is a comment on the scarcity of food.[1]

Food is an essential and continual element of life, so it does find

---

1. All song texts are from my Treasury of Nebraska Pioneer Folklore (Lincoln, 1967).

constant mention in pioneer accounts. Opinions regarding the fare's
quality, quantity, and ingenuity are frequently expressed and offer us a
broad and fairly accurate view of pioneer foodways.

Interviewers for the Federal Writers Project during the Depression
years sought out recipes from still-living pioneers. Regional and
county biographical sketches, like Emerson Purcell's *Pioneer Stories of
Custer County, Nebraska* (*Custer County Chief*: Broken Bow, 1936),
contain many references to foods. Finally, historians like Everett Dick
have included diet as a part of historic description.

A predominant feature of the early Plains frontier-years cuisine is,
of course, immigrant foods. Naturally, the first settlers, predominantly
European, continued to cook insofar as possible in keeping with the
traditions of their homelands. But the key words here are "insofar as
possible," for in a very short time whatever European supplies that
had been brought along had been exhausted and seldom was there
sufficient money to establish importation.

Furthermore, social pressures discouraged the day-to-day use of
immigrant foods; it was important to become "American" in language,
costume, and custom as soon as possible. Only rarely did pockets of
cultural conservatism persist. The results were: (1) a disappearance of
native foods and foodways; (2) substantial variance of basic ingredients, which resulted usually in a basic variance of the foodstuffs
themselves; and (3) relegation of immigrant foods to a ceremonial or
ritual status, which will be discussed in more detail below.

Classification of pioneer foods is very difficult. Should categories of
food be based on preparation? Or ingredients, or intent (in the case of
substitution foods), or source? If, therefore, my description of the
specifics of pioneer foodways seems undifferentiated, it is because I
have not been able to answer that question myself.

One needn't read very many accounts of migrants to the Plains
before it becomes evident that the foodstuffs in the wagon box were
notably regular inventory:[2] a sack or two of flour (perhaps the last
wheat flour that family would see for many seasons), a side of bacon,
a keg of molasses, or carton of loaf sugar.[3] A cast iron Dutch oven
was the most common and often the only cooking equipment, serving
as a pan, pot, and oven. Thrust into the lonely and barren Plains
environment, many adventurers became suddenly and acutely aware
of their own inadequacies in the "kitchen": "After being initiated into
the art of constructing biscuits in a Dutch oven, in the heroic act of

2. Emerson Purcell, *Pioneer Stories of Custer County, Nebraska* (Broken Bow,
1936), *passim.*

3. Sugar came in loaves that had to be dismantled with pincers.

eating them soaked in bacon fat and syrup, washed down with strong coffee, I achieved the sleep of exhaustion."[4]

Mari Sandoz, always a sensitive and accurate observer of pioneer temperament, commented on the preeminence of foods in *Old Jules*: "This year there were more women, not many, but more, and some of these were single. Whatever their status in Indiana, or Iowa, or York state [sic], where competition was keener, here they were all sought after as heiresses, or, more to the point, good cooks."[5]

A good many Plains foods were familiar to all comers and could be eaten out-of-hand—for example, wild plums and grapes. Others were new, and certainly the housewife's mode of preservation had to change to suit the conditions of the Plains. In *Pioneer Stories of Custer County, Nebraska*, Mrs. Elizabeth C. Sargent could write: "In the summers my sisters and I were kept busy gathering wild fruit of which there was an abundance. We were fortunate in having brought with us a supply of glass jars since they could not be bought here."[6]

But not many settlers shared that foresight. They had to adopt new ways of food preservation. Drying was certainly the most common method: "If store fruit were to be had at all, the staple was dried peaches or apples. In fact, everything was dried that possibly could be. Green beans, corn, rhubarb, berries, and even pumpkins were dried."[7]

In an effort to bring some variety to their family fare, women searched about to find new ways to make dried fruits savory:

> We had plenty of red plums, sweet and delicious and father brought them to the house by the pailful. The Indians had dried the wild fruits, then pounded their flesh into the meat to make *pemmican*. Father had learned how to do this, and we "jerked" dried some wild meat, then dried it that fall and beat the sweet plum fruit into the meat, then dried the powdery substance again. It was a real treat and would tempt any palate today. The plums were sweet when ripe and fresh, but it took their weight in sugar to put them up as fruit. However, since we had no fruit jars, and the canning process was only half-understood at that time, we spread the plums out on blankets or a wagon sheet on the ground and as they dried they shriveled into hard-as-stone form, in frosty blue colors. But they kept well, and it took only an overnight soaking to restore their juicy goodness. . . .
> The wild plums could be pitted and cooked to a thick mass. Spread thinly in pans, and dried in the sun like the others, they became a thick, tough, chewy fruit that we called "plum leather."

4. From H. Lomax's account of his arrival in Nebraska, Purcell, 2.

5. Mari Sandoz, *Old Jules* (Lincoln, 1962), 60.

6. Purcell, 10.

7. Everett Dick, *The Sod-House Frontier, 1854–1890* (Lincoln, 1954), 274.

Mother thought the yellow-orange plums made the best plum leather, but they were few and hard to find. The really small plums that grew best on the stunted bushes in sand draws we called "sand cherries." They were sweeter than the plums of orange-yellow coloring. Then there were wild gooseberries that made excellent pies, but would make you wrinkle your nose if eaten without sugar. And the grapes from the canyons made wonderful fruit ·dishes when sugar could be added. But like other fruit, we generally dried them with the seeds left within. Even the livestock ate these grapes that hung on the vines that were festooned over the smaller plum bushes.[8]

Chrisman and many other journalists (for example, Roy Sage, in *Pioneer Stories of Custer County, Nebraska*) mention robbing the six-foot-high stick nests of pack rats for their content of dried fruit. It was a simple matter to tear the nests apart, and, according to these accounts, forty or fifty pounds of clean, neatly dried fruit—grapes, chokecherries, and plums—could be gathered.

The pioneer housewife would be astonished to see the price tags on dried fruits today, and certainly the pioneer homesteader who made it through a hard winter on dried apples would find it hard to believe that today such fare is nearly considered a delicacy. In those days dried apples were tough and leathery, tobacco-brown and fly-specked. A pioneer poet in Gage County penned: "Spit in my ears and tell me lies, but give me no more dried apple pies."[9]

Meat too was dried, especially game like elk, antelope, and venison, which profit considerably from drying. Although smoked meat was common fare in European and eastern United States homelands, smokehouses were unusual indeed on the Plains, where wood was far too rare to be squandered by burning! The settler who resigned himself to cooking over a smolder of cow chips considered it a substantial step lower to smoke meats over the same fuel.

Indeed, in considering pioneer cookery, the whole concept of fuels must also be examined. The cook obviously had to accommodate her calculation to the kind of fire she had: from the gunpowder flash of twisted-grass "cats" to the slow smolder of cow chips. The accommodations *were* made, however, and excellent angel food cakes could be made in a Dutch oven over a corncob fire. Elaborate formulas were developed and a recipe might contain such instructions as: "Stoke the fire until you can hold your hand in the oven no longer than the count of five, then add five cobs everytime the fire dies down."[10]

---

8. Berna Hunter Chrisman, *When You and I Were Young, Nebraska!* (Broken Bow, 1971), 8–9.

9. Welsch, *Treasury of Nebraska Pioneer Folklore*, 310.

10. Fom Joyce Henry, North Platte.

During hard, hard times, when the corn was selling for a few cents a bushel, the pioneer family wound up eating the corn crop and little else but the corn crop. The irony was honed sharper by the fact that, since they couldn't sell the corn to buy other foods, they also couldn't sell it to buy coal. Hence, they had to burn corn in the stove to cook the corn for supper. Next to drying, perhaps the most common method for the preservation of both meats and fruits was pickling in a strong brine:

> The process of canning was not in use on a large scale during the frontier period, and, hence, the only other method of preserving food was by means of salt brine and boiling sweets. Tomatoes were placed in a barrel of strong brine, and kept submerged by weighted boards. When the housewife desired tomatoes for a meal, she took a few from the barrel and soaked them in cold water, changing the water frequently. When the brine was finally soaked out, the tomatoes were cooked.[11]

Meats were preserved in the same way: "These birds [field birds: prairie hens, quail, grouse] frequently found their way into mother's stone jar of heavy salt brine, and we could eat two or three birds at our table in one meal."[12]

Several sources also mention merely packing meat in a barrel with a heavy interlarding of salt; this included poultry and, especially, pork. Pork was also preserved by boiling it down ("trying") and then packing the well-cooked pieces of meat in the barrel in a matrix of the rendered tallow.

Fruits and berries might also be boiled down into a "butter," so that the heavy sugar content and sterilization would prevent spoilage. Jellies—preserved juices—were also very popular, especially because they provided much needed vitamins and variety during the long winter months:

> Where the silvery buffalo-berry bushes were solid clumps of yellow-orange, the tiny, shot-like berries in round clusters all along the thorny stems, Mary held the bushes back while Jules chopped them off, to be threshed with broomsticks over the sheet.
>
> Dishpans full of berries were taken to the river for preliminary washing, the worm-lightened fruit floated away, until all the pails were full. Then there was a day of jelly making in the big copper boiler and the wine press, until six- and eight-gallon stone jars were filled with the wine-red liquor to cool and set into firmest jelly for winter.[13]

11. Dick, 274.
12. Chrisman, 14.
13. Sandoz, 283.

Figure 1. Gardening was an essential part of almost every homestead—and the especial province of the farmer's wife. In 1888 the Nelson Potter family on Lees Creek, Custer County, posed in their garden for a photograph.

As suggested by several allusions in the Sandoz passage above, wine too was an important way of preserving the nutritious elements in wild fruits and berries for the winter months, and, incidentally, of providing nostalgic memories of lost days in a European homeland where the civility of a glass of wine was considered a matter of course.

Another paragraph from Mari Sandoz's work, *Old Jules*, mentions her father's home-made wine and other matters of pioneer foodways: "And as they planned they ate young prairie chicken flavored with wild garlic and roasted to the point of disintegration in the army kettle. And with it they drank deep red wine of the black currants from along the river."[14]

Indeed, when Jules Sandoz was first examining this new land, he was impressed by the wealth of wild fruit and its potentials. "Upon seeing a bush covered with plums and draped with burdened grape vines, Jules says, 'Fruit enough for a whole village, plum jell [*sic*], grape wine.' "[15]

14. Sandoz, 41.
15. Sandoz, 80.

Figure 2. In this windmill-irrigated garden (c. 1925) little had changed from the days of the sod house, but the farm improvements were better. Mother and children are picking peas.

The saddest tales, however, are those that come from times and places when there was not much concern about how to preserve food —because there was not much food to preserve.

Actually, food was never so abundant that there was not room for improvement. Even when there was plenty to eat, it rarely existed in variety:

> If frontier food was unhealthful it was not because of its richness and high seasoning, but rather on account of the sameness which made the menu monotonous and unappetizing. Corn was the staple article of diet. In the *Nebraska Farmer* of January, 1862, thirty-three different ways were given for cooking corn.[16]

As was later the case during the Great Depression of the 1930's, children ate whatever there was to eat, and usually lots of that, so that whole generations were produced with unmitigated hate for corn bread or oatmeal, or, later, peanut butter:

> That winter we lived for six weeks on cracked wheat raised along

16. Dick, 270.

with the rosin weeds.[17] This wheat had to be washed and kiln-dried in the oven, then taken by sled to the river across the channel on a willow raft, carried one and one-half miles down the river to Ben Griebel's corn crusher, and back home the same route, but at the end of six weeks this food still tasted 'rosin.' My lunch on my wood-hunting trips was mostly this cracked wheat bread and I even belched 'rosin.'[18]

And, of course, even sadder than the tales of time when there was only one kind food were those when there was no food at all:

> We got to John Applegate's the night of April 17. We asked him if we could stay. 'You get you can, if you have anything to eat,' he said. We told him we had meat and provisions with us, so we furnished the grub and Mrs. Applegate cooked our supper. Mr. Applegate had a wife and three small children, and that night at supper he gave his children some meat and they seemed to relish it hugely. They wanted more, so he gave them a second helping. Then they wanted more, and he said, 'No, you have had enough for tonight.' After supper, we were all outside and I told him to give his children all they wanted to eat, and he said he could not do it as they had not had any meat since last November and this was the 17th of April. Everything that was eatable in the house was a half pint of little potatoes and a pint of shorts meal [a by-product of wheat milling consisting primarily of chaff, bran, and coarse meal], nothing of any other kind, and Mrs. Applegate had lived on Indian turnips dug out on the prairie for three days.[19]

For the past two years I have been examining pioneer Plains humor[20] and my conclusion has been that the hardy homesteaders were able to laugh at even the most trying of hardships, and that perhaps it was this ability to laugh that made it possible for them to endure the hardships. Neither did the scarcity and monotony of food escape their wit—although, one must remember, the laughter was never without a tinge of bitterness:

> While they [Berna Chrisman's father and his friend] were gone on this trip, mother had nothing in the house to eat but corn meal. So she set up a menu that went something like this for the following four or five days:

17. [Also called compass plant, cup plant, or gum plant. Genus *Silphium*.]
18. Harry Gates, in Purcell, 165.
19. John Scott, in Purcell, 109.
20. For a discussion of this study and its fuller conclusions see my article "The Myth of the Great American Desert," *Nebraska History*, 52 (Fall, 1971), 255–265, or *Shingling the Fog and Other Plains Lies* (Chicago, 1971).

Breakfast: corn meal, fried
Dinner: corn meal, boiled
Supper: corn meal, baked

Breakfast: corn meal, fried
Dinner: corn meal, boiled
Supper: corn meal, baked.[21]

During my study of pioneer humor, I found that two of my favorite stories from Nebraska's past dealt with the scarcity of food during hard times. One was told to me by Warren Fairchild of Lincoln and dealt with a pioneer circuit-riding minister who stopped by a settler's dugout for supper:

> The meal was not elegant, but it was nicely served and there seemed to be plenty of ears of roasted corn to go around.
>   "Say," said the preacher, "I see this fine corn you've been serving and I wonder if the crops are as bad this year as I've been hearing."
>   "Parson," replied the homesteader, "You just et two acres of corn."[22]

A story related by Estelle Chrisman Laughlin again underlines the way everyday things could become precious in a time of little: "Another story I recall concerned the shortage of potatoes one year, being used as company fare only. On an occasion when Aunt Bettie Chrisman of Ansley ate dinner at our home she remarked to my father, 'My law, Genie, you all better save these potatoes for dessert!'"[23]

Much to their credit, many pioneers (and many of today's young people) discovered the food value of what are commonly called weeds:

> During the summer months weeds contributed much to our table. As in most countries, weeds—vegetables out of place, as some people call them—grew in profusion, creating lots of problems and entailing lots of work in their eradication or control. But in the O'Kieffe home our slogan was: "If you can't beat 'em, eat 'em." The names of three of these helpful little pests come to mind as I write, "pigweed," "Lambsquarters," and "pussley" [purslane]. . . . Mother had a way of slipping a small hunk of salt pork in the pot with the cooking weeds and, brother, that made the difference.[24]

Berna Hunter Chrisman gives virtually the same description of her mother's recipe for "weeds," and anyone who has tried "greasy greens" made of pigweed, purslane, or lambsquarters will agree heartily with these pioneers' descriptions. Sheep sorrel is a common green eaten in

21. Chrisman, 24–25.

22. This tale is adapted from Welsch, *Shingling the Fog and Other Plains Lies.*

23. Purcell, 56.

24. Charley O'Kieffe, *Western Story: The Recollections of Charley O'Kieffe, 1884–1898* (Lincoln, 1960).

the East and the South, but Gertrude Eubank Worley's description of sheep sorrel pie is, as far as I know, unique. She says, however, that it took so much sugar to sweeten the sour herb that it was prepared only rarely in their pioneer home.[25]

Sweetness was, in fact, one of those things that Plains homesteaders had to forego for a few years or improvise. On the eastern edges of the Plains there were enough maple trees for tapping and bee trees for robbing, but for most persons, when sweetness returned to their diets, it was in the form of sorghum molasses, which was welcome enough at first but its strong flavor soon palled and eventually the very smell of sorghum molasses was enough to turn a meal—or a day—into disaster.

Substitutions were attempted, probably, for every scarce commodity. Recipes were common for apple pie without apples, and anything that would turn brown under heat was roasted for coffee. Grains like corn, wheat, oats, and rye were especially common, and not always unpalatable: "[The Schreyer family] invited us to eat and for a drink they had coffee made of rye, which they had parched in the oven and ground in a coffee mill. It was the first rye coffee I ever drank and with cream it certainly tasted good."[26]

Eggs were frequently such precious commodities that the families that kept the hens could not afford to eat the eggs, instead taking them into town to trade for more necessary items and less valuable foods. Game bird eggs were gathered and when boiled served especially well as travel fare.

Butter too might be carried to town for trade while the family had to be content with the buttermilk. Berna Chrisman tells a story about butter that touches on the still-human nature of our frontier heroes and heroines. It was a common occurrence, she writes, that a mouse might fall into the butter churn if the lid was not firmly seated overnight. The housewife had to decide whether she would grit her teeth and serve the butter to her family (remembering that mouse all the while) or whether she should take it to town to trade off.

A Custer County sod house dweller suffered this unfortunate dilemma and decided to take the butter into town and trade it for some "unmoused" butter. The storekeeper obviously knew what was going on when she wanted to trade her butter for someone else's, but as she explained, the next purchaser could scarcely be hurt by what she didn't know. The grocer agreed, took her butter to the back room, trimmed it, stamped it with his mark, took it back out to the counter

25. Purcell, 133.
26. Albert Sprouse, in Purcell, 81.

and gave it back to the woman as her trade, smugly thinking to himself that she could scarcely be hurt by what she didn't know.[27]

Many accounts, on the other hand—especially later ones—wax eloquent about the groaning tables at happy occasions during the good years:

> A spot in some outlying part of the grove was selected as the meeting place for dinner. Then began the loading of pans and crocks containing great quantities of fried chicken, baked beans, potato salad, sandwiches, brownstone front cake and gooseberry and raspberry pie, the contents of the pies having been diligently gathered from canyons and creek banks by us children in happy anticipation. Lemonade was made with cold spring water in a huge tin tub brought along for that purpose. Sometimes a foresighted one who had ice put up brought a large chunk wrapped in straw and gunny sacking. The chunk of ice gradually diminished through the day, but our thirst never did.[28]

Even when meals remained humble and home-grown, they often made impressions on children that remain with them until today:

> I can't call up adjectives to describe the super quality of [corn] bread when eaten with 'cow butter' or ham gravy, with a glass or two of rich milk or buttermilk made in the old wooden churn. It was simply 'out of this world,' as the youngsters today would say. So, while we did not have frosted cakes, pies with two inches of meringue, and many other 'musts' of today, we had food which met the needs of growing, healthy bodies and we did not have to keep a bottle of vitamins from A to Z to keep us in good health.
>
> After a night of sound sleep we would be awakened in the morning to the tune of the coffee mill grinding the coffee for breakfast, or Mother sharpening her butcher knife on the stove pipe or a stoneware crock as she prepared to slice ham, bacon, or venison for breakfast as an accompanist to hot buttermilk biscuits, potatoes, or fried mush, which made a real meal on which to start a strenuous day. . . .[29]

Viewing the whole body of data, from which the above passages have been selected, leads to some interesting and curious conclusions, the most obvious (and perhaps most surprising) of which was the ease with which immigrants adopted "American" foods and the tenacity with which they maintained them in an uncooperative environment.

Native European foods quickly diminished to a ceremonial status,

27. Chrisman, 52–53.

28. Chrisman, 25–26.

29. Roger Welsch, *Sod Walls: The Story of the Nebraska Sod House* (Broken Bow, 1968), 146.

Figures 3 and 4. Perhaps because of his cheerful countenance the homesteader at top found himself the subject of a postcard (c. 1900), the title of which was "Hope and Contentment on the Claim." The bachelor below (c. 1886), while less ebullient, seems well satisfied with his simple evening meal. (Solomon D. Butcher Collection, Nebraska State Historical Society)

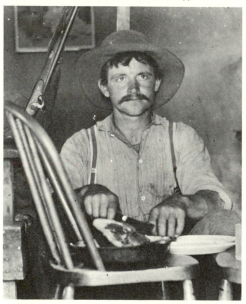

as did also the native languages, especially in the first American-born generation. They were eager to be all-American and therefore rejected non-American foods and languages—*except in a very important ritual sense.* This is still obvious today, where communities made up almost totally of one ethnic extraction or ethnically oriented families prepare ethnic meals and, perhaps, offer a meal prayer in, for example, Norwegian for special holidays like Christmas or festivals celebrating their ethnic origins.

In addition to sociological pressures motivating such foodway changes there was of course the lack of the basic ingredients necessary for the preparation of such food.

On the other hand, migrants with roots in American culture and migrant European families that had accepted American foodways clung tenaciously to them in spite of all manner of reasons to abandon or alter them. Note, for example, that the homesteader refused to turn from coffee to some more available potable—for example, herbal teas from native prairie grasses, weeds, or shrubs.

To me, the most surprising feature of pioneer Plains foods, however, is the nearly total absence of foods borrowed from the Plains Indians. There are references to borrowed Indian foods, of course, but they are inevitably foods borrowed many years before the Homestead Act—like turkey, corn, squash—and carried much earlier to the East Coast and even Europe. Foods borrowed by Plains homesteaders from Plains Indians are virtually nonexistent.

The occasional references to Indian foods like pemmican, *wasna*,[30] Indian turnips, and dried chokecherry patties nearly always underline the role of these foods as emergency survival foods. They were abandoned as soon as something "better" (that is, anything to which the settler was accustomed) was available. The few complimentary comments about these foods come from children, who obviously didn't know any better.

The frontier had exhibited a long history of borrowing from the Indians in other areas and at other times, of course. Indeed, many concepts and materials that facilitated westward movement had been borrowed from the Indian. Corn, squash, the canoe, snowshoes, and jerked meat had been borrowed early. It is even a possibility that the sod house, so intimately associated with the settlement of the Plains, was a borrowing from the Plains-Woodlands Indians encamped along the Missouri River.[31]

Place names were continually borrowed from Indians, names that

---

30. The Lakota Indian word for powdered dried meat (usually buffalo).
31. For an extended discussion of this possibility, see my book *Sod Walls.*

today are often the only evidence of mangled, dislocated, or erased tribes: Dakota, Nebraska, Kansas, Missouri, Nemaha, for example.

There can be no question of the advisability of borrowing such foods. These immigrant people, so used to wild arborial crops, teeming greenery, reliable supplies and communications, *had* to eat, and what they were used to simply could not be found here. On the other hand, even discounting the buffalo, Plains Indians had developed a thorough knowledge of edible plants that are available nearly the year around.

The prevailing hostilities and resultant lack of communication between the settler and the Indians might explain the anomaly in certain cases, but in Nebraska the Ponca, Omaha, and Pawnee were non-belligerents who had a long record of generosity in sharing their bounty and its sources.

Finally, one is further mystified by the pioneers' reluctance to adopt Indian foods as a permanent part of their menu after they had sampled them during times of famine and certainly discovered upon such experimentation that the foods were not inferior to those of the Anglo-American-Western European tradition and were not simply lesser substitutions but were in most cases admirable for reasons of their own individual savor and, in some cases, were delectable, needing apology to no chef.

Prejudices we have perhaps inherited from our pioneer forefathers stand in the way of our appreciation of the *sound* of milkweed soup, arrowroot tubers, or chokecherry broth, but the *taste* of such dishes usually dispels any hesitation to "dig in."

Some Plains Indian foods were already cultivated in other parts of the world—for example, Jerusalem artichokes were a staple in England—but found little favor with Plains settlers.

I once studied this cross-cultural phenomenon in another light, the Indians' tenacity to cling to traditional foodways in spite of overwhelming historical, cultural, and economic forces that appear to work against such survival.[32] The conditions seem to be identical despite the difference in the direction of the change being resisted.

My conclusions in regard to Omaha foodways were that the term "soul food" is a very real concept, not simply a romantic-nationalistic (or perhaps better, here, "cultural") catchword, not a figurative use of the term.

Plains Indians had provided me with the foundation for this assertion in their explicit declarations that at boarding schools Indian children surreptitiously prepared and ate simple Indian foods like

32. In a paper read before the American Folklore Society, Los Angeles, November, 1970, "Traditional Omaha Foodways," later published in *Keystone Folklore Quarterly*.

parched corn specifically to nurture their "Indianness," while other Indians told of school administration and governmental efforts to alter foodways with the expressed and motivating intention of destroying last vestiges of Indianness in their charges.

Implicit support for my contention is found in the survival of Indian foods as ritual and ceremonial objects revered for their importance in maintaining communication with a past, lost heritage.

It seems likely that emotions worked the same way on both sides of the frontier in view of the similarity of evidence and phenomena. For the pioneer, too, foods transcended physical nourishment. It was important to them, I believe, to abandon foods of their European origin (in addition to the reasons of scarcity of basic ingredients) in order to establish themselves as Americans and yet to retain some of the same foods as a ritual communication with the past. To adopt "American" foodways in the face of incredible pressures, because such foods constituted an affirmation of citizenship, was to some non-naturalized Americans abandoning a link to friends and family, civilization, and "normality."

Among the Plains Indian populations it is hard to judge at this point if the changes and their order are analogous. Language, clothing, and architecture remain but are fading fast *except ritually*, which also appears to be true of indigenous foods. A determination of the differences of degree between the two cultures will require some historical perspective.

MR. WESTFALL'S BASKETS:
TRADITIONAL CRAFTSMANSHIP
IN NORTHCENTRAL MISSOURI

Howard Wight Marshall

Any basket that is woven of split oak wood is a true folk artifact. While modern mass-production technology has all but replaced baskets with cardboard, plastic, or glass containers, it has never developed a method for actually making baskets. The only split oak baskets in existence, and ever likely to be, are handmade. Compared to most other containers these baskets are light, strong, reusable, and extremely durable. In pioneer America, as in many current traditional societies, baskets were used for carrying and storing eggs, fruit, flowers, laundry, and almost everything else from berries to babies. Nowadays the few traditional baskets still being made in America are bought for nostalgic or aesthetic reasons and used for such things as picnic lunches, sewing supplies, or magazines.

This essay describes the work, products, and environment of a maker of these true folk baskets. Unlike most of his fellow basketmakers, he does not employ any power tools or mechanized shortcuts. The tools and techniques of his craft are entirely traditional, having been passed down in his family for several generations. As folklorist Howard Wight Marshall points out, such a person is a producer of folk artifacts, not a performer of folklore. The importance of the study is the "total ethnographic picture" it gives of a folk artisan and his work. In addition, Marshall provides the historic-geographic, social, psychological, and economic contexts of the basketmaker in this outstanding documentation of a typical American maker of folk artifacts.

THIS PAPER CONCERNS Mr. Joseph Earl Westfall, aged seventy-two, of near Higbee, Missouri, in the rolling farm and timber prairie uplands of northeastern Howard County. Westfall is a craftsman who makes hand-riven white oak farm and market baskets using the technique practiced in his family for several generations and learned altogether through the traditional pipelines of apprenticeship and imitation. A look at the man and the technology in natural context may yield useful information about a skilled basketmaker who lives and works in an area supposedly devoid of practitioners of this craft.[1]

1. It is interesting to note that Earl Westfall lives not in the famous Missouri and Arkansas Ozarks, but rather in northcentral Missouri where a rich body of tradition remains uncollected by the serious folklorist. Westfall lives in a several-county region known to many of its residents as "Little Dixie."

The corpus of published material, whether scholarly or otherwise, on American material culture is still small, particularly in regard to acculturative processes affecting European-American tradition. An article of exceptional value by Henry Glassie serves as the model for this paper.[2] It is recognized that the simple description of a cultural process is no longer sufficient when attempting to understand a moribund craft, which until recently was essential to the functioning of the rural community and economy. Hence, while this paper covers the mechanics of basketmaking as practiced by Westfall, it also points toward the total ethnographic picture by noting pertinent data about the man in his social, cultural, and psychological matrix and about the position of basketmaking in relation to the traditional and the contemporary economic scenes. At the risk of seeming trite, it must be noted that Westfall seems to be the last craftsman still reasonably active in the production of split oak baskets made completely by hand using ancient tools and unimpeachably traditional techniques not only in the Little Dixie region of Missouri but very likely in a much broader geographic area as well. Even the most authentic of the highly-advertised Ozark basketmakers who cater to the tourist trade routinely employ modern power tools and other labor-saving devices. The nearest basketmaker familiar to Westfall as a proper craftsman lives in southcentral Illinois and no longer makes baskets on a steady basis.[3]

This paper is based on information gathered from many visits with the informant, spanning a period of four years, from the fall of 1969 to the summer of 1973. I first met Westfall at the annual Howard County "arts and crafts show" put on by the University Extension Office in Fayette, the county seat, in October of 1969. I was then a student at the University of Missouri, Columbia, and noticed a small item in a local newspaper announcing the event. My wife and I attended the fair expecting to enjoy the usual displays of decorated cakes, quilts, and assorted household and leisure crafts. But back in a corner, beyond the decoupage[4] table, sat Westfall, patiently weaving baskets from a pile of prepared stock.[5] We met the man, purchased a

2. Henry H. Glassie, "William Houck, Maker of Pounded Ash Adirondack Pack Baskets," *Keystone Folklore Quarterly*, 12 (1967), 23–54.

3. Westfall has corresponded with Clyde Thomas, who is nearly eighty and lives in southcentral Illinois and who produces traditional split oak baskets in a manner similar to that of Westfall. Like Westfall, Thomas could sell all the baskets he could make, but his age prevents the long and hard work necessary to turn them out. Lacking an apprentice, he seems to be the last of the basketmakers in his area.

4. [Popular (but not folk) handicraft in which designs or pictures cut from paper are glued to objects for decoration, then varnished.]

5. Until 1970 Westfall regularly took his wares to the Fayette show and demonstrated his craft. He sold few baskets, though, and the trip to Fayette took time and effort. Westfall seemed out of place at the affair and worked quietly in his corner.

peck-size egg basket, and were given directions to his house together with a tentative invitation to learn more about his work. Since that first meeting, I have been out to see Mr. Westfall regularly, each time gaining further comprehension of the basketmaker's trade.

The traditional basketmaker is not a folk performer, and his activity is not audience-oriented. He "just makes baskets," so an observer can expect no special privileges or old-timer discourse. The most satisfying interview situation is when Westfall is at work in his shop behind the house, where he feels fairly comfortable in talking about himself and where he may concentrate on the labor of his hands while attempting to answer the interviewer's odd sorts of questions.[6]

"We Was From Pokyhontas"

Joseph Earl Westfall was born in Randolph County, Arkansas, into a family of split oak basketmakers. His father, Lewis Jackson Westfall, and his grandfather, William Westfall, migrated into northern Arkansas from Illinois sometime before the Civil War, presumably to take advantage of the new markets opening up in the areas being settled. Lewis Jackson and William "just made baskets," and the craft almost totally accounted for the family's subsistence. Living in the small rural community of Pocahontas, the Westfalls provided neighbors and storekeepers with several different standard shapes and sizes of farm baskets, often in trade for various household supplies and staples in accord with the customary barter system of economic exchange. Although Westfall does not know whether his grandfather was the first basketmaker in the family, he believes that the Westfalls had made baskets in Illinois before the move to Arkansas.[7]

Lewis Westfall moved the family to Howard County, Missouri, when Earl was about fifteen years old—"before the first war" (World War I). There were "about a dozen" children in all, and each was involved in the production of baskets according to his ability, age, or

6. My visits always included a chat with Mrs. Westfall, herself a fine source of traditional farm lore, beliefs, foodways, and household wisdom. She naturally dominated the parlor conversations among the three of us; the house and environs are, after all, her domain. Born near Fayette, Mrs. Westfall is in her late sixties.

7. Westfall remembers little of his ancestry, but this is not remarkable. Mrs. Westfall, as wife and mother, is the repository of most information of this nature and recalled that Earl's grandfather was named William. Westfall is no story teller or performer and not accustomed to being questioned; he used to play the harmonica, but no longer has "the wind." He has been the subject of two good newspaper stories, one by Tom Hackward in the *Moberly Monitor Index and Evening Democrat* (December 1968) and the other by Dan Holman in the Boonville *Daily News* (July (1970).

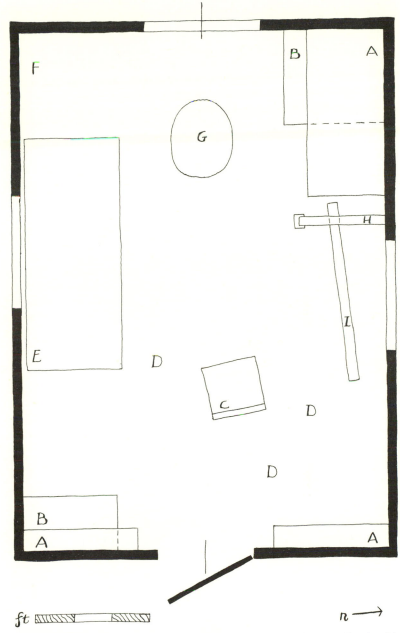

Figure 1. *Westfall's workhouse:* A. *high shelves (storage);* B. *tables (tools);* C. *slatback chair;* D. *lumber being worked up;* E. *army cot for resting;* F. *finished baskets, stovewood;* G. *King Heater sheet iron woodstove;* H. *ribber;* I. *shaving horse.*

size. After coming home from the nearby schoolhouse and after doing the routine chores, the children would spend most of the evening in the special room in the house where the baskets were "worked up." The first stage in the process, the splitting of the oak "sticks" down into "eighths," was done in the woodlot. There were enough hands available so that task specialization evolved naturally with each child performing a suitable job along a casual assembly line. Various jobs included the riving of "splits" for weaving onto the frames, shaving and assembling the "hoops" for the frames, making "ribs," and weaving the basket itself together. Lewis Westfall and the older boys attended to the rigorous labor of selecting the proper trees, felling them and then backpacking eight-foot sticks to the barn, and splitting them into eighths—first with a splitting sledge and iron wedge, then with sledge and hardwood "glut," and finally with a forged-iron froe. At the age of seven, Earl began to weave ribs onto frames as his first role in the process.

The Westfalls subsisted as basketmakers through the 1920s until the Depression brought about what amounted to the destruction of basketmaking as a self-supporting individual trade and of barter economy in America.[8] After the Depression Earl, unable to make a living solely from the family craft, sought employment on his own, and other family members either moved away or took "regular jobs" in the area. Earl's younger brother Everett eventually became the Higbee postmaster, and another brother went to Illinois where he now makes a good living as a plumber. Earl engaged in light farming on his acreage near Higbee "on the side" by keeping as many as nineteen head of black Angus cattle, putting up a hay crop, and sowing "a little corn." Until his retirement in 1955, he was formally employed by the F. M. Stamper Company in Moberly, a nearby city of thirteen-thousand. At Stamper's, a producer of prepared foods and the state's largest turkey producer, Westfall worked at various unskilled tasks such as operating a feather-drying machine. He also occasionally drove a coal truck hauling for local mining concerns and for himself.[9]

Earl's wife Ella Mae was "raised" near Fayette, Missouri. Westfall built their present one-story frame house in 1947. Except for assis-

8. Modern revivalists or preservationist "craft guilds" notwithstanding, barter economy had not flourished since the Industrial Revolution, but the special conditions of the 1930s made it possible for the trade and exchange of goods without cash to become active again.

9. The Moberly-Huntsville-Macon section of north Missouri has long been a major soft coal-producing region, and many farmers drove coal trucks part-time and operated their own small coal yards and mines. The bituminous coal in this area is obtained by strip mining now, and the leviathan Peabody Coal Company owns nearly all rights. For a description of these coal fields in the 1930s see Jack Conroy's novel *The Disinherited* (New York: Covici, Friede, 1933).

tance from his son Robert with pouring the concrete foundation, raising the walls, and other tasks beyond one man's capability, he designed and built the house entirely himself. He walked through the wooded acreage, selected the right oak trees, and hauled them to a neighbor's small sawmill to be "sawed out" into lumber. He recalls, "I just sat down under that big shade tree over there and looked over at the ground and decided what I wanted to do. . . . Anybody can build a basket can build house. . . . Only thing ever shook it was that earthquake in 1966." Westfall built everything on the place—house, barn, workhouse—except for the old chicken "brooder house" which is now used to stockpile finished baskets.

Like Glassie's informant William Houck, Westfall was able to devote full time to the production of baskets only after retirement from his job.[10] Westfall provided an Ozark souvenir entrepreneur with a carload of baskets nearly every month from 1955 until a severe heart attack in 1967.[11] The only retail outlet which has continued to stock his baskets over the years is Miles Skillman's old-fashioned grocery and dry goods store in Fayette.[12]

Westfall learned his craft for the most part by direct apprenticeship and imitation of his father's techniques. However, none of Earl's children or grandchildren have shown much interest in basketmaking, so the Westfall basketmaking tradition is moribund.

> HWM: You don't think a man can make a living at it anymore?
>
> WESTFALL: Oh, if a man was able to work and do a good day's work—'cause it's a slow job and you gotta put in long hours on it to make any money . . . , but he couldn't make nothin' like what he could make in a factory somewhere, you know, nothin' like that.
>
> HWM: Well, is that why young men aren't taking it up anymore?
>
> WESTFALL: Well, that's it. It takes a long time to learn it and learn how to do it—and these kids when they get out of *school*, they can go get them a job, you know, and make two-three dollars an hour, and they just won't fool with it. I *know*—I've got grandsons that's grown, and I haven't got ary one that makes baskets. None of 'em make 'em. And none of my brothers took it up either.

10. Glassie, pp. 24–25.

11. "Davis's" in Camdenton, Missouri, near the Lake of the Ozarks stocks many varieties of baskets, most of which are made by Ozark craftsmen who use a labor-saving device, a gauged drawknife, for making splits and whose baskets are "not as stout" as Westfall's. Davis, who has had as many as seventeen Ozark families working for him, would like to have as many Westfall baskets as Earl can provide.

12. Miles Skillman is in his late seventies; his father Marion sold baskets made by Earl's father. Skillman displays the baskets in his front window and does his best business in the small gift baskets Earl now makes.

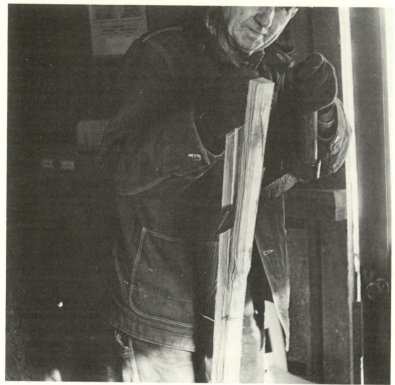

Figure 2. Using a froe, Westfall begins the process of splitting the basket lumber which will ultimately result in its reduction to thirtyseconds.

HWM: Well, it may not pay much, but I'd think it'd be a good way to live, you know, to make something fine with your hands. . . .

Westfall: Oh, sure, I *enjoy* makin' 'em, yeah. If it's somethin' you'd like to do, why that there's nice, you know, to be able to do it—but as far as makin' a lot of money out of it, I never seen anybody get rich makin' *baskets!*

Westfall's sister in Arkansas can still make baskets, but only when someone can go to the woods and get the sticks and split them out for her. She tried unsuccessfully to coax her brother into going to Arkansas to prepare a supply of basket "lumber" for her in 1970.

Westfall now spends much of his time putting split oak "bottoms" in settin' chairs brought to him by local customers. He works in his shop weaving baskets as his health and inclination dictate, but he is dependent on his son to bring in fresh sticks from the woods and to quarter them for him. He has no trouble selling his baskets and in fact can easily sell all he can produce.

THE WESTFALL BASKET

The first step in the basketmaker's routine is the selection of the "right tree." According to the specifications in the Westfall tradition, the tree must be white oak, about thirty years in age, straight-grained and free of knots, smooth-barked, and grown on the north side of the hill (sheltered from prevailing winds and harsh sunlight).

> HWM: Well, I guess it's pretty hard to pick out just exactly the right tree. . . . There's a lot of white oak around here. . . .
>
> WESTFALL: Well, yeah. Sometimes you go in the woods that looks like it's nice timber, and you can run over forty acres and not find a stick of timber that'll make a basket. Yessir. It's got to be so tough and straight-grained and no knots in it. It's got to be just right, or it won't work. If you don't get timber that'll *work*, I can't split it out and nobody else can.
>
> HWM: Can you tell just from *looking* at a tree?
>
> WESTFALL: No, you've got to take your ax and take a chip out of it . . . down towards the bottom of the tree. Just take a good chip out of it with your ax, and you can tell whether it's straight-grained, whether it'll split for you. The bark's got a lot to do with it. You can look at a tree and tell whether it's twisted or not, you know. Lotta times you can look at it and tell that it's too brash. Why, if you split it open, it'd just break . . . and of course that wouldn't be no good. It'd split good into a *post* or somethin', just to split it in bigger pieces like stovewood or somethin', it'd just pop open easy—but it won't make no basket.

Westfall's son Robert, who farms nearby, now fells his trees with a gasoline-powered chain saw, but a common double-bitted ax was invariably used in the past. A neighbor, Bill Perkins, fetched sticks from the woods for Westfall for years but is no longer fit enough for such work. Perkins' price for the work was one dollar per tree, or fifty cents if Westfall did the felling.

> WESTFALL: We use chain saws now. 'Course, I don't cut any myself. I wouldn't undertake to chop a tree or even to load it in on the truck. The boys—they go and cut it for me and carry it out or drag it out with a tractor and bring it here for me. And they split the logs down for me till they get it to where I can use the froe on

it, you know, into small pieces ("eighths"). I split the heart out of the eighth, and then it's all accordin' to how big the tree is. You'll split it into about four strips, uh, barrel-fashion, you see, and then you whittle that down smooth (with the drawknife on the shaving horse), and then use your pocket knife to split it with the growth then. A *growth* should make two splits—you can split the growth first; then that growth to work good should make two splits.

HWM: . . . do you do all that at one time—you don't let the wood sit awhile and season, or do you take it right in and weave it?

WESTFALL: No, you can take it right off the stump and work it if you cut it in the *fall* after the sap goes down. Now, my son-in-law come out last fall and cut me a bunch back in the woods—cut me about ten sticks. And that was the first of October, I mean of November, and I just worked the last of it up last week (May 1971), and it was still good. But that's after the sap goes down. Now, this summer when it gets warm weather and you go out and cut it and the sap's up in it, why then you better work it up inside of two weeks, or three weeks at the least, or it'll go bad on you.

HWM: You mean it dries too fast when the sap's still up?

WESTFALL: Yeah, and then it'll *sap-rot* on you too, you know— the white part it'll turn black after the sap comes up. . . . Oh, I cut it in the summer. It's just as good as any, that is if you go ahead and work it up and then let it dry out. It'll season out *after* you work it up.

HWM: I expect that's one thing that makes your baskets so stout. If you work them when they're real pliable, then they set, and they're just as hard as a rock then.

WESTFALL: Yeah, you can't bend 'em in after they get dry. . . . Well, after I get it split out sometimes, I split out enough for thirty-forty baskets and let it season out and then *soak* it in water to work it. The splits—they're *thin*, you know, and you can run them through a pan of water and they soak right up. But 'course the *ribs*—now you got to soak them a little, but you can't leave 'em in a pond overnight, or they'll turn black. You just have to run 'em through the water and let 'em soak up a little at a time, you see— 'cause I have now before put a bunch of that ribs in the pond, and, oh, they turned blue overnight.

MRS. WESTFALL: Well, you can let it *rain* over it.

WESTFALL: Yeah, you can throw 'em out—I like to make 'em when it's rainy weather, you know, if I've got a lot of stuff out, and you can throw it out in the yard and let the rain soak up. Works good.

Following the initial steps required in getting his "timber" ready to work up, Westfall prepares the ribs and weaves the baskets together in

his workshop.[13] The importance of selecting the right tree is illustrated in a humorous anecdote that Westfall tells about a greenhorn
to Missouri:

> I got a brother—he lives out in Colorado, and his son was by here
> awhile back. And now my brother—he lives out there. He used to
> make a few baskets after he married before he went out there, and,
> uh, 'course way *Colorado* is, there's no white oak out there—nothin'
> but pine, nothing to make 'em out of. And this boy—he'd been
> down to visit some of his kinfolk down in Rolla, and he cut one
> tree down there, a *blackjack*. And it was just as full of knots as it
> could be, and he cut two pieces off of one tree, and he had it out
> there on his car, and I said, "What's that there you got on the car?"
> And he said, well, he'd told Frank he'd bring back a piece of timber,
> and they'd make some baskets. And I said, "Well, you ain't a-goin'
> to make 'em out of *that* stuff!" And so I went down there. I had
> some timber, and I give him some good timber to take back with
> him. So he left them pieces a-layin' there. And I said, "You take
> that stuff out there, and Frank'll run you *off!*" Why just full of
> knots from one end to the other—that old blackjack stuff that grows
> limbs from the ground up! Why, you couldn't split it into stove-
> wood, let alone basket timber![14]

The tools Westfall uses are not unique to his trade, but are imple-
ments commonly found in the traditional farmer's toolshed until
recent times.[15] Westfall's collection of tools includes felling ax, iron
sledge and woodcutter's wedge for splitting sticks into quarters and
then into eighths,[16] a store-bought wood saw for shortening eighths
into proper lengths for splits, a forged-iron froe for further splitting of
eighths,[17] a common drawknife used with his homemade shaving

13. See the plan of Earl's workhouse. As Glassie has suggested, there is an interesting relationship between the craftsman and the layout of his workhouse. Westfall's workhouse is not extremely neat, but then "I don't like my workhouse too
clean 'cause it's too much of a job keepin' it thataway." Each object in the shop
does have its place, however, and the arrangement is functional.

14. "Blackjack" is the local dialect term for any of several varieties of the black
oak group, which is deemed inferior to the white oak family by traditional workers
in wood.

15. See Henry C. Mercer, *Ancient Carpenters' Tools* (Doylestown, Pennsylvania:
Bucks County Historical Society, 1929); W. L. Goodman, *A History of Woodworking Tools* (New York: G. Bell, 1964).

16. Westfall uses a homemade hardwood glut after the initial split is begun in
order to protect the wood grain from the damage by an iron wedge.

17. The froe is now the rarest, if not the most ancient, of Westfall's tool.
J. Geraint Jenkins, "Some Country Basketmakers," *Gwerin*, 3 (1961), 197, describes the British froe in terms applicable to Westfall's: "The froe, fromard, doll
axe, dill axe, or cleaving axe, is an L-shaped tool used by many woodland workers. . . .(the) blade is sharpened on one side only." Westfall's froe was made for
him many years ago by a blacksmith to his specifications, its cutting edge is sharp
enough to cleave properly, but not so sharp as to bite into and bruise the wood
being split. It has a hardwood handle tightly inserted into the iron handle loop.

Figure 3. After the lumber has been split, Westfall dresses down the bark and rough splittage with his drawknife.

horse to dress the long sticks smooth and flat prior to their being riven into splits,[18] and any of several different types of "pocket knives."[19]

After the sticks are split into eighths, Westfall saws them to the correct length for splits using a slender stick about five feet in length to measure. The eighths, split with the froe into sixteenths, are taken into the workhouse where the bark and rough splittage are dressed

18. This is similar to the spale basketmaker's drawknife described by J. Geraint Jenkins in *Traditional Country Craftsman* (London: Routledge and Kegan Paul, 1965), p. 48. Unlike the British, American basketmakers do not use a billhook or beetle although some use a maul or mallet roughly similar to the beetle. Westfall simply uses a handy piece of firewood to drive the froe down the cleavage. His shaving horse is not a regular designed one, but is a long piece of two-by-four board which he straddles forcing the stick being dressed tight against the wood frame in an elementary levering fashion.

19. No special knife is necessary, but the one used must have a strong handle and blade to withstand the force applied when starting the riving process and when scraping the splits down. Westfall has experimented with various knives, even a U. S. Navy "frogman knife" given to him, but he finds a common high-quality pocket knife with a six-inch blade sufficient. No knife of Earl's has lasted longer than a year or two of continuous use before the rivet connecting handle and blade has worn out. Westlake's hardware store in Moberly is Westfall's favorite knife supplier.

down on the shaving horse with the sharp drawknife being pulled smoothly with a short quick action. The froe is then used to split the dressed sixteenths into thirtyseconds. The basket frame hoops are made from thin splits approximately one inch in width, two of which are bent to an overlapping circular shape and tacked together with two or more brads.[20] The brads are the only items used in the process which come from a store. The hoops are then crossed at right angles and nailed together with one hoop half left for exposure after weaving to serve as the basket's handle. To save time in the lengthy process, Westfall assembles a number of different sized frames at once. Next, the splits are further riven by hand using a pocket knife to start the cleavage. The final splits for weaving around the frame and ribs of the basket are half the width of one year's growth of the tree (half an annual ring), approximately one-sixteenth of an inch in thickness, and of suitable width to the basket being made.[21] This last riving step required utmost skill and dexterity. The wood is gently pulled apart by hand over the left knee along the grain exactly. Both patience and long practice are required to keep the lengthening split's progress perfectly in the center of the growth. Haste or carelessness in this process results in splits either too wide or too thin in spots causing the finished basket to be misshapen and eventually to weaken and come apart. Westfall makes the ribs round by arduously whittling the rib stock down to a proper roundness and smoothness. The older method in his family was to pull the rib stock through the forged-iron "ribber," a plate secured to the upright posts which support the shaving horse with several small holes the exact size of the particular rib desired. Westfall demonstrated this traditional rib-making technique for me. However, he no longer works ribs in this way since jerking and pulling of the stick through the hole demands strenuous and exhausting activity. Each basket size requires a different number of ribs and weaving splits for its completion, but all of the various types employ only two hoops in the frame.

After the fiber and coarseness of the splits are scraped off with the knife, the process of weaving the splits around the ribs and frame begins with the rib ends being tucked into the weave. With the ribs set

20. Westfall uses storebought "three penny fine" brads ("little nails") which he purchases at Westlake's in quantities of five or six boxes at twenty-five cents a box. He has used two or three sizes over the years. The type of nails used makes no great difference to him, but such details of construction are often the only way the researcher has to determine the probable date of an artifact.

21. With this highly developed sense of proportion and fit, the craftsman perfectly scales his basket; the larger ones are reduced proportionately to scale in the smaller ones of the same shape. A mathematical ratio could be achieved by a measured comparison of several sizes and shapes.

into both sides, the weaving continues. Westfall uses a traditional "randing" stroke, similar to that used by the British spale basket-makers. The last step, like that in the creation of any handmade object, is to give the basket a good rap and a tug on the handle. The basketmaking process typifies the way in which traditional craftsmen make very efficient use of both time and materials in the transformation of natural object (tree) into cultural artifact (basket). Westfall wastes nothing save for a few bent brads and utilizes the whole oak tree. The "heart" of the tree is used for ribs—being too brash for splits—and the good white layers of wood form the frame and splits. What he discards in the preparation of basket stock he later uses to fuel his King Heater stove during the cold Missouri winter. The scraps from the shaving horse and pocket knife make excellent kindling.

Not surprisingly, the Westfall basket improves with age and often gains in dollar value. Westfall has witnessed a basket he made twenty years ago auctioned off at a country sale for ten dollars, an increase of eight dollars over the original price. As the white oak ages and "sets," it dries out, darkens, and becomes extremely rigid and "stout." West-fall notes with pride that he can stand on one of his baskets without breaking it and that such a test would destroy the weaker-constructed Ozark baskets sold at craft shops and tourist stops. His most popular basket now seems to be his "magazine basket"—actually the oldtime farmer's wood basket with flat bottom and open ends. Also popular is the small "Christmas basket" made especially for the seasonal market. In all, Westfall makes a wide variety of baskets: the market or stock-feeding basket, the clothes basket (made now only on request), the "picnic basket," the egg basket, the small novelty basket, and the magazine basket.

There is no special seasonal round in the basketmaker's activities, and the periods of the year when he is most active depend on the other duties he may have as farmer or laborer. Westfall makes baskets throughout the year, but due to his health and temperament he prefers the transitional seasons of mild weather, spring and fall. Since the basketmaker's stock need not be seasoned out, there is no necessity to work at certain periods of the year. Westfall prefers having a supply of sticks quartered and stored in his small single-crib barn so that he may work when he wishes. Timber that does lie unused long enough to season may simply be dampened and softened for the working-up process. Westfall depends on the forces of the natural environment to provide the suitable trees. He did plant a stand of good white oak saplings some twenty years ago, but doubts that he will live long enough to harvest the matured trees. After his heart attack in 1967, his doctor "gave" him "five years to live" providing he takes care of himself.

THE HISTORIC AND GEOGRAPHIC CONTEXT OF SPLIT OAK BASKETRY

The Westfall basket falls within even the most restrictive definitions of what is meant by "traditional" or "folk" craftsmanship. J. Geraint Jenkins posited three characteristics "inherent in craftsmanship," all of which well apply to Westfall:

(1) The craftsman is able to marry beauty and utility, combining good taste and usefulness.

(2) The true craftsman does not depend on complex machinery and equipment to complete his work.

(3) The true craftsman is not only able to work in an ancient tradition, but he is able to build on the foundation of history. The past provides a solid basis for his work.[22]

As Jenkins notes, the craftsman "came into being in order to fulfill society's need for a specialist who could supply it with its day to day requirements"[23] and has therefore since antiquity been of central importance to the functioning of society and economy, in which the countryman was largely self-sufficient. Further, "It is certain that the country craftsman contributed in no small way to the personality and character of localities. Many of the craftsmen worked in a tradition that varied tremendously from one region to another."[24] In another direction, E. P. Richardson in considering American folk painting—and by implication folk crafts as well—stated that it was

> . . . an unselfconscious, highly-developed, traditional craft. Its makers are not amateurs. They are extremely skilled craftsmen. The element of continuity is important: folk art's products follow an ancient and traditional sense of design. They are also made for use. Folk art is a skilled handicraft product intended for the enjoyment of simple people, rather than for the aesthetic delectations of the connoisseur. . . . Folk art has its own aesthetic and human values, but they are not the same values as those of conscious art. In American painting, true folk art is found only rarely.[25]

Jenkins places British crafts into three categories:

(1) The processing crafts where the craftsman is concerned with processing some raw material.

22. Jenkins, *Traditional Country Craftsman*, p. 3.
23. Jenkins, *Traditional Country Craftsman*, p. 1.
24. Jenkins, *Traditional Country Craftsman*, p. 2.
25. E. P. Richardson, *A Short History of Painting in America* (New York: Thomas Y. Crowell, 1963), p. 5.

(2) The service crafts where the craftsman is concerned with the repair and renovation of equipment.

(3) The creative crafts where the craftsman takes a raw material and converts it into a finished product.[26]

The Westfall basket is clearly type (3).

Unlike other types of woven baskets in the United States, the Westfall basket has little or no relation to native American technology or to Afro-American tradition. On the other hand, William Houck's process of making pounded ash baskets has a kinship with the technology and techniques that northeastern Indian tribes adopted from British immigrants in the early colonial phase of American history,[27] and the famed Gullah basket traditions of the Georgia Sea Islands are linked to West African influences. Westfall himself knows of no connection between his baskets and those of any peoples other than the British, but he and Mrs. Westfall recall seeing "Hope-eye Indians make baskets at the Missouri state fair" several years ago.[28]

Westfall confidently told me that basketmaking "came from the old Bible days," that is, from the Old Testament narrative of the child Moses hidden in the basket in the bulrushes.[29] For the Westfalls no better validation of one's family tradition could be found.

Little serious study of American basketmaking technology at least in the Anglo-American tradition has been done, so one may only speculate on the ever present problem of origins of the Westfall-type basket, it seems to me that the evidence argues for an origin resting with the varied traditional basketmakers of Great Britain as described by Jenkins and others. Split oak basketry is apparently more common now in the United States, particularly the Upland South, than it is in the British Isles where historical events and processes caused the loss of woodworking technology in general and basketmaking technology in particular in many areas. According to Jenkins,

> It is rarely that one associates hard and durable oak with the art of basketweaving, but nevertheless in the Furness district of Lancashire and in the Wyre Forest of Worcestershire coppice grown[30] oak

26. Jenkins, *Traditional Country Craftsman*, p. 7. (Note that Jenkins uses "creative" not to mean artistic embellishment or invention, but rather the action of creating an object from raw material. Most American craftsmen no longer practice their business in a traditional context and like blacksmiths fall into category (2).

27. Glassie, p. 44.

28. Regrettably, state fairs and festivals are accustomed to hiring exotic or unusual performers and displays to catch the visitor's eye. Some would argue that states might attempt in their nativistic fairs to represent more accurately their own cultures.

29. Exodus 2:3.

30. [Grown in a dense thicket (British usage).]

Figure 4. Westfall demonstrates the use of the forged-iron ribber. The strenuous and exhausting activity associated with this method of reducing basket ribs has caused it to be replaced.

provides the raw material for a once important industry, that of spale basketmaking. These tough, durable baskets, known in some parts of the county as *whiskets, slops* or *swills* are made of interwoven laths or spelks, and they are still widely used in the north and Midlands for carrying a great variety of products ranging from shell fish to coke and from animal fodder to cotton waste.[31]

Westfall's process and baskets bear comparison to those of certain of the British craftsmen.[32] Jenkins' description of the oak used could describe as well the oak selected by Westfall for his baskets, save that

31. Jenkins, *Traditional Country Craftsman*, pp. 47–48. American basketmakers use natural trees, not coppice grown timber.

32. Like dry stone walling, basketmaking is ancient, and no point of ultimate origin is likely to be pinpointed.

Westfall does not use coppice grown oak nor does he intentionally allow his timber to season out. The ancient technique of using the froe is also precisely Westfall's method: "The froe, after being started with sharp blows of the bettle, is levered up and down until the pole is completely split."[33] Although Westfall does not have a special shaving horse as does his British counterpart, his elementary apparatus is none the less efficient. Also, like that of the British spale basketmaker, Westfall's craft is "disappearing . . . like the osier basketmaker, the spelk maker depends almost entirely on skill and dexterity rather than on any elaborate equipment. By tradition it is a heriditary trade, which not long ago demanded an apprenticeship of seven years."[34]

THE SOCIAL AND PSYCHOLOGICAL CONTEXT

The making of baskets is a solitary job for Westfall, but traditionally this was not the case in his family. Basketmaking was a concerted effort with all family members taking either active or passive roles in the production of baskets. Despite the demise of basket technology as a self-sustaining trade and the resultant scattering of the Westfall family after the Depression, Earl still continued producing baskets, alone in his workhouse, with a radio baseball game or an occasional visitor or customer to break the monotony of a slow and tiring occupation. The making of baskets tends to preserve Westfall's sense of a proper position and functional role within the rural community. He discerns the inherent threat in the circumstances not only of the ebb of basketmaking and other "old time things," but in the ebb of his energies as well. The continued occupation of basketmaking helps to maintain a sense of security in a world which may seem hostile to him and what he "stands for." Westfall realizes that he is out of step with a modern world of technological progress and innovation, but he is proud of his life and his craft.[35] The fact of ever-accelerating "progress" is a concern to Westfall, but although technological change contributed to the end of his craft, it has not stilled his genius and love for his work.

Westfall has never doubted the essential masculinity of basketmaking. He knows the work to be very strenuous involving considerable

---

33. Jenkins, *Traditional Country Craftsman*, p. 49.

34. Jenkins, *Traditional Country Craftsman*, p. 50. One fears that, lacking apprentices, the Westfall basket tradition will go the way of the extinct British crafts discussed by Jenkins.

35. As with most people, Westfall does not freely verbalize or philosophize about his condition, but continues to live and be active within his accepted formalized patterns of behavior. Acceptance or rejection of modern concepts is psychologically operational, not theoretical.

expenditure of physical strength as well as requiring manual dexterity. Other types of folk baskets are commonly made by women, but a Westfall basket could be made start-to-finish only by an exceptional woman. Westfall's sister can weave the splits, and Mrs. Westfall has woven a basket or two, but few women could perform the rudimentary but critical preliminary tasks of selection, felling, and transportation of the oak tree to the work area, the splitting out of sticks of timber, and the riving of the larger splits. Moreover, the old ribbing operation requires enormous effort and strength to pull the rib stock through the iron ribber. People accustomed to the popular scene of Indian women weaving straw baskets or of the ladies' home companion basket weaving kits have little notion of how laborious the making of a basket is when done according to methods like that of Westfall, and the standard craft-show reactions of curious dilettantes both amuse and irritate the craftsman. While Westfall is talking of baskets or is in his workhouse, his manner is gentle, relaxed, and good-natured, but at the same time commanding, even aloof. To dispell any notions that his craft is without hazard or danger, he related this narrative which his father had told him:

> Well, they used to make barrels, and they shaved these little hickory poles for 'em—put the hoops around the barrel. And you'd curt a little hickory pole and split it open, and then they would shave that one side of that hoop, you see. And so he was a-shavin' that hoop, and his drawknife broke right in the middle. He hit a knot one cold mornin'—'course they have these drawknives just as sharp as a razor, you know—and the drawknife broke when he give a jerk on it to cut that knot, and the knife come back and just cut his sides—cut his whole sides out. Each piece of the knife, you see, he just give it a jerk like that (gesture), and it broke and just sliced him in two right there in his stomach.

It is clear that Mr. Westfall takes pride in his sturdy baskets, but he gives no hint of a boast. Jenkins' statement applies: the craftsmen "make something useful and durable without any unnecessary adornments and decorations. In the wake of this utilitarian purpose, there follows pride; the true craftsman's pride in creating something useful, but creating it with beauty and good taste."[36] Westfall's craft is no longer integral to the operation of the community, but he remains a respected figure, and his baskets are in demand. Williams observes that country craftsmen were once a bridge between gentry and farmer and

---

36. Jenkins, *Traditional Country Craftsman*, p. 4. Useless decoration shows "a deterioration of craftsmanship" in many cases. Westfall's baskets are devoid of adornment.

Figure 5. Raw material and finished product are piled outside Westfall's work-house. Westfall's repertoire of basket types includes six varieties.

channels for information, carrying news back and forth in their travels and trade.[37] Though most of the craftsmen no longer travel country circuits and few maintain shops and regular businesses, in America the blacksmith's shop often remains open as a gathering place for old-timers while not operating as a viable business enterprise.

The Economic Sector

Basketmaking as a livelihood for the Westfall family passed from existence after the Depression, but those "Hoover days" provided a last period of activity, however faint, for barter economy.

HWM: Would you mind telling about the Hoover days, as you say?

WESTFALL: Well, back in '29 is when times got hard, and then he'd (Earl's father) take a big load of baskets off, take 'em clean up in Iowa. And money was tight. You couldn't hardly sell anything for the money, so he'd trade for groceries and dry goods. And 'course with a big family you could use flour and sugar and coffee and beans and anything the grocer had, you know. You'd trade for just about anything. You really wouldn't get much money out of 'em, but they still lived good, you know.

HWM: Well, he really didn't have much cash, did he?

WESTFALL: Why, no. Out of a truckload of baskets he wouldn't get over twenty-five dollars in cash out of 'em. There just wasn't much cash to be had in them days.

HWM: I guess that would have been from '29 on up into the thirties?

WESTFALL: Yeah, up until Roosevelt was elected, you know. Then's when times started gettin' a little better. . . .

HWM: Well, what'd he have, an old Model-A or something he'd drive up there?

WESTFALL: Yeah, he had an old Chevrolet touring car, and he had a big frame on it and he'd pile 'em up on there and look like a haystack goin' up the road.

HWM: Was this something he built over the car?

WESTFALL: Yeah, he just built a frame over the back seat and let it stick out behind the car, you know. And he'd just pile 'em on there—tie 'em in bunches, nine or ten in a bunch—just keep pilin' 'em up on there. He used baling wire to tie 'em on with. Boy, he'd get goin' towards the wind, and it'd look like it was goin' to pull him over! . . . Yeah, I remember one time I went down in Henry County with a load, and I had an old Model-T that time . . . along

---

37. W. M. Williams, *The Country Craftsman* (London: Routledge and Kegan Paul, 1958), p. 180.

about '20—along there—and I had a big rack on it, a big load, and there was a strong south wind. And I tell you that old Model-T—I had to run in low part of the time. . . . Those baskets would scare a man and his horse half to death!

HWM: Did you do a pretty good trade in those days?

WESTFALL: Oh yeah, you could sell all of 'em you make. 'Course they wouldn't sell like they do now—didn't get near as much for 'em, of course.

HWM: How long was he gone when he went on those trips?

WESTFALL: Oh, he'd go up in Iowa—he'd stay three—four days. . . .

HWM: How come he picked Iowa to go to?

WESTFALL: Well, seemed like they sold better up thataway than they did—for one thing, there wouldn't be no basketmakers up in thataway much, you know, where down south it's just full of basket-makers at that time.

HWM: You mean down in the Ozarks?

WESTFALL: Yeah, and on down thataway where there's lots of basketmakers—'course anymore there's *not*. There's nobody much that makes baskets anymore. Just goin' to be a thing of the past. Goin' to be a day when there's just no baskets—handmade baskets— 'course people just can't make any money out of it unless they're retired or somethin' and just do it for a hobby. Why there's just not a-goin' to *be*.

Basketmaking never provided much more than a subsistence income for the Westfalls, but the father "done about as good as them other poor folks." Westfall's market now is both local farmers and the domestic commercial trade carried on for the most part through Skill-man's store in Fayette. Neighbors still like to use the baskets for farm chores like "gatherin' beans," and again Westfall can sell all he can make.

The Westfall baskets are the result of the functional determination of the object's form—the shape built to meet practical needs of ease of carrying, weight distribution, use, and handiness. Westfall's basket prices have changed over the years, but each increase in price was made after the passage of a certain time period and not in pace with economic shifts. Prices changed only when determined as absolutely necessary to bring the prices in line with Westfall's sense of economic value in comparison with other market goods.[38] Westfall knows that he is physically able to produce only a given number of baskets in a space of time and that that number of baskets is indeed small. In a full

38. Customers have often urged Westfall to increase his prices, but he has resisted doing so.

day's activity, he can now complete no more than two or three market baskets. Westfall realizes that to attempt to make more baskets in the same amount of time would be of no benefit, for the market would not significantly expand, he would not make any more profit, and his health would suffer from the added activity. Whether or not Westfall makes a profit from his labors is now largely incidental. Being retired from Stamper's in Moberly, he receives a monthly Social Security check sufficient to meet routine needs. And though not well off financially, Mrs. Westfall reminded me that they "ain't never been on no *relief!*" Even if it were possible to locate and train a staff of helpers and apprentices, Westfall would very likely not care to. The Westfall basket is a family craft, and if his progeny do not care to carry it on, he can do nothing about it. Moreover, to modernize or cut corners in his basketmaking process or in other ways to alter significantly the technology would be unthinkable. In addition to his sense of aesthetics preventing such modernization, it is really too late in his life for change. Modernization and innovation in the traditional Westfall basket process could occur only at the expense of his principles and his health. In addition, Westfall is an individual and the family patriarch, so a "company" making baskets would damage his feeling of self-reliance and independence. At the time of my last visit with Westfall, his supply of finished baskets was exhausted, and he doubted that he would "bother making any more."

During Westfall's lifetime basket prices have been determined by size rather than shape:

Type	1920 Price	1969 Price	1973 Price
Clothes	$2.00	$10.00	$12.00
Bushel	1.00 (9.00 per dozen to stores)	6.00	7.00
Small round			
Peck round			
Small egg	.50	3.00	3.50
Medium round			
medium oblong (egg)	.75	3.50	5.00
Picnic			
Magazine (wood)	.75	5.00	5.00
Christmas		1.00	2.00
CHAIR BOTTOMING			
Large rocking chair, back and bottom		25.00	25.00
Ladder-back chair, bottom only		7.00	7.00

It should be noted that changes in the economy occur in a discontinuous process, and "sectors of society . . . do not change at the same rate. There are always leads and lags."[39]

Figure 6. *Westfall uses a traditional "randing" stroke, similar to that of British* *spale basketmakers, when he begins the process of weaving the splits around* *the ribs and frame.*

There are two possibilities with regard to change in traditional craftsmanship: change in the artifact with no change in the artifact's function or no change in the artifact but change in its function. The Westfall basket fits the second, though imperfectly. While the basic form and technology in production of the baskets has remained constant over time, Westfall has adopted a new basket type to satisfy his customers' demand—the very small "Christmas basket" which has no traditional function but which is very popular as a gift item. Significantly, no compromise of aesthetics or standards was endured to produce this new basket type; it is simply a reduction in proportionate size from the standard market basket.

39. Manning Nash, *Primitive and Peasant Economic Systems* (San Francisco: Chandler, 1966), pp. 124–125.

CONCLUSIONS

Basketmaking came into existence on the frontier and elsewhere because of the availability of the necessary raw materials in addition to the functional need within the community for that sort of handy, durable container. Through the inevitable but rude progress of technology, traditional crafts which once supported life passed from thriving business into memory and dusty artifact. Only a few exceptional and tenacious craftsmen continued to work due either to personal will or to accident of location, environment, or economy. The rural crafts supporting the community which still survive are for the most part leisure activities such as lacemaking, quilting, and rag rug weaving. These considerations increase the value of Westfall and others like him who have persevered in the practice of their crafts in the face of certain extinction. Even while his relatives, children, and grandchildren have failed to follow the family craft of basketmaking, Earl Westfall until very recently has been no less interested in his work. In his dedication to what his hands create, Westfall appears at this moment as a rare individual, whose knowledge and recollections are of immeasurable worth to the folklorist as well as to other scholars, especially the cultural geographer, dialectologist, anthropologist, and local historian. The future of traditional craftsmanship in America is thus perceived to be uncertain.[40]

The folklorist must venture beyond mere description of traditional crafts to theoretical inquiries. The entire context of the situation must sooner or later be considered as an element in the organic, ecological whole of basketmaking. It remains for the thoughtful observer to comprehend and record such threatened aspects of the national cultural experience. In general, material folk culture is such an aspect. In particular, the craft of basketmaking, still vital in the workhouse and personality of Earl Westfall, is such an aspect.

HWM: What's the future of basketmaking?

WESTFALL: I don't think there is any. I don't think there's gonna *be* no more basketmakers. Oh, they'll always be baskets, but then they send 'em over here from China and India, I guess, and places like that where they weave these wicker baskets and things and get cheap labor, you know.

---

40. It must be noted that folklorists should no longer be only observers, but whenever feasible should attempt to give assistance to the craftsman. For example, there is no reason why the scholar cannot at least help locate sympathetic markets for the craftsman's work.

COYOTE TALES:
A PAIUTE COMMENTARY

Judy Trejo

This fine discussion of the performance and meaning of trickster tales in one American Indian family was the first of only a few articles in the Journal of American Folklore to include the tradition-bearer's own commentary. Most publications of Indian narratives in this journal and elsewhere have been either context-free (such as Dixon's article in Section 1) or loaded with details and observations from outsiders' views of the cultures they were studying. The insider's viewpoint, however, is indispensable for a reliable interpretation of folkloric materials and their functions; this is the "oral literary criticism" which Alan Dundes calls for in his essay "Metafolklore and Oral Literary Criticism" (in Section 4, below).

As Dundes points out, we cannot guess at the meanings of folklore, folk informants do not always agree with each other about meanings, and meanings may change in different contexts or over time. Therefore, one should not assume that Judy Trejo's explanations are "the meaning" of the four Coyote tales, even if, as she says, the lessons were "fairly clear to us." She denies, for example, that the first tale is "about cyclones," but on one level it is a tale explaining the presence of cyclones in one region and their absence in others. In a similar way the second tale accounts for the origin and spread of venereal diseases, and the fourth "explains" how Bobcat and Coyote came to look the way they do. Comparing Trejo's interpretations to the commentaries of non-Indian editors of such tales, we could conclude that the Indians make much less of these explanatory (or "etiological") aspects than outsiders do. For example, a literary folklorist might immediately classify the first story as a variant of "Pandora's Box," motif (C322.1. Bag of Winds), an explanation for weather phenomena, missing the point that it may also suggest to an Indian audience that "a person gets back only what he gives to others" or that one should be kind to those less fortunate than oneself. Perhaps such "morals" to the trickster stories seem strangely bland and sententious to "civilized" readers who find many of Coyote's deeds to be cruel, whimsical, and self-centered, but this is what an Indian says they mean to her people.

The third tale in this article violates an Anglo puritan notion of propriety and good taste. Most parents would hardly consider the toothed vagina motif suitable material for bedtime stories! Judy Trejo, is obviously at ease with this detail, however, referring to its casually as "a sort of Paiute garbage disposal unit." The student may be interested in the distribution and variations of the vagina dentata *in world folklore and mythology (see Motif F547.1.1.), which is possibly explained by Bruce Jackson's suggestion that it could be a folk reference to "a fairly common syndrome affecting the ovaries called systic teratoma." (See JAF, Vol. 84 [1971], pp. 341–42.)*

Judy Trejo's concluding reference to movie cartoons based on animal figures ignores the popular "Coyote and Roadrunner" series already in existence in which the coyote is invariably the loser, despite his constant trickery.

STORYTIME IN A PAIUTE HOME was an occasion to look forward to. Winter was reserved for grandfather's (*togo-o*) stories; if a family did not have a grandfather, the honor was given to the next oldest male in the family. Sometimes the father (*na*) or an uncle (*atze*) told these stories, or occasionally an older brother had the honor.

Grandmother (*mo-a*) and mother (*pia*) also had their turn at storytelling, but they, like the male members of the family, had their own special time for storytelling. Grandmother often told her stories to children (*tu-waki*) when she was left alone with them. Mother told her stories to her daughter (*pa-de*) when an appropriate occasion arose from which there was a lesson to be learned. When the female members of the family told stories, their stories often concerned the home life (*nauvi qua-to*). These stories were about how to gather and prepare food or how to deliver babies, and many stories were about death. Grandfathers and other male members of the family told stories about hunting, brave deeds, but, most of all, their domain was the great coyote (*e-tza*) tales.

In anticipation of hearing coyote tales, children eagerly did their evening chores—bringing in wood for the wood-burning stove and seeing that the water buckets were full. As grandfather settled himself in his favorite "sitting place" to roll a cigarette (*pahmo*) from a sack of Bull Durham, each child would find a cozy spot for himself and wait for grandfather to finish his smoke.

When it was commonplace for every Paiute home to use kerosene lamps and wood-burning cookstoves, the atmosphere for listening to coyote tales was an experience to be cherished forever. Things are no longer the same. Many homes are now endowed with a bare light bulb that hangs from the ceiling. Lost forever are the soft, playful shadows cast by the flame from the kerosene lamp.

After grandfather finished his smoke and one of the grandchildren considerately placed grandfather's "spit can" at his feet, and while deer (*tu-hucha*) jerky (*tuvasap*) was cooking in the oven, the stories began. All stories begin with Coyote.

I do not know whether all people were animals at one time or if all animals were able to communicate with people. This is one thing I have never understood, but all stories begin as follows: "Once long ago when we were all the same." This is the formula. In Paiute it is: "*Sumu onosu numeka nana quane ynas.*"

Once long ago when we were all the same our country was plagued with tornadoes and cyclones ["our country" means Idaho, Oregon, and Nevada]. Our people feared these terrible things [you can imagine how their fears were compounded since they believed that a simple whirlwind was the spirit of the dead who had returned to earth]. The animals and people were getting tired of being blown away at the most inconvenient places and times. Their lives were constantly in danger, and finally they called a meeting to decide what should be done about the tornadoes and cyclones.

Grandmother Owl (*mo-who*), presided at the meeting. Everybody gathered at the meeting since it was about a subject of common interest. Mother Bear (*piava woa-da*) was the first to volunteer. She said, "Let me gather the evil winds and take them far away because I'm the bravest and strongest among all of you."

Grandmother Owl replied, "No, Mother Bear, you are too fat and slow. I don't think you should be the one to take the evil winds away."

Rabbit (*kamu*) thought this was funny and laughed and laughed (*Su kamu yayshe e-nit-tze su eye kuha*). He said, "See, Bear, even with all your bravery and strength you are worthless to us at this time."

Nephew Bobcat (*to-who*) was the next to volunteer. He said, "Let me take it, let me take it, I'm very fast. I'm also very smart."

Grandmother Owl replied, "No, my nephew, you would never do. You are much too frivolous (*ea-ki suyqui sunami*), you play too much (*ea e-nit-tze te-a-tiad*), so therefore you cannot be trusted."

Sister-in-law Deer (*tu hucha adaze pia*) offered to take away the evil winds. She said, "I'm not foolish like my nephew Bobcat, and I'm very fast on my feet; I could chase the evil winds far far away."

Grandmother Owl thought a minute and replied. "No, my sister-in-law. I'm afraid not. You are much too gentle of heart; you would probably go a short distance and take pity on the evil winds and let them go."

Porcupine (*tza guidi*) said, "I've got the best idea. Why don't we all gather the evil winds and put them in a sack. After the sack is full I can put it on my back and take it far away."

All the animals liked the idea of putting the winds in the sack, but the idea of Porcupine carrying the sack on his back made everybody laugh. Grandmother Owl said, "Thank you, Porcupine. You have given us a good idea, but I'm afraid you would do more harm than good if you try to carry away the evil winds on your back. Why, the quills on your back would put holes in the sack, and when the evil winds escape we would have many more evil winds to worry about. Besides, you are much too slow."

Finally Badger (*who-na*) was chosen to take the evil winds away. The other animals chose him because he was the only one among them who could move quickly to avoid danger. He was envied and respected for his ability to dig a hole and disappear rapidly. All the animals got together and by using their various cunning tricks eventually had all the cyclones and tornadoes gathered into one big sack.

Early one morning Badger set forth with his evil bundle. How very careful he was as he trudged away from his beloved homeland. He did not have any trouble, and the day went well until he met Old Man Coyote (*Etza Waetz*).

When Old Man Coyote saw Badger, he sidled around him and said, "Oh, hello, Badger. Do you have something good to eat in that sack?"

Badger said, "No, Coyote, there is nothing good to eat in this bag. Now go away and don't bother me."

Coyote said, "Well, let me see then."

Badger said, "No, Coyote, I can't let you look in this sack because it contains all the evils of this land."

Coyote whined, "Please, Badger, we are friends, you can trust me. Can't I even have one little peek?"

Knowing that he would never get rid of Coyote, Badger gave up and handed Coyote the sack and quickly dug a hole and disappeared from sight. Coyote eagerly opened the sack, and much to his surprise a powerful wind blew him away, carrying him across the countryside and stopping where cyclones and tornadoes are now prominent.

My grandfather would then usually tell, without interruption or comments, the next tale.

One hot summer day, many years after the cyclones blew Coyote away, an unexpected thing happened. Coyote woke up from the dead. The crows (*a-da*) had been pecking at his eyes, and grass had grown between his toe pads. As he got up his bones rattled within his stinking hide because he had been dead for so long. Coyote said, "I wonder how long I have been dead." He was even surprised to see flowers poking out from between his ribs. His poor old tail was a tattered mess, and his hide was a sight to behold. One of the first things he wanted was a huge meal. He was so hungry he would have eaten a skunk (*pong-icha*) if one happened to be available. Coyote also wanted to go home, so he began his long walk back. He did not realize how far away his home was, and he really didn't care. His main concern was food.

The first creature he snuck [I say "snuck" because the Paiute word *wazi mia*, is the equivalent of the non-standard English "snuck"] up on was a beautiful fox. She was young and very innocent. Coyote watched her for a while and snuck up beside her and said, "I'm hungry, Fox Girl. Will you give a poor helpless coyote something to eat? I'm too old and feeble to hunt for myself."

One whiff of the dirty old coyote made her wrinkle her pretty nose in disgust. Fox Girl became angry and chased Coyote away with a stick. Fox Girl was very insulted: why, just whom did that dirty old coyote think he was talking to? Didn't he know that Fox Girl was the most beautiful of the dog family? She was too beautiful to be bothered by a smelly old coyote.

Coyote slouched away to feel sorry for himself. Later he bathed in a stream to wash away his filth. He did not spare the mud, for mud is a very good soap. On his way back to Fox Girl's house, Coyote really spruced himself up by rolling in a bed of clover [another culture might say he was "putting on the dog"]. "Now let her turn me away," Coyote thought to himself. "I used to be rather charming when I was here before," he said. The next time Fox Girl saw Coyote he was a far cry from what she had seen before. He sauntered up to her and turned his charm on immediately by telling her how beautiful her fluffy tail was [the Paiute equivalent is: *"How-ea pisha pitaviad"*]. Coyote told Fox Girl that her little black nose and pointed little ears made her the fairest female on four legs. Fox Girl was completely flattered. She fed him the best food she had to offer. After Coyote had eaten to his heart's content, he seduced the beautiful Fox Girl. Quite satisfied, he continued his journey. Fox Girl did not realize that Old Man Coyote had left her with a disease. Late she married, and through unfaithfulness the disease was passed on to others.

After the tale telling was over, we might discuss some of the tales, and we had our favorites among the animals. The meanings of the various stories were fairly clear to us. The lesson in these stories is not about cyclones and tornadoes or the seduction of a young maid by a dirty old man, but about conceit, self-centeredness, and sweet revenge. What the Paiutes have tried to teach their young is to be kind to the elderly regardless of how offensive they often appear. The Paiutes say that a person gets back only what he gives to others. So he should be kind to others and do all he can to help them. He should never let himself think he is too beautiful or too good to offer a kind hand, because if he is too conceited there will come a day when he will get his "come down." Incidentally, Paiutes refer to young Anglo boys who sneak around gawking at young Indian girls as coyotes (*e-etza*). Here follows another coyote tale.

Once long ago when we were all the same, Coyote was trotting through a canyon on his long journey home when he saw a flash of light up above him. He sneaked up the canyon wall to investigate.

What he saw almost blinded him, so he squinted until his eyes got used to seeing the forbidden parts of the two females he saw squatting on the ground. This was back in the days when the female genital organs still had teeth. The flash of light Coyote saw came from the sun reflecting on those teeth. [It was forbidden to look upon the female genitalia, and besides the female organ was a threat to the male.] The two females that Coyote was watching were eating boiled rabbit. As they stripped the meat off the rabbit bones, they would throw the bones underneath themselves, and the second set of teeth in their genitals devoured the bones hungrily [a sort of Paiute garbage disposal unit].

Coyote was just fascinated at what was going on. He decided to throw a piece of thorny rose bush under one of the females. The stick was quickly chewed up, thorns and all. Coyote said, *"Hea-te suda ma-ni"* [The Paiute equivalent of "Oh, my goodness, how awful!"] Coyote then decided to throw a piece of shale rock under the females. From his hiding place he aimed carefully and then— BANG! When Coyote hit his target all the teeth from the females' genital organs broke out as they crunched down upon the rocks. To this day the female genitalia have remained toothless.

Males should be eternally grateful to Coyote since the female is no longer a threat to man. Let the females have Women's Liberation. Regardless of what they demand they cannot regain their second set of teeth.

The fourth tale is about Coyote and Bobcat.

Once long ago when we were all the same, Coyote and Bobcat were brothers. They even looked alike. Their faces were the same since they were so closely related. They played together every day, and many times they played tricks on each other [playing tricks in Paiute is *nazoo tzame*].

One day after a hard day of play Bobcat became overtired and fell into a deep sleep. Coyote was leaning against a tree with a mean smile on his face. He was thinking up some kind of meanness to pull on his little brother the bobcat and thought to himself, "What can I do to my little brother that would be really funny? (*Hayu saqua ni oo yeagui?*) Suddenly an idea ran through his mind. "I know what I'll do," he said. "I'm going to fix his face so he won't be able to recognize himself when he wakes up. I think I'll make his face nice and round, and won't he look funny with sharp ears? Yuk, yuk, yuk, poor little brother of mine."

Coyote began by molding Bobcat's face until he was satisfied with the shape of it. Coyote laughed and laughed at what he had done. Then he grinned and tugged at Bobcat's ears until they became pointed. Coyote said, "My little brother doesn't look like me anymore; he looks more like a cat. Ha, ha, ha, he is the funniest thing I ever saw." Coyote rolled on the ground and laughed until he was so weak that he also went into a deep sleep.

While Coyote was sleeping, Bobcat woke up and went to the creek to get a drink of water. When Bobcat saw his reflection for the first time, he became frightened. "What a terrible creature that is looking at me from the water," he cried (*He e shu suda tavea d ni-ni-ea e vuni pini*). Quickly he moved, only to find that the creature moved when he did. So he reached up to touch his ears, and when he did this the creature in the water also touched his ears. Finally he realized that the funny looking creature he was looking at was himself.

He walked back to where Coyote was sleeping. As he stood looking down at Coyote, he realized that his own brother Coyote had done that to him. "So you want to play tricks on me, my big brother," Bobcat thought to himself. Suddenly he grabbed Coyote's face and pulled until he made it long and ugly. Then it was his turn to laugh, for Coyote no longer had a handsome face. Bobcat had managed to mold Coyote's face in such a way that Coyote was left with a very stupid expression. Bobcat laughed until he cried. Then he cried some more. Still, getting even with his brother did not leave him feeling good when it was all over. Since then Bobcat and Coyote have carried a grudge against each other, and to this day they avoid each other whenever possible.

This story carried an admonition for us not to do things to our brothers and sisters out of anger. Fights between brothers and sisters ended by grandfather saying, "All right, Coyote and Bobcat!" That stopped everything.

Let me conclude this paper by reminding you that, to the minds of some, coyote tales are a source of fatigue and boredom. In particular, John Greenway laments the frequent appearance of Coyote trickster tales during earlier years of the *Journal of American Folklore*.[1] However, I can testify that coyote tales are entertaining and that they served several useful purposes, including the teaching of proper behavior. Of course, if Greenway's statement about the chaps that cowboys wear[2] is any indication of his knowledge of the West, his response to the more complicated and abstract Old Man Coyote is understandable. Who knows? Perhaps a fortune will be made with the coyote, as one man of imagination made a fortune off a mouse (*pong-aze*) . . . or a duck (*puhu*).

---

1. John Greenway, ed., *Folklore of the Great West* (Palo Alto, Calif., 1969), 9.

2. Ibid., p. 180. [Greenway wrote that cowboys wore "monstrous great chaps with a gap in front that demanded the re-invention of the codpiece for the sake of decency," forgetting, apparently, that the chaps were always worn over sturdy pants.]

"HOGS ARE PLAYING WITH STICKS—BOUND TO BE BAD WEATHER": FOLK BELIEF OR PROVERB?

Ronald L. Baker

Professor Baker's opening remark that most American folklorists have collected texts without context is perfectly true, and this article provides a good object lesson in the importance of observing and recording social context as well as verbatim text. It also illustrates the ever-present possibility of collecting folklore simply by keeping alert for folk materials and practices that occur in daily life. Finally, the point is clearly made that the genre of an item of oral folklore may depend as much upon its use as on its content or structure.

Baker's description of the barber shop setting and the participants' roles is commendably detailed, even though it is limited to a few paragraphs. It is evident that the unexpected uttering of a folk saying was triggered by the old gentleman's "strange" behavior after his haircut (lingering to light up a cigar), the barber's imitation of the act, and the coincidental arrival of another cigar smoker. Thus the stage was set for a folk "performance" in a context previously found to be mostly barren of folklore. ("Performance" is used here to refer to a traditional remark being made to an audience of peers in response to a naturally occurring and appropriate situation.)

The sense of the newcomer's remark (clearly supported by the North Carolina example cited in footnote 4) is whimsically to equate portly cigar smokers with hogs, thus twisting the old belief-statement to a proverbial usage unrelated to weather signs. Even the fact that it was raining in Terre Haute, Indiana, on the day that Ronald L. Baker heard the saying is important in the understanding of the meaning in this context, since obviously then the saying could not function as a weather sign of rainy weather coming.

One cannot predict when a situation of this kind might occur, nor when a random bit of traditional lore remembered from printed sources may suddenly be heard in a natural context. The only preparation for such collecting is to read widely in published collections and to be alert for folk performances. Opportunities for observing folklore in everyday life might occur while shopping, riding in car pools or on public transportation, waiting in lines, during work breaks, or in social gatherings. The goal is not necessarily to find a great deal of folk material, but *rather to collect the context thoroughly, with a sensitive awareness of what is happening.*

AMERICAN FOLKLORISTS HAVE HAD a bad habit of recording only the texts of folklore and neglecting the social context of the items they collect. Collecting texts without context makes the fieldworker's job a lot easier, but it hardly adds to the folklorist's understanding of how, why, when, and by whom the various genres of folklore are performed in particular situations. Fortunately, most folklorists now realize they must report the cultural setting and function of folklore as well as the text itself.

An item of folklore I collected aptly illustrates the importance of recording both the text and context of folklore. A few years ago I encountered a variant of the widespread traditional weather belief that a hog with a stick in its mouth is a sign of bad weather. If I were to follow the examples of many encyclopedic presentations of American folklore, I would simply list the item and perhaps note that I collected it in Terre Haute, Indiana, on October 13, 1967, from a middle-aged Anglo-American male laborer who learned it as a child. Then I would cite an instance of the item in a standard collection of superstitions to prove its folk quality. For example, I might note that in *Ozark Superstitions* Vance Randolph says, "Any backwoods farmer will tell you that when a hog carries a piece of wood in its mouth there is bad weather a-comin' . . ."[1] Other parallels can be cited from North Carolina, Illinois, Alabama, and Europe.[2]

Certainly the folklore collector must prove the traditional quality of the material he collects by citing the standard collections and indexes, but the job of the professional folklorist does not end there. In fact, if only the annotated text is given, a reader might be misled about the possible use and setting of the text. If I merely listed and annotated the item that a hog with a stick in its mouth is a sign of bad weather, probably a reader would infer that the item was collected in a rural setting as an omen of unfavorable weather. But this is not the case. I

1. Vance Randolph, *Ozark Superstitions* (New York, 1947), p. 12.
2. See *The Frank C. Brown Collection of North Carolina Folklore*, ed. Wayland D. Hand (Durham, 1964), VII, 233, No. 6178; Harry M. Hyatt, *Folklore from Adams County, Illinois* (Hannibal, Mo., 1965), p. 28, No. 758; Ray B. Browne, *Popular Beliefs and Practices from Alabama* (Berkeley and Los Angeles, 1958), p. 208, No. 3480; *Handwörterbuch des deutschen Aberglaubens*, ed. Eduard von Hoffman-Krayer and Hans Bächtold-Stäubli (Berlin and Leipzig, 1927–1942), VII, 1483.

collected the item in an urban setting, and it was used to size up a social situation.

I collected the item in a busy barber shop in a Terre Haute shopping center on a rainy Friday afternoon. This particular barber shop I had found on two previous visits was not an especially good place to collect folklore. Businessman and students popped in and out, waiting only briefly for their turns in one of four barber chairs with their noses buried in wrinkled, two-or-three-month-old magazines. Unlike the casual shops of old, there were no loafers in this shop and little conversation. The little conversation there was usually centered around auto racing, a hobby of one of the barbers, or conservative politics, a hobby of each of the barbers.

On this occasion, however, the center of conversation of the four barbers, three college students, and a couple of businessmen was neither auto racing nor politics but a box of toilet articles the shop was giving to some lucky man whose name was to be drawn out of a box. "Better fill out a card; someone's gotta win; maybe it'll be you; won't that box look nice in your bathroom?" each barber repeated as a customer pulled himself out of a barber chair and examined his fresh haircut in a mirror by the cash register. One old gentleman took his barber's advice and wrote his name, address, and phone number on one of the blue cards and dropped it in a box wrapped like a birthday present but with a slot in the top for depositing the tickets. Then the old man did a strange thing; he did not leave the shop. Instead, he fired up a Dutch Master and leisurely seated himself in a fifth barber chair that did not have a barber. One of the barbers took his cue from the old man and lit a small stogie.

At that moment a short man of about forty-five traipsed in. Protruding through his brown T-shirt and resting on a wide brown belt stretched around green work pants was a rather large stomach—in fact, a real beer belly. This man, too, was smoking a cigar. As he shuffled across the floor towards a vacant chair, he immediately observed the pair of cigar smokers already in the shop. With two fingers he held up his own cigar for all to see, gestured toward the other cigar smokers, and said in a loud voice, "Hogs are playing with sticks—bound to be bad weather."

The performance of this widespread traditional item, however, was appreciated only by me, a student of folklore, who until that moment had only read the item in a number of collections of superstitions. The businessmen, students, and barbers apparently were not familiar with the rural belief that a hog carrying a stick in its mouth signifies bad weather. At least, there was no response. At any rate, consideration of the social context of this item shows that it was not used as a portent of bad weather; it had been raining all afternoon. Rather, the item was used metaphorically to "name" a situation, a function generally attributed to the proverb.[3] Moreover, this performance was not unique but traditional, for a similar setting and function of the item have been reported from North Carolina. In 1971 Talmadge Moose's pencil drawing "Rain" won first prize in the Gallery of Contemporary Arts 34th Southeastern Graphics Show. The drawing, recently reproduced in *North Carolina Folklore*, depicts a stout, cigar-smoking farmer standing before barren fields. A note accompanying the drawing explains: "During his growing-up years, the artist, a native of Albemarle, spent a lot of time hanging around his father's service station and grocery store on the Norwood Road in southern Stanly County. When someone came in, especially a farmer of portly stature and sporting an unaccustomed cigar, he would be given the tongue-in-cheek salutation 'I see it's gonna rain,' followed by some good-natured joshing. Country folks had an old saying, 'When pigs start toting sticks in their mouths, it's a sure sign of rain.' Later it was applied to farmers 'toting' a cigar."[4]

3. Roger D. Abrahams, "Introductory Remarks to a Rhetorical Theory of Folklore," *Journal of American Folklore*, LXXXI (1968), 150.

4. *North Carolina Folklore*, XX (August 1972), 106–107.

FOLKSONGS AND FUNCTION: SOME THOUGHTS ON THE AMERICAN LULLABY

Bess Lomax Hawes

In common with the essay that precedes it, Bess Lomax Hawes' study defines a folklore genre not by content or textual form but by context and use, here in particular by function. The lullaby is a peculiarly "functional" folksong type intended solely to be used to sing babies to sleep. It is a time-honored form of family folklore never likely to become obsolete, and consisting in the United States of what Hawes refers to as a "peculiar melange of materials." The examples discussed come mostly from two archives of student-collected material at California universities, but they probably would be similar to those in any other American folklore archive or family repertory. The analysis draws on cross-cultural comparisons with childrearing practices in Japan and the relative incidence of "chats" and "lulls" in each tradition.

As Hawes points out, the major lack in most archived texts is information about the exact context of performance of the collected items. Consequently, her description of the two-phase process of putting children to sleep is drawn from personal observations unrelated to the song texts, which are the data base for the study. Students interested in studying American lullabies should be careful to record as as much context as possible during actual "lulling" situations. Further, it would be instructive to study the specific kinds of interactions and communication between parents and children that are characteristic of other family folklore, such as bedtime stories, answers to children's questions, and the teaching of simple skills such as tying shoes or riding a bicycle.

Reference is made throughout this essay to mothers' interactions with their babies, but more could be said about the roles of fathers or even of older siblings, close relatives, and babysitters. (Footnote 21 points in this direction.)

Hawes' concluding ideas concerning the theme of spatial isolation of the baby in sleep-centered American lullabies should be applied to other forms of traditional parent-child communication, such a baby-bouncing rhymes, finger- and toe-counting rhymes, and nursery rhymes. Also, it should be noted how children themselves portray members of the family in their play rhymes and games (such as "Mother, May I?").

GENRE IDENTIFICATION AND DESCRIPTION is a problem much discussed by folklorists in recent years. Ultimately it is probably an unsolvable one, but—as in the fairy tales—the quest is likely the most interesting part of the story, for it leads one into intellectual confrontations with anomalies that one would otherwise probably avoid.

Some years ago, hearing of my interest in children's song, a young woman in her late twenties introduced herself to me and said that she had been brought up in Chicago and that her mother, a young widow, had sung her to sleep every night with the same song. And then, with the most extraordinary mixture of emotions on her face—half genuine sentimental reverie, half self-conscious amusement—she sang me what she herself identified as a "funny kind of lullaby":

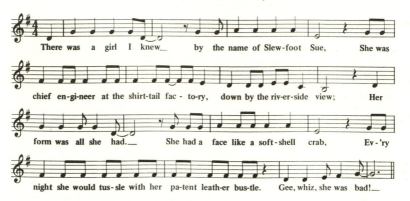

There was a girl I knew__ by the name of Slew-foot Sue, She was chief en-gi-neer at the shirt-tail fac-to-ry, down by the riv-er-side view; Her form was all she had.__ She had a face like a soft-shell crab, Ev-'ry night she would tus-sle with her pa-tent leath-er bus-tle. Gee, whiz, she was bad!__

I helped the young woman notate her song (she was pleased, because she wanted to preserve it for her own children), and today in the folklore archives at California State University at Northridge "Slewfoot Sue: a Lullaby" stares up at me whenever I open the lullaby folder, where it lies tucked in between fragments of Brahms, various "Rockabye Babies" and "Go Tell Aunt Rhodys," a few baby games like "This Little Piggy," and a couple of errant hymns.[1] All are labeled "lullabies" by their student collectors; I assume this must mean "songs associated with children going to bed."

When I had occasion, in 1970, to examine the folklore archives at the University of California at Berkeley, it was interesting to discover exactly the same peculiar melange of materials in its lullaby section. Slightly over half the songs included had texts that did not mention going to sleep at all; there were ten or so miscellaneous "children's"

---

1. My thanks go to Joanne Matthews for contributing her mother's lullaby to the California State University at Northbridge folklore archives in 1959. I would also like to express here my appreciation to Alan Dundes for permission to cite materials from the University of California at Berkeley archives and for helpful comments during my early work on this project.

songs about animals, birds, and the like; two infant games; a hymn; and several songs that can only be categorized as adult—for example, the following, collected in 1964 by Kathleen Whitney from a twenty-five-year-old woman of American Protestant background, who described it as her "favorite lullaby" (from the University of California at Berkeley folklore archives; tune not given):

> There's a man comes to our house every single day,
> Papa goes to work and the man comes to stay.
> Papa does the work, and mama gets the pay,
> And the man comes to our house every single day.

The use of such non-sleep-centered songs at bedtime does not seem to be entirely a middle-class or urban phenomenon; that is, it is not simply a function of the parent's lack of a "suitable" repertory. When I asked Mrs. Bessie Jones, a black lady from rural Georgia and mistress of a fine tradition of childrens' songs, what she used to sing babies to sleep, she told me:

> I sang to babies so much, just all church songs, you know, just sing and sing and sing, just anything I could think of. And at last one day, I jumped off on "Casey Jones." Mama come to the door, she say, "Well! I *never* heard nobody put no babies to sleep on 'Casey Jones'!" I had just sung on out . . . I had just sung and sung and sung, and he *wouldn't* go to sleep, so I got off on "Casey Jones"! I sing all *manner* of songs . . .[2]

And then I remembered singing my own babies to sleep. I happen to know quite a number of lullabies myself, and I come from a lullaby-singing family; but the song that always seemed to "work" best—my stand-by old reliable in times of stress—was the fine old Protestant hymn "I Am Bound for the Promised Land."

The classification problem suggested here is by no means a new one and can be simply stated: is a song a function of its lexical content or its social usage? Is a lullaby a song about going to sleep, or is it any song on any subject that is used to induce slumber? The dual allegiances, literary and anthropological, of the discipline of folklore announce themselves under the most trivial of circumstances; and I suppose that by the simple act of filing "Slewfoot Sue" under "lullaby" I have aligned myself irrevocably with the anthropological (or, at least, the functional) wing.

Of course, as far as the act of archiving goes, it doesn't really matter; you pay your money and you take your choice, and then you

2. Bessie Jones and Bess Lomax Hawes, *Step It Down* (New York, 1972), 5.

can settle back into what Gershon Legman has referred to as "the great peace of non-understanding."[3] But the functionalist position, as enunciated by Malinowski, is most demanding: "The functional view of culture lays down the principle that in every type of civilization, every custom, material object, idea and belief fulfills some vital function, represents an indispensable part within a working whole."[4] If this is true—and it seems at the least to represent a sensible working premise—it suggests by extension that there should be some degree of appropriateness between a function and the group of items a culture uses to fulfill that function. This quality of appropriateness may be found on the level of form, structure, content or stylistics; and the degree of appropriateness is easily recognized by carriers of the culture. Both Mrs. Jones and her mother, for example, seemed to feel a certain lack of congruence between the content and style of "Casey Jones" and the function of putting a baby to sleep.

The present discussion is an examination of the cultural norms governing the rather bizarre congregation of items that American adults choose to use in getting a young child or infant ready to go to sleep. Although the concentration will be mainly on problems of text, there are at least three stylistic qualifiers which must be mentioned as preliminary concerns.

The first is rhythm. American parents seem to rely heavily on a straightforward, non-complex, swaying meter, normally $\frac{4}{4}$, to produce a suitably quieting effect. This is not a pan-human trait; to cite only one contrastive example, A. M. Jones describes a method of soothing sleepless babies used by the Ewe people of West Africa, which relies on a complex and syncopated rhythm.[5] Clearly, Ewe parents can no more stand a crying baby than can their American cousins; the mother takes the baby's hands and the father his feet and they swing the child between them, hammock fashion, in a slow wide arc, with a pause at the top of every third swing. The movement is performed in what may be roughly described as duple meter,[6] and the accompanying song is essentially in $\frac{3}{4}$; when combined with the pause, the overall effect is of extreme syncopation. I have never tried it with an American baby. It seems likely, though, that by the age of three or four months an infant would be stimulated, rather than soothed, by such actions. All the American songs used as lullabies that I have tested can be slowed to our favorite, supremely regular, simple meters of either $\frac{4}{4}$ or $\frac{3}{4}$ time.

3. Gershon Legman, *The Horn Book* (New York, 1964), 285.
4. Abram Kardiner and Edward Preble, *They Studied Man* (New York, 1961), 173.
5. A. M. Jones, *Studies in African Music* (London, 1959), I, 22–23; II, 2.
6. [I.e., a meter divisible by 2, as 2/4 and 4/4 time.]

A second stylistic qualifier concerns the patterning of preferred phonemic choices, particularly those apparent in humming or in the use of nonsense syllables. Alan Lomax and the linguist Edith Crowell Trager have hypothesized that folksong areas can be partly defined in terms of vowel preference patterns. These basic patterns of assonance seem particularly evident in the texts of lullabies. Lomax remarks:

> Spain is a region of lullaby singing—often rare in other parts of the world. Each lullaby has a refrain consisting of a characteristic set of syllables. In recording scores of lullabies, I observed that the effect of lullabies on the child was to put it to sleep even when the singing took place during a recording session in the presence of the entire village. There was a marked change from northern to southern Spain in terms of the vowel set composing the lullaby refrain, and it occured to me that perhaps vowel preferences were implanted by mothers in their children during infancy and that these patterns helped to shape the development of adult folk song.[7]

Although the Lomax/Trager study centers primarily on adult folksong, it seems, on the basis of their extensive Spanish and other data, that the hypothesis may be verifiable. I am unable to pursue this interesting suggestion here, primarily because comparable data are simply not available; however, there are some associated observations to be made.

American lullabies, on the whole and in contrast to the situation described in Spain, fit our generally wordy adult singing style and do not really feature nonsense syllables. However, there is evidence both in the CSUN and the Berkeley archives that much non-verbal singing, usually described as "humming," takes place in the lullaby context. Brahms' lullaby is reported frequently, for example, but generally in fragmentary form, because apparently few people choose to remember the syrupy English translation. My hunch is that a number of other tunes are also typically sung without words and that nonsense syllables, such as "dee dee" or "na na," are used rather than strict humming. Unfortunately, it is the rare collector who reports such non-word-centered data. If more detailed collections were available, however, it would be surprising if it did *not* evince regional or subcultural patterning, in view of the longevity and persistence of some nonsense refrains in other genres of folksong.

A final stylistic qualifier reflects the relationship between singing and a larger pattern of social intercourse. A song is a communicative act, and to some degree "fits" the overall communicative style of the

7. Alan Lomax and Edith Crowell Trager, "Phonotactique du chant populaire," *L'Homme: Revue Française d'Anthropologie*, 4 (1964), 5. English translation courtesy of Alan Lomax, Columbia University.

society.[8] This point can be clarified by viewing comparative data, specifically, a cross-cultural study by William Caudill and Helen Weinstein, which details the results of an intensive examination of the interactional patterns between Japanese mothers and their infants below the age of four months, as contrasted with those of American mothers and their infants of the same age range.[9] In the course of this research, observers visited in the homes and noted the amount of time the various mothers spent feeding, holding, or rocking their babies, as well as the kinds of behaviors engaged in by the babies during these contacts.

In the sphere of oral communication, the babies' actions were classified as either "happy vocalizing" or "unhappy vocalizing," a reasonably obvious distinction. The description of the mothers' verbal behavior is, however, more complex. The overall category "mother talks to baby" was subdivided

> into *chats* and *lulls*. "Lulls" is a very delimited variable and means that the caretaker is softly singing or humming a lullaby, or making repetitive comforting noises, with the apparent intent of soothing and quieting the baby or getting him to go to sleep. "Chats" includes all other vocalizations to the infant, such as talking to him, singing to him in a lively fashion, and playing word games, such as "boo" and "goo" with him.[10]

It is here, in the mothers' behavior, that the culturally distinctive features emerge. Caudill and Weinstein report that, although Japanese and American mothers spend almost exactly the same total amount of time "talking to" their infants, their communicative styles within that overall category are significantly different. On the basis of adjusted mean frequencies, the ratio of "chats" to "lulls" for the Japanese mother was 79 to 22; comparable statistics for the American mother show a ratio of 120 "chats" to 3 "lulls"—a striking disproportion.[11]

In terms of the interaction between mother and child, there is a strong correlation between the American infant's happy vocalizing and

8. I am indebted for this general formulation to the research in cantometrics conducted by Alan Lomax. See Lomax, *Folk Song Style and Culture* (New York, 1969. [Cantometrics is an approach that attempts to relate stylistic and contextual aspects of folksong tradition in a unified interpretation.]

9. William Caudill and Helen Weinstein, "Maternal Care and Infant Behavior in Japan and America," *Psychiatry*, 32 (1969), 12–43. This study was confined to urban middle-class families in both Japan and the United States; corollary investigations, however, suggest that the results of the research hold true across class lines in both cultures and thus that cultural, rather than social, variations were exposed. See pp. 13–16.

10. Ibid., 23.

11. Ibid., 29.

the American mother's chatting, a relationship that is actually reversed in the Japanese data; that is, the Japanese mother's chatting correlates only with her infant's *unhappy* vocalizing. Caudill and Weinstein speculate that the chatting behavior may effectively be reserved by the Japanese mother for occasions when the baby needs distraction. They conclude in summary that the Japanese mother

> does more lulling and rocking of her baby. She seems to try to soothe and quiet the child and to communicate with him physically rather than verbally. On the other hand the American . . . mother in her care does more looking at and chatting to her baby. She seems to stimulate the baby to activity and to vocal response. It is as if the American mother wanted to have a vocal, active baby, and the Japanese mother wanted to have a quiet, contented baby. In terms of the styles of caretaking of the mothers in the two cultures, they seem to get what they apparently want.[12]

The wide range of subject matter selected by the American mother when putting her child to sleep becomes less puzzling. The chatting style of interaction, associated as it is with happy vocalizing on the part of the infant, is carried into the bedtime context. And, as the child learns to speak and can chat back and ask for what he wants to hear, he is already adjusted to a communication style with the parent that is far-ranging in subject matter, cheerful, and emotionally perhaps a bit dispassionate. In my own experience with putting two- and three-year-olds to bed, I found that at that age they actively resist anything that smacks of lulling, but are so enamored of the chatting style that they form possibly the most enthusiastically receptive audience in the United States for the myriad stanzas of the traditional ballad. Length —prolonging the pleasant contact—appears to be the major esthetic criterion for this age range.

On the basis of the foregoing stylistic criteria—simple meter, complex phonemic patterning, and the tendency toward verbal contact with the child on an adult and chatty level—"Slewfoot Sue" may not, after all, be a particularly bizarre or outlandish choice for a bedtime song. What is still unclear is the *exact context* within which the song was used. I have evidence, both from interviews and observation, that putting a small child to bed in the United States is often a two-phase operation: a period of chatting during which infant games may be played, miscellaneous favorite songs sung, or stories told; followed by a briefer time for lulling—singing sleep-centered or otherwise quieting songs, rocking, and the like. By the time the child is two or three, the second phase has almost always dropped out. Many parents, indeed,

12. Ibid., 31.

never lull at all, but simply chat with the baby for a while and leave him to fall asleep on his own.[13]

The chatting phase can, by definition, encompass a repertory of song unlimited in subject matter. The repertory used in the lulling phase, where it exists, is more difficult to ascertain, because American mothers, unlike the Spanish women whom Lomax describes, seem invariably to perform this function in spatial isolation with their babies. My hunch[14] is that a variety of songs are used, and that the two repertories are not as far apart in subject matter as might be supposed. Lacking any but the most fragmentary evidence, however, I must fall back on the literary criterion and make the straightforward assumption that when American parents sing songs that *talk* about going to sleep, they have actually reached the stage when they *want* the baby to go to sleep.

A brief essay by Theresa Brakeley provides a useful general summary of the textual content of the linguistically definable lullaby, though it is based on a vaguely described "world-wide" repertory.[15] Lullabies, according to Brakeley, say in great part "go to sleep, mother is here, you are safe, everything is all right. The all rightness of everything may be elaborated by a placid description of what the rest of the household is doing. Father has gone hunting, fishing, sheep-tending . . . ."[16] The peacefulness of the surroundings may be described; the safety of the child may be guaranteed by "invoking saints, angels, or guardian spirits"; and maternal admiration of the child or "a prophecy of his glorious future" may be expressed. Some lullabies include promises or bribes for good behavior; conversely, "threats,

13. For a striking example of a culturally contrastive attitude, see the German legend cited by Karl Wehran, *Kinderlied und Kinderspiel* (Leipzig, 1909), 14. According to this chronicle, Kaiser Friedrich II, for purposes of scientific research, allowed several children to be brought up in such a way that they never heard any human speech or song, in order to determine which language they themselves would choose to speak. The experiment failed to come to fruition, however; all the children died in infancy before they could possibly speak, since none could fall asleep without a lullaby.

14. The unfortunate number of "hunches" included in this paper are in part due to the syndrome Alan Dundes describes in "Text, Texture and Context," *Southern Folklore Quarterly*, 28 (1964), 251–265. As Dundes points out, social scientists normally report context without noting the specific texts in use, while folklorists all too often report only the texts, without reference to the contexts in which they occur.

15. Theresa C. Brakeley, "Lullaby," in *Standard Dictionary of Folklore, Myth and Legend*, ed. Maria Leach, vol. 2 (New York, 1950), 653–654. Other sources on lullaby content, equally generalized and of varying degrees of usefulness, include: Heinrich Ploss, *Das Kind in Brauch und Sitte der Völker* (Leipzig, 1884); Countess Martinengo-Cesaresco, *Essays in the Study of Folk Songs* (New York and London, 1886) 231–268; and Leslie Daiken, *The Lullaby Book* (London, 1959).

16. Brakeley, 653.

from the playful to the hair-raising" may occur. There are also some lullabies "complaining of the mother's lot, of the father's absence, neglect or drunkenness."

Against this generalized "international" picture, I have aligned a repertory of those American "true" lullabies (as defined by their lexical content) that are most frequently reported in some fifteen regional and national collections of American folksongs, as well as in the two archives previously mentioned, thus sampling both rural and urban areas. The method is sloppy but fair, I believe, considering the definitional problems. Few people would challenge as uncharacteristic the following list, which comprises those sleep-centered lullabies I have found to be the most frequently reported in the United States:

> "Rockabye Baby"
> "Bye Baby Bunting"
> "All the Pretty Little Horses"
>   sub-type: "Poor Little Lamb Cries Mammy"
>   sub-type: "Go To Sleepy, Little Baby"
> "Sleep Baby Sleep"
> "Baby's Boat's the Silver Moon"
> "Hush, Little Baby, Don't Say a Word"

The equally popular "Brahms' Lullaby" has been excluded since the large number of fragmentary versions in the CSUN archives indicates that by the time singers get through the second line "with roses bedight" they have generally given up on the words and started humming.

All the above clearly fit one or more of Brakeley's descriptions, except that there appear to be no expressions of "maternal admiration for the child or predictions of his glorious future" and no complaints about the mother's condition or the father's misbehavior. These themes are, it is true, represented in the overall corpus of American lullabies, but they occur in less widely known songs than those cited above. The absence of the two topics in the "most popular" list may be significant, as they are the most emotionally direct (the least "chatty") of all the subjects detailed by Brakeley.

Two of the songs ("All the Pretty Little Horses" and "Hush, Little Baby") might be categorized as containing bribes for good behavior. Their promises, on closer examination, are simple predictions: "When you wake, you shall have . . ." and "Papa's going to buy you . . ." Again, the emotional formulation is oblique, rather than direct. These two songs also suggest a future orientation, unlike most American lullabies, which are expressed in present tense and filled with descriptive terms about the surroundings and the activities of various people.

And it is here that we reach the single most characteristic quality in the lexical content of sleep-centered American lullabies: the spatial isolation of the baby. All the people around him in song are actually somewhere else—shaking dreamland trees, gone hunting, out watching sheep, or what have you. Baby, meanwhile, is up in a tree, or sailing off in a boat made out of the moon, or driving away with his "pretty little horses." When he does sleep, he is described as being in a place called "dreamland" which, wherever it is, clearly isn't his own bed; and he is variously requested or ordered to take himself to that "land of Nod" by the linguistic convention that requires English speakers to "go to sleep." Even the most widespread choice of a lulling nonsense syllable takes the form of a spatial metaphor; "bye bye," after all, means both "sleep" and "farewell."

Here again, some of the data developed in the cross-cultural study mentioned previously might be enlightening. Japanese and American mothers seem to spend almost the same amount of time in caretaking activities when their babies are awake. During the hours of sleep, however, the Japanese mother tends to continue her caretaking at a leisurely pace, and thus she scores high in such factors as rocking, carrying, and holding her sleeping baby. The American mother, on the other hand, only scores high in "looking at" her sleeping infant. This is because, as the investigators point out, she has ordinarily gone out of the room as soon as (or before) the baby has fallen asleep; she then returns from time to time to glance through the door at him.[17]

"When the bough breaks, the cradle will fall . . ." Perhaps it is not too fanciful to suggest that that moment of high spatial drama that concludes the most popular of all English-language lullabies simply presages, for the modern American baby, the closing of the bedroom door. There are not many other societies in the world besides ours that hold to the belief that babies should sleep alone.[18]

Now what is to be made of all this? In his groundbreaking essay, "Four Functions of Folklore,"[19] William Bascom pointed out that one of the functions of traditional oral expression is to allow the individual to say what is otherwise unsayable in his society, to release his feelings of hostility, tension, or anger in a depersonalized and therefore sanctionable way. In terms of this thesis, must we then conclude that American mothers are really expressing hostility toward

17. Caudill and Weinstein, 38–39.

18. William N. Stephens, *The Family in Cross-Cultural Perspective* (New York, 1963), 360. Also, see William Caudill and David W. Plath, "Who Sleeps by Whom? Parent-Child Involvement in Urban Japanese Families," *Psychiatry*, 29 (1966), 344–366.

19. William R. Bascom, "Four Functions of Folklore," *Journal of American Folklore*, 67 (1954), 333–349.

their infants when they chat away at them all day about miscellaneous topics and then put them to bed to the cheerful but impersonal lines of "Slewfoot Sue," or to a lulling refrain that actually suggests that the babies should go off somewhere else?

Maybe, but that's only one of the possibilities. There are, after all, two people present and in the "audience" when a lullaby is sung within context: the infant and the mother. I do believe that the lullaby singer feels tensions and that the songs she sings express those tensions with a kind of exquisite economy. But the source may be external or internal; the lullabying mother may in fact be singing as much to herself as to her baby.

Edmund Leach, among others, has pointed out that one of the first problems facing an infant is to discover the delimits of his own body, to determine what is himself and what is outside or separate from him.[20] I have wondered whether the post-partum mother does not face the same problem in reverse. Her infant, after all, once a part of her own body, is now permanently and forever separate.

This experience, of course, is common to mothers in all societies, but American culture puts what is clearly an abnormal degree of separation strain on the mother. On the one hand, she must train her baby to be the active, exploratory, happily vocalizing—in sum, independent—little character that our culture prefers. On the other hand, she must do this without assistance from anybody else because our society is most unique in its insistence that mothers—and mothers alone—take care of their babies.[21] Thus, she must simultaneously try to separate her baby from herself, making him independent, self-reliant, and strong (for in America, they say, every tub stands on its own bottom), while at the same time she remains in maximum physical proximity to him.

No wonder American mothers sing to their babies—and more especially, probably, to themselves—about separation and space and going very far away. I always found myself that rocking a baby to sleep was kind of a sad thing to do—not miserable or tragic or irksome—just a little bit sad, somehow.

It was remarked earlier that in terms of child-training, Japanese and American mothers "seem to get what they apparently want." Other investigations have indicated that this is profoundly true for cultures

20. Edmund Leach, "Anthropological Aspects of Language: Animal Categories and Verbal Abuse," in *New Directions in the Study of Language*, ed. Eric H. Lenneberg (Cambridge, Mass., 1966), 23–63.

21. Stephens, 366–370. It will be interesting to see if the lullaby repertory eventually reflects the trend, currently observable in many young families, for the father to take on a greater proportion of the caretaking activities, including putting the baby to sleep.

everywhere; overall, a society tries to produce the kind of individuals it needs for its own survival.[22] But—as expressed in an ancient Spanish proverb—there is another cultural law that seems equally universal: "Take what you want—but pay for it, says God."

The bill must be paid. If we want independent children, we must thrust them away from us, and, equally importantly, we must thrust ourselves away from them. The American lullaby is, I suggest—whether "chatty" or "lulling," whether the mother finds herself singing "Bye Baby Bunting" or "I Am Bound for the Promised Land," or even "Casey Jones"—on one of its deeper levels, a mother's conversation with herself about separation. And, as such, one of its most profoundly supportive functions is to make the inevitable and inexorable payment of our social dues just a little less personally painful.

22. Herbert Barry, Irvin L. Child, and Margaet K. Bacon, "Relation of Child Training to Subsistence Economy," *American Anthropologist*, 61 (1958), 51–63.

TALKING TRASH
IN THE OKEFENOKEE SWAMP RIM, GEORGIA

Kay L. Cothran

This study is an excellent example of the recent emphasis in American folklore studies on context and event rather than on texts and genre analysis. It deals with the activity known in the Okefenokee Swamp Rim area (and elsewhere in the South) as "talking trash," and in other regions by such terms as "kidding around," "shooting the breeze," or "bullshitting." While several distinct kinds of stories, including some with international distribution, may be identified in the transcriptions of the talk during such activities, the events are unified, as Kay L. Cothran shows, by the context of the situations in which trash is talked. The study, then, must be concerned not with recognizing types and motifs or collecting variants of known traditional tales, but rather with analyzing the talk and behavior of people in social situations; the people observed must include the folklorist too. Cothran provides revealing instances of her own influence on what was said in the collecting sessions, and she shows how even the nonverbal reactions of listeners were meaningful. In connection with these examples, it is important to read her theoretical essay "Participation in Tradition" reprinted in Section 4. Also, the student would do well to review a text of the traditional dialogue "The Arkansas Traveler" in order to understand fully the game of crafty answers and pretended dullness that some informants played with the folklorist during her research. (See James R. Masterson, Tall Tales of Arkansaw [1942; rpr. as Arkansas Folklore, Little Rock, Ark.: Rose Publishing Co., 1974], esp. chapter XIV "A Traveler, a Cabin, and a Fiddle.")

The differences between men's and women's folklore repertories and performance styles have seldom been mentioned in American folklore studies, so Cothran's observations (plus her study cited in footnote 20) are valuable starting points for further research. A relevant essay by another Southern woman is Rayna Green's "Magnolias Grow in Dirt: The Bawdy Lore of Southern Women," Southern Exposure, Vol. 4, No. 9 (1977). Besides pursuing this matter in their own fieldwork, students may wish to investigate the dynamics of other folk communicative events such as joke-telling sessions, songfests, and the occasions when proverbs or riddles are spoken.

In the pineywoods around the rim of the Okefenokee Swamp in southeastern Georgia and northeastern Florida, a cracker culture developed in the nineteenth century.[1] According to Bevode C. McCall,

> it represents a frontier "frozen" at the stage of animal husbandry. This is probably best explained in terms of two factors. First, the earlier migrants considered the area unsuited to agriculture, and, second, they lacked capital both in the form of slaves or of machinery with which they could exploit the natural resources. The general pattern of settlement was the lonely farmstead located in the pine barrens with a few acres of "cowpen" land on which vegetables and other foodstuffs were grown. The farmer also hunted for food, gathered wild fruits, and occasionally collected his wild cattle to drive to market.[2]

Early white settlement in the rim began in the 1830's, and cracker culture persists today as more than a memory culture but less than a full way of life. Now the area has several towns of considerable size, as well as crossroads villages and tiny homestead clusters. The black population is relatively small for a deep southern area, and there has never been an aristocracy of the sort found closer to the sea coast. Indeed, plantation agriculture appeared only in the present century in the form of pine forests feeding the forest industries: paper and pulp, naval stores, and saw timber.

The Okefenokee-rim cracker culture produced a number of exceptionally talented tellers of humorous stories. The last truly superior narrator, Len Griffis, died in 1968, but it is certainly too soon to consign the local storytelling tradition to folkloristic nostalgia. Even though it *may* be weaker than it once was, the tradition remains part of the cultural environment for most inhabitants of the rim, regardless of social class. Whether they like and practice humorous narration or scorn and avoid it, the tradition means something to them.[3] Thus they

---

1. The term *cracker culture* is used here without derogatory connotation, following the usage of several southern sociologists: Mozelle C. Hill and Bevode C. McCall, " 'Cracker Culture': A Preliminary Definition," *Phylon: The Atlanta University Review of Race and Culture*, II (1950), 223–231; John Gillin and E. J. Murphy, "Notes on Southern Culture Patterns," *Social Forces*, 24 (1951), 422–432; Bevode C. McCall, "Georgia Town and Cracker Culture: A Sociological Study" (Ph.D. diss., University of Chicago, 1954). The latter, not on microfilm, is largely unavailable; I am grateful to Ray Birdwhistell for loaning me his copy.

2. McCall, 108. See also Kay L. Cothran, "Such Stuff as Dreams: A Folkloristic Sociology of Fantasy in the Okefenokee Swamp Rim, Georgia" (Ph.D. diss., University of Pennsylvania, 1972; Xerox University Microfilms number 72–25, 557).

3. Kay L. Cothran, "Participation in Tradition," *Keystone Folklore*, 18 (1973), 7–13.

participate in it, positively or negatively. This article portrays the local tradition as I came to understand it through a year's fieldwork (1970–1971) and two shorter collecting trips, in 1966 and 1972.[4] Except for Kato Lambert, all informants are white. For prudential reasons some proper names have been replaced with randomly chosen letters of the alphabet.

One informant, Henry Harrison Lee, said that as a boy, perhaps fifty years ago, he used to go into Waycross (Ware County) from his home on Billy's Island inside Okefenokee. In town he heard men in leisurely conversation on street corners telling all sorts of wild stories about Okefenokee. Given the hazards of life around the swamp and the local men's love of playing and telling about practical jokes, at some time every man's life was a potential source of stories. Another source, of course, was international tradition.

Since the time when the hunting- and fishing-camp trade began to flourish, after Lem Griffis' camp was established during World War I, local men have traded tales with visiting sportsmen. Lem Griffis wrote down tales learned from customers and delved into such popular publications as *Captain Billy's Whizz-Bang* for more material. Over the years he and other storytellers have enjoyed seeing their fabrications published as fact by credulous science and travel writers, and the better performers in the rim themselves have carried their performances outside the conversational context into popular media. Lem Griffis appeared on television several times, wrote a column called "Tall Tales" for the Clinch County newspaper every week, and published a small booklet (now unavailable) of his humor. A good younger storyteller, Willie Fred Roberts, has been on radio in Nashville and has made a record.[5]

Earlier there was a passing reference to the "competence" of the storytellers. What are its evidences? Dorson has said that "the hallmarks of the American master narrator are his avid practice of entertaining auditors with allegedly true anecdotes, an extensive repertoire that embraces well-known native tales, and a local reputation that attests his skill."[6] Henningsen adds that tall-tale narrators "appear as heroes in their own stories, and . . . therefore are forced to create a certain harmony between the lies and their actual lives."[7] These

4. John Burrison, Georgia State University, and Kenneth Goldstein and Don Yoder, University of Pennsylvania, supervised and encouraged the research.

5. *Willie Fred Tells It Like It is* (Comanche LP 1000).

6. Richard M. Dorson, "Maine Master-Narrator," *Southern Folklore Quarterly*, 8 (1944), 279.

7. Gustave Henningsen, "The Art of Perpendicular Lying," *Journal of the Folklore Institute* 2 (1965), 186.

criteria—frequency of narrating and delight in it, size of repertory, local fame, and development of one's self into a literary and literal character—certainly apply in the rim. But these are markers of excellence, not competence per se, inasmuch as they pertain to tall-tale tradition only and not to "talking trash," a more varied activity that includes tall-tale telling.

Country men in the rim refer to the folklorist's tall tales as "lies" or "tall yarns." These stories and a number of other analytically (but not locally) distinct kinds of folklore belong to a larger kindred of talk appropriate to and defined by the male leisure activity known as "talking trash" or "telling lies." Trash ranges from small talk about the weather, the prospects for hunting season, the relative merits of brands of pickup trucks, whose dog just had pups, and so on through teasing, joke telling, and yarn spinning. The talk is unified by the event in which it occurs, if it is unified by anything. A more conservative-minded folklorist might wish to ignore portions of this loafing and lying behavior and to concentrate only on what is folklore—the tall tales, whoppers, and perhaps the experience stories—and then separate these into distinct genres. In terms of modern method, this would be a mistake. The talk varies, but it is unified by context.

A great many men in the rim can talk trash when the occasion for it arises; properly sociable men are expected to be able to do so. Many enliven trash conversation with a clever experience story. Thus competence in talking trash goes hand in hand with the essentials of male sociability. The master narrator, however, goes beyond basic essentials; he is a linguistic craftsman who works at his endeavor. His fantastic wit needs, indeed thrives on, the praise of other men. More than a good, sociable self, he needs a character, a fantasy world built of style, and language is the technique he uses to create these. If he needed to be a character for his own sake alone, he might be labeled a lunatic, but he is sought out by other men who share his need but perhaps not the drive or the gift to satisfy it without assistance.

What marked Lem Griffis as the foremost narrator in recent times was his great influence on other storytellers. All storytellers interviewed, from the well-known craftsmen such as Willie Fred Roberts and Will Cox to the ordinary sociable talkers of trash, admitted their admiration for Griffis and their use of him as a source of tales. Some narrators now tell stories about Griffis as a storyteller; one of these appears on Willie Fred Roberts' recording.

Separating kinds of stories will illustrate the variety of talk that is talking trash (it will be done simply for that purpose, not to attempt the formation of subgenres). Predictably, some talk is not trash; although not named locally, one can call it "serious" talk. This kind of

talk may include stories about one's ancestors' settling their homestead, exempla[8] in fundamentalist sermons, and tales of "haints"[9] and
witches. But trash and serious talk do not have mutually exclusive
contents. A disbeliever can narrate a "haint" tale to frighten someone
who does not know whether to take it seriously. The local people
appear to classify kinds of events rather than kinds of narratives. A
great part of the superior trash-teller's skill lies in his ability to manipulate ambiguities in the way events are defined. Thus a basically
factual experience story can take on qualities of fantasy in a trash
session, and a wholly fictitious "haint" tale can fit into a serious
conversation. In terms of content, one may say with Wittgenstein that
"the strength of the thread does not reside in the fact that some one
fibre runs through its whole length, but in the overlapping of many
fibres."[10]

In many if not most cases, the evaluation of the event as serious or
trash determines the evaluation of the language forms used during the
event. What complicates matters is that, on another level, the language
and nonverbal communication evaluate the participants in the event
and so make characters of them. Logically, one goes from the existence in the cultural repertory of a kind of event (talking trash),
through an actual instance of talking trash, and from there to the
functions of that instance for its participants.

Some kinds of trash are pure fictions, such as whoppers, those
hyperbolic descriptions that may be cliché similes on other occasions.
Jansen excludes whoppers from the category of tall tale because they
have little or no plot.[11] Because many whoppers are not technically
narratives, lacking temporal juncture, to avoid calling them "tales" is
not objectionable. One must be careful, however, not to allow such a
technical point to stand in the way of seeing the contextual kinship of
the whoppers with other kinds of trash. Whoppers are part of the core
of trash in the rim.

Another major kind of trash, the personal-experience story, could
be excluded from folklore altogether because many such items are
highly ephemeral and do not "go into tradition." Yet the *custom* of
narrating personal experience is traditional; again one must study what
happens, not just what one's definitions approve. Some personal-
experience tales, hunting stories for example, are partly or even largely

8. [Stories used as examples to illustrate moral or ethical principles. Singular
"exemplum."]

9. [Also "hants," from "haunts" or ghosts.]

10. Ludwig Wittgenstein, *Philosophical Investigations*, trans. G. E. M. Anscombe,
2nd ed. (New York, 1958), 32e.

11. William Hugh Jansen, "Abraham 'Oregon' Smith: Pioneer, Folk Hero, and
Tale-Teller," (Ph.D. diss., Indiana University, 1949), 185.

factual, while in other experience stories the balance of fact and fiction cannot be determined. In tales about lynchings, sometimes a part of trash, what actually took place has decidedly less significance than what is alleged, imagined, or wished to have happened. Stated in Burke's language, optative and indicative blend in these macabre tales.[12]

Dreams, wishes, myths, tall tales, whoppers, and other sorts of public and personal fantasy of course cannot be dealt with completely in terms of a fact or falsehood disjunction. A fantasy is neither true nor false. Rather, it has a particular degree of experienced reality or unreality, as prescribed by society or by a deviant individual.

In the case of talking trash, there are two kinds of "event" to consider: the event within which the talk happens (talking trash itself) and the event, actual or not, of which the story purports to be an account (the referent event). For each narrative cited, I estimate the degree of factuality, not because I am concerned with historical accuracy but because I want to show that (1) fact and fiction are not distinguishable with any degree of certainty in many if not most tales, (2) the truth of the tale has to do with the storytelling event—fantasy used to define oneself as a "character," and (3) analytically speaking, a true-false dichotomy does not apply to trash vis-à-vis its supposed referent event.[13]

The first, most obviously fictional kind of trash that can be distinguished is the simple whopper. If one whopper is told in isolation from others, it is usually embedded in an anecdote, so that what one gets is a story *about* telling a whopper. Will Cox narrated the following story from his days of employment at the Okefenokee Swamp Park near Waycross.

> I said, "Mr. Fleetwood, I'm gon' get rich offa that hooraw bush."
> He said, "How is that?"
> I said, "Well," I said, "I'll tell you." I said, "You know the honeybee won't suck the bloom on this bush."
> He said, "No," he knowed that, no kinda insect.
> I said, "That's right." Then I said, "When the good Lord made the world," I said, "He made all the plants and everything. When He started out, put the bloom on all of 'em, all the little insects was along with Him." I said, "When He come to this one, He put the bloom on it, honeybee jumped on it, jumped right back off." I said, "The good Lord told him he had to suck this bloom or work on

12. Kenneth Burke, "The Philosophy of Literary Form," in *The Philosophy of Literary Form: Studies in Symbolic Action*, rev. ed., abridged (New York, 1957), 4–7.

13. John J. Gumperz and Dell Hymes, eds., *Directions in Sociolinguists: The Ethnography of Communication* (New York, 1972), 326.

Sunday," and I said, "He's been working on Sunday ever since."
"Yeah," he said, "I reckon you right."
I said, "Yep," but I said, "I'm gon' get rich on it."
"By the way," he said, "How is that? How you figger on—"
I said, "Well," I said, "I got the honeybees crossed with lightning bugs and working at night. They can't tell no difference 'tween hooraw and huckleberry."
He just tuck his little bundle of tags and throwed 'em away off the walk, turn around and walk back. Told Mr. Elkins, says, "Dr. Hafford, that man you got down there, knows more about them bushes than I do." He says, "I'm not gon' mess with 'em."

In Lem Griffis' narrating routine at the fishing camp, he used physical objects as cues for whoppers, including his version of the one above.

See that honey a-sitting up there on the shelf? Well, I crossed my bees with lightning bugs, so they could see how to work at night, and they make a double crop of honey every year.

Ordinarily, whoppers are narrated in strings of related items, like the following from Lem Griffis. As the second excerpt shows, the string may be cumulative, building to a grand finale.

COTHRAN: Ever get cold down here?

GRIFFIS: Cold? Got so cold this last winter my hens didn't lay nothing but snowballs.

COTHRAN: Hoo!

GRIFFIS: One ole hen set on her nest fulla them snowball eggs and hatched out a covey of ice-cream biddies.

COTHRAN: Well, if it gets that cold, how hot does it get?

GRIFFIS: Oh, these old tree stumps, you can see 'em a-crawling in a shade. Yeah, got so hot this last summer my hens laid hard-boiled eggs.

COTHRAN: Does the weather ever get kinda bad down here?

GRIFFIS: Oh yeah. We have some monster winds down hyer. Bad winds. You know we had a storm pert' near several years ago that blowed the wash pot wrong side out, blowed it through the front yard so fast lightning struck at it three times and missed, twisted the well curb so crooked we had to draw the water with a corkscrew, scattered the days of the week till Sunday came up late on Wednesday evening.

Whoppers are extremely simple, structurally, and given a fertile imagination they are not difficult to generate. The typical whopper form is a grammatical frame with three slots. Slot 1 is filled by a

substantive ("One of my uncles . . ."), slot 2 by an intensifying phrase
(". . . he was so short and chunky . . ."), and slot 3 by a dependent
clause expressing an absurd consequence of the intensification (". . . till
every time he'd fall down he'd fall right back up again").

When such an expression is used as a cliché simile, the principal
change is attitudinal, not linguistic.[14] One is no longer talking trash.
A simile evaluates something, often with exaggeration, and cliché
similes can appear in a variety of conversational contexts. They are
intended to convey, by means of imagery and intensification, the
actual qualities of something or someone. In other words, the simile
evaluates that to which it refers: a short uncle, a cold winter, a hot
summer. That it does so via figurative language adds pleasure in style
to presentation of the referent. But the whopper, as part of talking
trash, underplays the referent's importance. The referent may not even
exist in the real world. Delight in style, in building a fantasy world in
which speaker and auditors become characters, takes precedence. As
Lem Griffis responded to my tongue-in-cheek questions with whoppers, we played a game of Arkansas Traveler. What our interchange
was really "about" was our make-believe relationship: naïve city-girl
versus canny old swamper.

The kind of trash that has been most studied is, of course, the tall
tale. It is a plotted narrative, which removes it from the realm of
"minor" genres. In the rim, tall tales are often combined in normal
narration, as in the following two well-known tales narrated by Lem
Griffis. The only factual elements here are that Griffis did have an
Uncle Paul and that some local saw timber has been used for crossties.

> Oh yeah, we have a good many snakes hyer, but you know, snakes
> they're terrible 'bout the fighting each other. Now when they run
> together to fight, they always fight until death, and when one kills
> the other, he always do swaller him, he never fails, always eats him.
> I saw two of 'em run together for a fight and they caught each other
> by the tail and went to swallering, and they swallered and they
> swallered till there wasn't anything but two heads there, and gave
> one more swaller, and 'twas no snake a-tall. We have some of the
> most deadly poison snakes here most any place in the world, I
> reckon. Uncle Paul, he come down to see us one time, and he walked
> with a walking cane. He went to carry one after he was ninety-six,
> and he was walking around through the woods out here, one of them
> poisonous snakes struck at his leg and hit that walking cane. He
> walked little ways further, noticed that walking cane to get—begin
> to get—heavy, and he looked at it and it was all swollen up. He
> couldn't carry but a little ways further, before it got so big and

14. Mody C. Boatright, *Folk Laughter on the American Frontier* (New York,
1961), 164–165.

heavy he just *had* to leave it. He thought lots of his walking cane, so next morning he went down to see about it. By that time it was swollen up till it was just an enormous size log. He notified feller to have a sawmill to come get that log and saw it up into lumber. But by that time it was swollen so large it couldn't be moved, but he moved his saw mill to it, and he sawed enough crossties out that swollen-up walking cane to build ten miles of railroad, and after he got his railroad built there come up a awful heavy rain, washed all the poison outa them crossties, and he gathered 'em up and sold 'em for toothpicks.

Because in this area, as elsewhere, tall tales are part of the wilderness guide's stock in trade, and because hunting and fishing once played a great part in economic life, it is not surprising that many locally popular tall tales have to do with hunting and fishing. In addition, many factual and partly factual experience stories deal with these topics. Thus in a talking-trash session one can hear tall tales like the Wonderful Hunt and fundamentally factual stories dressed with boasting. Stories from other occupations also occur. Former cowboys tell about the unusual feats of their favorite horses back in cattle-herding days, just as hunters brag about their best dogs.

Once one leaves behind whoppers and tall tales and moves to these experience-based stories, the interweaving of fact and fiction proves so smooth that one could not separate the two strands even if it were important to do so. Participants know that the tales are fantasies, told to pass the time, to entertain, to impress, to make people say, "He's a *character*, isn't he?" They know that the narrator's assertion that the tales are "true" is a convention of talking trash, but a narrator who seems to be unaware of the difference between talking trash and talking seriously worries them. If he does not size up a situation dependably, the auditors do not know what is going on. Are they characters, or are they themselves?

One elderly narrator in the rim appeared to be confused as to the nature of events. I was never able to decide whether he was simply senile, or did not bother to define his conversation as trash or not trash, or had never understood the difference. No matter which, he was not a competent talker of trash. The significant thing is not that I, an outsider, could not follow his intentions but that local people sensed something off key in his behavior. Regardless of how many realities a society allows, no matter how readily it permits people to shift or escape realities, to be sane one has to know and show where one is at the moment. The good narrator does not ignore boundaries between kinds of events; he plays with the unavoidable ambiguities of such boundaries. Lem Griffis delighted in giving a trash answer to a question posed seriously, throwing the interlocutor into momentary confusion as to how to evaluate the answer, but when the joke was over and his command of the situation was reaffirmed he gave a serious response.

Hunting and fishing tales based on experience concern both encounters with animals and animal behavior. The first example was narrated by Will Cox, the second by Rhoda Mizell Barber.

I remember one time when I was a boy, was in the swamp fishing with ole man Carter, ole man Tom Carter, and everybody would tell you that a alligator would drownd a bear in the swamp. So me and him was fishing, and *late* in the evening we saw a bear come up and start to swim the lake where we was fishing. There's a alligator, 'bout a nine-foot alligator laying right out in the middle of the lake. Before the bear got to him the alligator sunk. Went down under the water. We thought he was gone, running. But when the bear got right to where the alligator was, he just went right down and went under. The mud, leaves, and everything just boil up in the water. Directly the bear riz, and swum on to the other side and went on, and we went over there and pull the alligator out. He killed him. Busted him all to pieces. Tore him all up. Busted his bill all up.

[Uncle Lon Thrift] said that he was camping one time in the swamp and—they would always try to make it scary, you know, to me as a child it sounded more scary, I guess. He always tried to tell some great yarns that would be real scary, you know. And this time he was telling in particular about he was camping out in the swamp, and he heard the sort of a slapping, or cracking noise, you know, and he couldn't imagine, he'd never heard that sort of noise before in the swamp when he'd be in there, and he couldn't imagine what it was. And it came closer. And then it would come a little closer, and little closer, you know. And he thought he would be smart and go out part of the way to meet it, to see what it was instead of staying with his campfire, you know. And he could tell that it was coming down the run,[15] and he was standing near the run on the bank there, and he said that it was sort of light, you know, it wasn't real complete dark night, and he said he could see something on the water that was white, but it wasn't very large, and it was floating along, and all at once it would turn dark, and when it turned dark it would make that cracking noise. And it came a little closer and almost up to where he was standing, and he realized it was an alligator with his mouth open. And he was floating along on the water with his mouth open, and his big white tongue was showing, he said, and he couldn't imagine why he was slapping, but he was waiting for all the mosquitoes to fly in on his tongue and start eating and then he slap to and catch the mosquitoes. I wondered a lot of times if it was actually true.

15. [Path or passageway through woods or swamp.]

Mrs. Barber related this tale most effectively, but, as is the case with many rim women, she wondered about its factual truth. On the other hand, she recognized that the present event—scaring the children—took precedence for Uncle Lon. Mrs. Barber narrated another story learned from Uncle Lon, the ending of which left him stuck in a tree that was bending over into a mass of fighting dogs and ferocious wild hogs.

> BARBER: I don't know how he ever got out of that one. I don't think he ever told how he did get out of it.
> COTHRAN: I guess they ate him up, what do you think?
> BARBER: They probably did!

Something odd was going on in the session with Mrs. Barber. A woman was telling a man's stories to another woman. Nominally we were discussing men's stories and recording the ones she could recollect, but in addition we were carrying on an implicit talk about ourselves as southern women and about the southern men we have grown up with. Possibly the ending I supplied to the last story mentioned is the one Uncle Lon actually used, for it is a traditional ending for such a tale. In any case, the tale shrieked for resolution, like a hanging dominant seventh chord, and the tonic that snapped into my mind was not merely traditional but also quite relevant to our implicit woman-talk. We have grown up with men who do crazy things, or say they do, who tell wild stories, and if they think it is funny, well, so do we—but for different reasons. We see the stories as evaluations of our lives with our men. At the risk of waxing tractarian, I will return to the theme of women and trash at the conclusion of this article.

Through old southwestern humor, both literary and oral, runs a strong strain of humor involving cruelty and discomfiture. Country men in the rim play practical jokes, rough ones, with great relish. Practical jokes amount to nonverbal "lies," both when they work and when they misfire. Stories are told about practical joking, and in them people incorrectly evaluate what is going on and pay an embarrassing price for the error. No doubt such jokes are really played, but much of the fun is in the later narration of the victim's plight or of the biter's being bit.

Uncle Buddy Griffis, Lem's brother, told about jokes that the Griffis and Lee boys played on one another and on other boys. A favorite joke was to get some boy out near the Suwannee River bank so that a fellow perpetrator could leap out of the darkness with a sheet over his head, hooting and wailing like a haint. Once the Lee boys took another boy out into the woods, where one of the Lee brothers suddenly appeared in the dark carrying lighted corncobs in both hands and tucked into his boots. The frightened victim and the jokers ran away in real or mock terror, leaving Cliff Lee alone. When his corncobs burned out, he became scared himself and ran home. By the time he arrived he was more frightened than the victim and was covered with bruises, scratches, and insect bites.

Several of the rougher practical-joke stories hinge upon finding a corpse, usually that of a black person. According to Will Cox, a noted landowner once sent an injured black worker to a Clinch County physician. For some reason the worker tried to stab the doctor, who shot the black man dead, then packed the corpse in a crate and sent it to Valdosta. When the landowner received the crate at the train station, he pried it open and found the corpse with an attached note: "X, here's your nigger." Cox narrated another similar tale:

> 'Bout as good a joke as I ever pulled on anybody, Twin Trees Lumber Company built a mill in there around old Hopkins, and hauled her pine logs off. Hebard Cypress Company didn't cut the pine trees, they just cut the cypress, so Twin Trees bought the pine on these islands from 'em. They had a line, road come into the pond. They had a big pond dug, hit'd turn off around that big pond in there by that mill pond. So they had a dead nigger on the cab, had him covered up with a blanket, 'bout dark when they got in. And engineer when he come on in, told Hamp Mizell about it, the nigger on the cab, and told him to tell the night watchman, to go and call some people in there, take him off. So I was standing there, I told Mizell, I said, "No, don't tell him. I'll go tell him." So there while we's talking, the night watchman come by, and we told him that there was a man a-sleeping on the cab, wanted him to go wake him at four o'clock the next morning, he wanted to get out of there on the mail car going to the town. He said, "All right." And it was a-raining a little bit, rained all night most. So there *way* down yonder in that pond there next morning, pull that blanket off that man, tried to wake him up—it's a dead nigger under there, you know. We had to stay hid from that man for about a month along. He's mad enough to kill us.

The practical-joke story typically ends with the idea that the victim carries a grudge for some time afterwards.

Practical-joke humor in the rim is directly appreciated by country men and indirectly enjoyed, surreptitiously, by town men. Women enjoy practical-joke stories because they show that, as we suspected, men are just overgrown little boys with their pranks. Keeping men undersocialized has both advantages and drawbacks. An undersocialized man is unpredictable, sometimes brutal, but also controllable by cunning. He is less frightening if considered as a child. Women, then, see practical jokes as jokes on a group, men, as well as jokes on particular individuals, and their laughter may be gentle or bitter. Once

again, women's response to a form of masculine humor represents a
sizing-up of their own situation; it is refreshing to see men making
fools of each other, but the fact that they are wild enough to pull these
pranks sometimes makes daily life disconcerting.

Men tend to see practical jokes as jokes on individuals, unless the
person happens to be an outsider, one of "them," who needs to be
taken down a notch. In the latter case, men and women alike may be
victims, though among the in-group the victims are virtually always
male. Lem Griffis' trash-answers to the visitor's serious questions fell
into the area of verbal practical jokes:

> COTHRAN: Have you lived around here about all your life?
>
> GRIFFIS: Not yet.
>
> COTHRAN: Ohh! That's one on me!
>
> GRIFFIS: I was born here in a log cabin I helped my father to
> build.

Again the game was Arkansas Traveler. Griffis never showed any
actual hostility toward me as an individual, but he did not miss his
chance to strike at silly city-slickers through me. Willie Fred Roberts
also asserted control of the conversation by wrenching it from fact to
trash. When I earnestly asked him how one could tell when Lem
Griffis was "lying," he answered, "When he opened his mouth." Of
course in real daily life this was not true, but, when Lem was Lem the
Character, it certainly was.

Not all practical-joke stories have factual grounding. Lem Griffis
told the well-known traditional tale of the turtle put in a bragging
Texan's bed and explained as a Georgia bedbug. Lem cast himself as
the jokester and gave his fishing camp as the setting.

Rough stories are told about epic fits of anger and about foolish
members of other races. The humor once again hinges on pain or
discomfiture. My small amount of collecting among blacks in the rim
shows that such stories are not confined to whites, as demonstrated by
the third example to follow.

> GRIFFIS: There's a colored feller down hyer one day, down there
> standing on the banks of the river a-fishing, and he hooked one of
> them large Johnson bass, one of the blackfish we call 'em, we call
> 'em Johnson bass now [1966].
>
> COTHRAN: How come you call 'em that?
>
> GRIFFIS: Well, because they're black.
>
> COTHRAN: I see.
>
> GRIFFIS: And the fish was so heavy he couldn't pull it out a-back
> with his pole, so he was just a-walking backwards up the bank, drag-

ging him out, backwards went slick and his feet slip from under him, he fell in the river, turned his pole loose, and the fish went swimming, dragging the pole off, and this colored feller he crawled up on the bank, spit the water out of his mouth, and looked back at his pole a-being drug off by that fish, he said, "Now what I wanta know am dis: Is dis nigger fishing, or am dat fish niggering?"

According to Willie Fred Roberts, a man once came into Lem's camp with a black servant. The black was sent to the river for water, but he was afraid of an alligator floating there. The white man told him to go on back, because the alligator was just as scared of him as he was of it. "If that gator's as scared of me as I am of him," the black man answered, "Boss, that water ain't *fit* to drink." This is the only tale I collected that is even the least bit off-color. I do not doubt the existence of sexual and scatological tales in the trash of the rim, but men were unlikely to tell them to me.

Me, and Wesley Brown. I seen Wesley Brown and Mr. Sikes have one the prettiest foot races you ever seen. And Wesley Brown's a *big* man, and he run over a little sapling like one 'em little saplings out there, straddle it and went over it and bent it down, and Mr. Sikes was pushing him so close, Mr. Sikes run up on that sapling, Wesley Brown jump off that sapling. That sapling Mr. Sikes a-BIM! Mr. Sikes went to the commissary, told Mr. Hopkins, say, "Mr. Hopkins," say, "You'll have to hobble your niggers if you want me to catch 'em. That nigger like to kill me down there!" That sapling— that thing sure was funny. But boy, us was to have some times at Toledo.

The black narrator of this story, Kato Lambert, worked in the turpentine camps. Toledo was a tiny town in the rim.

Not surprisingly, tales about killings and lynchings may be told when talking trash. It is impossible to say now important they are in the repertory because they frequently incriminate the narrator and thus often may be kept secret from the outsider. At any rate, they are aggressive, fantastic, hyperbolic, and possess a macabre humor. Because they are intrinsically horror stories, the laughter they inspire may reflect considerable anxiety. These are hunting tales, after all, but the quarry is human. They combine fear of the dark, fear of surprise attack, fear that the customary rules of give-and-take may be violated by a hidden rapist or killer. In the whopper, tall tale, and ordinary experience story, all things are twisted out of shape and what cannot happen, happens. In the practical jokes and related tales the "boogers" leap out of the dark to frighten one half to death, and corpses appear where none ought to be. Trash is funny, sometimes innocently, sometimes in a way that strikes the outsider as cruel, weird, or both. Of course this kind of humor is not limited to the white South.

The killing and lynching tales that follow are tame compared to others I have heard elsewhere. Perhaps my storyteller, whose name must be omitted, left out the clinical details in deference to my age and sex. If the young lady wants stories, give her stories, and make them sensational, thrilling, but not revolting or indecent. The humor of the frontier, of the bush, of rims, raw places, slave quarters, and ghettos is a hard-bitten humor.

> I saw a lotta men get killed in there. Saw a fella X come in. A fella Y run a little drink stand and all there on the island. X's boy was standing right pretty close to that place, and his daddy was running the log engine. As he pulled in, Mr. Y picked up his gun, went to shooting at X's son. X stopped his engine, got off, and just walked right straight to him. Walked right up to him, took him by the shoulder, turned him around facing him, shot him right through the breast, killed him. Turn around, walked right back, got on his log engine, pulled it right on up, put his loads in the pass truck. Course X had killed a lotta men. He finally got killed right below the park, X did. Fella Z finally killed him. Shot him when he's on a wagon with a load of wood on the wagon. Z shot him right in the back, killed him.

All the characters in the foregoing story were whites.

> L sent one of his boys one time, my first wife's daddy, old man M, he was a boy, a nigger got sick working turpentine down there round his place, went and those still quarters was just about two miles from here back through these woods over here. So he put old man M on the horse and sent the nigger in, the nigger claimed he's sick. So he got the nigger home, he got off the horse, and that nigger got a piece of, picked up a piece of hoop iron, hit the boy, hit him all the way across the back with it, and hit at him twice, tried to kill him, tried to knock him off the horse, take horse away from him. The horse got away from him anyhow, carried the boy back in, and the old man got hold the horse, come back, nigger was gone. So that night, he got four more men with him. They went back over, and they hunt that nigger up. Hung him up in his shanty, took the old crossbeam that was in, just tied him up there, hung him round the neck where he'd die and left him hanging. Fella that run the turpentine still didn't know anything about it, you know, didn't make no noise all in the night, but he was a surprised man the next morning when them niggers found that other one down there hung up by the neck.

In the foregoing tale, unusually confused for this narrator, we see the practical-joke tale motif of finding the dead black.

Talking trash is done in prose, whether narrative like tall tales or descriptive like whoppers. Lem Griffis, however, regularly included in his performances some poems that he either created or re-created. The best known of these, "Hitler's Dream," was written in 1944, for a war-bond drive. Although there is no evidence that others learned this poem from his recitation and though other trash talkers used no poetry at all, I include it here partly because it has roots in tradition and partly because Griffis evidently felt that it belonged with his other humorous material. The poem is not completely original; it appears to be a minimal reworking of a World War I item called "Kaiser Bill's Dream," a fragment of which has been collected as a toast in Atlanta black tradition.[16] Chase mentions but does not print a prose form of the story collected in North Carolina.[17] The story attaches the motif of the man too wicked for both heaven and hell to Kaiser Wilhelm and then, at Griffis' hands, to Hitler.

> There's a story now current, though strange it may seem,
> Of that great man Hitler and his wonderful dream.
> Being tired of the Allies, he lay down in bed,
> And among the other things, he dreamed he was dead,
> And in a fine coffin was lying in state,
> With a guard of those Russians, the cause of his fate.
> He wasn't long dead, until he found to his cost,
> That his soul, like his soldiers, had surely been lost.
> On leaving the earth to heaven he went straight
> And, arriving up there, gave a knock at the gate.
> But St. Peter looked out, and a voice loud and clear
> Says, "Go on Hitler, we don't want you here."
> "Well," says Hitler, "that is very uncivil.
> I suppose after this I must go to the Devil."
> So he turned on his heel and off he did go
> At the top of his speed to regions below.
> When he got there he was filled with dismay.
> While waiting outside he heard Old Nick say
> To his imps, "Look here boys, I give you a warning.
> I'm expecting Hitler down here in the morning,
> But don't let him in, for to me it's quite clear
> He's a dangerous man, and we don't want him here.
> If once he gets in, there'll be no end of quarrels,
> And in fact I'm afraid he'd corrupt our good morals."
> "Oh Satan, my dear friend," Hitler then cried,

16. "Kaiser Bill's Dream" was collected by Rosa Jean Tomlinson from Mrs. Mary Minter, Atlanta, Georgia, 1967. Georgia Folklore Archives (Georgia State University), Number D36, ms. I would appreciate learning about other versions from readers.

17. Richard Chase, *Ameican Folk Tales and Songs* (New York, 1956), 21.

"Excuse me for listening while waiting outside.
If you do not admit me, where can I go?"
"Indeed," said the Devil, "I'll be damned if *I* know."
"Oh do let me in for I'm weary and cold."
Said Hitler, most anxious to enter Nick's fold.
"Let me sit in a corner, no matter how hot."
"No," said the Devil, "Most certainly not.
We do not admit people for riches or pelf.
Here's sulfur and matches. Make a hell for yourself,"
Then kicked Hitler out and vanished in smoke.
And just at that time Mister Adolf awoke.
He jumped out of bed in a shivering sweat.
He said, "Well, that dream I will never forget.
I won't go to heaven, I know very well,
But it's really too bad to be kicked out of hell."

Talking trash in the rim, then, is a diverse body of fantasy, narrated and acted out, linked together primarily by performance context and secondarily by thematic threads such as humor and aggressiveness. Cracker culture is damaged today: the open range no longer exists for hunting and stock grazing but has been converted into pine plantations and wildlife refuges. Talking trash, however, has not died. For the ordinary country man it is still a leisure-time activity, and at least one man, Willie Fred Roberts, seems destined to be a master narrator.

If talking trash is not "about" the events it superficially appears to narrate or describe, what *is* it about? Why does it promise to outlive the culture that cherished it? The answer, as hinted earlier, lies in its evaluative function.

Talking trash functions evaluatively in several ways. Some evaluations of human relationships and behavior may be found in the texts, which may praise or poke fun at characters. The talking itself, whatever the textual content, allows participants to make characters of themselves for the duration of the event. Trash is an acceptable fantasy realm in which a man can strut as a character, a real whopper of a self, while passing through illogic and fear to humor or excitement. Talking trash as a custom comes from a time when men did not work by the time clock but by cycles of nature. Talking trash today is an act of identification with that older way of life, and, whether one does it as a matter of course or as something of a rebellion, talking trash is a sneer at middle-class subservience to continuous gray work and a denial of that class's identification of the materially unproductive with the counterproductive.

Because talking trash exists in the expressive repertory of the community, one can characterize oneself either by liking and doing it *or* by rejecting it. As I have argued elsewhere, a person's refusal to practice a custom, or indeed any negative response to a custom, is an important datum, not a null in the data set.[18] A custom closely associated with a group to which one does not belong can still be a part of one's own expressive life, for one has to get along in the world with that other significant group. One has to size them up somehow. If to men talking trash is a means of expressing their "characters," to women talking trash represents the leisurely male life that supports the custom, of which they are well aware.

The evaluative function of talking trash comes out especially clearly in the points of contact between men's and women's language repertories. Women in the rim do not ordinarily narrate the stories and whoppers used by men, though they may use similes. Mrs. Barber was the only woman I met who can present men's stories at all well; she grew up as a tomboy among two good adult narrators, and she has extraordinary linguistic gifts. In her narrations, however, as previous examples show, the female point of view intrudes into her replication of men's stories.

The main thematic contact point between men's and women's storytelling, as one might expect, is humor about the opposite sex. Gibing stories are told both in single-sex groups and in mixed groups. Here women are not onlookers; they can match the men story for story.

I overheard several exchanges of gibing stories in mixed groups in the rim. A fundamentalist preacher once announced jovially to the gathering in the Clinch County cafe, where trash was regularly talked at the men's table, that he had preached a fine sermon telling women to obey their husbands. As the laughter subsided among the men, a gravel-voiced older woman at another table countered. She and her husband were driving down a back road one night and became stuck. He would not leave his precious car and ordered her to go for help through the dark, rain, and mud. She toiled a mile and a half to the nearest source of help, where, she said, "I was so give out and mad, I told 'em, 'Mr. Z is still stuck back there in a bog hole, and you can go pull him out if you want to. I don't care if you do or not. I don't care if you do or not.'" The preacher was definitely outgunned, as everyone in the cafe laughed.

On another occasion, a cafe regular was called to the phone to speak to his wife. He jokingly asked the gathering how she knew he was there. The owner responded that another man had once been called to the phone and wondered aloud who the caller might be. Others suggested that it might be his wife. Just as he took the receiver, lightning hit the line and knocked him flat. When he revived, he said,

18. Cothran, "Participation in Tradition."

"Yep, that was her." The story in context points directly at the fact that many women disapprove of their husbands' hanging around the cafe talking trash. And I suspect the men rather enjoy the disapproval; they can laugh about it, proving that the hens do not yet have them completely pecked.

The literature on tall tales documents the fact that women may contribute to men's tall-tale sessions even when they do not swap tales competitively.[19] In the rim, women may urge men to tell certain stories, generally ones making some man look foolish. They may add tag lines to stories: "Now wasn't that a crazy thing to do?" But there is more. Women may disappear into the kitchen and bang pans in an unmistakably disapproving manner while their husbands are narrating to that young woman from the city, who must be out of her mind to want to encourage that rubbish. Or they may go into another room and make no sound at all, creating a deafening volume of focused silence. This kind of behavior is part of the traditional orchestration of talking trash at home, not something merely opposed to talking trash. This fact cannot be emphasized enough: both man and woman in these instances are taking part in the talking of trash, one positively, one negatively. The woman's behavior is not "noise" damaging the session (although slamming screen doors do not facilitate transcription) but a predictable, significant part of the whole performance. It is data, not "bad rapport" with the wife on the collector's part.

Of course, a female fieldworker may be denied access to certain kinds of trash that a male fieldworker could record. This is a real problem, since we know a great deal about tall tales and relatively little yet about the forms that accompany them. But it is also the case that a female fieldworker on talking trash can get information, subtly, from the wives of narrators that a male could not get. Because this information is at the core of the tradition's social meaning rather than supplementary to it, we need it at least as much as we need a complete record of the kinds of language used in talking trash.

Thus, although I may have missed certain kinds of items, I obtained expressions of attitude toward the tradition. These expressions could be as loud as clattering saucepans, as clear as a note of laughter in the voice or as inaudible and yet as eloquent as a woman's listening to her husband's fancies. The best example of the latter in my data is worth giving at some length, as an example of the information a female fieldworker can obtain about this tradition and thus, I hope, as an encouragement to female folklorists to avoid limiting their work to all-female groups.

19. Herbert Halpert, "Tall Tales and Other Yarns from Alberta, Canada," *California Folklore Quarterly*, 4 (1945), 36.

The morning temperature had taken an unusual drop into the low twenties. I arrived at a dirt road branching off U.S. 1, in Charlton County, where an abandoned store stands near a house trailer and the Race Pond Church of God. I drove down this sandy road through a cattle break to my informants' house. The yard, a muddy area just beginning to dry out from earlier rain, had in it half a dozen mongrel dogs, a tiny puppy, a blue station wagon, a frowzy turkey, and numbers of ducks still asleep on one leg. Mrs. X let me into the house along with the cold puppy. When Mr. X finished reading a letter from his son in the military, we talked about hunting bears. His father was a bear hunter, so he grew up with the art. He preferred hunting bears to any other animal because "it tests your nerve" to crawl through the brush after a bear, hearing it blowing, puffing, and popping its teeth. We talked about kinds of dogs and methods of hunting. Mr. X liked to let the bear come directly at him so he could kill it with one point-blank blast. "If you miss, you're in trouble," I remarked. "You don't belong to miss," Mr. X smiled, and his wife repeated this, also smiling. He talked about the biggest bear he ever killed, the most he ever killed in one day, the meanest one he ever faced, the closest he ever came to being killed.

Once he hunted a bear at night. "That was silly," said his wife, casually. He had a two-cell flashlight, though. "That was silly, too." She had been sitting so as to form a triangle with Mr. X and me; as she evaluated his night hunt, she moved to sit behind him and to his right, so that I could easily see her face but he could not—not without turning his attention from me and thus physically requesting her response. What was she saying, contrapuntal to his narration, with body and face? Why did she shift from triangular opposition to him and me into a position of solidarity with me such that he would have to shift posture rudely in order to break it up? In words I can only crudely approximate her communication, for it was not coded in words and did not have to be so coded. Essentially, having decided to define me as "fellow woman" rather than as "encourager of foolishness," she was saying to and with me something like this: "Isn't he a hell of a wild old boy, and what's there to do besides bear it, banter with it, and even love it?" At any rate, Mr. X eventually found himself five feet from the bear only to find that it was not nearly as dead as he had supposed it to be. If there was ever a multifunctional grin, it was the one on my face at that moment, a grin for either of them and for both.

The previous day I had met Mrs. X alone when I first went to the house looking for her husband. I said I understood her husband hunted bears. "A little," she half-smiled, eyes cutting back-and-to, "a little." Mr. X's response to the same question the following day was linguistically identical, but his understatement, belied by his straight-forward glance, was that of trash-talking humorous modesty. Hers had been an understatement of the pride, wonderment, and humor of one who does a great deal of humoring. The entire interview lasted only twenty minutes, because Mr. X had to attend a funeral. His tales were typical; by that time in the fieldwork few textual surprises remained. Indeed there cannot be many textual surprises for the regular talkers of trash. What matters is the talking, the style with which it is done, and the company with whom it is done. The data that turned out to matter most came from moments conveying the feelings men have for men and the natural world and the feelings men and women have for one another—as in Mrs. X's mostly silent commentary not just upon the tales but upon a lifetime and a culture, unelicitable commentary given unelicited to another southern woman.[20]

20. There is probably something comparable to talking trash among women. See Kay L. Cothran, "Women's Tall Tales: A Problem in the Social Structure of Fantasy," *St. Andrews Review*, 2 (Fall and Winter, 1972), 21–27.

SYMBIOSIS OF JOKE AND LEGEND: A CASE OF CONVERSATIONAL FOLKLORE

Linda Dégh

It required a bilingual folklorist from a similar ethnic background who had wide acquaintance with published folk-narrative materials and long experience in fieldwork to write this sensitive analysis of the narrative art of Steve and Ida Boda, Hungarian-speaking immigrants in the Calumet Region of Northern Illinois and Indiana. But even the highly respected ethnic folk scholar Linda Dégh found that it was the storytellers themselves, over a period of several years, who brought her to understand the "symbiosis" of two different story types. Dégh uses this biological term to characterize the husband's humorous narrations and the wife's supernatural stories as not only coexisting but supporting each other in a conversational context.

While the story genres in the two informants' repertoires are listed, and several individual tales are furnished with type and motif numbers or references to analogues, such conventional annotations are subordinated to a close analysis of context, audience, and the interaction of the two star performers. Since the reported conversations were carried out in Hungarian, or in a mixture of Hungarian and English, the American reader is introduced in the essay to the "profoundly harmonious haven" of an ethnic household in the midst of a decaying industrial region. The importance of the quoted transcripts of conversations in the Boda home lies not in the individual stories that can be isolated and identified but in the smooth interplay of husband and wife, teller and audience, jokester and legend-teller, believers in the extranormal and skeptics. Their traditional texts, therefore, have meaning only in the proper traditional context.

Dégh gives a richly detailed description of the general setting in which the symbiosis occurs, including biographies of the married couple, the layout and use of their living space, traditions of hospitality, interaction with relatives and friends, foods, religious practice, and the role of mass media and popular culture. Within this larger scene is described the micro-context of daily conversations spiced with frequent and repeated stories. It would be instructive at this point for the reader to look again at Richard M. Dorson's essay that began this section, noting the much sketchier handling of context and the emphasis on collected texts, including a variant of the tale type "Clothing Caught in Graveyard" (see Dégh's footnote 10). Dorson, however, as we have observed, departed from mostly textual collecting since 1947; he is quoted at the beginning of Dégh's article because he was project director for

Indiana University's Folklore Institute research in the Calumet Region (an endeavor which emphasized the total context of folklore) and because this essay was published in a book of studies honoring him upon his sixtieth birthday.

The production of such a study at Indiana University where Stith Thompson led an important comparative school of folklorists for many years has almost symbolic importance, indicating .the "arrival" of the new contextual approach. At the same time, Dégh's continuing reliance on type and motif references might signal a symbiosis of the two seemingly opposed scholarly approaches to folk narrative research.

"The culture of Gary-East Chicago is largely an oral culture, in the sense that talk flows freely. Television has not displaced conversation."

(R. M. Dorson, "Is There a Folk in the City?" *Journal of American Folklore* 83 (1970):209.)

1.

IT WAS DECEMBER OF 1964 when I first met Steve Boda and his wife Ida. This was on my second field trip to the Calumet Region where I was collecting materials on Hungarian immigrant culture.[1] I visited the Boda couple following the advice of several community members. Still somewhat unclear about the ways, goals and potentials of research among ethnics in a complex, urban-industrial area, I was looking for tellers of stories in the way traditional folklorists had for the past century and a half. Entering the neat home of the Bodas I found not only the storytellers I wanted but also the direction I needed in researching Hungarian-American ethnic life. They turned out to be the most authentic and versatile guides to ethnicity, interethnic relations, the sustenance of traditions of adaptation, as well as the ensuing formulation of new folklore. I also learned from them the importance of carefully observing the story-performance that flowed naturally in their home. The Bodas led me to some theoretical conclusions concerning the specific nature of the folk legend.[2]

1. For summary statements of my participation in the Ethnic Research Survey of Northwest Indiana see: Linda Dégh, "Survival and Revival of European Folk Cultures in America," *Ethnologia Europea* 2–3 (1968–1969):97–107; Richard M. Dorson, "The Ethnic Research Survey of Northwest Indiana," *Kontakte und Grenzen—Probleme der Volks-, Kultur- und Sozialforschung. Festscrift für Gerhard Heilfurth zum 60. Geburtstag.* (Göttingen: Otto Schwartz, 1969), pp. 65–69.

2. See my earlier publication of a transcript of a legend-telling session: Linda Dégh and Andrew Vázsonyi, "Legend and Belief," *Genre* 4 (1971):289–94; and more particularly in "The Dialectics of the Legend," *Folklore Preprint Series* 1 (1973): on pp. 29–30 we referred to the Boda couple's example in describing the legend-polemy.

The situation I encountered on this first visit remained similar to those of visits I made for eight subsequent years. The only difference was seasonal change. The first visit came during an unusually cold winter. The lawn that in the summer months displayed the plastic statue of a sitting deer and a grazing fawn was frozen gray in front of the fenced yard. The previous flower garden and the vegetable patch so characteristic of Hungarian peasant immigrant homes[3] was reduced to dry twigs and empty shells. The plastic wrappings on the rosebushes and the barren fruit trees rattled in the icy wind under the leaden sky, forcing me to hasten towards the glass door on the side of the house which was coated with the vapor of kitchen steam, cigarette smoke and warm air from the oil furnace. The main entrance of the spacious red brick house was permanently blocked from the inside by a large buffet, the centerpiece of the front room used only on extraordinary festive occasions, such as receiving guests after family weddings or funerals.

The side door yielded immediately to my knocking and our host opened it, revealing the entire living space of the residents. This was the kitchen in which guests were received with warm hospitality and treated to food and drinks spiced with entertaining stories. But even on the rare occasions when the Bodas expected no visitors, the kitchen would be their living quarter until the late hours when they would retire to their bedroom, overcrowded with two large beds, two bed-stands, a sofa and a vanity. The bedroom wall was covered with landscape paintings and rustic old country scenes by an artist who was a relative of Aunt Ida who also "made it" in America.

Entering the kitchen, the visitor can see two other doors. One leads to the bathroom, conveniently located between the kitchen range and a large refrigerator, the other leads through a small passage to the living room, the bedroom and a staircase to the basement. The pantry is the only room in the finished basement that is in active use. Two other rooms had been leased to two working men. The pantry has a prominent role in food provisions as well as in the manifestation of loyalty to the old country and the reinforcement of intergroup relations. The products of the garden are lined up on the shelves, canned or dried by Aunt Ida, awaiting consumption. The seeds of special flowers and herbs are carefully stored for the next season and for exchange. There is a ring of procurement and exchange of the cherished *Székely* spices that are proudly distinguished from the common Hungarian kinds. The Bodas are prominent artists of the *Székely* cuisine, one of the symbols of ethnic solidarity in the old country as

---

3. Dégh, "Survival and Revival," p. 140.

well as in America. Whoever visits the homeland, the *Székelyföld*[4] allotted to Romania after World War I, must bring replenishment for the transplanted stock of savory, penny royal, tarragon, sweet basil, dill or anise. Seeds are also sent by mail, enclosed in ordinary letters, and the *Székely* clan within the Calumet Hungarian enclave keeps up a lively network of barter and mutual food sampling, in order to check out the best kinds for cultivation. Uncle Steve is as active in ethnic cookery as his wife. A former butcher, he still is the foremost authority in sausage making, and his masterpieces—home smoked bacon, ham and sausage—are hung from the pantry ceiling in an orderly row.

The kitchen is large, with sparkling white walls, ruffled curtains, furniture and cabinets, and stainless steel pots and pans. There is not much room to move around. A large oblong table occupies the main space in the center of the room, surrounded by chairs. The main chair is occupied by Uncle Steve at the head of the table, opposite the entrance door, with a white cupboard behind him and the bathroom door at his right. A chain smoker, Uncle Steve has a large ashtray in front of him and several packs of Lucky Strike cigarettes. Aunt Ida's place is before the refrigerator, the electric range and the sink, so that she can perform her kitchen duties with ease while participating in the conversation. She is a virtuoso in fixing delicacies quickly. If old friends arrive, it is her habit to start cooking. "I'm sure you are hungry," she says, "how about a nice pancake?" and without waiting for the answer she sets to work.

At the time of my first visit the couple was alone. The small stout bald man behind the table started to talk without being asked. Joke telling was a natural pastime for him. He was known to the neighborhood and among his peer group as a funny man who never missed an opportunity to crack a joke, or to make jocular remarks about anything that came to his attention. He introduced himself to me as a jokester as soon as I took off my coat and sat down.

MR. B.: "I bet[5] you haven't heard about that man here . . . he started to drink, got into real bad ways. His wife divorced him . . .

MRS. B.: That made bad worse, indeed, for him.

4. The Székely-land is located in southeast Transylvania. For the history of this Hungarian ethnic culture see Linda Dégh, *Folktales and Society* (Bloomington: Indiana University Press, 1969), pp. 3–4.

5. This as well as all following narratives and statements were told in Hungarian, interspersed with occasional English words. In my translation I tried to follow the original as closely as possibe and italicized the English words to show the variable degree of adaptation of loanwords in the different texts. The Bodas spoke a very captivating, archaic Székely dialect but used many English terms, as is typical of the industrial regions of the United States. In common speech as well as in folklore texts their Hungarian was mixed mostly with distorted English loanwords, as is usual within the peer group.

MR. B.: Two years later he went to see the *Reverend: 'Father,'* he says, 'you know what? I want to come back to the Church. I want to join in again.' 'How come? I haven't seen you for two years . . . you drank.' 'Yes, I did. But now I am good, I don't drink anymore.' So the Reverend tells him: '*All right.* I take you back. But go home first and come back again in a week. I will examine you from the Bible and I will see if you haven't forgotten your religion. If you can answer my questions, I will take you back.' So it happened. The man goes back to the Father, back to the minister, and the minister tells him: 'Where was Jesus Christ born?' And he says: 'In Pittsburgh.' 'In Pittsburgh?' 'Oh,' he says, 'hold it, I know! He was born in Bethlehem, *yes*,' he says, '*sorry*, I knew he was born someplace in Pennsylvania. Pittsburgh, or Bethlehem, I mixed up the two cities. I wanted to say Bethlehem.' He says, 'Go home, get out of here, go home, you do not belong here.' But the man insisted, 'I tell ya, I knew he was born in Pennsylvania, I just mixed up Pittsburgh with Bethlehem.' [He gives a big laugh and Mrs. B. heartily seconds.] But the Reverend did not take it, *no*. [Chuckle] 'Go home. Pittsburgh, not Bethlehem, you fool!' 'Sorry, I said I thought it was Pittsburgh but I knew it was in Pennsylvania.' [The couple laugh together.] *Yeah.* The Reverend did not take him back, *no*. The fool! This really has happened. The man was a Hungarian.

This brief anecdote had a tremendous effect on Aunt Ida. She could not stop laughing and could hardly catch her breath. She finally rose to her feet and reached out to tear a paper towel from the roll on the wall and wiped her eyes, and Uncle Steve was ready for some more. This time he did not continue with his favorite stories of local numskulls he had known, but picked one of his set of anticlerical jests. By staying with the topic of church and clergyman, he wanted to introduce himself as a critic of bigotry and hypocrisy. He went on, with a direct question:

MR. B.: Do you go to *church* every Sunday? [pointing at his wife] 'cause she does.

This was an unnecessary question. He knew that I met his wife through the minister of the Hungarian Presbyterian Church in Indiana Harbor, the most durable ethnic institution in the region. But Uncle Steve did not really expect an answer. He turned immediately to his view on churchmen. In later years I heard his argument many times, addressed to his churchgoing wife and her female friends of different denominations, as garnishings to his jokes about religious orders. These jokes usually emphasizing the mercenariness, greed, adulterous sex life, and unbecoming behavior of clergymen, expressed his reasons for anticlericalism. This time, he wanted to tell me why he does not attend the services with his wife:

> MR. B.: I am an honest man. I never took what did not belong to me. I believe in God, but I do not believe in going to church.[6] Still I have got as much *chance* to go to heaven as my wife. That's what I told this old *Reverend* who is now retired. And guess what did he say? '*Listen,*' so he says, 'Uncle Steve, you won't be admitted to heaven if you don't pay your dues to the Church.' Hey, that's the pastor, eh? Wise guy, *see*? Main thing I pay my dues to the church. *No sir.*

This was more than Aunt Ida could bear.

> MRS. B.: You know what? Go and get a piece of sausage. We'll talk while you are gone, *okay*? Bring a piece of sausage so that I can roast it. Yes, because we have real good smoked sausage. Real, home made, nothing you can buy in Bloomington groceries. We make it. I want to make a little *lunch* . . .

But Uncle Steve was hard to stop, once he was talking. In view of Aunt Ida's interjected comments and big belly laughs, I did not get the impression that she really wanted to stop him. I realized much later that her embarrassment was a pretense, a part she played in supporting his joke-telling. This time she had to go get the sausage from the pantry herself.

> MR. B.: This is a good *business*. The church, I mean. They want to grab everything they can. And they sure can as long as you are concerned with the thereafter. When I was in the hospital, the *nurse* asked me right away, '*Are you Catholic*?' 'No,' says I, '*I am re-tired.*' The Catholic Heaven isn't any better than the other.
>
> MRS. B.: [pointing to the tape recorder] Stop that, will you? Every word you say is recorded. Take care.
>
> MR. B.: Why should I? I don't mind. This doesn't kill me.

With a shrug he began to tell about a compatriot who became a Pentecostal minister:

> MR. B.: Smart man, I tell ya. He came to America long ago, he still was a child. They took him to Ohio. Now, he has an *office*, you

6. The religious belief of this rational thinker became apparent to me years later. At that time, he was seriously ill and underwent treatment in the hospital for seven weeks. After his recovery, on returning to his home and regular audience, he repeatedly told the story of his miraculous cure, without medicine. When the nurse brought him his regular medicine, God whispered to him, "Don't take the pill." And God healed him in His way. Uncle Steve was as distrustful of doctors as of clergymen. He did not believe in pills or in diets, he preferred traditional home remedies. He refused to eat the hospital food and had his wife bring his meals.

know, they send him letters, lined with twenty dollars, ten dollars. Yeah. Joe, my buddy told him, 'Look. You are a smart guy, that I can see. Do you really believe what you preach? You don't really believe, do you?' You know, this man was speaking in tongues. He can speak all tongues of the world—oh, hell. He is just talking, talking, talking and the folks just listening, listening, listening. 'And do you really believe what you tell them?' my buddy, Joe asked him. 'I bet, you don't.' But he makes big money. His son is a *foot doctor, a specialist*. And he's got a *home* worth forty thousand dollars, a new home. He is a millionaire, *sure*. Needn't work. He only talks. He can talk German too and these guys listen to him. They give him one percent of what they make. Those rich people in Akron, Ohio, there are those rich *tire companies*. Fifty-sixty thousand people work there; they make fifty-sixty thousand dollars on them. They all give to the church, yeah. Because he is a smart guy, you know, he knows how to talk to people and he milks them. The fools. All he does is, he preaches in church once a week, on Sunday, and then talks for half an hour on the *radio*. That's all he does. *You see?* Smart man.

By this time, Aunt Ida had fixed the sausage and we ate. But there was one more story to put down churchmen and exhaust the topic. This time it was Aunt Ida who reminded her husband:

MRS. B.: Why don't you tell how it was when you went to Heaven?

MR. B.: Ah, what?

MRS. B.: How did you bow to St. Peter?

MR. B.: Oh, that? The one *Reverend* said? Shall I tell it all?

MRS. B.: *Why, sure.*

MR. B.: *Okay.* Well, you know *Reverend* M. was from Transylvania. You know? We met at the *courthouse*, we had some *business* to settle and then we had a drink. There was another man there and we were drinking with the minister, you know. And he said: 'Now I'll leave you, but I'll tell you something before I go, *Mr. Boda.* You will never go to Heaven.' 'I won't? Why not?' 'Why not? Do you want to know why not? *Listen.* When your spirit goes up there, you go and you knock on the door of St. Peter [he knocks on the table three times], you say: "I am here, István Boda from earth, please, let me in." 'But,' he says, 'we cannot go there just like this, holding up our head high and proud and with a cigar in our mouth. Now, we must bow there, like this: 'I wish you a good day, Sir, St. Peter.' And when St. Peter will see you there, will see your bald head, he will believe that you went with your arse first. He will kick you so hard that you fall down to hell,' So. The minister said that. Just him, don't forget it.

MRS. B.: Well, you did not make an obeisance in greetings. [Chuckles]

MR. B.: Oh yes, I did, Didn't I greet him? And he told me not to forget to go to church on Sunday. I said. 'Sure, I'll go. You don't believe yourself. Why should I believe if you don't? What are you talking about?'

At this point the telephone interrupted the conversation. It did not take a minute and Aunt Ida excitedly hastened to the bedroom to turn on the television. The caller was Lizzie, a young neighbor woman who said that a pilot who talked to Martians was on the screen, telling about his experience. Unfortunately, the show was over by the time Ida turned the TV on and we never could learn what the planet-men said when their space ship made a crash landing near the Little Calumet River. However, this incident diverted the trail of our talk.

MRS. B.: I wish she had called sooner.

[I wanted to know what language the pilot could communicate with the Martians.]

MRS. B.: This is no problem at all. They had been in touch for so long through signaling that they can make themselves understood in English. Why couldn't Liz call earlier? She was too excited. What bothers me is that swampy place at the river . . . why, all strange things happen there?

[I ventured a question here, being ignorant of strange happenings in the area.]

MR. B.: [airily] No strange things ever happened there. There are some liars who try to scare others and she falls for that sort of thing. I've been on the road night after night but never saw a ghost. You and your friends!

MRS. B.: Don't say that. How about the house that burned down with the woman inside? Didn't Mr. Kiss the coalman see her in white, rocking her baby on the *porch?* And didn't your godson (a *police officer*) tell you about the woman who was killed by her husband right there? Wasn't it just seven years this *Halloween?* Don't you remember how many people waited out there to see her appear on the anniversary of the murder? The *policeman* saw her.[7]

MR. B.: They are all crazy like you and your lady friends.

MRS. B.: Here we go again! Look. You never believed us when we heard my *sister* cry . . . [Here she seemed to address herself entirely

7. The Vanishing Hitchhiker legend is generally known and localized to this area by residents of the Calumet Region. In 1965, Halloween was the time when the ghost was expected to appear because it was the seventh year of her death. Police had to disperse the cars of experience-hunters who blocked the highway from traffic. See the formulation of the legend by Mexican residents of the Region in Philip Brandt George, "The Ghost of Cline Avenue: 'La Llorona' in the Calumet Region," *Indiana Folklore* 5 (1972):56–91.

to me.] The only daughter of my *sister* died. And when she died, she was laid out at McGuan's[8] . . . there were four of us here in the kitchen. We fixed *lunch*. That the guests come, the relatives, so . . . everything was here. We ran to this door. There were four of us. We ran to that door; nobody there, nobody. *Well*, my *sister* came back later and we told her how much she was crying, it was her voice, we all recognized it . . . One was her daughter-in-law, the other was my daughter, my other sister and myself. There were four of us. We ran from one door to the other and nobody was there. When she came back: 'No,' she said, 'I wasn't here, I was at the *undertaker*, we had *pictures* taken.' Well, it was the spirit that cried just like my *sister*.

Mr. B.: Well, I can't believe this. No, I can't . . .

Mrs. B.: Don't say that because there were four of us. We are four who say it, all four of us ran to the door. If it would be only for me, they could call me a fool, or that I am raving, but all four of us ran; my daughter, my *sister*, we all heard her crying. And she was nowhere. This is something, a wonder . . .

Mr. B.: Nothing . . . [gesture of dismissal]

Mrs. B.: We should have written somewhere, to someone who understands this, who looks into such matters.

Mr. B.: Cheaters!

Mrs. B.: And I tell you another thing. When this girl died, it was so sudden. We celebrated March fifteenth in *church*.[9] While the program was on, they wanted me on the *telephone*. We didn't realize she was that sick. It came as a shock to me. The *Reverend* asked me if I wanted to make the announcement now or after the program? 'No,' I said, 'we should not make such an *excitement*, please, announce it after it's over.' Later we all went to the *home* of my *sister* to pay our respects. As we all were there, suddenly the door quietly opens and then nicely closes again. We go to the door, maybe someone is there? *Nobody*. No one . . .

Mr. B.: It was imagination.

Mrs. B.: *No, no, no, no!* It opened and closed.

Mr. B.: I don't believe in this.

Mrs. B.: *Now, wait a minute!* And before Betty died, some two weeks before, she was still at home, there was a sudden clattering sound in the house at night. My sister believed that the pastry board fell off the wall. But next morning the board was still on the wall, only that loud sound . . . Betty too . . . '*Mother*, what was it, *mother*? What was it?' And she said: '*I don't know*, maybe the

8. The local funeral parlor of Thomas McGuan.

9. National day of the Hungarian nation, commemorating the declaration of independence from Austria in 1848.

pastry board fell down!' And this clattering sound occurred two weeks before Betty died. All this . . . then . . . was related . . . I mean, this is really true. This is all true, everything I said . . .

Mr. B.: *Baloney.* They were dreaming.

Mrs. B.: There must be something. Really, this spirit thing. There is such a thing. We heard her cry, scream, she cried so much. Where and who did it? It must have been her ghost. I don't know how it can appear in body, in shape that I haven't seen. But in sound . . . Yes, I can prove it, we heard the voice clearly . . .

Mr. B.: How can somebody cry without having a body?

Mrs. B.: Come now. My sister can also prove it. *Yes.* We knew that *medium* in Hammond. She called the spirit: 'Come, my dear spirit, come, my dear spirit,' she said, she talked nicely to the spirit, and everything. Well, once it really came. We were seven around the table and our hands had to touch. Once then, the table started to rise . . .

Mr. B.: Someone was pushing, right?

Mrs. B.: Oh *no, no, no-no-no,* nobody was there. We touched the edge of the table. We wanted to prove that it is true, but a man didn't believe. She said then: 'Dear Spirit, if you are here, show us whom you don't like and press him against the wall.' Well, once the table moved right against the wall pushing the man to the wall. He was so scared that he ran away. I jumped up on the bed, didn't know how to flee, we were all scared, because the table was dancing. It was of fine wood, my grandpa made it. I'm telling you, this was true. Where is the spirit then? It must be somewhere. It must live some place. *My sister* cried, you see, who else could it be once she was not here?

Mr. B.: This is just a joke. Someone tried to trick you like it was with those two in our home town, Remember? One told the other: 'You know what? I bet you would not dare to go to the cemetery' . . . The *jackass* believed in ghosts.

Mrs. B.: *Ya,* midnight, twelve o'clock. *Yeah,* he said, 'Sure I dare.' And he took off and went to the cemetery when the clock struck twelve. And the other followed him and stuck the tail of his jacket with his knife to a grave so he could not move from there. He thought the ghost had caught[10] him.

Mr. B.: *See,* and he died of the scare. This was true.

Mrs. B.: Yeah. But his friend did it as a practical joke to . . .

Mr. B.: Look, I don't believe in ghosts and the likes but I would not go to the cemetery at midnight. Not that I would be afraid . . . No, I wouldn't go.

Mrs. B.: The devil wouldn't take you [chuckles].

10. Type 1676B, "Clothing Caught in Graveyard."

Mr. B.: Sure. You heard of the devil carrying the man on his back to hell? And the devil carries him and they are on their way. And there they meet the neighbor of this *Székely góbé*.[11] The neighbor tells him: 'How are you, friend, neighbor?' And he says: 'I could be worse than that.' And he says: 'How on earth could you be worse than that? Isn't it that the devil takes you to Hell?' 'Oh, I would be much worse if I had to carry the devil on my back to Hell. [laughs] I would be much worse!'

With this story Uncle Steve managed to engineer the conversation back to his humorous favorites while Aunt Ida modestly withdrew and switched from her role as active legend teller back to that of member of the anecdote-audience.

This small sample from the first tape recorded by the Bodas, is representative of their performance and interaction, and it displays their distinctive repertoires. During subsequent years I had many occasions to observe the Boda couple in different performance situations. I watched them at this first encounter, as they introduced themselves to me, heard them later perform for diverse audiences, and could observe them as their houseguest when no one was around and they recounted only to each other. I have re-recorded the stories several times under different *ad hoc*, contrived conditions and could determine the permanent and transient pieces of their repertoire, the new acquisitions as well as the rejections. No matter what the actual conditions were, there was a conspicuous interdependence in the conversational performance between the husband and wife. They seemed to be engaged in an everlasting, never-to-be-resolved debate, caused by two conflicting ideologies manifested by a rationalistic joke teller and a mystic-transcendentalist legend teller. Each time narration was cooperative; they gave cues to each other like actors in a theatrical play, they reacted with rebuttal or with supportive comments to each other's statements. Jokes and legends were alternately and interdependently told and it was seldom that one spoke up while the other was absent. This relationship can be called *symbiotic*. By this I do not mean only that jokes and legends get on well together under the same roof but also that they provide the necessary living conditions for each other.

2.

Usually Uncle Steve started to tell some stories—generally a string of anecdotes of some sort—until the opportunity came for Aunt Ida to take the lead. His telling aimed at entertaining, hers at stimulating

11. According to Hungarian folk concept Székelys are born tricksters: the "*góbé*" is the hero of many anecdotes.

discussion of extranormal[12] events. He liked to laugh and make other people laugh at comic situations not necessarily topical; she liked to report on supernatural incidents that captured her attention in normal daily life, made her wonder and eventually led to the legends she told. Steve and Ida Boda have been married for over fifty years and narration has always been part of their life together. No matter how different their personalities and interests, they could always reconcile conflicting ideas through discussing their differences in terms of stories. Uncle Steve was a carefree, happy-go-lucky man who liked his work, his food and his booze, and resolved his problems in life by a strong sense of humor. Whatever happened to him, no matter how disadvantageous it looked, he made it appear funny. It was not always others who played the dupe in his stories; he did not spare himself from ridicule. One of his funniest stories is about how his driver's license was suspended because of drunken driving on the wrong side of the highway. Even his arrest sounded like a hilarious experience. If one can believe relatives, friends and neighbors, Uncle Steve's easygoing way caused him much trouble and his wife, spoiling him immensely, often came to his rescue. She, on the other hand, was always the one who cared and worried, who saw the dark shades and the drama behind the facts of life. The loyal belief in traditional superstitions which she inherited from her beloved mother and grandmother obtained reinforcement through her friends with whom she talked of supernatural encounters, ominous predictions, dreams, signs and the horrors of violent death. Uncle Steve did not need to search for inspiration or assurance from others. He rather needed a stage on which he could play his role. People came to hear him and offered him raw materials to elaborate. Aunt Ida, on the other hand, went out of her way to find those who shared her interest, who told her new stories that she could add to her corpus, to take home and tell. The couple compared notes on new acquisitions, providing the necessary reactions: objection, rebuttal, banter, mockery on his part; embarrassment, astonishment, forgiveness, alleviation, hearty laughter on her part. This set a well-rehearsed pattern to be staged for their audience. If one can say that Steve Boda was the member of a joke-conduit and Ida Boda was the member of a legend-conduit,[13] one can also say that both acquired their materials in the specific way jokes and legends are learned in their cultural setting: the Székely ethnic was their donor

12. For the introduction of the term "extranormal" see Dégh and Vázsonyi, "Dialectics," p. 50.

13. For the description of the conduit see Linda Dégh and Andrew Vázsnoyi, "Hypothesis of Multi-Conduit Transmission in Folklore" in *Folklore Performance and Communication*, ed. D. Ben-Amos and K. S. Goldstein (The Hague: Mouton, 1975), pp. 211–14.

culture, just as its Calumet-colony became its current base. Each repertoire shows the chronology of its bearer's life history.

This life history is simple. It is the success story of modest working men who made the transition from a rural-peasant to an urban-industrial way of life, while accommodating their ethnic loyalties to a multi-ethnic environment. Steve and Ida Boda were born and raised in Udvarhely County, the very heart of Protestant *Székelyföld*. They were married in their home village and came to the United States with their small daughter in 1924. They were twenty-six and twenty-one at the time. For them, America was not a new adventure. Steve came first in 1921, to "look around" and then returned for his bride and together they joined a colony of compatriots who had arrived earlier. The Székelys, born entrepreneurs whose mass emigrations have been known to historians since the sixteenth century, were also among the earliest Hungarians who made the trip to America in search of labor.[14] Aunt Ida's grandfather tried his luck in the oilfields in the 1880s, her father Lajos Ferencz, worked from 1905 to 1910 at Pullman. He became a successful farmer in his homeland, adding more acres to his estate after three consecutive work periods in the South Chicago mills. Of his seven children only two remained home, the others settled in the Gary-Chicago area and raised their children and grandchildren to become prosperous Székely-Americans with strong loyalties to both the original and the adopted country. This double loyalty remains unchanged in the upcoming generation despite gradual loss of competence in the old cultural values. Kinship ties persist as a cohesive force in the ethnic community and lend respectability to the Boda couple.

In 1963 Uncle Steve retired from Inland Steel after twenty-nine years of labor. By this time his home was paid for in full, and he could also buy a lot for a family home for their daughter, Julie, and help build it. His income from pension, social security, and four rented rooms totalled $500 per month; enough for a comfortable life. The household budget allowed the luxurious cookery, feasting and generous treatment of guests—essential to the concept of the good life for the Boda couple. It also included obligations: sending packages to relatives in the old country, gift-giving to relatives and friends here at birthdays, namedays, Christmas or other occasions, and charities channeled through the ethnic church. Even extra hobbies for Mrs. Boda, playing bingo once a week and going to sales, could not exhaust the monthly income.

The Boda home, the permanent stage of story-performance, was located on the main street of the original Hungarian ethnic enclave of

14. Dégh, *Folktales*, p. 30.

Indiana Harbor. The audience of the storytelling was variable with a solid-core membership consisting of visitors who can be classified according to their frequency of their visits: (1) neighbors, (2) relatives, (3) friends within the local ethnic community, (4) old friends outside the local community.

(1) The primary audience. At the time of my fieldwork there were just a few Hungarian families living within walking distance: two old Székely couples, a half-blind widow, a young woman married to a Slovak, and a Slovak woman who spoke fluent Hungarian. Only two blocks away there was also a Hungarian couple, owners of a grocery store that catered to the needs of Mexican customers. But these were not the only steady neighborhood visitors, who could drop in any time of the day. There were Polish, Croatian, German, and also two Italian neighbors who regularly came by, in addition to the Mexican friends of the Bodas living further down the street. It did not make much difference who was what; the ethnic residents spoke the same broken English slang learned and homogenized in the Calumet mills, stores and streets. The immigrant generation retained its lifestyle, the multi-ethnic neighborhood of the Bodas shared their experience and world view, even if their American-born children and grandchildren departed from it. The Boda home was an ideal place to exchange common experiences. The favorites, however, were the Mexicans, the latest arrivals. They looked with respect at the Bodas who started their American career as they had—forty years ago. The old couple had a weakness for the Mexicans and they admired their cleanliness, modesty and hard work, which corresponded to their own inherited ethos. If there were no Hungarian refugees in need, they rented rooms to Mexican newcomers for a nominal fee. Uncle Steve used his old connections to get them jobs, Aunt Ida cooked for them, and when they decided to settle for good, bringing wife and children from Mexico, the Bodas babysat for them. Thus, neighbors were the most frequent casual visitors and listeners to legends and jokes. Women brought a sample of a new pastry recipe or a cut from a meat dish to taste, borrowed cooking ingredients, kitchen utensils, asked for some advice or just stayed to chat. Men more often came to listen and sit silently. The neighborhood relationship of the Boda couple was very similar to that of old world peasant narrators.

(2) The second class of visitors consisted of members of the family. For Székelys the degree of respectability still depends on the size and strength of a clan. The Boda-Ferencz kinship has a large American branch including blood and affiliated kins in different degrees, several of whom eventually came by for a visit on Sunday, holidays or after the working hours. Drawing up a family tree of Aunt Ida's lineage, I

noted forty out of seventy-one contemporaries who kept in touch, depending on their time and the driving distance.

(3) Friends within the local ethnic community were largely identical with the members of the ethnic church and the different action-groups, composed mostly of Aunt Ida's women-friends, who shared her fascination with the supernatural. These women were active in helping the church with bake sales. During noodle- or sausage-making in the church basement, they liked to exchange extranormal experiences. If they came for a visit to the home in connection with some project, legends were passed on in the atmosphere of an enjoyable controversy stimulated by Uncle Steve's disparaging remarks accompanied by seconding husbands.

(4) Old friends who moved away from the Calumet Region were occasional guests: former cronies of Uncle Steve and former roomers, protégés, and refugees of the Hungarian revolution of 1956 whom the couple sponsored and helped through the first critical years. Such people usually paid their visits during vacation time, accompanied by their families. It was an emotional journey for them. I understood how they felt when once Aunt Ida bade farewell to Andrew and me with these words: "Come back *home* soon, don't wait until next Christmas."

Evidently, the audience fluctuated from morning to evening. The actors were always ready to perform.

3.

Uncle Steve became a real homebody after his retirement. Seated at the kitchen table, as I found him for the first time, he was always available for receiving guests and telling stories to them. He hated to leave home and if he had to pay a visit—for a grandchild's birthday, the annual picnic, or other community affairs—he kept nervously looking at his watch and soon found someone to drive him home. Since his arrest twenty-five years ago, he has not driven a car and he has been satisfied to learn about the outside world through those who brought him the news. He never watched TV, but glanced through the daily paper for headlines and through the Hungarian weekly for obituaries. He depended altogether on oral communication. It was his wife who read the paper, watched the news on TV and used the telephone, meeting social obligations, attending weddings, baptisms and funerals. Funerals annoyed Uncle Steve in particular; he said:

> At the funeral of my brother-in-law, Uncle Takács started to wail, and to cry, 'O my Lord, this is the second this year, o my Lord!

Who's going to be the next to go, Steve?' 'Are you looking at me? You're old enough. Who will be next? Don't look at me.'

He often said his purpose in telling stories was "to have a good time," "to make people laugh" and "to frisk about." A real anecdote-teller, Steve Boda's style did not follow the strict rules of specific humorous narrative genres. He spoke rather liberally in a free conversational manner, setting his stories into realistic contexts. In this way, his anecdote style was similar to that of legends.[15] He often related his stories to situations with which he was familiar. They all took place in the *Székelyföld*, in the Calumet Region or in generally known cities like Budapest, New York, Cleveland or South Bend. His characters were Székely tricksters, Gypsies, Blacks, Irish, Scotch, or Jews, in addition to the general run of fools and tricksters. He often went so far with localization that he diluted the punchline of his stories by repeating incredibly stupid acts and utterances—as in the story quoted above of Jesus' birth in Pennsylvania. The response audience, with his wife as choir leader, encouraged him to involve himself in the tales. He would even go so far as to add his own judgments and personal opinions, giving the impression that the account was based on a real experience. In one of his "madhouse" jokes, localized in Logansport, Indiana, for example, a doctor went to see the patients:

'Come with me,' said the director. So they walked. There is a young man behind bars, shaking the bars. 'What's the matter with this, do you know?' the doctor asked. 'Poor man got married, he was married hardly a week . . . well, a *roomer* eloped with his wife. And he went crazy, because he loved her very much. The fool!' They walk, and walk. *Well,* there is another young man behind bars and . . . and he said: 'What?' He said, 'What is this?' 'This is, this is the one who eloped with his wife. He also went mad.' [Laughs. General laughter: six people are present.] *Yeah.* He went crazy. The fool. He deserved it, sure. Why did he have to bother? *What?*

Obviously, the success of this joke was enhanced by the audience's familiarity with earlier boarding house love-affairs within the ethnic group. Another comes still closer:

The man goes to the *bartender*: 'Hey, Joe, give me a *pint* beer.!' 'Man, you're drunk. Sorry, no beer.' 'No? You don't serve me?' 'No,' 'No look. I tell you, you are drunk, I tell you. You're drunk.' Well, you know, it was summer and the swinging door, you know, was open in the *saloon*. And he said: 'You know what? I am not

15. As described by specialists of humorous narratives: Hermann Bausinger, "Bemerkungen zum Schwank und seinen Formtypen," *Fabula* 9 (1967):118–36, Siegfried Neumann, "Volksprosa mit komischem Inhalt," *ibid.*, pp. 137–48.

drunk.' Well, um, a cat went out from the *saloon*. And its tail was up high and went out. And the man said the *bartender*: 'You know what? I am not drunk,' he says. 'I can even tell you that I can see that a one-eyed cat just came in, it has only one eye.' And the cat went out, not in, his tail was raised, *see*, he only saw this. The dupe. 'Get out of here you fool.' *Yeah*. I knew this man. This happened here, in Indiana Harbor. *Honest to God!*

The popularity of Steve Boda as a "funny guy" was not earned only by his repertoire of one hundred and fifty-eight humorous stories. In addition to these he liked to clown and make people laugh by citing grotesque situations, people's strange and funny sayings, word-games, puns, tricks and puzzles. He also liked to play practical jokes on his visitors. He often quizzed his guests: "How can you take a broom from a room with closed door and windows?" (by taking it to pieces and pushing the broom straws one by one through the keyhole). He always had some funny experience that had happened to him "just the other day." Once a public opinion agency asked him to watch a *"gangster picture"* on TV and polled him over the telephone. Uncle Steve hated the telephone and did not pick it up if his wife was around, but this time he did, and improvised a hilarious story around the conversation he had with the girl over the gangster picture. He poked fun at such everyday events; however, this kind of improvised humor did not enter the standard repertoire but remained short-lived and was easily replaced by another topical story.

The pieces of this standard repertoire, that could be ascertained by more than one recording and by repeated hearings during the period of our acquaintance, fall into the following categories.

(1) Anecdotes which were localized in the ethnically mixed Calumet Region or in the Hungarian ethnic community, within or outside of the Calumet; these deal with common concerns of the ethnic and non-ethnic population in the area.[16] (2) Traditional anecdotes (Schwänke) classified in the *Type* index; these were mostly numskull and trickster stories. All of these originated in *Székelyföld* and were learned in childhood and imported by the Bodas or their friends and relatives. New additions to the old stock were acquired from newcomers or from those who had visited back home. (3) Short, punchline jokes or diverse nature and origin: obscene (mostly in Hungarian or Székely urban or rural setting), political (related to topical events both in Hungary and in America), ethnic and racial (partly fashionable, widespread American, and partly local banters from Calumet).

16. Many fall into the "dialect story" category; see Richard M. Dorson, "Dialect Stories of the Upper Peninsula," *Journal of American Folklore* 61 (1948): 113–150.

When the couple was alone, they always spoke in Hungarian, although the language of the stories varied according to their origin. Even if a pure Hungarian audience was present, stories were told in a characteristic mixture of English and Hungarian, depending on the setting and the actors. If actors in a story were English speakers, they were cited in English and then repeated in Hungarian translation, mixed with distorted loanwords. A part of a story told at an evening get-together after two neighbor women mentioned something about the ignorance of hillbillies will illustrate Uncle Steve's English style.

This lengthy story is about a simpleton who came from Kentucky to work for Inland Steel but who worked at Youngstown unwittingly because he could not read the sign and caught the wrong bus every morning:

'Yeah, listen,' he said, 'you are good people, see? Come, and,' he says, 'look me up.' And I say, 'How should I look you up? Where do I find you?' 'You know what?' 'What?' 'You know where Louisville, Kentucky?' You know, Louisville is a big city. I say: 'I been there.' 'You know, when you come to Louisville, Kentucky?' so should I stop like this. This was a jackass, see?' 'When you get there,' he says, 'that we go to the country, reach four corners, you know, four corners?' I say: 'Me know me side.' 'Ok. Here a drugstore, right hand side, there a drugstore. And on the left side, left, that's a left hand, see, there are saloon. There's a stockhouse and you turn that way, left at the saloon. You don't go straight, don't go left, you just turn right and you go, aaa— let's see, about two or three miles and then about two or three miles just go fast and don't go right, go left again. Turn left and about a mile and a half and then you stop. And you look. See, my wife she has lived there but we have no gas, we burn wood and you see the smoke above my chimney: that's my house.' 'Well, if I go, I'll never find it. Well, there are other places too with smoke in the chimney, 'Oh no.' I say' 'I never catch you that way!' He says: 'Just come, where the smoke comes that's my house.' Well, I say 'where is your house, in what street?' 'Oh,' he said, 'no name, no street, no number, nothing, nothing. Where you see the smoke, that is my house.'

At this point Aunt Ida could not keep silent. She did not like her husband to put down a former buddy who stayed with them for a while and felt that he had to say something nice about Southern migrants. Actually she felt bad also because an Appalachian family rented their basement rooms.

MRS. B.: These here are no such ignorants. Their *brothers* and *sisters* are all *teachers*, and one is in *college*. And the other is a very rich man in Florida. He is the poorest among them. But they are very fine people. And they love to be with us so much because he can save much of his good earnings. They are used to us and the little girl is always here in the kitchen. She loves my cooking very much, better than that of her mother, she says her mother cannot cook so well. If I make some stuffed cabbage, I have to give her some. She just loves it. Baked sausage, too . . .

4.

If Uncle Steve is the entertainer in the husband-and-wife team, Aunt Ida is a firm believer and the possessor of mystic knowledge. Unlike her rationalist husband, she is driven by an insatiable hunger to seek the secret powers that govern human life and death, destiny and continual contact with the dead. Her curiosity is inexhaustible, she is always looking for people to share her interest, people who can tell her about similar observations. Her primary inspiration, however, came from within, from the extranormal experiences she has had since early childhood. She has a large stock of stories on second sight, precognitive dreams, sighting of ghosts in various shapes, encounters with evil spirits and witches, evil eye, sickness and healing by magic.

As a legend teller Aunt Ida, always persuasive, is heated by her own conviction. She calls for response, stimulates the skeptic to argue and the believer to testify. Her style is captivating, dramatic; her language is more artistic than that of the average legend-teller. The essential story in Mrs. Boda's legends is usually preceded or followed by her reflections concerning its truth. "What makes that you think of someone and then he will come to you?" "How would this be possible if there would be no way for a ghost to return?" "How would you explain my dream of three rivers of blood that warned me of the car accident of my three relatives next day, but at different places?" "If you say charms do not help, how could my mother cure the sick horse the vet gave up, just by commanding the disease to get out of its body?" All her life Aunt Ida had been in touch with professional healers, seekers, palmists and clairvoyants in whom she had great confidence. A "knowing woman" told her from a book a week before her wedding was to take place, with an unwanted young man, that her family will not go through with their plan to force the marriage. She liked to visit magic practitioners in need. When she worked in a canning plant in Kansas City during the Great Depression, a seer predicted her near fatal sickness and surgery. She consulted a Negro clairvoyant in Gary after her sister died. The woman lit a candle, prayed and started to talk Hungarian, without knowing what she was saying, because the dead sister spoke through her. Aunt Ida knew a

Croatian, a Gypsy and a Mexican clairvoyant in the Calumet Region but there were also several among her friends and relatives who had ESP, could read from cards and had precognitive experience of some kind. She knew all the legends that had currency in the Region.

Ida Boda's legend repertoire and knowledge of related beliefs and activities can be traced to the archaic system of folk religions characteristic of the culture in which she was born. Some of her stories occurred in the environment of her native village. They happened to people she knew, or people she had heard of, who had died before she was born. Some of the stories came from the personal experience of close or distant relatives, but most of them came from her mother and grandmother, who must have been as much attracted to supernatural belief as she is. The wrongdoers and the victims of these legends were known as local villagers. Certain topics were the main concerns of the peasant women: the milk witch,[17] the changeling, bewitching of babies, and domestic animals, horseshoeing the witch, witches' Sabbath, demon as lover, treasure hunt. Mrs. Boda also has a number of stories about local healers who miraculously cured people whom doctors could not help. She could recite magic prayers that were several centuries old.[18] One which she claims her mother learned from a Catholic priest gave her goosepimples. In spite of the strong ties of these legends to the Székely land, they have not faded from memory, but were kept within the standard repertoire because of the constant company of women who had a similar Old World peasant indoctrination. Apart from the classic European legend themes, she inherited a sensitivity that is not necessarily and narrowly culture-bound but can exist in changing social situations. It is the interest in second sight, precognition, spiritualism and dream visions that has continually kept its topicality in the modern industrial environment. Aunt Ida had many prophetic visions and tragic dreams. One particularly impressed her: she saw her mother's funeral at the same time that her mother died in the old country.

Mrs. Boda had three overwhelming experiences that she never could forget. She repeated these whenever she could grab the floor from her husband. All three are characteristic of her personality as a legend teller and revealing of the consistency of folk belief patterns despite the change of cultural values. One is about the death of her first-born child by the effect of Evil Eye in the old country. The other is about her miraculous rescue from suspicion of theft by a Kansas City Clairvoyant who told her where to find the missing money. The third is

17. [A person who could magically dry up the milk in cows.]
18. Irmgard Hampp, *Beschwörung-Segen-Gebet. Untersuchungen zum Zauberspruch aus dem Bereich der Volksheilkunde.* (Stuttgart, 1961).

about the already quoted spirit crying at the door. The legends formulated from these experiences were of general interest for the audience that reacted in accordance with the rules of legend communication. For Aunt Ida, the most effective and lasting was the memory of the crying dead imitating her mother's voice at the door. In addition to this, she recounted several other ominous death signs related to the premature death of her young niece. I have heard these separate stories quite often and recorded them three times, always in the presence of a different audience. The supportive behavior of the listeners, countering Uncle Steve's negative attitude, was interesting. This situation illustrated the merger of Old World tradition with modern American supernaturalism.

Nothing can better demonstrate legend performance in its proper context of controversy than to quote here two brief sections from a tape-recorded session. In this particular case, Mrs. Boda was joined by a close friend, Mrs. Ethel Deme, as co-proponent of legends and their belief-ingredients, while Uncle Steve acted as the usual *advocatus diaboli*.[19] Mrs. Deme is also from the *Székelyföld* but from a different district; the Bodas did not know her in the old country. She lost her husband twenty years ago and now lives with her daughter's family. Like Aunt Ida, she is active in church work and the two women meet regularly. After Sunday services she sometimes lunched with the Bodas. The following sample was taken from an all-afternoon conversation and is representative of the communication of legends anywhere where they are alive.

Mrs. D.: Why do we have always to think of the person of whom we will hear news? Even my daughter believes this is so.

Mrs. B.: Me, too. Last night I went to bed and my poor dead *niece* came to my mind because I laid on my side. Poor Betty could not turn around, she was always on her back. The middle board immediately fell from my bed. It never did. With a big noise it fell under the bed. I got such a scare, I shuddered. It make a big clack under the bed.

Mrs. D.: There are no board beds today . . .

Mrs. B.: No-*no*, not the board, there is a board under the *spring* that supports the *spring*. But it clapped so strong and I was so frightened. Wasn't it that her spirit came back and sat on the spring?

Mrs. D.: Sure thing, one never knows.

Mrs. B.: It made such a terrible noise. Poor Betty, she could never lay on her side . . .

19. [Devil's advocate, i.e. one who defends the less popular side of a question for the sake of argument.]

Mrs. D.: And the board fell.

Mrs. B.: And I had that horrible feeling . . .

Mrs. D.: Hm. These are true . . . these noises.

Mrs. B.: This was true.

Mrs. D.: Even my grandchildren believe in this, Lyn, the daughter of my daughter. If there is some clap in the house, she knows this is a danger sign. If a mirror or a picture falls from the wall, it is no good . . .[20]

Mrs. B.: Yes, Mrs. Davis told me . . .

Mrs. D.: I heard it in the radio. It was also in a book.

Here the conversation is interrupted by Uncle Steve who enters with a glass of goat's milk that was ordered for him because it has less fat than cow's milk. With disgust he occasionally utters a 'ba-a' to express his opinion on the topic of the two women.

Mrs. B.: Well, my mother went to town, to Udvarhely with her godmother and as they are on the way back, the town was so about fourteen kilometres from us, it was far for a walk and she asked my mother: 'Well, how do you want to go home, in a sieve or on foot?' And my mother said, 'No I won't go in the sieve.[21] So they went on foot. But it was rumored that when it was the coldest winter and women were spinning, these have just disappeared somewhere and soon they brought back ripe red cherries. They put them on the table for the spinning women, the ripe red cherries, in winter. In winter. And they were witches. They speedily went to Turkey,[22] brought the cherries and placed them on the table. *Yes.* My mother said this and she never told a lie, she always used to tell this to us.

Mr. B.: In what did they go? In a sieve?

Mrs. B.: *Yes.* She asked: 'Do you want to go in the sieve?' Somehow they turned themselves into spirit shape . . .

Mrs. D.: Broom . . broom?

Mrs. B.: They flew somehow. And she said: 'Hoopla, I be where I want to be' with the broom.

Mr. B.: The English says: *bullshit* . . .

Mrs. D.: They said broom-riding old witch . . .

Mr. B.: The American calls what you are talking about *bullshit*.

Mrs. B.: Well, *I don't know* . . .

Mr. B.: Aaaah, there is no such thing.

Mrs. B.: You see that the big . . .

20. E 765.4. Life bound up with external event; M 341. Death prophesied.
21. G 241.4.3. Witch travels in sieve.
22. D 1531.5. Witch flies with magic aids.

MR. B.: An American, tell this to an intelligent American, he will call it *bullshit*.

MRS. B.: Listen, scientists are looking into this, isn't that so? You hear me? They directly look after such things to find out . . . well . . .

MRS. D.: We went to do our work in the fields. My father got up early and my mother went to milk the cow. And it came out from a big dark cloud. Its tail stayed outside. But it was huge. That snake-dragon.

MR. B.: Dragon!?

MRS. D.: My father was not a liar.

MR. B.: Seven-headed dragon? What?

MRS. D.: My father saw it, it was very early, it hardly dawned, the clouds laid on the mountains.

MR. B.: Did it have two heads in front? [jokingly]

MRS. D.: My father did not see its head only when its waist slid from one cloud into the other. And there was a horrible rain that morning. My grandmother predicted of this—she still lived then. 'Dear son,' she said, 'rain will stop.' Because it rained for six weeks and they could not do any work in the fields. Because he saw the snake-dragon.[23] My father said that. And he did not like superstition, he did not want to listen to such talks, no. But he saw the snake-dragon.

MRS. B.: They toll the bells so that the clouds dissolve . . .[24]

MRS. D.: In Erzsébetváros the great Armenian, no the Greek church, was dedicated that if the bad weather comes . . .

MRS. B.: They always tolled the bells when the storm came . . .

MRS. D.: The bells are consecrated for that, otherwise it would not help. I was a young woman, o my God, as I remember, poor hens were all flooded in the pen . . . it was hoeing time. . . .

MRS. B.: My dear mother stood on the porch and when the storm came, she crossed the sky and prayed the prayer she learned from the priest whom I told you about and I remember . . .

MR. B.: But you still know how the prayer went?

MRS. B.: Oh yes. 'They set out . . . be off, be off to Venice, take three drops of the milk, three drops of the blood of Virgin Mary, take it to faraway snow-covered mountains where you could not harm anybody, anything . . .!' But there was more to it and then she crossed herself in the name of the Father, the Son and the Holy

23. The snake dragon, often associated with the *garabonciás* in Hungarian mythology, raises storms, as in nos. 63 and 64 in Linda Dégh, *Folktales of Hungary* (Chicago: The University of Chicago Press, 1965). [A *garabonciás* is "a supernatural being believed to be born as an extraordinary child which acquires magic powers through a trance." *Folktales of Hungary*, p. 353.]

24. D 2141.1.1. Church bell rings as protection against storm.

Ghost, Amen. And then the cloud dissolved nicely. I really know this.

MR. B.: Ida! Ida, listen.

MRS. B.: No, he does not believe anything.

MR. B.: Now, wait a minute. If there were so many smart people in the world, you hear me: in the whole world that it comes . . . when the radio warns ahead that the tornado is coming, take care, if there would be such a man who could stop it . . .

MRS. D.: No, man could not do that . . .

MR. B.: Noooo, naaa, you can pray as much as you want, once it comes, it takes everything.

MRS. D.: Oh, but it avoids many places.

MR. B.: Oh well, but not because you say all this hocus-pocus. To hell.

MRS. B.: This is a prayer.

MR. B.: Prayer is *all right* but not to take away the storm.

MRS. D.: But the prayer can help.

MR. B.: It would not. The English say: *bullshit* of this kind of talk. Ah. Pray or curse is all the same.

MRS. D.: I don't like this kind of talk . . .

Leaving the home of the Boda couple, one becomes suddenly aware of the enormous distance that separates the surrounding inscrutable, noisy, polluted industrial town from this profoundly harmonious haven within it. There are many good reasons for the perfect harmony between Ida and Steve Boda: mutual love and respect for each other, warm relationship with children and grandchildren, appreciation of faithful friends, popularity within the peer group and, of course, the feeling of being well provided for. But the folklorist can see a significant dimension of the couple's union: the capability of turning their happy, successful marriage also into the creative, successful symbiosis of their narrative art.

Analysis and Interpretation
of American Folklore

Analysis is inevitable in any folklore collection or study, and it takes place at every stage of research. The very acts of collecting, classifying, archiving, and annotating folklore are analytical to the extent that the researcher has in mind a concept of folklore and folklore genres as he or she records, sorts, and files material. In a sense, our scholarly categories and definitions have been created out of the free-flowing stream of traditional utterances and behavior patterns that are observed and "collected" from peoples' everyday interactions. Even our idea of "tradition" is based on a concept of what aspects of culture we will select for study. Not all folklore collectors and archivists have verbalized their conceptual frameworks, of course, but the analysis of folklore takes place just the same. It is clear, then, that every folklore study—including each of the selections in this reader—is in some ways analytical and interpretive. The particular studies in this section are set apart simply because the goal of analysis is enunciated explicitly and is followed more or less systematically.

Some modes of folklore analysis illustrated here (not necessarily only one theory per selection) are historic-geographic, rhetorical, esthetic, structural, psychological, symbolic, and functional. Most authors have gathered material from the field themselves, while several have cited printed sources and folklore reference works to annotate their examples. While the question of origin of a certain type or variant of folklore is discussed by many of the scholars, most of them are more concerned with using the results of their analysis to explain the appropriateness of the folk traditions studied to aspects of American or regional character. The conclusions drawn from folklore provide insights into popular culture, frontier history, age-group differences, and immigration. Different approaches to different genres are illustrated with the essays on folktales and legends, folksongs, and dances. A wide range of folk traditional settings is included, from backwoods Anglo-American settlements to modern urban gestures, jokes and games.

Many of the recently published studies in Section 3 show the influence of theoretical essays included in Section 4.

METHOD IN THE HISTORY AND INTERPRETATION OF A PROVERB: "A PLACE FOR EVERYTHING AND EVERYTHING IN ITS PLACE"

Archer Taylor

Stith Thompson and Archer Taylor were the two major American proponents of the comparative approach to folklore study usually known as the "historic-geographic" or "Finnish" method. Thompson specialized in folk narrative analysis, and Taylor's emphasis (although he also made narrative studies) was on proverbs and riddles. This brief note which appeared in the international journal devoted to paremiology (proverb study) is an example of the approach of the typical comparative folklorist. It focuses on texts gleaned from the standard published collections. (In a folktale or folksong study, archives of unpublished texts would be consulted as well.)

By comparing various occurrences of the proverb, the scholar tries to determine its original form, paths of dissemination, and patterns of variation. As Taylor showed, an acceptable explanation of a proverb's origin must be based on localized and dated examples, and not simply a reasonable explanation that seems to fit the general meaning of the saying as Marshall McLuhan's theory operated. Since many familiar proverbs have traditional origin stories that circulate orally, a student could follow Taylor's method, trying to validate or to dispute the various suggested explanations.

The same passage in Ecclesiastes which Taylor believed must underlie the English proverb is quoted by Dan Ben-Amos in "Toward a Definition of Folklore in Context" (reprinted in Section 4) as part of his discussion of the "contextual conventions that set folklore apart." This usage seems to show that the quotation itself, not only its derivative forms, can be used proverbially in English.

THE ENGLISH PROVERB "A place for everything and everything in its place" is a convenient text on which to base some remarks about the historical study and interpretation of proverbs. We may begin with examples of the proverb. These are surprisingly few in number and recent in date. We learn this from the standard English collections: G. L. Apperson, *English Proverbs and Proverbial Phrases* (London, 1929), *The Oxford Dictionary of English Proverbs* (2d ed., Oxford,

1948), and Burton E. Stevenson, *The Home Book of Proverbs* . . . (New York, 1948), to which we may add such collections limited in time or space as Morris P. Tilley, *A Dictionary of the Proverbs in England in the Sixteenth and Seventeenth Centuries* (Ann Arbor, 1950), which does not include our proverb, and Archer Taylor and Bartlett Jere Whiting, *A Dictionary of American Proverbs and Proverbial Phrases 1820–1880* (Cambridge, Mass., 1958), which illustrate restrictions in regard to time or place. These are the chief sources of the information used in the following remarks and will not be cited later except for special reasons.

Historical and other studies in proverbs are much complicated by the fact that collectors usually do not indicate where they found their texts and what the dates of the texts may be. An illustration of the value of this information is readily seen in the interpretation of the comparison "like a bull in a china shop," for which see Archer Taylor, *Proverbial Comparisons from California* (Berkeley, 1954), p. 22. No example of this older than the nineteenth century has been cited and it appears to be unknown in other than English use. This situation is explained by the fact that a bull actually invaded a London china shop in 1773. This explains the lack of early examples and the limitation of the saying to English use.

Let us now turn to the proverb with which we are concerned: "A place for everything and everything in its place." Marshall McLuhan has recently explained it as an allusion to printing and the necessity of returning type to its box when it has been used; see his *Understanding Media* (1964). To be sure, the linotype and other modern procedures dispense with all this and his ingenious explanation must consequently imply the invention of the proverb, if it is to be readily understood as an allusion to a printing shop, at some time before the middle of the last century. The explanation does not rest upon evidence but is expected to win the reader's assent as being obviously true. Explanations of this sort are all too numerous in the case of proverbs for which examples ranging widely in time and place are lacking or have not been collected and studied.

During the last half-century a considerable number of dated and localized examples of our proverb have become available. The first examples appear to be those in Thomas C. Halliburton, *Nature*, I, 164 (1855) and some other popular novelists who wrote in the next dozen years. In 1875 Ralph Waldo Emerson quoted it in his *Journals*. The span between Halliburton and the other novelists is great enough to assure us that the proverb was currently used after the middle of the nineteenth century. Samuel Smiles an author of moralizing and didactic works, wrote in *Thrift* (1875): "Order is most useful in the management of everything . . . Its maxim is, A place for everything and everything in its place." This suggests the direction in which we should look for the origin of the proverb. And we are confirmed in doing so by such a maxim as that cited by the forgotten novelist Elizabeth Hamilton who wrote in *The Cottagers of Glenburnie* (1808. See V.S. Lean, *Collectanea*, III, 448): "Do everything in its proper time, keep everything to its proper use, put everything in its proper place." We shall return to this bit of advice from an orderly housewife. Such modern variations as "A niche for everything and everything in its niche" (1936) and "A tidy person with a place for everything and everything in its place" (1941) are clearly allusions to the household. For examples showing the wide use of our proverb see V.S. Lean (*Collectanea*, III, 401) with a citation from England (1902), B.J. Whiting from North Carolina (1950), see *The Frank C. Brown Collection*, I, 459; Austin E. Fife from Virginia (1952); Owen S. Adams from California in 1948 (*Western Folklore*, IX, 142), and Frances M. Barbour in 1965 (*Proverbs and Proverbial Phrases from Southern Illinois*, Carbondale, p. 142). The standard collections cite these (which have been cited to show wide distribution) and more—enough to establish the general currency of the proverb.

If we look abroad, we find no example of our proverb in Danish, Swedish, and Finnish or in Modern Greek and Italian, as friends experienced in collecting and studying proverbs tell me. This fact should awaken once more doubt of an explanation based on printing practice. If this explanation were correct, we would expect to find an example in German and in languages in which German proverbs are familiarly used. This is not the case. Arguments from both history and geography compel us to look in another direction.

The direction in which we should look has already been suggested, but before insisting on it, let us note a simpler version of the idea incorporated in it. The very simple proverbs "There is a place for everything" and "Everything in its place" are familiar enough to me in daily use, although I do not find them recorded in English collections. Hans Christian Andersen used such a proverb in 1853 as a title for a short story: "Alt paa sin rette plads (Everything in its right place.)" Such a saying lends itself easily to expansion as we find in the Danish "Hvert paa sin sted, og pispotten paa skabet," which I need not translate, was reported as early as the end of the seventeenth century.[1] We see a different expansion in the verses of a minor English poet:

---

1. Aage Hansen, ed., *Aldmindelige danske ordsproge* (Copenhagen, 1944), No. 10789. This collection was first printed at Copenhagen in 1682–1688. See also N. F. S. Grundtvig, *Danske ordsprog og mundheld* (Copenhagen, 1845), No. 1231; E. Mau, *Danske ordsprogs-skat* (2 vols., Copenhagen, 1879), No. 9557. I am indebted to I. Kjær for the references and other good counsel.

> "There is a place for everything
>   In earth, or sky, or sea,
> Where it may find its proper use,
>   And of advantage be,"
> Quoth Augustine, the saint."[2]

The origin of "There is a place for everything" is not far to seek. It is a variation of the ancient "Omnia tempus habent, et suis spatiis transeunt universa sub caelo" (To everything there is a season, and a time to every purpose under the heaven. Ecclesiastes 3:1). This may very well have been known to St Augustine, if we insist upon identifying the versifier's ascription. However this may be, this notion is often found in collections of proverbs (see Stevenson, *Home Book*, pp. 2051:1, 2328:5). However this may be, Montaigne and many others used the idea, and Chaucer credited it to Solomon. More interesting and more important than such details (which prove the wide use of the proverb) is the fact that it was easily expanded. We have already noted an instance in the previously quoted maxim recorded by Elizabeth Hamilton. Similar expansions that Stevenson quotes are the eighteenth-century "Every Thing has its Time, and that Time must be watch'd," Thomas Jefferson's "There is a time for all things; for advancing and for retiring" (1821), and Thomas Babington Macauley's There is a time for everything—a time to set up, and a time to pull down" (1832).

The inferences to be drawn from my discussion are various and obvious enough. We cannot safely study the meaning, origin, and history of a proverb without having at our disposal a generous stock of parallels from as many times and places as possible. As far as the available evidence goes, "A place for everything and everything in its place" is a proverb of rather recent origin in England. It is a derivative of "Everything in its place" or "There is a place for everything." This has a counterpart in a still older and still more widely known "There is a time for everything." Proverbs about time and place are closely related to each other and are easily modified by adding details.

2. John Bartlett, *Familiar Quotations*, 11th ed., Boston, 1939, p. 706. [From the poem "Augustine's Philosophy", by Benjamin Breckinridge Warfield (1851–1921).]

THREE MEDIEVAL TALES AND THEIR MODERN AMERICAN ANALOGUES

Shirley Marchalonis

Annotating folktale texts and comparing different variants of the same theme can yield interesting results, even when few hints of context or performance style are available. In this instance there were few type or motif references to aid the scholar, but medievalist Shirley Marchalonis was able to match similar stories from old published sources to recent American fables (moral tales which often have animal characters) and to an exemplum (a tale used for teaching, often in a sermon). The features that changed and those that remained constant through the centuries correlate to historical and cultural aspects of the two periods and the various countries involved.

The consistent change in all three stories is the loss of the religious framework characteristic of medieval literature and lore. The false conversion tale, of course, continues to deal with religion, but it lacks a specific stated "moral" summary. It is only one of many modern jokes about Jews and Christians that often center on priests, rabbis, and ministers. Some of these jokes may be linked to older prototypes via the type or motif index. The most consistent feature of the modern variants seems to be adaptation to a particular group and its concerns.

Although the citation of analogous examples and the comparative analysis is well done in this article, the presentation of the modern folklore variants is somewhat weak. "The Fatal Hairdo" story is referred to only in a summary form, and no oral source is credited for the text of the Jewish joke. Context is given only for the black American tale of Sister Goose. Most folklore students should be able to collect their own texts of "The Fatal Hairdo" and possibly of the other two tales, or at least of some similar modern tales. In any such project it should be borne in mind that verbatim texts and close descriptions of the context of storytelling are important to the full interpretation of the tales. The kind of summary treatment of several texts quoted from folklorist Kenneth Jackson (footnote 10) gives only intriguing hints of materials that might be useful for further comparative studies.

THE OCCASIONALLY EXPRESSED OPINION that a technological and television-ridden world is destroying folklore is one that does not stand up to close examination. Not only are new folklore items constantly generated, but older pieces, changed perhaps by time and circumstances but still recognizable, continue to exist. This paper will be concerned with two fables and an exemplum from the Middle Ages and their current American analogues.

The first of these is the tale known to folklorists as "The Fatal Hairdo."[1] The story in its modern version is associated with the time of massive, structured hair styles held in place by heavy applications of hair lacquers. According to the story, a high school student whose hair was arranged in one of these beehives or balloons became mysteriously ill in school one day. Usually the illness involved fainting; sometimes the teacher or another student saw blood running down the girl's neck. She was rushed to the hospital, where she died. After her death the doctors discovered spiders (or other insects) nested within her hairdo; she had been poisoned by their bites.

Obviously the tale is topical in that it depends upon certain social conditions—specifically, on fashion—to give it meaning. Although it is told as a sensational story, there are certain didactic elements implied: if the girl had washed and combed her hair more often, rather than holding her hairdo together with hairspray, she would not have died.

In the *Speculum Laicorum*, a late thirteenth-century collection of English exempla, there is a very similar story; the version given here is that of G. R. Owst:

> There is a sermon story of a certain lady of Eynesham, in Oxfordshire, 'who took so long over the adornment of her hair that she used to arrive at church barely before the end of Mass.' One day 'the devil descended upon her head in the form of a spider, gripping with its legs,' until she well-nigh died of fright. Nothing would remove the offending insect, neither prayer, nor exorcism, nor holy water, until the local abbot displayed the holy sacrament before it.[2]

A slightly different version appears in Robert of Brunne's *Handlyng Synne* (1308).[3] A lady who was proud of her appearance and especially of her elaborate hair arrangements and headdresses ("Moche

---

1. A version of this story is given in Jan Harold Brunvand, *The Study of American Folklore* (New York: Norton, 1968), pp. 322–323 [2nd. ed., p. 377]. See also Kenneth Clarke, "The Fatal Hairdo and the Emperor's New Clothes Revisited," *Western Folklore* 23 (1964): 249–252, where the story is used as a base for satire.

2. G. R. Owst, *Preaching in Medieval England* (Cambridge: Cambridge University Press, 1926), p. 170. Owst's source is the *Thesaurus Exemplorum. Fascicule V: Le Speculum Laicorum. Edition d'une collection d'exempla composée en Angleterre à la fin du XIII° siècle*, ed. J. Th. Welter (Paris, 1914), Chapter LX, Item 5. I have not been able to see this work.

3. Robert of Brunne, *Handlyng Synne*, ed. Frederick J. Furnival. *EETS* 119 (London: Kegan Paul, Trench, Trubner & Co., 1901), pp. 113–116.

she loued feyre tyfing,/ Of here hede, ouer al þyng," 3243–44) died, and after her death she appeared to her husband's faithful squire. She led the young man to an open place,

> As þey hadd stondë but a þrowe,
> Come furþ deuylys þat fast gun blowe;
> With þem þey broght a brennyng wheyl,
> þat on her hede was set eche deyl.
> þys whel þat was set on her heuede,
> Brende here alle, þat noght was leued.
> Efte she ros, when she was brent,
> And had þe same turment,
> And brende ryȝt as she dede before;
> To se þat peyne hys herte was sore.[4]
>   (3271–80)

The purpose of the lady's visit is to warn her husband and the squire against the pride and vanity that have caused her punishment. In still another version, a "Lady vain of her hair appears after death to one of her husband's grooms, tormented by devils putting toads and scorpions on her head and burning her to ashes."[5]

Toads, scorpions, and spiders, as well as fire, are associated with devils and hell. Consistently in these tales the punishment is retributive: the lady's sin of pride (the first of the Seven Deadly Sins, as the medieval audience would know) is focused on her head and therefore that is where her torment is directed. Death and damnation are the results of pride, and the ghost appears as a warning to others. The lady whose interest in her hairdo makes her constantly late for Mass is more fortunate than the others, for she is given a chance to repent and change her behavior.

The twentieth-century version of the story is still an exemplum, although the didacticism is implicit and cleanliness has replaced godliness as the operative force. Without laboring an obvious point, it

---

4. [Free translation:
> When they had stood there a while,
> Devils came and began to rail at her;
> They brought with them a burning wheel,
> That was set on her head.
> This wheel set on her head,
> Burned there so nothing was left.
> At once she rose, when she was burned,
> And still had the same torment,
> Burning just as before;
> Seeing which pain his heart was sore.]

5. Listed in J. A. Herbert, *Catalogue of Romances in the Department of Manuscripts in the British Museum* (London: Longmans and Co., 1910) as MS Royal 8 F. vi ff 1–23, 24b–25. See also Frederic C. Tubach, *Index Exemplorum, FFC* 204 (Helsinki, 1969), p. 197 (#2489).

may be safe to say that the change illustrates—if illustration were necessary—that the medieval theocentric universe has given way to the scientific and sterile twentieth century. The high school girl with the nest of spiders in her hair offends contemporary standards of behavior just as the proud medieval ladies offended contemporary belief. In both cases the story acts as warning and example.

The second item is current in oral tradition as a Jewish joke:

> There was once a Jewish manufacturer who thought his business would do better if he became a Christian. He did convert and his business prospered until he was a very rich man. At last he decided that he did not want to be a Christian any longer. He gave a dinner party one Friday night and invited his parish priest. The main course was roast beef.
>
> The priest said, 'You know I can't eat meat on Friday—and neither can you.'
>
> For answer the Jew took some water and sprinkled it on the meat. 'There,' he said, 'now we can eat it.'
>
> When the priest exclaimed, the Jew said, 'Well, that's what you did to me, and it didn't work any better on me than it does on the roast beef.'[6]

Compare this joke with one of the *Moral Fables* of Robert Henryson, one of the best of the fifteenth-century Scottish Chaucerians. His story is entitled, "The Taill how this forsaid Tod [fox] maid his Confession to Freir Wolf Waitskaith."[7] The fox, Lowrence, after waiting for night so that he may hunt, sees in the stars that his omens are foreboding. He therefore wants to make his confession. At this point Friar Wolf appears and agrees to hear the confession. Asked if he repents, the fox admits that he can only repent the many hens and lambs he has not yet eaten; he cannot promise to stop because necessity causes him to steal and eat animals; he won't accept punishment because he acts according to his nature. Friar Wolf absolves him anyway, with one provision, " 'Thou sall' (quod he), 'forbeir flesch untill pasche,[8]/ To tame this Corps, that cursit Carioun;/ And heir I reik the full remissioun' " (723–25).

The fox goes to the water's edge, but while he is puzzling over the difficulties of fishing, he sees a kid, which he immediately seizes:

> Syne over the heuch unto the see he hyis,
> And tuke the Kid be the hornis twane,

6. With the relaxation of Roman Catholic rules concerning fasting, it is possible that this tale might lose some of its force.

7. *Robert Henryson: Poems and Fables*, ed. H. Harvey Wood (London: Oliver and Boyd, 1958). All citations are to this text.

8. [Easter.]

> And in the watter outher twyis or thryis
> He dowkit him, and till him can he sayne:
> 'Ga doun, Schir Kid, cum up Schir Salmond agane!'
> Quhill he wes deid; syne to the land him drewch,
> And off that new maid Salmond eit anewch.[9]
>
> (747–53)

Having eaten the kid, the fox lies in the sun, "Straikand his wame against the sonis heit,/ 'Upon this wame set wer ane bolt full meit'" (759–60). The keeper promptly shoots him in his full belly, and Lowrence's last words are characteristic: " 'Me think na man may speik ane word in play,/ Bot now on dayis in ernist it is tane'" (770–71).

Each of Henryson's thirteen fables is followed by a "moralitas" which interprets the tale in moral and usually theological terms. While the moralitas that follows this tale is grim in its message (prepare for a death which may come without warning), the tale itself is lighthearted and charming. Even the satire is fairly gentle: Lowrence's answers to the Friar are humorously logical, as his baptising and transformation of the kid is humorously illogical. There are certainly serious satirical elements in the tale: the fox's confession is inspired by fear and the notorious laxness of the friars guarantees a too-easy absolution. The moralitas makes these points and turns the tale into a moral-theological lesson.

Between the fifteenth-century beast fable and the modern version of the story is a long period which can to some extent be bridged. Kenneth Jackson reports being told the story by Peig Sayers, an Irishwoman from whom he collected many tales in 1930.[10] He then goes on to say:

> Now when I got back to London on this occasion it happened that I was dining with my old friend Ifor Evans, late Principal of this College. Another guest was a member of the Roumanian Embassy, who astonished me by repeating this self-same story and declaring it had actually occurred in Roumania. A few days later I spoke of this to my neighbor at High Table at my college, G. C. Coulton, the medieval historian. 'Oh,' said Coulton, 'that's an old story,' and he

9. [Free translation:

> He went over the cliff, down to the sea,
> And took the kid by the two horns,
> And into the water twice or thrice
> He ducked him, saying,
> "Go down Sir Kid, come up again Sir Salmon!"
> Until he was dead; then he drew him to land,
> And from that new-made salmon ate his fill.]

10. Kenneth Jackson, *The International Tale and Early Welsh Tradition* (Cardiff: University of Wales, 1961), p. 7.

referred me to an eighteenth century source where it is related of a
Turk in Italy. Some years later I happened on exactly the same
thing told in Australia about a missionary and an Australian aborig-
ine who wanted to eat meat on Good Friday. Finally, when I was
studying Yiddish as a language and a source of folkelore some years
later I discovered a Yiddish version about a Jew and a priest in
Poland, very remarkably close to the Irish one I heard on Blasket
Island. I have little doubt that the tale is in fact of Jewish origin.

In spite of the fact that the characters change, the stories describe
the same basic situation, although in the "joke" version the changing
of meat to fish is the point of the tale and in Henryson's fable the
transformation leads to something else. Jackson's conclusion that the
tale is Jewish in origin may be questioned, though neither proved nor
disproved. The "false transformation" can be a true conversion, as C.
Grant Loomis, in his book *White Magic*, explains:

> Upon numerous occasions, particularly upon fast days, it was found
> convenient to turn meat into fish. A chicken's leg became fish when
> a cardinal tried to accuse Thomas of Becket of eating flesh on a feast
> day. He appropriated the leg and carried it to the pope, but when
> he opened his kerchief, a fish fell out. Under other circumstances,
> fish was changed into meat. After Ciaranus blessed a side of bacon,
> it became a number of different foods, such as bread, vegetables, fish,
> honey and oil.[11]

The motif is D476.3.4 "Meat miraculously turned into fish on a
feast day."[12] It is a fairly common concept in serious religious writings of the Middle Ages. It is easy to imagine a humorous inversion of
the miraculous transformation; all that is essential is a protagonist
who is either a non-Christian or a cheerful hypocrite like Lowrence
the fox. It is of course not possible to know who first saw the comic
potential, but I find it very difficult to agree with Richard Bauman's
insistence that the joke was not in oral tradition in Henryson's time.[13]
Given the widespread knowledge of the idea and a society in which
oral communication was more prevalent than written, it is difficult to
believe that the story was not told. That it has not been recorded does
not mean that it did not exist.

The current version of the third tale comes from black American

11. C. Grant Loomis, *White Magic* (Cambridge, Mass.: Medieval Academy of
America, 1948), p. 79.

12. Stith Thompson, *Motif-Index of Folk Literature* (Bloomington: Indiana
University Press, 1955–58).

13. Richard Bauman, "The Folktale and Oral Tradition in the Fables of Robert
Henryson," *Fabula* 6, ii (1963): 108–124. Bauman suggests a source in the appendix to the fables of Gualterius Anglicus (see note 13) but I have not been
able to see the appendix.

folklore. Professor Sterling A. Brown of Howard University tells the story of Sister Goose,

> . . . one of those fine individualistic people. She had courage. She had intelligence. She wouldn't let anybody kick her around (something like the New Negro). One day she was paddling on the lake and it was fine. She was just paddling on the lake. It was a beautiful day, like today, and she was just swimming on the lake. All of a sudden she gets too near some reeds and Brer Fox reaches out and grabs her. He says, 'Uh-huh, I got you! You swimming on my lake,' she says, 'Un-nuh! This ain't none of your lake. . . . I got civil rights. . . . I got just as much right to swim on this lake as you got!' Brer Fox says, 'No you ain't. It's my lake. I'm goin' to kill you. I'm goin' to execute you. I'm goin' to pick your bones!' Sister Goose says, 'Oh, no, you can't kill me. You can't pick my bones. I'm goin' to take you to court.' So she took the fox to court. And in the court the Sheriff was a fox, the jurymen were foxes, everybody who came to see the trial—all were foxes. The prosecuting lawyer was a fox and the defending lawyer was a fox. So they tried her. They gave her a fair trial. They executed her. And they all sat around and picked her bones.[14]

A version of this story collected in 1923 uses heavier dialect and omits the references to the New Negro and Civil Rights.[15] It ends with a moral:

14. Sterling A. Brown, "The Background of Folklore in Negro Literature," *Mother-Wit From the Laughing Barrel*, ed. Alan Dundes (Englewood Cliffs, N.J.: Prentice-Hall, 1973), p. 43.

15. A. W. Eddins, "Brazos Bottom Philosophy," *Publications of the Texas Folklore Society* 2 (1923): 31. Also collected in *The Book of Negro Folklore*, eds. Langston Hughes and Arna Bontemps (New York: Dodd, Mead and Co., 1958), p. 13. This version is a little different from the one told by Sterling A. Brown:

Ole Sis Goose wus er-sailin' on de lake, and ole Br'er Fox wus hid in de weeds. By um by ole Sis Goose swum up close to der bank and ole Br'er Fox lept out and cotched her.

'O yes, ole Sis Goose, I'se got yer now, you'se been er-sailin' on der lake er long time, en I'se got yer now. I'se gwine to break yer neck en pick yer bones."

"Hole on der', Br'er Fox, hold on, I'se got jes' as much right to swim in der lake as you has to lie in der weeds. Hit's des' as much my lake es hit is yours, and we is gwine to take dis matter to der cotehouse and see if you has any right to break my neck and pick my bones."

And so dey went to cote, and when dey got dere, de sheriff, he wus er fox, en de judge, he wus er fox, and der tourneys, dey wus fox, en all de jurymen, dey wus foxes, too.

En dey tried ole Sis Goose, en dey 'victed her and dey 'scuted her, and dey picked her bones.

Now, my chilluns, listen to me, when all de folks in de cotehouse is foxes, and you is des' er common goose, der ain't gwine to be much jestice for you poor culled folks.

Now, my chilluns, listen to me, when all de folks in de cote is foxes, and you is des' der common goose, der ain't gwine be much jestice for you pore culled folks.

In Henryson's "Taill of the Sheep and the Doig," the dog unjustly accuses the sheep of owing him money for bread and takes him to court. The judge who presides over the court is a wolf. Officers of the court are a raven, a fox, a kite, and a crow. When the sheep protests the unfair treatment, the judge has the court select two arbiters, who turn out to be a bear and a badger. Judgement is made in the dog's favor, and the sheep, at the beginning of winter, has to sell his fleece to pay the debt. The moralitas ends with the lines, "We pure pepill as now may do no moir/ But pray to the, sen that we are oprest/ In to this earth, grant us in hevin gude rest" (1318–20).

There are at least two analogues for this story, one in an obscure collection of Aesopic fables called the *Anonymous Noveletti* of Gualterius Anglicus (English Walter) and a later one in Caxton's *Aesop*.[16] The Latin version is brief:

Canis traxit in causam coram indice Ouem et peciit ab ea panem suum, quem ei tradiderat, ut menciebatur. Oue uero negante assunt Milius, Vultur et Lupus, pro Cane et contra Ouem falsi testes. Iudex igitur uidens testes, condempnauit Ouem ad reddendum debitum. Ipsa igitur iniuste condempnata, non habens unde solueret, licet instaret hiemps, uendidit uellus suum, et sic nuda remansit.
Sepe fidem falso mendicat in (h)ertia teste,
Sepe dolet pietas criminis arte capi[17]

Caxton's version is longer and less stark in its tone.[18] Henryson's

16. *Les Fabulistes Latin*, ed. Leopold Hervieux (Paris, 1883; repr. New York: Burt Franklin, 1964), p. 384.

17. I would like to thank William Edward Walton, III, of the Pennsylvania State University for his assistance with this translation.

A dog brought a sheep into the presence of a judge in a lawsuit and asked the court for his bread which the sheep had taken that he might eat it. The sheep denying this to be the truth, a kite, a vulture and a wolf were present, false witnesses for the dog and against the sheep. The judge, therefore, hearing the witnesses, condemned the sheep to return the debt. The sheep, therefore, unjustly condemned, although winter was approaching sold his fleece, and thus went about naked.

Often want of skill begs faith of false witness
Often piety suffers pain (when) seized by the artfulness of crime.

18. *Caxton's Aesop*, ed. R. T. Lenaghan (Cambridge: Harvard University Press, 1967), p. 76:

Of the men chalengynge whiche euer be sekynge occasion to doo some harme and dommage to the good/ saith Esope such a tale/ Somtyme was a dogge/ which demaunded of a sheep a loof of brede that she borowed of hym/ And the sheep ansuerd that neuer she had none of hym The dogge made her to come before the Iuge/ And by cause the sheep denyed the dette/ the dogge prouysed and broughte with hym fals wytnes/ that is to wete the wulf/ the

precise source may have been the Latin version, but the fact that the story appears in Aesopic collections indicates that it was fairly well known.[19]

All thirteen of Henryson's *Moral Fables* are beast fables.[20] In this genre animals behave both according to their own nature and as human beings, a seeming paradox from which the form draws its strength. It was a popular form, and particularly useful for exemplum literature, for it drew on the concept of man standing between the angels and the beasts in the great chain of being, capable of moving in either direction. The beast fable exploits the man-beast relationship; for example, the fox can ask for absolution like a man, but when he explains that he steals and kills because it is his nature to do so he is right as an animal but wrong as a human being. The form carries its own humor, which is the humor of sudden deflation,[21] and it is perhaps that built-in humor that made the beast fable useful for social criticism, especially in a day when criticism of institutions could be equated with treason.[22] The tale of the sheep and the dog is pure social criticism. It is a grim story, very short and direct, the least humorous of the thirteen fables. The attack is against corruption of institutions; the sheep represents the poor, victimized by the very

---

myland & the sparhawk/ And whanne these wytnes shold be examyned and herd/ the wulf sayd to the Iuge/ I am certayne & me remembreth wel/ that the dogge lend to her a loof of brede And the Myllan went and sayd/ she receyued hit presente my persone/ And the sperowhawk sayd to the sheep/ Come hyder why denyest thow that whiche thow hast take and receyued/ And thus was the poure sheep vaynquysshed/ And thenne the Iuge commaunded to her that she shold paye the dogge/ wherfore she sold awey before the winter her flees and wulle for to pay that/ that she neuer had/ And thus was the poure sheep despoylled/ In suche maner done the euylle hongry peple whiche by theyr grete vntrouthe and malyce robben and despoyllen the poure folke.

19. While there is no way of being precise about a medieval author's source, any version of the story must be considered, especially if it is known to have been current. The Aesopic tales were undoubtedly told as well as written; it seems logical to assume that Henryson, a schoolmaster, knew both literary and oral versions. I am not able, however, to agree with Bauman's suggestion that Henryson wrote the *Moral Fables* for his pupils. The literary quality and the sophistication of the work suggest that he had a wider audience in mind.

20. [For other examples, see the American Indian Coyote stories in the essays by Dixon (Section 1) and Trejo (Section 2).]

21. For example, in the "Taill of the Uponlandis Mous, and the Burges Mous," the city mouse, searching for her sister, behaves in a perfectly human fashion, until she calls out to her sister to "Cry peip anis!" Her words suddenly remind the reader that these are mice, not women. The fox basking in the sun after a good meal is like a comfortable man, but the keeper's arrow is the logical end for fox, not man.

22. John Langland, *Piers the Plowman*, ed. W. W. Skeat (Oxford: The Clarendon Press, 1906), Passus I.

institution set up to protect them.[23] Specifically, the sheep is denied justice. In most cases, and in other fables, the dog is the sheep's protector; here he falsely accuses the sheep for his own gain. He is supported by a court made up of the sheep's natural enemies.[24]

It is true that for the medieval exemplum writer the final word is religious: the misery of life on earth will give way to rest in heaven for the good man. The medieval victim had the dubious comfort of knowing that eventually his oppressors, being sinful, would suffer more than he. That is why the sheep is not killed: he instead must suffer the Edinburgh winter without his protecting wool. Death would release him from misery.

The hope offered at the end of the moralitas does not affect the tale. In the stark narration there is never any possibility of justice for the sheep being tried by his natural enemies. Bauman feels that the tale is bare and unembellished because Henryson's source did not inspire him.[25] I would suggest instead that Henryson is doing exactly what he wants to do, and that his style reflects his content. No two of his fables are alike, and the thirteen as a whole combine to present a picture of the world comprised of different points of view. This fable presents the world as the oppressed see it: stark and merciless.

Underneath the surface humor of the story of Sister Goose the world is equally stark and merciless. The tale is not, under any circumstances, a "funny" story; it is extremely bitter whether told in the grim brevity of Henryson's Middle High Scots version or traditional Southern black dialect.

Henryson constructs his story by presenting a series of unembellished facts. The sheep is accused and the events unfold: it is impossible to have any hope that the sheep will win. Even the request for arbiters is an act of desperation, for what kind of arbiters will Judge Wolf appoint? The two versions of the Sister Goose story given here rely strongly on contrast for their effect—Sister Goose paddling happily on the lake against the suddenness of her fate; vigorous dialogue followed by swift exposition—to create the startled recognition that makes the story effective. The version of the story with the reference to Civil Rights is probably the stronger of the two, for Sister Goose really does seem to have a chance in court—but she is killed and eaten anyway, and her bones are picked.

23. The identity of the sheep with the poor is established in the moralitas; however, it was a standard identification.

24. To complete the picture of the poor man as a helpless victim in a world of wrong, the moralitas draws upon two topoi, God is Asleep and The World Turned Upside-Down. See Ernst Curtius, *European Literature in the Latin Middle Ages* (New York: Pantheon, 1963).

25. Bauman, p. 118. "Henryson pads out his version with legal jargon, but the tale leaves an impression of sparseness nevertheless."

The trial is the core of the story. The literal form of justice is observed in both the fifteenth and the twentieth centuries, even though both dog and fox have the physical equipment to take what they want.[26] Justice is not found where it should be found. The five hundred years between Henryson and black America have made only superficial changes in the story.

More change has occurred in the false conversion tale: it is no longer a beast fable and it has become an end in itself rather than an episode on the way to an end. Yet it retains certain qualities: a tone of genial humor, a delight in cleverness—both the fox and the Jew are quite pleased with themselves—that involves outwitting someone, and finally an inversion of the concept of baptism and transformation.

Henryson's version displays another strength of the beast fable: the ability to point a lesson through the man-beast relationship. Lowrence is charming and his story is told with humor and warmth, almost with affection. Nevertheless, he is wrong and he is punished. As fox he preys on his natural food and meets his fate in the keeper's arrow; as man he behaves like a beast and the result is that unpredictable bolt from heaven that is the underlying force of the theological level of the *Moral Fables*. The beast in man pleads his nature as an excuse, but man's responsibility is to control his nature, to overcome the beast and move toward the angelic. The fox is not evil; he is instead the man who loves the "pleasant vices" and who sins through love of pleasure and through choosing the easy way. The tale is entirely concerned with individual, rather than social, behavior; ease and pleasure are the attacking forces, not a corrupt institution. Even though the friars are certainly shown as a contributing factor to Lowrence's eventual fate, they are not castigated in the tale. Tone, style, and content of this fable have other concerns, especially warnings against the dangers of pleasure. The fox's charming hypocrisy, which seems to amuse him as much as it amuses us, provides him with a good dinner at the same time that it leads him to the death that he accepts with philosophical humor.[27] Other verisons, without the beast-fable frame and the theological message, focus on a situation that is funny in itself.

For medievalists examination of these jokes is most rewarding. Francis Lee Utley says, "A recently collected oral version with a history going back to the Middle Ages might well outweigh the evidence of the literary document . . . because if not closer in time it is closer in content and motivation, and can better explain Chaucer's [or

---

26. As in the story of the wolf and the lamb, when after the lamb argues logically and correctly the wolf simply kills and eats it. Henryson also tells this tale.

27. It should always be remembered in dealing with the Middle Ages that death itself is not punishment, but damnation is. Lowrence's facile and meaningless confession and false penance condemn him to hell.

any medieval author's] donnée."[28] For the folklorist—and I do not mean to suggest that these two categories are or should be mutually exclusive—this kind of examination is a starting point. Certainly it demonstrates the vitality of folklore, if that needs to be proved: five hundred years is a long and healthy life.

Perhaps one of the most provocative questions raised by this kind of examination is why one story remained a beast fable and the other did not. A possible answer suggests itself if we accept folklore as controlled fantasy which offers a way of dealing with material that must be repressed.[29]

The beast fable was useful as a means of conveying a point obliquely, often for the sake of the narrator's safety. Even by the end of the fifteenth century the church was losing its enormous power. As time went on a joke against church doctrine did not have to stay underground, and the humor of the situation could surface safely. The same is not true of the story of Sister Goose. As a form of black humor, it is still essentially underground. When Sterling A. Brown told the story, he was a black man talking to a black audience. The conditions upon which the tale depends are still present, though the externals are different: the contrast between the fact and the form of justice. Whether the tensions involve justice for blacks in a white society or justice for the poor in a semi-feudal society with immense power in the hands of a few, they are the same kinds of tensions. It is safer, therefore, to talk about sheep and dogs and geese and foxes.[30]

The passage of time and the differences in ideas and beliefs have caused these three stories to change, or to adapt to different worlds. The religious framework for all three is gone, yet each manages to retain its flavor: the fatal hairdo story is still a warning, the false conversion tale keeps its genial tone, and the tale of Sister Goose is still bitter and ironic. Perhaps the most striking thing about an examination such as this is the evidence it offers of the vitality of folklore and its ability to adapt and change as the world in which it functions changes.

28. Francis Lee Utley, "Some Implications of Chaucer's Folktales," *Laographia* 22 (1965): 589.

29. This idea comes from Professor Alan Dundes, for whose encouragement and advice I am extremely grateful.

30. I suspect that the search for versions of this story between the fifteenth century and today would be difficult, since by its nature the tale seems to be essentially an underground one. If it could be found I would expect it to be part of the folklore of an oppressed group.

THE MIGRATORY ANECDOTE
AND THE FOLK CONCEPT OF FAME

Mac E. Barrick

This study demonstrates the folkloric nature of a minor narrative genre by demonstrating the variations on a few themes, the traditional attachment of these themes to well-known individuals, and the folk acceptance of apocryphal stories that are often circulated in printed or broadcast media. Generally an individual knows only the version of a migratory anecdote which is attached to a specific person, and so he may regard it as a true story and nontraditional. The folklorist establishes the traditional quality of the story by gathering many applications of the same anecdote to various persons in different times and countries. But this is a big and sometimes frustrating task, as suggested by Mac E. Barrick's documentation; a specialist in Spanish literature, he has had to be familiar not only with published folklore collections but also with writings in popular newspapers and magazines, with joke books, and even with television comedy programs (see footnotes 8, 19, and 31).

The "folk concept of fame" that Barrick mentions seems to describe the career of a somewhat eccentric person from a folksy background rising to national or international prominence. The migratory anecdote attributed to such people (and perhaps "folk hero" is too limited a term for them) is typically one which is believable because it seems to sum up that person's eccentricity and folksiness. The stories are accepted as authentic because they are clearly true to our expectations of such people, and the earliest examples seem to be the truest simply because they came first and are probably reprinted the most. Also, as Barrick points out, when such a person tells some of these anecdotes in public, then it is an easy step for the story to be incorporated into others told about him (or her).

Students might seek, in oral tradition and publications, other anecdotes about figures in American history listed by Barrick. Or they might find out who are the more recent subjects of such anecdotes: Billy Carter, Elvis Presley, Bob Dylan? Are there anecdotal subjects who do not fit the pattern Barrick suggests: Henry Kissinger, W. C. Fields, Barbara Walters? What are the migratory anecdotes concerning film and rock stars, athletes, popular authors, and local celebrities? Some personal anecdotes from the academic world are mentioned in Barre Toelken's essay "The Folklore of Academe" in The Study of American Folklore, and references to other relevant studies are given in the same book on pages 123–24 and 37 (the folklore of folklorists).

Barrick has provided a number of additions to his original notes especially for this reader.

THE MIGRATORY ANECDOTE IS a little studied form of folklore. The initial problem that arises in any discussion of the genre is whether it should be considered folkloric at all. Despite Archer Taylor's definition of this genre as an oral one,[1] most anecdotes today circulate as printed texts, usually in collections compiled from earlier sources. Yet even if the folk do not create anecdotes, they do propagate them, and a study of the forces that influence that propagation may shed some light on the processes of folklore creation and development.

Anecdotes often have some basis in fact, but in many cases the historical details have been changed or the material is completely fictitious. Both Archer Taylor and Jan H. Brunvand have remarked on the strong affinity between anecdote and legend.[2] Like legends, anecdotes tend to be familiar to a larger audience than that actively engaged in narrating them, but unlike legends, anecdotes tend to circulate as intact units, in a relatively unvarying form. This is probably because they are, at least in the United States, usually brief narrative settings for clever sayings and retorts. Like legends they do tend to be localized or to be adapted to the character of a protagonist familiar to the narrator. It is this constant shifting of protagonist that complicates the study of individual anecdotes, because heretofore most collections of these personalized narratives have been organized around the central figure rather than the thematic content.[3] Little allowance is thus

1. "An anecdote is a brief narrative current in oral tradition that tells something unusual about a person, an event or a thing. It may involve quotation of a witty remark or a description of a remarkable situation." See Archer Taylor, "The Anecdote: A Neglected Genre," in *Medieval Literature and Folklore*, ed. Jerome Mandel and Bruce A. Rosenberg (New Brunswick, New Jersey: Rutgers Univ. Press, 1971), p. 223.

2. Taylor, pp. 226–227. In *The Study of American Folklore* (New York: Norton, 1968), p. 94 [2nd. edn., p. 114], Jan Harold Brunvand writes, "The *anecdote* is a short personal legend, supposedly true but generally apocryphal, told about an episode in the life of either a famous individual or a local character." Cf. Evan Esar's facetious definition: "An anecdote is a brief account of an incident that has never occurred in the life of some famous person." See *The Humor of Humor* (New York: Branhall House, 1952), p. 32.

3. For example compare the collections of Alfred H. Miles, *One Thousand & One Ancedotes* (New York: Whittaker, 1895), and Edmund Fuller, *Thesaurus of Anecdotes* (New York: Crown, 1942). Though it contains fewer than 1800 stories, the latter has been reprinted as *2500 Anecdotes for All Occasions* (Garden City, New York: Dolphin, 1961). Miles's collection is primarily character-oriented while Fuller's, though the anecdotes are tied to specific persons, is organized according to theme, with cross-referencing by idea and proper name.

made for the occurrence of the same anecdote with differing characters. One example, usually the one assumed to be earliest, is accepted as authentic, the rest being dismissed as apocryphal and therefore of no value. But the folkloric value of anecdotes lies specifically in these so-called apocryphal variants.

For example, three anecdotes published by Vance Randolph in his *Hot Springs and Hell* continue to appear frequently in jokebooks, newspaper columns, and other published sources. The first, "The Governor Said Manure,"[4] which the informant attributed to Jeff Davis[5]—though Randolph noted that it was told on many politicians, is now related (and printed) with Harry Truman as the central figure. Gershon Legman collected a text of it in Washington, D.C., in 1952 and published it in *Rationale of the Dirty Joke* without naming Truman, but the implied reference is obvious:

> In another joke on the same politician not strictly relevant here, the politician's daughter complains to her mother that her father has disgraced the family by saying 'manure' instead of 'fertilizer' in presenting medals for roses at the Ladies' Horticultural Club. "It's all right, dear," says her mother, "it's taken me years to get him to say manure."[6]

In a book review published in *Saturday Review/World*, John P. Roche noted that the story had been told to him by a Secret Service agent in 1966:

> One morning the President—trusty Secret Service man in tow—walked out the French doors into the rose garden, where Bess was entertaining a group of friends from Missouri. After the amenities, Truman looked at the rosebushes with a critical eye, said, "Bess, they need manure," and returned to his office. A friend remonstrated with Mrs. Truman: "Bess, the President of our country shouldn't say 'manure'; he should say 'fertilizer.' " "Dearie," replied 'the Boss,' "do you have any idea how long it took to get him to say 'manure'?"[7]

A curious parallel appeared more recently in an English joke collection:

> A Fermanagh farmer's son brought his girl-friend home for tea, and during the meal his father, a big, rough man, talked of nothing but work on the farm.

4. Vance Randolph, *Hot Springs and Hell* (Hatboro, Pennsylvania: Folklore Associates, 1965), p. 9.

5. [Jefferson Davis (1808–1889), President of the Confederate States of America (1861–1865).]

6. Gershon Legman, *Rationale of the Dirty Joke* (New York: Grove, 1968), p. 339.

7. *Saturday Review/World*, 23 February 1974, p. 22.

"John, tomorrow we'll have to spread dung in the top meadow," he said. "And the day after that we'll have to spread dung in the corner field. And then you'll have to go over to Hagan's and get another load of dung so that we can get the potatoes planted."

After his girl-friend had left the son complained to his mother, "That was very embarrassing, Ma. Could you not get Da to say 'manure' or 'fertiliser,' if he must talk about such things at the tea-table."

The mother shook her head.

"Sure, it's taken me years to get him to call it 'dung'," she sighed.[8]

The origins and date of this Ulster variant cannot, of course, be traced from this reference, but from the euphemisms used and suggested as improvements, it would seem to antedate the American texts. The word "dung" is considerably less acceptable in polite society than "manure"—the suggestion being in the American texts that even "manure" is vulgar and should be replaced by "fertilizer." One wonders how long "fertilizer" will remain proper before being replaced by something like "organic nutrient."

The second anecdote in Randolph's collection, "Preachers Around the Fire,"[9] has a great number of parallels with a wide variety of protagonists. Randolph's story does not identify any of the participants, but the story has on other occasions been associated with Lorenzo Dow, Ulysses S. Grant,[10] the Archbishop of Canterbury and his sons, and Lincoln.[11]

8. Ken Nixon, *Best Ulster Jokes* (London: Wolfe, 1970), pp. 14–15. J. M. Elgart (*More Over Sexteen* [n.p.: Grayson, 1953], p. 118) published a joke version eliminating the personal reference and ending: "Daughter, I believe in letting well enough alone. It took me 27 years to teach him to say 'manure.'" Other joking variants were used in the cartoon jokebook *Gaze*, June, 1958, p. 69, and on TV's Hee Haw, July, 1976.

9. Randolph, p. 57. [A boy tells the preachers what he dreamed hell looked like: "Just like it is here. I mighty nigh froze. The preachers was so thick, I couldn't get near the stove."]

10. [Dow: "Primitive Methodist" itinerant evangelist (1777–1834), the subject of many anecdotes; Ulysses S. Grant: 18th President of the United States (1822–1885).]

11. For Dow, see Emelyn E. Gardner, *Folklore from the Schoharie Hills, New York* (Ann Arbor: Univ. of Michigan Press, 1937), p. 38; reprinted by Benjamin A. Botkin, *A Treasury of American Anecdotes* (New York: Bonanza, 1957), p. 187. For Grant, see Bennett Cerf, *The Life of the Party* (Garden City, New York: Doubleday, 1956), p. 193. For the Archbishop, see Kurt Ranke, *European Anecdotes and Jests* (Copenhagen: Rosenkilde and Bagger, 1972), p. 126. For other British variants, see E. M. Wilson, "Some Humorous English Folk Tales," *Folk Lore*, 54 (1943), 259–260; and Alfred Williams, *Round About the Upper Thames* (London: Duckforth, 1922), p. 41. For Lincoln, see the note in Randolph, p. 207, to which add Keith W. Jennison, *The Humorous Mr. Lincoln* (New York: Bonanza, 1965), pp. 36–38. Cf. also Baughman motifs X312.1 and X459(d). George Dunkelsberger in *The Story of Snyder County* [Pa.] (Selinsgrove, Pa.: Snyder Co. Hist. Soc., 1948) relates the same story about a local halfwit.

The third anecdote, "A Superfluous Speech,"[12] has had an even more varied circulation. Randolph's text ascribes the incident simply to an "Arkansas politician." An apocopated version in *Scholarly Books in America* associates the incident with an unnamed Senator:

> A Senator has just finished a campaign speech. An ample lady rushes up to congratulate him. Here is their conversation:
> Ample Lady: "Senator, your speech was absolutely superfluous!"
> Senator: "Why thank you, Madam, I intend to have it published posthumously."
> Ample Lady: "Wonderful, wonderful; the sooner the better!"[13]

After the death of Adlai Stevenson in July of 1965, several newspapers reprinted the anecdote as an example of his wit. Subsequent examples[14] omit the "superfluous" malapropism completely, dwelling instead upon the punchline. The story has apparently lost its anecdotal quality and has become a folk jest with no personal reference (cf. Motif J1803. *Learned words misunderstood*). In the case of public speakers like Stevenson, it is readily apparent how a joke or story told as an illustrative or diverting anecdote might be interpreted by the audience as a personal experience, but this would account for only a few of the migratory anecdotes in current circulation.

One such widely adapted story is regularly updated on appropriate occasions. It involves a man returning to his rightful position after years of political imprisonment or exile. In his first address after his return, he dismisses the injustice of his detainment with a few seemingly original and well chosen words, "As I was saying before I was interrupted. . . ." The story has been published on several occasions with Eamon De Valera, the Irish political leader, as the protagonist.[15] In another variant, Stanley Woodward, sports editor of the *New York Herald Tribune*, returning to the paper after an eleven years' absence, began his first column with the words, "As I was saying when I was so rudely interrupted."[16] Oral versions of the story collected in recent years concern a French politician returning to Paris after its liberation

12. Randolph, pp. 74–75.

13. *Scholarly Books in America*, 6 no. 2 (October 1964), 8.

14. *The Pennsylvania Gazette*, 65, no. 7 (April 1967), 4, reprinted a variant from *The Catholic Digest* involving a pastor and a female parishioner. In Clyde Murdock, *A Treasury of Humor* (Grand Rapids, Michigan: Zondervan Books, 1967), pp. 77–78, neither speaker is identified, but in a version in the Williamsport (Pennsylvania) *Grit* (16 August 1970, p. 32), the figures are again a congressman and a female admirer. In "My Favorite Jokes," *Parade*, 8 August 1971, p. 19, Emil Cohen makes himself the protagonist of the joke.

15. Fuller, no. 771; Bennett Cerf, *Try and Stop Me* (New York: Simon and Schuster, 1944), p. 262.

16. *Time*, 10 December 1965, p. 84.

in World War II, and Father Curran, president of Catholic University in Washington, who was dismissed and restored to office after the student riots in the Spring of 1969. The original—or at least the oldest—version of the story relates to Fray Luis de León, Spanish poet and educator, who was arrested by the Inquisition in 1572 and returned to his lecture hall in January of 1577, beginning with the words *"Dicebamus hesterna die"* ("As we were saying yesterday"). Yet even this version seems to be apocryphal, not being recorded for years after the event.[17] Who then was the original speaker? That is not the important matter here. What is important is that the story was so familiar and so expressive of a universal experience that it could be adapted to a great variety of situations and people for over four hundred years of recorded history. Unlike the historical facts which are buried in libraries and forgotten, the anecdote has remained for many people an authentic and memorable detail in the life of Fray Luis de León, Eamon De Valera, or Father Curran.

The study of anecdotes is further complicated by the fact that newspaper columnists and collectors of anecdotes frequently update their material by attributing it to colorful public figures currently in the news. Formerly, publicity agents adapted appropriate stories to fit their clients and fed the stories to columnists and reporters in order to keep the clients' names before the public. Academic public relations officers occasionally still do this, as evidenced by the story of a computerized scheduling system that routinely assigned classes to the men's room in one of the buildings, an event which supposedly occurred on several campuses from Texas to Pennsylvania.

Whether the result of action by professional writers and humorists or of the natural vagaries of folkloristic change, certain names occur regularly as the referents of anecdotes. In England, Samuel Johnson, George Bernard Shaw, and more recently Winston Churchill have been the most popular subjects of anecdotes. Churchill, like Shaw, was a master of the clever retort, and many of the anecdotes concerning him are based on fact.[18] Some have become sufficiently well known so as to be almost proverbial:

Lady Astor is reported to have said to Churchill, "Winston, if you were my husband, I would poison your coffee."

17. See Angel Valbuena Prat, *Historia de la literatura española,* I (Barcelona: Gili, 1950), 573; Pedro Salinas, *Reality and the Poet in Spanish Poetry* (Baltimore: Johns-Hopkins Press, 1940), p. 103.

18. Churchill's one-time bodyguard Walter H. Thompson states that Churchill "was never stingy in giving his enemies an abundance and variety of copy. Everything he said was either quotable or misquotable." See *Assignment: Churchill* (New York: Popular Library, 1961), p. 42.

"If you were my wife, Nancy," replied Churchill suavely, "I would drink it."[19]

However, Churchill's famous statement about Sir Stafford Cripps, "There but for the grace of God, goes God,"[20] is often attributed to others—for example, H. J. Mankiewicz referring to Orson Welles.[21] It is noteworthy that the phrase Churchill is parodying, "There but for the grace of God go I," has likewise been attributed to a variety of figures, including John Bradford, John Bunyan, John Wesley, and Sherlock Holmes.[22] Some Churchill anecdotes, like the following, seem apocryphal:

> ADMIRER—Winston, that fat belly of yours would look better on a pregnant woman!
> CHURCHILL—It has been, my boy—and she is![23]

This does have a similarity in tone to another story that seems authentically Churchillian:

> On one occasion, a young woman of glib tongue sought to have some fun at the expense of the corpulent statesman.
> "Mr. Churchill," she said, "there are two things about you that I dislike very much."
> "What are they?" inquired the vociferous man.
> "Your politics and your mustache," replied the inexperienced woman.
> "Well," answered the indomitable Churchill, "don't worry about

19. Isaac Asimov, *Treasury of Humor* (Boston: Houghton Mifflin, 1971), p. 136. Cf. John O'Hara, *The Horse Knows the Way* (New York: Random House, 1964), p. 118: " 'Is there anything in it—like arsenic?' 'I'd have put some in last night willingly,' she said. 'And as Churchill said to Lady Astor, I'd have drunk it.' " The story has appeared occasionally in jokebooks, e.g., Henry M. Kieffer, *More Laughs* (New York: Dodge, 1923), p. 118; in January, 1976, John Henry Faulk used it as a joke on *Hee Haw.*

20. Leon A. Harris, *The Fine Art of Political Wit* (New York: Dutton, 1964), p. 174; see also *New York Times Book Review,* 28 November 1971, p. 54.

21. Max Wilk, *The Wit and Wisdom of Hollywood* (New York: Atheneum, 1971), p. 146.

22. Burton Stevenson, *The Home Book of Proverbs, Maxims and Familiar Phrases* (New York: Macmillan, 1948), 1017: 14. The phrase lies currently in that undefined area between familiar allusion and proverb. See John O'Hara, *Ten North Frederick* (New York: Random House, 1955), p. 74: "There but for the grace of God go I"; and Joseph Wambaugh, *The Blue Knight* (Boston: Little, Brown, 1972), p. 154: "There on the sidewalk, but for the gods, sleeps old Bumper Morgan."

23. Cited by D. Cook in *American Notes and Queries,* 6 (1968), 119. The same story was collected by Gershon Legman with no personal reference to Churchill (see Legman, p. 591). It also appears in J. M. Elgart, *Over Sixteen* (1951; rpt. New York: Signet, 1968), p. 36.

these two things—you are not likely to come in contact with either."[24]

The last story corresponds closely to the American folk attitude depicting Churchill as an immoral, untrustworthy man, at odds with the Protestant ethic.[25]

In American anecdotes, Lincoln is by far the most popular subject, followed closely by Mark Twain and more distantly by Calvin Coolidge and Thomas Edison. Dozens of compilations of stories involving Lincoln have been published, some of them in his own lifetime.[26] In general collections he figures prominently in a large percentage of anecdotes.[27] Lincoln, perhaps wisely, welcomed the association of his name with humorous anecdotes and often, on seeing such a story in print, would make it his own by retelling it himself. Such is the case with the story of "two Quaker women in a railway coach during the war, and one saying, 'I think Jefferson Davis will succeed.' 'Why does thee think so?' asks the other. 'Because Jefferson is a praying man.' 'But so is Abraham a praying man,' the other says. 'Yes,' the first woman concluded, 'but the Lord will think Abraham is joking.' "[28] On a few occasions common folk jests which do not seem to fit the character of Linocln are ascribed to him:

Abraham Lincoln (according to the story) attended a charity bazaar, and tendered a twenty-dollar bill in payment for a bunch of violets. Receiving no change, he reached over the counter to pat the girl's breasts. "What are these, my dear?" he asked. "Why they're my

24. E. V. White, *Let's Laugh* (Denton, Texas: White, 1940), p. 78; Fuller, no. 503; Thompson, p. 61; and *National Enquirer*, 26 August 1975, p. 10.

25. Churchill was caricatured in several obscene comic booklets during the 1940s; see Donald H. Gilmore, *Sex in Comics* (San Diego: Greenleaf, 1971), III, 158–159. Cf. the following story collected in Duncannon, Pennsylvania, in June of 1966: "Churchill came to visit Roosevelt. He came about two o'clock and all the hotels was closed so Roosevelt said he could stay in the spare room. So during the night he come out in the hall and seen Churchill coming out of his wife's room, so he said, "That'll be enough of that.' And he said, 'Yeah, it wasn't no good noway.' " Churchill was known to parade naked at night during his stays at the White House; see J. M. Orndorff, Jr., "Those Summers in the White House," *Saturday Review*, 20 July 1968, p. 40.

26. For example, *Old Abe's Jokes Fresh from Abraham's Bosom* (New York: Dawley, 1864); A. K. McClure, *Lincoln's Yarns and Stories* (Chicago: Winston, 1911); Anthony Gross, *Lincoln's Own Stories* (New York: Harper, 1912); and Jennison, *The Humorous Mr. Lincoln*, already cited.

27. Lincoln is mentioned in over one hundred of the anecdotes in Fuller's *Thesaurus*; see also Harris, pp. 94–110.

28. Harris, p. 102. The story is often reprinted, for example in *Baer's Almanac* (Lancaster, Pennsylvania) for 1969, with the note: "Abraham Lincoln is said to have felt this the best story he'd ever read about himself."

breasts, Mr. Lincoln." "I see," he said; "everything is so high around here, I thought they might be your buttocks."[29]

The folk picture of Lincoln as a tall, sober man delivering the Gettysburg Address belies the real man. Lincoln was quite capable of this type of humor, but unfortunately few examples of it have been recorded.

Politicians would do well to be concerned about the stories being told on them. Leon Harris shows how Franklin D. Roosevelt was able to manipulate public opinion in part through the adroit use of humorous stories, though an equally important series of jokes in oral tradition depicted him in a less than positive light.[30] Anecdotes about Adlai Stevenson, portraying him as a highbrow with little of the common man about him, and jokes about Spiro Agnew[31] certainly did little to help their political careers. The many bitter jokes about Edward Kennedy and Chappaquiddick[32] will undoubtedly be an important factor in any political campaigns in which he figures.

Comparison of the characters of Lincoln, Twain, Coolidge, and Truman yields some indication of the reason for their popularity as folk heroes. Each was possessed of a certain eccentricity or idiosyncrasy that made him a likely referent for any stories reflecting that eccentricity. A story about an ugly man might easily be applied to Lincoln,[33] just as any anecdote involving taciturnity might come to be associated with Coolidge.[34] All of these men have another trait in

29. Legman, p. 245. Legman collected the story in California in 1942 and notes that it was ascribed to Lincoln in *The New Anecdota Americana* (1944). The story is Baughman's motif J1499.13(g). A version collected in Carlisle, Pennsylvania, in 1968 has a customer in a store amazed at the price of peanuts ask the clerk, "What's that mark on your chin?" "That's a dimple, why?" "Oh, I thought it might be your belly-button, as high as your nuts are." Cf. George G. Carey, *Maryland Folk Legends and Folk Songs* (Cambridge, Maryland: Tidewater Publishers, 1971), p. 61; and Bennett Cerf, *The Laugh's on Me* (Garden City, New York: Doubleday, 1959), pp. 388–389.

30. Harris, pp. 134–159.

31. For example: "Vice President Agnew was called upon to greet a delegation of Navajo Indians, and he said, 'Welcome to our country.'" (Johnny Carson, NBC-TV, 6 March 1969).

32. "New Kennedy Lore," *Folklore Forum*, 3 (1970), 65, 71; *Newsweek*, 2 June 1975, p. 25.

33. See John Q. Anderson, "For the Ugliest Man: An Example of Folk Humor," *Southern Folklore Quarterly*, 28 (1964), 199–209.

34. Two Coolidge anecdotes are sepecially well known: (1) Coolidge attends church without his wife. Later she asks him what the subject of the sermon had been. "Adultery" (or "Sin") is the reply. "What did he say about it?" "He's against it." See Bennett Cerf, *Try and Stop Me*, p. 261; E. D. Asselin, *New England Laughs* (Middlebury, Vermont: Vermont Books, 1963), p. 28; and George F. Will's syndicated newspaper column, appearing in the Carlisle, Pennsylvania, *Evening Sentinel*, 3 July 1975. (2) A lady sitting beside Coolidge at a dinner remarks that she had made a bet he will say more than two words. He says, "You lose." See Fuller, no. 813; Asimov, p. 71; and Allen R. Foley, *What the Old-Timer Said* (Brattleboro, Vermont: Greene, 1971), p. 54.

common, and that is a close affinity to the folk mentality in matters of birth, speech, and sentimentality. When a suitable figure, like a Davy Crockett, a Lincoln, or a Truman, a man with whom the folk can identify, rises from their ranks to national prominence, they quickly make him the protagonist of their legends and anecdotes. When one of their number "makes it" in the world of the upper crust, their own hopes for ultimate success are buoyed. By identifying with these men, by knowing some personal detail about them, as contained in these anecdotes, they share vicariously the experience and the reputation.

"THE LANE COUNTY BACHELOR":
FOLKSONG OR NOT?

Jan Harold Brunvand

This study began as a concise review of a few well-known published versions of a Western folksong for a lecture to demonstrate to students what might be learned even from a few texts. Another goal was to show the influence of folksong collectors and editors on the interpretation of their materials. But the project snowballed as more and more information came in from folklorists, librarians, and the residents of Lane county, Kansas, itself. As data accumulated it became clear that the tampering hands of well-meaning editors and poets on the records of folk tradition had been much busier than suspected. Still the song-texts themselves, viewed historically and geographically, preserved enough information to support a positive answer to the question "Folksong or not?" I hope this is a worthy example of D. K. Wilgus's "individual song history" approach. (See "The Future of American Folksong Scholarship," Southern Folklore Quarterly, 37 [1973].) Incidentally, even if the answer to the title question had turned out to be "No," this would have been a useful result of the research.

THE FOLKSONGS OF HOMESTEADERS on the Great Plains have received relatively little study by American folklorists.[1] Such songs are not deficient as documents of social history, for the numerous texts of a homesteaders' song like "Sweet Nebraska Land" with its variations as "Dakota Land," "Kansas Land," and so forth are just as revealing of Western American events and attitudes as are songs like "The Old Chisholm Trail," "The Mountain Meadows Massacre," or "Sam Bass," all of which have been traced and discussed. Probably, pioneer farm-

1. The major modern students of Western American folksongs are Austin E. and Alta S. Fife of Logan Utah, to whom I owe a great debt of gratitude. They generously furnished me with numerous references and many copies from their copious achive. Items integrated into their personal collection are labelled FAC (Fife American Collection) below; other excerpts from their collections are individually identified in notes.

I also thank the following for sending me important information and texts: Joseph C. Hickerson, Head, Archive of Folk Song, The Library of Congress; Rachel Christopher, Reference Librarian, Forsyth Library, Fort Hays Kansas State College; Professor Samuel J. Sackett, Fort Hays Kansas State College; Richard Gilbar, Reference Librarian, University of Kansas Libraries, Lawrence; R. J. Tillotson, Shields, Kansas; and Ellen May Stanley, Dighton, Kansas.

The Interlibrary Loan section of the Marriott Library, University of Utah, was most helpful in locating and borrowing several scarce publications.

ers' folksongs have been slighted simply because swatting fleas in sod houses has seemed less intriguing to scholars than driving dogies up the trails or pulling hand carts across the plains or describing a life of crime.

Particularly neglected among Western pioneer songs are the lyrical pieces. Ballads, such as "Joe Bowers," have attracted much attention, while songs centering on feelings rather than plot, like "Little Old Sod Shanty on the Claim," usually rate only generalized headnotes in the folksong collections. One such lyrical folksong of the plains settlers which prominent anthologizers like Sandburg, Botkin, and Lomax have included is generally known as "The Lane County Bachelor" or "Starving to Death on my Government Claim." Sung to the tune of "The Irish Washer Woman,"[2] this lilting piece renders into rustic verse common experiences of life in a homestead shack, such as those in the third stanza of the first example: "How happy I feel when I crawl into bed,/And a rattlesnake rattles a tune at my head" and so on.[3] Surely we have here a clear instance of Mody Boatright's claim for a "buoyant" strain of frontier humor which employed "extravagant burlesque of the outsider's conception of the frontier" and which projected a resilient pioneer spirit rather than bleak despair.[4] And surely it is worthwhile to learn more about a song which writers on American folklore frequently cite as a typical example of the Western folk worldview[5] and which authoritative Western folklorists have characterized as "probably the most widely sung of the 'sodbuster' ballads."[6]

It needs to be reiterated, however, that "The Lane County Bachelor" is not a ballad, or at least it has not been indexed as such in the standard syllabus of native balladry. G. Malcolm Laws, Jr., did not

2. Sigmund Spaeth in *A History of Popular Music in America* (New York: Random House, 1948) writes that the first American printing of "Yankee Doodle" (1795) used it as the finale for a medley that included "The Irish Washer Woman" (page 17). It is among the tunes that "Pa" plays on his fiddle in Laura Ingalls Wilder's *Little House On the Prairie* (1935; rev. ed., New York: Harper and Row, 1971), p. 68. For a recently-collected traditional rendition, see *Cowboy Songs*, Vol. II, a disc issued by the Arizona Friends of Folklore (Flagstaff, Ariz. [1972]), Side B, No. 3.

3. A similar description in prose is quoted in Robert C. Steensma, "'Stay Right There and Toughy it Out': The American Homesteader as Autobiographer," *Western Review*, 6 (1969), 16, from Martha L. Smith, *Going to God's Country*, a woman's chronicle of life on the Great Plains spanning the years 1890 to 1910.

4. *Folk Laughter on the American Frontier* (1949; rpt. New York: Collier Books, 1961), p. 169.

5. See Russell Ames, *The Story of American Folksong* (New York: Grosset & Dunlap, 1955), pp. 52–53, and Jan Harold Brunvand, *The Study of American Folklore: An Introduction* (New York: W. W. Norton, 1968), p. 292 [2nd. edn., p. 347].

6. Austin E. and Alta S. Fife, *Cowboy and Western Songs: A Comprehensive Anthology* (New York: Clarkson N. Potter, 1969), p. 58.

see fit to include it in his section "Ballads of Cowboys and Pioneers," nor even in his appendix list of the less structured "Ballad-Like Pieces," although the song was printed by several of the authors Laws drew upon, and it has as much narrative content as, say, "The Dreary Black Hills," which is in Laws' syllabus.[7] Lacking Laws' listing, one must gather published examples without the convenience of a special bibliographic aid.

We may assume at the outset that the major reference in the song is to the Homestead Act of 1862 under the provisions of which vast stretches of the Great Plains were opened in 160-acre parcels to anyone willing to pay a ten-dollar fee, reside on his claim, and cultivate it for five years. Details in the various texts of the song jibe well with the hardships of farming in these parts during the last three decades of the nineteenth century when inept administration of the lands combined with plagues of insects and a run of miserable weather to test the pioneers' mettle. The song fits these historic circumstances; we lack clear proof of it being widely sung on the plains early in the homesteading period, but there is reasonably convincing evidence for a tradition by the 1880's and the turn of the century.

Lane county in the song is the one in west-central Kansas (the only other in the U.S. being in Oregon). From Lane county, Kansas, we get the longest early version of the ballad. This is the "Kepner text" given in full below as it was written down and dated March 8, 1891, by Ed Kepner of Dighton, Kansas, and given in 1933 to the library at Fort Hays Kansas State College. The text remained there for some twenty years before being published in the *Dighton* [Kansas] *Herald*[8] in the early 1950's after a Lane county resident accidentally discovered Vance Randolph's 1941 Library of Congress recording of an Arkansas version. At that time Ed Kepner delivered a copy of his manuscript to the newspaper for publication, and finally in 1961 it was also published in a local commemorative booklet[9] and in a scholarly collection of Kansas folklore,[10] then again in a general collection of Western folksongs in 1968.[11]

7. See *Native American Balladry* (Philadelphia: AFS Bibliographic and Special Series, vol. 1, 1950; reissued, 1964).

8. I have two undated xerographic copies of clippings from the *Dighton Herald* sent to me by Ellen May Stanley; she writes that they date from the 1950's.

9. *An Historical Record of Lane County, Founded June 3, 1886* [Dighton], 1961; second printing, 1976), sent to me by Ellen May Stanley, pp. [23–26].

10. See Henry H. Malone, "Folksongs and Ballads," in S. J. Sackett and William E. Koch, *Kansas Folklore* (Lincoln: University of Nebraska Press, 1961), pp. 146–148.

11. Richard E. Lingenfelter, Richard A. Dwyer, and David Cohen, *Songs of the American West* (Berkeley and Los Angeles: University of California Press, 1968), p. 459.

The Lane County Bachelor

The Kepner text:

1. Frank Baker's my name and a bachelor I am,
   I'm keeping old batch[12] on an elegant plan.
   You'll find me out west in the county of Lane,
   I'm starving to death on a government claim.
   My house it is built of the natural soil,
   The walls are erected according to Hoyle.[13]
   The roof has no pitch but is level and plain,
   And I always get wet when it happens to rain.

   > Hurrah for Lane County, the land of the free,
   > The home of the grasshopper, bed bug and flea
   > I'll sing loud its praises and tell of its fame,
   > While starving to death on a government claim.

2. My clothes they are ragged, my language is rough,
   My bread is case-hardened both solid and tough.
   The dough it is scattered all over the room,
   And the floor it gets scared at the sight of a broom.
   My dishes are scattered all over the bed,
   They are covered with sorghum and Government bread.
   Still I have a good time and live at my ease
   On common sop-sorghum, old bacon and grease.

   > Then come to Lane County, here is a home for you all,
   > Where the winds never cease and the rains never fall,
   > And the sun never sets but will always remain
   > Till it burns you all up on a Government claim.

3. How happy I feel when I crawl into bed,
   And a rattlesnake rattles a tune at my head,
   And the gay little centipede, void of all fear,
   Crawls over my neck and down into my ear.
   And the little bed bugs so cheerful and bright,
   They keep me a-laughing two-thirds of the night.
   And the gay little flea with sharp tacks in his toes,
   Plays "Why don't you catch me" all over my nose.

12. [A bachelor keeping house for myself.]
13. [Proverbial phrase meaning "in a proper manner"; refers to the famous rulebook for card games compiled by Sir Edmund Hoyle (died 1769).]

Hurrah for Lane County, hurrah for the west,
Where farmers and laborers are ever at rest.
For there's nothing to do but to sweetly remain
And starve like a man on a Government claim.

4. How happy am I on my government claim,
For I've nothing to lose nor I've nothing to gain.
I've nothing to eat and I've nothing to wear,
And nothing from nothing is honest and fair.
Oh, it is here I am solid and here I will stay,
For my money is all gone and I can't get away.
There is nothing that makes a man hard and profane,
Like starving to death on a Government claim.

Hurrah for Lane County, where blizzards arise,
Where the winds never cease and the flea never dies.
Come join in the chorus and sing of its fame,
You poor hungry hoboes that's starved on the claim.

5. No, don't get discouraged, you poor hungry men,
For we are all here as free as a pig in a pen.
Just stick to your homestead and battle the fleas
And look to your Maker to send you a breeze.
Now all you claim holders I hope you will stay
And chew your hardtack till you are toothless and grey.
But as for myself I'll no longer remain
And starve like a dog on a Government claim.

Farewell to Lane County, farewell to the west,
I'll travel back East to the girl I love best.
I'll stop in Missouri and get me a wife
And live on corn dodgers the rest of my life.

The evidence is good that a real Frank Baker did homestead in Lane county and there composed the words to the song which begins with his name, fitting his lyrics to a well known fiddle tune. Mrs. Bessie Prose Young, an old resident of the county, responded to a query from the Lane County Historical Society in 1944 giving the exact section numbers that Frank Baker homesteaded and the name of the other bachelor he lived with; she noted that "[he] composed a number of songs for our literary society."[14] Clint Hanna, in 1957 a Lane county college student doing research on the song, spoke to

14. Xeographic copy of a handwritten letter from Bessie Prose Young to Esther Hineman, March 4, 1944, sent to me by Ellen May Stanley.

several old residents who remembered Frank Baker; Hanna concluded that the song was written between 1886 and 1891.[15] It is believed by most who have investigated the matter that Baker had left the county early in the 1890's,[16] none of his relatives remain there or are known of elsewhere. In any case, Lane county residents have no doubts about his existence or his composition; their historical society even started a Lane County Bachelor Contest in 1974 to choose the local man who most resembles the person in the song, awarding him prizes such as a framed photo of the first sod house built in Lane county and a package of sunflower seeds. The contest is held annually during the Lane County Fair.[17]

I accept the Kepner text for its length, date, detail, coherence, location, and apparent solid link to an actual Western homesteader as a very likely base text for the whole tradition. It stands up well as a clever and well-organized folk poem, and it can plausibly explain all other known variants. The name "Lane county" appears in versions far removed from western Kansas, but that is where the only possible actual location may lie. The spirit of the song is cheerful (matching its tune), and the language is sprinkled with proverbial commonplaces (like "according to Hoyle") and with nicely ironic touches, such as "an elegant plan" (the Homestead Act itself?) and "nothing from nothing is honest and fair."

Corroborative evidence for its authenticity is furnished by other early western Kansas and Oklahoma texts, all shorter and exhibiting variations typical of oral tradition. Raymond Tillotson of Shields [Lane county], Kansas, found an undated pencil copy of thirty-two lines of the song among the papers of his father, a pioneer settler in the county. Folklorist S. J. Sackett has suggested that the gaps, spellings, and lack of line divisions here raise the possibility of its having been taken down from oral rendition.[18] Curiously, the Tillotson text's unique closing reference to *Topeka* has been printed twice as the ending of the Kepner text, which actually names *Missouri*.[19] Here is the last stanza of the Tillotson text as it was written:

15. Quoted in *An Historical Record*, p. [23].

16. However Ellen May Stanley found this entry in the diary of a Lane County pioneer, dated July 19, 1897: "Walter and Frank Baker came awhile this afternoon." There is no evidence that this is the composer of the song. (Letter dated July 27, 1976.)

17. Xerographic copies of *Dighton Herald* (1974), *Garden City Telegram* (1974) and *Hutchinson News* (1975) sent to me by Ellen May Stanley.

18. Malone (in Sackett and Koch), pp. 148–149.

19. Both Malone and Lingenfelter, Dwyer and Cohen print the Topeka version. The *Dighton Herald* and the Lane county *Historical Record* print the Missouri version, which is also as Austin Fife reports it (FAC II 408).

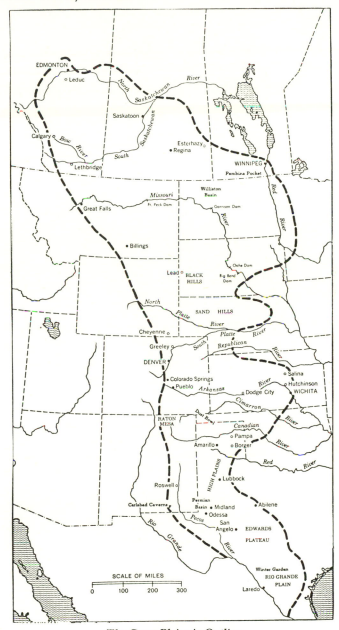

The Great Plains in Outline

Now all those good people
I hope they will staye &
chew there hard tack till they
Are toothless and gray
But as for My Self I'l Nolonger
remain and starve like a dog
on a gov clame
I'm going to leave the
West & travel back east to the
girl I love best I'll stop
in Topeka and get Me a
wife & there shall I stay
the rest of my life

Another handwritten text six lines shorter than the Kepner text was sent about 1889 to the North Topeka *Mail* but was only published in 1939 in the *Kansas Historical Quarterly*.[20] The first stanza reads:

frank baker is my name
and a bachelor I am
ime keeping old bach
just like a man
youl find me out west
in the county of ford
a starving to death
on a government clame

The wording throughout includes many slight variations suggestive of oral transmission ("Hoyle" is spelled "hoil," for example), but the order of stanzas and choruses is very close to the Kepner text with the exception of the county name, which is Ford county (southeast of Lane county, the location of Dodge City). Sackett has collected a modern fragment of the song in Hays, Kansas; it retains the Lane county reference but begins with another personal name: "Waterson's my name and a bachelor I am."[21] A striking change in this text is in the "according to Hoyle" section:

My house it is built of the Lane County soil,
The walls are erected of the best kinds of soil.

repetitious, and certainly no improvement on the Kepner text, but probably derived from a faulty memory of it.

20. See Myra E. Hull, "Cowboy Ballads," *KHQ*, 8 (1939), footnote 23, pp. 52–53. Other unusual wordings include "whitling sap sorgum potatoes and greas," "play rattle logketchem all over my nose," "where the wind is never clenched and the fall never dies," and "ile stop in mosoura."

21. FAC II 538. Collected from Charles C. Waterson, eight lines plus a four-line chorus.

An important early Great Plains text of the song was collected by a most unlikely chance in Kentucky. In 1907 Josiah H. Combs of Transylvania University, Lexington, collected a full sixty-line text from Dr. Ernest Smith, a transplanted Oklahoman, living in Knott county, Kentucky.[22] Combs included eight lines of the song in his 1925 doctoral dissertation at the University of Paris,[23] and he published it complete in 1939 with piano accompaniment in a song folio titled *Folk Songs from the Kentucky Highlands*,[24] a designation that hardly fits! Ernest Smith used his own name in the opening stanza, a practice Combs identified as traditional with the song. The first stanza and chorus of the Combs text are as follows:

> Ernest Smith is my name; an old bachelor I am;
> I'm keeping old batch on an immigrant plan.
> You'll find me out West on the high-road to fame,
> A-starving to death on a Government claim.
> My house it is built of rich, fertile soil;
> My walls are engraved acccording to Hoyle.
> My roof has no pitch, but it is level and plain;
> And I'm sure to get wet if it happens to rain.

> Hurrah for B. County, the land of the free,
> The home of the bed-bug, grasshopper, and flea!
> I'll sing out its praises and tell of its fame,
> While starving to death on a Government claim.

While the subject matter of the Kepner text is intact, virtually every stanza has minor verbal variations on the order of "immigrant plan," "high-road to fame," "crew of all fears," and the unrhymed lines:

> There's nothing that makes a man solid and firm,
> Like starving to death on a Government claim.

an obvious variation in the direction of poorer wording from Kepner's version. The name "B. County" in the choruses is glossed by Combs as "Beaver County," which lies in the Oklahoma panhandle south and

22. See Hubert G. Shearin and Josiah H. Combs, "A Syllabus of Kentucky Folk-Songs," *Transylvania University Studies in English*, 2 (Lexington, Kentucky: Transylvania Printing Company, 1911), p. 15.

23. *Folk-Songs of the Southern United States*, D. K. Wilgus, ed. and tr. (Austin, Texas, American Folklore Society Bibliographic and Special Series, vol. 19, 1967) p. 78; listed in appendix as no. 171, p. 223.

24. (New York: G. Schirmer), "Schirmer's American Folk-Song Series, Set 1," pp. 32–34. Other curious wording includes "scarce hardened," "robbers and beggars," "help tell its fame," and "fatten your fleas."

west of Lane county, Kansas. Even more suggestive of a direct traditional link between these states is the concluding chorus:

> Farewell to B. County, farewell to the West!
> I'll travel back *North* to the girl I love best;
> I'll go *back to Kansas* and marry a wife,
> And live on corn-dodgers the rest of my life.
>
> [Italics supplied]

The earliest known publication of "Starving to Death on my Government Claim" was another from Oklahoma collected in 1908, one
year after Combs' text; it appeared first in John A. Lomax's famous
book *Cowboy Songs* (1910) under the title "Greer County."[25] Its
thirty-six lines begin, "Tom Hight is my name, an old bachelor I am,"
and the rest differs considerably from the Kepner text, both in structure and in phraseology.[26] The most striking new wordings are
"country of fame," "elegant plain," "natural sod/according to hod,"
and in the final stanza a desire to "quit corn bread for the rest of my
life," since this Oklahoma bachelor had been eating "corn dodgers" all
along instead of hardtack or government bread.

The actual Greer county, Oklahoma, is directly south of Lane
county and near the Texas border. The song "Greer County" has the
earmarks of an interesting oral variation of the longer song, but neither John A. Lomax nor his son Alan ever commented on it in terms
of this larger traditional context as they republished their text, often
with inexplicable variations.

Reprinting it first as twenty-four lines in their book *American
Ballads and Folk Songs* (1934), they footnoted the song only "Text
from *Cowboy Songs*."[27] But a comparison shows that not only have
we lost an even dozen lines (all of stanzas two, three, and five), but
also some of the wording has been revised. In stanza one, for example,
"county" has replaced "country," bringing the phrase to its normal
form. In *Folk Song: U.S.A.* (1947) the Lomaxes titled their song
"Starving to Death on a Government Claim," adding a piano arrangement plus the information that "John A. Lomax first recorded this sod-
shanty complaint in 1908 from that hardy old Western cowboy and
homesteader, Tom Hight, who could sing ballads all night and never

---

25. Rpt. ed. (New York: Macmillan, 1922), pp. 278–279.

26. Material corresponds with the Kepner text as follows: St. one (lines 1–4) +
ch. one + st. one (5–8) + st. four (1–4) + st. three (1–4) + st. five (5–8) + st.
two (1–2, 7–8) + ch. four (1–2) + ch. two (2–4) + ch. five.

27. (New York: Macmillan), p. 434.

repeat.[28] However, the relationship between the text now presented and their supposed 1910 original becomes even more curious. This time there are thirty-two lines, since stanzas two and five have been restored; but now six has been shifted ahead of four. In stanza one the term "country" is back, but elegant "plan" has replaced "plain." The "natural sod" of 1910 has been altered to "national soil" and rhymed with the familiar "according to Hoyle." In the last line "corn dodgers" have replaced "corn bread." Finally, in 1964, Alan Lomax in the *Penguin Book of American Folk Songs* presents his latest thirty-two line revision of the song, still presumably drawn from his father's earliest fieldwork, but now under the title "My Government Claim" and fitted out with a new piano arrangement.[29] He chooses the same stanzas as appeared in *Folk Song: U.S.A.*, but now stanza eight has been moved up to penultimate position and rewritten "cry quits on corndodgers the rest of my life." We have "county of fame" back again, but "elegant plan" remains.

What might we conclude from this amazing history of a supposed single folksong text recurring in the works of two folklorists upon whom we are forced to rely for many important traditional items? Obviously, as John O. West also found in his investigation of a related matter in the Lomax corpus, there is strong evidence for tampering with the text beyond the limits of emendations or clarifications.[30]

In 1964 in Ethel and Chauncey O. Moore's book *Ballads and Folk Songs of the Southwest*[31] a version of "Greer County" was published coming from a singer in the town of Mangum [Greer county], Oklahoma. But it seems impossible to credit their statement that "it was composed by a singing schoolteacher named George Crawford, who conducted classes in the AV schoolhouse on the AV Ranch before Oklahoma became a state" (that is, before 1907). Not only are there earlier and better authenticated texts, but this one is almost exactly John A. Lomax's 1910 version, with Tom Hight, "country of fame," "cornbread" and all. Either the informant has made some reference to the

28. (New York: Duell, Sloan, and Pearce), p. 227, song on pp. 238–239. The same book with the same pagination also appeared in 1947 as *Best Loved American Folk Songs* (New York: Grosset & Dunlap). John Lomax also mentioned collecting songs from Tom Hight in his *Adventures of a Ballad Hunter* (New York: Macmillan, 1947), p. 48. This one seems closest to the text recorded by Pete Seeger on *Frontier Ballads* (New York: Folkways FP 5003, n.d.). It was also reprinted without credit to Lomax but with only a few changes (such as inserting the name Lane county) in Paul Glass and Louis C. Singer, *Songs of the West* (New York: Grosset & Dunlap, 1966), pp. 34–35.

29. (Baltimore: Penguin Books), p. 111.

30. See "Jack Thorp and John Lomax: Oral or Written Transmission?" *Western Folklore*, 26 (1967), 113–118.

31. (Norman: University of Oklahoma Press, 1964), pp. 282–285.

book *Cowboy Songs*, or Crawford wrote it for Tom Hight, or this is
an unusual instance of communal re-creation of folksongs failing to
operate in oral tradition. It is also interesting that the Moores give
"Bee County" as a local variant of the song's title; there is no Bee
county in Oklahoma. Likely this is the "B. County" of Combs' version, that is, Beaver county, where, incidentally, Tom Hight himself
told Lomax that he had participated in singing contests during his
boyhood—another nice hint of southward migration of the song from
Lane county down into Oklahoma.[32]

Now, where *did* John (or Alan) Lomax get different versions of the
song? Unfortunately, as D. K. Wilgus has written, "even with the help
of the Lomax manuscripts it is not possible to reconstruct all the links
between the folk versions and the printed texts."[33] Austin Fife in-
spected the Lomax papers but found no original text taken down from
the lips of Tom Hight, but only a few "extra stanzas" sent to John
Lomax after the publication of *Cowboy Songs* by Professor Hubert G.
Shearin, who was a sometime collaborator on folksong research with
Josiah Combs of Transylvania University.[34] These stanzas are recognizable as coming from the Combs' "Ernest Smith" version, complete
with the very revealing "North to Kansas" chorus, but Lomax seems
not to have noted this clue, although he may have plucked "according
to Hoyle" and other wording from this very text.[35]

We recognize so far from the late 1880's up to around 1907–08 a
movement of the song southward from Lane county, into north and
central Oklahoma, thence coming to the attention of certain professors
in Texas and (very oddly) in Kentucky. Next let us briefly review
other directions of migration. Ben Gray Lumpkin of the University of

32. See John A. Lomax, *Adventures*, pp. 49–50, describing Tom Hight writing
to him twenty-five years after singing folksongs for him in an Oklahoma City hotel
concerning his memories of singing "near Beaver City in the old neutral strip, or
No Mans Land, just north of the Texas Panhandle."

33. *Anglo-American Folksong Scholarship Since 1898* (New Brunswick, N.J.:
Rutgers University Press, 1959), p. 158.

34. See note 22. The texts sent by Shearin are numbered in the Fife collection
JL 8 and 145.

35. Some scraps of more recent Oklahoma oral tradition of the song do exist.
Fife's collection includes three fragments from archival sources: 1) FAC II 454,
"Frank Baker" in "Woodward county" (close to Beaver county, northwestern
Oklahoma), eight lines, Oklahoma City Library, dated December 27, 1949; 2)
FAC II 110, a single chorus sent by George W. Boswell, Austin Peay State College,
Clarksville, Tennessee, January, 1959, labeled "Clay county, Oklahoma" (no such
county in that state), said to have been collected in 1952, and 3) FAC II 131, two
isolated stanzas from Charles M. Gould Collection, University of Oklahoma Library; source on faculty of University of Oklahoma from 1900, died in 1949.
In an apparent case of Oklahoma references moving north, the Fife collection
also contains a 1959 text from Kathy Dagel of Augusta, Kansas, which is a slightly
shortened version of the Lomax "Tom Hight/Greer County" version. (FAC 518)

Colorado collected a thirty-line text in Boulder in 1961.[36] The singer said she learned it in her family about 1910, and it seems to be the Kepner "Frank Baker" text severely worn down by years of traditional circulation or faulty memory. Nebraska folklorist Louise Pound had collected a much more complete text—fifty-eight lines—in the opposite direction, from an informant in Hot Springs, South Dakota, back in 1914.[37] The only two lines of the Kepner text·not found here are those concerning the sharp-tack-toed fleas in stanza three. It had bacon and *cheese* (rather than "grease") in the bachelor's menu (agreeing with Lomax) and refers to chewing the "hard *rag*" where "hard tack" is expected; other variations are minor. When Louise Pound's text was recently reprinted in Roger L. Welsch's book *A Treasury of Nebraska Pioneer Folklore*[38] and then again in Welsch's *Sod Walls: The Story of the Nebraska Sod House*,[39] a presumption is conveyed that this very text of the song was orally circulated in Nebraska, which is, of course, probably not true. (Welsch also mentions North Dakota as a place where the song was sung, without citing examples, and none has come to my attention.)[40]

At about this point it is convenient to mention that sheet music and four stanzas of words for "Starving to Death on a Government Claim" were copyrighted in 1912 by O. S. Grant.[41] While a few phrases of the folksong tradition are recognizable here ("according to Hoyle," "Home of the grasshopper, bedbug and flea," and so forth), most of it is completely different and brings in such illogical references as "sagebrush and cactus." The opening line is completely original: "Don't ask me my name, a honyocker[42] I am," and the conclusion follows suit:

> Some day Uncle Sam will say, "well done,"
> Here is a deed to the homestead that you have won.

We come now to probably the best known version, certainly the most widely reprinted, and heretofore the most mysterious as to

36. See *Colorado Folksong Bulletin*, 1:1 (January, 1962), 3.

37. "Folk-Song of Nebraska and the Central West: A Syllabus," *Nebraska Academy of Sciences Publications*, 9:3 (Lincoln, 1915), 30–31, and *American Ballads and Songs* (New York: Scribners, 1922), pp. 178–180.

38. (Lincoln: University of Nebraska Press, 1966), pp. 46–48.

39. (Broken Bow, Nebraska: Purcells, Inc., 1968), pp. 170–173.

40. *Sod Walls*, p. 170.

41. (Washington, D.C.: H. Kirkus Dugdale Co., Inc.). Xerographic copy furnished by the Archive of Folk Song, Library of Congress.

42. Defined as "a farmer, c. 1877–1941" in Harold Wentworth, *American Dialect Dictionary* (New York: Crowell, 1944). A 1941 supporting quotation from the *Saturday Evening Post* reads " 'Honyocker,' the Yankee neighbors called them [immigrants from central Europe.] 'Honyocker' came to be . . . generally applied to any farmer who tries to raise grain and livestock in the high prairies of the Northwest."

source: Carl Sandburg's[43] full sixty-line text from his 1927 book *The American Songbag* attributed rather vaguely to Iowa and Nebraska.[44] Its opening sentence as printed, because of the name used and the spelling of a contraction, makes it immediately recognizable: "My name is Frank Bolar, 'nole bachelor I am." Once again the order of stanzas and choruses is very close to the Kepner text, the name "Lane county" is preserved, and the variations in wording are mostly those which oral tradition may account for. If we focus on just four of these changes which appear for the first time in this version (plus the opening line already quoted), we can easily trace the specific influence of Sandburg on later writers and singers—mostly writers. These changes are: 1) *"national* soil" (instead of Kepner's "natural" soil), a reading which appeared in a Lomax reprinting twenty years later; 2) "My *head* is case-hardened" (instead of my "bread"); 3) "A rattle-snake rattles his *tail* [instead of a tune] at my head"; and 4) *"tack/ back"* as the rhyme in the flea couplet, instead of "toes/nose" (Kepner's text being rearranged). Texts naming Frank Bolar as the bachelor may be scored from zero to four with regard to these wordings, a higher score suggesting likely derivation from Sandburg. In brief, and chronologically, the reprintings (and I have probably missed some) are as follows:

1930—Sandburg's text reprinted straight (score four) in a work on *Kansas* folksongs. (No source given.)[45]

1932—One stanza and chorus printed in a songbook, *The Cowboy Sings* (score one; other relevant stanzas lacking). No source.[46]

1937—Full Sandburg text (score four) except for last chorus. (Source: "Old Song.")[47]

1942—Three stanzas and choruses (score three) printed with numerous dialect respellings and piano music. (No source.)[48]

1944—Reprinted with credit to Carl Sandburg (score four) in Benjamin Botkin's first *Treasury*.[49]

43. [American poet, biographer, and folksong collector (1878–1967).]

44. (New York: Harcourt, Brace, and World), pp. 120–122.

45. Edna Reinbach, *Music and Musicians in Kansas* (Topeka: Kansas State Historical Society, 1930), pp. 24–25.

46. Kenneth S. Clark, ed. (New York: Paull-Pioneer Music Corp., 1932), p. 71.

47. Ruth A. Barnes, *I Hear America Singing: An Anthology of Folk Poetry* (Chicago: John C. Winston Co., 1937), pp. 85–86. Although other texts in the book are labelled *The American Songbag*, this one is not; the first line alone shows variation—"*lone b*achelor I am."

48. Satis N. Coleman and Adolph Bergman, *Songs of American Folks* (New York: John Day, 1942), pp. 32–34.

49. *A Treasury of American Folklore* (New York: Crown, 1944), pp. 314–316.

1946—A University of Kansas M.A. thesis on "Northwest Kansas Folksongs": Sandburg's text (score four) except for dropping "Lane County" and substituting "this county." (Source: "A well known homestead song.")[50]

1961—Published as sung by Manhattan, Kansas, professor William Koch; full Sandburg text (score three).[51] (Two shorter versions recorded by Koch for Austin Fife in 1959 score only two, and one of these has the name as "Frank Boor." Koch is quoted: "I do not know where I got this version"; the chance seems good that he has mixed an oral-traditional family version with his reading knowledge of Sandburg and perhaps other writers.[52]

1967—The William Koch published text (score three) credited as such and printed with piano arrangement and some minor spelling changes. (Source: "Words anonymous.")[53]

The only two properly validated oral-traditional versions I have been able to find that relate to the Sandburg text were these: 1) From Westminster, Colorado, 1962. While it does name Frank Bolar as the bachelor, it scores only one on other distinctive traits, agreeing with the Kepner readings elsewhere;[54] 2) Twenty-four lines included on a 1973 recording made by the Arizona Friends of Folklore in Clay Springs, Arizona; it has the name "Frank Bole" and scores two (out of a possible three for the stanzas included).[55]

Carl Sandburg's 1927 headnote says that his text came from Edwin Ford Piper, concerning which source D. K. Wilgus has raised the general complaint that later folksong researchers lack further information about his collection.[56] Piper was a midwesterner, a student of Kittredge's[57] at Harvard, who then returned to teach at the State University of Iowa. He dedicated his book *Barbed Wire and Other Poems* in 1917 "To the memory of my father and my mother, pioneers in Nebraska in the year Eighteen Hundred and Sixty Nine."[58]

50. Milred M. McMullen, *The Prairie Songs: Northwest Kansas Folksongs*, M.A. thesis, University of Kansas, Lawrence, 1946, pp. 133–135.

51. Bill and Mary Koch, "Kansas History and Folksong," *Heritage of Kansas*, 5 (1961), 10–11.

52. FAC I 531, II 127.

53. Irwin Silber and Earl Robinson, *Songs of the Great American West* (New York: Macmillan, 1967), pp. 224–228. The illustration with this text shows a man standing in the doorway of a *log* house.

54. See *Colorado Folksong Bulletin*, 2 (1963), 33.

55. *In an Arizona Town*, AFF recording No. 33-3 (1973).

56. Wilgus, *Anglo-American Folksong Scholarship*, pp. 215–216.

57. [George Lyman Kittredge, influential literary and folklore scholar.]

58. (Iowa City: The Midland Press, 1917).

The Fifes, following the lead in Sandburg, tracked down in Ames, Iowa, Piper's "very haphazard array" of clippings and handwritten notes on American folksongs, and they estimate that he made this collection from about 1909 to 1917.[59] In their 1969 book *Cowboy and Western Songs* the Fifes first published Piper's unaltered original, which (as the manuscript shows) he collected from one "H. Cooper" (no date or place indicated).[60] What is most fascinating about this text is that it reveals how Sandburg the poet, *not* some anonymous folk muse, was responsible for two out of the four distinctive features I have traced; in other words, Piper scores only two on our Sandburg scale of four. Piper has "natural," not "national" soil; and "bread," not "head"; both agreeing with our old friend Kepner. Also interesting is that there are two other shorter versions of the song in the Piper collection which display unique (probably oral) variations:

1) Another "Mr. Cooper" text which names "Frank Baker"(!) and has unique lines like, "Whenever it happens I want to be fed,/I eat up some hard tack and dry gingerbread."[61]
2) An "Oklahoma version" which names "Fred Barber" and "the county of Wood" (north Oklahoma, right on the Kansas border), the latter rhyming with "A starving to death on my government goods."[62]

The first sound recording of "The Lane County Bachelor" was made in 1941 by Ozark folklorist (note, not *folk!*) Vance Randolph who sang it in a very unpolished manner for the Library of Congress Folksong Archive. The thirty-six line rendition was issued on an LC disc,[63] printed in Randolph's *Ozark Folksongs*,[64] and recently reprinted.[65] Randolph learned the text in Hot Springs in 1917 from an informant who had learned it from a family living near Fayetteville, Arkansas. (We are not surprised to find this city in the extreme northwest corner of the state, near Oklahoma and Missouri.) While its length is close to Lomax's version, the wording is nearer to Kepner's, including even the "back east to Missouri" closing which would not

59. Letter from Alta Fife dated January 21, 1975.

60. The text is numbered PC-F 116 in the Fifes' collection; the publication is in Fife and Fife, *Cowboys and Western Songs*, pp. 58–61.

61. PC-F 118 is written in black ink on lined paper; PC-F 119 is the same text typewritten on plain paper.

62. PC-F 117, typewritten on plain paper and labelled "The Homesteader" with "Starving to Death on a Govt. Claim" in pencil.

63. Duncan Emrich, ed., *Songs of the Mormons and Songs of the West* (Washington: Library of Congress. AAFS L30 [n.d.]), side B, no. 2.

64. Vol. II (Columbia, Mo.: State Historical Society, 1948), pp. 190–191.

65. Duncan Emrich, *American Folk Poetry, An Anthology* (Boston: Little, Brown, 1974), pp. 627–629.

make sense in Fayetteville. The name had evolved to "Frank Taylor". In general, Randolph's text represented a reduction by two-fifths of all the essentials of the long Kansas original—nothing inconsistent with the usual workings of oral tradition nor suggestive of interference from print. (It may be noted here that the only vulgar stanza ever associated with the song is a mere couplet recalled by Austin Fife from farmhands singing near Idaho Falls, Idaho, in the 1920's, and brought to mind by Fife's hearing of this Randolph record.) [66]

One final unpublished text brings the record of oral tradition for the song up to 1925. In that year Harvey W. Cable, Presho, South Dakota, a reader of the column "Songs Old Men Have Sung" in *Adventure Magazine* sent his handwritten version to the writer of that column, the important American folksong collector Robert W. Gordon.[67] This version begins:

> John Biggs is my name, an old batchelor I am,
> You'll find me out west on an elegant plan.
> You'll find me out west in that country of fame
> Starving to death on a government claim.
>
> Hurrah for Mills county the land of the free,
> The home of the grasshopper, bedbug and flea,
> I'll tell of its praises, I'll sing of its fame
> While starving to death on a government claim.

Cable wrote that this was "a song I have heard sung by several different men." Mills county is a placename found only in Iowa and Texas. The order of material agrees with the Kepner text, but some wording is reminiscent of Lomax: "country of fame," "according to hod," and "live on corndodger no more in me life," for instance. A few lines are unique, such as "from nothing to nothing I've harvested air." It seems possible that either the Great Plains oral tradition stemming from Kansas was influenced by someone's reading Lomax's *Cowboy Songs*, or else Cable may have had some Texas singers among his acquaintances.

The remaining handful of texts is marginal in terms of locale, date, and details; these all seem to show printed influence or are self-conscious parodies. Others are simply too fragmentary or anonymous to trace to any clear folk source. For example, the Canadian version,

66. FAC I 875: "My name is Frank Taylor, my cock is a whaler,/My bollix weigh forty-nine pounds."

67. Xerographic copy of item 881 in the Gordon MSS, Library of Congress. Dated January 10, 1925, on Harvey W. Cable's own letterhead. A reply from Gordon thanking Mr. Cable, dated Feb. 15, 1925, from Cambridge, Mass., is also part of item 881. Gordon remarked on the "several points of difference which interest me greatly."

"The Alberta Homesteader," collected in 1958 in Ontario (?), simply relocates the events and furnishes appropriate details of Canadian weather and crops.[68] A 1951 unpublished recording of a singer from Albuquerque, New Mexico, turns out to be pretty close to the Lomax text and is credited to Greer county, "a little county down in Texas."[69] A 1959 Arizona text is an obvious southwestern parody which omits the sod house description and adds ranching and Spanish-American touches: "I'm going to Old Mexico and get me a wife,/And live on tortillas the rest of my life."[70]

Last of all, in the two large but very miscellaneous northwestern collections of folksong notebooks and clippings which Austin Fife discovered, a few random texts occur. In the Stella Hendron collection from Kooskia, Idaho, there are three undistinguished and unidentified handwritten or typewritten texts plus one with unique military language and references to "Camp Borden" (wherever that is).[71] In the Pacific Northwest Farm Quad collection (Spokane, Washington) Fife found two texts, one a fragment apparently based on Sandburg, the other probably related to one of the many that follow from Kepner.[72]

In analyzing this maze of material, much of it of rather doubtful accuracy and unknown origin, I have had an advantage over previous commentators of possessing every important published text of the song plus back-up material from archives and private collections.[73] I have

68. Edith Fowke, Alan Mills, and Helmut Blum, *Canada's Story In Song* (Toronto: W. J. Gage, 1960), pp. 144–145, 221. Referred to by Edith Fowke in "American Cowboy and Western Pioneer Songs in Canada," *Western Folklore*, 21 (1962), 252.

69. FAC I 181. Copied from the collection of Donald Robb, University of New Mexico, Albuquerque, May, 1959.

70. FAC II 422. Copied from mss. in University of Arizona Folklore Archive; collected in February, 1948; said to have been written and sung by Clyde Baldwin at Nogales radio station.
A Utah parody, "The Contented Bachelor," was recorded about in the early 1950's by the Rhythm Wranglers of Vernal, Utah; it was reissued on *The New Beehive Songster*, Vol. II (Salt Lake City, Okehdokee Records, 1976), pp. 8–9 of accompanying notes. This version begins "My name is Tex Ross an old bachelor I am," but the tune is different and the details are local. Only at the very end does the parody return, with the line, ". . . go right on starving along with the rest."

71. In the Fife collection these are numbered Hendron 625, 626, and 1182. "Hurrah for Camp Borden" is Hendron 399. Another item from the Lomax files in the Fife collection, JL 473, is a similar parody apparently from the Petersburg, Virginia, Federal Reformatory Camp. Beginning "McGee is my name, an old bachelor I am," it furnishes details of prison life. Most likely the composer had a Lomax published text in hand.

72. Numbered PNFQ 240 and 436 in the Fife collection.

73. Two published versions I have been referred to have not been located, so far. These are in Carson J. Robison, *World's Greatest Collection of Mt. Ballads and Old Time Songs* (Chicago: M. M. Cole, 1930), pp. 30–31, and as sung by Bill Bonyun on Folkways record FC 7402.

tried to deduce from these sources when oral tradition created variations and when the hand of an editor or writer was at work. It has
been possible to estimate fairly reliably the influence of printed versions upon oral performances. The patterns that develop are quite
clear, and conform closely to what residents of Lane County, Kansas,
have maintained for some time.[74] That is, the song seems to have
originated with one of their own pioneers and achieved considerable
popularity elsewhere in the west, both through folk and published
circulation.

The main reliable early western traditional texts consist of just nine,
by my count; they range from late nineteenth-century Kansas (Kepner, Tillotson, and Ford County) down into Oklahoma by 1907–08
(Lomax) and north through Iowa and Nebraska (Piper) and as far as
South Dakota (Pound) in the 19-teens. Probably via Oklahoma the
song found its way, before 1920, into Arkansas (Randolph) and even
Kentucky (Combs), but by 1925 printed influence was already becoming evident (Cable). Altogether the song has been associated with
twelve states (mostly of the Great Plains) and Western Canada. Of
thirty-three texts known to me (of which eight are fragmentary), only
thirteen have been published, but these have been reprinted, often
without credit, a total of thirty-six times. Lomax's version (published
six times in different variations) continues to be heard from singers in
Oklahoma and further southwest up to the present. After 1927 Carl
Sandburg's revision of one of Piper's texts (published eleven times so
far) influenced some oral versions of the song. Beyond these two, the
most often reprinted texts have been Kepner's and Pound's (four
each) and Randolph's (three). In recent years and at the furthest
periphery of the song's distribution, printed influence (especially from
Sandburg) is the major trend, and parodies are sometimes composed.
Possibly Pete Seeger's recording[75] or Randolph's have been influential
on some folk singers, bypassing the paths of both oral and printed
circulation.

It is deplorable, but true, that almost every step of the way collectors and editors of the song have altered or obscured the record.
These efforts range from the obvious falsifications by the Lomaxes and
the poetic (or possibly just careless) rewordings by Sandburg down to
the many unacknowledged reprintings and resingings of previously
published texts which have tended to inflate the count of supposedly
verifiable traditional versions. But I am greatly impressed at the same
time by the crucial importance of just a few first-hand written records
of the song taken down by college professors and early folk listeners

74. See Clint Hanna's summary in *An Historical Record*, p. [25].

75. See note 28.

alike. Also, the sheer good luck of several texts being preserved and rediscovered raises the whole question of what else lies unnoted in private files or has been lost forever.

In any case, "The Lane County Bachelor" does exhibit sufficient distribution, variation, and folk-group possession to be termed a valid example of Western folksong. Although it does not prove to have been common knowledge among the early homesteaders themselves, still it comes from the folk, and it handles authentic materials of Plains pioneer life in a manner consistent with frontier humor. Probably its misadventures in the hands of self-styled folksong authorities are not unlike what has happened to many another American folksong. All I can say, in conclusion, is:

> There's nothing that makes a man hard and profane,
> Like tracking a song to the county of Lane.

"MARY HAMILTON"
AND THE ANGLO-AMERICAN BALLAD
AS AN ART FORM

Tristram P. Coffin

The aesthetic approach to Anglo-American ballads in a way was where folklore study began in American colleges and universities. If folklore appeared nowhere else in the curricula of the 1920s through the '40s, there were always at least some "Old English ballads" in the literature surveys. Many of the earliest college folklore courses were taught by passionate lovers of ballad poetry who were self-taught folklorists. This changed, however, as folklore graduate programs took hold in the 1950s, and folklorists with backgrounds in anthropology were trained. Whatever their theoretical orientations, American folklorists by the 1950s began to reject the study of ballad texts without tunes and to criticize the undue emphasis on a few "masterpieces" of English or Scottish balladry to the neglect of other folksong types and other folklore genres. The most obvious legacy of the earlier approach was the lodging of most folklore courses in English departments forever after.

In this 1957 article Tristram P. Coffin is still concerned with the literary merits of some Anglo-American ballad texts; they are, in his opinion, "the greatest single art form that oral tradition has produced." In a fine piece of comparative analysis he shows how these ballads became masterpieces through the influence of oral transmission. His phrase, the "emotional core," has come to express an axiom of ballad-variation study—that the evolutionary process of folksong communication and performance may eventually eliminate the dross, leaving only the pure gold. As plots are simplified, lyrical qualities are enhanced and "universal emotions" remain strong in the best examples of ballad art.

Coffin pays lip service to ballad music but offers no examples or interpretation of the role of the music in ballad change or art. An essay by another folklorist published the same year, however, does make a thorough analysis of the interaction of words and music in another of the aesthetically satisfying English ballads in America. See George List, "An Ideal Marriage of Ballad Text and Tune," Midwest Folklore, Vol. 7 (1957).

Anglo-American ballad poems are the texts of ballads, printed without music and judged by the literary standards of Anglo-American culture.[1] These texts, comprising the greatest single art form that oral tradition has produced, are seldom discussed as art by the amateurs and anthropologically-trained researchers who work with them. As a result, most teachers and many scholars think of Anglo-American ballad poetry as something a bit unusual in the realm of human endeavor, something a breed apart from "conscious" arts like drama, concert music, poetry in print. Today, it is frequently assumed that such ballad poetry "just happens" or that the folk, working in communion, have mystically borne what we recognize as great literature. Yet we know better. We know things don't "just happen"; and we know the old "communal theory of ballad composition" to be almost completely wrong. It seems long past high time that the whole subject of the Anglo-American ballad text as art was brought up for review.

MacEdward Leach has characterized all ballads as follows:

> A ballad is story. Of the four elements common to all narrative—action, character, setting, and theme—the ballad emphasizes the first. Setting is casual; theme is often implied; characters are usually types and even when more individual are undeveloped, but action carries the interest. The action is usually highly dramatic, often startling and all the more impressive because it is unrelieved. The ballad practices rigid economy in relating the action; incidents antecedent to the climax are often omitted, as are explanatory and motivating details. The action is usually of a plot sort and the plot often reduced to the moment of climax; that is, of the unstable situation and the resolution which constitutes plot, the ballad often concentrates on the resolution leaving the listener to supply details and antecedent material.
>
> Almost without exception ballads were sung; often they were accompanied by instrumental music. The tunes are traditional and probably as old as the words, but of the two—story and melody—story is basic.[2]

Leach's definition would be disputed by few folklorists. Add to his points the idea that ballads are individually composed, and are most often fed down to the folk from a somewhat more highly educated stratum of society, and one has a good picture of the ballad as modern scholarship sees it. Ballads, thus, are widely considered to be plotted narratives, rising from relatively trained minds, taken over and fos-

1. This paper, an extensive development of a study read at the meeting of the AFS in Bloomington, Ind., 28 July 1950, was read at the AFS meeting in Washington, D.C., 28 December 1955. Throughout, the word "ballad" should be read as meaning the "Anglo-American ballad," although the remarks are pertinent to the ballads of Western Europe in general.

2. *The Standard Dictionary of Folklore, Mythology, and Legend*, ed. Maria Leach (New York, 1949–1950), I, 106.

tered by the folk until they become the verses and masterpieces that our collectors uncover.

The word "plotted" is of particular significance. It shall be a main purpose of this paper to suggest that plotting is vestigial, rather than vital, in the make-up of Anglo-American ballads. Unified action is a sign of the trained artist from the time of Homer through the Renaissance to the twentieth century.[3] Such organization of narrative tends to distinguish a man with training in the traditions of Western European literature from the ignorant or primitive. Plotting is honored by the tradition in which the Anglo-American ballad is born, but there is little evidence to support a contention that the folk, in whose oral heritage the ballad lives, care very much at all for unified action. Their myths and their tales lack unified action, except as a vestige. Generally, the folk tend to discard plotting in favor of something one might call "impact" or "emotional core."

Leach, as other writers on the ballad, stresses action as the most essential ingredient. I feel, however, that Anglo-American ballads stress impact over action and retain, in the long run, only enough of the original action or plot unity to hold this core of emotion in some sort of focus. In our ballad, details are kept and discarded to fit the core, and little real attention is paid to plot consistency or structure. Plot is present, but in the background. The emotional core, a part of the musical as well as the textual meaning of the song, is emphasized and cherished.

To understand the process by which an Anglo-American ballad becomes a poem, one must go into the problem of "emotional core" in some detail. It is essential that we understand what our folk consider a ballad to be and how it should be sung. Two things are certain: to our folk a ballad is song, not poetry; for us ballads become poems because certain variants (often by sheer chance) measure up to Western European aesthetic standards.

A ballad survives among our folk because it embodies a basic human reaction to a dramatic situation. This reaction is reinterpreted by each person who renders the ballad. As an emotional core it dominates the artistic act, and melody, setting, character, and plot are used only as means by which to get it across. This core is more important to the singer and the listeners than the details of the action themselves. For while a singer is often scrupulous not to change the version of a song as he sings it, he shows little interest in the consistency or meaning of the details he is not changing. Ballads resemble gossip.

3. Even the revolt against plotting that has taken place in much 20th century literature shows a definite consciousness of plotting.

They are transmitted like gossip, and their variation comes about in much the way gossip variation occurs.

The thesis presented above accounts for a number of the unique qualities of folk art and, through these qualities, designates the pattern of development that our ballads take over a stretch of time.

1. That many singers actually miss the point of the ballad action may well be because they focus attention on the emotional core of the song rather than on the plot detail. For example, about six years ago I published a paper dealing with an Arkansas version of "The Drowsy Sleeper."[4] My informant considered "The Drowsy Sleeper" to be an incest tale, but the woman who had taught the song to him had considered it a suicide-love story. Although the factual detail was the same (actually all the words were the same) in both texts, my informant had changed the emotional core that these details went to make up.

2. Such focus on the emotional core of a song may also account for the fact that the folk tolerate contradictions and preposterous images in their songs. So lines like "he mounted a roan, she a milk-white steed, whilst himself upon a dapple gray" and "up spoke a pretty little parrot exceeding on a willow tree"[5] survive even from generation to generation.

3. Finally, if we accept the thesis of the "emotional core," the difficulties encountered by all scholars who attempt to define the Anglo-American ballad are accounted for. Every text of every ballad is in a different stage of development and derives from a different artistic environment. The details of the action are never precisely conceived. As a result, there is nothing exact enough about a ballad to define.

As an Anglo-American ballad survives in oral tradition, the details become conventionalized so that songs of the same general type (love songs, ghost songs, etc.) tend to grow more and more alike, to use more and more of the same clichés. As Moore said, "In a way, the ballad resembles the proverb: there is nothing left in it which is not acceptable to all who preserve it by repetition. The simple ballads, which have served a general public, are non-technical in diction, whereas the modern songs of special classes . . . are highly technical. The same levelling process destroys whatever individual character the original poem may have."[6] And (p. 400), "After a painstaking study

4. "The Problem of Ballad Story Variation and Eugene Haun's 'Drowsy Sleeper,' " *Southern Folklore Quarterly*, XIV (1950), 87–96.

5. See, respectively, Arthur K. Davis, *Traditional Ballads of Virginia* (Cambridge, Mass., 1929), p. 188, and J. Harrington Cox, *Folk Songs of the South* (Cambridge, Mass., 1925), p. 18.

6. John Robert Moore, "The Influence of Transmission in the English Ballads," *Modern Language Review*, XI (1916), 404–405.

of the subject, I have yet to find a clear case where a ballad can be shown to have improved as a result of oral transmission, except in the way of becoming more lyrical." Moore's words, along with other things, have led me to believe that the life of an Anglo-American ballad can be charted somewhat like this:

Stage 1. A poem, created by an individual, enters or is retained in oral tradition. This poem has three major parts: an emotional core, details of action, frills of a poetic style that are too "sophisticated" for the folk. At this stage the poem is frequently not for singing and may well be closer to literature than to musical expression. The Frazer broadside of "Sally and Billy" or "The Rich Lady from London" (the song so often cited erroneously as Child 295) offers a relatively modern example:

> 'Tis of a young sailor, from Dover he came,
> He courted pretty Sally, pretty Sally was her name,
> But she was so lofty, and her portion was so high,
> That she on a sailor would scarce cast an eye.
>
> .   .   .
>
> "So adieu to my daddy, my mammy, and friends,
> And adieu to the young sailor for he will make no amends.
> Likewise this young sailor he will not pity me,
> Ten thousands times now my folly I see."[7]

So, of course, do any number of other newspaper, almanac, and broadside texts.

Stage 2. This is the "ballad" stage. The frills of sub-literary style have been worn away by oral tradition; some of the action details have been lost. Any so-called "traditional" ballad can serve as an illustration of Stage 2, although in the cases of both "Sally and Billy" and "Geordie" the American texts are close enough to print so that the transition from Stage 1 to Stage 2 is not complete. In fact, a majority of American songs lie in the area between the first two stages and were in the process of evolving toward traditional balladry when hindered by print and the urbanization of the folk. Some songs are born at this mid-point, to be sure. Individuals like Booth Campbell or Sir Walter Scott, who are used to singing or working within the conventions of folk tradition, may compose songs that never pass through Stage 1, that are traditional in language and detail at their birth.[8]

7. Broadside in the Yale University Library. See the Claude L. Frazer Collection, 2:5.

8. Narrative accretion may occur during Stage 2 also. But the addition of narrative detail in Stage 2, even when two whole ballads fuse, offers only a temporary setback to the steady movement toward Stage 3—lyric or nonsense.

Stage 3. In this final stage the ballad develops in one of two ways. Either unessential details drop off until lyric emerges, or essential details drop off until only a meaningless jumble, centered about a dramatic core, is left. The so-called "degenerate" ballad (and that is a poor term) is either a lyric or a nonsense song. The Scarborough text of "Geordie" beginning,

> Come bridle me up my milk-white steed.
> The brownie ain't so able, O.
> While I ride down to Charlottetown
> To plead for the life of my Georgie, O.[9]

shows the start of a development toward something like the lyrical "Rantin' Laddie" that is given in toto below:

> Aft hae I played at the cards an' dice
> For the love o' a rantin' laddie, O,
> But noo I maun sit in the ingle neuk
> An' by-lo a bastard babbie O.
>
> Sing hush-a-by, an' hush-a-by,
> An' hush-a-by-lo babbie, O,
> O hush-a-by, an' hush-a-by,
> An' hush-a-by, wee babbie, O.
>
> Sing hush-a-by, an' hush-a-by,
> An' hush-a-by-lo babbie, O,
> O had your tongue, ma ain wee wean,
> An A gae a sook o' the pappie, O.[10]

In much the same way the nonsensical Wisconsin "Sally and Billy" that begins with the meaningless lines,

> There was a ship captain
> That sailed on the sea.
> He called on Miss Betsy;
> Pretty Polly did say
> You go to the sea captain
> And grant me love or ruined I'll be.[11]

has its counterparts in "Bessy Bell" nursery rhymes and the amazing Texas version of Child 84, "Boberick Allen."[12] Both lyric and nonsense stages develop, of course, from forgetting. Yet it is significant to

9. Dorothy Scarborough, *A Songcatcher in the Southern Mountains* (New York, 1937), p. 213.

10. Phillips Barry (with Fannie H. Eckstrom and Mary W. Smyth), *British Ballads from Maine* (New Haven, 1929), pp. 303–304.

11. *JAF*, XLV (1932), p. 54.

12. *Publications of the Texas Folklore Society*, VII, p. 111, or X, p. 149.

note that it is the detail, not the emotional core, that is forgotten. The emotional core may be varied or modified, but it is the essential ingredient of any one song as long as that song exists.[13]

Ballads in Stage 3 and ballads in the process of moving from Stage 2 to Stage 3 are the only Anglo-American ballads that can meet the requirements of Western European poetry.[14] While it is certainly true that collectors are always finding Anglo-American ballads with complete or nearly complete plot unity, the variants that subordinate plot detail and focus on the emotional impact are the variants that are accepted as art. To become great poetry, our ballads must lose so much of their original style, atmosphere, and detail that they must become lyrics as well.

Which of our ballads will meet the requirements of Western European poetry as they move toward lyric is governed by chance. A balance attained in oral tradition between stress on plot unification and stress on emotional impact gives some texts a magnificent half-lyric, half-narrative effect. Individuals, coming in series, often generations apart, change lines, phrases, and situations to fit their personal fancies and to render what they consider to be the song's emotional core before giving the ballad back to oral tradition. Some of these individuals are untrained geniuses, a few may be trained geniuses like Burns or Scott, most are without artistic talent. The geniuses give us the texts, or parts of texts, that measured by Western European standards are art. Their efforts are communal in the sense that there are usually many "authors" working on the tradition of any one song or version of a song. But it must be remembered that often these geniuses live decades apart, handle the song separately, and store it in an ineffectual oral tradition in between. Oral tradition is an aimless thing. It will stumble into art—but not with any sort of consistency.

The widely anthologized Child A version of "Mary Hamilton"[15] is an example of an Anglo-American ballad poem that has gained artistic acceptance. The plot of the song is quite simple. Mary, Queen of

13. It should be noted that a composition can move back up these stages at any time that an individual inserts morals, sentiment, and other poetic frills. Parodists, broadside-writers, and the like, frequently made such changes, particularly in the 18th century. The Civil War parodies of "Lord Lovel" as printed in many Southern collections, and the moral version of "The Three Ravens" printed in *JAF*, XX (1907), 154, serve as examples. It is also true that a song may be composed at any one of the three stages, even at the lyric or nonsense stage; (see many of the minstrel tunes).

14. American ballads, which, as stated above, are usually in the process of moving from Stage 1 to Stage 2, are generally thought of as inferior to Child ballads when measured by Western European poetic standards.

15. See Child's *The English and Scottish Popular Ballads*, III, 384. The text is not printed here, to conserve space.

Scots, has four maids-in-waiting, each selected for her virginal name and her beauty. One of the maids, Mary Hamilton as she is called in the ballad, not only flaunts the conventions of society by having an affair with the Queen's husband, but is unfortunate enough to bear a child as fruit of this indiscretion. She attempts to destroy the baby, is caught, tried, and hanged for murder. Characterization and real setting are almost nonexistent, but the emotional core of the ballad is given great emphasis. This core, the tragedy of beauty and youth led astray, the lack of sympathy within the law, the girl's resigned indifference to her lot, are driven home with full force.

Only the first five of the eighteen stanzas that make up Child A are devoted to the rumors of Mary Hamilton's pregnancy, the courtship by Darnley, the murder of the child, and the Queen's discovery that she has been deceived. This juicy copy could not be dispatched more decorously had Mary of Scotland written the lines herself. The next five stanzas are devoted to the trial and conviction of Mary Hamilton, although again no effort is made to capitalize upon dramatic potentialities. Mary Hamilton, somewhat ironically, decides to dress in white, laughs and cries conventionally before and after the trial, and has her misfortune symbolized by losing the heel to her shoe. If the folk as a whole really cared about plot it is doubtful that the narrative possibilities of these events would be so ignored.

Stanzas 11–18, almost half the text, show what really interested the folk who preserved the Child A variant. Stanzas 11–18 deal with material that reflects the girl's feelings as she stands on the gallows waiting to die. The first ten stanzas have remained in the song only because they bring into focus the last eight. The folk recognize that the emotional situation brought on by the seduction and subsequent murder is the artistically vital part of the ballad.

That these stanzas are primarily cliché stanzas is not of importance. They are admirably suited to the emotional situation at hand. Mary tells the sentimentalists that congregate at every hanging not to weep for her, her death is her own doing. She calls for wine in a burst of braggadocio. Her toast mentions her parents, and her mood changes. Mary becomes sentimental herself, and the ballad draws to its end in four heart-rending stanzas. This is the essence of the story: the beauty and youth of a girl snuffed out by law.

It is true that one can turn the page in Child and read the B text to discover that Mary Hamilton would not work "for wantonness and play" and that Darnley came to the gallows to ask Mary Hamilton to "dine with him." But these details, as the ones in Scott's composite version,[16] do nothing to increase the impact of the emotional core.

16. Sir Walter Scott, *Minstrelsy of the Scottish Border* (Edinburgh, 1833), II, 294 (Child I).

Nor does it matter that Mary Hamilton was really a girl in the Russian court of Peter the Great and that, besides Seaton and Beaton, Livingston and Fleming were the names of Mary of Scotland's other Maries. A girl is a girl, the law is the law, in any age, in any place.

As an Anglo-American ballad survives in oral tradition more and more of the plot material can be expected to vanish, until only a lyric expressing the emotional core is left. Barry's collection from Maine (see n. 10) includes, page 258, the following variant of "Mary Hamilton":

> Yestre'en the queen had four Maries,
> This nicht she'll hae but three;
> There was Mary Beaton, an' Mary Seaton,
> An' Mary Carmichael an' me.
>
> Last nicht I dressed Queen Mary
> An' pit on her braw silken goon,
> An' a' thanks I've gat this nicht
> Is tae be hanged in Edinboro toon.
>
> O little did my mither ken,
> The day she cradled me,
> The land I was tae travel in,
> The death I was tae dee.
>
> They've tied a hanky roon me een,
> An' they'll no let me see tae dee:
> An' they've pit on a robe o' black
> Tae hang on the gallows tree.
>
> Yestre'en the queen had four Maries,
> This nicht she'll hae but three:
> There was Mary Beaton, an' Mary Seaton,
> An' Mary Carmichael an' me.[17]

Here is a lyric poem with but the merest suggestion of plot. Only the facts that the girl was one of the Queen's favored maidens and is now about to die remain clear. Yet the emotional core, girlhood and its beauty snuffed out by law, is as clear as it was in Child A.

It is certain that the Maine lyric did not evolve from Child A (or some similar text) merely through the miracles of forgetting and fusing alone. A member of the folk, or some learned poet, framed Mary's lament with the "Beaton and Seaton" stanza. Perhaps this poet, or another, purposefully discarded some of the plot detail as well. These points are relatively unimportant. The basic thing is that "Mary Hamilton" as it is found today is almost always a lyric and that the tendency to preserve the core and not the plot of the song is typical.

17. [*Nicht*, night; *braw*, fine; *ken*, know; *een*, eyes; *tae dee*, to die. (Scottish dialect).]

The tendency is also typical of the American song "Charles Guiteau"—an example of mediocre poetry. Here the murderer of James A. Garfield waits for his death with the "little did my mither ken" cliché on his lips. The lines are just as adequate for a nineteenth century assassin as they are for a medieval flirt, and the folk have sloughed nearly all the plot detail included in the original sub-literary text; but "Charles Guiteau," unlike "Mary Hamilton," never passed through the hands of a genius or series of geniuses who could lift it above sentimental verse.

In the hands of A. E. Housman, the "Mary Hamilton" situation was touched by a great poet. "The Culprit," the poem that opens with the lines "The night my father got me / His mind was not on me,"[18] tells of the musings of a man about to be hanged. It is in reality a restatement of the emotions Mary Hamilton expressed in stanzas 11–18 in the Child A text. Why the youth is on the gallows, how he got there, are too clinical for Housman's poetic purpose. Like the folk singer who shaped "Mary Hamilton" and even "Charles Guiteau," Housman did not clutter his lyric with action detail.

Beyond the observations made on the Child A "Mary Hamilton" lie similar observations that can be made on the Scott "Twa Corbies," the Percy "Sir Patrick Spens," the Percy "Edward," the Mackie-Macmath "Lord Randal," and the other most widely anthologized of our ballads.[19] All of them are basically lyrics. In each case there is a full plot, now lost forever, that the folk have seen fit to discard. A realization of the importance of the "emotional core" to the folk is essential to a sensitive evaluation of Anglo-American ballad poems. The teacher, the critic, the poet, even the researcher, must know that in certain ballad variants there is to be found a fine blend of plot residue and universal emotion that produces priceless offspring from mediocre stock. An Anglo-American ballad may look like narrative. At its birth it may be narrative. But its whole life proceeds as a denial of its origin.

18. A. E. Housman, *Collected Poems* (New York, 1940), p. 114.
19. See Child for the texts of "The Twa Corbies," "Sir Patrick Spens," "Edward," and "Lord Randal" mentioned.

"MILLER BOY,"
ONE OF THE FIRST AND LAST
OF THE PLAY-PARTY GAMES

John Q. Anderson

Here a folklorist recalls his earlier role as folk performer in the now obsolete tradition of play-party games, a form of traditional recreation in which the participants sing and dance simultaneously. Once widely collected and published, American play-parties remain today only in a few people's memories and in some instances as fiddle tunes or children's games. John Q. Anderson's reminiscences document what was apparently the last stage of play-party survival in the original form of this practice in the Texas Panhandle region. He gives a text and tune, the manner of play, and a good description of the social context in which play-parties were performed. Of special interest is the account of how the nature of the participants in any given game helped determine the leader's choices of stanzas to sing. Anderson's footnotes fill in the historical background for "Miller Boy," and he comments on this game's original symbolism and satire.

In comparison to Ida M. Cromwell's "Songs I Sang on an Iowa Farm" in Section 1, this report offers both detailed comments from the informant and good comparative study by the folklorist—in this instance, one and the same person. But it also reflects a male bias, since the thoughts of the girls about play-party games are not discussed.

ALTHOUGH THE PLAY-PARTY was dying out in most areas of the nation by 1900,[1] it was very much alive in the Texas Panhandle long after that time. "Miller Boy" was one of the swinging games that continued in Wheeler County, where I grew up, as late as the mid-1930s.[2]

1. W. E. Richmond and William Tillson, in the notes to their revision of Leah Jackson Wolford's *The Play-Party in Indiana* (1917) (Indianapolis, 1959), say that the period of the play-party was "from around the Civil War to its heyday before 1890, after which it declined" (p. 237).

2. Under the various names—"Old Miller," "Jolly Miller," "Happy Miller"— the game appears in these collections published in the *Journal of American Folklore*: Mrs. L. D. Ames, "The Missouri Play-Party," 24 (1911), 295–318; Goldy Hamilton, "The Play-Party in Northeast Missouri," 27 (1914), 289–303; Emelyn E. Gardner, "Some Play-Party Games in Michigan," 33 (1920), 91–133; Arthur P. Hudson, "Ballads and Songs from Mississippi," 39 (1926), 93–194; Vance Randolph, "The Ozark Play-Party," 42 (1929), 201–32; Paul G. Brewster, "Game-Songs from Southern Indiana," 49 (1936), 243–62. "Miller Boy" also appears in

"Miller Boy" was more popular than others of the games for two reasons: it was a "cheating" game which allowed participation by extra boys without dates, and the three changes of pattern in the game allowed more opportunity for "cheaters" to "steal" partners.

Here is the Texas Panhandle version of "Miller Boy":

Hap-py is the mil-ler boy who lives by the mill; The mill turns a-round with its own free will; Hand on the hop-per and the oth-er on the sack La-dies step for-ward and the gents step back.

       2. Happy is the miller boy who lives by the mill;
            The mill turns around with its own free will;
            Hand on the hopper and the other on the sack—
            Hold to your partner and turn right back.

       3. (Repeat the first three lines of No. 1)
            Ladies to the center and the gents fly the track.

Couples formed a double circle, boys on the inside, girls on the outside. Each boy stood beside his partner with his left hand grasping her left hand and his right arm over her shoulder, holding her right hand. This position permitted quick reversal of direction at the appropriate call. All extra boys—and there were always extra boys at Panhandle parties—stood inside the ring. As the leader sang the first part of Stanza No. 1, the players moved clockwise, skipping in time with the song. At the call, "Ladies step forward," each girl moved up to become the partner of the boy ahead—unless a boy (a "cheater") from the center of the ring stepped in and claimed her as partner. In that event her former partner moved to the center of the ring and himself became a "cheater." Since the point of the game was to provide opportunities for the "cheaters" to "steal" partners, the pattern in Stanza No. 1 was most often called.

R. E. Dudley and L. W. Payne, Jr., "Some Texas Play-Party Songs," in *Round the Levee*, ed. Stith Thompson, *Publications of the Texas Folklore Society*, 1 (1916), 7–34; Wolford, pp. 179 and 285–86 (1959 ed.); John H. Cox, "Singing Games," *Southern Folklore Quarterly*, 6 (1942), 183–261; and eleven versions in *The Frank C. Brown Collection of North Carolina Folklore* (Durham, 1952), I, 110–13.

But the leader, aware of the suspense he commanded, would sometimes skip the anticipated pattern and call, "Hold on to your partner and turn right back" (Stanza No. 2)—to the chagrin of the "cheaters." Now, however, the girls were inside the circle and more accessible to the "cheaters." The leader next provided the expected move for the "cheaters" to grab partners by calling again, "Ladies step forward." Soon, though, the leader returned the circle to its original clockwise revolution before he called, "Ladies to the center" (Stanza No. 3) and sent all the boys to the outside of the circle to race around the girls gathered in the middle. At a whistle, the whirling mass halted as boys grabbed partners. The circle was again formed with the "cheaters" in the center, and the whole maneuver repeated as long as the players desired.

Compared to other published versions of "Miller Boy," this Texas version is more flexible because the leader had three options as against one that existed in the same game as played elsewhere in the nation.[3] Only Oklahoma versions offered two.[4] Furthermore, the Texas version allowed for several "cheaters" instead of only one. Such flexibility permitted the leader to maneuver his group more readily. He knew which couples were "sparking" and wished to be together, and he would teasingly separate them as often as possible. He did not forget the "cheaters," for he himself became one when his partner was stolen. "Miller Boy" remained popular at parties because it pleased everyone —boys who had dates and those who did not.

Even though the Panhandle version of "Miller Boy" provided variety, it preserved the outlines of the traditional game whose history reaches back to an English ancestor.[5] The symbolic motion of the turning mill wheels was retained, although the milling of grain was no longer within the experience of the players. Also, whatever satire of

---

3. Most versions reported from other areas of the United States give only one change, "Ladies step forward," and list only one boy in the ring as the "miller" who stole partners.

4. B. A. Botkin, *The American Play-Party Song* (New York, 1963, first published in 1937), includes two versions of "Miller Boy" collected in Oklahoma with two changes—"Ladies step forward" and "Hold to your partner and turn right back."

5. William Wells Newell, *Games and Songs of American Children* (New York, 1963, first published in 1883), mentions "Round and Round, the Mill Goes Round" as a seventeenth-century English dance and "The Happy Miller" as a song in D'Urfey's *Pills to Purge Melancholy* (1707). W. Chappell, *The Ballad Literature and Popular Music of the Olden Times* (London, 1859, 2 vols.), says that the tune of "The Jolly Miller" was used in several ballad operas (II, 666), and he includes two stanzas of a version used as a drinking song (II, 668). Alice B. Gomme, *The Traditional Games of England, Scotland, and Ireland* (London, 1894, 2 vols.) lists seven versions of the game called "Jolly Miller" which she describes as being very much like the American play-party game (II. 290–93).

greedy millers that existed in the English forerunner of the song[6] no longer was meaningful to these players. With youthful lack of concern for the past, my contemporaries and I knew nothing of the origin and meaning of "Miller Boy"—or any others of the swinging games for that matter. We were unaware of holding on to folk games that had already died out elsewhere in the nation. We kept the games because they entertained us. "Miller Boy" was the best "cheating" game we knew, and so we played it with gusto.

A typical Panhandle party (they were never called "play-parties") included no more than about twenty young, unmarried people; rarely did married people play, even if they had married young, as most did. Six or seven couples and four or five unattached young men made up the group. Since the games were played out-of-doors, parties were held from spring to fall, when weather permitted. They were held at night and at private homes, never at schoolhouses as reported elsewhere in the nation. Formal invitations were never issued; instead, one or two young men would "get up" the party simply by riding on horseback to each home in the community and telling the families that a party would be held at so-and-so's house on a certain night. Everyone was invited, although some families never attended. Simple refreshments were sometimes served, but never liquor. Parties began about dark and ended before midnight.

Along with the ever popular "Miller Boy," a Texas Panhandle party of the 1920s and 1930s would include such partner games as "Ju-Tang," "Ten Little Indians," "Tideo," and "Little Brown Jug," along with such non-singing games as "Snap," "Three Deep," and even the children's games "Drop the Handkerchief" or "Needle's Eye," if the group tired of swinging games.

The community in which I attended parties was much like those Botkin described in Oklahoma in the 1920s in which he did his research on the play-party.[7] Dominated by a large ranch, my community included no more than fifteen to twenty families. The one-teacher school, in the middle of a ranch pasture, served as a meeting place for the union Sunday School and for church services held by preachers of different Protestant denominations on various Sundays of the month. People in the area were about equally divided between those who had religious prejudices against dancing and those who did

6. Commenting on origins of the game, Lady Gomme says (II, 292) that the miller, who paid himself in kind for corn ground, was an object of satire in ballads and medieval writing. She speculates that the custom of "grabbing" for sweethearts and wives may be reflected in versions of the game in which the miller makes "his grab."

7. B. A. Botkin, "The Play-Party in Oklahoma," in *Follow De Drinkin' Gou'd, Publications of the Texas Folklore Society,* 7 (1928), 15–17.

not—the very situation that had led to play-party games in the first place.[8] Square dances in private homes were even more popular than parties, and my family attended both dances and parties. My father was a fiddler who reared his own string-band of sons and daughters who accompanied him on guitar and mandolin. Among my earliest memories (about 1920) is traveling in a farm wagon to dances for which the family band played. Members of my family were also in demand at parties because we could sing. My older brothers and sisters were married and gone by the time I was fifteen, and it was about that time that I sang for parties, three and four hours at a time, all the while playing the games with the group.

By the middle of the 1930s my area of the Panhandle was part of the Dust Bowl, and those families who had not already gone to California with the Okies were battling drouth and depression. But the young people found entertainment where they could, at either dances or parties, because there was seldom money to buy gasoline to drive Model-T or Model-A Fords over thirty miles of ranch roads to nearby towns to attend movies. But even this remote area could not long escape changes that ended the play-party forever. The local school was consolidated with a larger one and the community no longer had a gathering place. A transcontinental highway (Route 66) was paved through the county, and along it sprang up dance halls and other places of amusement. Though only the "tougher" element in the community attended these public dances, others came to think of their parties and dances as old-fashioned and backward and so dropped them. Consequently, the play-party, in one of its last strongholds in the United States, came to an end before 1940, for reasons that Botkin had noted as early as 1928: ". . . the play-party was doomed to die a natural death," he said, "to pass with the conditions that created it. Wherever the invading tide of modern amusements found ingress, the play-party was engulfed; and wherever the resistance of the church was weakened, the play-party was assimilated by the dance from which it sprang."[9]

Thus "Miller Boy," with a history that reached back to seventeenth-century England and with an exceptionally vigorous tradition that made it a favorite in the United States, ended with the death of the swinging games. In the cold print of books and articles, there is little to suggest the vitality, the rustic fun, and human warmth that once characterized "Miller Boy," one of the best "cheating" games.

8. See Botkin, "The Play-Party in Oklahoma," and Wolford, *The Play-Party in Indiana*, p. 114.

9. Botkin, "The Play-Party in Oklahoma," p. 14.

THE FIDDLE TUNE:
AN AMERICAN ARTIFACT

Louie W. Attebery

In common with John Q. Anderson in the preceding study, Louie W. Attebery (at least in part) is both informant and scholar in his analysis of American square-dance fiddle tunes and their cultural significance. He is interested in these dance tunes for their structural patterns and for their performance context in the Lower Snake River Valley of Idaho; both of these aspects, he writes, "are richly suggestive of the American character." Attebery's review of fiddle tune and square dance history provides examples of American practicality and adaptability, but the original point of his essay is the analysis of these "artifacts" as true products of a distinctive American culture. However, like Anderson, Attebery found that square dances and fiddle tunes lost much of their original function and vitality as the frontier gave way to civilization. The Lower Snake River Valley was one of the last places where these traditional amusements survived in traditional forms.

Referring to American Studies specialist John A. Kouwenhoven's ingenious argument for twelve "distinctly American" artifacts, Attebery cites counterparts to several of the proposed items and their attributes in the society he grew up in. He shows that fiddle tunes and the square dances they accompanied have at least four qualities in common with the items on Kouwenhoven's list: foreign antecedents, a strong repetitive basic beat, a quality of endlessness, and an adaptive capability. The question might be raised, of course, whether the same qualities might be found in some other borrowed folk "artifacts" of American culture, such as ballads, holiday customs, or children's games.

There are many publications that furnish more technical information about the musical qualities of American fiddle tunes; one useful article is Marion Unger Thede's "Traditional Fiddling" in Ethnomusicology, Vol. 6 (1962). Attebery himself provides the cultural background for the artifacts discussed here in "Rural Traditions of the Snake River Valley," Northwest Folklore, Vol. 1 (1966).

AMONG MY NOTES on rural traditions of the Lower Snake River Valley is an account of a progressive square dance held in the first decade of this century. Both the dance itself and the music to which it was performed are richly suggestive of the American character, if one is.

careful in drawing his inferences. In addition to what the dance and its music may reveal positively about American culture is the likelihood that with the fading of the frontier these artifacts also went into a decline. They ceased to be generally viable. Underlying the argument of this paper, then—that the fiddle tune and the square dance show something of our Americanness—is this additional notion that the frontier provided a particularized setting in which the two artifacts could thrive.

Two assertions need to be made about the word *artifact* in order to make clear its use in the context of this paper. An artifact may be recognized by its uniqueness to the culture in which it is found, or it may be recognized by its unique employment in the culture which has borrowed it from some other cultural group. Thus the free verse structural antecedents of *Leaves of Grass* have been identified variously as the polyrhythms of the German poet Heine, the Semitic prosody of the Hebrew psalmists,[1] and the "free verse" of Matthew Arnold.[2]

Even so, Whitman's poem *is* an American poem, and it is a good example to use in support of the second assertion about artifacts—that they may sometimes be recognized by the unique use to which they are put by the adopting society. If the assertion is not granted, then it becomes very difficult to talk about an American culture exclusive of native Indian materials. Nearly everything else is ultimately traceable to transoceanic sources. Yet the music for a hoedown, and the hoedown itself, is American. They can be considered American artifacts when their European origins are remembered and their American applications, refinements, and adaptations are made as clear as current scholarship will allow.

Let me cite the tradition of the progressive square dance as it was recorded in the memory of Mrs. Victoria Schweitzer.[3]

"I began teaching in Barren Valley in 1909. I was nineteen and just out of Indiana. There was a shortage of women in that community and a lot of cowboys. They nearly danced our legs off. One Friday noon a cowboy I knew rode up in a buggy to the little schoolhouse and dismissed the children. He told me we were going to the Diamond Ranch for a dance, and we'd have to leave early to make

1. Louis Untermeyer, ed., *The Prose and Poetry of Walt Whitman* (New York, 1949), p. 19. Untermeyer's case for the Biblical influence is a strong one. He expresses doubt, however, that Whitman knew Heine's multirhythmic poetry.

2. Richard Chase, "Whitman and the Comic Spirit," in Leo Marx, ed., *The Americanness of Walt Whitman*, Problems in American Civilization (Boston, 1960), p. 121. Chase's point that "no culture is perfectly unique" needs to be kept in mind. He, too, mentions Heine as a "free verse" forerunner of Whitman.

3. Interview, summer 1958.

it. We drove the fifty miles in good time and danced all night. When daylight came we had breakfast, then drove out to Bud Smith's for a turkey feed. After dinner the whole crowd went on up to Brown's Ranch on the mountain [Steens Mountain] and danced all Saturday night. We finally got back home late Sunday night. We must have covered close to two hundred miles."

Here, indeed, are the three essential elements: the frontier, the hoedown or square dance, and its essential partner the fiddle tune.

It is probably common knowledge that the fiddle tune and the square dance have foreign precedents, prototypes, or forebears, call them what you choose. Anyone who has ever listened to a bagpipe chanting a Celtic jig or reel has heard an important part of the musical tradition lying behind the fiddle tune. Not only do fiddle tunes consist, in part, of such traditional melodies as the jigs and reels, but also many fiddle pieces employ an open string which in certain passages provides a musical effect paralleling the effect of the drone pipes sounding behind or under the melody being played on the chanter.

Granted that names by which the tunes go are the most casual, least permanent things about them, as, indeed Samuel Bayard has noted,[4] it may well be with a change in title that change in content is signalized. The Revolutionary War undoubtedly contributed a share of anti-British sentiment which was very likely expressed in renaming many traditional tunes. It is likely, too, that the War of 1812 furthered the process. Through this procedure of naturalization "Lady Walpole's Reel" became "The Boston Fancy,"[5] "The Breeches On" became "Leather Breeches,"[6] and "The Walls of Liscarroll" became "Muddy Water."[7] Other names given to tunes descended from these still await collection, making Bayard's complaint of 1944 still valid: "We know little about instrumental folk music in the United States, and study of it cannot go far because the tunes themselves remain largely uncollected."[8]

Perhaps a brief look at the square dance will through analogy enable us to draw valid inferences in the absence of scholarship. The tone here is set by S. Foster Damon in an extended essay "The History of Square Dancing" in *Proceedings of the American Antiquarian Society*: "Wherever it is found, the American square dance has grown

4. Samuel Preston Bayard, *Hill Country Tunes: Instrumental Folk Music of Southwestern Pennsylvania* (Philadelphia, 1945), p. xxiv.

5. John Tasker Howard and George Kent Bellows, *A Short History of Music in America* (New York, 1957), p. 316.

6. *Bayard*, tune 16.

7. *Bayard*, tune 43.

8. *Bayard*, p. xi.

from its historical roots into something like nothing to be found else-where in the world."[9]

Common sense and reflection would lead us to surmise that the presence of French soldiers and the gratitude we felt to France in the Revolutionary War crises would create a market for things French, among them, certainly, French dancing. Scholarship here supports surmise, for French forms were the originals for our square dances.[10] Generally, the two varieties of imports, the quadrille and the cotillion, were respectively elegant, formal, city-oriented dances relying upon art music, and roisterous, country-oriented dances relying upon tradi-tional tunes.[11] And it is the cotillion that is the direct ancestor of our square dance.

To become an American square dance, the cotillion needed only a few refinements. One of these was the introduction of the role of the *caller,* said to have been the product of "some smart American about the time of the War of 1812."[12] Apparently the role of caller evolved from the dancers' reliance upon the fiddler for instructions. He ceased to be merely an accompanist, for he could now, in a sense, create the dance by varying the figures at any moment, perhaps to keep the dancers alert by inventing new patterns or by simply calling out at random whatever popped into his head.[13] Appearing about 1870 was another refinement, the singing call.[14]

During this time of naturalization of the cotillion, the traditional English, Scottish, and Irish tunes must have been experiencing a paral-lel development and adaptation. Some of the titles, as noted earlier, were changed to fit local manners, vocabulary, and attitudes. And because fiddle tunes are folk art,[15] that is to say they are generally of

9. V. 62, Part I, April 16, 1952, p. 97.

10. Damon, "The History of Square Dancing," p. 69. The point is arguable. To repeat fn. 2, no culture is perfectly unique. We often forget that ideas, attitudes, and art forms have been exchanged across the Channel for hundreds of years. A reference in *The Spectator* to the superior morality of French dancing would sug-gest that mutual influence makes categorical statements about French origins de-batable. In addition to the wartime experience of 1776 and 1812, linguistic evi-dence seems to support a significant French contribution to the American square dance. See J. S. Baker, "French, Scotch, and Merry English," *American Speech,* XXXI (1956), 148–149.

11. Damon, p. 82.

12. Damon, p. 80.

13. Damon, p. 80.

14. Damon, p. 90.

15. Many art musicians borrow consciously from the folk tradition. The situa-tion is reversible for occasionally an art song will be picked up by folk musicians, absorbed, modified, and preserved in tradition after it has ceased to be viable as an art song. Johann Christian Fischer (b. 1733, d. ?) composed a popular minuet and a hornpipe about 1780 in London, according to Damon, "The History of Square Dancing," p. 74. "Fischer's Hornpipe" is still standard fare with many fiddlers who perform annually at the Weiser, Idaho, fiddlers' festival and contest.

unknown authorship, learned and transmitted by ear and imitation rather than notation, in the nature of things variants developed, indeed, are still developing as I can affirm after having heard fiddle tunes in the early thirties and those in the national fiddling contests at Weiser, Idaho.[16] The process clearly is still going on.

The point of all this is that the naturalization of both the French cotillion and the traditional tunes of the British Isles reveals that Americans are adaptable and of a practical turn of mind that allows them to take advantage of anything about them that they find engaging.[17]

This is a safe generalization. It is also jejune. Hopefully, neither safe nor jejune is the assertion that fiddle tunes (and the square dance, their excuse for being) demonstrate a distinctly American concern for *process* in *the manipulation of a series of simple and infinitely repeatable units.*

In John A. Kouwenhoven's by now well-known essay "What Is American about America?" twelve artifacts appear as "distinctly American—not likely to have been produced elsewhere."[18] I would add two more, for it seems to me that the fiddle tune and the square dance show the same kind of American quality that Mr. Kouwenhoven finds in his twelve artifacts: the Manhattan skyline, the gridiron town plan, the skyscraper, the Model T Ford, jazz, the Constitution, Mark Twain's writing, Whitman's *Leaves of Grass*, comic strips, soap operas, assembly line production, and chewing gum. The list, we are reminded, reflects the pluralism of our nation, yet there is a unifying quality that extends through all twelve. That quality, if I read Kouwenhoven correctly, is that all twelve when reduced to their lowest common denominator consist of simple and infinitely repeatable units, with the process of repetition guaranteeing their viability.

The skyscraper and the gridiron town plan which makes the Manhattan skyline possible are surprisingly similar. The skyscraper was created by the development of the cage or skeleton construction. We all have surely seen this type of building process: with each additional floor another cage—steel girders employed vertically and horizontally

16. For details on this activity see Barre Toelken, "Traditional Fiddling in Idaho," *Western Folklore*, XXIV (October, 1965), 259–262.

17. There may be some serious consequences to this American practical mindedness: William Whyte (*The Organization Man*, New York, 1956) insists that it is a great hazard that we continue to ignore the theoretical. See especially Chapter Sixteen, "The Fight Against Genius."

18. Kouwenhoven's remarks appeared originally in *Harper's* Magazine, July, 1956, as "What's American about America?" but have been republished in slightly different form in Harold F. Graves and Bernard S. Oldsey *From Fact to Judgment* (New York, 1957, 1963). It is the latter version hereinafter summarized and modified and to p. 133 that the reader is referred for the context of the quotation.

—is added, creating a three dimensional gridiron. As the skyscraper is a vertical gridiron capable of towering *upward* thrust, so the typical American town plan is a horizontal gridiron capable of dynamic *outward* thrust. The pattern of streets and blocks was inherent in the square townships, sections, and quarter sections imposed upon our expanding nation by the Ordinance of 1785.[19]

One of the big differences between an American town and its European counterpart is the capability of expansion of the former, the capacity for the streets and blocks to be extended as the gridiron expands with the growth of the town. This is not the case with the European town, medieval in origin, whose growth was restricted by a complicated and closed system of land holding and, more importantly, by the presence of the town wall.[20] To gain room within the limitations of the town wall, medieval builders were forced to construct overhangs, second or third or fourth storys that actually extend over the streets. And the streets, of course, were stopped by the wall.

But in America, no such limitations existed, and in theory our streets are open-ended, with the great highways which criss-cross our land merely their extensions east and west, north and south. This fact makes it possible for the megalopolis to exist: growing cities simply push their way out and incorporate smaller entities without disturbing the gridwork of streets and blocks of either.

To remind you of the basic similarity of the skyscraper and the city gridiron, let me repeat that both consist of simple and infinitely repeatable units, steel cages on the one hand, streets and blocks on the other. How large can a city become? The availability of water may be the only limiting condition. How high can a skyscraper go? Frank Lloyd Wright was supposed to have said that if someone wanted a building a mile high, he would design it. In other words, these two artifacts are not limited by any internal logic or rationale. They can go out and up, if not forever, at least a "mighty fur piece." And when they have gone high enough, a penthouse or an excrescence containing elevator machinery signalizes not a conclusion but a halt. This, Kouwenhoven reminds us, is not the case with a Gothic cathedral or a Greek temple whose architecture demands completion, fulfilment, rounding off. "Topping out" is the way we used to refer to this concept when we were finishing a stack of long hay.

19. [The ordinance established the pattern of Western land surveys, setting the grid of townships, sections, and fractions of sections as the norm for the American landscape.]

20. Lewis Mumford, *The City in History: Its Origins, Its Transformations, and Its Prospects* (New York, 1961). The reader will find remarks on the limitations imposed by the city wall, an interesting medieval symbol, on pages 289 and 304, among others.

The Model T, with its system of interchangeable parts, fits into this notion of simplicity and infinitely repeatable units if one remembers that the old Fords were never really finished products. When a new gadget came out to improve the performance of the vehicle, it could be added without disturbing the essential simplicity of the car or the interchangeability of its parts. I remember the Ruckstell axle, sometimes installed even before the newly purchased Ford left the dealer's, that aided substantially in negotiating the steep Mann's Creek Grade.

The Ford, then, could be modified (indeed, automobiles today regularly undergo this process), changed, altered without damaging the integrity of the unit. And this is very close to one of the claims folklorists always advance to justify calling a given item folklore: it exists in variant forms. I am not prepared at this point to argue that hotrodders are perpetuating a folk tradition by souping up and decking their cars, even though I suspect that these teenagers are the vectors of a viable folk process. I further suspect that an analogy could be drawn between this Ford refinement and the modifications which art music undergoes when it is absorbed into the folk medium.[21]

Jazz, that interesting hybrid of African rhythms and slavery and freedom, features a strong $2/4$ or $4/4$ beat, a simple rhythmic gridiron capable of infinite expansion on which or around which the improvisations occur. No matter how wild the break from the basic melody, no matter how florid the solo performance as instruments compete for the lead, there is always a return to the $4/4$ beat and to the melody. Then, too, the matter of completeness figures here. Just as there is no logical conclusion or summation necessary for a skyscraper, there is no single point in a free wheeling jazz selection which, when reached, is the climax, conclusion, or moment of structural fulfillment.

But jazz musicians are human and cannot play on forever. They have devised, therefore, a variety of rather artless stopping points— penthouses if you will—where they arbitrarily close off the piece. With art music, however, there is a climactic point to which the whole piece has built and which, when reached, says in effect, "That's it." The jazz musicians' coda is, to the contrary, an admission of their inability to do more than halt temporarily the flow of simple and infinitely repeatable units.

Two more observations remain before I suggest ways of considering the fiddle tune in the same light which has been shed on these American artifacts. The first observation concerns the United States Constitution.

The Constitution is a product of the Age of Enlightenment, and

21. See note 15.

among European ideas antecedent to the creation of such a document are, certainly, Locke's notion of federative power outlined in the sixth chapter, "Of the Constitution of England," in Book XI of the *Spirit of the Laws*; Montesquieu's trio of legislative power, executive power, and the power of judging[22]; and Rousseau's social contract. I have already noted that fiddle tunes have European ancestors and have insisted that this fact does not denigrate them as American artifacts. So it is with the Constitution. And to link it to the other items showing Americanness, it is only necessary to point out that this document consists of articles and sections which can by amendment be extended to accommodate itself to whatever exigencies need to be met. It provides for a federation of separate units, as few as thirteen but not limited by internal logic or necessity to fifty.

The common characteristic of process, the quality of the continuation of simple and infinitely repeatable units, is shared, says Kouwenhoven, by comic strips, soap operas, assembly line production, and chewing gum. Whatever your favorite comic strip, it is never concluded. Its basic structural unit is the panel (a simple and infinitely repeatable unit). One adventure or sequence ends, but before the reader has a chance to reflect, he is engaged in the process of another. Like Tennyson's brook,[23] Orphan Annie threatens to go on forever. Not even the death of a writer necessarily stops the flow of panels, for the syndicate, which holds the copyright, can find another talent. And so with soap operas; properly sponsored, *The Long Hot Summer* and *Peyton Place* will go on and on and on, a series of especially simple and infinitely repeatable units.

It has already been established that the fiddle tunes which Victoria Schweitzer danced to through the course of a memorable two days of frolic had foreign antecedents. So had the Constitution, and jazz of the southern Mississippi owes a debt to Africa.

The second attribute which the fiddle tune shares with other American artifacts is the rhythmic structure, a basic duple beat either $\frac{2}{4}$ or $\frac{4}{4}$. So, we noted, has jazz. And no matter how many flourishes and pizzicatos and glissandos, no matter how intemperate the bowing, the fiddler has to keep to the beat and return to the tune. His dancers insist.

It is a commonplace observation that Mark Twain was a gifted

22. For a discussion of stimuli operating on the formation of the U.S. Constitution, see Francis D. Wormuth, *The Origins of Modern Constitutionalism* (New York, 1949), especially Chapter XX, pp. 191–206.

23. [The poem "The Brook" by Alfred, Lord Tennyson (1809–1892) contains the refrain, spoken by the brook, "For men may come and men may go, / But I go on for ever."]

storyteller. Part of the craft defies description, but certainly part of it depends upon the judgment to know when the basic "beat" can be abandoned for details of local color and when the story must get back to what the characters are doing. There are real possibilities in "That reminds me of the time me and Ole Bob went huntin' over on Skillet Creek. . . ." But listeners are frustrated if the narrative continues: "I remember that was the fall of the spring old May calved out in the slough where Smith's horse, the one with the string halt that he traded Deefie Johnson out of. . . ." Twain knew all this; indeed he discusses it in his "Autobiographical Dictation" and also in *Life on the Mississippi*. And the good fiddler senses the saturation point which forces him to keep the beat and return to the tune no matter how inspired his improvisation.

The third consideration is perhaps the most interesting. Like jazz, like the town gridiron, like the skyscraper and *Huckleberry Finn* and all the rest of these artifacts, there is no internal logic or necessity—arkitektonike—that insists upon a stopping place. How long can a fiddle tune be played? The only consideration here is a coincidental human one: how long can a fiddler's arm hold out? Or what has convention decided shall constitute a set? The tune itself can continue indefinitely—the process is the important thing—and fiddlers, like jazz musicians, have constructed highly artificial codas signalizing the ending of a piece. Otherwise the repeatable musical phrases on their rhythmic grid *would* go on infinitely. The most common coda, I suppose, is the rhythmic formula, "shave and a haircut, six bits," or "shave and a haircut, bay rum."

Fourth and finally, the setting in which the tunes were played and the use to which they were put (accompaniment for a country frolic) qualify them as American artifacts. This is the American refinement and adaptation I spoke of, and some remarks by Damon are pertinent:

> When America became nationally conscious of its folk dancing, it discovered that each little community had its own way of doing the traditional dances, just as each fiddler had his own way of playing the tunes. There was no standard, no book which stated what was correct; there was no right or wrong—there was only better or worse.[24]

One of the remarkable features in the performance of traditional dances in the Lower Snake River Valley might well be the progressive square dance. How it suggests the American concern for process is too obvious for comment. What the nineteen year old Victoria Schweitzer experienced is somehow symbolic of the process of replacing the fron-

24. Damon, p. 96.

tier with civilization. And the fiddle tune and square dance flourished as long as there was a frontier, either geo-historical or cultural, for they played an important part in providing entertainment which had to be either home made or done without.

As recently as thirty years ago there was still, in some respects, a cultural frontier in the Lower Snake River Valley along Monroe Creek where I grew up. No antibiotics, no paved road, indeed, not even a gravelled one, and no electricity. Consequently there was a good deal of do-it-yourself-or-go-without entertainment, and the square dance and fiddle tune were very much alive. In this same locale today the fiddle tune survives in a shadowy kind of existence through an annual fiddle festival and contest. Although it is a coelacanthine existence when compared with its former vitality, it does provide the opportunity to study, to know, and to enjoy this once most engaging folk art.

Whatever else can be said about fiddle tunes and square dances, they help make us aware that we have been a people fascinated by activity, by movement, by process.

ON GAME MORPHOLOGY:
A STUDY OF THE STRUCTURE
OF NON-VERBAL FOLKLORE

Alan Dundes

The characteristic patterning of folklore is evident in most examples and studies presented in this reader, and some of the preceding essays have examined the form ("morphology") of folk materials along with their content, style, function, or context. In the early 1960s closer structural analysis of folklore gained favor in the United States, but many of the best publications which used this approach did not deal with American folklore or are too lengthy and technical for reprinting here. Alan Dundes' article on the structure of children's games is a notable exception; it is clear, concise, and based on relatively familiar examples of American children's games. Dundes also outlines the essential goals and methods of structural analysis and provides a basic bibliography of earlier studies and some explanations of needed terms.

The word "motifeme" was introduced by Dundes for use in the structural analysis of folktales; it signifies the generalized units of narration that make up a plot (villainy, pursuit, capture, etc.). In games the same motifemes seem to appear as acted-out patterns rather than merely as sequential plot elements. Thus, Dundes writes that "a game is, structurally speaking, a two-dimensional folktale"; that is, both the hero's and villain's plot functions occur at the same time in a game. But, unlike folktales, games usually have unpredictable outcomes.

Dundes' emphasis on the importance of studying non-verbal folklore as well as the verbal genres is still valid, but his concern is less necessary now than it may have been in 1964 because American folklorists have since taken up the study of customary and material traditions with much energy and interest. Still, most of his examples of structural counterparts in verbal and nonverbal forms have not yet been followed up in thorough studies, leaving even beginning folklore students ample opportunity to apply these ideas to their own projects.

ARE CHILDREN'S GAMES, a form of non-verbal folklore, and folktales, a form of verbal folklore, structurally similar? I am suggesting in the following article that they are and also that there are many other non-verbal analogues to verbal folklore forms. Consequently, the definition of folklore should not be limited to verbal materials.

Although structural analysis, as an effective means of descriptive ethnography, has been applied to a number of types of folklore expression, it has not been employed in the study of children's games. Yet games, in general, and competitive games, in particular, are obviously patterned. In competitive games, the participants are aware that play is governed by definite limiting rules. The application and the interrelationship of these rules result in an ordered sequence of actions by the players, and these action sequences constitute the essential structure of any particular game.

In order to delineate the structure of a game, or any other form of folklore, one must have a minimum structural unit. Only with such a unit can there be any precise segmentation of the continuum of game action. As a trial unit, I propose to use the *motifeme*, a unit of action which has been used in structural studies of folktales.[1] One obvious advantage of employing the motifeme is that if game action can, in fact, be broken down into motifemes, then it would be relatively easy to compare the structure of games with the structure of folktales.[2]

Before examining the pronounced similarities in game and folktale structure, it is necessary to emphasize one important difference between the two forms. The difference is dimensionality. The folktale is concerned with conflict between protagonist and antagonist, but the sequence of plot actions is unidimensional. Either the hero's actions or the villain's actions are discussed at any one moment in time at any one point in the tale. Vladimir Propp, a Russian folklorist, made, in 1928, a thought-provoking examination of fairy tales and devised a distribution of functions (motifemes) among the *dramatis personae* of the tales.[3] He noted, for example, that functions VIII (villainy), XVI (struggle), and XXI (pursuit) belong to the villain's sphere of action. Certainly, functions IV (reconnaissance) and V (delivery) in Propp's

1. See the author's "From Etic to Emic Units in the Structural Study of Folktales," *Journal of American Folklore*, 75 (1962), 95–105; and "Structural Typology of North American Indian Folktales," *Southwestern Journal of Anthropology*, 19 (1963), 121–130.

2. A recent interesting study by John M. Roberts, Brian Sutton-Smith, and Adam Kendon, "Strategy in Games and Folk Tales," *Journal of Social Psychology*, 61 (1963), 185–199, demonstrates that folktales and games are strikingly similar models of competitive situations and that folktales with strategic outcomes are positively correlated with the occurrence of games of strategy in given cultural settings. However, the comparison of game and folktale content was limited to a generalized consideratoin of "outcomes." The delineation of game structure should facilitate this type of cross-cultural study.

3. Vladimir Propp, *Morphology of the Folktale*, edited by Svatava Pirkova-Jakobson, translated by Laurence Scott, Publication Ten of the Indiana University Research Center in Anthropology, Folklore, and Linguistics (Bloomington, 1958), pp. 72–75. Propp's study was also issued as Part III of the *International Journal of American Linguistics*, XXIV, No. 4 (1958), and as Volume 9 of the Bibliographical and Special Series of the American Folklore Society.

analysis are villain and not hero actions. In games, however, one finds a contrast: there are at least two sequences of actions going on *simultaneously*. When A is playing against B, both A and B are operating at the same time, all the time. This is theoretically true in folktales, but only one side's activities (usually the hero's) are described at a given point in the tale. A folktale is, therefore, a two-dimensional series of actions displayed on a one-dimensional track, or, conversely, a game is, structurally speaking, a two-dimensional folktale.

In his notable discussion of folktale morphology, Propp drew particular attention to function VIII, villainy. In this function, a villain causes harm or injury to one member of a family by abducting a person or stealing an object, etc., thus creating the actual movement of the folktale.[4] At the same time, he astutely observed that a folktale could begin with the desire to have something or a deficiency or lack as a given ground-rule. In the analysis, Propp considered lack (function VIIIa) as morphologically equivalent to villainy (function VIII). If a folktale did not begin with a state of lack, then a state of lack could be created by an act of villainy. This same distinction can also be applied to the structure of many games. A game can begin with an object which is missing, or the object may be hidden before play begins. In some games nothing is missing, but the initial portion of game action (corresponding to Propp's "initial" or "preparatory" section of the folktale, functions I–VII) brings about the requisite state of lack or insufficiency. In games of the first type, an individual may hide from the group (as in "Hare and Hounds") or the group may hide from an individual ("Hide and Seek"). In games of the second type, an individual or object may be abducted or captured, which also results in a lack. This happens, for example, in the child stealing game of "The Witch." Other characteristics shared by both folktales and games will become apparent in the following discussion of several specific games.

In "Hare and Hounds,"[5] the boy chosen as the Hare (the choosing by counting out rhymes or other means may be construed as pre-game activity) runs away to hide. Usually a fixed time span, a specific number of minutes, or counting to some arbitrary number, marks the formal beginning of the chase, much as the iteration of an opening formula marks the passage from reality to fantasy in the beginning of a folktale. In fact, some games actually have opening formulas such as "Ready or not, here I come." The game, then, begins with a lack, the missing Hare. The quest, so popular in folktales, is equally popular in

4. Propp, p. 29.

5. Alice Bertha Gomme, *The Traditional Games of England, Scotland, and Ireland*, Vol. I (New York, 1964), 191.

games. The Hounds attempt to find and catch the Hare, just as the hero in folktale seeks to liquidate the initial lack (function XIX).

Note, however that two sets of actions, or motifeme sequences, are involved in the game. One action is from the point of view of the Hounds, the other from the perspective of the Hare. The sequences include the following motifemes: lack, interdiction, violation, and consequence.[6] In one motifemic sequence, the Hounds want to catch the Hare (lack). They are required to catch him before he returns "home," a place agreed upon previously, (interdiction). If the Hounds fail to do so (violation), they lose the game (consequence). In the second motifemic sequence taking place simultaneously with the first, the Hare wants to go "home" (lack), but he is required to arrive there without being caught by the Hounds (interdiction). If he fails to do so (violation), he loses the game (consequence). It is possible to win the game, by liquidating the lack, by either of two actions: catching the Hare or returning "home" safely. But it is impossible for both Hare and Hounds to win and also impossible for both Hare and Hounds to lose. Here is another point of contrast with folktales. In folktales, the hero always wins and the villain always loses. In games, however the outcome is not so regular or predictable: sometimes the Hare wins, and sometimes the Hounds win. As Caillois has pointed out, one characteristic of competitive games is that the opponents are equal and, in theory, each opponent stands the same chance of winning.[7]

6. One should remember that an interdiction is a negative injunction. Compare, for example, "Don't open your eyes" with "Keep your eyes closed." It should also be kept in mind that one form of consequence can be lack, while another form can be liquidation of lack (Propp's functions VIIIa and XIX). Brian Sutton-Smith in "A Formal Analysis of Game Meaning," *Western Folklore*, 18 (1959), 13–24, lumps game action into a cover-all term, "The Game Challenge." While he does discuss the structure of game time and space, he does not really conceive of games as linear structural sequences of actions nor does he appear to be aware that there are two distinct sets of action sequences in the game he analyzes, "Bar the Door," one set for the person who is "it," the central player, and one set for the children who attempt to run past "it" as they go from one base to the other.

7. Roger Caillois, *Man, Play, and Games*, translated by Meyer Barash (New York, 1961), 14. The double set of rules existing in games makes their analysis somewhat different from the analysis of folktales. Sometimes the two patterns are distinct in that there is no rapid change from one set of rules to the other for an individual player. In baseball, for example, the rules of "offense" apply for the team at bat until three men have been put out. Similarly, the rules of "defense" for the team in the field apply for the same period. At the end of the period, the teams exchange places (and rules). However, in other games, such as basketball or football, the rules can change at any time. In football, an intercepted pass or a recovered fumble by the team on defense immediately transforms the defense team into an offense team, and the same action immediately transforms the team previously on offense to a defense team. In "How many miles to Babylon?" described in Paul G. Brewster, *American Nonsinging Games* (Norman, 1953), 52–53, players who attempt to run from one end of a rectangular space to another may be caught by the player in the middle; they now belong to that player and aid him in catching others trying to cross the field.

The game of "Hare and Hounds" might be structured as follows:

	Lack	Interdiction	Violation	Consequence
Hare	wants to go home	without being caught by Hounds	is caught (isn't caught)	loses game (wins game)
Hounds	want to catch absent Hare	before he arrives back home	do not catch Hare (do catch Hare)	lose game (win game)

The double structure is also illuminated by comparison with analogous folktale structure. From the Hare's point of view, one could say there was a hero pursued (function XXI) and that the hero is rescued from pursuit (function XXII), assuming the Hare wins. The game-folktale analogy is even closer in those versions in which the Hare is required to leave signs, such as strips of paper, to mark his trail. In folktales, when the hero runs from his pursuer, he often places obstacles in the latter's path. These objects mark the trail, but also serve to delay the pursuer. From the point of view of the Hounds, i.e., with the Hounds as heroes, the Hare appears to serve as a donor figure, inasmuch as the dropped slips of paper are "magical agents" (identified as function XIV) which aid the hero-Hounds in liquidating the initial lack.[8] The donor sequence, then, is another point of similarity between games and folktales.[9]

In a popular American children's game which Brewster calls "Steps,"[10] the leader, or "it," aids the others in reaching him (to tag him) by permitting various steps, such as baby steps, giant steps or umbrella steps. In this game, the donor figure grants the privilege of using certain "magical" steps. The fact that the magical aid is not granted until the hero is tested by the donor is also a striking parallel to folktale morphology. After the donor, ("it") permits the number and type of steps, (e.g., four baby steps), the recipient ("hero") is required to say "May I?" If the latter passes the politeness test, he is permitted to take the steps which bring him closer to his goal. How-

8. It is quite likely that magical gestures such as touching a certain tree, crossing one's fingers, or assuming a certain "safe" position (such as squatting in "Squat Tag") are analogous to the host of magical agents which protect protagonists in folktales.

9. [Propp designates one key character in folktales as "the donor, or more precisely, the provider . . ." This figure enters in stage 12 of Propp's 31-stage outline of the functions of dramatis personae of folktales to provide an object or agent (usually magic) with which the hero is able to overcome obstacles and succeed in meeting the challenges of the tale.]

10. Brewster, *op. cit.* 164.

ever, should he neglect to express the etiquette formula, the donor will penalize him by ordering him to step backwards, thus moving him away from the goal. More often than not in folktales, civility or politeness to the donor will provide the needed magical agents while discourtesy deprives the would-be hero of these same agents.

In some games, the presence of a donor sequence appears to be optional rather than obligatory, as is also true in folktales. In "Thimble in Sight"[11] an object, such as a thimble, is hidden. Actually, the object is supposed to be visible but not obvious. The children seek to discover or notice the object (lack). As each child does so (lack liquidated), he indicates his success by exclaiming a verbal formula such as "rorum torum corum," much as the successful player in "Hide and Seek" announces his return "home" with the phrase "Home free." (These verbal formulas would appear to be analogous to closing formulas in folktales.) In this form of "Thimble in Sight" there is no donor sequence but in some versions, the hider aids the thimble-seekers by giving helpful clues such as "You're freezing" or "You're cold," when the seeker is far away from the quest-object, and "You're warm" or "You're burning," when the seeker is close to the object. In such versions, the seeker could presumably request assistance from the donor by asking, "Am I getting warm?" Nevertheless, since the game can be played without the donor sequence, it is clear that the sequence is structurally not obligatory.

The frequency of the donor sequence in games and folktales also demands attention. One would suspect, for example, that since the donor sequence is comparatively rare in American Indian folktales, as compared with Indo-European folktales, the donor sequence would be infrequent in American Indian games. The presence or absence of such a sequence might even be correlated with magic and religion. If a person can make magic or seek a religious vision as an individual, then the need for a donor might be less than in those cultures in which experts or intermediaries supply magic or religion.

So far, mention has been made of a number of games in which the initial lack is part of the given. The game's action does not begin until an object or person is removed or secreted. "It" may absent himself in order to produce the initial lack situation. However, in "The Witch" the lack is the result of "it's" abducting someone.[12] In this game, the parallel to folktale structure is also apparent. A mother leaves her

11. William Wells Newell, *Games and Songs of American Children* (New York, 1963), 152; Brewster, *op. cit.* 46.

12. Gomme, *op. cit.*, Vol. II, 391–396. For a New York State version called "Old Witch," see Anne Gertrude Sneller, "Growing Up," NYFQ, Vol. XX, No. 2 (June 1964), 89–90 (Editor).

seven children, named after the days of the week (Propp's function I, "One of the members of a family is absent from home"—still bearing in mind that Propp's morphological analysis was made of folktales and not games). Before leaving, the mother tells her children, "Take care the Old Witch does not catch you" (function II, "An interdiction is addressed to the hero"). The witch enters and the children do not take heed (function III, "The interdiction is violated"). The witch pretends that the children's mother has sent her to fetch a bonnet (function VI, "The villain attempts to deceive his victim in order to take possession of him or of his belongings"). The child goes to get the bonnet (function VII, "The victim submits to deception and thereby unwittingly helps his enemy"). The witch abducts one of the children (function VIII, "The villain causes harm or injury to one member of a family"). The mother returns, names her seven children, and thus discovers that one of her children is missing. The remaining children cry, "The Old Witch has got her" (function IX, "Misfortune or shortage is made known"). The sequence of motifemes is repeated until the witch has abducted all the children. This action is analogous to the repetition of entire moves in folktales, e.g., elder brothers setting out successively on identical quests.

The mother then goes out to find the children (function X, "The seeker agrees to or decides upon counteraction," and function XI, "The hero leaves home"). The mother encounters the witch and asks her for information about the whereabouts of her children. In the standard ritual dialogue, one finds possible traces of the standard donor sequence, as identified by functions XII–XIV. In this game, the witch functions as donor. The mother finally arrives at the place where her children are being held captive (function XV, "The hero is transferred, reaches, or is led to the whereabouts of an object of search"). This function or motifeme is of great significance to the structural analysis of both games and folktales. Propp remarks (page 46), "Generally the object of search is located in another or different kingdom." Anyone familiar with children's games will recall that many make mandatory the penetration of the opponent's territory. In "Capture the Flag" (Brewster, pages 69–70), the object of the search is the opponent's flag, clearly located in the "enemy's kingdom."

Now the mother discovers her lost children (function XIX, "The initial misfortune or lack is liquidated"), and mother and children pursue the witch. The one who catches the witch becomes the witch in the next playing of the game. In folktales, a pursuit often follows the liquidation of the initial lack, but more commonly the villain pursues the hero (function XXI, "The hero is pursued"). The hero inevitably escapes (function XXII, "The hero is rescued from pursuit"). Propp remarks that "a great many folktales end on the note of rescue from pursuit." The same might be said of games. In many games, "it," or the villain, is the one who pursues the "hero"-seekers after the latter have obtained the quest-object, such as the flag in "Capture the Flag." Of course, one reason why the game of "The Witch" is similar to folktales is the fixed nature of the outcome! The witch never wins, just as the villian in folktales never wins.

Critics have been skeptical of Propp's morphological analysis on the grounds that he limited his material to Russian fairy tales. Competent students of the folktale, however, are aware that most, if not all, of the tales Propp analyzed can, in fact, be classified according to the Aarne-Thompson system[13] as tale types. Others complain that Propp was too general and that his functions apply to literary as well as to folk materials. It is true that Propp's concept can be correlated to the plot structure of *Beowulf* and to most of the *Odyssey* (Cf. his functions XXI to XXXI with the end of the *Odyssey*). Clearly, the game of "Old Witch" contains a number of Propp's functions and, in one sense, the game appears to be a dramatized folktale. Moreover the "Old Witch" game bears a superficial resemblance to the Aarne-Thompson tale type 123, "The Wolf and the Kids." But what is important here is that the morphological analysis of folktales appears to apply equally well to another genre of folklore—traditional games, thereby providing further confirmation of the validity of Propp's analysis.

When one perceives the similarity between the structure of games and folktales it is also possible to see parallels among special forms of the two genres. For example, one type of folktale is the cumulative tale. In these tales (Aarne-Thompson types 2000–2199), one finds chains of actions or objects. Usually, there is repetition with continual additions. In ballads this stylistic feature is termed "incremental repetition." Stith Thompson, in his discussion of tales of this type, noted, but without further comment, that they had "something of the nature of a game."[14] This game-tale analogy is obvious in "Link Tag" in which "it" tags someone. The tagged person must take hold of the tagger's hand and help him tag others; the next one tagged joins the first two and so on.[15] (The same structure is obviously found in those folk dances in which couples or individuals form ever-lengthening chains.)

13. [Antti Aarne and Stith Thompson's *The Types of the Folktale*, 2nd rev. edn. (Helsinki: *Folklore Fellows Communications*, no. 184, 1961) is the standard catalog of folktale types consulted by folklorists for classification of European and European-derived folktales.]

14. *The Folktale* (New York, 1951), 230 and 234.

15. Brewster, *op. cit.* 67.

Another sub-genre analogy might be trickster tales (or jokes) and pranks. In trickster tales and in most pranks or practical jokes, the primary motifemes are fraud and deception (Propp functions VI and VII) so there can even be an exact identity of content as well as form in folktales and games.[16] For example, in some versions of tale type 1530, "Holding up the Rock," a dupe is gulled into believing that he is holding up a wall. But "Hold up the wall" is a hazing stunt at Texas Agricultural and Mechanical College, in which, according to one report, a student is required to squat with his back against a wall as if supporting it.[17] A more surprising example is the prank analogue of tale type 1528, "Holding Down the Hat," in which victims were fooled into grabbing feces concealed under a hat.[18] Perhaps the greatest similarity in trickster tale and prank morphology is their common parodying of standard folktale and game structure. Instead of liquidating an actual lack, a false lack is feigned. Thus the unsuspecting initiate is sent snipe-hunting, armed with a sack and a flashlight, or an apprentice is persuaded to seek some quest-object which, according to the occupation group, may be striped paint, a board-shortener or a left-handed monkey wrench.

The morphological similarity between game and folktale suggests an important principle which may be applied to other forms of folklore. Basically, these different forms derive from the distinction between words and acts. Thus, there is verbal folklore and non-verbal folklore. The distinction is made most frequently with respect to myth and ritual. Myth is verbal folklore or, in Bascom's terms, verbal "art."[19] Ritual, in contrast, is non-verbal folklore or non-verbal art. Myth and ritual are both sacred; folktale and game are both secular. (Whether all games evolved from ritual is no more or less likely than the evolution, or rather devolution, of folktales from myths.) Whereas folklorists have, for some time, known of the similarities between myth and ritual, they have not recognized the equally common characteristics of folktale and game. Moreover, they have failed to see that the verbal/non-verbal dichotomy applies to most, if not all, of the standard genres of folklore. The proverb, clearly an example of verbal folklore, has for its non-verbal counterpart the gesture. They are functionally equivalent as both forms may sum up a situation or pass judgment on a situation. Riddles are structurally similar to proverbs in that both are based upon topic/comment constructions, but they are

16. *Ibid.*, 120–126.

17. Fred Eikel, Jr., "An Aggie Vocabulary of Slang," *American Speech*, 18 (1946), 34.

18. James R. Caldwell, "A Tale Actualized in a Game," *JAF*, 58 (1945), 50.

19. William R. Bascom, "Verbal Art," *JAF*, 68 (1955), 245–252.

distinct from proverbs in that there is always a referent to be guessed.[20] Non-verbal equivalents include a variety of difficult tasks and puzzles. The distinction between proverbs and riddles applies equally to gestures and non-oral riddles. The referent of the gesture is known to both the employer of the gesture and his audience *before* the gesture is made; the referent of the non-oral riddles is presumably known initially only by the poser.[21]

Superstitions are also illuminated by this verbal/non-verbal distinction. Folklorists have long used terms such as "belief" and "custom" or "practice" in discussions of superstitions. In this analysis, practices or customs would be examples of non-verbal folklore since actual physical activity is involved. The distinction may even apply to folk music. If folk narrative, for example, is set to music, it would then be termed folksong; if a game were set to music, it would then be termed folk dance. (Note that the etymology of the term "ballad" supports this distinction.)[22] I am *not* implying that folksong derives from folk narrative or that folk dance derives from game but only suggesting that these supposedly disparate genres have much in common. For example, the basic sequence of lack and lack-liquidated found in folktales and games is also found in folk dance. In many dances, a couple is separated, or from the man's point of view, he has lost his partner (lack). The remainder of the dance consists of reuniting the separated partners (liquidating the lack).[23] Moreover, the leaving of home and returning home occurs in folktales, games, folk dances and folk music.

20. Robert A. Georges and Alan Dundes, "Toward a Structural Definition of the Riddle," *JAF*, 76 (1963), 113 and 117.

21. For examples of non-oral riddles, *see* Jan Brunvand, "More Non-Oral Riddles," *Western Folklore*, 19 (1960), 132–133. Note that this form of folklore is defined negatively, in terms of the presumably primary verbal form: riddles. In the same way, the term "practical joke" represents a qualifying of the primary term "joke," which is also verbal. Even the term used here of "non-verbal folklore" continues the same bias in favor of the primacy of verbal forms. At least gestures are not called non-oral or non-verbal proverbs.

22. [The word "ballad" comes from the Old French *ballade*, a musical piece accompanied by dancing. It was long thought that English ballads—narrative folksongs—originated with a "singing-dancing throng," but later ballad scholars rejected this theory in favor of one positing individual authors and communal re-creation of ballads and other folksongs.]

23. In the structure of folk dance, the same distinction is found of beginning either with a state of lack or causing a state of lack by an act of villainy. Some dances have an "it" who is without a partner (lack) and who seeks to obtain one (lack liquidated). Other dances begin with couples, but during the dance one or more couples become separated (lack) and reunite only at the end of the dance (lack liquidated). For an interesting study of dance morphology, *see* Olga Szentpal, "Versuch einer Formanalyse der Ungarischen Volkstanze," *Acta Ethnographica*, 7 (1958), 257–334; also Gyorgy Martin and Erno Pestovar, "A Structural Analysis of the Hungarian Folk Dance (A Methodological Sketch)," *Ibid.*, 10 (1961), 1–40.

Structurally speaking, it does not matter whether "home" is a house, a tree, a position on a dance floor or a note.

The techniques of structural analysis should be applied to genres of folklore other than games and folktales. These forms, from the design of quilt patterns to tongue-twisters, can be defined structurally. One would guess that such analyses will reveal a relatively small number of similar structural patterns underlying these apparently diverse forms.

Specifically, I have tried to demonstrate that at least one non-verbal form of folklore, children's games, is structurally similar to a verbal form, the folktale. If, then, there are non-verbal analogues (e.g., games) for verbal folklore forms (e.g., folktales), then folklore as a discipline cannot possibly be limited to the study of just verbal art, oral literature, or folk literature, or whatever similar term is employed. Kenneth Pike has observed that "Verbal and non-verbal activity is a unified whole, and theory and methodology should be organized or created to treat it as such."[24] It is time for folklorists to devote some of the energies given over to the study of verbal folklore to the study of folklore in its non-verbal forms. Compared to folk narrative and folksong, such forms as folk dance, games, and gestures have been grossly neglected.[25] Admittedly there are complex problems of transcription but surely they are not insuperable.

24. *Language in Relation to a Unified Theory of the Structure of Human Behavior*, Part I (Glendale, 1954), 2. These categories of "verbal" and "non-verbal" folklore are arbitrary distinctions which do not necessarily reflect objective reality. Obviously jump rope rhymes, counting out rhymes, and finger rhymes involve both words and actions.

25. Alexander Haggerty Krappe, for example, in his *The Science of Folklore* (New York, 1930), gives these forms short shrift. The unfortunate trend continues. One looks in vain for extended mention of these forms in annual folklore bibliographies, works in progress lists, and surveys of folklore research.

PLAIN AND FANCY:
A CONTENT ANALYSIS OF
CHILDREN'S JOKES
DEALING WITH ADULT SEXUALITY

Rosemary Zumwalt

Zumwalt's study surveys and analyzes the image that one group holds of another as revealed in folk traditions. The informants are modern American children, the group pictured consists of adults, the genre is jokes, and the subject is sex. The content of these jokes which she quotes from the oral tradition of young white middle-class California girls is startling, especially in comparison to the bland nature of most "children's folklore" published in storybooks. The classification and analysis of the jokes, however, goes beyond their titillating surface features to the deeper patterns of metaphor and symbol. However, it is possible that Zumwalt has generalized too freely from limited data; other folklorists should attempt to validate her suggested meanings of children's sexual humor with studies of other groups' jokes.

The title joke of this study is a good example of how folk tradition itself may suggest the scholar's best approach to interpretation. The terms "plain and fancy" used by the child clearly symbolize the typical relationship between child and adult in these stories, at least as regards sex. Also, the opening joke is in the traditional "kids say the darndest things" form, a familiar device adults use to displace their concern with a sensitive topic by putting a discussion of it into a child's mouth. (Remember the proverb, "Out of the mouths of babes we hear the truth.") It should be noted too that this is the only joke discussed that did not come from a child; instead, it is about a child who asks a question that is not answered. Perhaps this shows that adults telling the joke realize how curious children are about sex, but also recognize that they may be getting no answers to their questions about it.

The form of Zumwalt's presentation is much like William Hugh Jansen's in his article on "The Surpriser Surprised" in Section 1—each text is followed by interpretation. Zumwalt, however, is concerned with a number of different narratives on one theme, not with the life history and possible origin of a single plot and its subtypes. But both studies show how economically and directly the folk texts state their meanings in contrast to the sometimes circuitous nature of scholarly explication. The two-line Tarzan gesture joke is a good example; a child's performance of it (four words, two gestures) conveys everything that the folklorist needs several lines to summarize.

It is unfortunate that there is so little commentary on these texts from the informants themselves. Without this "oral literary criticism" it is impossible to say just how much of the jokes these little girls understand and what they are merely repeating from their sources (who may be older children). For example, in the jokes in which adults respond to questions about sex with roundabout answers that later backfire when the child repeats them, we wonder if the seven-to-ten-year-old girls recognize the satirical treatment of adult obtuseness. On the other hand, do the children sometimes appreciate the jokes at levels that are lost on an adult analyst? A comment from an older child reveals that this particular type of joke is discarded as children grow up; an obvious question, then, is "What jokes do the older children tell about sex?" One example concludes this study, pointing the way to further research.

A little girl was taking a shower with her mother. She looked up at her mother, and said, "Mommy, why am I so plain, and you're so fancy?"[1]

The mother makes no reply, and the little girl remains ignorant and naked. But other jokes from children's oral tradition draw conclusions about adult sexuality. Some continue to watch passively, but with new understanding of their parents' sexual prowess. Others participate with their parents on a sexual plane. And still others suggest action, or worse, take action, destructive to their parents' sexual superiority. However, there is a gulf between the plain and the fancy, the child and the adult, no matter what course of action is taken. And this gulf between the adult, and his or her sexual powers, and the child, and his or her impotence, is never bridged even in the laughing world of the dirty joke. The adult remains fancy (if mutilated), and the child remains plain, yearning for the fancy frills.

With the exception of the opening joke, all of the jokes presented were collected from little girls of the white middle class, who ranged in age from seven to ten. The children, all close friends of the author, were familiar with my interest in children's folklore, and volunteered the jokes along with numerous other items of their folklore. The children who tell these jokes classify them as dirty or nasty because

---

1. Personal communication from middle-aged, white, male, maintenance-person; Yountville, California; 1973. Told to the informant by his eight-year-old daughter in 1953.

they deal with sex. This sexual element in children's folklore has been ignored in most folkloristic studies, a phenomenon most evident in the major works on children's folklore.[2]

In the beginning, there was Tarzan and Jane:

> Tarzan and Jane were walking through the forest, when Jane got very hot. "Can I take off my top?" asks Jane. "Sure," says Tarzan, "I'll take mine off, too." And so he takes off his shirt. And they walk on. And later, they get so hot that Jane has to say, "Would you mind if I just take off my pants?" "O.K.," agrees Tarzan, "I'll take mine off too." Then they look at each other. Tarzan asks Jane, "What are those things?" And Jane answers, "Those are my lights." "And what's that between your legs," he asks. "That's my socket," she says. "But what's that between your legs, Tarzan?" asks Jane. "Oh, that's my plug!" Pretty soon, they reach a cave, and they say, "It's dark in here, very dark in here! Is there any light?" And Jane says, "Oh, I know a way that we can turn on the light! You put your plug in my socket, and then that will make my lights turn on!"[3]

Tarzan and Jane discover each others' sexuality as they penetrate the solitude of a hot forest. They are removed from the social restraints that govern the little child who tells this joke. Tarzan and Jane do not live in a city; they are not surrounded by neighbors or family: they are enveloped in solitude, perhaps sharing the quiet, hot forest with animals, who likewise lack social restraints. Tarzan himself is half-way between the world of animals and the world of men. The little girl who told me this joke referred to Tarzan as the "ape-man". And in another rhyme of children's oral tradition, Tarzan appears as:

2. Herbert Halpert discusses the censorship of children's folklore in his article "Folklore and Obscenity: Definitions and Problems": "Because the major books in this field, in English, have been edited for a general audience, there is still no complete treatment of children's lore in England or the United States [*Journal of American Folklore*, 75 (1962): 193]. Martha Wolfenstein, in her book *Children's Humor*, provides an exception to the trend of deleting all sexual matters from discussion (Glencoe, Illinois: The Free Press, 1954). Gershon Legman also includes a discussion of children's jokes in his book, *Rationale of the Dirty Joke* (New York: Grove Press, 1968). The first chapter of his book is entitled "Children," and contains a mixture of jokes told by children and jokes told about children. William Fry, in an article published in *Medical Aspects of Human Sexuality*, entitled "Psychodynamics of Sexual Humor: Sexual Views of Children," [(September, 1974): 77–80.] discusses this discrepancy between sexual jokes told by children and sexual jokes told about children. Claude Gaignebet, author of *Le Folklore obscene des enfants*, offers a very recent and complete treatment of children's obscene folklore. (Paris, 1974.)

3. Personal communication from eight-year-old girl; Santa Cruz, California; 1972.

> Tarzan, the monkey-man,
> Hangin' on a rubber band,
> Lost his pants.
> It was full of ants.[4]

In another version of this rhyme, Tarzan gets up some momentum on his rubber band:

> Tarzan, the monkey-man,
> Hangin' on a rubber band,
> Went right past the garbage can.
> Man! That's Tarzan![5]

This man-animal Tarzan is paired with Jane, not only in the dirty joke quoted above, but also in the following joke:

> Me, Tarzan!
> You, Jane![6]

The child performing this body-joke pounds his chest on the first line, and then, on the second line, pounds the air about six inches out from his chest to indicate Jane's voluptuous breasts. Tarzan is manly, and flat-chested; Jane is womanly, and full-breasted.

Now we will once again accompany the ape-man (or monkey-man) Tarzan, and his girl friend, the full-breasted Jane, on their walk through the forest. Tarzan and Jane discard their shirts. But this does not cool them off. Instead, they get hotter, and must take off their pants. As they discard their clothes in the heat of the wild, they gain heat, and their sexual knowledge increases. They have penetrated the forest, gone deeper into the heat, and acquired sexual familiarity when they arrive at the end of their walk at a dark cave. This walk has been a crescendo of oppositions and tensions. They have come from outside to inside; from the outer edges of the forest to the cave; from light to dark; from the cooler to the hotter; from ignorance to partial sexual knowledge. And their solution to the build-up of these oppositions and tensions, a light for their darkness, is ultimate sexual knowledge of one another.

Tarzan and Jane discovered the power of sex; sex gave them heat and electrical energy. A sexually immature child is denied this tremendous power. But this same child can vicariously share the pleasures of his parents' bed through voyeurism:

A little boy asked his mother if he could take a shower with her. She said, "Yes, if you don't look up or down." So in the shower, he

4. Nine-year-old girl; Santa Cruz, California; 1972.
5. Seven-year-old girl; Santa Cruz, California; 1972.
6. Eight-year-old girl; Yountville, California; 1973.

looked up, and said, "Mommy, what are those?" The mother said, "Those are my headlights." Then he looked down, and he said, "What's that?" And she said, "Oh, that's my garage!"

And then the little boy went to his father to ask if he could take a shower with him. And the father said, "Yes, if you don't look down!" In the shower, the boy looked down, and asked, "Daddy, what's that?" And the father answered, "That's my car."

Then the little boy asked, "Mommy, why don't you turn on your headlights, so Daddy can put his car in your garage?"[7]

The mother of this joke shares the power of illumination with Jane; her breasts are headlights. When they are turned on, the car can find the way into the garage. The mother lights up, the father drives in, and the little boy watches!

Another little boy begs to take a shower with his parents. His questions are the same, but the parents' answers are different. The little boy of this dirty joke goes beyond suggestion to an actual sharing of the parents' sexual bed:

There's this little boy, and he wanted to take a bath with his dad. And his dad said, "If you promise not to look under the curtain." And then he took a shower, and he looked under the curtain. And he said, "Dad, what's that long hairy thing?" And the father says, "That's my banana."

Then he asks his mom, "Can I take a shower with you, Mom?" She says, "If you promise not to look under the curtain." And then they get into the shower, and he looks under the curtain. And he says, "Mom, what's that thing?" And she says, "That's my fruit bowl." And he says, "Mom, can I sleep with you and Dad?" And she says, "Yes, if you promise not to look under the covers." And he looks under the covers, and says, "Mom, Dad's banana is in your fruit bowl!"[8]

The little boy approaches his father first. Apparently, the father does not think it quite right that his little boy should share the shower with him, for he stipulates that the little boy not look under the shower curtain. The little boy breaks his promise, and is surprised by what he sees. His question, "Dad, what's that long hairy thing?," indicates that he has never seen his father naked before. And his father's response, "That's my banana," indicates, once again, the father's reluctance to be entirely open about sex. Of course, the little boy, assuming he is anatomically complete, should have a banana too. But his father's is long and hairy, and quite transformed from his own.

When the little boy received the information he needed from his

7. Eight-year-old girl; Yountville, California; 1973.
8. Ten-year-old girl; Yountville, California; 1974.

father, he went to his mother to see if he could take a shower with her. The mother is also reluctant to share her nakedness with her son, because she also stipulates that her son must not look under the shower curtain. But the little boy, whose curiosity is only partially fulfilled, looks under the curtain. And he finds that his mother has a fruit bowl which he has never seen before.

With his full knowledge of anatomy, the little boy is allowed to share his parents' bed with them, once again only if he follows a certain rule, not to look under the covers. In the shower and in the bed, the nakedness of his parents must be hidden from his inquisitive eyes.

But the little boy has no intention of following his parents' rules, in the shower or in bed. He looks under the covers, and the sexual elements are united; the banana is in the fruit bowl. In this joke, apparently the father with his banana is the aggressor, since the little boy alerts his mother, "Mom, Dad's banana is in your fruit bowl."

In the following dirty joke, the sex of the aggressor is reversed: it is the mother's sexual organ which searches out the father's:

> There was a boy and he asked his mother if he could take a shower with her. His mother said yes, if he didn't look up or down. So in the shower, he looked up and he said, "Mommy, what are those?" And so his mommy told him they were headlights. So then he looked down, and he said, "What's that?" And she said, "Oh, that's my gorilla." So then she said, "Go bug your father."
>
> And so he went to his father and asked him if he could take a shower with him. So his father said, "Yes, if you don't look down." So in the shower, he looked down, and he said, "Daddy, what's that?" And his father said, "Oh, that's my banana."
>
> And so in the night, they were all ready for bed, and the little boy said, "Mommy, Daddy, can I sleep with you?" And so they said, "Yes, if you don't look from side to side." So in the night, he looked from side to side, and he said, "Mommy, Mommy, turn on your headlights! Your gorilla's eatin' daddy's banana!"[9]

In this joke, the mother has all of the sexual power. The father is equipped with a banana, which can be devoured by a hungry gorilla. And the child fears that his father is about to lose his banana to just such a gorilla. But there is electrical power to light the dark in this joke too. If mommy will just turn on the headlights, certainly the flood of light will allow daddy to retrieve his banana, and hopefully it will all still be there. The mother is the gorilla, symbol of uncontrolled sexual drive. The father is the gorilla's favorite food, and the little boy sounds the alarm, saving his father from castration.

9. Nine-year-old girl; Santa Cruz, California; 1972.

The children of the three preceding dirty jokes learn about their parents' sexual organs in the wet nudity of the shower. Their parents' bodies, in the fruit of maturity, are so transformed from their own bodies, that these children do not recognize their own sexual organs in those of their parents. They can look up; they can look down; and they can look from side to side. But they are not ready to do more than look!

The little girl of the following joke looks, asks questions, and then makes a suggestion:

> This girl and her mother and father were taking a bath together. They were pretty poor. And the little girl asked her mother, "What are those things?" "Those are my oranges." "Oh," said the little girl. And she asked her father, "What's that?" "That's my bun, and that's my hot dog."
>
> And so, when they finish the bath, they find out that they didn't have a thing to eat for dinner. And the little girl suggested, "Let's cut off Mommy's oranges and Daddy's hot dog and buns!"[10]

The little girl is attempting to derive nourishment from the traditional source. She is hungry, and she looks to her mother and father to provide the food. Her parents have failed her on a purely economic level; the home is without food, and the family is without money. This is the practical framework of the joke. But within this framework, the sexual tensions pull. In her hunger, the little girl suggests that they cut off "mommy's oranges and daddy's hot dog and buns," a sexual meal to satisfy her sexual appetite. This dinner will be served equally: each will eat a portion of the mother's and father's organs. For the mother and the father, however, this meal would be sexual suicide, as the mother's body will not grow new oranges, and the father's body will not produce a new hot dog and buns. In a mutilated state, the parents will be reduced to the asexual state of their daughter. But the parents' asexual state would be permanent, and the daughter's would be temporary. She, in her youth, will grow and develop; her parents, however, would scar and wither, if the suggested dinner were to be served. While the parents would be making a suicidal feast, the little girl would be enhancing her power. She would see the destruction of her parents' sexual superiority, and their sexual food would become her dinner. She could ingest her mother's breasts, father's penis and buttocks; and through the ingestion of parental sexuality, perhaps she would hasten her own sexual development.

In all of the previous jokes, the children have been in the position of passive voyeurs. They could look, they could ask questions, they could

10. Eight-year-old girl; Santa Cruz, California; 1972.

make suggestions; but they could not act. The little girl of the following joke sheds the passive role, and through a series of threats, succeeds in sleeping with her father, having sexual play with him, and castrating him:

> There's this little girl and she says to her father, "Can I take a bath with you tonight?" And so the father says, "No, you can't! Go do it with Mother." And she says "If you don't let me, I'll scream!" And he let's her. And during the bath, she says, "What's that?" And he says, "That's my dolly." "Oh," she says.
>
> And then after the bath, she says, "Daddy, can I sleep with you?" "No, go sleep with Mommy." "No, if you don't let me, I'll scream!" "O.K."
>
> And so in the morning, the mother comes and sees that there is blood all over the room. And she said, "What happened?" And the little girl says, "Papa said that that thing was his dolly. And it was a birdy that spit at me. And so I crushed its eggs and broke its neck."[11]

In this joke, the little girl definitely wants to have sexual knowledge of her father. The father tries to avoid the aggressive curiosity of his daughter, saying "Go do it with mother." The little girl will not accept this alternative. And she threatens to use the recourse of the spoiled child; she will scream if she does not get her way. The threat of this scream gets her into the bathtub with her father, where she discovers his dolly. The little girl then decides she wants to sleep with him. Once again the father tries to avoid the daughter's sexual aggressiveness, but he relents. The daughter climbs into bed with her father and during the night decides to play dolls. Her gentle touch changes the doll into a bird that spits at her. She punishes this aggressive action on the part of her father's dolly-bird by breaking its neck and crushing its eggs.

The little girl's father, who should be the one to maintain the moral order, submits to the demands of his daughter. He lets her in his bath, in his bed, and lets her play with his dolly. He is passive, and his passivity allows this sexual encounter to progress beyond the boundaries of voyeurism of the previous jokes. The daughter, who is after all the innocent, the ignorant, the virgin, must punish her father—she castrates him. (At the same time that the daughter is innocent and ignorant, she is sexually aggressive and demanding. She is the destructive virgin.)

The mother, who has been ignorant of this incestuous encounter, enters the room in the morning. She finds her daughter and her husband in bed, and the room drenched in blood. The mother and daugh-

11. Eight-year-old girl; Santa Cruz, California; 1972.

ter have switched places and the results are disastrous. The child has destroyed both her father's sexual prowess, and her mother's sexual pleasure. She has gained sexual knowledge of her father, punished him for it, and eliminated the possibility of an active sex life between her mother and father—all in one night, and all under the veil of innocence!

In all of the jokes presented, there is a general ignorance about sexual anatomy. The body of the adult is unknown to the child, transformed from his or her own, with the fancy frills of maturity. In order to gain knowledge of the adult's body, the child must ask the names for the sexual organs. The parents avoid a direct, truthful response, and instead give fanciful names to the sexual parts.

In addition to the general ignorance about sex, and frequent avoidance of body exposure, there is often an interdiction associated with viewing the naked body. The mother tells the child not to look up or down, and the father tells the child not to look down. The parents tell the child not to look under the shower curtain, and in bed, the child is told not to look under the covers or from side to side. These interdictions are always broken, and the child gains access to the sexual realm of the parent.

The fanciful names given to the sexual organs are associated either with power, food, or animals. This association extends to the sexual activity as well. Jane has lights for breasts, as do two of the mothers. Jane is unique in that she has a socket, whereas Tarzan, of course, has the necessary plug. All of these images are electrical, and therefore powerful. Another image of power is the father's penis: it is a car. When the woman has lights for breasts, she has the ability to turn them on; either to facilitate sex, or to prevent it.

The sexual organs offer a variety of food. The father has a banana in two of the jokes. The mother has a fruit bowl for a vagina, and oranges for breasts. And the father has a hot dog and buns. The association of food with sexual organs places sexuality at an oral level. The father's banana is in the mother's fruit bowl, or a meal is suggested of mother's oranges and father's hot dog and buns. The oral is, in this case, both sexual and edible.

In addition to the oral aspect of sexuality is the animal aspect. Tarzan the monkey-man and the gorilla, in the shape of mother's genitals, make appearances in two of the jokes. The other animal, whose weakness is its undoing, is father's dolly-bird.

In these jokes, sexuality entails a certain amount of aggression. Mother should wake up, because dad's banana is in her fruit bowl; mother should turn on her headlights, because her gorilla is eating father's banana; the hungry daughter suggests that they cut off her parents' sexual organs for dinner; and the angry daughter destroys her father's dolly-bird.

In all of the jokes, the child feigns innocence of sexual matters. The parents' answers, instead of being direct and honest, attempt to perpetuate the child's ignorance, and to deny the child's sexuality. The child, however, sees through the artifices of the parents, and exposes the true nature of their sexuality. Gershon Legman, in a discussion of other versions of the bathtub-shower jokes, says, "In all forms of the . . . joke, the wonderful humor of the child is the mocking of the parents' evasions, which are somehow so foolishly phrased . . . that precisely the action that is intended to be hidden or prevented is the one that must logically follow."[12]

The bathtub-shower jokes have the greatest appeal for prepubescent children. Once the child's body matures, the jokes lose their impact, and are discarded and forgotten. As one fourteen year old boy told me, "Yeah, I used to know a lot of jokes like that. But you sort of grow out of them."

Another form of the joke which is told by teen-agers rejects the childhood categories of genitalia:

> This little boy walks into the bathroom, and he catches his mother naked. She was a little embarrassed. He said, "Mommy, what's that?" And she says, "Oh, that's where God hit me with an axe." And the little kid says, "Got you right in the cunt, eh?"[13]

All of the versions of this joke filed in the archives of the University of California, Berkeley, were told by the informants when they were teenagers. Clearly, this is a reversal of children's feigned ignorance, and an expression of explicit sexual knowledge on the part of the teenager. I would argue that this reversal of the categories by the teenager supports the contention that the bathtub-shower jokes presented in this paper are in the domain of the prepubescent child.

In the shower (or in the forest), and in the parental bed, the child discovers the nature of adult sexuality. It is powerful, at times aggressive, at times pleasing, and at times disastrous. At all times, the child is set apart from the ripe, sexually mature body of the parents. The fancy frills will not grace the child's body until the years pass, and his memory of the plain body has faded.

12. Gershon Legman, *Rationale of the Dirty Joke,* (New York, 1968), 53.

13. From the Archives of the Folklore Department, University of California, Berkeley. Collector: twenty-year-old male. Informant: eighteen-year-old female who learned the joke at the age of sixteen in Vermont, c. 1964.

CUT-EYE AND SUCK-TEETH:
AFRICAN WORDS AND GESTURES
IN NEW WORLD GUISE

John A. Rickford and Angela E. Rickford

The way John and Angela Rickford characterize many studies of African-American "survivals" in folk tradition should seem familiar to most readers, because for a long time the same kinds of assumptions dominated American folklore research in general. The scholars' quests, they say, have often been limited to searching for "the unusual and the exotic." This is comparable to the widespread belief that the best and oldest folklore texts are always archaic examples found in the most remote and folksy settings. But this "reasonable" assumption often proves false, as the Rickfords demonstrate here in their study of a minor aspect of black American tradition and its African prototype. They traced two extremely simple and commonplace gestures used by American blacks back to Africa, using evidence easily gathered from urban blacks met in the course of their studies in Philadelphia. The resulting article is somewhat like Alex Haley's Roots but on a much smaller scale.

A comparable study based on material tradition is described in John Vlach's "Shotgun Houses," Natural History, Vol. 86, no. 2 (February, 1977).

In the New World, things African are usually associated with the unusual and the exotic. Thus *cumfa*, with its frenzied drumming, would seem a natural candidate for inclusion in any list of African "survivals." So also would a folktale or folksong which included several lines of obscure incantation. Or a word which made use of very un-English phonotactics, like *kpoli*, or was matched against a more standard equivalent (*nyam* versus *eat*).

Our suspicions would be particularly aroused if the cultural or linguistic item were rarely used, if, for instance, we "got" it for the first and only time from the aging grandchild of some erstwhile slave, now living an isolated life far from the masses of the people. For academics and laymen alike, it is of such stuff that true New World Africanisms are made.

In keeping with this pattern of intuition and reasoning, we never attached any historical significance to *cut-eye* and *suck-teeth*. The gestures to which these refer are performed daily in our native Guyana by all kinds of people, in urban center and rural area alike. And the compounds we use to describe them could hardly be more ordinary, composed as they are of simple English words—*cut, eye, suck,* and *teeth.* With such unpromising clues to go by, it is hardly surprising that we used them every day without giving any thought to their source.

However, while doing graduate work in Philadelphia in 1971, we happened to notice a curious division between Americn Whites and Blacks with respect to these very gestures. While the Blacks would "cut their eyes" and "suck their teeth" in much the same way that people did in our native community, Whites apparently never did, and were often ignorant of the meanings of these gestures when they were directed at them.

On the basis of this chance observation, we began to consider the possibility that both the gestures and the words we used to describe them might represent African "survivals," and we began to study more systematically the extent to which they were used and recognized across three broad areas: the Caribbean, the United States, and Africa. This paper reports on the results of this investigation.

We shall first briefly describe the methods we used to obtain data on these areas and then summarize the findings for *cut-eye* and *suck-teeth* under separate headings. In the conclusion, we discuss some of the larger implications and research directions which grew out of our research.

METHOD

Data on the use of *cut-eye* and *suck-teeth* in the Caribbean area were obtained from several sources. For the detailed physical and ethnographic descriptions of the gestures in Guyana we drew mainly on our own observations and experience, supported by comments and criticisms from fellow Guyanese. For other areas in the West Indies, we first consulted available dictionaries and glossaries,[1] then carried out our own interviews with several West Indians, representing Antigua, Barbados, Haiti, Jamaica, Trinidad, and St. Kitts.

Data from the United States are based on original fieldwork conducted by the authors. Within the framework of a questionnaire de-

---

1. These include *Dictionary of Jamaican English,* ed. Frederic G. Cassidy and Robert B. LePage (London: Cambridge University Press, 1967); Frank Collymore, *Notes for a Glossary of Words and Phrases of Barbadian Dialect* (Bridgetown: Advocate, 1970); J. Graham Cruickshank, *Black Talk, being Notes on Negro Dialect in British Guiana* (Georgetown, Demerar: Argosy, 1916); Carlton R. Ottley, *Creole Talk of Trinidad and Tobago* (Port of Spain: Ottley, 1971); and the glossary in Hyman Rodman, *Lower-Class Families in the Culture of Poverty in Negro Trinidad* (New York: Oxford University Press, 1971).

signed to explore linguistic and cultural differences between Black and White Americans, we asked the following question:

> Now we want to consider some things that people say and use a lot. Do you know what the following things mean (in terms of the actions and "social significance"):
> (1) To "cut your eyes" on someone_____
> (2) To "suck your teeth"_____ [2]

In each case, the informant was asked to give a physical demonstration and to discuss the meaning freely. A corpus of seventy American informants was interviewed, in Philadelphia, Boston, and New York. Thirty-five of these were Black, and thirty-five were White. Within each group, there were eighteen males and seventeen females. Informants represented a diverse range of native geographical backgrounds, including Pennsylvania, New York, California, Alabama, Georgia, Illinois, and Massachusetts.

Our African data were limited by the small number of accessible informants, and by the fact that so few dictionaries of African languages had entries classified in terms of English. Nevertheless, among students at the University of Pennsylvania and in Guyana, we managed to locate speakers of the following languages: Twi, Temne, Mende, Igbo, Yoruba, Swahili, Luo, Banyang, Krio, and Cameroon Pidgin. They were first asked if they were familiar with the gestures, and then asked to provide data on their use and equivalent terms from their native languages if any existed.

CUT-EYE

In Guyana, *cut-eye* is a visual gesture which communicates hostility, displeasure, disapproval, or a general rejection of the person at whom it is directed. The very existence of a well-known term for this particular gesture indicates its centrality in the wide range of gestures in the culture, not all of which have comparable verbal labels.

The basic *cut-eye* gesture is initiated by directing a hostile look or glare in the other person's direction. This may be delivered with the person directly facing, or slightly to one side. In the latter position, the person is seen out of the corners of the eyes, and some people deliberately turn their bodies sideways to achieve this effect. After the

---

2. Discussion of some of the other items which appeared in this questionnaire and provided evidence of sharp discontinuities in the linguistic competence of Blacks and Whites is contained in J. Rickford, "Carrying the New Wave Into Syntax—The Case of B. E. BIN" in *Proceedings of the Second Annual Colloquium on New Ways of Analysing Variation*, ed. Roger Shuy (Washington, D.C., 1975).

initial glare, the eyeballs are moved in a highly coordinated and controlled movement down or diagonally across the line of the person's body. This "cut" with the eyes is the heart of the gesture, and may involve the single downward movement described above, or several sharp up-and-down movements. Both are generally completed by a final glare, and then the entire head may be turned away contemptuously from the person, to the accompaniment of a loud *suck-teeth*. See Figure 1 for the main stages of this sequence.

Part of the effectiveness of a *cut-eye* as a visual "put-down" lies in its violation of what Erving Goffman has called the "information preserve" of the individual, one of his important "territories of the self."[3] The information preserve is "the set of facts about himself to which an individual expects to control access while in the presence of others," including "what can be directly perceived about an individual, his body's sheath and his current behaviour, the issue here being his right *not to be stared at or examined* (emphasis ours)."[4] As Goffman goes on to point out, since staring constitutes an invasion of informational preserve, it can then be used as "a warranted negative sanction against somebody who has misbehaved."[5]

A *cut-eye* provides even more of a "negative sanction," since one not only invades, but with the eyes, rummages up, down, and about in another's preserve. It is as if the recipient has no power to prevent this visual assault, the very fact that someone else's eyes can run right over him like this proclaiming his worthlessness. The "cut" is made even deeper when the eyes are finally turned away—the implication here being that the victim is not even worth further attention.

This kind of visual "put-down" or "cut-down" comes to the fore in "buseings" or fierce arguments between two or more protagonists, especially between women. The argument is waged as much with words as with eyes, each protagonist "cutting up the eyes" on the other in a threatening and belligerent fashion. But there may not be any verbal argument at all. In any situation where one wishes to censure, or challenge someone else, or convey to him that he is not admired or respected, a *cut-eye* may be conveniently employed.

Thus an old woman rebuking an eight-year old for hitting her younger brother on the street might receive a *cut-eye* from the child (challenging her authority to intervene) in response. Similarly, a male who whistles at a female may be met with a cold *cut-eye* suggesting that she does not appreciate this form of greeting, and that he fails to

3. Erving Goffman, *Relations in Public* (New York: Basic Books, 1972), pp. 28–61.

4. Ibid., p. 39.

5. Ibid., p. 61.

Figure 1. Sequence of movements in a cut-eye. *Note accompanying suck-teeth (in this case, closure is made with the tongue against the alveolar ridge).*

win her interest or favor. In both these cases, the recipient is guilty of some infringement of what the sender considers his "rights," and the provocation for the *cut-eye* is clear (whether others consider it justified or appropriate is another matter).

Sometimes however, the "misbehavior" which earns someone a *cut-eye* is not as obvious on the surface. The recipient need not have said or done anything to the person who directs the gesture to him. But there is something in the way he dresses, looks, or behaves, which, while not necessarily intended, rubs someone else the "wrong way." This is particularly true if others around interpret the situation as one in which the recipient is trying to "show off." If, for instance, someone drives up in a big new car or arrives at a party in expensive clothes on the arm of a well-known figure, others around might cut their eyes on that person as a way of suggesting that they are not really impressed. The *cut-eye* is a way of saying "you're no big thing at all, not to my mind at least."

In fact, however, it frequently is the case that the recipient *is* someone in a situation which many people, including the sender, respect and envy. Thus, while the gesture might express genuine resentment and dislike, it is sometimes an attempt to nullify the appeal of another's attributes or circumstances when these are precisely what the sender would like to have. This is clearer when the sense in which people also talk of cutting their eyes on *something* is considered. A woman who sees a prohibitively expensive dress in a store window might report to her friends that she had to "cut her eyes" on it and walk away. The phrase is used here to symbolize a rejection of something one would really like to have, but cannot or should not, because of personal circumstance.

The gesture of *cut-eye* is performed most frequently (and most skillfully!) by women. Men do not use this gesture as often and may experience real difficulty in trying to imitate the darting, highly co-ordinated movement which women can control. The gesture is often used when the other party in an encounter, conversation, or dispute, is enjoying his "turn" to talk, and may prompt the latter to interrupt his turn to give a more powerful *cut-eye* or some form of verbal retort in return. One common verbal retort is "Look, *cut-eye* na a kill daag" (*"Cut-eye* doesn't kill dogs"). This acknowledges that an invasion or affront has been made but attempts to vindicate the recipient by claiming that it can do him or her no bodily harm.[6]

Another pattern can be seen in a turn-of-the-century description of a classic type of court dispute.[7] In the course of giving his testimony, the complainant notices that the defendant has "cut his eye" on him. He interrupts his testimony to ask, "A who you a cut you yiye pon?" ("Who are you cutting your eyes on?"), to which the defendant simply replies, "you see um" (which is roughly equivalent to "If the shoe fits, wear it!"). In this particular incident, the exchange was followed by further verbal provocation and retort which is often called "shot-ting" or "rhyming" in Guyana, "talking broad" or "rhyming" in other Caribbean territories.[8]

The physical and ethnographic account of *cut-eye* given above still does not tell the whole story, but we have attempted to make it reasonably detailed, partly because of the limited data available on patterns of nonverbal communication generally, and also because we hope it might be more easily recognizable elsewhere by other research-ers. As we ourselves discovered since beginning this study, it is cer-tainly known and used in other parts of the Caribbean. The term is listed in the *Dictionary of Jamaican English* for what is clearly the same gesture with the same meaning:

Cut-Eye: to catch (someone or something) with the eyes, then quickly close them and turn or toss the eyes aside. The purpose of

---

6. Compare one of the standard rejoinders to *verbal* insult or mockery:
   "Sticks and stones can break my bones,
   But words can never hurt me."

7. Michael "Quow" McTurk, *Essays and Fables in the Vernacular* (George-town, Demerara: Argosy, 1899).

8. Roger Abrahams, "The Training of the Man in Words in Talking Broad," in *Rappin' and Stylin' Out*, ed. Thomas Kochman (Urbana: University of Illinois Press, 1972), pp. 215–240.

the action may be to avoid temptation . . . but it is usually directed against another person . . . and is usually insulting.[9]

The editors also add that the action may combine insult and temptation into provocation, and they cite the following definition from Miss Joyce Nation:

> To cut one's eyes is to toss one's head away from a man's glance in a contemptuous but sexually provoking fashion: Little girl to a little boy, "You come a me yard" (cutting her eyes) "come if you name man."[10]

While this "provocative" use of *cut-eye* is also found in Guyana, it is usually distinguished from the more hostile use of the gesture in very subtle ways, involving different privileges of co-occurrence with other paralinguistic features or "kinesic markers."[11] The difference may reside in nothing more than whether the *cut-eye* is accompanied by a slight smile, or by a *suck-teeth*, and sometimes males misread the meaning of a female's *cut-eye*, to their own embarrassment.

The term, the gesture, and its meaning, as discussed above were all instantly recognized by the various West Indians whom we interviewed. From Karl Reisman (personal communication), we also learned that it can be frequently observed in Antigua. A Haitian informant provided a dramatic demonstration of the gesture as soon as it was mentioned and explained that it was known in Haiti as "couper yeux"—literally "to cut (or cutting) the eyes." We find it very striking that the Haitian expression for this gesture should consist of morphemes which literally refer to *cut* and *eye*. The same phenomenon may be observed in Saramaccan (example provided by Ian Hancock): *a ta koti woyo*—"she's cutting eye." These examples seem to suggest different New World relexifications of an expression which existed either in one or more African languages or in a Proto-Pidgin, and which included morphemes for *cut* and *eye*. We will return to this point briefly when considering the data from African languages.

The results of our questionnaire investigation of familiarity with *cut-eye* in the United States were more dramatic than we expected. As Table 1 indicates, almost all the Black informants were familiar with the term. Among the "meanings" volunteered were "a look of disgust";

9. Cassidy and LePage, p. 139. Compare also the brief descriptions in Collymore, p. 38, and Cruickshank, p. 31.

10. Miss Nation's contributions to the *Dictionary* were made on the basis of her analysis of the spontaneous conversation of Jamaican children.

11. This is one of the useful terms for the basic units of contrast in body-motion communication derived from Ray L. Birdwhistell, *Kinesics and Context* (Philadelphia: University of Pennsylvania Press, 1970).

TABLE 1: NUMBER OF AMERICAN INFORMANTS FAMILIAR WITH
CUT-EYE ACCORDING TO RACE AND SEX.

Sex		Blacks		Whites
Males	(n = 18)	16	(n = 18)	2
Females	(n = 17)	17	(n = 17)	2
Total	(n = 35)	33	(n = 35)	4

"expression of hostility"; "to threaten"; "act of defiance or disapproval"; "bad feelings"; "when you're mad at someone"; "to show you
don't like somebody." All the Black women understood the term and
were able to perform the gesture easily and expertly.

Two of the Black men were not familiar with the term. The other
sixteen, although clearly aware of the meaning of the gesture, could
not execute it as skillfully as their female counterparts, and they kept
excusing themselves by saying, "Mostly women do that." As we have
noted above, this situation is paralleled in the Caribbean. Some of the
men felt it would be a "cop-out" for a man to keep using this gesture
to express his feelings—physical or verbal expression ("sounding")
would be the more masculine thing to do. Barring this, one should
simply "keep one's cool"—remain silent, apparently unperturbed.

As Table 1 also indicates, *cut-eye* as a lexical item and as a cultural
form of behavior is almost totally unknown to White Americans. Only
four of the thirty-five White informants displayed familiarity with the
term. Of these, three said "to stare at someone," and one suggested "to
look at someone out of the corner of the eye." These are good descriptions of the initial stage of the gesture, but not of the complete sequence. And in none of the cases could a White informant execute the
full gesture.

Sixteen Whites plainly admitted that they had never heard the term
before and had no idea of its meaning. The other fifteen in the sample
provided idiosyncratic and highly varied responses: "expression of
religious ecstasy"; "to go to sleep on someone"; "to stop looking at
someone"; "expression of horror"; "to look at someone attractively for
a long time." This sharp divergence between the responses of Blacks
and Whites is all the more revealing because many of the Black
informants were middle-class individuals completing their college education and might otherwise be considered highly acculturated to the
mainstream American culture.

Some of the Black informants mentioned that "rolling the eyes" is
sometimes used instead of "cutting the eyes" in Black American com-

munities to refer to the very same gesture. This is confirmed in Keith Johnson's description of "rolling the eyes" among American Blacks, which accords with our own description of *cut-eye* in Guyana on several points.[12] Unless it omits certain details, however, the following description from another researcher would suggest that the physical movements involved in "rolling the eyes" might be slightly different:

> If a girl in a lounge does not want to be bothered when a cat comes up to rap, she might lift up one shoulder slightly, rolling her eyes upward in her head as though saying, "what a drag!"[13]

Whether or not this is the case, note that the meaning and usage of the gesture still register dislike, disapproval, or hostility. The fact that the general public usually associates "rolling the eyes" with ingratiation and "Uncle Tom" behavior (an image partly propagated by television and the cinema) suggests that Blacks might have endowed the gesture with a systematic ambiguity which they exploited to permit safe and subtle expression of their more genuine feelings. As we shall see later, *suck-teeth* can be similarly used with a strategic ambiguity.

Before presenting the results of our research on *cut-eye* with African informants, we feel a few remarks are in order. Several scholars have attempted to pinpoint the African languages which, for various historical reasons, may be assumed to have had the greatest influence on the New World pidgins and creoles. The lists are somewhat different from one scholar to another, and the relative importance of particular languages (like Wolof) is a matter of some dispute.[14]

The absence of universal agreement in this area is sometimes problematic. When considering possible etymologies for New World forms, it can be difficult to determine which languages must be examined and what weight must be assigned to the evidence of one language as against another. However, this problem is not always as critical as it might seem, because as many observers have noted, many New World Africanisms go back to generalized features of West Africa, even of sub-saharan Africa as a whole.[15] Given the mul-

12. Kenneth Johnson, "Black Kinesics—Some Non-Verbal Communication Patterns in the Black Culture," *Florida Foreign Language Reporter* (Spring/Fall 1971), 17–20.

13. Benjamin Cooke, "Non-Verbal Communication among Afro-Americans—an Initial Classification," in *Rappin' and Stylin' Out*, pp. 32–64.

14. Compare the list of "key" languages in Lorenzo Dow Turner, *Africanisms in the Gullah Dialect* (Chicago: University of Chicago Press, 1949), with the list in David Dalby, "The African Element in American English," in *Rappin' and Stylin' Out*, pp. 170–186.

15. On this point, see Mervyn C. Alleyne, "Acculturation and the Cultural Matrix of Creolization," in *Pidginization and Creolization of Languages*, ed. Dell Hymes (Cambridge, England: Cambridge University Press, 1971), pp. 175–176, and Ian F. Hancock, *A Study of the Sources and Development of the Lexicon of Sierra Leone Krio* (Ph.D. Thesis, University of London, 1971), p. 652.

tiplicity of areas from which slaves were taken, it is easy to see why this might have been so. "Survivals" were more likely to survive if they were supported by the common experience of Africans from several areas and tribal affiliations, rather than restricted to a single group.

We cannot claim to have exhausted all the "key" languages in the lists referred to above. However, the picture which emerges from the languages for which we do have data is that the concept of a *cut-eye* or *suck-teeth* gesture is familiar in several areas of both West and East Africa, and it is described by a verbal label in many of the languages spoken there.

The Mende, Banyang, and Luo examples make use of morphemes with the literal meaning of "cutting the eyes" or "sucking the teeth," and thus provide the kind of models we would need to classify our New World compounds as straight cases of loan-translation. However, we are in no position to claim that any one of these provided a particular immediate source. Neither Banyang (a "minor" language spoken in Cameroon) nor Luo (an East Coast language) are normally rated as "key" languages where the business of seeking etymologies for New World forms is concerned. Mende certainly is a "key" language in this sense, but several others for which we do not have data may provide equally plausible prototypes for loan-translation. The whole point of our discussion is that all this is not crucial. We shall probably never know which language or languages provided the immediate source; wherever the particular description of "cutting the eyes" may have come from, it received support from the fact that what it referred to was familiar everywhere.

All of the African informants with whom we talked, for instance, recognized the *cut-eye* gesture immediately. They provided the following equivalent expressions:

Twi: *obu ma ni kyi*—"He breaks the backs of the eye on me."[16]

Yoruba: *mólójú*—"making expressions with your eyes to show disapproval."[17] R. Abraham also lists *mónlójú* cross-referenced to mọ́n (D.2) under which the following items are listed: (I) ó *mọ́njú*—"he looked away contemptuously." (II) ó *mọ́n mi lójú*—"he looked at me in scorn." (III) *àwòmọn jú*—"a scornful look."[18]

16. This metaphorical reference to "breaking the back of the eye" is evocative of the straining of the eye muscles which one actually feels when delivering a good *cut-eye.*

17. For all Yoruba examples cited in this paper, v́ = high tone, v = mid tone, v̀ = low tone, and v ' = mid-high rising tone.

18. R. C. Abraham, *Dictionary of Modern Yoruba* (London: University of London Press, 1958), pp. 423, 427.

Cameroon Pidgin: *no kɔt yɔ ai fɔmi*—"Don't cut your eyes on me."
Banyang: *a kpot a mek ne me*—"She cut her eyes on me."
Luo: *kik ilokna wangi*—"he is cutting his eyes."
Swahili: *usinioloka macho*—"to roll one's eyes."

The last two languages provide an interesting comparison. They are both spoken in Kenya, Swahili as the more widespread and better known East African lingua franca. The terms in Luo and Swahili correspond to the two American variants: to "cut" and to "roll" the eyes respectively. Data from other languages may provide other possible sources for the alternation between these terms.

SUCK-TEETH

Suck-Teeth refers to the gesture of drawing air through the teeth and into the mouth to produce a loud sucking sound. In the basic *suck-teeth* gesture, the back of the tongue is raised toward the soft palate and a vacuum created behind a closure formed in the front part of the mouth. This closure may be made with the lower lip against the upper teeth (as in Figure 2), or with the tip or blade of the tongue just behind the upper teeth, on the alveolar ridge (as in Figure 1, although not clearly seen). When the closure is suddenly relaxed, air outside the mouth rushes in audibly.

The gesture is accomplished by the same velaric ingressive mechanism used to produce the "clicks" of Khoisan and Southern Bantu languages.[19] The differences lie mainly in the fact that the closure for "clicks" may be formed at several other points in the mouth, and that while "clicks" are stops—produced by one sharp release of the closure, a *suck-teeth* is more like a prolonged fricative—after the closure is relaxed, air continues to rush in turbulently through the narrow opening.

There are all kinds of minor variations in the way the gesture is produced. It can be made with the lips tensely pouted, or with them spread out, or pulled to one side. There are variations in the duration and intensity of the sound produced depending on the tightness of the closure and the pressure of the inrushing air. These variations depend to some extent on personal habit, but are governed also by the sit-

19. Peter Ladefoged, *Linguistic Phonetics* (Los Angeles: UCLA Press, 1967), and D. Westerman and Ida C. Ward, *Practical Phonetics for Students of African Languages* (London, 1933).

Figure 2. A suck-teeth made with the inner surface of the lower lip pressed against the upper teeth.

uation—how angry one is, whether one is in a place (like a church) or in company (a circle of parents' friends) in which a loud *suck-teeth* might be frowned on. In general however, the longer and louder the *suck-teeth*, the more forceful and expressive its "meaning."

Suck-teeth, also known in Guyana and the Caribbean as *stchoops* (*-teeth*) or *chups* (*-teeth*), is an expression of anger, impatience, exasperation or annoyance. It shares some of the semantics of *cut-eye* and, as mentioned before, is often used in combination with the latter. It can be more open and powerful however, and it is considered ill-mannered in certain situations. For instance, while people of all ages do it when something annoys them or someone makes them angry, its use by children in the presence of their parents or other adults is considered rude and insubordinate. As J. Cruickshank noted in 1916: "A sulking child is told sharply, 'Wha you suck you teeth fo?' . . . With eyes lowered and lips pouting, it pictures disgust, discontent—rebellion with the lid on."[20]

The prohibitions against the use of this gesture are sometimes justified by the claim that it means "kiss my ass" or "kiss my private parts." This meaning may have become attached to it because of the close resemblance between the sound made in producing a *suck-teeth* and the sound sometimes made for "calling off" a girl on the street. This latter sound is made with pouted lips (the teeth not involved as

20. Cruickshank, p. 50.

articulators), and is supposed to represent a forceful kiss (among other things). It has much cruder sexual connotations than other ways of attracting a girl's attention (like whistling, or saying *pssssss*), and these seem to be attached also to the *suck-teeth* sound.

To avoid actually sucking the teeth in situations where it might be considered vulgar or ill-mannered, people sometimes say the words *stchoops* or *chups* without making the sound itself. Other interjections like *cha, cho,* or *shoots* may also be used, and children in particular will purse or pout their lips as if preparing to make a *suck-teeth,* but again, without making any audible sound. The advantage of this latter strategy is that it can be carried out behind the back of a reproachful adult without fear of discovery or reprimand.

Interviews with informants from Jamaica, Trinidad, Barbados, Antigua, and even Haiti (where, we understand, it is sometimes referred to as *tuiper* or *cuiper*) confirmed familiarity with this oral gesture, its meaning, and the social prohibitions against its use as outlined above. In Antigua, according to Karl Reisman (personal communication), *stchoops* to describe the action of sucking one's teeth is convergent with the word for "stupid," and the ambiguity is well exploited ("Wuh yuh *stchoopsin* yuh teeth fuh? Yuh *stchoops* or wuh?"). This reinforces the negative social connotations of the gesture.

The West Indian dictionaries and glossaries all contain some reference to *suck-teeth* or the alternate terms *stchoops* and *chups*. The *Dictionary of Jamaican English* defines *suck-teeth* as "a sound of annoyance, displeasure, ill nature or disrespect (made) by sucking air audibly through the teeth and over the tongue."[21] Hyman Rodman refers to it as an "expression of disdain or mild disgust," and gives as an example of its usage: "When I suggested that she visit them, she said *stchoops.*"[22]

Frank Collymore, writing on Barbados, describes it as indicative of distrust or sulking, but attempts also a more detailed classification of the different kinds of *chupses* or *suck-teeth* which is worth reprinting:

(i) the *chupse* of "amused tolerance," used in retort to some absurd remark or statement, a sort of oral shrugging of the shoulders; (ii) the *chupse* "self-admonitory" when the chupser has done something of which he has no occasion to be proud; (iii) the *chupse* "disdainful," accompanied by a raising of the eyebrow; (iv) the *chupse* "disgusted," in the performance of which the eyebrows are almost closed; (v) the *chupse* "sorrowful," in reality a series of quickly emitted chupses, the

21. Cassidy and LePage, p. 428.
22. Rodman, p. 235.

head being shaken slowly from side to side; (vi) the *chupse* "offensive and abusive"; (vii) the *chupse* "provocative," a combination of (iii), (iv) and (vi) which often leads to blows.[23]

This description certainly seems to justify the statement, attributed by Collymore to the lead-writer of the *Barbados Advocate*, that "the *chupse* is not a word, it is a whole language . . . the passport to confidence from Jamaica to British South America."[24]

The immediately preceding statement appears, however, to have set too closely the northern limits of the area in which *chupse* or *suck-teeth* is known. This is clear from Table 2, which reveals that many Black Americans are also familiar with it.

TABLE 2: NUMBER OF AMERICAN INFORMANTS FAMILIAR WITH
SUCK-TEETH ACCORDING TO RACE AND SEX

Sex	Blacks		Whites	
Males	(n = 18)	10	(n = 18)	0
Females	(n = 17)	14	(n = 17)	1
Total	(n = 35)	24	(n = 35)	1

If we compare Table 2 with Table 1, it is clear that Black Americans are slightly less familiar with *suck-teeth* than with *cut-eye* (nine persons who recognized the latter failed to recognize the former). But the recognition rate is still quite high (68.5%), with the Black females again slightly in the lead.[25] Among the "meanings" given by Black informants were: "when disgusted"; "act of defiance, disapproval"; "sign of frustration"; "impatience"; "to show disappointment."

What is particularly striking about Table 2, however, is that only *one* White American, a woman, was familiar with *suck-teeth*. Twenty-six of the White informants did not even attempt to suggest possible meanings, and the eight who did were far off the intended track: "to shut up"; "to stammer"; "to express that you like food"; "after eating to clean teeth." This last "meaning" was suggested by four informants, and in fact is the only one given for "sucking the teeth" in the *Oxford English Dictionary*. Under entry 10b for the verb *suck* is listed: "to apply one's tongue and inner sides of the lips to (one's teeth) so as to extract particles of food."

23. Collymore, pp. 30–31.
24. Ibid.
25. Some of the Black females pointed out that "titting your teeth" is sometimes used instead of "sucking your teeth" for the same gesture.

Now while West Indians rarely speak of "sucking the teeth" in this "Standard English" sense, they sometimes use it as a cover or excuse for the everyday *suck-teeth* of annoyance or insubordination. For example, a student who responds to the teacher's instructions to write an essay in class with an inadvertent *suck-teeth*, might claim as she approaches him with an icy stare, that he was just "trying to clear out his teeth." Given the demonstrated divergences between what Black and White Americans most commonly understand by this gesture, it is not at all difficult to imagine that many a slave might have been able to use it on his masters with equally feigned innocence, to express feelings of exasperation and rage for which there was no other outlet.

As early as 1951, Richard Allsopp had observed that "words exist in West and East African languages which contain a sound produced by sucking air between the teeth. What connection this may have with sulking or defiance, however, as it does in our (Guyana) dialect, I do not know."[26] It is not clear from this whether Allsopp is referring to the famous "clicks" of certain African languages (which so far as we know, have no connection with rudeness or defiance). However our interviews with African informants some two decades later confirmed that they were in fact familiar with the gesture, and that many of their languages had verbal labels referring to it. Some of the African informants pointed out spontaneously that "sucking your teeth" in front of your parents was very rude, likely to earn you a slap or a whipping. This is, as we pointed out before, also true of Guyana and the rest of the Caribbean.

The African equivalents for *suck-teeth* which we collected were the following:

Mende: *i ngi yongi γofoin lɔ nya ma*—"He sucked his teeth on me" (literally, "He his teeth sucked me on").[27]

Temne: *tós nè*—"to suck to self"

Igbo: *ima osò*—"to make a sucking noise with the mouth"

Yoruba: *ḳpòše '*—(vb.) "to make a sucking noise with the mouth"

          òše '—(n.) "sucking noise made with the mouth"[28]

26. Richard Allsopp, "The Language We Speak," *Kyk-Over-Al*, 3, no. 11 (October 1950), 25.

27. We wish to thank Richard Allsopp for contributing this example.

28. R. C. Abraham, p. 490, describes *òṣe'* (1a) as "a sign denoting unhappiness." I. O. Delano, *A Dictionary of Yoruba Monosyllabic Verbs*, 2 (Ile-Ife, Nigeria: Institute of African Studies, University of Ife, 1969), p. 91, glosses *pòṣé* thus: "to express impatience or dissatisfaction by saying 'pshaw.'"

Luo: *ichiya*—(vb.) "to make suck-teeth noise"
           chiyo—(n.) "suck-teeth noise"

Krio: *no sɔk yu tit pan mi*—"Don't suck your teeth on
           me"
           no sɔk tit mi—"Don't suck-teeth me"

Cameroon Pidgin: *no sɔk yɔ tif fɔ mi*—"Don't suck your teeth on
           me."

There is the possibility too that *chups* and *stchoops* also have their roots in an African expression for the gesture involving the word "suck." We had always assumed that these were merely onomatopoeic creations for the sound made in sucking one's teeth. But as Hancock points out (personal communication), the Papiamentu and Sranan expressions for the gesture include a morpheme *tšupa*, which is very similar, of course, to *chups* or *stchoops*. It may derive from the Portuguese *chupar*, which, not surprisingly, means "to suck." But it is also significant that in Gambian Krio ("Aku"), the term for *suck-teeth* is *tšipú*, adopted from Wolof. As Hancock himself was the first to suggest, the Caribbean forms *chups* and *stchoops* may possibly represent a convergence of the Portuguese and Wolof forms.

If *chups* and *stchoops* turn out to be more than mere onomatopoeic New World creations, so also do the other equivalents or substitutes mentioned above: *cho, chu,* and *tcha.* There is first the possibility that these are merely abbreviated forms of *chups.* But there are other possibilities. The *Dictionary of Jamaican English* describes *cho* (with variants /cho, cha, chut, chu/) as "an exclamation expressing scorn, disagreement, expostulation, etc.," and provides two possible West African sources: "Ewe *tsóò*—interjection of astonishment, anger, impatience, disappointment," and "Twi *twéaa*—interjection of uttermost contempt."[29] The editors add that "English *tcha* can hardly be the source," because the earliest citations for *tcha* in the *Oxford English Dictionary* are later (1844, 1887) than the Jamaican attestations (1827, 1835).[30] In fact, far from being the source, English *tcha* may well be a later reflex of the Ewe or Twi interjections, perhaps via the Caribbean forms *cho* and *cha.*

This expanding network of possible African derivations which grew out of our original research into *suck-teeth* does not end here. After reading an earlier version of this paper, Ian Hancock mentioned that the Yoruba have a term (*šumú, šùtì*) for the gesture we discussed above of pursing the lips for a *suck-teeth* without actually making the sound. We wrote back, without taking it too seriously, that people

29. Cassidy and LePage, p. 441.
30. Ibid.

sometimes refer to this in Guyana as *faul biti maut* ("mouth shaped like a fowl's behind"). When Hancock replied excitedly that speakers of Krio in Sierra Leone also use this very metaphor—*luk we yu de mek yu mɔt lɛkɛ fol yon* ("look how you make your mouth like a fowl's behind"), we felt the similarity could hardly be due to coincidence. Once again we were struck by the pervasiveness of the African influence which lurks behind so many of the symbols, patterns, and institutions we manipulate in the New World from day to day.

CONCLUSION

Cut-eye and *suck-teeth* provide clear evidence that "Africanisms in the New World may reside not only in the exotic, but also (and perhaps more frequently) in the commonplace. In general, the identity of such items will not be obvious, either to "natives" or "outsiders." However, it may be revealed by careful attention to disparities in usage between Whites and Blacks, and to the recurrence of the same patterns in different communities which have sizable African-derived populations.

To discover other nonverbal patterns, we need to be interested not just in rare and elaborate rites, but also in the more "ordinary" rituals involved in everyday behavior: how people walk and stand; how they greet and take their leave of each other; what they do with their faces and hands when conversing, narrating, or arguing, and so on. Karl Reisman has come across some examples of just this type in Antigua quite recently,[31] and of course Herskovits had suggested several others over three decades ago which still warrant further investigation.[32]

In terms of linguistic survivals, we can translate the need to look for the commonplace into an increased alertness for loan-translations and cases of convergence between English (or other European) and African forms. Like *cut-eye* and *suck-teeth*, these will look like ordinary English words; sometimes it is only the subtlest "non-English" shades of meaning and usage which will help to give them away.[33] In fact, where a particular form and meaning have become generalized to

31. Karl Reisman, "Cultural and Linguistic Ambiguity in a West Indian Village," in *Afro-American Anthropology*, ed. Norman E. Whitten Jr. and John F. Szwed, (New York: Free Press, 1970), pp. 132–133.

32. Melville J. Herskovits, *The Myth of the Negro Past* (New York: Harper, 1941).

33. On this point, see Frederic G. Cassidy, "Multiple Etymologies in Jamaican Creole," *American Speech*, 4 (1961), 211–214, and Jay G. Edwards, "African Influences on the English of San Andres Island, Colombia," in *Pidgins and Creoles: Current Trends and Prospects*, ed. David DeCamp and Ian F. Hancock (Washington, D.C.: Georgetown University Press, 1974), pp. 1–26.

almost every part of the English-speaking world,[34] we will not have even this clue. Difficulties of this sort (and others) can make the search for loan-translations and convergences more harrowing than the search for direct loans of the *nyam* and *goober* type.

On the other hand, the very English facade which makes them difficult to recognize today has undoubtedly helped them to survive in larger numbers. Like *cut-eye* and *suck-teeth* they may be actively used even among those people who are striving most consciously toward the prestigious "standard" language and culture, and in whose speech direct African loans like *nyam* are unlikely to be found.

There is an additional significance to the study of loan-translations and convergences. As Dalby has suggested, they must have been invaluable in the creation and maintenance of a subtle code by means of which slaves could communicate with each other without fear of detection or punishment by Whites.[35] From our suggestions above, too, of the ways in which the gestures discussed in this paper might have been passed off with more acceptable "meanings" (*cut-eye* as ingratiation, *suck-teeth* as the effort to remove food from the teeth), it is clear that the code was not restricted to linguistic material. Both verbal and nonverbal resources were utilized for its creation, *Cut-eye* and *suck-teeth*, Africanisms both as words and as gestures, are themselves evidence of this.

Other examples abound. Reisman notes the existence of a side-up turn of the head in Antigua which seems to be of African origin; it is used today as a greeting, but it also resembles a Euro-American head-gesture which might have been used as a command ("Come over here!") in the plantation environment.[36] Investing the latter gesture with the "African" interpretation of a salutation would have provided a measure of personal satisfaction, "a way to redress the harshness of the slavery situation."[37] Similar to this is the story told to us by Richmond Wiley, a native of the South Carolina Sea-Islands, of a slave who used to answer his master's queries and commands with the words "You-ass, sir!" The insult, so obvious to his fellow slaves, was passed off on the master as the slave's slurred pronunciation of "Yes, sir."

More urgently and directly communicative was the way slaves would raise the spiritual refrain "Wait in the Water" from one plantation to the next to warn a runaway that bloodhounds were on his

34. Like "O.K.," the informal signal of assent or agreement, which is discussed in David Dalby.

35. Ibid., p. 174.

36. Reisman, pp. 132–133.

37. Ibid., p. 133.

trail—a signal interpreted by the masters as their expression of religious zeal. In all these cases, the existence of public and more "acceptable" interpretations is exploited by Blacks for the communication of more private or "unacceptable" meanings.[38] The value of Africanisms in this more general strategy is that they provided one of the sources (though not the only one) of its fuel.

As we hope this paper has itself been able to demonstrate, there is more to be done with "Africanisms" than presenting them in a list with possible sources. Viewed from the standpoint of different cultures and social groupings in both the present and the past, they have much to tell us about how peoples of African descent adapted to the experience of the New World, and how much they were understood by their social and political superiors. Finally, as we should like to stress again, the most telling Africanisms from this point of view might involve the most ordinary items of everyday behavior—how that person is looking at you across a room, or what that woman is yelling down the street.[39]

38. Reisman, ibid., provides the most detailed discussion of the different ways in which all kinds of linguistc and cultural symbols in Antigua have been subject to a process of remodelling and reinterpretation which allows them to "mediate at least two sets of cultural identities and meanings."

39. This paper represents a revised version of a paper entitled "Cut-Eye and Suck-Teeth" originally prepared in June 1973, and circulated in mimeo. We wish to thank Karl Reisman and Ian Hancock, who helped with data collection and provided both encouragement and criticism. We should also like to thank many Americans who participated in our questionnaire, and the various West Indian and African informants, too numerous to mention by name.

THE GERMAN-RUSSIAN HOUSE
IN KANSAS: A STUDY IN
PERSISTENCE OF FORM

Albert J. Petersen

The analysis of material folk traditions in the United States has been strongly influenced by cultural geography, particularly the studies and teaching of Fred Kniffen, who provided the hypothesis tested in the following essay. Albert J. Petersen, also a geographer, viewed traditional artifacts—in this instance, houses—against a background of immigration and settlement patterns, use of land and natural resources, and the persistent forms of traditional structures. He found that the houses of German-Russian settlers in western Kansas retained certain formal features of design even when they were constructed of stone instead of wood in the United States; but the preferred building material was eventually used, even when others were more plentiful and less expensive. Such is the strength of people's attachment to traditional cultural norms.

The area covered in this study is just east of that where the native American ballad "The Lane County Bachelor" (discussed earlier in this section) developed at about the same time (1870s and 1880s). The immigrants' attitudes that are evident here might be compared to those discussed by Aili K. Johnson in "Lore of the Finnish-American Sauna" above. The documentation and analysis of folk architecture is discussed in Chapter 18 and Appendix C of The Study of American Folklore where many relevant sources are cited. But Petersen's study is distinct from all of these because it closely examines one kind of artifact peculiar to a single group in a small area.

The study illustrates several kinds of data needed for folk architectural analysis—measured plans, distribution patterns, identification of variations on the basic pattern, an account of the succession of materials employed, historical background, etc. The adherence of German-Russians to their traditional Old World housing seems fairly extreme, for not only did they build a distinctively foreign sod-house type, but they valued frame construction to such a degree that some even covered their stone houses with wood siding. While this last practice is analogous to other Americans covering log houses with clapboards, it seems carry higher prestige value than wood. (Mormon settlers in Utah, for instance, usually regarded solid stone or brick houses as much finer and more desirable than log, frame, or adobe houses, even though the latter were cheaper, easier to build, and quite durable in the relatively arid climate.)

While this is an admirable study of traditional artifacts themselves, it does not deal with other German-Russian folklore and oral history. For example, the reasons given by informants for the use of mud-grass nogging are merely summarized without comment or analysis. And apparently no older people in the communities were asked about the lack of the traditional Russian kriliz or antechamber on the houses; instead the researcher simply guesses that its absence is attributable to "somewhat milder winter conditions" on the Great Plains. This is not a wholly satisfactory explanation. Kansas winters are often very severe indeed, and people that cover stone houses with wood siding for esthetic reasons might also leave off a traditional appendage for some other less-than-practical cause. (Perhaps the antechamber looked too much like an outhouse, or prevented a good view from the kitchen, or seemed "too Russian" for American use.)

Some wedding and holiday customs of the German-Russians of Kansas are described in S. J. Sackett and William E. Koch's Kansas Folklore (Lincoln: University of Nebraska Press, 1961).

THIS STUDY CONCERNS the most basic aspect of human habitation— the unit of dwelling. Although the house is only one way in which a culture manifests itself in the visible landscape, it is a reflection of both the social and economic systems on the most fundamental level.

The genesis of this study was an idea expressed by Fred Kniffen. In describing settlement patterns in Louisiana, Kniffen observed that the "form" of traditional structure tends to persist even after construction materials change.[1] This paper is a testing of Kniffen's hypothesis, in an immigrant agrarian-village culture on the Great Plains.

The culture under consideration in this study originated in the eighteenth century German Rhine Palatinate. During the reign of Catherine the Great, it replanted itself on the steppes along the Russian Volga. After a century of life on the Russian steppe, many of the Germans, now referred to as German-Russians, emigrated to the plains of western Kansas. Arriving during the winter of 1876, they established six agrarian villages (Fig. 1).

At first they constructed temporary shelters on the chosen village sites. The first dwellings were semi-dugout sod houses. Although often attributed to the American experience, the German-Russian sod dwell-

---

1. Fred Kniffen, "To Know the Land and Its People," *Landscape*, Vol. 9 (1960), p. 22.

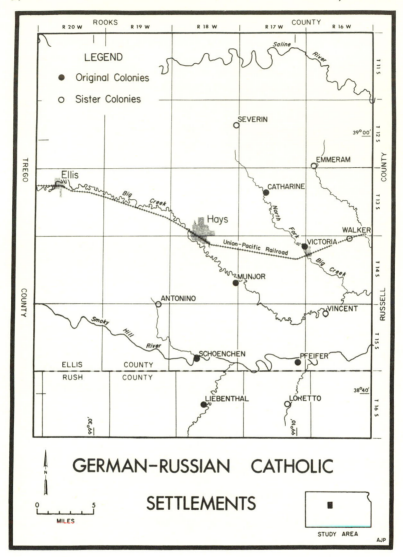

Figure 1. German-Russian Catholic village settlements in Ellis and northern Rush Counties, Kansas, date from 1876. The villages still retain much of their Old World character.

ing, or *semljanken*, actually had its origins on the Russian Volga.[2] Unlike American sod houses, the *semljanken* was set three feet in the ground. The walls were built of sod, projecting several feet above ground level.[3] The interior walls were plastered with a combination of mud mixed with dried prairie grass.

This mud-grass mixture was also pressed into molds and made into sun-dried bricks. The use of these bricks was common on both the Volga and Kansas landscapes. The mud-grass brick was used for interior partitions in Kansas German-Russian dwellings until the 1940s. As an exterior building material, the inferior quality of local clay relegated the mud-grass brick to the same eventual extinction as the sod slab.

Associated with lower economic status on the Volga, the German-Russian sod dwelling was considered as only a temporary shelter. On the Kansas landscape the *semljanken* disappeared within a decade, and permanent shelters were constructed of wood or stone.

Within the German-Russian village, frame structures were preferred, and those who could afford to purchase lumber did so. However, the most common building material in the early village was limestone. The stone was available in the local area and was free to those who wished to expend the labor quarrying it.

Although building stone was unavailable on the Volga, the German-Russian was familiar with brick construction. Upon his arrival in Kansas, he came into immediate contact with stone structures built by the railroad and the military. Scottish immigrants, who had settled earlier in the vicinity of the German-Russian villages, hired many young German-Russians to work in their stone quarries. As a result, the German-Russian adapted his previous knowledge to newly acquired techniques and stone structures were erected within a year of their settlement.

The earliest stone structures were cemented with a simple clay-mud, as had been the case with brick construction on the Volga.[4] However,

2. Lother Konig, *Die Deutschtumsinsel an der Wolga*, Dulmen in Westfalen, Germany: Verlag Laumann, 1938, p. 125.

3. Rev. Matthew Pekari, *History of St. Catherine's Parish: Catherine, Kansas 1876–1942*, Hays, Kansas: St. Joseph's College and Military Academy Press, 1942, p. 12; also see: B. M. Dreiling, *The Golden Jubilee of the German-Russian Settlements of Ellis and Rush Counties, Kansas*, Hays, Kansas: Ellis County News Publishers, 1926, p. 23.

4. For a more detailed description of the German Volga dwelling see; Albert J. Petersen, *German-Russian Colonization in Western Kansas: A Settlement Geography*, Unpublished Ph.D. Dissertation, Louisiana State University, 1970; Gottlieb Bauer, *Geschichte der deutschen Ansiedler an der Wolga seit ihrer Einwanderung nach Russland bis zur Einführung der allgemeinen Wehrpflicht (1766–1874)*, Saratow: Buchdruckerei "Energie," 1908, and Robert Low, *Deutsche Bauernstaaten auf russischer Steppe*, Berlin-Charlottenburg: Ostlandverlag, 1916.

the limestone blocks did not lend themselves to protective whitewash-
ing, as did brick, and the mud quickly washed away (Fig. 2). Within

*Figure 2. Early exterior stone construction with mud cementing weathered
away. (Pfeifer, Kansas)*

a few years, the German-Russian learned to mix lime with sand to
make a more substantial mortar. Since stone buildings were double-
walled, 18 inches thick, the interior walls continued to be cemented
with clay-mud, a practice which prevailed until after the introduction
of Portland cement.

While the early stone structures gave evidence of a crude, simplified
masonry, those constructed after 1900 show the influence of expert
techniques (Fig. 3). The use of quality masonry necessary for the
massive church structures in each village was a result of one man,
Father Emmeram Kansler. Kansler had been a stonemason in Germany before becoming a Capuchin priest.[5] Arriving in Kansas in- the
late 1890s, Kansler traveled from village to village supervising the
construction of religious buildings. His influence was apparently carried over to stone dwellings. Those structures in the Kansas villages
that exhibit fine masonry have been constructed since 1899.

5. Mary Eloise Johannes, "A Study of German-Russian Settlements in Ellis
County, Kansas," *Catholic University of American Studies in Sociology*, Vol. 14
(1946), p. 62.

Figure 3. Expert limestone construction was a consequence of a Catholic priest who had been a mason in Germany and was sent to the villages in the late 1890s. This masonry work dates from 1908. (Near Victoria, Kansas)

Although stone structures dominated the early village landscape (Fig. 4), such construction was not particularly popular with German-Russians in Kansas. As soon as the family was financially able, it chose to build with lumber. Many earlier stone dwellings were subsequently covered with wood siding (see Fig. 5), while others acquired frame additions. The frame structure was constructed on a footing of flat limestone slabs (Fig. 6). Essentially, the entire structure was secured to the footing by its own weight.

To give the frame structure additional weight and stability against the strong Kansas wind, the exterior walls were packed with a stone and mud-grass nogging (Figs. 7 and 8). The nogging was packed from inside as the interior wall was being constructed. While the nogging was similar to half-timbering construction common to Western European folk architecture, the stone and mud-grass nogging seems to be more directly associated with the German log structure and the Russian Volga experience. In his description of the evolution of the German Volga dwelling, Konig reports that moss and mud used earlier for chinking log structures was later used to fill the walls of frame

Figure 4. *The oldest stone dwelling in Liebenthal, Kansas, depicts many German-Russian dwelling characteristics such as the hipped roof with offset chimney and the absence of a front door.*

Figure 5. *A stone structure constructed in 1878 and later covered with wood siding. Wood construction was preferred as a stylistic form. (Victoria, Kansas)*

Figure 6. Limestone-slab footing under a frame structure. The flat slabs served as a footing for the structure as well as support for floor joists which were not an integral part of the frame construction itself. (Pfeifer, Kansas)

dwellings occupied by the poor.[6] While such construction was employed for its insulating qualities on the Volga, it is impossible today to assess whether the same was true of the stone-mud nogging in Kansas. A consensus of informants did not attribute its use to insulating the dwelling, but older German-Russian informants credited such construction with giving the structure stability in the wind.

Many frame dwellings built as late as 1940 utilized the stone-mud nogging. It is a construction feature peculiar to the early German-Russians and is unknown to the younger generation.

The architectural form of the traditional German-Russian dwelling in Kansas retained the character of its Volga origins despite changes in building material imposed by the new environment, the form of the traditional German-Volga *einfaches Haus*, or "simple house," was re-established on the Kansas landscape with only minor variation (Fig. 9). Rectangular in form, the *einfaches Haus* was divided into four rooms of equal size.[7] This single-story dwelling varied somewhat in size, with a length of 12 to 18 meters and a width of 6.5 to 10 meters.

6. Konig, *op. cit.*, p. 125–126, notes that the German log dwelling with dovetail notching was chinked with a combination of stone, mud, and grass. Log structures did not appear on this Kansas landscape.

7. Karl Stumpp, *The German-Russians: Two Centuries of Pioneering*, Bonn, Germany: Atlantic-Forum, 1964, p. 56.

Figure 7. *An abandoned frame dwelling with a stone-mud nogging. The nogging was packed from the inside as the interior walls were being constructed. The reason for the use of such nogging is unclear but it is generally believed that the nogging gave the structure weight to prevent it from being blown off its footing by the strong Kansas winds. (Pfeifer, Kansas)*

Figure 8. *A close-up view of the stone-mud nogging in Figure 7.*

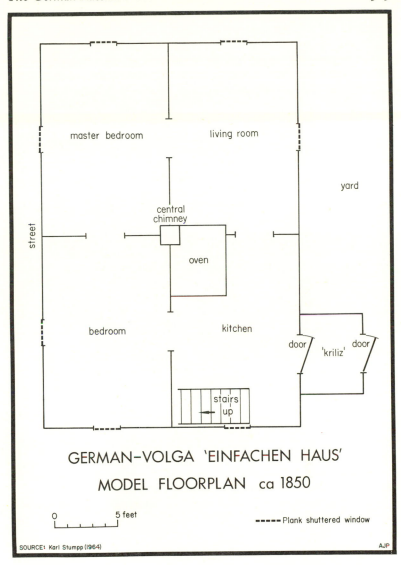

master bedroom   living room

central
chimney

oven

bedroom   kitchen

yard

door   'kriliz'   door

stairs
up

street

GERMAN–VOLGA 'EINFACHEN HAUS'

MODEL FLOORPLAN ca 1850

0   5 feet

▬▬▬ Plank shuttered window

SOURCE: Karl Stumpp (1964)   AJP

Figure 9. A model German-Russian floor plan derived from the Russian experience. A central oven was used for cooking and heating. All pre-World War II dwellings utilized this simple floor plan.

A single entrance opened upon a small antechamber or *kriliz*, which served as a coatroom during the winter.[8] The *kriliz* was not an integral part of the structure, but was added as a shed-roof appendage.

The dimensions of the interior rooms varied with the size of the structure and the family, but the basic four-room plan was universal. Despite its rather limited size, the *einfaches Haus* provided shelter for an extended patriarchal family which might include three or four married sons, their wives, and their children. Excepting the kitchen, the use of the other rooms varied with family size. All the young children shared the small attic which was reached by stairs through the kitchen.

Although many dwellings had a roof with two end gables, the most popular style on the Volga *einfaches Haus* was the hipped roof with a single dormer overlooking the street to provide natural light for the attic (Fig. 10). This style prevailed on the Volga dwelling but was never used on outbuildings.[9] With Volga gable roof dwellings, Konig notes that one end gable with a window "always faced the street."[10] The same roof orientation was found in the Kansas study area.

The entire dwelling was heated by a large brick oven situated in the central corner of the kitchen. A central chimney heated the other rooms as well as the attic. The chimney had a generalized central location, although a direct vertical flue often placed the exterior projection of the chimney several feet off from the center of the roof.

Excepting the *kriliz* or antechamber, the German-Russian dwelling on the Kansas landscape was identical in form to its Volga counterpart. Although many of the Kansas dwellings have a shed-roof antechamber, most dwellings appear to have been constructed without this unique Russian architectural feature. One can only hypothesize on the reason for the abandonment of such an appendage, but certainly the somewhat milder winter conditions of the Kansas area must have been an important factor.

As family size and affluence increased, additions were often made to the original four-room structure. Although such additions gave to the German-Russian dwelling and "L" or "T" shape, all newly constructed dwellings retained the simple rectangular, four-room floor plan. While

8. Martin Hagin, "Dehler: ein Wolgadeutsche Siedlung," *Heimatbuch der Deutschen in Russland*, (1966), p. 80.

9. While roof structures were essentially ignored in the literature, a preference for hipped roof construction on the German-Russian dwelling was observed in the Kansas study area by the author. Examination was then made of the drawings and photographs contained in the German Volga studies.

10. Konig, *op. cit.*, p. 127.

Figure 10. A simple German-Russian dwelling of frame construction with single dormer overlooking the street. (Catharine, Kansas)

later German-Russian structures increased in size, the ground floor retained its Old World orientation, and additional rooms were added by increasing the structure by a half or a full story (Fig. 11).

The German-Russian preference for the hipped roof and dormer was retained. All the early structures had the heavy plank-shuttered window; and the early architrave, or molded frame above the window, is identical to that found on the Volga. The single entrance in the rear of the dwelling is a feature of German-Russian architecture that was retained until the post-World War II period. Almost without exception, the older dwellings conspicuously lack a front door (Fig. 10). In many structures with a front door, close examination reveals evidence of later remodeling.

Persistence of form has been a characteristic of the German-Russian dwelling. While the theory of limited possibilities is certainly applicable to dwelling construction on the American Great Plains of the late nineteenth century, it would seem to apply to building material and not to style and form. Kniffen has observed that housing reflects "cultural heritage, current fashion, functional needs, and the positive and negative aspects of the noncultural environment."[11] My

11. Fred Kniffen, "Folk Housing: Key to Diffusion," *Annals of the Association of American Geographers*, Vol. 55 (1965), p. 549.

Figure 11. A one and one-half story stone dwelling. The increased size of the structure was a recognized indicator of family affluence. (Victoria, Kansas)

study of the German-Russian house type of the pre-World War II period supports that conclusion. Analysis of the evolution of the German-Russian house type tends to indicate cultural heritage as being the dominant shaping force.

It is not my intent to suggest that the German-Russian village in Kansas universally retains an Old World dwelling form. A visitor would notice the addition of several red or yellow brick structures possessing the style of the contemporary "development" house. All new homes are constructed on this American model and yet the traditional house type still dominates the landscape as a relict feature.

Some Theoretical Perspectives in American Folklore

Beginning in 1888—when the American Folklore Society was founded partly to collect the "fast-vanishing relics" of folk tradition—until well into the mid-twentieth century, the research emphasis was upon gathering material, indexing, annotating, and pursuing historical or comparative analysis. Most American folklore studies were of oral texts, to the neglect of folk music, customary lore, and material folk traditions. There was little systematic study of context, performance, function, meaning, or the relation of folklore to its cultural environment. The 1930s and 1940s were decades of important fieldwork and documentation, but the analytic perspectives of American folklorists were still primarily literary or historical, like those of the European folklorists whom they emulated. These were also the years in which some popular American writers began to interpret our folklore as an expression of national character, often with chauvinistic overtones and with limited knowledge of the foreign analogues of much American lore. The 1940s saw the first large-scale popularizing of American folklore, and was also the period of the creation of American fakelore.

American folklorists' changed attitudes and increasing influence began to be evident in the mid-1950s as scholars came to realize that the continued accumulation of texts without context could never advance folklore study very far. Nor would the public ever truly understand American folklore if only fakelore writings were well known. Quite obviously, it was time for a change. By that time the revised edition of Stith Thompson's Motif-Index of Folk Literature was available, the Type-Index revision was well under way, some American ballad syllabi had been compiled, and many standard regional and genre collections were being published with scholarly annotations. As the graduate programs in folklore established in the 1950s grew, they helped to accelerate and upgrade undergraduate folklore teaching across the country. American folklore theory had begun to feel the influence of theories *in anthropology, ethnography, cultural geography, linguistics, psychology, and other fields. In December, 1950, Stith Thompson gave an optimistic midcentury appraisal of American folklore study at the annual meeting of the Modern Language Association, and in the next few years it became clear that his basic reading of the situation was sound.*

In 1957 Richard M. Dorson, Thompson's successor as director of the folklore graduate program at Indiana University, delivered a paper titled "A Theory for American Folklore" which was later published in the Journal of American Folklore as a sort of theoretical background for his new textbook American Folklore (University of Chicago Press, 1959). After rejecting seven existing bodies of theory and methodology as insufficient for the full analysis of American folk traditions, Dorson proposed a new approach adapted to several unique qualities of United States history and civilization. His suggested major themes were colonization, the westward movement, immigration, aborigines and slaves, regionalism, democracy, and mass culture. He recommended close cooperation between the academic fields of folklore and American Studies. In a 1968 address (published in the Journal of American Folklore in 1969) Dorson reviewed the reaction—or rather lack of one—to his Theory among American folklorists. As he put it, "The seven sinful schools kept on sinning with increased vigor." While structural, psychological, symbolic, and other approaches were gaining in favor among American folklorists, few scholars took a broad American Studies approach. The only three "searching analyses" the Theory received were made by non-folklorists, and they were answered with "polemic rejoinders" by Dorson. Yet he also found reasons for encouragement in the appearance since 1957 of "fresh and exciting works of scholarship . . . which relate folklore to central themes in American history," and he surveyed several of these. Both of these papers by Dorson ought to be read by any serious student of American folklore; they are conveniently reprinted in his American Folklore and the Historian (Chicago, 1971) and hence do not need repeating here.

The essays in the final section of this reader begin roughly at the time when American folklorists were discovering ways of interpreting their folklore based on a synthesis of general folklore theory, influences from other scholarly traditions, and unique aspects of the folk traditions of the United States themselves. The arrangement of selections is chronological—from 1963 to 1973 (these are publication dates; some papers were read earlier)—and the material was chosen to suggest a dialogue between the various viewpoints that are characteristic of recent American folklore research. Except for the third selection (my own summary of progress since Thompson's midcentury statement), the essays all propose new perspectives, freshly coined terms, and innovative views of the possibilities for original research in American folklore. The concluding selection discusses possible overlapping of folklore research with a related area of scholarship.

This handful of recent publications by American folklorists is only a sample of the voluminous writings that have been devoted to theory, but the ideas they put forward are typical of the larger concerns of those scholars who are currently collecting and analyzing American folklore.

FOLKLORE IN CULTURE:
NOTES TOWARD AN ANALYTIC METHOD

Roger D. Abrahams

Published in 1963, this essay was one of the earliest calls by an American folklorist for a unified and up-to-date scholarly approach to the study of folklore. In it Roger D. Abrahams rejects the chaos of "special pleading" and "insular analytic systems" of past scholars, and he suggests a merging of the best features of many diverse approaches. "Salvation," he writes, "lies in eclecticism." Without rejecting totally the goals and methods of the traditional historic-geographic or comparative study of folklore, Abrahams argues strongly for more attention to the anthropologists' concerns for cultural context, performance, and function. He advocates better analysis of folklore style, structure, and rhetorical purposes in given cultures and situations. These are goals, he stresses, which will require reference to such outside fields as sociology, linguistics, and psychology.

Abraham's concept of what constitutes folklore avoids the idea of a relatively pure oral tradition disseminating specific genres of material from generation to generation. Instead he emphasizes that folklore is involved in dynamic situations of contrast and of process within cultures. Folklore embodies what he calls "the conflict between stability (tradition) and change"; it continually has to accept both "innovation and stability." In other words, folklore manages to be both conservative (clinging to older forms and themes) and new (incorporating present subjects and concerns), and it exists only in the context of specific cultural uses by interacting groups.

Like the earlier Swedish folklorist C. W. Von Sydow (and others not mentioned here, such as Stith Thompson), Abrahams employs a biological metaphor for studying folklore. Thus, folklore is viewed "organically, as a living process. . . . It lives and dies or mutates." The local variation of a particular folk story or other item is termed an "oikotype," using Von Sydow's version of the scientific term "ecotype" (an isolated subtype of a biological species). Similarly, cultures are not static entities, but are full of instances of "dynamic polarity" involving sex, age, strength, status, wealth, and the like. By implication, then, the eclectic folklorist must be just as "alive" as his subject—that is, broad-minded and flexible enough to "utilize as many methods as possible to illuminate data under study."

Unfortunately, this exciting general essay is entirely theoretical, offering not a single example of actual folklore analysis. Both folktales and folksongs are alluded to, but no specific texts or performances are put through the new analytic method. We are never shown exactly how folklore "echoes the special preoccupations of the group in which it is found." Abrahams writes of fitting various "polarities" into general categories, and he mentions that rhetorical functions of folktales are "mirrored in the dramatic antagonism of the story," but he withholds any specifics or examples. His ready acceptance of the concept of oiko-types is not supported by references to any localized tales or songs that can be identified and analyzed. Nor does he name any of the genres of folklore which supposedly express the tellers' thoughts better than others.

These lacks, however, were liquidated shortly in several other important publications by Abrahams in the later 1960s which are cited below in my essay "New Directions for the Study of American Folklore" (see footnotes 26, 31, and 36). To these should be added his article "Folklore and Literature as Performance," Journal of the Folklore Institute, Vol. 9 (1972), pp. 75–94. Furthermore, Abrahams' influence as a writer and a teacher (at the University of Texas) is evident in the works of many younger American folklorists of the 1970s. See, for example, Frank Hall, "Conversational Joking: A Look at Applied Humor," Folklore Annual, Vol. 6 (1974) and other articles published in this graduate student journal of the University of Texas.

In 1978 Abrahams became president of the American Folklore Society.

FOLKLORE, LIKE ANY OTHER humanistic discipline, must utilize as many methods as possible to illuminate data under study. It is rightly then called an "eclectic discipline." Yet as any folklorist will admit, this area has been more prone to special pleading and less to a catholic approach than almost any other. Sociology, literature, psychology, anthropology, history, economics all have recently used knowledge or methods from the others in order to bring new light to their disciplines. Folklore, on the other hand, has become the whipping boy for anthropologists and has provided data for a number of insular analytic systems. But no consistent effort has been made either to analyze folklore on its own terms or to develop a methodology which is coherent, comprehensive, empirical, catholic, and thoroughly analytic. Certain pleaders see traditional lore as quaint vestiges of the past (and this long after the antiquarian movement has run its gamut); others view it as data through which we can anatomize the oral process, but of little intrinsic worth beyond this. Still others see it as a bearer of enigmas, the solving of which will give us clues into the history of the race, or of the individual psyche. And most firmly, one group regards it as a minor and mishandled aspect of culture.

It is the purpose of this paper to show that a potential order exists in this chaos, and salvation lies in eclecticism—the use of as many points of view as possible to cast light on folklore and the culture within which it exists. As illustration, I will discuss the use of the anthropological and comparative approaches, how they have been used on folklore matters in the past and how their use can be expanded, and then treat some other approaches that I feel complement the traditional ones. Throughout, I will be speaking in terms of analyzing folk narrative, but I believe the method which I am attempting to develop could be expanded to include any piece, or series of pieces, of folklore.

Folklore is, as the anthropologists would have us believe, but one facet of culture. It is a series of artifacts which obey culture's general laws, those generated by the conflict of innovation and stability, and complicated by the interactions of different groups. The traditional process, oral transmission, which folklorists have been claiming as their own, is but one argument of an evolutionary theory of history which sees forms and ideas as mutable but not radically changeable.

Too often, because the theoretical ideal of pure oral transmission loomed before his eyes, the folklorist has seen himself as dealing with sacrosanct matters, lore transmitted from the pure "golden age" of the primitive past of Indo-European culture by word of mouth, and thus divorced from contemporary discourse, except as vestige. But recent scholarship has slowly erased the concept of a pure process of oral transmission; increasingly we are led to see the influence of the written and the printed, the recorded word, upon pieces of traditional literature. As these preconceptions are being modified, we must realize concurrently that folklore is not only not made up of sacrosanct antiquities, but is in fact a very live cultural phenomenon, subject to the same processes as other things cultural, and therefore available to the same type of analysis as other similar humanistic studies.

Every agency, artifact, and entity within a culture is potentially capable of reflecting the whole of the constructs of that group. But in order to so reflect, it must be presented within some context of the culture from which it emerged.[1]

Folklore is an important aspect of any culture, and one which yields

---

1. "The full significance of any single element in a culture design will be seen only when that element is viewed in the total matrix of its relationship to other elements" (Clyde Kluckhohn, *Mirror for Man* [New York, 1956, Signet edition], p. 11).

much illumination through its study. It is a prime example of the variety and incredible breadth to which man is capable of giving form. As with any object or concept, every work of folk creation or transmission is an artifact potentially capable of providing great insight into the story of its culture, because that work, in both its form and its function, reflects the preoccupations and values of those who create and transmit it. Folklore represents or reflects the functional unity which man in groups can create for himself. This unity is not delusive, one which speaks for all time of permanence, but rather represents a constantly shifting, but nonetheless effective, dialectic unity—one that relies for its existence on contrarieties, on balanced oppositions:

> The various forms of human culture are not held together by an identity in their nature but by a conformity in their fundamental task. If there is an equipoise in human culture it can only be described as a dynamic, not as a static equilibruim; it is the result of a struggle between opposing forces.[2]

Any study of folklore must be presented so that the "opposing forces" can be isolated and understood; otherwise the lore will not be comprehended except insofar as the dynamic unity it illustrates approximates that of the culture of the reader. This is simply extending the anthropological method of presenting material in as full a cultural context as possible, at the same time as insisting, with some anthropologists, that culture produces artifacts which are not only of passing interest as artifacts, but of lasting value as evidences of process; and it is these anthropologists who are interested in process rather than structure to whom we must turn to develop our concepts and methodology. Although it is perhaps less important, it is hardly unnecessary to present a collection of folklore with a full description of its cultural context to the group from whom it was collected. Such data can serve as an index to the preoccupations and problems of that group, the things that provide the oppositions in this dynamic unity. These are matters which should be explored in any group, especially one's own.

A glaring instance of the failure of method has been studies of Anglo-American folksong. Because the collectors and commentators have been deluded into thinking that the culture from which these songs have sprung is enough like ours that the songs function self-evidently, or because they simply haven't cared about such matters, and because this group has viewed the song predominantly as an artifact, we know very little about the individual and social patterns of the rural people of England and the United States among whom these

2. Ernst Cassirer, *Essay On Man* (New York, 1944), p. 279.

songs are living and changing. What we do know of the aesthetics of this group indicates that their values and modes of appreciation, as well as their societal and familial structures, are in many important respects different from our middle-class standards. Thus we can only partially comprehend such large questions as the importance of improvisation and "rewriting" on these songs, the necessity of social situation upon the form and subject of the songs, the effects of cliché, commonplace, and formula upon the writing and transmission of the songs, and most important, the relationship of social convention to song convention, and the use of these constructs to outline the strategic or rhetorical roles of the songs.

It is vitally important to present any corpus of lore with some analysis of the conflicts which exist within the culture that produce this dynamic unity, and to attempt to relate the lore, as strategies within this universe of conflict, to the conflict (or unity) itself. To do so is to recognize that dialectic produces not only conflict but synthesis, and that exploration of such matters is going to explain not only much about the lore itself, but also much about the process of that group. Even if the analysis presentation is not wholly correct, it can be corrected toward illumination; lack of any analysis precludes even this possibility. Though we recognize the fact that most of us collect because of our acquisitive compulsion, our burden must be greater than a simple presentation of our acquisition.

This procedure does not have to be as difficult as it seems at first. The oppositions present in different cultures, the polarities that create the dynamic unity to be described, are usually those that fit into general categories. And the enumeration and subsequent consideration of the common areas will at least guarantee a modicum of proper analytic approach.

The study of folklore itself inherently contains one pair of oppositions, the analysis of which can cast much light on the lore itself and its creation and transmission: the conflict between stability (tradition) and change. Any study of a body of collected lore should contain at least some discussion of the place of improvisation and the improvisor within the group from which the material has come. Improvisation can be a traditional mode itself. Though folklore is by its nature traditional, therefore conservative, the influence of conscious change, or innovation, is not alien or inimical to any group. The creative individual within the folk community has been pointed out too often to ignore him any longer.

The opposition of permanence and innovation is by no means the only dynamic polarity that exists universally. There are numerous other pairs which exist to varying degrees of importance in every culture or society. Certainly the biological differences of male and female cause polarities to exist in all groups, delineating the relative positions of men and women. A similar opposition exists between generations which, in one way or another, will affect the constructs of a group. Furthermore a hierarchic set-up may exist other than those above based on strength, verbal ability, inheritance, caste system, or any of a number of other "mysteries" which may cause other oppositions.

If these oppositions exist in all groups to some extent, then they must find expression; government, religion, economic system, marriage practice, family pattern will illustrate these forces, it is true, but it is often only in the realm of folklore that these oppositions find their expression in words.

Viewed in this way, folklore functions purposefully. Though we may not agree with their individual applications, Freud and Marx and their followers have clearly shown that there is no such thing as nondirected actions within the context of culture. This is especially true of any formal grouping of words (a class into which folklore certainly fits). Nothing exists because of form alone. Though there may be forms whose functions are outmoded, they will cease to exist if no function at all is assumed by the form. And the function of words is more than to entertain or communicate. Words exist to persuade, court, control. Viewing society agonistically or dialectically, words in formal arrangement then exist primarily for rhetorical purpose.[3]

Thus the folk narrative is a rhetorical expression of the dialectical unity of the culture, and the oppositions that naturally exist in any dialectical enterprise are mirrored in the dramatic antagonism of the story. But just as there is a dialectic structure of the narrative, so we must look for its synthesis, or in proper dramatic terms, transformation or regenesis. And this transformation as an approved resolution of the struggle will be value-laden, and therefore something that we can look to for significance. So, in this immediate way, dialectic reflects dramatic, and an analysis of one in terms of the other, if only analogically, will be valid. But basically these matters are more literary than anthropological and will be returned to later.

To analyze the strategic effect of any piece of folk-literature is to consider its function. However, by insisting upon such considerations I am not espousing any strict functionalist approach. Rather I am concerned with viewing folklore organically, as a living process. In fact,

3. Cf. Kluckhohn, p. 115: "Mainly language is an instrument of action. The meaning of a word or phrase is not its dictionary equivalent but the difference its utterance brings about in a situation." See also Kenneth Burke's *Rhetoric of Motives* (New York, 1953), to which I am indebted throughout this rhetorical discussion, both for terms and concepts.

we can profitably look at each piece of folklore as an organism. It lives and dies or mutates. It has the primary attributes of an organism: it acts both as a receptor and an effector, and the two functions act not separately but in equilibrium. It is a receptor because it is sensitive to outside stimulus, both in inherited forms and the dialectics of the group. It is an effector because it reacts to these stimuli in such a way that a change occurs, a mutation in the chain of causation.

The mutating "organism" or piece of lore reflects its history in its very constitution. And it also echoes the special preoccupations of the group in which it is found. But the "organism" also acts as a genera-tor, not only embodying but also furthering through the strength of its position the values implicit in its construction. Thus the lore is not just a result of past and present forces upon it, but is also able to affect its own future. This accounts for the conservatism of folklore (and other cultural phenomena).

As form and function do act jointly, it is often hard to separate them. Certainly when viewing oral literature from its rhetorical base it is not difficult to see how its persuasive purpose is going to influence its ultimate form. But, as mentioned, cultural necessities are mutable, can and do change. With their function gone, pieces of folklore will naturally fade and disappear. But any piece of lore has both form and function and the form may be able to achieve other cultural functions and therefore continue to exist, though in a different place in the life of that group.

> Any given culture trait can be fully understood only if seen as the end point of specific sequences of events reaching back into the re-mote past. Forms persist; functions change.[4]

It is important to investigate such forms historically in any collec-tion of texts, but in a way that present rather than past function is stressed; for one can ascertain function now, but can only hypothesize what uses might have been in the past. On the surface, this would seem to gainsay the method of the comparative folklorists, but it is not intended as such. The analytic direction of the comparative approach is wholly laudable and quite serviceable. It is the sort of conclusion toward which they are driving that seems to me to be questionable, not the way in which they arrive there.

Briefly, the followers of the comparative method take one specific story (or gesture or song, etc.) and by amassing all of the collected variants in as many languages and areas as possible, arrive at some idea of the pattern of the dissemination of the tale and, ideally, at an hypothesis as to where it first arose. Theoretically, if enough studies of

4. *Ibid.*, p. 56.

this sort were made we would be able to place these dissemination patterns in some sort of perspective and thus be able to arrive at a general dissemination pattern on an empirical base.

The comparativist is concerned primarily with the story as a series of motifs often found in conjunction with each other. They reduce the story to a diagrammatic structure of the movement of these motifs. Therefore no consideration is made of the style of the individual collected version, its genre, its cultural content, or even its point. It matters not at all even whether such a story is serious in one area and humorous in another. It is only the story *pattern* with which they are concerned.

It is not within the scope of our study here to point out at any length the ultimate distracting fact of the law of diminishing returns in relation to this method. Much more work goes into amassing the incredible number of versions and variants of a tale than is warranted by the limited conclusions with which the comparativists have emerged. Nor shall we pursue the argument that any collected text is a mistake of history and not, therefore, necessarily representative, as the comparativists would have us believe. More apposite to our discussion are the misconceptions which such a method fosters.

The major misconception that concerns us is, of course, the idea which emerges that tales *are* reducible to motif formulae, thus eliminating the meat and keeping the bones. (The bones won't decay, but the meat may!) Further, the comparative approach fosters the idea that tales by their very nature are international, and thus are able to cross cultural and linguistic frontiers with ease.

But as C. W. Von Sydow and other theoretical comparativists since have pointed out, we should not delude ourselves into thinking that tradition is an easy process. Because we have a large corpus of tales of international currency from numerous regions and in various languages, we should not assume that this dissemination was achieved at any small cost. For a piece of oral literature to transcend the bounds of language and culture, a strong impulse must exist (usually in the form of an emigrating traditional story-teller) and an ability for that bit of lore to adapt itself (or more properly, to be adapted) to the values of the new group. Often enough, this transition has been effected with a modicum of cultural changes. Any study of an international tale-type will indicate this.

On the other hand, for every story that has made this transition, there are certainly many that have not. The problem of culture is one that is far more complicated than simply one of language. In order for a story to make a transition between two cultural groups there must be some element in it that will appeal to the specific sensibility of the culture into which it is entering. This element (or elements) may or may not correspond to the "emotional core"[5] of the story as it was told in the area from which it is coming. If it does correspond, the story may enter oral currency in the new area in much the same form in which it was told in the old. If, however, it is different, there is a good chance that the story will mutate because of the inevitable change of emphasis that will occur in the new situation, creating a new and local form of the story. One can not help realizing that changes which occur in the migration of a story happen as much because of a disparity of cultures as of language.

Though the comparativist has realized the existence of the local variant he has chosen to ignore for the most part its implications in favor of the broader historical-geographical study. However, a full appreciation of these local changes that may occur as a tale crosses a linguistic and/or cultural frontier is perhaps the greatest asset of the comparative approach for the student of the folklore of a specific group. For it is by comparing the forms and style of a story among other groups that we are best able to arrive at a knowledge of the "cultural imperatives" that operate upon stories in the group from whom the collection was made.

Von Sydow, in his considerations of the problems of transmission within the method of the comparativists, saw this potential weakness and attempted to compensate by a formulation of a theory of "oiko-type." He said that, as important as the study of the forms of a story are, in search of its archetype, just as important is the form which this story attains when it reaches a specific area and achieves a distinct manner. This local variation he called the "oikotype." Von Sydow was concerned with the organic nature of the folktale, as most compara-tivists have not been:

> One of the most serious deficiencies in the study of folk tradition has been that investigators have, to a far too great extent, been con-tent with extracts, instead of seeing their information as part of a natural, living whole. In questions of belief and custom this has led to their concentration overmuch on chance similitude, and neglect-ing to find out if there was any deeper connection.
>
> The same fault has been committed in folk-tale research. To be able to survey your material you have, of course, to use extracts; but if you are content with them without bothering about the original, you will not be able to treat your material critically but will get in-volved in purely schematic methods which will almost certainly lead you astray. But it is not enough to study folk-tales as tales only. It is

5. [This term was introduced into folkloristics by Tristram P. Coffin in his essay on the ballad "Mary Hamilton" reprinted in Section 3.]

also necessary to make oneself familiar with the use of folk-tales, their life in tradition, their transmission and spread.[6]

Von Sydow here has hit upon a very important principle, and one that the anthropologists have spent much time developing (probably independent of his remarks). He has explicitly recognized the organic quality of folklore, the fact that lore does not live in schemae but in the mouths of individuals existing within groups. But he has been schooled in the comparative method and his schism is only minor (especially in view of the fact that he doesn't seem to have carried his preaching into practice). He sees the local variant, the oikotype, as important, not because it gives us insight into the dynamic unity of the group, but because it allows us to understand more fully patterns of dissemination. His object is not to show the interrelationship of forms of various tales within a specific locale, but rather to show that tales, in their complex travels tend to assume local forms.

But the oikotype is a notion that has value beyond pointing out the way in which tales change as they travel. If one can isolate an oikotypal form of one tale in one region or among one group, why not similarly note oikotypes of other tales in the same group and then analyze what makes them oikotypical? This should cast much light on that group and on their attitude and approach toward life, language, and expression.[7] Thus the methods of the anthropologist and the comparativist could be made complementary.

Similarly, a literary approach can be made a useful tool for folkloric analysis, adding distinctions where the comparative and anthropological methods stop. Folk-literature, if properly distinguished from written works, can be illuminated by internal analysis. There are the important concerns of genre, style, structure and content, form and feeling, and objective intent and subjective reaction to be utilized in discussing the traditional narrative in its relation to the culture in which it is encountered. It is important to point out the prevalence of specific genres, for instance, and to attempt to investigate what it is about this form that appeals to the audience or so aptly encompasses the thought and style of the teller.

Most of these structural matters can be discussed only in regard to individual stories, or stories as told by one informant, or those which conform to one type or genre within a group. But just calling a folktale a "traditional narrative" is qualifying it in a literary manner.

---

6. C. W. Von Sydow, *Selected Papers on Folklore* (Copenhagen, 1948), p. 44.

7. Theoretically it would be possible, if enough oikotype studies were made, to look at an individual traditional narrative or other piece of folklore and to tell approximately where it came from just from internal evidence. Thus this procedure could become predictive as well as descriptive.

"Traditional" indicates that, because of oral change, it has no recognizable author. And "narrative" indicates that the strategies it utilizes will be from the point of view of the embodied story. It is just this consideration of rhetoric which provides us with the greatest benefit of a literary approach.

As Kenneth Burke has so forcefully shown, on the hint from Freud (and many others before him), there are few literary motives which cannot be shown to be strategic in conception and nature.[8] Most consciously conceived sets of words exist for a purpose, and the essence of this purpose is to convince. Words exist to produce action. Any convincing is in the interest of future action. It is true that the more reflexive and complex the words and word relationships become, the greater the aesthetic effect, and the greater the distance created between the words and the potential actions.

The strategy involved in the traditional story is not so complex however; it is usually one of attempting to induce action through a portrayal of action. Which is not to say that the story will induce immediate action. Rather, the tale will in most cases direct our emotions toward values which it approves or disapproves, and thus guide future action. But it is not my purpose here to outline all of the possible strategies inherent in the telling of a folktale; I am merely pointing out how a literary approach to narrative lore can yield some results otherwise unattainable.

There are further literary or linguistic considerations that would contribute to this analysis. Style and content analysis exist somewhere between standard literary and linguistic approaches, for literature looks to the larger elements of word progressions, and linguistics to the smallest. It is as necessary to point out certain words (important to the individual or the group) which are given more persuasive weight in a traditional narrative, and to answer why and how they achieve such values, as it is to analyze key words and concepts in a work of *belles lettres*. It is also important to attempt to discover syntactical patterns of individual informants and of groups and to attempt to relate these patterns to technical and aesthetic values. This is saying that it is obligatory to attempt to make some consideration of the aesthetics of the group and the individual performers within it.

Perhaps even more important is the consideration of narratives as contrastive phenomena, a wholly linguistic matter. If it is agreed that

---

8. [Abrahams applies some of literary critic Burke's ideas about literature to folklore analysis in his article "Introductory Remarks to a Rhetorical Theory of Folklore," *Journal of American Folklore*, 81 (1968), 143–158, and in subsequent writings.]

construction of the narrative involves a playground much like life but not exactly lifelike, then it is necessary to establish how the contrast between the playground and life is conveyed. This should be provided by an analysis of contrastive devices of language: that is, how the method of constructing word groups, narrating, speaking, delivering, differs from everyday speech patterns.

The literary aspect of the method under development is capable of pointing out the materials of structure, and to some extent what makes it cohere. But there still remains the problem of establishing the relationship between the fictive playground and the agonisms of life and this is where the method of the psychologist helps us most greatly. For psychology tells us the importance of the fictive experience as a release mechanism in expression of matters otherwise repressed. To discuss the story in emergent symbolic psychological terms is to see the tale as a physical embodiment of an internal experience. And when the experience can be shown to be extrapersonal the narrative achieves psychological importance for the group as well as the individual. Thus we can relate the implicit values of the story to the lives of those in the group. Further, psychological studies have shown us the importance of two major folkloristic matters, form and repetition, in the creation of pleasure (or release from anxiety).

However, as with other disciplines, we must deal not only with the strengths of an approach, but also with its insularities. Psychology, perhaps more than any other discipline, has produced single-minded theories. Freud, Jung, and Adler, all developed systems of thought which cast much light on folkloristic matters, but because of their preoccupations, more than because of their actual formulation. We are indebted to Freud because his theories insist on the facts of rivalry between members of families, especially between father and son. Similarly Jung has shown the importance of the struggle for individuality or a sense of individualness in the lives of everyone, while Adler's preoccupation with the search for control or power has been equally illuminating. But as many have pointed out, alliance with any of these theories asks us to buy much more of the system of the individual teacher than we otherwise might want.

Both Freud and Jung ask us to accept forms as explanations, when we are really asking for processes. To recognize that a story fits into the Oedipal pattern, the Electra pattern, or any of the number of Jungian archetypal patterns does not necessarily explain how that story achieved its form. It simply gives us some notion as to what its psychological function may be, and even then, as Herskovits has pointed out, "It is . . . only one of the causal factors, and not *the* causal factor."[9] This does not destroy the usefulness of even the most insular psychological approach.

Recognizing that the method being developed looks for answers in terms of process rather than through categorization by simple recognition of form, it is possible to accept the theories for what they can tell us about the process which the texts illustrate. If a story fits into the "quest archetype" or the "oedipal pattern" this may point out important relationships between life within the group and that specific fictive experience.

But the applicability of psychological theory to the analytic method being pursued goes beyond a discussion of narrative structure as a reflection of psychic development. Ultimately we are perhaps more indebted to the psychological approach for the articulation of a proposition of purposive tendency of all expression. If the idea can be accepted (and indeed it must), that all methods and modes of expression exist for some purpose, conscious or unconscious, then perceptive psychological analysis will be able to lay bare the force behind the expression, and more fully expose both the form and the function in which the expression has been embodied. And, because everything is viewed as having intention, one can gain some insight into the problem of where value resides within a group by noting at which places the group reacts to the fictive experience, for through reaction we can see tendency. And the effectiveness of strategy of course relies on the effective manipulations of just such reactions. Where people laugh, cry, howl, or make any other physical manifestation is the place in which some soft spot in their psychic lives has been hit. And from just such moments we can begin to judge why certain values have been developed, and how these values and these soft spots have ultimately affected the form of the piece. Until recently the value of the psychological approach to any cultural matter has been suspect, because psychological investigation has been so concerned with the abnormal personality, that is, with psychopathology. Recently however works have been published which investigate the normal personality in its development.[10] These studies are important because, though they don't neglect the psychic life and especially the development of the ego, they lay equally heavy stress on two other factors which enter into the process of normal identification: group experience and

9. Melville and Frances Herskovits, *Dahomean Narrative* (Evanston, 1958), p. 95. They note further that both are notoriously unscientific in their inability to refer their theorems to empirical cultural proof, but rather must rely on them as articles of faith.

10. See especially Erik Erickson, *Childhood and Society* (New York, 1950), and *Identity and the Life Cycle* (New York, 1959); John H. Rohrer and Munro S. Edmonson, editors, *The Eighth Generation* (New York, 1960).

somatic development. The use of psychological technique can help us relate the individual with his group, the teller with his story, and the story with its audience. Further, it allows us to correlate physical development with psychic, and thus to more fully understand the nature of the folklore of different age groups. It is through psychological investigation, then, that we have one of our clearest insights into cultural imperatives and their operations in any culture.

The major problem in finding acceptance for such an analytic method as this is the distrust that anthropologists and folklorists have for each other's methods. Folklorists will undoubtedly find it too anthropological and vice versa. This friendly distrust has been to the detriment of both groups. Folklorists have consistently erred in not considering their collected lore in view of the important cultural considerations of the group from which the lore came. Anthropological recordings of 'texts' have, for the most part, ignored the comparative method of analysis until recently, an approach that helps much to define cultural imperatives through contrast with other groups. Is it not just as revealing to show how a group has changed a story, or tells a story differently, as to point out other ways in which the cultural imperatives are reflected? But those anthropologists who have been concerned with tales have not been so much concerned with the process of culture.

What is being espoused then, is an eclectic manner of analyzing folklore. Primary in a proper study should be the placing of the lore in context. We can achieve this aim not only by inclusion of relevant ethnological data, but also by expanding the idea of the oikotype to include analysis of lore from both a comparative and an intracultural point of view. Further, formal, psychological, and sociological considerations should be utilized wherever they illuminate. Analysis should not be engaged in where internal examination of the pieces of folklore is forgotten or slighted in favor of an historic or cultural approach. The formal matters considered by the comparativists must be extended so that they include not only motifs but also genre, style, structure in general. The matters of process of the anthropologist must be expanded so that they may embrace the same formal preoccupations, but in such a way that structure is understood in its fullest interrelation with function. (Theoretically at least we should be able to compare both form and function in the ideal oikotypical approach.) And finally any approach should be considered which might cast light on the corpus of folklore being studied.

METAFOLKLORE AND
ORAL LITERARY CRITICISM

Alan Dundes

Like Abrahams and many other American folklorists who completed doctoral studies in the 1960s, Alan Dundes was determined to change the focus of folklore scholarship from the description of surviving frag- ments of past cultures to the study of "the present context of folklore." Dundes in this article advocates that analysis of "metafolklore" (folk- lore that is actually about folklore) and "oral literary criticism" (in- formants' own comments about their folk traditions) as an aid to interpretation of folklore. He supports these theories with examples of contextual and interpretive data from fieldwork in American and foreign folklore.

A particularly important point in this essay is that the meaning of a piece of folklore cannot be guessed at reliably by an outsider; it is essential to ask bearers of folklore what traditions mean to them. What follows from this situation is the truism that "the meaning" of folklore is almost always multiple, depending upon context, use, and the indi- vidual performer and audience.

Metafolklore, as Dundes suggests, is no more difficult to collect than other folklore, and students might try to see how many further examples they can find in present circulation or in published collec- tions of folklore. For example, besides the non-standard "Knock Knock" joke Dundes quotes, there is the metafolkloristic prank "I know a new 'Knock Knock.' You start it!" (This as a catch, since the person who starts a "Knock Knock" has to be able to insert the "right" answer in the slot following "who's there?") Proverb parodies and the punning punchlines of Shaggy Dog Stories often function as negative reflections on the older serious use of proverbs as comment and advice. There are folktales about riddle-telling, graffiti about graffiti, folksong references to songs and singers, anecdotes about noted storytellers and their tales, and so forth.

Dundes' illustration of the multiple meanings of the phrase "to have an axe to grind" calls to mind other varying applications of pro- verbial speech to specific situations. In a related example, some people who misunderstand the metaphorical expression "to whet [sharpen] your appetite" as "to wet your appetite" use the phrase only literally and have a before-dinner drink in mind. When "eat, drink, and be merry" is spoken as ". . . make merry," it may mutate to "make Mary" with a new meaning. And I have found the saying "a rocky [or long] row to hoe" and "a long road to go" combined in print as "a rocky road to hoe," which telescopes the suggestions of difficulty and inter minableness in one magnificent mixed metaphor.

One advantage—or danger—of most of Alan Dundes' writings about folklore is the seductive quality of prompting the reader to endless matching of his examples. Many folklorists stop, however, with symbolic interpretations where no final proof can be· found for the suggested meanings. The readers of this reader will have to judge for themselves if Dundes' proposed explanations for nursery rhymes are acceptable; but, if not, then what alternative interpretations can be offered? An interesting example of evaluating such multiple meanings of a familiar fairy tale is found in an essay influenced by Alan Dundes; see Alan C. Elms, " 'The Three Bears': Four Interpretations," Journal of American Folklore, Vol. 90 (1977).

THE THEORETICAL ASSUMPTION that folklore was limited to a survival and reflection of the past was a crippling one for the study of folklore in context. For if in fact folklore did reflect only the far distant past, then clearly there was no point in bothering to attempt to collect· the *present* context of folklore. A past-oriented folklore collector would tend to regard his informants as relatively unimportant carriers of precious vestigial fragments, fragments which might prove useful in the central task of historically reconstructing the past. For the execution of historico-comparative studies, one needed only minimal information concerning the place and date of collection. It is clear that for the kinds of theoretical and methodological questions that nineteenth century folklorists were asking, e.g., "what was the original form of an item of folklore and what were the genetic relationships between various forms or subtypes of that item of folklore?", place and date of recording were sufficient.

In the twentieth century with the increasing amount of ethnographic fieldwork, it became glaringly apparent that folklore reflected the present as well as the past and that there was certainly a context in which folklore was used. Nevertheless, custom is strong even among scholars and the "butterfly" or "object-curio-collecting" philosophy has continued. Long lists of proverbs are published in folklore journals accompanied by no explanation of either use or meaning. Anthropologists append to their ethnographies a token section consisting of folktales and myths but with little or no comment on their relationship to other aspects of the culture. The "object-collecting" philosophy is itself a survival of the antiquarian days of folklore studies. Folklore texts

without contexts are essentially analogous to the large numbers of
exotic musical instruments which adorn the walls of anthropological
or folk museums and grace the homes of private individuals. The
instrument is authentic as is the folklore text, but the range of the
instrument, the tuning of the instrument, the function of the instrument, and the intricacies of performing with the instrument are rarely
known.

It was Malinowski who was most vociferous in calling for context.
In his important 1926 essay "Myth in Primitive Psychology," he repeatedly pointed out the fallacy of collecting mere texts, calling them
mutilated bits of reality. Here again is the notion of folklore as fragments, but not fragments of the past, fragments of the present. In one
formulation, Malinowski observed, "The text, of course, is extremely
important, but without the context it remains lifeless."[1] More recently,
Bascom has continued the call for context. Auguring well for future
folklore field research is Goldstein's praiseworthy concern for context
in his valuable *Guide for Field Workers in Folklore.* He specifically
lists "folklore processes" as one of the principal kinds of folklore data
to be obtained in the field.[2] In another recent development in the
study of folklore context, it has been suggested that the ways and
means of using folklore are just as highly patterned as the materials of
folklore themselves. The identification of the rules for the use of an
item of folklore, or the "ethnography of speaking folklore" as it has
been termed, suggests that to the "laws" of form (Olrik) and the
"laws" of change (Aarne) may be added the "laws" of use.[3] The
discovery of such laws or rules opens a new area of folklore research.

The current interest in the collection of context, however, has partially obscured the equally necessary and important task of collecting
the meaning(s) of folklore. One must distinguish between *use* and
meaning. The collection of context and preferably a number of different contexts for the same item of folklore is certainly helpful in
ascertaining the meaning or meanings of an item of folklore. But it
cannot be assumed that the collection of context per se automatically

1. Bronislaw Malinowski, *Magic, Science and Religion* (Garden City: Doubleday, 1954), p. 104.

2. William R. Bascom, "Four Functions of Folklore," *Journal of American
Folklore,* 7 (1954), 333–349; Kenneth S. Goldstein, *A Guide for Field Workers in
Folklore* (Hatboro, Pa.: Folklore Associates, 1964), p. 23.

3. See E. Ojo Arewa and Alan Dundes, "Proverbs and the Ethnography of
Speaking Folklore," *American Anthropologist,* 66:6, Part 2 (1964), 70–85. For
the laws of folklore form, see Axel Olrik's classic paper "Epic Laws of Folk
Narrative," in *The Study of Folklore,* ed. Alan Dundes (Englewood Cliffs, N.J.:
Prentice-Hall, Inc., 1965), pp. 129–141. For the laws of folkloristic change, see
Antti Aarne, *Leitfaden der Vergleichenden Märchenforschung,* Folklore Fellows
Communications No. 13 (Hamina, 1913), pp. 23–29.

ensures the collection of meaning. Suppose a folklorist collected the following Yoruba[4] proverb:

> A proverb is like a horse: when the truth is missing, we use a proverb to find it.[5]

Let us assume that he also collected the typical context of this proverb in which it is employed in an introductory capacity prior to uttering another proverb which was designed to settle a particular dispute. The introductory proverb announces to the audience that the arbitrator is planning to use a proverb and reminds them of the great power and prestige of proverbs in such situations. But from this text and context, does the collector know precisely what the proverb means? What exactly is meant by comparing a proverb to a horse? While the meaning(s) of a proverb are unquestionably involved in an individual's decision whether or not the quotation of that particular proverb is appropriate in a given context, the folklore collector may miss the meaning(s) even though he has faithfully recorded text and context. One cannot always guess the meaning from context. For this reason, *folklorists must actively seek to elicit the meaning of folklore from the folk.*

As a terminological aid for the collection of meaning, I have proposed "oral literary criticism."[6] The term is obviously derived from "literary criticism" which refers to a host of methods of analyzing and interpreting works of written literature. Even a beginner in literary criticism soon discovers that there are alternative and rival interpretations of one and the same work of art. The identical phenomenon occurs in the case of folklore which for the sake of the discussion we may call "oral literature" (although this unfortunately tends to exclude nonverbal folklore). For each item of oral literature, there is a variety of oral literary criticism. This is an important point inasmuch as folklorists, despite the fact that they are accustomed to thinking of variation in the texts of folklore, often wrongly assume that there is only one correct meaning or interpretation. There is no one right interpretation of an item of folklore any more than there is but one right version of a game or song. (We must overcome our penchant for

---

4. [West African people of southwestern Nigeria.]

5. In Yoruba, the proverb is:

Òwe	l'eṣin	ọ̀rọ̀:	bi	ọ̀rọ̀	bá	sonù
proverb	is horse	word	if	word	got	lost

òwe	l'a	fi	ńwá	a		
proverb	is we	use	finding	it		

For the proverb and its explanation, I am indebted to E. Ojo Arewa.

6. Alan Dundes, "Texture, Text, and Context," *Southern Folklore Quarterly*, 28 (1964), 263; Arewa and Dundes, *op. cit.*, p. 73.

monolithic perspectives as exemplified in monotheism, monogamy, and the like.) There are multiple meanings and interpretations and they all ought to be collected. One could ask ten different informants what each thought a given joke meant and one might obtain ten different answers. It is difficult to determine the gamut of interpretation because there has been comparatively little collection of oral literary criticism.

The interpretation which is made is inevitably from the collector's point of view. There is nothing wrong with analytic as opposed to native interpretations, but the one does not eliminate the need for the other. Unfortunately, in a few instances, the analyst-collector suggests that his interpretation is really the natives' own interpretation. Melville Jacobs, for example, tries to "see the literature as it appeared to Chinooks,"[7] but one wonders if the Chinooks would have agreed with Jacobs' interpretations. Jacobs has reconstructed oral literary criticism but this may not be the same as the oral literary criticism he might have collected. The nature of his criticism is revealed in his discussion of Clackamas Chinook[8] humor when he speaks of his methodology. ". . . I enumerated 130 instances in the Clackamas collection *where I was certain* that an audience at a folkloristic recital responded with smiles or laughter" or ". . . I took each of the 130 fun situations and attempted to pinpoint each fun-generating factor or stimulus to humor *which I believe* to have been present in them" make the analytic bias clear.[9] Jacobs was not present at a Clackamas Chinook tale-telling session—he collected the tales from a highly acculturated informant in relative isolation—and he can give little more than educated guesses. Even in our own culture, it would be difficult to guess whether or not a "funny" story got a laugh and more particularly to know just at what points in the joke laughs were stimulated. One must not only record laughter (distinguishing types of laughter—a giggle, a belly-laugh), but one must try to find out what was funny and why the audience members laughed or did not laugh.

It is not easy to collect oral literary criticism. Much of it has probably never been consciously formulated. Yet the meanings and traditional interpretations of folkloristic materials are transmitted from individual to individual and from generation to generation just as is folklore itself. But some types of oral literary criticism are easier to collect than others and it might be well to mention them first.

One source of oral literary criticism comes from folklore itself

---

7. Melville Jacobs, *The Content and Style of an Oral Literature* (Chicago, 1959), p. 3.

8. [Northwest American Indian group.]

9. *Ibid.*, pp. 178–179. Italics mine.

rather than directly from the folk. There are a limited number of folkloristic commentaries on folklore. As there is a term "metalanguage" to refer to linguistic statements about language, so we may suggest "metafolklore" to refer to folkloristic statements about folklore. Examples of metafolklore or the "folklore of folklore" would be proverbs about proverbs, jokes about joke cycles, folksongs about folksongs and the like. Metafolklore is not necessarily intra-genre. There are proverbs about myths, for example. The previously cited Yoruba proverb would be an instance of metafolklore. It is a folkloristic commentary about a folklore genre, namely, the proverb. "A proverb is like a horse: when the truth is missing, we use a proverb to find it." This clearly indicates an attitude towards a key function of proverbs in Yoruba culture, the function being the determination of truth in problem situations or disputes. Of course, since metafolklore is still, after all, folklore, it is necessary to elicit oral literary criticism of the metafolkloristic texts themselves. The meaning of the Yoruba proverb, according to one informant, is that by mounting a horse, as opposed to goats, sheep, dogs, and other animals found among the Yoruba, one can quickly obtain a superior perspective. From the back of a horse, one can see further than one can from the ground and the immediate local problem may be seen in a new and better light. A proverb is like the horse inasmuch as it also provides a speedy and efficacious means of getting above the immediate problem-situation and of placing it in a perspective which is more likely to result in finding a just and proper solution.

An example of a metafolkloristic joke is the following: It was a dark and stormy night and this guy goes up to this old farm house. He's a salesman and he says to the farmer, "I'm a salesman, my car broke down, and I need a place to stay." And the farmer says, "That's all right, but there's just one thing, we have no extra rooms to spare so you'll have to sleep with my son." And the salesman says, "Oh my God, I must be in the wrong joke." Here is a folk comment on the nature of the traveling salesman joke cycle. Invariably the jokes involve the seduction of the farmer's daughter and/or wife. In most jokes in the cycle, as you may know, the farmer explains to the salesman that he can stay but that the only available space is in his daughter's room. This is thus a joke about a joke cycle and it draws attention to one of the critical content features of the cycle. Once again, one could elicit oral literary criticism of this bit of metafolklore. One might find, for example, that the substitution of homosexuality for heterosexuality is particularly significant in the light of our culture's taboo against homosexual activities. The mere suggestion of such activities to a traveling salesman, the epitome of unrestrained heterosexual impulse, is so shocking as to call a halt to the story. In other words, at the very mention of homosexuality, the American male wants out because this activity is "wrong": the salesman is in the *wrong* joke. (The breaking out of the joke is analogous to the breaking of the "fourth wall" in theatrical parlance. Actors normally regard the proscenium as the fourth wall of a room. Occasionally, an actor will break the convention and will speak directly to the audience. Some plays, like this traveling salesman joke, specifically call for the breaking of the conventional vehicle.)

Sometimes the metafolklore may comment on the formal features rather than on the content of folklore. For example, consider the following metafolkloristic joke based upon the "knock, knock" cycle.

Knock!
Who's there?
Opportunity.

Here attention is drawn to the distinct characteristic reduplicative opening formula of jokes in this cycle: knock, knock. The use of just one "knock" is incorrect, but is rationalized by reference to a proverb: "opportunity only knocks once." Such parodies of and plays on folkloristic forms can be useful sources of the folk's own attitudes towards their folklore.

Another source of overt literary criticism besides metafolkloristic texts consists of the asides or explanatory commentary made by raconteurs as they tell tales or sing songs. These asides are sometimes unwisely eliminated by the overscrupulous editor but they should not be. Two examples from a Potawatomi[10] informant may illustrate the nature of these asides. At the beginning of one tale, my informant said, "Well there was once, there was a little boy. There was always a little boy, you know, and . . ."[11] The line "There was always a little boy" is a folk confirmation of one of the important characteristics of certain folktales, namely that the protagonist is a little boy. Such a comment might be particularly valuable if the folklorist-collector did not know in advance what kinds of tales were in his informant's repertoire. The comment indicates that there are a great many tales with little boys in them and it also serves to authenticate the particular tale he is recounting. It is as if to say that traditional tales must have little boys in them as protagonists and so in this traditional tale I am about to tell there is this required stereotyped character.

10. [Midwestern American Indian group.]

11. This first example was published, see Alan Dundes, "The Study of Folklore in Literature and Culture: Identification and Interpretation," *Journal of American Folklore*, 78 (1965), 139. The second example has not yet been published.

Another self-critical aside made by my informant came in a version of *Big Turtle's War Party*. In the mock plea (Motif K 581.1, drowning punishment for turtle) episode, the villagers are devising ways to kill the captured turtle. First they discuss throwing him into a kettle of boiling water, but the turtle threatens to splash the water and scald their children. Next, the villagers suggest tying him to a tree and shooting him with buckshot—at which point the narrator observed "I don't know whether they had any buckshot in those days or not" before concluding with the final throwing of the turtle into a river à la the tarbaby rabbit into the briar patch.[12] This commentary challenges the historical accuracy of the tale. Given the time setting of this American Indian tale—when animals were like people, the occurrence of such an obvious acculturated element of material culture as buckshot upset the sensibilities of my sensitive storyteller. However, he did not deny or alter the traditional tale as he knew it. He merely inserted a partial disclaimer, thereby expressing his own parenthetical doubts.

The problem with metafolklore and with the raconteur's asides is that they provide at best only an incomplete picture of the folk's evaluation of their folklore. For some folklore, no metafolklore has been recorded; for some genres few asides have been published. What is needed is the rigorous and systematic elicitation of oral literary criticism. A tale or song might be treated by the folklorist-collector much as a modern psychiatrist treats a dream. As the psychiatrist asks his dreamer-patient to "free associate" and to comment on the various elements in the dream, so the folklorist-collector should ask his informant to "free associate" in the same manner, attempting to explain or comment on each element in the tale. Too often the text-hungry folklorist immediately after the recitation of a tale or song will say, "That's fine, do you know any more like that . . ." and he will not patiently seek to have the informant provide a folk exegesis of the tale just told. Perhaps the collector should consider the item of folklore collected as a projective test or should we say "projective text" and in that event he should ask the informant to make up a story about the story.

Even more desirable would be to elicit the oral literary criticisms of both raconteur and audience. The meaning for the tale teller is not necessarily the same as the meaning for the audience or rather the different meanings for different members of the audience. It is incred-

12. [The motif of punishing the turtle by throwing it into a river (its home) is analogous to the conclusion of the famous folktale of the rabbit and the tarbaby best known in Joel Chandler Harris's "Uncle Remus" version collected from blacks. After Bre'r Rabbit is trapped by the doll made of sticky tar, he begs not to be thrown into a briar patch for punishment, and of course that is where his captors do throw him—right where he has lived all his life.]

ible that folklorists speak of *the* meaning of a folktale. Moreover, the existence of multiple meanings suggests communications blocks. One might assume that if A and B, members of the same culture, both know a given folklore text that this text serves as a strong bond linking A and B. However, if A and B interpret the text differently, then A's addressing it to B might result in misunderstanding rather than understanding. The following may serve to illustrate multiple meanings.

There is a folk metaphor (proverbial phrase) "to have an axe to grind" and to me it means to have a bias as a lobbyist might have. If I said, "Watch out for so and so, he has an axe to grind," I would be warning against accepting what that individual said at face value inasmuch as his words or actions would be influenced by what I considered to be a vested interest. Archer Taylor told me that he thought the metaphor connoted the asking of a favor inasmuch as it takes two men to grind an axe, one to spin the whetstone and the other to hold the axe. Thus if one individual came to another and announced that he had an axe to grind, he would be asking the other person to stop what he was doing and help him grind the axe. The dictionary supports this interpretation by saying "to have an object of one's own to gain or promote."[13] However, there is another traditional meaning of this metaphor, the meaning of "grudge". According to informants, "to have an axe to grind" is similar to having a "bone to pick" with someone. One informant related that if he had neglected to do one of his assigned household chores, say taking out the garbage at the end of the day, the next morning his mother would say to him "I've got an axe to grind with you, you didn't take the garbage out last night." The informant explained that "I've got an axe to grind with you" meant "There's going to be friction, i.e., sparks were going to fly, just as sparks fly when an axe is ground." (I discovered that my wife also uses this meaning. Our neighbor's dog occasionally knocks over and rifles our garbage can. My wife indicated that she would think it appropriate to call up our neighbor and say, "I have an axe to grind with you," meaning there was something she was angry about.) Here then are two distinct interpretations of the same folk metaphor.

In some instances the meaning may be fairly constant, but the evaluation of the common meaning may vary. For example, the proverb "A rolling stone gathers no moss" means that a person who moves around from place to place, not staying in any one place for

13. *Webster's New World Dictionary of the American Language*, College Edition (Cleveland and New York, 1960). This is the meaning found in *The Oxford Dictionary of English Proverbs* (2d ed.; Oxford, 1948), p. 17; Archer Taylor and Bartlett Jere Whiting, *A Dictionary of American Proverbs and Proverbial Phrases 1820–1880* (Cambridge, 1958), pp. 10–11.

very long, will never belong to a place, or look as though he belongs to that place. The oral literary critical difference concerns whether this is good or bad. In the older tradition, it was bad and the proverb might be cited to keep someone from roaming too far and wide, to urge him to stay at one place. But in modern usage, at least in some quarters, the accumulation of moss is considered to be a negative characteristic and the "rolling stone" is conceived of as the ideal unencumbered life. Admittedly these differences could be gleaned from printed contextual instances of the proverb in novels and newspapers, but the point is that folklore collectors ought to obtain direct oral interpretations of the proverb at the time of collection.

As has been noted, it is not always easy to elicit oral literary criticism. The folk know and use folklore without bothering to articulate their esthetic evaluations. For some types of oral literary criticism, e.g., symbolism, an indirect method of eliciting might be recommended. The problem in symbolism is that the folk may not be completely conscious of the one or more symbolic meanings of an element of folklore. This is understandable in view of the fact that it is often the taboo activities and ideas which find expression outlets in symbolic form. If the folk consciously recognized the symbolic significance of the joke or folksong element, this element might not be able to continue to serve as a safe, socially sanctioned outlet. (Cf. the popular belief that analysis of a work of art interferes with or ruins one's enjoyment of it.) Fortunately, much of the symbolism in folklore is baldly stated and may be obvious enough to some of the members of the culture concerned. But the study of symbolism would surely be greatly advanced if symbolic interpretations of folklore were obtained from the folk rather than from Freudian folklorists. No one likes to accept an *ex cathedra* pronouncement that a shoe can symbolize female genitalia. Even the folkloristic "evidence" such as is provided by nursery rhymes among other genres leaves the issue in some doubt.

> There was an old woman who lived in a shoe
> She had so many children she didn't know what to do.

People don't live in shoes and the possible connection between a woman's living in a shoe and having lots of children requires explanation. The sequel verse: "There was another old woman who lived in a shoe, she didn't have any children, she knew what to do" suggests the sexual nature of the symbolism with the implicit statement that a knowledge of contraceptive measures can allow a woman to live in a shoe and not have children. One might also consider the possible symbolism in:

> Cock a doodle doo!
> My dame has lost her shoe
> My masters' lost his fiddling stick
> And doesn't know what to do.[14]

Maybe there isn't a reference to a woman who has lost her vagina matched by a man who has lost his phallus, but if not, the logical connection between a shoeless dame and fiddle-stick-less master remains to be seen. But the point is that one should not guess at such interpretations, one should go to the primary sources and ask the folk. Let field data prove or disprove armchair guesswork. What does the shoe suggest to the informant? Can the informant draw a picture of the old woman and her shoe? Perhaps a modified Thematic Apperception Test based upon the nursery rhyme (or other folklore) can be devised and administered. While it may be true that not all informants will be equally facile in articulating oral literary criticism, some will be able to do so. Even a passive bearer of tradition (as opposed to the active bearer who tells the tale or sings the song) may be able to contribute an interpretation. Folklorists should be just as anxious to collect variant interpretations of a folksong's meaning as they are to collect variants of the folksong's text![15]

As a final argument for the collection of oral literary criticism, I would note the interpretation of the word folklore itself, especially among the folk. The meaning of "folklore" in the phrase "That's just folklore" is similar to one of the meanings of myth, namely falsehood, error, and the like. I suspect that it is this pejorative connotation which has encouraged some folklorists to consciously avoid the term, substituting instead "verbal or spoken art," "oral or folk literature,"

14. The rhyme of the old woman who lived in a shoe is number 546 in the canonical *Oxford Dictionary of Nursery Rhymes*, ed. Iona and Peter Opie (Oxford, 1951). The Opies suggest (p. 435) that "the shoe has long been symbolic of what is personal to a woman until marriage." The Opies do not mention the sequel verse which dates from the 1890's in American Ozark tradition. See Joseph C. Hickerson and Alan Dundes, "Mother Goose Vice Verse," *Journal of American Folklore*, 75 (1962), 256. As for the "Cock a doodle-doo" rhyme, number 108 in the Opies' collection, one finds not even an oblique circumlocutory hint of any symbolic interpretation. Nursery rhymes should really be studied further. One wonders, for example, why the three blind mice (Opies' number 348) tried to run after the farmer's wife. If it were an Oedipal theme, then the cutting off of the presumptuous mice's tails would be appropriate symbolic castration.

15. It should be mentioned that recently a number of folklorists have observed that the meaning of the folklore to the folk must be investigated. For typical statements see G. Legman, *The Horn Book: Studies in Erotic Folklore and Bibliography* (New Hyde Park, N.Y.: University Books, 1964), p. 285; Goldstein, *op. cit.*, (Hatboro, 1964), pp. 23, 106, 140. Linda Dégh, in a description of the future tasks of folklore collectors (written in Hungarian) urges folklorists to leave the explanations to the storyteller and the members of his audience, see *Ethnographia*, 74 (1963), 1–12.

and many others. More serious is the fact that this "folk" interpretation of the word "folklore" makes it difficult for the discipline of folklore and its practitioners to gain academic status. If folklore is error, then a Ph.D. in folklore is the height of folly, and the notion of a whole discipline devoted to error is unthinkable in the academic context of the search for truth. To use the term folklore without an awareness of the folk interpretation of the term is unwise.

One final point concerns the necessity for the continued and repeated attempts to elicit oral literary criticism. It is a commonplace that each generation reinterprets anew its folklore, but do we have records of these interpretations and reinterpretations? Sometimes the text is altered to fit new needs, but probably it is the interpretation of texts which changes more. The task of collecting oral literary criticism from a folk can never be completed any more than the task of collecting folklore from that folk can be. Even if both texts and interpretations remained almost exactly the same over a long period of time, this would still be well worth knowing. It might be an important index of the overall stability of that folk. Here also is an opportunity to use the scores of texts without commentary which line library shelves and archives. These texts may be taken *back into the field* and folk *explication de textes*'s[16] sought. Our goal for future folklore collection should be fewer texts and more contexts, with accompanying detailed oral literary criticisms.

16. [A term in literary criticism meaning a detailed explanation of all nuances of a text, particularly of poetry.]

NEW DIRECTIONS FOR
THE STUDY OF AMERICAN FOLKLORE

Jan Harold Brunvand

The following is an attempt to reappraise the development of the twentieth-century American folklore scene since Stith Thompson's optimistic survey at the midcentury. My purpose was not only to summarize the gains of nearly twenty further years of research, and gather bibliography, but also to identify problem areas, appraise recent theoretical departures, spot trends, and attempt to surmise where the "new directions" in folkloristics might lead us. Whether I was successful in anything beyond the summary and bibliographic tasks is debatable, but at least the essay provides a convenient account of the primary concerns of American folklorists in recent years and where their research findings have been published. The discussion brings Thompson's survey down to the late 1960s, and I have not updated it or extended it further for this reprinting. I continue to believe that American folklore studies are best characterized as eclectic, vigorous, growing, and promising, but still plagued with definitional dilemmas. Nothing I have seen since becoming editor of the Journal of American Folklore in 1976 has changed my mind on these points.

Since no one else, to my knowledge, has taken up my suggestion of examining "social situations . . . that call for a traditional statement or gesture," I would hope that some folklore students might find that project worthwhile.

NINETEEN YEARS AGO TODAY Stith Thompson, America's leading folklorist, addressed this forum on much the same topic as mine.[1] On December 27th, 1950, in New York, Professor Thompson spoke to the Popular Literature Section of the Modern Language Association on "Folklore at Midcentury."[2] First he glanced with tolerant amusement at the enthusiasts who were attracted to academic folklore conferences: folk singers, storytellers, students of jazz and hillbilly music, and writers of children's books. Next he traced progress in collecting, archiving, advancing theories, and publishing folklore. Then Thomp-

---

1. A slightly different form of this paper was read at the annual meeting of the Modern Language Association in Denver, Colorado, U.S.A. on December 27, 1969. The revision of this paper was a preliminary stage in my study of modern Folklore in social and cultural contexts which was supported by a grant in 1970 from the John Simon Guggenheim Memorial Foundation.

2. *Midwest Folklore*, 1 (1951), 5–12.

son stressed the need to formulate a better definition of folklore, and he emphasized the relationship of folklore theory, method, and materials to other disciplines. Some of his observations were startling; he said that "We have not at all decided what we mean by folklore . . . there is now no agreement by American folklorists as to what we are talking about." Thompson further remarked that "In some ways we seem to go in circles, so that the hard-won assumptions of one generation cease to be valid in another and we have to go back and debate the same problems that our ancestors thought they had settled." Concluding, Thompson spoke positively; he said, ". . . we will doubltess have a great deal of debate . . . before we know definitely where we are going . . . [but] there is so much vigor in folklore studies that we may well be optimistic about their future in the United States during the new half-century."

Whether nearly two decades later this optimism seems justified is debatable. Many American folklorists deny that we now know definitely where we are going. Most problems Thompson saw then have remained. Folklore theory and the relations of folklore to other disciplines are continually being debated. The basic definition of folklore has not yet been formulated to anyone's complete satisfaction. And one gets the strong impression from current folklore journals that we are still going in circles. For instance, in recent numbers of the *Journal of American Folklore,* as controversy raged between younger scholars over definitions of folklore,[3] one senior statesman of the field wrote in an article that "If we have to start all over again on basic definitions there is perhaps little point in trying to communicate."[4]

Spectators on the American folklore scene since the midcentury have described much confusion. Speaking to the English Folklore Society in 1950, an American folklorist admitted:

> [My colleagues] are only just feeling their way toward a common ground, and the present moment sees much heated controversy as to aims and methods. The annual meeting frequently dissolves into scowling circles of members defending their own and lampooning their neighbors' definition of folklore.[5]

3. Roger L. Welsch, "A Note on Definitions," *Journal of American Folklore,* 81 (1968), 262–264; Richard Bauman, "Towards a Behavioral Theory of Folklore: A Reply to Roger Welsch," *Journal of American Folklore,* 82 (1969), 167–170; Roger D. Abrahams, "On Meaning and Gaming," *Journal of American Folklore,* 82 (1969), 268–270; Jan Harold Brunvand, "On Abrahams' Besom," *Journal of American Folklore,* 83 (1970), 81.

4. Richard M. Dorson, "A Theory for American Folklore Reviewed," *Journal of American Folklore,* 82 (1969), 235.

5. Richard M. Dorson, "Folklore Studies in the United States Today," *Folklore,* 62 (1951), 363.

In 1961 another card-carrying American folklorist charged that most college courses in this subject "survive on sentiment and nationalism alone."[6] In 1965 at the Yugoslav-American Folklore Seminar a speaker from the States began, "One is tempted to suggest that there have been almost as many American concepts of folklore as there have been American folklorists."[7]

American Folklore Society presidential addresses are characterized by recurring unfulfilled dreams. In 1950 the retiring president observed that "trying to define folklore seems to be a favorite pastime of its devotees."[8] In 1955 the AFS president's topic was "Undeveloped Areas in American Folklore", and he had a long list.[9] In 1958 the keynote was that "the mandate to synthesize our work grows greater year by year."[10] The most biting denunciation of past scholarship was Melville Jacobs' 1964 presidential speech. After demolishing the prevailing scholarly approaches to folk narratives, Jacobs concluded that the only hope for "measurable advance" lay in a beginning completely anew "by as many folklorists as can manage to reorient themselves."[11]

The most hopeful state-of-the-discipline message from a recent American Folklore Society president was Richard M. Dorson's in 1968. He had proposed a "Theory for American Folklore" in 1957 which was discussed in a symposium at the time[12] and then provided the frame for his textbook two years later.[13] Dorson's "Theory" rejected specialized approaches to American folklore and urged viewing it against the full background of American civilization. In 1968 Dorson conceded that his formal "Theory" had quickly dropped out of sight, apart from his own book, but in a new group of "fresh and exciting works of scholarship" he found evidence of what he called "a predominantly humanistic folklore method, concerned . . . with the

6. Tristram P. Coffin, "Folklore in the American Twentieth Century," *American Quarterly*, 13 (1961), 526–533.

7. Alan Dundes, "The American Concept of Folklore," *Journal of the Folklore Institute*, 3 (1966), 226–245.

8. A. H. Gayton, "Perspectives in Folklore," *Journal of American Folklore*, 64 (1951), 147–150. These AFS presidential addresses are usually published a year or two later in *JAF*.

9. Herbert Halpert, "Some Undeveloped Areas in American Folklore," *Journal of American Folklore*, 70 (1957), 299–305.

10. Wayland D. Hand, "American Folklore After Seventy Years: Survey and Prospects," *Journal of American Folklore*, 73 (1960), 1–11.

11. Melville Jacobs, "A Look Ahead in Oral Literature Research," *Journal of American Folklore*, 79 (1966), 413–427.

12. John Ball, Ed., "A Theory for American Folklore: A Symposium," *Journal of American Folklore*, 72 (1959), 197–242.

13. *American Folklore* (Chicago, 1959).

reality of interpreting the human spirit in its manifold cultural settings."[14]

My own feeling is that although the study of American folklore has appeared to advance only by fits and starts for the past two decades, this period has shaped the direction of future research, so that presently we are progressing better than ever before in the eighty-two year history of organized American folklore research towards a new science of folklore in this country.

There has been real and measurable progress. Several graduate programs have become well entrenched, and advanced degree holders in folklore are flowing from these mills.[15] Consequently, undergraduate folklore courses are multiplying and improving.[16] A field collector's guide for American folklore was published in 1964.[17] The "folksong revival" boomed in the '50's and busted in the '60's, leaving its scholarly tracks behind when the American Folklore Society published in 1968 a history of Country-Western music.[18] Partly a spin-off from folklore studies is the academic respectability of American popular culture. The European folklife movement which emphasizes customary and material traditions reached the States in 1965 when a Folklife Committee was established by the American Folklore Society, followed by publication of important area studies in American folklife.[19] Over the past twenty years folklorists' share of the grants and fellowships pie has become more generous.

One significant development has been for the American Folklore Society to hold its annual meetings independently. The last year we met with the Modern Language Association was 1964, and the last year with the American Anthropological Association was 1965. Since then we have swung out into our own orbit, and the group has been alive and well in Boston, Toronto, Bloomington, Atlanta, and Los

14. "A Theory for American Folklore Reviewed," *Journal of American Folklore*, 82 (1969), 244.

15. See Richard M. Dorson, "The American Folklore Scene, 1963," *Folklore*, 74 (1963), 433–449.

16. See Robert J. Adams, "A Functional Approach to Introductory Folklore," *The Folklore Forum*, 1 (1968), 1–3 and Tom Burns, "Involving the Introductory Student of Folklore in the Functional Analysis of the Materials He Collects," *The Folklore Forum*, Bibliographical and Special Series No. 2 (1969), 13–27.

17. Kenneth S. Goldstein, *A Guide for Field Workers in Folklore*, Memoirs of the American Folklore Society, No. 52 (Hatboro, Pennsylvania, 1964).

18. Bill C. Malone, *Country Music, U.S.A.*, Memoirs of the American Folklore Society, No. 54 (Austin, Texas, 1968).

19. Henry H. Glassie, *Pattern in the Material Folk Culture of the Eastern United States*, University of Pennsylvania Monographs in Folklore and Folklife, No. 1 (Philadelphia, 1969); Austin E. and Alta Fife and Henry H. Glassie, *Forms Upon the Frontier: Folklife and Folk Arts in the United States*, Utah State University Monograph Series, No. 16 (Logan, Utah, 1969).

Angeles. The number of members who come to our annual potlatch of
jobs and ideas allows us to hold double and triple simultaneous sessions of papers for three days.

I felt confident enough in the stability of the discipline to publish in
1968 an introductory textbook called *The Study of American Folklore*[20]—a title as audacious as Child's The *English and Scottish Popular Ballads.* The book is notable for what it gets away with: a formal
definition of folklore, a detailed classification of genres, and numerous
examples of sub-categories. I included chapters on folklife subjects,
along with sample studies of customary and material folklore. I quoted
more currently viable folklore than archaic tradition, and I even
smuggled in samples of anti-social and obscene folklore. The book was
calmly accepted and is used in classes from Berkeley to Slipper Rock.
If this does not seem remarkable, consider that in 1949 twenty-one
members of the editorial board for a "standard dictionary" of folklore
could not even agree upon a common definition of the term.[21]

I certainly do not believe that my textbook has ended all debates in
American folklore studies. In fact it has started some new debates, and
one of the latest published comments on it contends that its "greatest
weakness . . . is in the area of definitions."[22] But I do see evidence
here that if American folklorists have not yet sighted precisely where
they are going, they are at least *possibly* on the verge of doing so, or
they are *at least* moving forward together. This, I think, is largely
because the earlier concepts of folklore in the United States are now
generally recognized to be outmoded.

As Richard Dorson has pointed out, "In the United States, folklore
has customarily meant the spoken and sung traditions."[23] It is not
that Americans are deficient in behavioral or material traditions, but
only that most students of American folklore emphasized the spoken
word. Since the early folklorists had backgrounds in philology, the
study of American folklore became verbal-centered and abstractly
analytical. In the majority of past American folklore studies the subject matter was "texts," the methodology was comparative and historical. Thus, the carefully transcribed words of verbal folklore variants
were systematically classified and compared in order to attempt to
discover their place and time of origin and their paths of dissemination. The steps for such studies were worked out by European and
American folklorists in the historic-geographic method, which yielded

20. *The Study of American Folklore: An Introduction* (New York, 1968).

21. See *Funk and Wagnall's Standard Dictionary of Folklore, Mythology, and
Legend,* 2 vols. (New York, 1949).

22. Roger D. Abrahams, "On Meaning and Gaming," *Journal of American
Folklore,* 82 (1969), 268–270.

23. *American Folklore,* p. 2.

interesting—if limited—results for folktales, and was applied occasionally to riddles, ballads, and children's games.

But the historic-geographic method really did not fit American folklore well, not even purely verbal lore. Our traditions lack the time-
depth and the relative freedom from the influence of mass communications that such studies require for validity. Besides, American folklorists' interest has turned less to the history of folklore items and
more to their contemporary functions and meanings. Therefore, it is
not surprising to find that the only full-scale study of this type made in
the United States with national material was Thompson's own analysis
of an American Indian myth.

One characteritstic direction that studies have taken is toward the
analysis of texts in social and cultural contexts.[24] Recent American
folklore scholars have studied folklore agianst the background of a
region,[25] a racial or religious group,[26] an occupation,[27] a social-
economic class,[28] or an aspect of the popular culture.[29] Another new
approach is studying the customary occasions for folklore transmission, such as the social contexts for dispensing proverbial wisdom,
riddle sessions, joke-telling situations, folkgame behavior, and especially the functions of folklore in such settings.[30] Still other approaches developing in the United States recently include the structural, psychological, or rhetorical analysis of folklore.[31]

24. Alan Dunes, "Texture, Text, and Context," *Southern Folklore Quarterly*,
28 (1964), 251–265.

25. Austin E. and Alta Fife, *Saints of Sage and Saddle: Folklore Among the
Mormons* (Bloomington, Indiana, 1956).

26. Roger D. Abrahams, *Deep Down in the Jungle: Negro Narrative Folklore
from the Streets of Philadelphia* (Hatboro, Pennsylvania, 1964); Jerome R. Mintz,
*Legends of the Hasidim: An Introduction to Hasidic Culture and Oral Tradition
in the New World* (Chicago, 1968).

27. Mody C. Boatright, *Folklore of the Oil Industry* (Dallas, Texas, 1963).

28. Archie Green, "John Neuhaus: Wobbly Folklorist," *Journal of American
Folklore*, 73 (1960), 189–217.

29. Alan Dundes, "Advertising and Folklore," *New York Folklore Quarterly*, 19
(1963), 143–151; Charles Keil, *Urban Blues* (Chicago, 1966); Tom Burns,
"Folklore in the Mass Media: Television," *The Folklore Forum*, 2 (1969), 90–106.

30. William Bascom, "Four Functions of Folklore," *Journal of American Folk-
lore*, 67 (1954), 333–349; William Hugh Jansen, "The Esoteric-Exoteric Factor in
Folklore," *Fabula*, 2 (1959), 205–211; Alan Dundes, "The Number Three in
American Culture," in *Every Man His Way*, Ed. Dundes (Englewood Cliffs, New
Jersey, 1968), pp. 401–424.

31. Alan Dundes, "From Etic to Emic Units in the Structural Study of Folk-
tales, *Journal of American Folklore*, 75 (1962), 95–105; Dundes, "On Game
Morphology: A Study of the Structures of Non-Verbal Folklore," *New York
Folklore Quarterly*, 20 (1964), 276–288 [reprinted above, pp. 334–344]; Butler
Waugh, "Structural Analysis in Literature and Folklore," *Western Folklore*, 25
(1966), 153–164; Roger D. Abrahams, "Introductory Remarks to a Rhetorical
Theory of Folklore," *Journal of American Folklore*, 81 (1968), 143–158; Abra-
hams "A Rhetoric of Everyday Life: Traditional Conversational Genres," *Southern*

It is encouraging for the future that the liveliest present folklore journal is published by graduate students. The *Folklore Forum* began in 1968 at Indiana University as an eight-page mimeographed leaflet. It grew quickly, and even spawned a separate "Bibliographic and Special Series" by the end of the year. In 1969 the *Forum* added book reviews, campus representatives at the other folklore centers, and an annual prize for outstanding scholarship. Articles in the *Folklore Forum* have treated such topics as folk games and game theory, folklore in the mass media, and the growth of modern legends. This is the only American folklore journal in which editorial stands are taken and in which problems of teaching folklore courses in the university are regularly discussed.

Further evidence of progress among American folklorists lies in the continuing debate over the definition of folklore. Players in the definitions game now understand that we are through with the strictly literary, thematic, analytical concepts of folk genres.[32] Under the influence of anthropology, sociology, psycholinguistics, and communications theory, those who would formulate a better definition are now doing it in terms of interpersonal relations, interaction rituals, or other communicative processes.

With luck, a definition might be arrived at without the social-science jargon that led one recent writer to suggest this: ". . . a set of parametric dichotomies as a means of defining the realm of folklore communication in such a way that it can be related to other kinds of behavior at the level of each cut."[33] What he is advocating here is simply finding some rules for slicing the traditional behavior away from the rest in any given culture. A better statement of the same approach comes from a provocative article on "ethnic genres." The author suggests that "It is possible to consider an ethnic [folklore] genre as a verbal art form which consists of . . . thematic and behavioral attributes . . . [and their position in] the folkloric system."[34] From this base the folklorist would examine a performance of folklore items, just as a linguist does spoken usage, in order to isolate the patterns of traditional language and behavior that belong to each total transmission situation, and then to write a descriptive "grammar of folklore."

Folklore Quarterly, 32 (1968), 44–59. For recent American folklore theory in general, see also Richard M. Dorson, "Current Folklore Theories," *Current Anthropology*, 4 (1963), 93–112 and Alan Dundes, "Metafolklore and Oral Literary Criticism," *The Monist*, 50 (1966), 505–516. [reprinted above, pp. 404–415]

32. Dan Ben-Amos, "Analytical Categories and Ethnic Genres," *Genre*, 2 (1969), 275–301.

33. See Bauman, as cited in footnote 3.

34. See Ben-Amos, as cited in footnote 32.

For instance, we might study what the social situations are that call for a traditional statement or gesture of consolation. What the unwritten rules are by which we unselfconsciously select the "correct" responses from our total traditional repertoire.

If an acquaintance suffers a loss or a disappointment, we might cry tears of sympathy, slap him on the back, lay a hand on his shoulder, or cross our fingers so it doesn't get worse, because (we vaguely remember) "bad luck comes in threes." Some situations call for telling an encouraging anecdote, or a story about worse cases, or a joke. Folk sayings appropriate for such times may reflect physical gestures:

> Chin up!
> Thumbs up!
> Keep a stiff upper lip.

Or they may offer advice:

> Don't take it so hard.
> Have a good cry.
> It could be worse.

Or they may consist of sententious maxims:

> Every cloud has a silver lining.
> Into each life some rain must fall.
> If at first you don't succeed, try try again.

Or they may advise resignation:

> What will be will be.
> Take it as it comes.
> It's just one of those things.
> That's life.
> Nobody's perfect.

Or they may even be satirical:

> That's the way the ball bounces (or the cookie crumbles)
> If at first you don't succeed, try try a gun.
> Things are tough all over.
> Don't tell me your troubles.
> Tell it to the Marines.

This study would describe the consolation of folk philosophy and would distinguish such tradition-directed behavior from practical aid, professional help, spiritual counsel, psychological compensation or other non-folk mechanisms. Probably no one presently can fully describe such an unselfconscious traditional system, even though we could all instantly detect a foreigner's or a child's clumsy mistakes in the system. In such an area we learn from experience and we perfect through trial and error a sense of which responses the members of our society will accept as proper expressions of consolation. We have a whole battery of other stereotyped responses regarded as appropriate for other situations, whether congratulations, or danger, or embarrassment, or frustration, or alienation, or self-awareness, or insecurity, or whatever. Folklore, in these contexts, is seen to be much more than just recreational songs, stories, or sayings. It becomes meaningful, functional, and relevant to daily living.

As American folklorists continue to explore clusters of traditional words and behavior patterns, they will increasingly want to use or adapt the techniques of other humanistic studies and of the social sciences. In a perceptive article published in 1963, University of Texas folklorist Roger D. Abrahams has suggested that American folklorists rightly have used many methods to study diverse kinds of materials, but that the total discipline as it is practiced in this country is not, as it might appear, chaotic, but rather, eclectic. As Abrahams put it, "salvation lies in eclecticism—the use of as many points of view as possible to cast light on folklore and the culture within which it exists."[35] Abrahams followed this article with a book and a series of articles that developed in practice his basic ideas.[36] The emphasis in his (and others') most recent work is on modern folklore as *process*—a living process in which there is a continual "conflict between stability and change"; the scholar proceeds by trying to "look at each piece of folklore as an organism [which] lives and dies or mutates" according to people's changing needs for it.[37] This, I believe, shows where the action is in current studies of American folklore.

In contrast, I will indicate one example that strikes me as a wrong direction for future studies. John Wilson Foster of the University of Oregon has published an article titled "The Plight of Current Folklore Theory."[38] Foster stated that basic in any definition of folklore are the concepts of a "tendency to persist" versus a "tendency to transform"—"conservation" versus "dynamics." He suggested that studies of biological evolution suggest a methodology for folklore research. Then he and a colleague published a follow-up piece in which he proposed a set of terms from biology to apply to folklore—*ecological*

35. "Folklore in Culture: Notes Toward an Analytic Method," *Texas Studies in Literature and Language*, 5 (1963), 98–110. [reprinted above, pp. 390–403]

36. See the book cited in footnote 26, the articles cited in footnote 31, and "The Complex Relations of Simple Forms," *Genre*, 2 (1969), 104–128.

37. Abrahams, "Folklore in Culture" (see footnote 35), pp. 101–102.

38. *Southern Folklore Quarterly*, 32 (1968), 237–248.

succession, panmictic type, convergence, radiation, and so forth.[39] In the first place, both the stability and change concept and the biological analogy were present, as illustrated above, in Abrahams' 1963 article (which Foster does not cite) and, in fact, even in earlier European writers (as Abrahams carefully points out). In the second place, Foster unlike Abrahams has made no effort yet to demonstrate his theories in practical studies, but rather seems to be trapped in his own rhetoric. He merely proposes impressive new (or rather, borrowed) terms like *ecological isolation* or *variant flow* for workable familiar terms like *regional folk group* or *oral transmission.* Sometimes Foster defines one metaphor using another; for example, he defines *ecological niche* as "a *constellation* of environmental factors" and he defines *texture* (that is, style) as the " '*coloration*' of a folklore item." I suggest that the terms and basic methods of folklore analysis should not come from any science except those that study cultures, and especially from linguistics, anthropology, literary criticism, psychology, and sociology. The progressive direction that American folklore studies are taking is not towards such totally new reorientations of our thinking, but rather towards a successful integration of the humanistic and anthropological approaches to folklore that existed in past scholarship. Thus, I believe that Stith Thompson was right in 1950 suggesting that the eclecticism and the vigor of American folklore studies promised them a secure future.

The picture in the crystal ball, then, looks like the following to me, and in another twenty years or so someone else will have to say whether I saw it clearly or not:

We should soon have an acceptable definition of folklore to reflect our general tacit agreement that folklore is that part of our culture which displays a measure of traditional stability balanced by dynamic change and informal transmission from person to person. The future student of the American folk and their lore will have to collect and handle this data like a traditional folklorist, but he will also have to penetrate into its human dynamics like a sociologist, read the language of texts like a psycholinguist, learn to sense implied meanings like an unselfconscious native informant, explicate style and structure like a New Critic,[40] and explore contexts like a cultural anthropologist. A truly comprehensive approach—which I see emerging now in current American folklore research—requires considering folklore

---

39. J. Barre Toelken and John Wilson Foster, "A Descriptive Nomenclature for the Study of Folklore," *Western Folklore*, 28 (1969), 91–111.

40. [Member of the group of mostly American literary critics who advocated close reading and explanation of the texts themselves as the best way to interpret literature.]

simultaneously as a mirror of culture, a projective screen for personality, a response to individual needs and desires, and an artistic expression with its own structures and aesthetics. The study of American folklore should, in short, reveal how individuals project and reflect upon and even modify the ethos of their own culture by means of that unofficial, traditional, and ever-varying part of culture which we loosely call "folklore."

TOWARD A DEFINITION OF
FOLKLORE IN CONTEXT

Dan Ben-Amos

The first number of the Journal of American Folklore for 1971 was devoted to publishing a collection of thirteen theoretical papers (edited by Richard Bauman) titled "Toward New Perspectives in Folklore." This special JAF issue, also published as a book in 1972 by the University of Texas Press, signaled a turning point in the study of folklore in the United States; it provided what Bauman called a "reorientation from the traditional focus upon folklore as 'item' . . . [and] an emphasis upon performance as an organizing principle." The following essay by Dan Ben-Amos was the first paper in the collection, and it has been probably the most influential and most frequently quoted American folklore study of recent years. In fact, Ben-Amos's attempt to settle American folklorists' definitional problems had been vigorously debated even before its publication. The notes and responses cited in footnote 3 of the preceding article ("New Directions for the Study of American Folklore") all refer to a preliminary version of this paper read at the 1967 annual meeting of the American Folklore Society.

Ben-Amos was a spokesman for many younger American folklorists of the 1960s who abandoned the item-oriented definitions of folklore held by many of their teachers for the "folklore in context" approach advocated by anthropologists and sociologists. The use of the word "toward" in the titles of several recent papers indicates a tentative acceptance of the "new perspectives," or at least an uncertainty about just where the reorientation may eventually lead. Many writers had criticized past definitions of folklore, but Ben-Amos offered the most complete and consistent critique and the most inclusive new definition. He is careful to distinguish his approach from that of other recent writers who have proposed methodologies based on folklore as a process; Roger D. Abrahams' approach, for example, as represented in the first essay in this section, does not satisfy Ben-Amos's demand for a method "not only to study but to define folklore in its context." (See his footnotes 37 and 38 and the related discussion.)

The definition which Ben-Amos proposes is that "folklore is artistic communication in small groups"—eliminating the once necessary terms "tradition" and "oral transmission." And having dispensed with these dimensions of folklore, Ben-Amos is ready to discard the usual approach to folklore study of collection, classification, and analysis. In short, his article is nothing less than revolutionary.

The debate goes on about Ben-Amos's program for future studies and the entire new approach to folklore study which it represents. Certainly a number of fundamental questions remain unanswered, including "How 'artistic' is an obscene gesture or a strong negative stereotype expressed in a joke or saying?" (or are these genres no longer folklore in the new scheme of things?); "Who is communicated with if a superstitious person knocks on wood or performs some other private ritual? (or is it the original communication of these actions to him that is folklore?); and "Just how large or small is a 'small group'?" (or does it matter?). Questions within questions and problems on top of problems—it is not likely that American folklore studies will stagnate in the next decade or for a long time.

DEFINITIONS OF FOLKLORE are as many and varied as the versions of a well-known tale. Both semantic and theoretical differences have contributed to this proliferation. The German *Volkskunde*, the Swedish *folkminne*, and the Indian *lok sahitya* all imply slightly different meanings that the English term "folklore" cannot syncretize completely.[1] Similarly, anthropologists and students of literature have projected their own bias into their definitions of folklore. In fact, for each of them folklore became the exotic topic, the green grass on the other side of the fence, to which they were attracted but which, alas, was not in their own domain. Thus, while anthropologists regarded folklore as literature, scholars of literature defined it as culture.[2] Folklorists themselves resorted to enumerative,[3] intuitive,[4] and opera-

1. For a discussion of each of these terms see respectively Gerhard Lutz, *Volkskunde: Ein Handbuch zur Geschichte ihrer Probleme* (Berlin, 1958); Åke Hultkrantz, *General Ethnological Concepts* (Copenhagen, 1960), 243–247; Manne Eriksson, "Problems of Ethnological and Folkloristic Terminology with Regard to Scandinavian Material and Languages," in *Papers of the International Congress of European and Western Ethnology Stockholm* 1951, ed. Sigurd Erixon (Stockholm, 1955), 37–40; Trilochan Pande, "The Concept of Folklore in India and Pakistan," *Schweizerisches Archiv für Volkskunde*, 59 (1963), 25–30. For a general survey of this problem see Elisée Legros, *Sur les mons et les tendances du folklore* (Liège, 1962).

2. Compare, for example, the definitions of Melville J. Herskovits and William R. Bascom with those of Aurelio Espinosa and MacEdward Leach in *The Funk and Wagnalls Standard Dictionary of Folklore, Mythology, and Legend*, ed. Maria Leach and Jerome Fried (New York, 1949), 398–400.

3. William Thomas, "Folklore," in *The Study of Folklore*, ed. Alan Dundes (Englewood Cliffs, N.J., 1965), 5; Alan Dundes, "What Is Folklore?" in *The Study of Folklore*, 1–3; Samuel P. Bayard, "The Materials of Folklore," *Journal of American Folklore*, 66 (1953), 9–10.

4. Benjamin A. Botkin, *A Treasury of American Folklore* (New York, 1944), xxi; Francis Lee Utley, "A Definition of Folklore," in *Our Living Traditions: An Introduction to American Folklore*, ed. Tristram P. Coffin (New York, 1968), 3–14.

tional[5] definitions; yet, while all these certainly contributed to the clarification of the nature of folklore, at the same time they circumvented the main issue, namely, the isolation of the unifying thread that joins jokes and myths, gestures and legends, costumes and music into a single category of knowledge.

The difficulties experienced in defining folklore are genuine and real. They result from the nature of folklore itself and are rooted in the historical development of the concept. Early definitions of folklore were clouded by romantic mist and haunted by the notion of the "popular antiquities," which Thoms[6] sought to replace. Implicit in these definitions are criteria of the antiquity of the material, the anonymity or collectiveness of composition, and the simplicity of the folk—all of which are circumstantial and not essential to folklore. The age of a song, for example, establishes it chronologically; the identification of the composer describes it historically; and its association with a particular group defines it socially. Each of these factors has an explanatory and interpretive value, but none of them defines the song as folklore. Thus, the principles that united "customs, observance, superstitions, ballads, proverbs, etc." in Thoms' initial definition of folklore were not intrinsic to these items and could only serve as a shaky framework for the development of a scientific discipline concentrating upon them.

Subsequent attempts to construct a definition that would hold together all these apparently diversified phenomena encountered a difficulty inherent in the nature of folklore. On the one hand, folklore forms—like mentifacts and artifacts—are superorganic in the sense that once created their indigenous environment and cultural context are not required for their continuous existence.[7] Background information may be essential for the analytical interpretation of the materials, but none of it is crucial for the sheer existence of the folklore forms. Tales and songs can shift media, cross language boundaries, pass from one culture to another, and still retain sufficient traces of similarity to enable us to recognize a core of sameness in all their versions. Folk art objects can outlive their users and even exist when their culture as a whole has become extinct, so that they are literally survivals of ancient times. A folk musician nowadays can perform for millions of people on a television network, in a style and manner that

5. Francis Lee Utley, "Folk Literature: An Operational Definition," *Journal of American Folklore*, 74 (1961), 193–206. Reprinted in Dundes, *The Study of Folklore*, 7–24.

6. [W. J. Thoms coined the word "folklore" in 1846, and his ideas are often taken as a starting point when redefining the term to suit modern needs.]

7. For a discussion of the implications of the concept of the superorganic see David Bidney *Theoretical Anthropology* (New York, 1953), 129–131.

approximate his own singing and playing in the midst of his own small group, thus extending his art far beyond his social circle. In sum, the materials of folklore are mobile, manipulative, and transcultural.

On the other hand, folklore is very much an organic phenomenon in the sense that it is an integral part of culture. Any divorce of tales, songs, or sculptures from their indigenous locale, time, and society inevitably introduces qualitative changes into them. The social context, the cultural attitude, the rhetorical situation, and the individual aptitude are variables that produce distinct differences in the structure, text, and texture of the ultimate verbal, musical, or plastic product. The audience itself, be it children or adults, men or women, a stable society or an accidental grouping, affects the kind of folklore genre and the manner of presentation.[8] Moreover, the categorization of prose narratives into different genres depends largely on the cultural attitude toward the tales and the indigenous taxonomy of oral tradition. Thus, in the process of diffusion from one culture to another, tales may also cross narrative categories; and the same story may be myth for one group and *Märchen*[9] for another. In that case the question of the actual generic classification of the tale is irrelevant, since it does not depend on any autonomous intrinsic features but rather on the cultural attitude toward it. Finally, unlike written literature, music, and fine art, folklore forms and texts are performed repeatedly by different peoples on various occasions. The performance situation, in the final analysis, is the crucial context for the available text. The particular talent of the professional or lay artist, his mood at the moment of recitation, and the response of his audience may all affect the text of his tale or song.

Thus, definitions of folklore have had to cope with this inherent duality of the subject and often did so by placing the materials of folklore in different, even conflicting perspectives. In spite of this diversification, it is possible to distinguish three basic conceptions of the subject underlying many definitions; accordingly, folklore is one of these three: a body of knowledge, a mode of thought, or a kind of art. These categories are not completely exclusive of each other. Very often the difference between them is a matter of emphasis rather than of essence; for example, the focus on knowledge and thought implies a stress on the contents of the materials and their perception, whereas the concentration on art puts the accent on the forms and the media of transmission. Nevertheless, each of these three foci involves a different range of hypotheses, relates to a distinct set of theories about

8. See Linda Dégh, "Some Questions of the Social Function of Story-telling," *Acta Ethnographica*, 6 (1957), 91–147.

9. [German word for folktales, commonly called "fairy tales" in English.]

folklore, and consequently leads toward divergent research directions.

However, since knowledge, thought, and art are broad categories of culture, folklorists have had to concentrate mainly on distinguishing their subject matter from other phenomena of the same kind. For that purpose, they have qualified folklore materials in terms of their social context, time depth, and medium of transmission. Thus, folklore is not thought of as existing without or apart from a structured group. It is not a phenomenon *sui generis*. No matter how defined, its existence depends on its social context, which may be either a geographic, linguistic, ethnic, or occupational grouping. In addition, it has required distillation through the mills of time. Folklore may be "old wine in new bottles" and also "new wine in old bottles"[10] but rarely has it been conceived of as new wine in new bottles. Finally, it has to pass through time at least partially via the channels of oral transmission. Any other medium is liable to disqualify the material from being folklore.

Further, folklorists have constructed their definitions on the basis of sets of relations between the social context, the time depth, and the medium of transmission on the one hand, and the conception of folklore as a body of knowledge, mode of thought, and kind of art on the other, as illustrated in the following table.

	Social Context	Time Depth	Medium of Transmission
Knowledge	Communal possession	Antiquity	Verbal or imitative
Thought	Collective representation	Survival	Verbal
Art	Communal creation or re-creation	Antiquity	Verbal or imitative

It is possible to distinguish three types of relations between the social context and folklore: possession, representation, and creation or re-creation. Basically, a literal interpretation of the term "folklore" sets up the first type of relationship. Accordingly, folklore is "the learning of the people,"[11] "the wisdom of the people, the people's knowledge,"[12] or more fully, "the lore, erudition, knowledge or teaching of a folk."[13] This view of folklore as the lore shared by the whole group communally applies, in practice and theory, to different degrees of public possession. First, folklore can be the sum total of knowledge

10. Botkin, xxi–xxii.

11. Charlotte Sophia Burne, *The Handbook of Folklore* (London, 1931), 1.

12. Y. M. Sokolov, *Russian Folklore* (New York, 1950), 1.

13. Ralph Steele Boggs, "Folklore: Materials, Science, Art," *Folklore Americas*, 3 (1943), 1.

in a society. Since no single member of the community has a complete command of all its facets, folklore in this sense must be an abstract construct based upon the collective information as it is stored with many individuals, "the whole body of people's traditionary beliefs and customs."[14]

Secondly, and in contrast, folklore has been considered only that knowledge shared by every member of the group. This definition excludes any esoteric information to which only selected experts in the community have access, since it restricts folklore to "popular knowledge"[15] alone. In that case, folklore is the real "common property"[16] of the community. Thirdly, this real communal lore can be expressed by the group at large in "collective actions of the multitude," as Frazer defines it,[17] including public festivities, rituals, and ceremonies in which every member of the group partakes. Lastly, folklore can be restricted to customs and observances that each individual adheres to in the privacy of his home, though all the people in the society abide by them. Although this last interpretation is theoretically possible, no definition has limited the scope of folklore so narrowly.

The construction of the second set of relations between folklore and its social context is based upon British evolutionary theory and French sociological anthropology. Accordingly, folklore represents a particular mode of collective and spontaneous thought, as André Varagnac has formulated his definition: "Le folklore, ce sont des croyances collectives sans doctrine, des pratiques collectives sans théorie."[18] In that case, the actual customs, rituals, and other observances are representations of the mode of thought that underlies them. The notion of collective thought in the context of definitions of folklore has several connotations. First it refers to the average, unexceptional thought that lacks any marks of individuality, "conventional modes of human thought."[19] Secondly, it implies the particular thinking patterns of primitive man, as they were conceived by early folklorists and anthropologists. Edwin Sidney Hartland, for example, defined tradition, the subject matter of the science of fairy tales, as "the sum total of the psychological phenomena of uncivilized man."[20] In that sense, folklore is "the expression of the psychology of early man" as it concerns any field, either philosophy, religion, science or history.

14. James G. Frazer, *Folklore in the Old Testament*, vol. 1 (London, 1919), vii.
15. Espinosa, 399.
16. Bayard, 8.
17. Frazer, vii.
18. André Varagnac, *Définition du Folklore* (Paris, 1938), 18.
19. Boggs, 1.
20. Edwin Sidney Hartland, *The Science of Fairy Tales* (London, 1891), 34.

All these aspects of thought are represented collectively in the folk-lore of the people. The conception of a special mode of thinking pertaining to primitive people was developed by Lévi-Bruhl as "the collective representation." Folklore, as other social facts, is a manifestation of this particular mode of thought. It expresses the particular mystique that characterizes primitive mentality in its perception of natural and social reality. Although Lévi-Bruhl's theories are no longer accepted without reservations, they still serve as a basis for defining folklore, as exemplified in Joseph Rysan's, "Folklore can be defined as the collective objectifications of basic emotions, such as awe, fear, hatred, reverence, and desire, on the part of the social group."[21]

When the principal of collectivity or communality is applied to the definition of folklore as art, reference is made particularly to the creation of folk literature. Two concepts have been developed in that regard: communal creation and re-creation. The first—whose main exponent in America was Francis Gummere—implies that folk songs, especially ballads, are a product of communal creation.[22] This notion, long discarded, is not as absurd as Miss Louise Pound would have liked us to believe.[23] Although its particular application to the origin of the ballad is rather doubtful, it is possible to conceive of such a process in relation to other kinds of folklore. Paul Bohannan reports a case of communal creation in the decoration of a walking stick and of other objects. Many members of the group, including the anthropologist himself, contributed to the formation of the wooden pieces.[24] Some of my own informants, composers of songs from Benin City, Midwestern Nigeria, admitted readily, and without perceiving the theoretical difficulties such admissions impose upon us, that they often composed a song alone, but that the group of singers to whom they belonged reworked it afterwards until everybody was pleased. However, by now the notion of communal creation has been completely discarded from any definition of folklore and replaced, when applicable, by the concept of communal re-creation. Archer Taylor, for example, incorporated the concept explicitly into his definition of folklore.[25] Actually this process is implied in the notion of oral transmission and the variability of the text. The concept of re-creation differs from that of creation only in regard to the duration of the

21. Joseph Rysan, "Is Our Civilization Able to Create a New Folklore?" *South Atlantic Bulletin*, 18 (1952), 10.

22. Francis B. Gummere, *The Popular Ballad* (New York, 1908).

23. Louise Pound, *Poetic Origins and the Ballad* (New York, 1921).

24. Paul Bohannan, "Artist and Critic in an African Society," in *The Artist in Tribal Society*, ed. Martin W. Smith (New York, 1961), 85–94.

25. Archer Taylor, "Folklore," *Funk and Wagnalls Standard Dictionary of Folklore, Mythology and Legend*, I, 402.

creative moment. The main feature of folklore remains the same: verbal art is the sum total of creation of a whole community over time. Actually, when this hypothesis itself is challenged, the notion of passive creativity is introduced. Accordingly, the audience reaction is as much a part of the act of creation as the active imagination of the folk artist.[26]

By its very nature, the notion of communal re-creation involves a relationship between folklore and a second factor—time depth. The persistence of the materials in circulation in a culture, "bequeathed from generation to generation,"[27] has become the determining criterion for the identification of folklore items. For Thompson "the idea of tradition is the touchstone for everything that is to be included in the term folklore."[28] According to this notion, however, there cannot be any innovation in tradition, and if there is, it still has to "live in people's mouth for at least several generations."[29] This conception of folklore was contained in the original definition of Thoms and maintained by folklorists up to the present time. Francis Utley, who made a content analysis of the definitions in the *Funk and Wagnalls Standard Dictionary of Folklore, Mythology, and Legend*, found the great preponderance of the term "tradition" to be unchallenged by any other concept.[30] The idea of tradition refers to folklore both as knowledge (the "wisdom" of the past) and as art (old songs and tales). In relation to thoughts and beliefs, the relative time depth qualifies folklore even further. It designates the materials as survivals, as implied by the evolutionary theories of Edward Tylor[31] and Andrew Lang.[32] In that case, "folklore" applies only to that item in culture that had vital currency in previous stages of human evolution and either survived the changes of time and became "a lively fossil"[33] or remained alive among those segments of society least exposed to the light of civilization.

Of the three factors, it is the medium of transmission that has been

26. See C. W. von Sydow, *Selected Papers on Folklore*, ed. Laurits Bødker (Copenhagen, 1948), 11–43; Walter Anderson, *Kaiser und Abt, die Geschichte eines Schwanks*, FFC No. 42 (Helsinki, 1923), 397–403.

27. Boggs, 1.

28. Stith Thompson, "Folklore at Midcentury," *Midwest Folklore*, 1 (1951), 11.

29. Richard M. Dorson, *Bloodstoppers and Bearwalkers: Folk Traditions of the Upper Peninsula* (Cambridge, Mass., 1952), 7.

30. Utley, "Folk Literature: An Operational Definition," 193.

31. *The Origins of Culture*, paperback edition, vol. 1 (New York, 1958), 70–159.

32. "Introduction," in *Grimm's Household Tales*, vol. 1, trans., Margaret Hunt (London, 1884), xi–lxxv.

33. Charles Francis Potter, "Folklore," *Funk and Wagnalls Standard Dictionary of Folklore, Mythology, and Legend*, 401.

the most persistent in folklore definitions. Almost from the beginning, the most accepted characteristic of folklore—whether conceived of as knowledge, thought, or art—has been its transmission by oral means. In order for an item to qualify as folklore, the prime prerequisite is that it have been in oral circulation and passed from one person to another without the aid of any written texts. When a visual, musical, or kinetic form is considered, the transmission can be through imitation.[34] The basic assumption is that this particular form of transmission introduces some distinct qualities into the materials, that would be lost otherwise. In this sense, folklore as a discipline preceded Marshall McLuhan in declaring "the medium is the message."[35]

The criterion of oral tradition has become the last citadel of folklore scholars in defending the uniqueness of their materials. When the theories about communal creation collapsed and the doctrine of survivals fell through, scholars were able to hold firm to the idea that folklore is "verbal art," "unrecorded mentifacts," and "literature orally transmitted."[36] This conception of folklore was hailed both by anthropologists who worked in nonliterate societies and by scholars of literature, who found it an operational distinction separating folklore from literature. Although folklorists concede that the purity of this transmission has often been contaminated by literary texts, the final standard for the identification of materials as folklore is the actual circulation, even once, through verbal media.

In spite of its popularity, the criterion of medium of transmission has not defined what folklore really is; it has merely provided a qualifying statement about the form of circulation. Moreover, such definitions impose a preconceived framework upon folklore. Rather than define it, they establish certain ideals as to what folklore should be. These attempts to reconcile romantic with empirical approaches actually have held back scientific research in the field and are partially responsible for the fact that, while other disciplines that emerged during the nineteenth century have made headway, folklore is still suffering growing pains.

It is still necessary to ask, "What is it that circulates verbally and is transmitted through time within a distinct social entity?" This rhetorical question in itself reflects the wrong direction that various attempts to define folklore have taken. They have searched for a way to de-

---

34. Boggs, 1.

35. Marshall McLuhan, *Understanding Media: The Extensions of Man*, paperback edition (New York, 1964), 23–39.

36. See Bascom, "Verbal Art," *Journal of American Folklore*, 68 (1955), 245–252; Elli-Kaija Köngäs-Maranda, "The Concept of Folklore," *Midwest Folklore*, 13 (1963), 85; Utley, "Folk Literature: An Operational Definition," 204.

scribe folklore as a static, tangible object. The enumerative definitions consisted of lists of objects, while the substantive definitions regarded folklore as art, literature, knowledge, or belief. In actuality, it is none of these and all of them together. Folklore does contain knowledge, it is an expression of thought, formulated artistically, but at the same time it is also a unique phenomenon which is irreducible to any of these categories.

In order to discern the uniqueness of folklore, it is first necessary to change the existing perspective we have of the subject. So far, most definitions have conceived of folklore as a collection of things. These could be either narratives, melodies, beliefs, or material objects. All of them are completed products or formulated ideas; it is possible to collect them. In fact this last characteristic has been at the base of the major portion of folklore research since its inception. The collection of things requires a methodological abstraction of objects from their actual context. No doubt this can be done; often it is essential for research purposes. Nevertheless, this abstraction is only methodological and should not be confused with, or substituted for, the true nature of the entities. Moreover, any definition of folklore on the basis of these abstracted things is bound to mistake the part for the whole. To define folklore, it is necessary to examine the phenomena as they exist. In its cultural context, folklore is not an aggregate of things, but a process—a communicative process, to be exact.

It should be pointed out that this conception of folklore differs substantially from previous views of folklore as a process. Focusing upon the dynamics of transmission, modification, and textual varia-tion,[37] such views perpetuated the dichotomy between processes and things. They stressed the transmission of objects in time and society and allowed for a methodological and theoretical separation between the narrators and their tales. These views of folklore are logically justified, since after all there is a distinction between the man and his songs, the child and his games. But the ever increasing emphasis on the situational background of tales, songs, and proverbs that developed from Malinowski's functionalism into Hymes' "ethnography of speak-ing,"[38] enables us not only to study but to define folklore in its

37. See for example Francis Lee Utley, "The Study of Folk Literature: Its Scope and Use," *Journal of American Folklore*, 71 (1958), 139; Roger D. Abrahams, "Folklore in Culture: Notes toward an Analytical Method," *Texas Studies in Liter-ature and Language*, 5 (1963), 102; [reprinted above, pp. 390–403] Kenneth S. Goldstein, "Experimental Folklore: Laboratory vs. Field," in *Folklore International: Essays in Traditional Literature, Belief, and Custom in Honor of Wayland Debs Hand*, ed. D. K. Wilgus and Carol Sommer (Hatboro, 1967), 71–82.

38. Dell Hymes, "The Ethnography of Speaking," in *Anthropology and Human Behavior*, ed. Thomas Gladwin and William C. Sturtevant (Washington, D.C., 1962), 15–53.

context. And in this framework, which is the real habitat of all folk-lore forms, there is no dichotomy between processes and products. The telling is the tale; therefore the narrator, his story, and his audience are all related to each other as components of a single continuum, which is the communicative event.

Folklore is the action that happens at that time. It is an artistic action. It involves creativity and esthetic response, both of which converge in the art forms themselves. Folklore in that sense is a social interaction via the art media and differs from other modes of speaking and gesturing. This distinction is based upon sets of cultural conventions, recognized and adhered to by all the members of the group, which separate folklore from nonart communication. In other words, the definition of folklore is not merely an analytical construct, depending upon arbitrary exclusion and inclusion of items; on the contrary, it has a cultural and social base. Folklore is not "pretty much what one wants to make out of it";[39] it is a definite realistic, artistic, and communicative process. The locus of the conventions marking the boundaries between folklore and nonfolklore is in the text, texture, and context of the forms, to apply Dundes' three levels for the analysis of folklore in somewhat modified form.[40]

The textual marks that set folklore apart as a particular kind of communication are the opening and closing formulas of tales and songs and the structure of actions that happen in-between. The opening and closing formulas designate the events enclosed between them as a distinct category of narration, not to be confused with reality. As the Ashanti[41] storyteller states most explicitly, "We don't really mean to say so, we don't really mean to say so," referring to the imaginary nature of the story.[42] Tales, however, do not necessarily relate to denotative speech as fiction does to truth. A folkloristic historical narrative, such as a legend,[43] is nevertheless formally distinct from a chronology of events. This contention, admittedly, requires further research. However, the phrase "it is like in a folktale"—which people employ whenever reality duplicates the sequence of actions in an artistic narration—attests to the awareness of a particular folktale structure. Also, other genres such as proverbs and riddles have distinct syntactic and semantic structures that separate them from the regular

39. George M. Foster, "Folklore," *Funk and Wagnalls Standard Dictionary of Folklore, Mythology and Legend*, I, 399.

40. Alan Dundes, "Text, Texture and Context," *Southern Folklore Quarterly*, 28 (1964), 251–265.

41. [African people of central Ghana.]

42. R. S. Rattray, *Akan-Ashanti Folk-Tales* (Oxford, 1930), x.

43. As defined by William Bascom, "The Forms of Folklore: Prose Narratives," *Journal of American Folklore*, 78 (1965), 3–20.

daily speech into which they are interspersed. Furthermore, these artistic forms are culturally recognized categories of communication. They have special names or identifying features distinguishing them from each other and from other modes of social interaction, pointing to the cultural awareness of their unique character.

Each of these forms may also have distinct textural qualities that separate them from other kinds of communication. These can be rhythmical speech, musical sounds, melodic accompaniment, or patterned design. In a sense, this is a reverse argument for the arts. Accordingly, a message is not considered artistic because it possesses these qualities, but it is these textural features that serve as markers to distinguish it as artistic. Since folklore forms are often interspersed in the midst of other modes of social interaction, they require such textural marks to single them out and prevent mistaking them for what they are not. Thus the telling of a story may necessitate a distinct speech pattern, such as recitative, and the saying of a proverb may involve a shift in intonation.[44]

Finally, there are contextual conventions that set folklore apart. These are specifications as to time, place, and company in which folklore actions happen. "To everything there is a season and a time to every purpose" (Eccles. 3:1). Narratives can be told during the daytime in the market place, the country store, and the street corner; or at night in the village square, the parlor, and the coffee-house. Songs and music have other occasions when they are performed. Although such specifications may have other functions, such as confining folklore to leisure and ceremonial activities, they also separate art from nonart in cultures that otherwise lack a complex division of time, space, and labor. In a sense, they provide a spatial, temporal, and social definition for folklore in culture.

These communicative marks of folklore do not necessarily exist on all three levels—text, texture, and context. The identification of social interaction as folklore by the people who tell the stories, sing the songs, play the music, and paint the pictures may be in terms of only one or all of these three. In any case, for them folklore is a well-defined cultural category.

Although folklore is a distinct category in terms of social interaction patterns and communication media, it is not necessarily recognized by the culture as a separate concept. In fact, within the cognitive system its forms may be classified into such apparently unrelated categories as history, tradition, dance, music, games, and tales. The reason for this categorization is inherent in the nature of the folk-

44. See George Herzog and Charles G. Blooah, *Jabo Proverbs from Liberia: Maxims in the Life of a Native Tribe* (London, 1936), 8.

loristic communication itself. Folklore, like any other art, is a symbolic kind of action. Its forms have symbolic significance reaching far beyond the explicit content of the particular text, melody, or artifact. The very syntactic and semantic structure of the text, the special recitative rhythm of presentation, and the time and locality in which the action happens may have symbolic implications for which the text itself cannot account. Consequently, it is quite plausible that in their classification of these materials people will use as a criterion not the symbolic mode of the form but its reference. Legend, for example, often signifies a chronological truth; myth symbolizes a religious truth; and parable implies a moral truth. A definition, according to these references, would regard them as history, religion, and ethics respectively. However, if their actual cultural mode of communication is the key for definition, then all these forms are but different phases in the same process of folklore.

The allowance for a possible disparity between ethnic taxonomy and behavior implies that, in a certain instance, the definition of folklore in its context depends upon actual modes of communication and not necessarily upon the particular cultural concept of them. There may be an overlap between the analytical view, which depends upon observation, and the internal interpretation, which results from participation; however, for the purpose of a cross-cultural application of this definition the analytical approach to the material must have methodological priority.

Similarly, the acceptance of the possible disparity between the analytical and the cultural views in regard to processes of social interaction permits the extension of the scope of folklore beyond the limits imposed upon it by the concept of verbal art. As an artistic process, folklore may be found in any communicative medium: musical, visual, kinetic, or dramatic. Theoretically, it is not necessary for the people themselves to make the conceptual connection between their melodies, masks, and tales. From the cultural point of view, these may well be separate phenomena unrelated to each other and not even existing in the same situation. Sufficient is the cultural recognition of their qualitative uniqueness in relation to other modes of communication in the respective media of sound, motion, and vision. The factor of rhythm changes human noise to music, movement and gesture to dance, and object to sculpture. Thus, they are artistic communication by their very essence. Furthermore, they are recognized as such by the people, since there are definite contexts of time and place in culture in which these actions are permissible. In the case of music and dance, there is no need to differentiate them from nonart communication. Their artistic qualities are intrinsic and essential to their very existence. There is, however, some necessity to distinguish these media as folklore. The distinguishing factor would be the particular social context of folklore.

As a communicative process, folklore has a social limitation as well, namely, the small group. This is the particular context of folklore. The concept of the small group, so popular among sociologists in the early fifties,[45] somehow bypassed the ranks of folklorists, who preferred the more romantic, even corny, term "folk." Since, in America at least, the connotations of marginality and low socio-economic status that once were associated with the term "folk" have long been abandoned,[46] the concept of "folk" has become almost synonymous with the group concept. A group is "a number of persons who communicate with one another, often over a span of time, and who are few enough so that each person is able to communicate with all the others, not at second-hand through other people, but face-to-face."[47] A group could be a family, a street-corner gang, a roomful of factory workers, a village, or even a tribe. These are social units of different orders and qualities, yet all of them exhibit to a larger or smaller extent the characteristics of a group. For the folkloric act to happen, two social conditions are necessary: both the performers and the audience have to be in the same situation and be part of the same reference group. This implies that folklore communication takes place in a situation in which people confront each other face to face and relate to each other directly.

It is necessary to remember at this point that even when a certain literary theme or musical style is known regionally, nationally, or internationally, its actual existence depends upon such small group situations. In these cases the tellers know their audience and relate specifically to them, and the listeners know the performer and react to this particular way of presentation. Of course this familiarity is often relative to the size of the general reference group. A storyteller who has a regional reputation may entertain people whom he does not know as intimately as he knows the people in his own village. Yet, even in such cases, both the performers and the audience belong to the same reference group; they speak the same language, share similar values, beliefs, and background knowledge, have the same system of codes and signs for social interaction. In other words, for a folklore communication to exist as such, the participants in the small group

45. For a critical survey of these studies see Robert T. Golembiewski, *The Small Group: An Analysis of Research Concepts and Operations* (Chicago, 1962).

46. See Boggs, 1–8; Kenneth W. and Mary W. Clarke, *Introducing Folklore* (New York, 1963), 1; Dundes, "The American Concept of Folklore," *Journal of the Folklore Institute*, 3 (1966), 229–233.

47. George C. Homans, *The Human Group* (New York, 1950), 1.

situation have to belong to the same reference group, one composed of people of the same age or of the same professional, local, religious, or ethnic affiliation. In theory and in practice tales can be narrated and music can be played to foreigners. Sometimes this accounts for diffusion. But folklore is true to its own nature when it takes place within the group itself. In sum, folklore is artistic communication in small groups.

Two key folklore terms are absent from this definition, namely, tradition and oral transmission. This omission is not accidental. The cultural use of tradition as a sanction is not necessarily dependent upon historical fact. Very often it is merely a rhetorical device or a socially instrumental convention. The combination of a narrative content concerned with olden times with the cultural conviction in the historicity of tales necessitates a presentation of the stories as if they were handed down from antiquity. Further, in past-oriented cultures, the sanction of tradition may be instrumental to the introduction of new ideas; and tales may serve as the vehicle for that purpose. Thus, the traditional character of folklore is an accidental quality, associated with it in some cases, rather than an objectively intrinsic feature of it. In fact, some groups specifically divorce the notion of antiquity from certain folklore forms and present them as novelty instead. Thus, for example, the lore of children derives its efficacy from its supposed newness. Often children consider their rhymes as fresh creations of their own invention.[48] Similarly, riddles have to be unfamiliar to the audience. A known riddle is a contradiction in terms and cannot fulfill its rhetorical function any more. In fact, riddles may disappear from circulation exactly because they are traditional and recognized as such by the members of the group.[49]

In both cases the traditional character of folklore is an analytical construct. It is a scholarly and not a cultural fact. The antiquity of the material has been established after laborious research, and the tellers themselves are completely ignorant of it. Therefore, tradition should not be a criterion for the definition of folklore in its context.

There are methodological reasons as well for releasing folklore from the burden of tradition. The focus on those items alone that have stood the test of time cannot provide us with a systematic understanding of the principles of diachronic transmission, selection, and memorization of folklore. Since the criterion of tradition determines a priori the selection of items, any research into these problems lacks the

48. See Iona and Peter Opie, *The Lore and Language of Schoolchildren* (Oxford, 1959), 12.

49. Kenneth S. Goldstein, "Riddling Traditions in Northeastern Scotland," *Journal of American Folklore*, 76 (1963), 330–336.

"control data" to check its conclusions. After all, the study of transmission requires the inquiry into the principles both of forgetting and of remembering. Thus, even the study of tradition itself should demand that we broaden the scope of folklore and not limit it to time-proven tales and songs alone. The artistic forms that are part of the communicative processes of small groups are significant, without regard to the time they have been in circulation. The statement that "all folklore is traditional, but not all traditions are folklore"[50] might well be revised to "some traditions are folklore, but not all folklore is traditional."

Furthermore, if folklore as a discipline focuses on tradition only, it "contradicts its own raison d'être."[51] If the initial assumption of folklore research is based on the disappearance of its subject matter, there is no way to prevent the science from following the same road. If the attempt to save tradition from oblivion remains the only function of the folklorist, he returns to the role of the antiquarian from which he tried so hard to escape. In that case, it is in the interest of folklore scholarship that we change the definition of the subject to allow broader and more dynamic research in the field.

The same applies to the notion of oral transmission; an insistence on the "purity" of all folklore texts can be destructive in terms of folklore scholarship. Because of the advent of modern means of communication, folklorists who insist upon this criterion actually saw off the branch they are sitting on. They inevitably concentrate upon isolated forms and ignore the real social and literary interchange between cultures and artistic media and channels of communication. In reality, oral texts cross into the domain of written literature and the plastic and musical arts; conversely, the oral circulation of songs and tales has been affected by print. This has long been recognized, and yet it has been a source of constant frustration for folklorists who searched for materials uncontaminated by print or broadcast. The notion of folklore as a process may provide a way out of this dilemma. Accordingly, it is not the life history of the text that determines its folkloristic quality but its present mode of existence. On the one hand, a popular melody, a current joke, or a political anecdote that has been incorporated into the artistic process in small group situations is folklore, no matter how long it has existed in that context. On the other hand, a song, a tale, or a riddle that is performed on television or appears in

50. Compare William R. Bascom, "Folklore and Anthropology," *Journal of American Folklore*, 66 (1953), 285.

51. Dell Hymes, "Review of *Indian Tales of North America—An Anthology for the Adult Reader*, by Tristram P. Coffin," *American Anthropologist*, 64 (1962), 678.

print ceases to be folklore because there is a change in its communicative context.

This definition may break away from some scholarly traditions, but at the same time it may point to possible new directions. A major factor that prevented folklore studies from becoming a full-fledged discipline in the academic community has been the tendency toward thing-collecting projects. The tripodal scheme of folklore research as collecting, classifying, and analyzing emphasizes this very point. This procedure developed as a nineteenth-century positivistic reaction to some of the more speculative ideas about folklore that prevailed at that time. Since then, however, the battle for empiricism has been won twice over. Folklore scholarship—which developed since the rejection of unilinear cultural evolutionism and the solar and psychoanalytical universal symbolism—has had its own built-in limitations and misconceptions. These resulted in part from the focus on facts. Because of the literary and philological starting point of folklore studies, the empirical fact was an object, a text of a tale, song, or proverb, or even an isolated word. This approach limited the research possibilities in folklore and narrowed the range of generalizations that could be induced from the available data. It might have been suitable for Krappe's notion of folklore as an historical science that purported to reconstruct the spiritual history of man,[52] but it completely incapacitated the development of any other thesis about the nature of folklore in society. Consequently, when social sciences such as anthropology, sociology, and psychology came of age, they incorporated folklore into their studies only as a reflection and projection of other phenomena. Folklore was "a mirror of culture" but not a dynamic factor in it, a projection of basic personality, but not personality in action. Once viewed as a process, however, folklore does not have to be a marginal projection or reflection; it can be considered a sphere of interaction in its own right.[53]

52. [Alexander Haggerty Krappe, *The Science of Folklore* (1930; repr. New York: W. W. Norton, 1964).]

53. A shorter version of this paper, titled "Folklore: The Definition Game Once Again," was read at the American Folklore Society Annual Meeting in Toronto, November 1967. My wife, Paula, helped me in many ways in preparing this paper for print.

PARTICIPATION IN TRADITION

Kay L. Cothran

One modern American folklorist advises us to drop the concept of tradition (see the preceding), and another says to hang on to it—but with a difference. In this concise essay, Kay L. Cothran gives part of the theoretical background for her study of "talking trash" (pp. 215–235) and she redirects the concern of "rhetorical folklorist" such as Roger D. Abrahams and Dan Ben-Amos from the definition of folklore to developing a sound field methodology and an analytic strategy for folklore study. Cothran stresses that while earlier folklorists may have slighted context in their emphasis upon texts in oral tradition, some modern folklorists probably overemphasize context to the neglect of tradition. And what is tradition? Cothran suggests this definition: "the rules by means of which a given context is made sensible." More simply put, she writes that tradition is "our way . . . our system."

One advantage of studying "participation in tradition" is that it reminds researchers that even as students of culture they never escape culture itself; every social interaction, including collecting folklore, involves us in cultural norms, roles, and choices. The ways we choose to study folklore are as much a part of our culture and its traditions as the folklore artifacts we choose to study. Thus, everything—including the folklorist—is part of the context. (This is beautifully demonstrated in Cothran's study above.)

This essay should be required reading for any student folklore collector who says to his or her instructor, "I can't seem to collect much of anything; no one knows many proverbs [weather signs, jokes, pranks, etc.]." Would it not open new lines of inquiry and new goals for fieldwork to be reminded that there are positive and negative degrees of participation, that "a 'no' means just as much as a 'yes'?" Then, perhaps, the project goal might be shifted from making a "collection" to investigating topics more like these: "Participation and Non-Participation in April Fool's Day Pranks" or "Proverbs Recognized, Used, Parodied, and Rejected" or "The Reactions of Ethnic Minority Members to Folk Humor Directed Against Them." Cothran herself published an imaginative study of some traditional American eating behavior in an article titled "Talking with Your Mouth Full: A Communications Approach to Food Rules," Tennessee Folklore Society Bulletin, Vol. 38 (1972).

The concept of "rules" is important here, as it is in many other recent theoretical essays. Searching for a "grammar of folklore" or a set of behavioral rules to explain how the dynamics of tradition and context operate is a strong concern of current American folklore scholarship. But the only generalizations that can be made about such rules at this point are that while they appear to be tremendously complicated in sheer number and detail, they may be essentially very simple in their underlying structures.

Another good recent essay that attempts to bridge modern theory and practice in folklore study is Gerald Cashion's "Folklore, Kinesiological Folklore, and the Macro-Folklore Complex," *Folklore Forum, Bibliographic and Special Series, No. 12 (1975).*

OUR DISCIPLINARY PREDECESSORS tended to overemphasize the notion of tradition as antiquity's dead weight, as deterministic and anesthetic. Perhaps, as Ben-Amos suggests, we can jettison the word "tradition" and think better in terms of esthetic technique.[1] And yet, as Orenstein observes,

> human beings would probably not persistently guide their behavior by social rules if the rules did not appear to them to transcend their immediate interactions. It would be . . . a society of the totally insane in which each interaction were undertaken in conceptual isolation from others, each thought to terminate in the realization of its own discrete goals.[2]

The rhetorical folklorists have demonstrated the importance of context in understanding folklore. We do not find the significance of folklore by looking inside the item, so to speak, but rather by referring to context. But how do we understand context? By looking only at its inner dynamics? Or by looking also for those next-level rules which make this context into an instance of a kind of context recognizable by participants and observers alike. There is a context of context, if you will. There is tradition: the rules by means of which a given context is made sensible, by means of which further contexts are made possible. Tradition—not antiquity and orality, but "our way, our means, our categories, our system."

I prefer the expression "participation in tradition" to "having folklore" and "being folk." My thinking depends upon two related ideas about tradition. First, Birdwhistell writes that "an individual does not communicate; he engages in or becomes part of communication."[3]

1. Dan Ben-Amos, "Toward a Definition of Folklore in Context," in *Toward New Perspectives in Folklore*, ed. Américo Paredes and Richard Bauman (Austin and London, 1972), pp. 13–15. [reprinted above, pp. 427–443].

2. Henry Orenstein, "Death and Kinship in Hinduism: Structural and Functional Interpretations," *American Anthropologist* 72 (1970), p. 1371.

3. Ray L. Birdwhistell, "Contribution of Linguistic-Kinesic Studies to the Understanding of Schizophrenia," in *Schizophrenia: An Integrated Approach*, ed. Alfred Auerback (New York, 1959), p. 104.

Far from choosing to communicate or not-communicate, people take part in communication willy-nilly because we are social, cultural beings. Abrahams distinguishes folklore approached as part of culture from folklore approached as a personally useful entity.[4] I prefer to conceptualize folklore as not just a product of human action—a part of culture or a means of acting—but as simultaneously and reflexively an environment and a set of techniques of human social activity that can change the environment or perpetuate it.

We can approach folklore, or to be more precise we can apply the concept of folklore, not only as an isolate, something people have, but also as action, something people do. We can see it as both a way and a means, as something people live in and through. In a sense we do not have traditions so much as we inhabit them. We participate in traditions because we are what we are.

Second, rejection of any particular tradition, such as gospel songs, witch beliefs, or downhome food, amounts by an ironic twist to participation in that very same tradition. We know a man as much by what he rejects as by what he embraces. Through both he presents and defines his social selves. Intention and consciousness are not at issue, because I am not speaking in psychological terms. Participation in a particular tradition is not something one can stop doing in a snap. Ceasing to participate in a particular tradition ordinarily takes longer than one lifetime. Participation in a tradition does not entail approval of that tradition. There exist, then, both positive and negative degrees of participation in a particular tradition, no matter how allegedly homogeneous the group. This idea is not at all new, for Durkheim distinguished between positive and negative rituals, and Goldstein and Browne recognized that disbelief in the total forgetting of traditional beliefs constitute folklore behavior.[5]

From the ideas of participation in tradition and positive/negative degrees of participation, follows the methodologically important, though ethically odd, idea that an informant gives me data whether or not he wants to do so. If, for example, he knows tall tales or likes them and talks about them at length, he provides me with data. His participation in this tradition could be called positive. If, on the contrary, he refuses to talk, tries with smiling face to keep me away from tall tale narrators, or he leaves the room and emits a deafening, disapproving silence, he or she still gives me data about himself or herself

---

4. Roger D. Abrahams, "Personal Power and Social Restraint in the Definition of Folklore," in *Toward New Perspectives in Folklore*, ed. Américo Paredes and Richard Bauman (Austin and London, 1972), p. 16.

5. Kenneth S. Goldstein, "The Collecting of Superstitious Beliefs," *Keystone Folklore Quarterly*, 9 (Spring, 1964), pp. 13–22.

as a member of a local society and about the symbolic value and social distribution of tall tales. This participation we could call negative. The rules of tall tale tradition specify how one behaves if he dislikes the tradition.

The negative is as real as the positive, not just analytically but in the data. Kenneth Burke says that "there are no negatives in nature . . . this ingenious addition to the universe is solely a product of human symbol systems," adding that "so far as the actual state of affairs is concerned, some situation positively prevails, and that's that."[6] But, as he goes on to show, once we cross from the nonsocial order into the order of human symbol systems, whether personal or public, we have to deal with a very real negative.

When I question an informant by word or action, a "no" means just as much as a "yes." There is a world of difference between a "no" response, the symbolic negative, and a "null" response, the occurrence of absolutely nothing. Not-tall-tale is not equivalent to nothing-at-all. We could not see this distinction when all we did was folklore collecting. If Jack had no folklore or was not folk, we marked him off and went on to the next house. He was a null, instead of a significant no. But if we look at folklore from the point of view of social communication, we see that there are no nulls, even though a null response is mathematically possible as a limiting case. Consequently, in approaching folklore as social communication, we must deal not just with good, bad, and indifferent performers, as when collecting items. We must deal not just with performers and audiences as analyzable into clearly distinguishable, psychologically motivated teams, as in doing small-group rhetorical analyses. We must also deal with people who do not appear to the naive eye to be involved in the tradition at all, or who even appear to be trying to stamp the tradition out.

Through our discipline's history, many of us have taken something like the following view of "the folk": "We differ from them. We can deal with them, as long as they don't sound too much like us, or we don't sound too much like them." We invented a partly imaginary group called "the folk," who had moribund traditions called "folklore," from which we could stand at safe social distance, never realizing that by separating ourselves from folklore we in fact participated in the very traditions we tried to fend off. It would be instructive to know how many folklorists today consider "the folk" to be a social real rather than a Redfieldian ideal type.[7]

6. Kenneth Burke, "Definition of Man," in *Language as Symbolic Action: Essays on Life, Literature, and Method* (Berkeley and Los Angeles, 1968), pp. 9–10.

7. [Anthropologist Robert Redfield proposed definitions of folk societies in *The Little Community* and *Peasant Society and Culture* (both 1956; pub. together by Univ. Chicago Press: Phoenix Books, 1969).]

As long as we confined our attention to the merry or degenerative peasants, rednecks, foreigners, and primitives, we could succeed in deceiving ourselves about the nature of our enterprise. We could imagine that we were not dealing with ourselves. As some of us now study urban folklore and do folkloristic ethnographies including all social classes in a locality, we find that in the old sense of the term there is no folk. Even "the folk" as an ideal type loses much utility. What we have before us as always, although we could not admit it because we, too, are social creatures participating in our traditions, is complex human social life with its many resonant traditions. Our predecessors who pronounced various tale traditions or indeed folklore as a whole to be dead or terminally ill, expressed a wish and not a fact. There are reasons why folklorists have certain concepts or nonconcepts of the folk and of folklore, reasons that are part of the disciplinary and larger social traditions in which we participate.

Finally, to date, few folklorists have even tried to do participant-observation fieldwork, but most of us by now interview informants as well as collect from them. Most of us also probably assume that "we" ask questions and "they" give answers—snip-snap, push-pull—in a stimulus-response dyad. If we are a bit more sophisticated, we hold that "we" bring up the matter of a given genre, and "they" respond in some way positively, negatively, sometimes both. This is how one punctuates what people do in something called "an interview." But if we take the matter of participation in tradition seriously, we see something very different. We have not question and answer but interaction packed with symbols radiating in indecently multiplicitous directions, involving a social unit that resolutely defies reduction to "us" and "them." There is no S, no R,[8] but an ordered continuum. No folklorist, no informant, but participants in tradition.[9]

8. [Simulus-Response, basic terms of experimentation in behavioral psychology.]

9. This paper is a slightly revised version of one read at the 1972 meeting of the American Folklore Society in Austin, Texas. Gregory Bateson has employed the expression "context of context" in nonfolkloristic but nonetheless helpful writings: "Minimal Requirements for a Theory of Schizophrenia," *A.M.A. Archives of General Psychiatry* 2 (1960), pp. 477–491; "Double Bind, 1969," *Steps to an Ecology of Mind* (New York, 1972), pp. 271–78; "The Logical Categories of Learning and Communication," ibid., pp. 279–308. He also lends support to the contention that we must attend to negative participation in tradition when he notes "the information content of *quiescence*. The quiescence of an axon *differs* as much from activity as its activity does from quiescence. Therefore quiescence and activity have equal informational relevance." ("The Cybernetics of 'Self': A Theory of Alcoholism," *Steps to an Ecology of Mind*, pp. 318–19).

FOLKLORE AND HISTORY:
FACT AMID THE LEGENDS[1]

William A. Wilson

The last selection in this reader was originally presented by a prominent American folklorist before an audience of specialists in a different academic field. William A. Wilson summarizes some of the goals of modern folklore scholarship and discusses the relevance of folkloristics to the related discipline of local history. He refers to certain misunderstandings by nonfolklorists of the nature of folklore study, and concludes with a hopeful view of future developments of the field, especially in terms of interdisciplinary cooperation.

Wilson makes particular reference to the history and historical folklore of Utah Mormons, a group with a rich heritage of oral, customary, and material folk traditions (although he includes only oral lore in this discussion). Paradoxically, while Utah folklorists have had a strong interest in the historical aspects of their subject, Utah historians have not been much aware of the usefulness to their own work of folk traditions. This address at an annual meeting of the state historical society was intended to encourage a greater exchange of data and ideas.

The oral history projects which have become widespread in recent years, have generally been limited to interviews with notable personages; historians have seldom assigned the same value to the oral traditions of common people. But Wilson cites studies and examples to show that some factual history may be preserved in tradition; perhaps even more important, folklore gives a view of "cultural fact" (values and attitudes) and of the people's own beliefs about what happened in the past. With examples of modern Utah folklore, he demonstrates that current values are mirrored just as clearly now as the pioneer viewpoint was contained in pioneer lore. There are also different perceptions of history evident in the folklore from within and outside a group. For example, non-Mormons (and non-Utahans in general) may know some of the exoteric lore concerning the early Mormon practice of polygamy, but three of Wilson's best examples of legends give an esoteric view of polygamy seen from inside the institution by wives themselves.

Readers interested in the general subject of folklore and history should consult the sources cited in Wilson's footnotes. Readers particularly interested in Mormon folklore should consult his article "The

1. This paper was originally presented at the Twentieth Annual Meeting of the Utah State Historical Society in September 1972.

Paradox of Mormon Folklore" in Brigham Young University Studies,
Vol. 17, No. 1 (1976).

A SHORT TIME AGO one of our university librarians declared that the
Special Collections Library probably would not be interested in acquir-
ing the burgeoning collections of folklore that are beginning to crowd
me out of my office because "Special Collections is interested only in
authentic historical documents." Now as a folklorist I would like to
dismiss such a statement as simply the careless comment of an unin-
formed individual; but, unfortunately, the sentiment behind the statement is one I meet on all sides, among laymen and academicians alike.
Indeed, though many of my friends consider the materials I work with
great fun, they are constantly taken aback by the notion that the
materials could be put to any serious scholarly use. And, whatever an
authentic historical document actually is, to many of these people, as
to our librarian, an item of folklore obviously is not one. Though
historically oriented folklorists have for some years now been defending judiciously used folklore texts as valuable historical source material,[2] we have evidently not come far from the day of George
Laurence Gomme who in 1908 began his book *Folklore as an Historical Science* with these words: "It may be stated as a general rule
that history and folklore are not considered as complimentary studies.
Historians deny the validity of folklore as evidence of history, and
folklorists ignore the essence of history which exists in folklore."[3]
Today, with closer ties between the Folklore Society of Utah and the
Utah State Historical Society having just been established, I should
like to follow Gomme's path and argue once again for the "validity of
folklore as evidence of history."

FOLKLORE AS ACTUAL FACT

In spite of the reverence historians in the past have paid written,
dated documents and in spite of repeated warnings that serious scholars
should eschew oral traditions of the folk, such oral traditions do at

---

2. For good summaries of the attitudes of past historians and other scholars
toward folklore and history, see William Lynwood Montell, "Preface," *The Saga
of Coe Ridge: A Study in Oral History* (Knoxville, 1970), vii–xxi, and Richard M.
Dorson, "The Debate over the Trustworthiness of Oral Traditional History," *Folklore: Selected Essays* (Bloomington, Ind., 1972), 199–224, also Dorson's *American
Folklore and the Historian* (Chicago, 1971).

3. George Laurence Gomme, *Folklore as an Historical Science* (London.
1908), 1.

times capture and retain actual historical fact. For example, two archaeologists, David M. Pendergast and Clement W. Meighan, collected from the Paiute Indians of southern Utah oral traditions about a Puebloid people who had once occupied the area with them and then moved away. The stories squared with archaeological evidence from eight hundred years in the past, giving accurate accounts of economic institutions, material culture, physical stature of the people, and intertribal relations.[4] The Indians knew more about the archaeological sites than their white neighbors, said the authors, because

> it is their land, they have been here for thirty generations or more, their ancestors saw these communities when they were living villages, and the old people talked about it to their young.[5]

Similarly, Frederica de Laguna, using carbon-dating tests, corroborated native traditions dating from 1400 telling of habitable periods of the Yakutat Bay. "Other natives' statements," said Laguna, "about the stages in the retreat of ice in the Yakutat Bay during the late eighteenth and nineteenth centuries are in complete accord with geological evidence."[6] Ballads and folksongs, often considered pure poetic fictions, have also contained historical data. Russian folksongs give valuable insight into the time of Ivan the Terrible,[7] and recent research has shown that the Scottish ballad, "The Battle of Harlaw," which recounts the battle in 1411 between the highland and lowland Scots, has preserved the details of that battle more accurately than have the sober histories.[8]

To be sure, folk history often views the past from an ethnocentric point of view, but so, too, do professional historians. In a fascinating study of the retreat of the British army in Afghanistan from Kabul to Jalalabad in 1842, Louis Dupree compares the accounts of the event recorded in British written histories with those preserved in the oral traditions of the Afghans and finds both sides equally lacking in objectivity. "Both Afghan and British contemporary writers on the First

4. David M. Pendergast and Clement W. Meighan, "Folk Traditions as Historical Fact: A Paiute Example," *Journal of American Folklore*, 72 (April–June 1959), 128–33.

5. Clement W. Meighan, "More on Folk Traditions," *Journal of American Folklore*, 73 (January–March 1960), 60.

6. Frederica de Laguna, "Geological Confirmation of Native Traditions, Yakutat, Alaska," *American Antiquity*, 23 (April 1958), 434.

7. Y. M. Sokolov, *Russian Folklore*, trans. Catherine Ruth Smith (New York, 1950), 350–51. See also Carl Stief, *Studies in Russian Historical Song* (New York, 1957).

8. David D. Buchan, "History and Harlaw," *Journal of the Folklore Institute*, 5 (1968), 58–67.

Anglo-Afghan War," says Dupree, "reinforce the social values of their perspective societies and defend national or tribal honor."[9]

About the only historians to make extensive use of oral traditions to reconstruct the past have been students of Black African history, forced to these traditions by the paucity of written documents.[10] In the United States where we have had literate people to record what has taken place in our country from the days of the first settlers the historian has had little truck with the folklorist. Still, in many areas of our past where written documents are scarce or nonexistent the historian could learn much from the lore of the folk. As John Bettersworth has pointed out,

> traditionally history has never troubled itself too much with the people as such. It must concern itself with kings and presidents; with movements and forces; and with wars, which Malthus[11] tells us are a way of getting rid of excess people. But everyman rarely gets attention unless he chops off a king's head, or is one of the anonymous hangers-on in a movement, or becomes a statistic in a plague, or gets buried under a pile of granite as the Unknown Soldier.[12]

The same point was made at the turn of the century by Finley Peter Dunne through his fictional character Mr. Dooley:

> I know histhry isn't true, Hinnessy, said Mr. Dooley, because it ain't like what I see ivry day in Halstead Sthreet. If any wan comes along with a histhry iv Greece or Rome that'll show me th' people fightin', gettin' dhrunk, makin' love, gettin' married, owin' th' grocery man an' bein' without hard-coal, I'll believe they was a Greece or Rome, but not before. Historyans is like doctors. They are always lookin' f'r symptoms. Those iv them that writes about their own times examines th 'tongue an' feels th' pulse an' makes a wrong dygnosis. Th' other kind iv histhry is a post-mortem examination. It tells ye what a counthry died iv. But I'd like to know what it lived iv.[13]

And here is where folklore comes into play. It can tell us what the people lived of. In 1855 John Little, an escaped slave who had fled to Canada, said, "Tisn't he who has stood and looked on, that can tell you what slavery is—'tis he who has endured."[14] Folklore brings us

9. Louis Dupree, "The Retreat of the British Army from Kabul to Jalalabad in 1842: History and Folklore," *Journal of the Folklore Institute*, 4 (1967), 69.

10. See Jan Vansina, *Oral Tradition: A Study in Historical Methodology*, trans. H. M. Wright (Chicago, 1965).

11. [Thomas R. Malthus (1766–1834), English economist who theorized about the disastrous effects of unchecked population growth on limited world resources.]

12. John K. Bettersworth, "The Folk Imperative," *Phi Kapa Phi Journal*, 52 (Winter 1972), 31.

13. Finley Peter Dunne, *Observations by Mr. Dooley* (New York, 1902), 271.

14. *Life Under the "Peculiar Institution": Selections from the Slave Narrative Collection*, ed. Norman R. Yetman (New York, 1970), 1.

the record of those who have endured through the major movements of American history—from colonization to industrialization, from the day of trapper and homesteader to that of the factory worker and sophisticated suburbanite.

Think for a moment of folk medicinal practices in early Utah. We smile today at the credulity of the pioneer farmer who anointed his sick oxen with consecrated oil or at the naivete of the pioneer mother who made a poultice of cow manure to put on the inflamed arm of her son dying from blood poison.[15] But then our survival does not depend upon a healthy draft animal; and when our children are ill we can take them to the doctor for a shot of penicillin. Early Utahns, however, had only their own resources to fall back on. Or think of the pioneer family settled at last in Cottonwood in Salt Lake Valley but then asked to pull up stakes once more and move on to southern Utah. They sang:

> Oh, once I lived in Cottonwood, and owned a little farm.
> But I was called to Dixie,[16] which did me much alarm:
> To raise the cane and cotton, I right away must go:
> But the reason why they called on me, I'm sure I do not know.

Once in Dixie, weary and destitute, they cried:

> I feel so weak and hungry now, there's nothing here to cheer
> Except prophetic sermons which we very often hear.
> They will hand them out by dozens and prove them by the book—
> I'd rather have some roasting ears to stay at home and cook.[17]

To know the history of medicine in Utah without experiencing the struggles of those who lived without it, or to know the history of settlement without feeling the mental anguish of the Dixie immigrant, or to know the history of irrigation without living the accounts of violence and bloodshed between neighbors fighting desperately for the same water—to know only these things is to know only half our history, the dehumanized half. As Theodore Blegen says, it is the folklore and the grass roots history that "break through the crust of figures and graphs to the living realities that alone can give them

15. Unless otherwise noted, all items of Utah folklore discussed in this paper are located in the Brigham Young University Folklore Archives, c/o English Department.

16. [In the 1860s Mormon president Brigham Young "called" many families to settle in southern Utah to help disperse the Mormons throughout "Zion." The region came to be known as "Dixie" because of its mild climate and the early attempts to raise cotton there.]

17. Printed in Thomas E. Cheney, ed., *Mormon Songs from the Rocky Mountains: A Compilation of Mormon Folksong*, Publications of the American Folklore Society, Memoir Series, vol. 53 (Austin, 1968), 118–19.

Figure 1. Grasshoppers' Descent upon Salt Lake Valley. (Grasshoppers figure prominently in early Utah farming lore. From John W. Clampitt, Echoes from the Rocky Mountain *(1890).)*

significance."[18] The figures and graphs tell us what people did; folklore tells us what they thought and felt while they were doing it.

In Utah the two most promising areas for folk-historical research are probably local history and ethnic history. A recent book by W. Lynwood Montell, *The Saga of Coe Ridge: A Study in Oral History*, provides an excellent methodology for those who would use folklore to help unravel the histories of their communities when the written record is skimpy.[19] In Utah ethnic studies where, as a recent issue of the *Utah Historical Quarterly* pointed out, there are many gaps,[20] we should follow the lead of Helen Z. Papanikolas. Her study of "Greek Folklore of Carbon County"[21] and her comments on Greek folklore in other publications tell more about what it has been like to be a Greek in Utah than do the more traditional surveys.

18. Theodore Blegen, *Grass Roots History* (Minneapolis, 1947), 14.

19. See footnote 2.

20. "In This Issue," *Utah Historical Quarterly*, 40 (Summer 1972), 207.

21. Helen Z. Papanikolas, "Greek Folklore of Carbon County," *Lore of Faith and Folly*, ed. Thomas E. Cheney (Salt Lake City, 1971), 61–77.

FOLKLORE AS CULTURAL FACT

A significant contribution of folklore to historical research is the insight it gives into social structure and social values and attitudes. Malinowski taught us some time ago that myth is a sort of aesthetic correlative of social organization, a mirror for culture, reflecting and justifying social practices and changing as those practices change.[22] Thus, one wishing to know what is going on in a group should look to its myths and legends. New developments in the Mormon legend of the Three Nephites—those ancient Book of Mormon prophets believed by Mormons to still be walking the earth—make this fact clear.

I have recently compared some six hundred accounts of Nephite appearances which I have collected since 1964 with those accounts recorded by Austin Fife and Hector Lee before World War II.[23] The stories have not diminished, as some have thought, but have merely changed to reflect the social environment. Stories that once took place in pioneer or village cottages with a country road winding pleasantly by now occur in urban centers with the freeway sounding noisily in the background. Thus, where at the turn of the century a Nephite might have appeared to a nursing mother with caked breasts and recommended tobacco boiled in lard, he now actually enters a hospital, operates on a woman the doctors have been unable to treat, and removes a "black-colored growth" from her stomach; where he might have earlier brought food to a starving homesteader, he now appears to the proprietor of an A & W root beer stand and warns him to close on Sunday; and where he might once have rescued a beleaguered cowboy from a cattle stampede, he now appears along the roadside to pull an injured Mormon missionary from a pileup of cars on a Los Angeles freeway.

Also interesting are the themes that occur in the stories. Though the stories tell of numerous different events, they have in recent years tended to cluster around three major themes: welfare, missionary work, and genealogical research. As Mormons will know, these are the three points of emphasis of the Priesthood Correlation Program initiated in 1964. To the exhortations of church authorities have been

22. Bronislaw Malinowski, "Myth in Primitive Psychology," *Magic, Science and Religion and Other Essays* (Garden City, N.Y., 1948), 91–148.

23. Austin E. Fife, "The Legend of the Three Nephites among the Mormons," *Journal of American Folklore*, 53 (January–March 1940), 1–49; Austin E. Fife and Alta S. Fife, *Saints of Sage and Saddle: Folklore among the Mormons* (Bloomington, Ind., 1956), 233–49; Hector Lee, *The Three Nephites: The Substance and Significance of the Legend of Folklore*, University of New Mexico Publications in Language and Literature, no. 2 (Albuquerque, 1949).

added the witnesses of the ancient Nephite apostles, testifying to the faithful of the validity of the correlation program and prompting them to obey its dictates. Thus, folklore both reflects and reinforces social organization and practice.

Folklore elso reflects social values and attitudes, giving good insight into the mind of the people. Because of this, Allan Nevins, founder of Columbia University's oral history program, has argued that the oral historian should collect and study not only the personal reminiscences of people who have experienced important events but folksongs and legends as well. "In our more recent history," he says, "the legends of pioneer settlements, mining camps, lumbermen, and the cowboys of the western range, whether in prose or ballad, are by no means devoid of light upon social and cultural history."[24] I would argue that in many instances folklore will throw more light on this history than will the recorded memories of individuals. And it will do so because folklore is transmitted orally and because in this transmission it changes— the very circumstances that cause many scholars to look on folklore with suspicion. If it changes from its original form, how, they ask, can it have any historical validity?

The answer lies in the nature of the change. In gauging group values, historians are concerned with getting representative opinions, attitudes typical of the group rather than of deviant members within it. But every member of society in some ways deviates from social norms: and every individual view of events is just that, an *individual* view. Hence the need for broad sampling of opinion, something not always easy when many of the people from a period being studied are either dead or have lost from memory details of earlier years.

Folklore, on the other hand, provides a sort of automatic random sampling. No matter what the origin of a folklore item, it will, if it is to survive, move from the individual expression of its originator to the communal expression of those who preserve it, sloughing off as it passes from person to person and through time and space the marks of individual invention, and in a short time reflecting quite accurately the consensus of the group. This is a process which folklorists call communal re-creation, in which the creation of one person becomes finally the creation of a community. To say this is not to deny the creative talents of those who tell the stories. Each tale teller is also an individual, and no two tellings of the same story will ever be quite the same. At the same time, few tellers, in their attempts to add something of themselves to the stories, will depart very far from the consensus value center of the audience whose stories they tell and whose ap-

24. Allan Nevins, *The Gateway to History* (Boston, 1938), 66.

proval they seek. As Abrahams and Foss say, "the traditional performer is synthesizing the group, reaffirming its values, giving it a feeling of community. His aim is a normative one, and his arguments will thus be conservative, in favor of the status quo."[25] For example, in 1966 two Mormon missionaries in Canada had a frightening experience which they interpreted as possession by evil spirits. Three years later one of these missionaries, now a member of my folklore class, collected versions of his experience from returned missionaries from the same field. The further the story had moved from its original source, the more the missionaries in the story, who had done nothing wrong, were converted into rule-breaking elders. One informant's comments are particularly instructive: "I think that it was late at night and that the elders hadn't been livin' the mission rules very well, and they were sort of apostate elders anyhow—kind of the haughty kind. *That sort of thing never happens to ya if you're livin' your religion.*" Thus the story was reshaped by its tellers to reflect and reinforce the group belief that wayward missionaries subject themselves to the power of Satan.

A short time ago Richard Bushman, speaking about this problem of recording attitudes and beliefs, wrote:

> The present generation would also dearly love to know the opinions and feelings of the poor and the slaves. One hundred and fifty years ago hardly anyone thought it worth the effort to record their thoughts. Now we must laboriously collect materials from scattered sources, speculate on the implications of the skimpy materials we do have and try to answer questions our generation is asking in order to make the past relevant for us.[26]

Here we see the historian so devoted to the written word that he misses the oral evidence that exists all around him. The thoughts and feelings of the slaves *were* recorded—by the slaves themselves in the songs, tales, jokes, and anecdotes that have survived to the present day. In them we find a constant dissatisfaction with the society they live in and a growing disposition on the part of many toward violence as a proper means to effect social change. For example, Brer Rabbit, who symbolizes the weak black man in his conflict against more powerful white men,[27] resorted in the earlier tales to clever tricks to

25. Roger D. Abrahams and George Foss, *Anglo-American Folksong Style* (Englewood Cliffs, N.J., 1968), 10.

26. Richard L. Bushman, "Faithful History," *Dialogue: A Journal of Mormon Thought*, 4 (Winter 1969), 15.

27. For a discussion of the symbolic role of Brer Rabbit in Negro folklore, see the comments of Sterling A. Brown and Arna Bontemps in *Black Expressions: Essays by and about Black Americans and the Creative Arts*, ed. Addison Gayle, Jr. (New York, 1969), 8–9, 30–31.

outwit the stronger but less intelligent Fox and Bear. But in a recently collected text, Brer Rabbit, when not invited to a party held by the other animals, forces his way in with a shotgun, eats all the food, dances with Lion's wife, rapes Ape's wife, defecates on the floor, then leaves, with the other animals wondering what hit them.[28] We would do well, I think, to heed such stories.

What is true of missionary folklore, and Black folklore, is true also of other groups and of our own state. If we are to know the heart and mind of our people, we must know their folklore. As Austin Fife has noted, the folksongs of a Mormon community "would be more useful than any single document in describing the morale of the community at any particular period in history."[29]

But as we seek to understand a community we must at the same time be prepared to see into hearts that are not always pure. People are often so accustomed to thinking of folklore as the prettified, sugary stories of a romanticized folk that they are shocked when they come in contact with vulgar lore. But folklore reveals us not only at our best but also at our worst. If we are vulgar, our lore will be vulgar. If we are racist, our lore will be racist. We Utahns do not always get along well together, and our lore reflects our points of stress. When the Mormon church was under pressure recently for its position on the Negro and when Brigham Young University athletic teams were the object of violent demonstrations, I heard again and again that a high church official had reputedly said that what we really needed now were some bigger seagulls. And the favorite riddle-joke at the time was: "Do you know why crows are black?" "No, why?" "Because they wouldn't eat crickets."[30] But the Mormons, too, are maligned. At a Catholic school not long ago a popular kind of joke was the Polack joke, except that it was not a Polack joke—here in Mormon Utah it had become the Mormon joke. Question: "How many Mormons does it take to change a light bulb?" Answer: "Five. One to hold the light and four to turn the house." Some of the items slurred both Mormons

---

28. Roger D. Abrahams, *Deep Down in the Jungle: Negro Narrative Folklore from the Streets of Philadelphia*, 1st rev. ed. (Chicago, 1970), 72–73.

29. Austin E. Fife, "Folklore and Local History," *Utah Historical Quarterly*, 31 (Fall 1963), 321.

30. [In the summer of 1848 the Mormons' crops were saved from a plague of crickets by the timely—and many believed miraculous—arrival of great flocks of seagulls. The event is commemorated by a statue dedicated to the seagull, now Utah's state bird, in Salt Lake City's Temple Square. On the other hand, crows—and some people—are black as punishment for an ancient wrong, according to Mormon tradition. In 1978, the Mormon church adopted a new policy admitting male blacks to the priesthood, thus defusing considerably the old jokes, although a new cycle of black-Mormon jokes has already begun to circulate, further supporting some of Wilson's ideas.]

and Negroes. Question: "Why did Missouri get all the Negroes and Utah get all the Mormons?" Answer: "Missouri had first choice."

We worry today about television and movies and wonder what effect they are having on our children in teaching them to accept drugs and violence. A historian from a later day studying this problem might find it instructive to look through archives for some of our present children's lore (and one of the folklorist's tasks is to record and file data for future historical analysis). For example, my seven-year-old son came in the house the other day singing lustily:

> Marijuana, Marijuana.
> L.S.D., L.S.D.
> Scientists make it; teachers take it.
> Why can't we? Why can't we?

And his songs seem increasingly to reflect the violence of the age. Children delight in parody. One of their favorites has been the parody of "On Top of Old Smoky":

> On top of spaghetti, all covered with cheese,
> I lost my poor meatball when somebody sneezed.
> It rolled off the table and onto the floor,
> And then my poor meatball rolled out of the door.
> It rolled in the garden and under a bush.
> And now my poor meatball is nothing but goosh.

But the neighborhood children now sing:

> On top of old Smoky all covered with blood,
> I shot my poor teacher with a forty-four slug.
> I went to her funeral.
> I went to her grave.
> The people threw flowers,
> But I threw grenades.

And to the "Battle Hymn of the Republic" they sing:

> O mine eyes have seen the glory of the burning of the school.
> We have tortured all the teachers,
> And we broke the Golden Rule.
> We are marching down the hall to hang the principal.
> Our truths are marching on.

> Glory, glory halleluah!
> Teacher hit me with a ruler.
> I met her at the door with a colt forty-four,
> And she ain't gonna teach no more.

Now I do not believe that my son and his friends are about to shoot their teachers and hang the principal. But I do believe that we live in a society where violence has become so commonplace that we, and especially our children, have become inured to it—indeed, derive satisfaction from it—and I believe that these songs reflect that fact. The songs of pioneer Utah reflected the values and attitudes of our forefathers and they continue to reflect our values and attitudes today.

FOLKLORE AS THE PEOPLE'S FACT

Perhaps the most important value in folklore study is its use in determining what the people believe about their past. Here I am concerned with those stories which a group of people regard as true and which they tell about themselves.

I am often asked if I ever try to trace the stories I study back to their ultimate origins. The answer is yes, but more often than not the search leads to that body of tales which have a national or international distribution and simply get attached to given localities. For example, the following story is told of Butch Cassidy:

Figure 2. Legendary Butch Cassidy (Robert LeRoy Parker), central character in many Utah tales, worked for Charley Gibbons at Hanksville. Gibbons's photograph, courtesy of Charles Kelly.

Butch Cassidy went to see an old couple in a small southern Utah town one evening. They told him that they were going to lose their farm the next day because the had been unable to pay the money they owed to the local banker. Butch told them not to worry because he could handle the situation. After a delightful evening of conversation, he gave them the money to bring their account up-to-date. A representative from the bank came the next day to take over the couple's farm and was very surprised when they handed him the money. After he left their house, he was riding along on his horse down a lonely road. Butch and his boys held him up and took the money back.

The same story is told of Jesse James[31] and belongs to the larger category of Robin Hood-type stories in which so-called outlaws fight a greedy establishment on behalf of the exploited poor.

Like Butch Cassidy, the redoubtable Mormon divine J. Golden Kimball is the subject of many localized anecdotes. The following is typical:

There was to be an impressive tour given to some dignitaries from other lands. J. Golden Kimball was assigned to the tour as a guide. They first took a bus trip to the important historical sites in and around Salt Lake City. Brother Kimball would constantly remind the visitors how fast buildings were put up by the industrious Mormons. Every time he would say so, one of the dignitaries on the tour would say, "Oh, is that right? In our country we could do it in half the time." J. Golden began to get madder and madder as the dignitary persisted to offer such comments. The tour was to end by having the bus drive around Temple Square. Then the dignitary asked, "What is that building there?" as he pointed at the temple. "Damned if I know," said J. Golden. "It wasn't there yesterday."[32]

In Baughman's *Type and Motif Index of the Folktales of England and North America*, this story is Type 1920s.[33] In a version of the story from the East, the visitor is an Englishman, the tour guide a Negro worker, and the building built in one day the Empire State Building.[34] I would guess that at least half of the stories told about J. Golden Kimball have, like this one, originated elsewhere.

Other Mormon stories can also be traced out of the region. For

31. Richard M. Dorson, *American Folklore* (Chicago, 1959), 241–42.

32. Printed in Jan Harold Brunvand, *A Guide for Collectors of Folklore in Utah* (Salt Lake City, 1971), 57.

33. Ernest W. Baughman, *Type and Motif Index of the Folktales of England and North America*, Indiana University Folklore Series, no. 20 (The Hague, 1966), 61.

34. Leonard W. Roberts, *South from Hell-fer-Sartin: Kentucky Mountain Tales* (Lexington, Ky., 1955), 150–51.

example, the widespread story of the hitchhiking Nephite who warns Mormons on the way to a temple to get in their year's supply of food is simply a Mormon adaptation of "The Vanishing Hitchhiker," a popular legend known throughout the United States.[35] And even those stories which seem to have originated within the church change as circumstances change. The once-popular story of a Nephite who delivers to a starving missionary a loaf of his mother's bread exists now only in fragmented versions. Missionaries no longer go out without purse or script, and while they may get hungry, they don't starve. Hence the old story speaks to no real need. But in recent years it has received new dress. According to one account, a stranger appeared to a lady in Roosevelt and asked for a sandwich. The lady, whose husband was serving in the Korean conflict, gave him one; later a stranger presented the husband in Korea the same sandwich. I would not be surprised to find the story now attached to Vietnam.

One might argue that the examples I have just given discredit much of what I have been saying. If much of what we call Utah folklore cannot be traced back to actual events and, indeed, has often not originated in Utah at all but exists in scattered versions known in many cultures, how, one might ask, can this material be of value to the historian? But what we must remember is that what actually happened is often less important than what we think happened. We are motivated not by actual fact but by what we believe to be fact. And if we believe something to be true, that belief will have consequences in our lives and the lives of others. As Henry Nash Smith has shown, the Homestead Act was based in part on the myth of the West as a virgin land, as a garden spot where the sturdy yeoman had only to sow and then to reap abundantly.[36] My grandfathers, both homesteaders, paid a dear price for that myth as they tried to support ten and thirteen children on 160 acres of Idaho and Utah dust.

The essential truth of folklore, then, is something that goes far beyond the question of fact or fiction. The fact that the Butch Cassidy story is "historically inaccurate" does not change the more important fact that the story is true to the economically pinched farmer who tells and believes it and that it therefore shapes his attitude toward banks and bankers and for a brief moment at least gives him vicarious victory over what he sees as the cold, impersonal institution that stands always ready to drive him from his land. Similarly, the essential

---

35. This legend has been analyzed by Richard K. Beardsley and Rosalie Hankey in "The Vanishing Hitchhiker," *California Folklore Quarterly*, 1 (1942), 303–35, and "A History of the Vanishing Hitchhiker," *ibid.*, 2 (1943), 13–25, and by Louis C. Jones in "Hitchhiking Ghosts in New York," *ibid.*, 3 (1944), 284–92.

36. Henry Nash Smith, *Virgin Land: The American West as Symbol and Myth* (New York, 1950), 138–213.

truth of the J. Golden Kimball stories lies not in their actually having happened but rather in Kimball's delightful irreverence for things that deserve irreverence—sham, hypocrisy, self-righteousness—and in the fundamental earthiness of the man. In him we find something of ourselves and through him—a real human being, not a stick figure or a paragon of virtue—many find hope for their own salvation. And the essential truth of the Nephite stories again lies not in their actual truth or falsity but in the vision they give those who believe them—a vision of a God who loves them, takes a personal interest in them, and, if they will follow Him, will send aid in time of need.

This impact of folk history on the lives of those who believe it is clearly illustrated in the folklore of polygamy, an issue that still today stirs more feelings than almost any event in Utah history. The lore of polygamy is endless, reflecting both the harmony and disharmony of that "peculiar institution." The following three stories all reflect the disharmony:

> Mother used to tell this story about a prominent family who lived in Ephraim. The first wife of this fella had quite a few children. She was heavy set and not too attractive. Later her husband married a younger, more attractive girl. Now their house was set up in such a way that to get to the kitchen you had to go through the bedroom. One day the first wife had to pass through the bedroom, and she was carrying some slop for the pigs. As she passed by the bed, her husband threw back the covers, gave his second wife a nice swat and said to the first wife, "See, Mary Jane, what a nice shape she has." Well, it made the first wife so mad that she threw the pig slop on both of them.

> This story really happened to my doctor's grandmother. She had twelve children. One day his grandfather brought this new woman home. Well, she didn't want it. She even had to give up her good bed and go upstairs with the twelve children. That made her good and mad. So she got together the twelve children and got them each to take turns filling the big chamber pot, if you know what I mean. The ceiling of the bedroom downstairs was made of planks of wood with big slots in between them. She dumped the chamber pot between the planks onto the bride and groom below, took the twelve children, left the house, and never came back.

> [Though told in first person, this story is nevertheless a traditional account.] There was a time when he was courting another woman and I knew it. He hadn't told me, but I knew it and knew who it was. He'd get all spruced up in an evening and go out to see her. This particular evening I knew where he was going. I pressed

Figure 3. Bringing home a new wife (a Mormon cartoon). The folklore of Polygamy seems virtually endless. This cartoon from the famous Rose Collection is by an unidentified artist. Gift of Charles Kelly.

his clothing and put a clean shirt on him, and I brushed him down and got him all ready to go. We used to have a bench by the door, and as he was leaving, I said to him, "Well, aren't you going to kiss me goodbye?" He said, "Yes." So he sat me down on his knee and made a real good job of kissing me goodbye. This was my chance— I pee-d, and I soaked him through, through everything.

In all three of these stories the first wife appears in a favorable light, the second wife (or woman) as an interloper, and the husand as a callous individual with little regard for his first wife's feelings. In all three stories the first wife comes out victorious. It is interesting that all three of the stories were told by women. When I asked my own wife why she liked the stories, she said "because they got what they deserved." However well polygamy may have worked during polygamous times, most modern Mormon women, I believe, identify with the first wife in these stories, applauding her way of handling a problem they themselves would not want to live with and taking comfort from the fact that even "back then" the demands of poetic justice were sometimes met.

But folk history need not take us back to the days of the pioneer fathers. Much of it is only as old as yesterday yet still plays an important role in our lives. My last example comes from late 1969 and early 1970, from the months preceding the April General Conference of the Mormon church. As noted above, during this time the church, because of its position on the Negro, was being criticized and sometimes threatened by outside groups. At the same time some apocryphal prophecies about racial wars and the bloodshed to come in the last days were widely circulated. As a result, many Mormons became convinced that Black-white conflict was imminent and that the violence would reach its peak during the April conference. Stories that justified this belief spread like wildfire throughout the Intermountain region. The following account is typical:

> Did you hear about the kids who were on their way to California and got jumped by some Blacks as they stopped for something to eat? I think it was in Nevada somewhere. Anyway, they were going to eat. They stopped and were jumped by some Blacks who happened to see their BYU sticker on their car. They messed up the car and drove it off the road and then beat up the guys and did who knows what to the girls. It's weird that they would do that just because they saw a BYU sticker, don't you think?

Other stories claimed that cars with Utah license plates were not safe out of the state, that carloads of Blacks were on the way to Salt Lake, that the Black Panthers were sneaking into the city with guns, that all the hotels around the temple were filled with Blacks, that the Lake Shore Ward Sacrament Meeting had been interrupted by Blacks, that the SDS and the Panthers[37] planned to blow up Mountain Dell Reservoir, that Black children were to sell candy bars filled with broken glass, that two bombs had been planted on Temple Square, and that Blacks would storm Temple Square during conference.

Conference came and went—peacefully. The stories proved to be groundless. But in the days before the conference they had a powerful influence on many people. Some formed defense groups; others stored guns and ammunition; and some who had planned to travel from out of state to conference remained home. For a few who still believe the stories the threat of invasion has not been ended, merely delayed—and folk history, rather than actual history, continues to govern their lives.

In summary, folklore throws light on aspects of our history which have been little illuminated by the written record; it provides valuable insight into the attitudes and values of a people in the past; and it

37. [The Black Panthers and the SDS (Students for a Democratic Society) were militant civil rights groups active in the 1960s.]

teaches us what the people believe their history to have been and thus helps us better understand the motivations which govern their lives in the present. Few folklorists, I think, would wish to disparage the work of serious historians. What we would like to do is recommend additional approaches to the study of our history and to suggest that when one learns how to look, he will find amid the legends many valuable facts, facts that one day even our librarian may find historically authentic.